THE
TEST

THE
TEST

A SEEKER'S JOURNEY TO THE
MEANING OF LIFE

DEAN DAVIS

REDEMPTION◆PRESS

© 2010, 2013 by Dean Davis. All rights reserved.

Published by Redemption Press, PO Box 427, Enumclaw, WA 98022

No part of this publication may be reproduced, stored in a retrieval system, or transmitted in any way by any means—electronic, mechanical, photocopy, recording, or otherwise—without the prior permission of the copyright holder, except as provided by USA copyright law.

The author of this book has waived the publisher's suggested editing and proof reading services. As such, the author is responsible for any errors found in this finished product.

All scripture quotations, unless otherwise indicated, are taken from the New King James Version®. Copyright © 1982 by Thomas Nelson, Inc. Used by permission. All rights reserved.

ISBN 13: 978-1-63232-027-8

Library of Congress Catalog Card Number: 2008906992

Thomas Aquinas once wrote, "Within every soul there is a thirst for happiness and meaning." I gratefully dedicate this book to the One who has filled my life with both, and to seekers everywhere who are earnestly looking for the same.

Once to every man and nation
Comes the moment to decide,
In the strife of truth with falsehood
For the good or evil side.
Some great cause, some great decision,
Offering each the bloom or blight,
And the choice goes by forever,
'Twixt that darkness and that light.
—*James Russell Lowell*

    I wanted to make the films so that young people would begin to ask questions about the mystery. Not having enough interest in the mysteries of life to ask the question, "Is there a God or is there not a God,"—that, for me, is the worst thing that can happen. I think you should have an opinion about that. Or you should be saying, "I'm looking. I'm very curious about this, and I'm going to continue to look until I can find an answer. And if I can't find an answer, then I'll die trying."
—*George Lucas*

We are not trying to please men,
but God, who tests our hearts.
—*Paul of Tarsus*

CONTENTS

Table of Charts and Diagrams........................... xi
Acknowledgments...................................... xiii
Prologue xv

Part 1: Life: A Mess or a Test?
   1. Life: A Mess or a Test? 1
   2. Hints of a Heavenly Hope: Nature 25
   3. Hints of a Heavenly Hope: Conscience 39

      One Man's Journey: A Seeker is Born 53

Part 2: In Search of the Teacher
   4. In Search of the Teacher 63
   5. Window on a World of Signs 89
   6. First Look..101
   7. The Great Debate 127
   8. Second Look.......................................155

      One Man's Journey: Good News From a Distant Land 197

Part 3: The Teacher on the Questions of Life
   9. What is the Ultimate Reality?........................207
  10. What is the Origin of the Universe, Life, and Man?.........227
  11. What, If Anything, Went Wrong?....................259
  12. What, If Anything, Can Be Done? 293
  13. What is the Meaning of Life? 321
  14. How Should We Live? 333

15. What Happens When We Die?..........................349
16. Where is History Heading?...........................365
17. How Can We Find Trustworthy Answers to
    the Questions of Life?..............................385

    One Man's Journey: A Furnace For Gold...................401

Part 4: The Teacher on the Test
18. Is Life a Test? 415
19. If So, How Can We Pass?............................435

    One Man's Journey: The Thrill of Them All................455

APPENDICES
1. Traditional Evidences for the Divine Inspiration
   of the Bible 467
2. The Unity of the Bible 469
3. Ten Signs of a Teacher Come From God 473
4. The Biblical Worldview 477
5. The Naturalistic Worldview.........................483
6. The Pantheistic Worldview: Eastern Religion 487
7. The Pantheistic Worldview: The New Age.............491
8. The Islamic Worldview..............................495

Endnotes...509

Select Bibliography 565

TABLE OF CHARTS AND DIAGRAMS

1. The Probationary Order 20
2. The Objective Moral Order 45
3. Modern Philosophy. 71
4. The Attributes of God 214
5. The Biblical Beginning 229
6. The Six Days of Creation 234
7. Adam's World 270
8. Salvation History. 297
9. The Days of the Messiah. 306
10. Salvation is Out of This World 312
11. A Meaningful Life 331
12. The Three Ages. 367
13. The Clash of the Kingdoms 368
14. The Last Days 370
15. How the Teacher Teaches All Mankind 399
16. Traditional Evidences for the Divine Inspiration of the Bible . . . 468
17. Ten Signs of a Teacher Come from God 474–475
18. The Biblical Worldview 480–481

19. The Naturalistic Worldview 484–485
20. The Pantheistic Worldview: Eastern Religion. 489–490
21. The Pantheistic Worldview: The New Age 492–493
22. The Islamic Worldview. 505–508

ACKNOWLEDGMENTS

IN MY LONG journey to the completion of this book I did not walk alone. Here I am pleased to acknowledge the rich contributions made by special friends and loved ones who stood faithfully by my side.

Many thanks to my new friends at Redemption Press. I am truly grateful for your sincere and generous efforts to get this book back in print. May the Lord bless you all as you embark with Him on this fresh adventure in Christian publishing!

Heartfelt thanks to my old friend Steve Carver, who produced the diagrams, charts, and tables that you will find in the pages ahead. Steve is that rarest of combinations: an imaginative artist, a skilled technician, and an all around great guy. He also has a great sense of humor, one that has refreshed me with the healing virtues of laughter for many years.

Thanks also to my good friends Hugh McCann and Joe Ferrante, busy pastors who generously gave of their valuable time to read and critique this long manuscript. While I have gladly incorporated many of their suggestions into the final product, I feel certain that Hugh and Joe would want me to remind my readers that final responsibility for the contents of this book is mine alone.

I want specially to acknowledge the vital contributions of my parents, Don and Leona Davis. Without their moral and practical support over the last decade, my life-long dream of writing big books on the great questions of life would have remained just that. Dad and Lee, thank you for your special part in making the dream come true.

The final words of appreciation belong to my dear wife, Linda. While the philosophy of religion is not exactly her cup of tea, it appears—for some strange and wonderful reason—that I am. Hence, her constant love and encouragement throughout the years it has taken me to finish this challenging project. Hence also my amazed gratitude, not only to her, but to God, who prepared such an excellent cup of tea for me!

PROLOGUE

RETURN WITH ME now to a beautiful spring morning in 1999, and to the teacher's lounge of a small elementary school located in Santa Rosa, California. Class is shortly to begin. As if oblivious to that fact, a middle-aged man—a substitute teacher—is standing alone, lost in thought before the faculty bulletin board. His eyes are fixed upon a little poster that reads as follows:

> **THIS LIFE IS A TEST.**
> **IF IT HAD BEEN A REAL LIFE**
> **YOU WOULD HAVE BEEN GIVEN INSTRUCTIONS**
> **ON WHERE TO GO AND WHAT TO DO.**

At first the man cannot help but laugh. Indeed, an involuntary "Amen!" almost escapes his lips. How many times—especially in recent years—has he ached for greater clarity about his direction in life? How many times has he felt that it was somehow hidden in darkness, engulfed in silence? Yes, he finds it comforting to know that others have experienced the same struggle, and healing to be able to laugh out loud with them about our common plight.

Yet as the true meaning of the poster begins to sink in, the man's laughter quickly fades. One by one, insights fill his mind, slowly carrying his thoughts into the depths.

First, he recognizes that for all its humor this poster is either an implicit plea for help, or an explicit cry of despair. *"The author,"* he reasons, *"is saying that human life can never be real, for real life would come with instructions—presumably at the mouth of a divine creator who would tell us what he wants us to know and what he would have us to do. Yet the author*

XVI   THE TEST

obviously believes there are no such instructions, probably because he believes there is no such creator. He thinks we are alone in the universe, and that human existence is an absurd 'test'—a trial run for a real life that, tragically enough, will never come."

As he ponders this gloomy conclusion, faceless people begin to appear at the edges of his imagination. First, he sees the anonymous author of the poster, and also the anonymous teacher who put it up in the lounge. Just behind them he thinks he sees a mass of anonymous "baby-boomers," multitudes of skeptical souls whom the author and the teacher quite likely represent. Next there arises a huge cloud of high schoolers, many of whom he has taught, and some of whom he knows have already embraced the poster's formula for despair. Then comes a smaller cloud, this time of little children; children too young and too unspoiled to get the joke, but who soon might—and might take it to heart—unless someone can get to them first with an alternative message of hope. Finally—as if through the lens of his own past experience—he catches an unsettling glimpse of millions upon millions the world over; of the famished and fearful faces of all who have ever given up on the very possibility of "real life."

But this is not the end of his reverie. For now he is struck by a very different kind of thought, and along with it, a delightful irony. To begin with, he realizes that this poster—so clearly designed to poke sardonic fun at a life without meaning—actually contains the hidden key to discovering what that meaning is! Or so he reckons, since in recent years he himself has become convinced that life really is a test!

Mulling that thought afresh, he recalls once again his own long and difficult journey: the early years of disillusionment with philosophy; the chilling specter of a world without "instructions;" the subsequent years of spiritual awakening, questing, and far-flung religious experimentation; the dreadful season of crisis and collapse; the climactic months of resolution and renewal; the ensuing years of struggle, healing, study, service, widening insight, and ever-deepening joy.

And thus, with his grateful mind fully returned to the present, he makes his final response to the poster before him: *"Yes, life is a test, but not an empty trial run; not a mockery of life as it should be. Instructions HAVE been given. We HAVE been told where to go and what to do. Real life really IS possible—if only we are willing to take the test."*

Then, with the bell just about to ring, a sudden recollection brings yet another irony to his attention, an irony that both surprises and encourages him. Yes, in recent years he has been thinking about life as a test. But more than this, he has been trying to write of it as such. Indeed, there is already a book, painfully slow in taking shape, almost languishing. Standing before the poster, feeling once again the anxious longing of all who must take the test, he therefore wonders: *"Is this morning—this moment— a work of Providence? Is it a confirmation of the value of the book? Could it even be an exhortation to finish it?"*

Ever the mystic, he answers "yes" to all of the above. Quickly, then, he removes a 3x5 card from his brief case and jots down the words of the poster *verbatim*. Tucking it safely away in his shirt pocket—giving both it and his heart a little pat of satisfaction—he resolves once again to finish the book, and also to make good use of this remarkable event. *Perhaps*, he says to himself, *I could even use it in the prologue*.

For the moment, however, he must rush off to his classroom and teach the fourth graders. As he does, he finds himself hoping that somehow he will be able to relate—even to these ten-year-olds—the simple truths that have gripped his heart once again: life really is a test; instructions really have been given; and for all who are willing to follow the instructions and take the test, there awaits the unspeakably precious prize of *real life*.

PART 1

LIFE: A MESS OR A TEST?

CHAPTER 1

LIFE: A MESS OR A TEST?

IN OUR DIFFICULT journey through this world it is always possible—and sometimes quite helpful—to experience a change in perspective. The following story about the ancient Mongol king, Genghis Kahn, supplies a memorable illustration of this important truth.

Having just returned from the rigors of the battlefield, the victorious Kahn decided to refresh himself with a day of hunting in the mountains. At sunrise he therefore exited the city with his courtiers at his side, his eager hounds before him, and his faithful hunting falcon perched upon his wrist. But alas, despite high hopes for a great day of sport, the little party came upon no game at all. Meanwhile, the weather grew hot and the men and animals irritable. Finally, the exasperated king decided to dismiss his entire retinue: if he could not hunt, at least he could enjoy a solitary ride through the forest. He even bade farewell to his beloved falcon: at the flick of his wrist she rose into the air and disappeared towards home.

But once again, events seemed to conspire against the king, for now he discovered that he had forgotten his water. Indeed, by mid-afternoon the thirsty traveler could think of little else but finding a spring or a creek where he could refresh himself with a drink. Happily, the trail finally brought him to a rocky hillside where Kahn rejoiced to see a thin trickle of water descending from somewhere above. Immediately he leaped from his horse, took out his cup, placed it beneath the trickle, and watched impatiently as the water entered his vessel one precious drop at a time.

After a long half hour, the cup was finally filled. Carefully, the king reached his hand down, picked it up, and set it to his lips. But before he had tasted even a drop, something extraordinary happened. The air whirred all around him, the sun was lost in shadow, a cry pierced his ears, and—to his utter amazement—his own trusty falcon knocked the cup out of his hands!

"What in the world has gotten into her?" muttered the puzzled monarch as he watched the bird disappear to the rocks above. But there was nothing for it. All he could do was start again.

And so, after another long wait, the thirsty traveler once again reached down for an even more coveted cup of water. But just as before, the agitated falcon suddenly appeared out of nowhere, flew straight at her master, and dislodged the cup from his trembling grip. "Enough!" cried the infuriated ruler, pulling out his sword and cursing the bird as it fled back to the rocks above. "Come and see what I will give you if you dare to reward me thus a third time!"

The time would come soon enough. Only moments later, with barely a mouthful of water in the cup, Kahn reached down his with his left hand to pick it up, while in his right holding his sword at the ready. It happened just as expected. Once again the falcon streaked down from above, intent on keeping the cup from the king's lips. But this time he was prepared. He met the attacking bird with three great slashes of his blade, one of which nearly cut her in two, bringing the winged hunter, bloodied and dying, to the ground.

"And now see what you have done to yourself!" cried the king who, for all his fury, could not help but grieve the loss of his beloved hunting companion. It wasn't long, however, before he yet again noticed his thirst, and also the astonishing fact that his fallen cup had somehow lodged itself in a crevice. Try as he might, he could not pull it out.

"What is the meaning of all this?" murmured the incredulous ruler. "Why can't I, the great monarch of all Mongolia, even get so much as a miserable drink of water?" And so, driven by powerful thirst and stubborn pride, he resolved to climb the hillside and get a drink from the hidden source above.

The climb was not easy, but at last he reached the top. And there, only yards away, he spied a shallow pool of unappetizingly murky water. "But it's wet, for all that," said the king to himself. "I'll remove that big branch, kneel down, and have my drink at last!"

As he drew near, however, Kahn met with a sudden shock. The "big branch" was not a branch at all, but the decaying carcass of an enormous viper. Poised above the dark water, his eyes glued to the grisly sight, the king suddenly understood everything. The serpent had died by the pool. The water was fouled and deadly. The falcon knew it and had tried to warn him. And he, in stupidity and anger, had killed a wise and faithful friend.

Forgetting his thirst, a sad and greatly humbled Genghis Kahn descended the hillside. He tenderly buried the falcon's dead body in the ground, whispered a mournful good-bye, mounted his horse, and headed home.

Lessons to Learn

This poignant story contains three important lessons that serve well to introduce our theme in the present chapter.

First, the emperor's misadventure teaches us that *we are all vulnerable to misperceptions*, to wrong perspectives on what we see, hear, and experience. In particular, we learn here that it is all too easy to base our judgments about a given situation on faulty or insufficient information. Indeed, the sad end to Kahn's tale reminds us that a single piece of new information can altogether revolutionize our perspective, enabling us to see a real friend in an apparent enemy.

Secondly, the story underscores *the importance of slow, thoughtful, and complete investigation*. It tells us that if we desire to get at the truth of a matter, we simply cannot afford to let our initial impressions—or our corresponding emotional reactions—push us into a judgment we may live to regret. Yes, Kahn's falcon was behaving "badly" relative to his desire for a drink. But if only he had paused a moment to remember her intelligence, love, and faithfulness, he would soon have realized that such behavior was completely out of character. It was behavior that required further investigation and a better explanation. As it happened, however, Kahn allowed dark clouds of impatience, selfishness, and anger to obscure important truths that he himself already knew. He paid a terrible price for his mistake.

Finally, the story teaches us *the importance of being open to fresh perspectives*. Such open-mindedness becomes a cherished value in all who recognize our vulnerability to misperceptions, the danger of impulsive responses, the importance of good information, and the need for careful investigation. If Kahn had been such a man, humbly open to a perspective different from his own, his falcon would have lived to hunt another day.

And now, as we prepare to think together about the meaning of life, please permit me to ask a rather personal question. Does it ever seem to you that our world—religiously and philosophically considered—is like a crazed falcon, maliciously trying to prevent you from slaking your spiritual thirst in a dry and weary land? To be more specific, does it ever seem to you that the world of religion and philosophy is an indecipherable and purposeless mess; that the contending voices of priests and pastors, rabbis and roshis, mullahs and imams, scientists and skeptics, philosophers and pundits, all are so much screeching—a sure sign that human existence is not only meaningless, but a species of madness itself?

If so, I understand (and later on will explain why). But because I do understand, I want all the more to urge you to think again about the three lessons we have just learned: 1) we are all vulnerable to misperceptions, 2) we are therefore wise to investigate things carefully, and 3) we are also wise to be open to fresh perspectives. For my message in this chapter (and throughout the entire journey ahead) is simply this: despite appearances to the contrary, the world into which we have been born is *not* a religious and philosophical mess. It is *not* a crazed falcon on the attack, intent on robbing us of our last few drops of sanity, purpose, hope, and joy. Indeed, upon careful investigation—*and with the benefit of a sudden change of perspective*—it turns out to be something very much better, and very much more encouraging. It turns out to be a friend rather than a foe; a friend that is coming to test us rather than torment us; a friend that would lead us *to* the water of life rather than keep us from it.

But lest we get ahead of ourselves, let us begin our journey at the beginning. Let us first turn inward for a closer look at the *source* of all our religious and philosophical hunger and thirst: the provocative, persistent, and sometimes quite painful "ultimate questions" that dwell in the depths of the human heart.

A Heart Full of Questions

Many have been the definitions of man, but none was ever more cryptic—or penetrating—than that of the French philosopher Blaise Pascal. Pascal declared that *man is a thinking reed.* In so doing, he clearly directs our attention to *thought* as the essence of man. Outwardly, says Pascal, there is little to distinguish us from a reed by the riverside. Inwardly, however, there is much. For though the reed presumably has no inward life at all, man is almost wholly identified by the mysterious inward flow of ideas, words, images, emotions, and decisions that pass through an equally mysterious "self," thereby enabling him to interact with the outside world. For Pascal, then, it is man's thought-life that makes him unique among all creatures. It is the very essence of his humanity.

But perhaps this definition needs some refining. Why? Because we know that the higher animals also possess a certain kind of thought-life, yet this in itself does not make them human. It appears, then, that what makes man unique is not the *fact* that he thinks, but rather the *kind* of thoughts that he alone is able to think—e.g., scientific, mathematical, musical, historical, artistic, etc.

Now all this brings us closer to a good definition, but I would argue that we still need to refine things a bit further. For it is clear that all men

LIFE: A MESS OR A TEST?

do not experience all kinds of thought, or at least not to the same degree. I, for example, experience very few thoughts about home improvements or landscaping, as my frequently frustrated wife will readily testify. Two of my daughters think of classical music day and night; my two sons would scarcely give it the time of day. When my former college friends get together, one of them gushes about tomorrow's Internet technology; yet even as he speaks, another's eyes glaze over until the conversation turns at last to poetry or ecology. Yet all of us are equally human.

There is, however, one stream of thought that all of us seem to experience. This stream—usually referred to as religious or philosophical—begins to flow at different times and in different ways for different people. Still, it is safe to say that sooner or later all of us find it carrying us in one direction or another. To be more specific, I would say that a person begins to experience this kind of thought when he starts to ponder one or more of the *questions of life*. These I define as the big religious and philosophical questions—what folks sometimes call the "ultimate" or "higher order" questions—that we humans have pondered, discussed, debated, and occasionally even fought and died for all throughout our history on the earth.

So then, if I had to improve upon Pascal's definition, I would modify it by saying that *man is a thinking reed whose thoughts are continually drawn upwards into the questions of life.*

Now before commenting further, let me be specific about what I think these questions are. Based upon a close examination of the recurring themes of philosophy and religion—and also of the constant musings of my own heart—I would suggest that the following nine questions constitute the irreducible core of the questions of life.

1. *What is the ultimate reality, the source of the universe and all that is in it?*

This question deals with what philosophers call *metaphysics*, the study of that which lies *above* or *behind* the universe, life, and man. As we shall see, it is the single most important question of life, primarily because it forces us to grapple with closely related questions about the existence and nature of an ultimate spiritual reality (god), and (assuming god exists) the exact character of his relationship to the world.[1] The importance of this question is also seen in the fact that the answer we give to it will exert a profound influence on the way we answer the other eight questions of life. More on this in a moment.

2. What is the origin of the universe, life, and man?

This question—the focus of *cosmogony*—lies at the heart of a much broader discipline called *cosmology*, the study of the origin, structure, purpose, and destiny of the universe. It is deceptively simple, since it involves a number of closely related matters that are of great interest and importance. For example, in thinking about origins we need first to determine what exactly "the cosmos?" is. Is it just the "time-space-energy-matter continuum" that modern scientists speak of, or might it include invisible spiritual elements as well? Is the universe eternal, or did it have a "true beginning"—a moment in time, or at the beginning of time, when it came into being? If it did have a true beginning, who or what brought it into being? And if it came into being, how and when did it reach its present form: more or less instantaneously, or over long ages of evolution and/or progressive creation? Down through the millennia—and never more so than today—people have disagreed about the answers to these basic questions of cosmogony. But all agree in asking them, for all sense that crucial keys to the *meaning* of the universe, life, and man may well lie hidden in the mystery of their origin and beginning.[2]

3. What (if anything) went wrong? Why are evil, suffering, and death present in the world?

This too is a cosmological question. It is rooted in the universal human feeling that things are not as they should be or could be. It wants to know where this feeling comes from, and what it signifies. It asks if natural (i.e., physical) and moral evils are simply unpleasant parts of reality as it happens to be, or whether they represent departures from an ideal state intended by a divine creator, a state somehow lost or as yet unattained.

4. What (if anything) can be done?

This question lies at the heart of what philosophers and theologians call *soteriology*, the study of "salvation." Moved by a spirit of hope, it asks what, if anything, can be done to mitigate or eliminate the evil, suffering, and death that are in the world. It wonders if things can ever return to a lost state of perfection, or advance to a possible or promised state of perfection—and what such a state might look like. Also, it wants to know who is responsible for whatever degree of salvation may be possible: god, man, or the two somehow working together.

LIFE: A MESS OR A TEST?

5. *Do the universe, life, and man have a purpose, and if so, what is it?*

This question—a favorite among youth—falls under the heading of *teleology*, the study of the *goal*, *end*, or *purpose* of the universe, life, and man. The central issue here is whether man is alone in the universe and therefore the only source of whatever purpose he may have, or whether there is a supreme being who has a specific purpose (or set of purposes) for his creatures. On the assumption that there is such a being, teleology goes on to ask what his purposes are and how they may be discovered, so that human beings may live a purposeful and fulfilling life.

6. *How shall we live?*

This question takes us into the controversial realm of *law* and *ethics*. It too involves a number of closely related questions. Where do feelings of right and wrong come from? What is the basis for personal moral standards and civil law? Are these phenomena merely cultural conventions? Are they part of an evolutionary process? Do they reflect divinely ordained absolutes by which all people must live if they hope to have a clear conscience and a just society? If such absolutes do exist, why can't we all agree on what they are? Assuming that they exist, how can we find out for sure what they are? How can we become better people, the better to live up to them? And what can be done when we find that we have *not* lived up to them; when we have wounded our conscience and desire to find a balm for its healing? All of this and more are involved in the little question that looms surprisingly large in our lives: how shall we live?

7. *What happens when we die?*

This is the central question of *personal eschatology*, the study of what happens to the "inward" part of a human being—the self or soul—at the moment of death and thereafter.[3] Understandably, most religions devote considerable attention to this question, since man is not just curious but deeply concerned about his eternal destiny. Do the lights go out? Is there a heaven, a purgatory, or a hell? What about reincarnation and other spiritual realms? Some say we cannot know the answers to these questions till we die. Others argue that we can and must. But all of us know that we have a date with this most intimate and disturbing of all the questions of life.

8. *Where is history going?*

Here is the core question of *cosmic eschatology*, the study of the destiny and final state of the universe. Once again, many related questions are involved. Will our orderly universe inexorably follow the Second Law of Thermodynamics to heat death and final disintegration? Is the cosmos progressing towards some divinely predetermined goal? Does it move in a straight line towards a single end, or in cosmic cycles, perhaps endlessly retracing exactly the same steps according to a law of eternal recurrence? Most importantly, does mankind have an eternal future, or is human history a mere "cry in the streets," a cry that will soon fall silent and never be heard again? Many assert that we simply cannot know the answers to such questions, while others contend that the very persistence of the questions strongly suggests otherwise.

9. *Can we find trustworthy answers to the questions of life, and if so, how?*

If this is not the most urgently felt question, it is certainly the most fundamental. How can we discover trustworthy answers to the other eight questions unless we are convinced that such answers exist, and unless we know how to find them? Here, then, is where a thoughtful seeker's journey logically begins: with what the philosophers call *epistemology*, the study of the possibility and sources of reliable philosophical knowledge. In particular, the seeker must ask, "Are there any good reasons to believe that I really can discover the truth about the questions of life? If so, where exactly should I turn to find this truth? Should I look to natural science, philosophy, mystical experience, or to some kind of divine revelation? And if to divine revelation, how shall I know *which* revelation, since there are so many of them in the world, and since they so plainly contradict each other at so many important points? As these penetrating questions reveal, the ninth question of life clearly has first claim on seekers everywhere as they begin their difficult journey to religious and philosophical truth.

Crucial Characteristics of the Questions of Life

Are you now in a panic? Do all these questions—and all the questions within the questions—threaten to overwhelm you? If so, that is quite understandable, especially if you are just beginning to wrestle with the questions of life. But not to panic. Instead, let us take a moment to remember the lessons we learned from Kahn and his falcon. In particular, let us

LIFE: A MESS OR A TEST?

consider the possibility that a little investigation into the *characteristics* of the questions of life might well produce a helpful change in perspective, a change that could not only calm your heart, but actually encourage and stimulate it for a great quest.

But what exactly are the characteristics that we need to consider? Here I will focus on three of the most important, showing that the questions of life are *universal*, that they are *existentially urgent*, and that they *supply the framework or infrastructure for our worldview*.

Universal

Observe first that the questions of life are *universal*. That is, they arise in every human heart. We can see this by looking back in time, out across the whole wide world, and deep into the recesses of our own minds. We can see it in the tomes of the philosophers, the scriptures of the holy men, and the inquiries of little children. We can hear it on talk shows, in coffee houses, and in the whisperings of our inmost thoughts. To be sure, these questions assert themselves differently in different lives. Some folks wrestle with many, others with only one or two. Some ask them early in life, others later. In some cases, the questions hit like lightning; in others, they arise slowly, like a storm or the break of day. But sooner or later all people have a date with the questions of life. These are "family matters," the great themes over which the whole human race has ever entered into its most interesting and important discussions.

Existentially Urgent

The questions of life are also *existentially urgent*. By this I mean that we care, and care deeply, about finding the answers. Indeed, I am inclined to think that the questions themselves may be characterized as a kind of mental offshoot; that they are the conceptual flower of a plant whose taproot sinks deep into inmost ground of human need and desire. This is why finding the answers is so important to us: we feel that our security and well-being depend upon it.

A personal illustration may help to clarify my meaning here.

Back in 1970, at the very beginning of my own spiritual journey, the question that mattered most to me was the nature of the ultimate reality. At that time, I had reached an intellectual conclusion that the ultimate reality was "Big Mind"—an impersonal Mind or Spirit, of which the whole world (including me) was but a manifestation. In other words, I had become a pantheist: I believed that all is one, all is mind, and all is god.

But this was only the beginning of my quest. For though my intellect was satisfied to "know" that Big Mind was the ultimate reality, my heart needed something more. I wanted personally to *experience* Big Mind as the ultimate reality. This is why I began to practice yoga, meditation, and other spiritual disciplines. I wanted to align my "heart"—my personal inward experience—with what was going on in my head.

My point here is that the questions of life are best understood as *existential questings*. In other words, they are aspirations not only of the intellect, but of the whole person, undertaken with a view to the felt well-being of the whole person. Thus, in asking about the ultimate reality, a seeker is actually questing for a (deeper) personal connection with that reality. In asking about the purpose of life, he is actually hungering to know his own purpose, and to walk in it. By thinking about how he should live, he is actually yearning to find a life-style that is good, and therefore safe, honorable, and worthy of a reward. In considering death and the afterlife, he is really hoping for personal inward assurance about what awaits him on the other side. And so on.

If we are wise, we will never underestimate the existential urgency associated with the questions of life. What else can explain the fact that people think about them so often, investigate them so earnestly, hold their conclusions about them so tenaciously, promulgate their convictions about them so energetically, and at times even fight, suffer, and die for what they believe about them? Yes, the questions of life must lie extremely close to the core of our humanity. Indeed, because this is so true, they must, in some sense, be matters of life and death.

A Framework for Our Worldview

The questions of life also *supply a framework for our worldview*. To appreciate this fascinating characteristic, we need first to understand what a worldview is. By way of preliminary definition, let us simply say that a worldview is *a way of looking at reality as a whole*. To use a humble analogy, a worldview is rather like a pair of glasses: it is a set of religious and philosophical concepts through which we can behold and interpret the world around us, and by which we can also navigate our way through it.

Very importantly, this illustration helps us to see the true goal of religion and philosophy. Suppose that I am looking at a rose through a pair of sunglasses. I am seeing the rose, but I am not seeing it as it really is, since the tincture in the glass has more or less distorted my perception of the flower before me. Analogously, I may be looking at reality through a given set of philosophical concepts—a given worldview—but that is no

LIFE: A MESS OR A TEST?

guarantee that I am seeing reality as it really is. What if my concepts are too few? What if some or all of them are false? In such cases, I will have an inadequate and/or distorted perception of the world around me. Here then is the implicit goal of all our philosophical questings: to find the one complete set of true philosophical concepts through which we can see reality without distortion or tincture; through which we can see reality as it really is. In other words, the true goal of philosophy is to discover *the one true worldview*.

This brings us once again to the questions of life. For it is clear that if we desire to find the one true worldview, we must first have some idea about the number and nature of the concepts that make it up; we need to know exactly how many lenses are required for an adequate "pair" of philosophical glasses. Just here is where the questions of life prove so helpful. Why? Because it turns out that *they are philosophically comprehensive*. That is, they express and sum up pretty much the full spectrum of mankind's religious and philosophical interest. But if this is so, it follows that a full set of answers to the nine questions of life will offer us a comprehensive look at reality. In other words, the questions of life supply the proper framework for any viable worldview. Indeed, this is so true that we may now offer a far more extended and much more useful definition of a worldview: *A worldview is a way of looking at reality as a whole based upon a particular set of answers to the questions of life*. And this implies, of course, that *the one true worldview is a way of looking at reality as whole based upon the one set of true answers to the questions of life*.

This characteristic of the questions of life—that it supplies the framework for our worldview—is fabulously useful to a seeker. Above all, it helps him to know exactly what to look for in a given religion or philosophy. For example, if there really is one true worldview—and if this or that particular religion/philosophy is it—then it must answer most, if not all, of the nine questions of life. Moreover, it must do so such a way that each of the nine answers logically *harmonizes* with the other eight, (for how can a true worldview contain answers that are falsified by contradicting themselves). And finally, the answers given by the one true worldview must speak to the deepest fears and longings of a seeker's heart. That is, in addition to giving him total truth, they must also offer him personal well-being. Indeed, of all the benefits of the one true worldview, this is surely the most important, since it is primarily the quest for personal well-being that animates our search for truth. We see, then, that for many reasons a good understanding of the questions of life will greatly help the seeker to be a shrewd evaluator of worldviews!

Speaking as a bush-league philosopher, I myself have come to believe that the one true worldview is, in fact, the holy grail of all religion and philosophy. As these two age-old disciplines abundantly testify, there is something in man that incessantly longs for the highest, widest, and deepest possible perception of reality as it really is. The questions of life both initiate the search for this vision and point the way. Question by question, answer by answer, we would mount up to that lofty intellectual vantage point from which alone we can at last survey reality as a whole. And again, we aspire to this not only because we desire to *see* reality as it really is, but also because we desire to *relate* to it as it really is. Deep in our hearts we sense that finding the one true worldview is a very special kind—indeed, the ultimate kind—of coming home.

Summing up, on our journey thus far we have unearthed not a little evidence to suggest that man is best defined as a thinking reed—a reed that thinks, above all else, about the questions of life. By their universality, their existential urgency, and their mysterious tendency to inspire an earnest search for the one true worldview, these questions commend themselves as belonging to the very essence of our humanity. And if this is so, a sobering conclusion follows: our *response* to those questions becomes an important measure—perhaps the *most* important measure—of our humanity. In other words, how we deal with the questions of life will in large part determine our success as human beings.

Suppose, then, that someone suddenly awakens to the profound importance of these questions. And suppose that he sincerely desires to respond to them. What then? Well, for starters I would say that he should rejoice: a noble journey—full of purpose and rich with promise—is about to begin. But just as soon as I had extended my congratulations, I would also begin to urge him to get himself into excellent philosophical shape. For as we are about to see, in our seemingly messy world, the way of a seeker can be hard.

A World Full of Contradictory Answers

Perhaps as never before, there is a world of philosophical diversity right at our doorstep. Whether in our neighborhood, school, or place of work, we have all met people who relate differently to the questions of life. Some think about them much, others very little (or so it may seem). Some are confident about their answers, others tentative. Some are vocal about their conclusions, others private. Most importantly, some hold one point of view, some hold others. *Lots* of others!

This situation should give us pause. Yes, as adults we have grown accustomed to such diversity, and have (for the most part) mastered a set of social rules by which we can deal with it fairly comfortably. But imagine for a moment that you are now encountering it afresh, as you first did when you were a child. It comes as quite a shock, does it not, to realize that the people around you—including even your closest friends and relatives—do not view the world in the same way? Indeed, is it not disturbingly evident that something is seriously wrong? Surely we all *ought* to agree; yet it is painfully evident that we do not. To look this philosophical situation straight in the face is to see immediately that it is scandalous.

As he begins his search for truth, an adult will often experience the scandal anew. It is deeply troubling to him, for now he realizes with fresh force that corresponding to his heart full of questions there is *a world full of contradictory answers!* Suddenly, as if to mock his newborn desire for truth, conflicting viewpoints are seen popping up everywhere! Moreover, these viewpoints are usually trumpeted—and sometimes even enforced—by men and women who seem to be more intelligent, more educated, more prestigious, and ever so much more confident than he. A mad falcon indeed!

Let me illustrate this point by again citing from my own experience with regard to the question of the ultimate reality.

From my tender years and right up to the present I have repeatedly encountered teachers who concur with the late Carl Sagan, boldly asserting that the physical cosmos is all there is, was, or ever shall be. This is the view of the *philosophical naturalist*. However, as a student of Eastern religions I was taught on the highest authority that the so-called physical universe is, contrary to all appearances, a dream: a spiritual phenomenon, a manifestation of Big Mind. Here is the view of the *pantheist*. However, in still other venues I have had people assure me over and again that the ultimate reality is an infinite personal god; a god who formerly created and presently sustains the universe; a god who is metaphysically separate from the world, yet remains intimately and intricately related to it. This is the view of the *theist*. And what is true about the answer to the first question of life is just as true for the answers to all the rest: naturalists, pantheists, and theists cannot agree on a single one!

Now this vexing state of affairs raises an important philosophical question, one of great concern to the seeker whose heart burns for truth about ultimate issues. Is our world in a state of spiritual and intellectual chaos? Does the multitude of contradictory answers prove that there are no answers at all? Or could it be that upon closer examination the apparent chaos reveals a hidden order and purpose beneath the troubled surface of things? To ask this question more picturesquely, does the unsettling fact of religious and philosophical diversity show that life is a *mess* or a *test*?

Before cutting the falcon in two, we had better try to find out.

Life: A Mess or a Test?

In a world full of competing answers to the questions of life, some people have always concluded that life is a mess. We remember, for example, the ancient Greek skeptics and sophists, or the famous 16th century French essayist, Montaigne, whose motto was, "What do I know?" But if we look at the big picture—scanning, say, the last 2500 years of Western Civilization—we realize that skepticism has not been the dominant philosophical mood at all. To the contrary, the vast majority of philosophers, theologians, scientists, and artists were quite confident that they could know what is universally true, beautiful, and good. They may have disagreed in their representation of these realities, but all concurred that the realities are indeed real and that man is meant to know them.

Until today. Today the dominant mood—at least in the West—is indeed one of philosophical skepticism. As we shall see later, this condition is traceable to a number of causes: a rejection of divine revelation as a viable doorway to truth; the failure of modern philosophy to arrive at a compelling vision of truth; the influential writings of various postmodern (i.e., skeptical) philosophers; and an ever-shrinking, electronically connected world, in which the striking diversity of man's religious and philosophical outlooks is more or less continually "in our face." For these and other reasons, truth has truly fallen upon hard times. Moreover, this is not happening only among the intelligentsia. According to Mr. Gallup, 66% of Americans now agree with the statement, "There is no such thing as absolute truth."

Here, then, is the "postmodern mind" in a nutshell: objective truth and moral absolutes simply do not exist. And as Mr. Gallup just told us, many today have embraced this mind. This is why we often hear people say, "It may be true (or wrong) for you, but it's not for me." Or, "If it works for you, good. But it doesn't work for me." This is why postmodern philosophers tell us that "truth" is relative to the language, history, culture, and even the biology of the people who hold it. It is also why they now refer to the great systems of philosophy and theology as "all-encompassing stories" or "meta-narratives." Such stories, they say, have no basis in reality, but are mere verbal constructs by which the human animal seeks to give meaning to the meaningless, to impose order on chaos, and to gain power over one's neighbor. For them, "truth" is not really truth, but *ideology*; it is an opiate for the muddled masses, and a cattle prod and a cudgel in the hand of the oppressor.

This perspective—which I will call *the mess perspective*—generates an ethic all its own. The new ethic asserts that in the past particular religions and philosophies may have had some survival value, but that in today's shrinking, volatile, and dangerously armed world we dare not take them too seriously. Indeed, the best solution is that we all should "come of age," exchanging our childish fantasies of moral and philosophical certainty for the hard currency of peaceful coexistence. Let us therefore abandon our quest for trustworthy answers to the questions of life. Let us surrender our hopes of ever finding the one true worldview. Let us simply bow uncomprehendingly before the great mystery of being. Let us live and let live, tolerating each other's stories and never again trying to force ours upon anyone else, whether by physical might, reasonable argument, or passionate persuasion. In short, however disappointing or frustrating it may seem, let all the family of man now accept and get used to the fact that life is a mess.[4]

In the pages ahead, we will examine the postmodern viewpoint in greater depth. Here, however, I want to propose a different and far more encouraging take on mankind's religious and philosophical diversity. I call it *the test perspective.* According to this view, life is a test set before us by an "unknown god." He himself has put the questions of life into our hearts, as well as an abiding hope of finding the answers. But for wise reasons he has not made those answers self-evident. Unlike the questions themselves, the answers are not innate; they are not planted within. Moreover, he has allowed a certain amount of religious and philosophical error to creep into his world, thereby setting the stage. What will his human creatures do now? Will they listen to their hearts and begin sorting through the various philosophical options till they find the truth? Or will they use the existence of options as an excuse not to seek truth but to do what they want? As each of us decides, the unknown god is watching. If we seek, he will help us. If we find, he will reward us. The test is on. Our part is as simple as it is important: we must love the truth enough to seek it, and we must keep on seeking it until we find it.

Signs of a Test

Most folks would probably agree that this is indeed a more hopeful way of looking at life in a philosophically diverse world. They would like to know, however, if there are any good reasons to believe it is true. I believe there are. Indeed, I seem to see the signs of a test all around us. Let us therefore pause to consider a few of the most important here.

Natural Hunger and Thirst

The first sign is the familiar mystery of *natural hunger and thirst*. In the natural world there is obviously an objective reality that corresponds to our hunger: food. Similarly, there is an objective reality that corresponds to our thirst: drink. Observe also that we often have to seek out food and drink, and can usually find them if we want them badly enough. Do these simple facts of daily life have a message for us? Is the natural world teaching us something important about the spiritual? Does our hunger for truth correspond to an objective reality? In other words, does it imply that objective truth really exists? And does it imply that objective truth will supply spiritual nourishment, refreshment, and pleasure if and when we seek it out and find it?[5]

The Telltale Make-up of the Human Mind

The second sign that life may be a test is equally familiar and equally mysterious: *the telltale make-up of the human mind*. How is it that we are all endowed with such amazing faculties as thought, language, intuition, reason, and conscience? How is it that we are free to train these faculties on the questions of life? How is it that many of us do so with a spirit of intellectual curiosity, a sense of existential urgency, and a fragile yet persistent confidence that solid answers may indeed be found? Also, how is it that we are surrounded by other minds, with whom we may seek, discuss, and debate the possible answers, if we so desire? Viewed from one angle, it certainly looks as if mankind has been equipped for a search for truth. The tools are in us and around us. Our part, it would appear, is simply to use them.

The Manageable Messiness of the Religious/Philosophical (R/P) World

To appreciate this sign, we must dig a little; but once having seen it clearly, it does indeed seem both real and impressive. The idea here is that the R/P world is not nearly as messy as our postmodern friends would have us believe. Indeed, upon close inspection we find that it is actually quite simple and orderly.

We have already seen, for example, that *the questions of life are relatively few and easy to understand*. Quantitatively, nine questions are hardly overwhelming. Qualitatively, they are readily understood by virtually everyone: children and youth ask them all the time, even if we adults cannot answer them all the time.

LIFE: A MESS OR A TEST?

Also, *the possible answers to the questions are few and easy to understand.* For example, to the question, "What happens when we die?" religion and philosophy repeatedly return to three basic options: the lights go out (the view of naturalism), the soul reincarnates (the view of pantheism), or the soul goes immediately to heaven, purgatory, or hell (the view of theism). We may not like some of these answers, or find them equally plausible, but no one can say they are too numerous or difficult to comprehend. And what is true for the question of the after-life is true for all the other questions as well.

Of special interest is the fact that *the possible worldviews are VERY few, and also fairly easy to understand.* Now at first blush, this statement might sound absurd, since we all know that our world veritably overflows with religious and philosophical systems. However, what many people do not realize is that these systems, like plants or animals, can easily be *categorized*. The basis for the categorization is the response that each system gives to the question of the ultimate reality. And as we saw earlier, in the end there are really only three viable views of the ultimate reality. According to the naturalist, the ultimate reality is matter, or, in the jargon of modern physics, the "time-space-energy/matter continuum." According to the pantheist it is "Big Mind"—an impersonal divine Spirit. According to the theist it is God—an infinite personal Spirit. *Thus, in the end there are really only three basic worldviews*. And for a seeker overwhelmed with worldview options, that is good news, indeed!

Let me illustrate the great usefulness of this characteristic of worldviews. Suppose you are a college student. Over the course of your undergraduate education you are asked to read the writings of Thales, Democritus, Epicurus, Lucretius, T. Hobbes, D. Diderot, C. Darwin, T. and J. Huxley, L. Feuerbach, K. Marx, V. Lenin, J. Stalin, Mao Tse Tung, J. Dewey, S. Crane, J. London, B. Russell, S. Freud, J. P. Sartre, A. Camus, B. F. Skinner, I. Asimov, C. Sagan, S. Gould, and R. Dawkins. Along the way you learn that some of these men called themselves *atomists*, others called themselves *materialists*, and still others called themselves *dialectical materialists*, *communists*, *existentialists*, or *secular humanists*. Sound confusing? It's bound to—until you realize that all embraced the same basic worldview: naturalism.

Or again, suppose your studies bring you into contact with the teachings of Gotama, Lao Tzu, Heraclitus, Plotinus, B. Spinoza, C. Berkeley, G. Hegel, A. Schopenhauer, R. Emerson, H. Thoreau, W. Whitman, Sri Ramakrishna, Swami Vivekananda, J. Krishnamurti, A. Watts, H. Hess, J. D. Salinger, S. Peck, K. Wilber, D. Chopra, or G. Zukav. You then learn that some of these men called themselves *Hindus*, others called themselves *Buddhists*, and still others called themselves *metaphysical idealists*, *New Agers*, or *cosmic humanists*. And this too could look pretty intimidating—until you realized that all these thinkers embraced the same basic worldview: pantheism.

Or again, your education may introduce you to the thought of Abraham, Moses, Isaiah, Jesus, Paul, Augustine, Mohammed, Anselm, T. Aquinas, M. Luther, J. Calvin, B. Pascal, I. Kant, Voltaire, J. Rousseau, C. Wesley, B. Warfield, Baha'u'llah, F. Dostoyevsky, A. Solzynitsin, F. Schaeffer, and C. S. Lewis. Along this road you learn that some of these men called themselves *Jews*, others *Christians*, and still others *Muslims*, *Deists*, *B'hai*, etc. Yet despite all the apparent diversity, every one of them would gladly affirm that they embrace a theistic worldview.[6, 7]

Now it is true that down through the years a handful of philosophers and theologians have proposed still other views of the ultimate reality.[8] Such thinkers, however, constitute a very small minority. The conclusion, then, is that on the surface of things the R/P world does indeed look fairly messy. If, however, we take time to investigate beneath the surface we find a surprising and intriguing simplicity. *We find that there are really only three basic worldviews, each revolving around one of the three basic answers to the question about the ultimate reality.* Such knowledge is most helpful to a seeker, since it greatly reduces his worldview options, simplifies his search, and focuses his attention on the ultimate philosophical question: the nature of the ultimate reality.[9, 10]

The Internal Coherence of Worldviews

We turn now to still another sign of the manageable messiness of the R/P world, a sign that I have already touched on, but one that here merits special attention. I have in mind the fascinating philosophical fact that our assumptions concerning the nature of the ultimate reality will necessarily shape the answers that we give to the other questions of life. In other words, in any coherent worldview, the answers to the questions of life are *logically related* to the view of ultimate reality presupposed. Indeed, we may fairly say that a given understanding of the ultimate reality will *generate* a particular set of answers to all the other questions, and therefore determine the essential character of the resulting worldview.

To illustrate this important point, let us look again at naturalism.

For the modern philosophical naturalist, the ultimate reality is the time-space-energy-matter continuum. There is no god. Accordingly, the universe cannot have a "true" or "absolute" beginning. That is, it cannot have come into being out of nothing, for it is inconceivable that something should come from nothing. Therefore, on naturalistic premises, the universe *must* be eternal, as indeed most naturalists teach. Moreover, since there is

LIFE: A MESS OR A TEST?

no god or divine creator, we may be sure that there is no heaven or hell, no angels, no human or animal spirits, and no supernatural life force animating nature. Where would such spiritual realities come from, if not from a spiritual creator? Thus, the naturalist's view of the ultimate reality profoundly shapes his idea of the beginning.

Similarly, in the naturalistic universe we cannot say that anything "went wrong," since there is no god or creator to define what is normal or abnormal, natural or unnatural, right or wrong. In other words, for the naturalist "evil" does not really exist, and suffering and death are simply part of the way things are. Many things may be painful and unpleasant, but nothing is "wrong" or "went wrong."

And what of salvation? Well, on naturalistic premises it is certain that we cannot look to a non-existent god for help. Therefore, unless visitors from outer space arrive to assist us, we have but one hope: ourselves. That is, through the wise use of science and technology, we must become our own saviors. How far we can go in rolling back (what people call) evil, suffering, and death no one knows. It is, however, all but certain that whatever our gains, they will only be temporary since the Second Law of Thermodynamics assures us that our earth, sun, galaxy, and universe must finally return to dust. Yet even this is not too great a concern, for when our (spiritless) human body dies, the lights go out once and for all. We will never see anyone or anything again.

And what of the meaning of human life? Obviously, there is none, since a transcendent purpose in life can only be found in a transcendent purposer: namely, god. If, then, naturalistic man is to have a purpose, he must become his own god by heroically *creating* one for his own existence, as indeed certain existentialists have urged. Much the same is also true concerning the moral standards by which man is to live. Since there is no divine lawgiver, no absolute moral laws can exist. Therefore, for survival's sake, man must *create* his own set of standards by which the race can go along and get along until the bitter end.

More could be said, but I think my point is clear. Worldviews are *orderly* intellectual constructs. Like planets revolving around the sun, their answers to the questions of life revolve around their understanding of the ultimate reality. Indeed, as we have just seen, their understanding of the ultimate reality actually generates, or at least profoundly shapes, these answers. Again, this characteristic of worldviews is most helpful to seekers. It shows them that the R/P world is simple, reasonable, and orderly—and also that they are wise to think long and hard about the nature of the ultimate reality!

So then, is life a mess or a test? This is a question every seeker must answer for himself. For my part, I judge that the evidence for the test perspective is weighty. It includes the lesson of natural hunger and thirst, the telltale makeup of the human mind, and the surprisingly manageable messiness of the R/P world. Yes, at first glance this world looks pretty chaotic. But upon closer examination we find that it is rich with order

---

THE PROBATIONARY ORDER

I. A SPIRITUALLY EQUIPPED HUMAN BEING...

- A. Intuition
- B. Reason
- C. Language
- D. Community and communication
- E. Conscience
- F. Hope

II. CHALLENGED BY THE QUESTIONS OF LIFE...

- A. Innate questions
- B. Curiosity about the answers
- C. Existential urgency

III. IGNORANT OF THE ANSWERS...

- A. The answers are not within
- B. To find them we must look without

IV. SITUATED IN A MANAGEABLY MESSY RELIGIOUS AND PHILOSOPHICAL WORLD...

- A. The questions are few and easy to understand
- B. The possible answers are few and easy to understand
- C. The possible worldviews are *very* few and easy to understand

V. AND FREE TO SEEK THE TRUTH OR NOT!

Let the Test begin!

and design, so much so that it seems far more appropriate to call it a maze than a mess.

A maze, however, requires a maze-maker. It demands *a person with a purpose*, someone who is watching from without, or perhaps even waiting within. What I am suggesting, then, is that all the signs we have just discussed point to the existence and activity of a divine Person, an unknown god. He is the one who plants hunger and thirst for the truth in our hearts. He is the one who spiritually equips us to seek it out. He is the one who has ordered the R/P world in a manageably messy way. And if all this is so, one thing more becomes crystal clear: he has placed us all in a *probationary order*. In other words, the unknown god is putting us to a test: a test of our love of the truth.

Children, Stay Busy!

In order to understand the idea of a probationary order better, consider the following parable.

Suppose that one fine morning a group of third graders enters their classroom and takes their seats. As they sit down, each student notices on his desk a wooden puzzle frame, emptied of its contents. The empty frame has slots for nine wooden puzzle pieces. Beside each frame there is a small pile of about thirty pieces. As the students look around the room, they realize that the teacher is not there. Nevertheless, she has left a note on the board:

> Good morning, children.
> I'll be back in a few moments.
> Please stay busy at your desks until I return.

What will the children think? What will they do? What would *you* think and do? I ask these questions because the elements of this scenario correspond fairly closely to the human condition as seen through the test perspective.

Corresponding to the empty puzzle frame is our innate capacity for a worldview, our capacity for a coherent and beautiful picture of reality as a whole. There is, you might say, a worldview-sized frame on the desk of every human heart, just waiting to be filled.

Similarly, the nine slots in the wooden puzzle correspond to the nine questions of life. They represent nine empty holes in our understanding of reality. They are nine intellectual and spiritual voids waiting to be filled by a vision of truth, so that we can see and enjoy the big picture that we intuitively know to be there.

The thirty or so puzzle pieces stand for the possible answers to the questions of life, answers that "pile up on our desk" as we interact with a world full of naturalistic, pantheistic, and theistic options.

As for the situation in which the children find themselves, it too corresponds quite closely to ours. They do not know if the pile of thirty puzzle pieces contains the nine they need; similarly, we do not know whether a world full of conflicting answers contains the true answers we need. Also, the children do not know why there are more pieces than they need; similarly, we do not know why there are so many possible answers, some of which *may* be true, and some of which *must* be false.

There is, of course, one (important) point at which our analogy breaks down: the children know they have a teacher. Indeed, she has left them specific instructions on the board, even if they are a bit cryptic. It is, then, highly probable that they will quickly take counsel among themselves, size up the situation, and "stay busy" working on their puzzles. True, a few may not get the message—or want to get it—and will therefore take up activities more to their liking. Most, however, will work. They know the teacher is coming back soon, and they want to be ready when she does.

As I said, at this point our analogy breaks down, yet in a most illuminating way. For while the children all know they have a teacher who has arranged this interesting situation, many of us who have entered the classroom of life have never paused to consider whether or not a divine Teacher might have arranged it as a kind of test. This is, of course, the perspective—or shift in perspective—that I am very much trying to encourage here. For as soon as you experience this shift, you see immediately that a divine Teacher really does exist. You see that he really has put a puzzle on every desk, and pieces beside every puzzle. You see that he really has written instructions on the board, better even than those given to the children in our parable. And because of all this, you know exactly why you are here and what you are supposed to do.

In short, you are well on your way to discovering the meaning of life!

Blessings of the Test Perspective

The thought of our being on probation can be intimidating, for it is only natural to wonder what will happen if we fail the test. However, the same thought can be profoundly encouraging, since it means that while our life in this world may indeed be philosophically burdensome, it is definitely not absurd. Indeed, when viewed from within the test perspective, a previously messy life is suddenly revolutionized, charged with *meaning, adventure,* and *hope*.

The meaning of life—or at least its first and foremost meaning—is clearly to take the test successfully. It is to seek, find, obey, and enjoy the truth—the unknown god's truth—about reality as a whole.

The adventure of life is to overcome every obstacle standing in the way. And surely there will be some obstacles, since a test is not a test unless there are difficulties. On the other hand, surely those difficulties can be overcome, since a test is not a test unless it can be passed. Here, then, is yet another blessing of the test perspective: by encouraging seekers with the possibility of success, triumph, and ultimate reward, it lifts their lives out of the realm of the absurd and into the realm of adventure.

As for hope, it has now become manifold and rich. If we really are on probation, it means that we really *can* find true answers to the questions of life; that we really *can* find the one true worldview; that our spiritual hunger and thirst really *can* be satisfied, and our deepest fears and concerns laid to rest. Indeed, it may even be that we can meet the divine Tester at the heart of the maze, and there receive both commendation and reward for a test well taken and a job well done!

Yes, the test perspective can revolutionize our whole outlook on life in this world, turning a mad falcon into a loving friend. But are there any other reasons to believe that an unknown god really exists, and that he really is putting us to the test?

Happily, the falcon is still overhead. Let us follow her a little farther and see.

CHAPTER 2

HINTS OF A HEAVENLY HOPE: NATURE

ON THE FIRST leg of our journey we discovered that the human condition—religiously and philosophically considered—looks curiously organized, designed, and purposeful. It looks like a test. But if our life really is a test, there would have to be a divine tester—an "unknown god"—working in our hearts and our world, putting us on probation. To the spiritually hungry, such prospects bring great hope. If an unknown god is indeed putting us to a test, then surely he can enable us to pass it; surely he can reveal to us the answers to the questions of life, as well as satisfy the spiritual longings and anxieties associated with them. In short, for earnest seekers, the very real possibility that we live in a probationary order is a welcome *hint of a heavenly hope*.

These folks would like to know, however, if there are any other such hints, any other indications that there really is an unknown god who is testing our love of religious and philosophical truth. I believe there are; indeed, I believe there are a great many. However, at this stage of our journey it is best to focus on two in particular: nature and conscience. In the next chapter, we will deal with conscience. Here we will deal with nature, or what is often called "the natural order." As we are about to see, both of them are big topics, and fabulously rich with hints of a heavenly hope!

Spiritually Significant Characteristics of the Natural World

By *nature* I mean the universe, life, and man; or rather, the distinctly *physical* side of the universe, life, and man. In other words, my focus in the pages just ahead will be on what most folks call *the physical world* (but what pantheists call the *phenomenal* world). In examining this world, we will look at three of its most fundamental characteristics: dependency, order, and man-centeredness. As we are about to see, each one is chock full of spiritual significance; each one supplies us with *many* provocative hints of a heavenly hope.

Dependency

We begin our examination of nature with a look at one of its subtler characteristics: *dependency*. The idea here is that nature, in manifold ways, clearly *relies upon something beyond itself* in order to be what it is, something *spiritual*. It is quite impressive to see the many different ways in which this is so.

Existence

Consider first the most immediate characteristic of the natural world: its existence. When we scan the starry vault of heaven, or pause before majestic mountains, or delight in beautiful flowers and wild animals, it is only natural for us to wonder just how these things got here and why they continue to exist. If proof were needed for this, one need only to consider the case of little children who—sometimes to the chagrin of their parents—vocalize such wonder and ask such questions all the time. They do so, I would argue, simply because they are human, and because all humans, standing before the mighty edifice of nature, are innately aware that *the things of this world cannot explain their own existence*. Did the rose create itself? Did the robin call herself into being? No, the existence of such individual things self-evidently depends upon something beyond themselves. Furthermore, we know intuitively that the "something" cannot be nothing, for nothing cannot create or sustain anything. So then, the "something" must be a *super* something; that is, it must be something transcendent, something non-physical, something spiritual—something bigger, older, smarter, and more powerful than anything *in* the universe, or even than the universe as a whole. In short, the something must be a spiritual supreme being—the being who brought all lesser beings into being, and now upholds them in being. This being is the independent one upon whom all depends; the uncaused cause of a caused cosmos; the giver of the gift of existence to all that is. True, little children do not typically express their wonder in the kind of philosophical language I have just used. But poets and philosophers do. And I would argue that they do so precisely because they themselves are still children at heart, striving to articulate a hidden wisdom that is lodged deep within every person, whether young or old. The message of the hidden wisdom is simply this: A physical world that *is*, points to a spiritual supreme being who formerly *caused it to be,* and who even now *causes it to be here.*

Cohesiveness

Next, we have the cohesiveness of nature. Whether we think of a molecule or a galaxy, a pebble or a mountain peak, a butterfly or a human brain, all physical beings manifest this fascinating property: at least for a season, they cohere or hold together in a given form and at a given density. As a rule, this cohesiveness does not strike us as particularly noteworthy, but modern physics has told us that it should. Today we know that even the smallest physical objects contain enough compressed energy to blow whole cities sky high! But how could such explosive power have been tamed into existence as a humble, ongoing, physical thing? And how can it *continue* to exist as a cohesive physical thing? Certainly the object's underlying physical energy does not perform this two-fold miracle. What, then, does?

The mystery of cohesiveness becomes even more intriguing when we focus our attention on living beings. According to the Second Law of Thermodynamics, the natural tendency of *all* things is to dissipate energy and therefore decay, or lose physical integrity. Living beings supply a real time illustration of this fundamental truth. When an animal dies, its tissues quickly turn into formless dust. In other words, at the moment of its death a hidden principle of cohesion departs, a principle that *grew* the body and *held it together* in its unique form all throughout the course of its life. But what is this principle? Well, whatever it is, it is not material in nature, since according to the Second Law of Thermodynamics matter left to itself only decays. It must, then, be spiritual. Moreover, this spiritual principle must be both powerful and intelligent, since it lays hold of lifeless matter, organizes it, and animates it, thus enabling the living being to swim upstream against the current of the Second Law until the day of its death. Could it be, then, that living beings cohere and endure because they are held in the hand of a living god?

Motion

Spiritual dependency is also exhibited in the motions of things. Pretty much everywhere we look, things are moving. In fact, even things that appear to be stationary are really moving, if only at microscopic levels. But *why* do they move? Intuitively, one feels that they should be at rest; that rest is the natural state or condition of things. Indeed, the Second Law of Thermodynamics declares that this is exactly where all things are headed:

towards absolute rest; the perfect stillness of the grave, brought on by a gradual loss of all kinetic energy. Thus, motion and the Second Law of Thermodynamics raise some important philosophical questions: How did moving things get moving in the first place? And what keeps them moving? Again, the cause cannot be the things themselves. But if that is so, then only one alternative remains: Something—or someone—must have *set them in motion*, and must also be *keeping them in motion*. So again—this time before the mysterious phenomenon of motion—we encounter a powerful, omnipresent supreme being; a being whom Aristotle glimpsed when he referred to the unknown god as "The Unmoved Mover."

In passing, it is well worth noting that certain peculiarities of cosmic motion point rather dramatically to a Prime Mover. For example, according to the modern nebular hypothesis, our solar system was "created" when gravity acted upon a swirling cloud of gas and dust so as to produce the sun, its several planets, and their 72 moons. Astronomers know, however, that this popular view is beset with grave difficulties. For example, on this premise all the planets should spin in the same direction: in fact, three rotate backwards. All the moons should orbit their planets in the same direction: in fact, eight or more orbit backwards—and Jupiter, Saturn, Uranus, and Neptune all have moons orbiting in both directions! Moreover, all the moons should orbit in their planet's equatorial plane: in fact, many are in inclined orbits. Such anomalies are significant. Not only do they frustrate the nebular hypothesis, but they also unveil a divine creator who reminds of us his presence, power, and sovereign discretion through the things—and the motions of the things—that he has made.[1]

Life

More than any other kind of being, living beings exhibit spiritual dependency. What is it that causes a living being to grow, cohere, move, eat, reproduce, work, play, etc.? What is it that keeps its heart pumping blood, its lungs drawing air, or its brain organizing the raw data of sensation into meaningful perceptions of the world? The reply of the naturalist is: chemically generated energy. But this view frustrates common sense. Yes, most of us are prepared to admit that organic life *involves* chemicals and energy in special arrangements and activities. But few of us will admit that this is *all* it involves. When, for example, we observe our pet cat stalking a bird, or arching its back beneath our outstretched hand, or circling our feet at dinnertime, we do not naturally ascribe the motions of her body to firing synapses and twitching muscles. No, we ascribe them to a *metaphysical* principle animating the cat, whether it be her soul or something beyond

… HINTS OF A HEAVENLY HOPE: NATURE 29

her soul. This is the intuitive view of life—that it "rides" on chemistry, and takes hold of chemistry, but that it cannot be reduced to chemistry alone. Life, then, is a distinctly spiritual principle or power. When it is present, it turns lifeless matter into a living being. When it departs, it turns a living being into dead matter. In short, living beings depend upon life, life is spiritual, and life therefore points to a living god.

To sum up, we have glimpsed through the dependency of the natural world the hand of an eternal, powerful, and living god; a god who brought the universe into being, keeps it in being, holds it together, sets and keeps its various physical objects in motion, and sets and keeps its living beings in life. Thus, dependency in nature is a very big hint of a heavenly hope.

Order

Once, during the early years of my search for spiritual truth, I thought I saw the face of god himself. The vision occurred on a pier in Santa Cruz, California. Walking along, browsing the merchandise in different stalls, I came to a store that featured seashells. Shrewdly enough, the owner had put the sorted shells into open bins, so that his customers could pick them up and inspect them. On this particular day, I did so with an unusual sense of wonder and awe. As if for the first time, I saw the variety, intricacy, and beauty of the shell's design—not only of their shapes, but also of the various patterns of color printed upon them. Though these shells reposed silently in my hand, the delicately wrought cones, cowries, murex', whelks, nautilus', clams, conches, and scallops all seemed to be shouting aloud: "We have a creator and he is here!" As a young pantheist, I felt as though I were looking him in the eyes.

My experience that day serves well to introduce the second fundamental characteristic of nature: order. A short definition of this philosophically rich idea will reveal why order is of outstanding spiritual significance. We meet order, says Mr. Webster, when we encounter *differing objects integrated into a system according to a definite plan*. This excellent definition highlights the main elements of any order. First, there is *multiplicity*—a finite number of different parts or objects. Second, there is *unity*—a perceivable oneness, integrity, or systematic quality that characterizes the multiplicity. Thirdly, there is *arrangement*, the element that creates the unity. Note carefully, however, that any old arrangement will not do. For order to exist, the arrangement must be according to a definite plan. In other words, it must display the fourth element of any order: *design, or rationality*.

This last is, of course, the spiritually significant aspect of an order. When we come upon a multiplicity of objects arranged in an intricate and beautiful design, we immediately experience an inescapable awareness that an intelligent person with a purpose—a designer—has been on the scene. *Order* implies and reveals *design*; design implies and reveals a designer, *a person with a purpose*. They are a little trinity, so that you cannot have the first without the other two. And when we look at a crystal, a conch, a cricket, a cuckoo, a crocodile, or a chemist, we know immediately and undeniably that the Person who purposefully created them was not human, but divine.

Order in nature is, then, a fingerprint of the divine. But to understand and appreciate this quality more deeply, we must consider several different characteristics of order as it appears in the natural world. As we are about to see, each one lifts up its voice in a unique way to proclaim the existence and attributes of the unknown god.

Pervasive

First, we find that order is pervasive. It is present in the tiniest building blocks of nature—the atomic elements—which are composed of orderly arrangements of protons, neutrons, and electrons.[2] It is also present in the largest objects in nature: those vast cosmic pinwheels and clouds that we call galaxies and galactic clusters, all of which are composed of orderly arrangements of stars. And it is present in all the objects in between. Great or small, organic or inorganic, all the things that we call things are, in fact, *systems*, orderly arrangements of component parts. Furthermore, these little systems are always part of bigger systems; and the bigger of bigger still, until at last we reach the biggest system of all, the cosmos itself. Order pervades the parts, and order pervades the sum of the parts, or the whole. Could such all-pervasive order have arisen by accident?

Manifold

Secondly, order in nature is manifold. That is, it appears in many different forms. For example, we find order in the *structure* of things, the unique way in which the component parts of a given system are related to one another. Think, for example, of the structure of a spiral galaxy, or of a snowflake, or of the many different kinds of crystals (e.g., isometric, tetragonal, hexagonal, etc.).

Similarly, we find order in the *form* of things: the regular shapes, colors, and symmetries that nature brings to our eyes, helping us effortlessly to distinguish a crow from a crawdad, or a dog from a dove. Just to see them is to wonder in whose fecund intellect nature's myriad structures and forms were conceived.[3, 4]

We also observe order in the *motions* of things. The sun, the moon, the planets, the comets, the stars and galaxies—all are set in orderly courses; all obey mysterious, mathematically describable natural laws. Objects upon the earth obey such laws as well, responding in scientifically predictable ways to being hit, hurled, dropped, drawn, spun, repelled, or otherwise moved along. Surely it cannot be without spiritual significance that such laws operate regularly in the physical universe. Do they not point to a rational lawgiver, one who has imposed a fixed, scientifically discoverable order upon the motions of things?

Also, we find order in the *behaviors* of living things. Across many species we repeatedly observe the same basic activities: breathing, drinking, foraging, eating, growing, playing, mating, sheltering, storing, migrating, etc. Can anyone reasonably doubt that other kinds of natural law are at work here, distinctly biological laws that constrain the movements and activities of all living beings? But who laid down these laws, who invented these behavioral patterns? And what, if anything, do they all mean?

As ecologists well know, nature's orderliness also appears in the *relationships that exist between things*. Plants and trees depend upon the sun and the soil. Mice, rabbits, and grasshoppers depend upon the plants and the trees. Foxes and falcons depend on the mice and the rabbits. Bacteria and fungi depend on the waste of foxes and falcons, and also upon the flesh of their dead bodies. Soil depends upon the nutrients that the bacteria and fungi produce from these. And so the complex cycle continues. Moreover, living beings are also symbiotically related to each other for purposes of reproduction, shelter, protection from predators, mobility, guidance, work, enjoyment, and more. And what is true of the earth's ecosystems is true of the cosmos as a whole: it too is an arrangement, a vast network of inter-related and inter-dependent beings. Did this massive skein of inter-dependency really arise by accident, or was it at the hand of a wise, powerful, and omnipresent Person with a purpose?

Complex

Thirdly, order in nature can be quite complex. Not infrequently we see this with the naked eye, especially among living beings. A peacock feather, an asparagus fern, the whorls, ribs, and spires of a crown conch— all inspire us to wonder over the incorporation of such intricate detail into such simple beauty. And what shall we say of the veritable worlds of complexity dwelling within our very bodies: our eyes, ears, and brains? When Darwin thought about them, he trembled.

But even this is not all. For now, with the advent of modern biological research at the cellular and molecular level, our wonder has been elevated to a state of awe. Indeed, I think it quite safe to say that for all practical purposes this new research has *proven* the existence of a superhuman intelligence at work in the cosmos. Of course, most scientists will not admit this publicly, but they all know it is true. Consider, for example, the following excerpts from a newspaper interview with an anonymous American molecular biologist (J), whose work with human DNA is designed to identify genetic controls for diseases:

J: I'm a bit like an editor, trying to find a spelling mistake inside a document larger than four complete sets of Encyclopedia Britannica.

G: Do you believe that the information (accidentally) evolved?

J: George, nobody I know in my profession believes it evolved. It was engineered by "genius beyond genius," and such information could not have been written any other way. The paper and ink do not write the book! Knowing what we know, it is ridiculous to think otherwise.

G: Have you ever stated that in a public lecture or in any public writings?

J: No, I say it just evolved. To be a molecular biologist requires one to hold on to two insanities at all times. One, it would be insane to believe in evolution when you can see the truth for yourself. Two, it would be insane to say you don't believe in evolution. All government work, research grants, papers, big college lectures—everything would stop. I'd be out of a job, or relegated to the outer fringes where I couldn't earn a decent living.

G: I hate to say it, but that sounds intellectually dishonest.

J: The work I do in genetic research is honorable. We will find the cures to many of mankind's worst diseases. But in the meantime, we have to live with the elephant in the living room.

G: What elephant?

J: Creation design. It's like an elephant in the living room. It moves around, takes up an enormous amount of space, loudly trumpets, bumps into us, knocks things over, eats a ton of hay, and smells like an elephant. And yet (in order to work and earn a living) we have to swear it isn't there! [5]

Intelligible

Order in nature is also marked by intelligibility. This characteristic is especially important, since it helps us to understand *why* nature is orderly. As we have already seen, the forms, motions, causes, and probabilities of things and events are ordered. Because they are, scientists can understand them. The geologist can describe and categorize crystals in terms of geometric shapes. The biologist can describe and categorize animals, birds, fish, reptiles, and insects in terms of common forms and behaviors. The astronomer can categorize the various kinds of heavenly bodies, and describe their motions, usually in terms of formulas derived from conic sections. The statistician can describe the likelihood of certain events by means of the laws of probability. In short, nature is intelligible because its forms and motions carry the imprint of certain ideal patterns or principles, usually mathematical.

But where exactly do these ideal patterns and principles exist? Yes, they exist in the minds of the scientists who discover them. But surely they existed *before* science discovered them, for nature bore their imprint long before the scientists ever looked upon her face with understanding. The conclusion, then, is that the patterns and principles governing nature exist pre-eminently in the mind of god, who first uses them to shape and control nature, and then reveals them to the minds of men as they study his world.[6]

But *why* does the unknown god want these patterns and principles to be understood? Part of the answer obviously involves their utility: they can help us humans master nature and thereby enrich our lives. But the other part of the answer—and the part that most intrigues me—is even more arresting: nature is intelligible *because the unknown god likes to show—and show off—his intelligence to other minds like his own!* Interestingly, this was precisely the conviction of astronomer Johannes Kepler, who said that God had purposely equipped us with mind and intellect, so that we might "think God's thought after him." Through the intricate and beautiful forms, motions, behaviors, and relationships of things, this god would excite the spirits of his human creatures to the contemplation of the most exciting thing he knows: himself! Moreover, he would do so in hopes of moving them to yet another kind of contemplation: the contemplation of the questions of life. For surely the intelligibility of nature hints at the intelligibility of religious and philosophical truth. And if religious and philosophical truth is intelligible, then surely, with god's help, it too can be found.[7]

Beautiful

Finally, order in nature is characterized by beauty. This is what stopped me in my tracks as I gazed, with wonder and delight, at the seashells on the pier at Santa Cruz. But what exactly is natural beauty? Perhaps the best way to reach an understanding of this mysterious phenomenon is to examine what our *experience* of beauty involves. When we do, we see first of all that beauty involves a measure of order—and often a very high degree of order—in the object observed. Muse, for example, upon a Golden Rectangle, the proportions of which (1x1.62) so delighted the Greek's sensibility that their architects used it in the design of temples. Ponder the form, flight, and iridescent feathers of a hummingbird. Consider the manifold geometry of the interior of a chambered nautilus. Contemplate a 3-D model of a strand of DNA. Why do we find all these little universes so beautiful? It is because their component parts are so harmoniously organized, and because they are organized according to an *idea* or *rational plan* so brilliant that it excites in us both pleasure and admiration.

Here, then, we meet two further components of our experience of natural beauty: *pleasure* in an orderly creation, and *admiration* for the one who created it. But where do such aesthetic feelings come from? Surely not from mere molecules banging around in our brain! No, the pleasure we feel must have a non-physical, or spiritual origin. What's more, a little reflection suggests that in the end this can be none other than *the creator's own pleasure* in his own genius and his own handiwork, graciously breathed into our hearts as we look upon the wonders of his world! The same principle applies with respect to our feelings of admiration: this is nothing less than the creator's admiration of himself—and an invitation to us that we should admire him as well. In short, it would appear that the purpose of beauty in nature is to woo us to the worship of nature's god.[8]

But what of ugliness in nature? Does not this unwelcome interloper refute a spiritual interpretation of beauty? No, it does not, for intuitively we know that ugliness in nature is simply a departure from the beautiful norm. A sand dollar is ugly (though never altogether ugly) because it is not normal—because it has been chipped or defaced by wind and sea. A rose is ugly because its once normal leaves are now wilted, diseased, or torn away. The stereotypical witch is simply a beautiful woman whose nose is abnormally crooked, whose chin is abnormally long, and whose back is abnormally hunched—all because her heart is abnormally wicked. Yes, natural ugliness is problematic, for we cannot understand why deformity has stricken our otherwise beautiful world. But the mere presence of deformity does not cancel the spiritual significance of beauty. For again, we know intuitively that the beautiful form is the normal form; that these forms exist as patterns and ideals in the mind of a beautiful god; and that one day—god willing—the ideal and the real shall become one.

Down through the years, seekers have probably regarded the orderliness of nature as her single loudest hint of a heavenly hope. It is easy to see why. Order so pervasive, so manifold, so complex, so pleasing and so admirable inclines the human heart not only to acknowledge a supreme being, but also to worship him for his infinite intelligence, artistry, and beauty.

Man-Centeredness

We come now to our third and final characteristic of nature, it's man-centeredness. Here I have in mind the striking adaptation of the vast majority of natural things to the sustenance of life, especially human life. Indeed, the more we reflect upon the intricacies of the cosmos, the more we are brought irresistibly to the conclusion that the vast system of nature exists for one fundamental purpose: the physical and spiritual nurture of living beings, and especially of the human race.

There are, of course, many today who resist this conclusion, but the evidence favors it nonetheless. In fact, modern science has uncovered hundreds of phenomena indicating that the earth, the solar system, and the universe itself have all been *fine-tuned* to support life on our planet. We now know, for example, that life could not exist if the sun were a different color, or a different mass, or a little closer to the earth, or a little farther from it. The same is true of the moon: if it were only 50,000 miles nearer, ocean tides would engulf nearly all the earth's land mass twice a day; if slightly farther, life in our stagnant seas would die. Similarly, if the earth's gravity, magnetic field, crustal thickness, oxygen/nitrogen ratios, and water vapor and ozone layers were only slightly different, all life would perish. Which is more reasonable: to say that this manifold fine-tuning arose by mere chance or by the hand of a divine Fine Tuner?[9]

Think also of the abundance of nature's *provision*. Why, for example, are the sun, moon, and stars not only beautiful, but also useful for marking time, guiding ships, moving tides, growing fields and forests, lighting days, warming bodies, and so much more? Why so many fruits, grains, nuts, meats, and vegetables, all so nourishing to the flesh and so pleasing to the palate? Why so many trees for shelter, so many plants for fabric or medicine, so many metals for structures, so much gas and petroleum for fuel or plastic? Why the fantastically serviceable gifts of electricity, radio waves, or nuclear energy? Why so many insects, birds, fish, and animals to enrich us with the fruits of their labor, not to mention the pleasure of their company? This list could go on, with each new item displaying yet again the benevolence of an unknown god who is concerned not only for the sustenance, but also for the happiness of man.

It is, of course, all too true that nature sometimes displays an evil countenance; that it can sometimes turn against man so as to wound and destroy him through flood, famine, pestilence, storm, earthquake, and more. Here again we confront the troubling reality of "natural evil," a mysterious principle that disrupts and injures the wholeness of the physical realm. Obviously, its presence in a god-sustained world requires an explanation. Indeed, we have already seen that this is one of the "ultimate questions" that perennially resound in the human heart.

Later on we will consider this problem at some length. Here, however, it suffices to point out once again that the presence of natural evil in the world is not incompatible with the existence or goodness of an unknown god. In part, we see this from the fact that nature's beneficence towards man is certainly the rule rather than the exception. We also see it in the fact that our innate expectation from nature is of good, not evil. Rarely, if ever, do we hear folks saying, "What went right? Why is there so much goodness, joy, and life in the world?" No, it is only evil that surprises and offends. In other words, it is human nature to view nature as a friend. Friendliness, however, is not a quality that inheres in lifeless matter but in living persons. Is there, then, an unseen Person—a friend to humanity— working through nature, speaking through nature, telling us that he is there, that he cares, and that evil will not have the last word?

Summing up once again, we have found that science confirms what common sense readily believes: nature is anthropocentric, the universe is tailor-made for man. But if it is tailor-made for man, there must be a divine Tailor. Interestingly, not a few modern scientists are ready to affirm this very thing. Dr. Robert Jastrow, for example, states that, "The anthropic principle is the most theistic result ever to come out of science."[10] Why? Because the anthropic principle gives us a glimpse of a wise, powerful, and benevolent creator; a creator who designed the cosmos with the welfare and joy of his human children in mind; a creator who thereby signals to us that he is here and that his human children do well confidently to seek him out.[11]

Conclusion

The natural order brings a message of hope to all seekers. Its three main characteristics—dependency, order, and man-centeredness—enable us clearly to discern the existence and activity of a spiritual supreme being. Though at this stage of our journey we must still call him the "unknown god," we have found that nature actually tells us quite a bit about him: that he is wise, powerful, and good. Here, then, is hope. For if he is wise, powerful, and good enough to sustain the whole natural order, surely he is wise, powerful, and good enough to sustain a probationary order as well. And if indeed he has created a probationary order—if he really is putting us to the test—then surely he is wise, powerful, and good enough to enable us to pass it.

Conscience: a subjective faculty that is attuned to an objective reality existing beyond itself.

CHAPTER 3

HINTS OF A HEAVENLY HOPE: CONSCIENCE

IN OUR JOURNEY towards the meaning of life, we have come upon two impressive hints of a heavenly hope: the probationary order and the natural order. Now we are about to meet a third. The one who will introduce it is a friend to some, an enemy to others, and a familiar companion to us all. I am speaking of the specifically moral dimension of human thought and feeling that we call *conscience*.

What exactly is conscience? For many folks, the word conjures images of the famous Disney character, Jiminy Cricket, therefore eliciting thoughts of an invisible ethical umpire perched upon our spiritual shoulder, evaluating all we do (or plan to do) in thought, word, and deed. I would agree with this notion, but I would also argue that in order to understand conscience most fully, we must see it as something *more* than a subjective faculty. Rather, we must see it as *a subjective faculty that is attuned to an objective reality existing beyond itself*. In the paragraphs ahead I will refer to that reality as *the objective moral order* (OMO). Unlike the natural order, the OMO is spiritual rather than physical, invisible rather than visible. Nevertheless, as we are about to see, it is just as big, just as complex, and just as real as the material universe itself!

In order to introduce the idea of the OMO, let me relate another experience from the early years of my search for spiritual truth.

Back in the mid-sixties, during my freshman and sophomore years at college, various kinds of hallucinogenic drugs were readily available on campus. I myself was frequently tempted to try one in particular, a new consciousness-expanding drug called LSD. I was a philosophy major. I was beginning to think about god. And I was intrigued by the fact that some of my friends had said they experienced god through taking LSD; that they had seen, first hand, "the truth" that all is one, all is mind, all is god.

39

For the first time in American history, pantheism was taking deep root in American soil. LSD led the way.

But all was not well. For as intrigued as I was with this new wave of pantheistic mysticism, something deep inside warned me against taking the drug. In part, I was afraid of having a bad trip and damaging my brain. In part, I was skeptical that a genuine religious experience could be chemically induced. But beyond this, there was still another concern: somehow, taking LSD didn't seem to be *right*. To take it, I felt, would be to violate some invisible rule of religious and philosophical fair play; to take an illegal short cut in the race to truth.

More than anything else, it was this—the testimony of my conscience—that finally moved me to go to my philosophy professor and ask him what he thought about my taking LSD. He was, I should add, a very intimidating figure, and I was deathly afraid even to knock on his office door. But I did so, anyway. Why? Because I feared the *consequences* of doing the wrong thing, and also because I wanted to enjoy the *benefits* of doing the right thing. And if my professor could help me distinguish the one from the other, well, surely that was worth a moment or two of abject terror. Thankfully, it turned out he was quite welcoming, and also quite clear on the matter: he thought it was wrong to take LSD, and spent considerable time with me explaining why. I am happy to report that despite repeated opportunities to do so in the years ahead, I followed his counsel. If only I had dealt with other college temptations as successfully as I did this one!

Now in this ethical vignette we see something important: a young man enmeshed in the OMO and trying to align himself with it properly. This is, of course, something we all do every day of our lives. But do we all acknowledge the objective existence of this order? Do we understand its several elements? Do we appreciate their spiritual significance? Because these matters relate directly to our search for hints of a heavenly hope, we must take a moment to examine them more closely.

Elements of the Objective Moral Order

Let us begin our journey into the realm of conscience by considering the three main elements of the OMO: moral law, moral obligation, and (the law of) moral cause and effect.

Moral Law

The first and central element of the OMO is *moral law*. By this I mean a universally recognized set of transcendent moral standards for all human

HINTS OF A HEAVENLY HOPE: CONSCIENCE

attitude, thought, word, and deed. Essentially, this law is prescriptive. That is, it prescribes for us the ethical ideal. It tells us positively what we should be, think, feel, and do. But in setting forth the positive, it also implicitly condemns the negative. Going back to my collegiate quandary, I felt I *should* seek spiritual truth through study and reflection, but *should not* seek it by taking LSD. Similarly, we all know we should be kind, not cruel; generous, not selfish; courageous, not cowardly; honest, not deceitful. We feel we should obey our parents, respect our elders, be faithful to our mates, remain loyal to our friends, etc. Precepts like these are embedded in human hearts everywhere, enshrined in sacred writings everywhere, and (usually) honored by people everywhere. None of us practices them perfectly. A few of us defy them openly. But all of us know they are there, and all of us know they are right.

Moral Obligation

This brings us to the second element of the OMO, *moral obligation*. Upon close inspection, we find that this is not simply a feeling, but *an objective fact that bestirs a feeling*. Think again of my struggle over LSD. For some reason, I felt that I ought not to take it. My feeling—what might be called the voice of conscience—told me that it was an objective fact that I *ought not* to take LSD; that I *ought not* to jeopardize my mind or my brain; that I *ought* to seek truth through the proper channels of study and reflection. This is no different from the feeling that I ought to arrive at work on time, or be faithful to my wife, or pay all my taxes. Such moral intuitions teach us that when our conscience perceives a moral law, it also perceives a moral obligation to obey that law. When we do obey, we enjoy the feeling of being in right relationship with the OMO. On the other hand, when we break a moral law, our conscience immediately registers the wrong, and then communicates to our heart a fresh moral obligation to make things right, to try to heal the breach and thereby be reconciled to the OMO once again.[1]

Importantly, this sense of moral obligation is the hidden impulse behind the formation and maintenance of all levels of government. First and foremost, moral obligation tells me that I ought to govern myself, try to keep the moral law, and make suitable amends when I fall short of its demands. It also moves me to do my part in governing the world around me. If I am a father, for example, I know I ought to teach my son the importance of honesty and diligence; I ought to praise him when he practices those virtues; I ought to correct, encourage, and discipline him when he does not. I have similar obligations towards my wife, friends, and colleagues—and they to me. Such mutual accountability is the *sine qua non* of any successful relationship. And what is true in the personal realm is true in the civic also: I must do what I can to uphold the moral standards that make for a wholesome community life. In short, moral obligation moves us to administer the moral law at all levels: in our own life, in our personal relationships, and in our community, nation, and world.

Law of Moral Cause and Effect

The third element of the OMO is itself a further law, *the law of moral cause and effect*. This law, intuitively known by all, states that every good action is necessarily and justly associated with a reward, while every evil action is necessarily and justly associated with retribution. My awareness of this law was one of the reasons I went to see my philosophy professor: I wanted to know the right thing to do because I felt a certain danger in doing the wrong, and a certain confidence about the benefit of doing the right. Here, then, is a most interesting characteristic of conscience: it faithfully issues both promise and warning. From this we learn that conscience, like Jiminy Cricket of old, is definitely "on our side"—that it does not want us to run afoul of the law of moral cause and effect, but rather wants us to remain safely (and happily) within the proper boundaries of the OMO.

Just as we all know that a law of moral cause and effect exists, so too we all know that it *ought* to be implemented. Here again we meet the spirit of moral obligation. It is not enough for us simply to declare the moral law. No, it is clear that we must also apply and even enforce the moral law by a wise system of praise and reproof, reward and punishment. This is primarily in the interest of simple justice, but also in the interest of encouraging future good and deterring future evil. Every parent, teacher, and judge understands—or should understand—this mandate. The family of man, as presently constituted, simply cannot function or endure without a system for the administration and enforcement of the moral law at all levels of society.

It is true, of course, that every human system for the administration of justice is flawed, since human beings themselves are flawed. But even if a given system fails—even if it is forced into the service of evil itself—we know intuitively that the law of moral cause and effect will never fail. We know that a higher law is *always* at work in the universe, ensuring that justice will be done, whether in this life or the next. This truth, acknowledged by world religion and common sense alike, is proverbial. No one gets away with murder. You play, you pay. What goes around, comes around. Whatsoever a man sows, that also shall he reap.

Here, then, are the main elements of the objective moral order within which our conscience operates, and from which it (and we) cannot escape: 1) a moral law consisting of universally binding standards, the sum of which constitutes the ethical ideal for all men; 2) a sense of moral obligation to hold ourselves and others accountable to this law; and 3) a further law of moral cause and effect, by which obedience to the moral law should and will be rewarded, and by which disobedience to that law should and will be punished.[2]

The Objectivity of the Moral Order

With all this as background, we come now to the crucial question: how exactly does the OMO supply a hint of a heavenly hope? The answer, I would suggest, is tucked away in the mystery of its objectivity. When we say that something exists *objectively*, we mean that it exists not just "in our heads," but also "out there," and "in reality." In other words, it exists on it's own, independently of our minds.

To get a feel for this important distinction, imagine that you are looking at a beautiful sunset. Now unless you are a pantheist, you naturally assume that the sunset is really there, and that it would still be there even if you closed your eyes, got knocked out, or dropped dead. You readily admit that through the mysterious operation of your senses your mind is somehow *attuned* to the sunset; but you are not at all likely to admit that your mind has *created* the sunset. Here, then, is the intuitive, common sense way of looking, not just at sunsets, but at the whole natural world: we believe that the world is really there even when we're not perceiving it. We readily grant that we may indeed become conscious of the world, but not that the world is a creation of our consciousness—or even of the unknown god's.[3]

Such, I would argue, is the case with the OMO. True, its elements are not physical, so that we cannot perceive them through our five senses. But that does not mean that they are not objectively real; that they are not really "out there." No, it simply means that they are "out there" in a non-physical way—a spiritual way; and it means that our minds interact with them through a non-physical sense different from our other five senses. Note carefully that this is precisely our attitude towards the moral realm. No matter what we may *say* about moral absolutes or the origin of conscience, as a matter of fact we all assume that some things *really* are good, that other things *really* are evil, that we *really* ought to cleave to the good and shun the evil, and that just rewards and punishments *really* should and do follow the choices we make. In other words, in real life we interact with the OMO just as we do with the natural order. We do not view it as a creation of our consciousness, but as an objective reality with which our distinctly moral consciousness (i.e., our conscience) often and necessarily interacts.

Consider still another illustration. Suppose that your worst "friend" dares you to walk the ridge of Farmer Jones' barn. Not wanting to appear the coward, you accept the challenge. However, just as you are starting to climb the ladder, you hear a still small voice within, warning you that no amount of "guts" is going to cancel the physical law of gravity or the dire consequences of a fall. Listening to this voice, you realize immediately that you are free to walk the roof if you wish, but wise if you don't.

Now segue from the physical realm to the moral. This time suppose you are a married man stuck in an unhappy marriage, and that your cute secretary is now showing definite signs of romantic interest. In other words, you are being tempted to challenge the moral law against adultery. Before you do, however, you hear another kind of voice whispering within, warning that no amount of passion (or cover-up) is going to cancel the law against adultery or the disastrous consequences of breaking it. Listening to this voice, you realize that you are free to challenge the law concerning adultery, but that it would probably be wiser to walk the ridge of Farmer Jones' barn.

In this humble illustration we see not only the objectivity of the moral order, but also its spiritual significance. If the several elements of the moral order really do exist "out there," that fact obviously raises the question as to where "out there" really is. And there is, of course, really only one answer that immediately, intuitively, and reasonably commends itself to us: "out there" is *in god*. The moral order exists in god, and he in us, in such a way that he makes known to us his moral laws, our moral obligations, and the certainty of moral cause and effect—all so that we might freely obey him and enjoy his blessing. In short, the objective existence of the moral order is rooted in the objective existence of god.

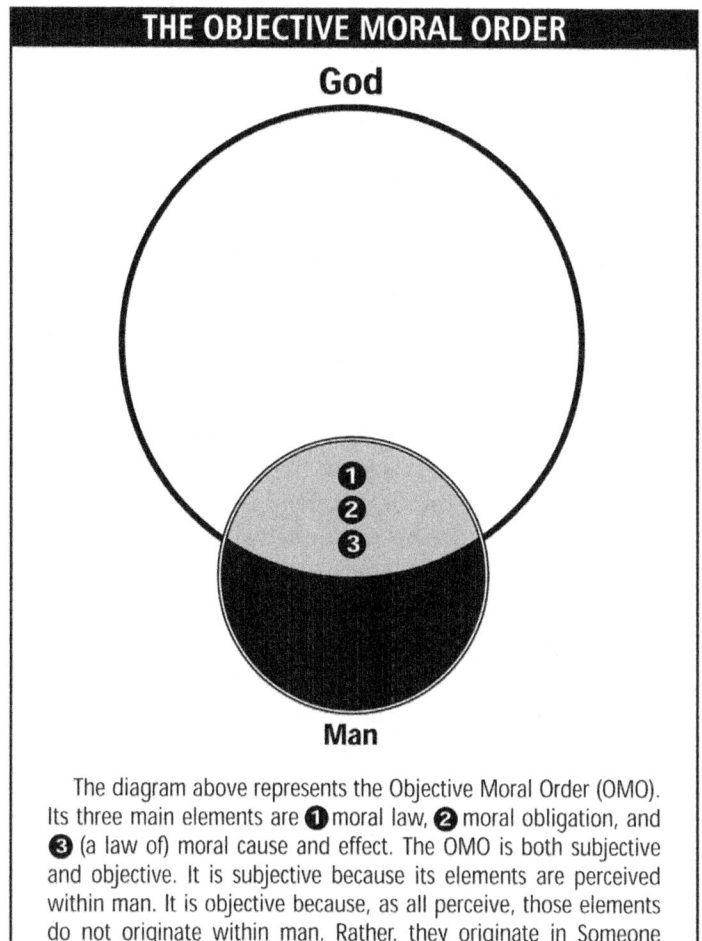

> **THE OBJECTIVE MORAL ORDER**
>
> **God**
>
> ❶
> ❷
> ❸
>
> **Man**
>
> The diagram above represents the Objective Moral Order (OMO). Its three main elements are ❶ moral law, ❷ moral obligation, and ❸ (a law of) moral cause and effect. The OMO is both subjective and objective. It is subjective because its elements are perceived within man. It is objective because, as all perceive, those elements do not originate within man. Rather, they originate in Someone who is over man, and ever speaking to man, so as to bring man into perfect, life-giving conformity with His moral law. In short, conscience bears witness to an objective reality beyond itself; to an Unknown God who creates and sustains the OMO so that all might live well, and therefore in close communion with Him.

The Postmodern Challenge

In a moment we will discuss the implications of these ideas for seekers. Here, however, it is important to pause and acknowledge a well-known fact of contemporary life: naturalistic and postmodern philosophers definitely do not look kindly upon the idea of an OMO. Indeed, they energetically deny that such an order even exists.

For the naturalist, this conclusion flows logically from his basic philosophical premise: there is no god. Now if his premise is correct, then clearly there is no one to create and administer an OMO. Hence, for the naturalist, what men call morality must simply be a species of biological impulse, somehow "designed" by the evolutionary process for the physical preservation of the race.[4] What alternative does an atheist have?

Similarly, postmodernists (who are nearly always naturalists masquerading as skeptics) argue that a single, universally binding moral order *cannot* exist because different moral orders, embedded in different cultures, *do* exist. They point out, for example, that in some cultures polygamy is a badge of honor, while in others monogamy is the sacred norm. Similarly, in some cultures vengeance and retaliation are the duties of true men, while in others non-violence and turning the other cheek are sure signs of the wisdom from above. Who, then, is to say which way is right? Indeed, who is to say there *is* a right? Postmodernist Paul Feyeraband takes this line of reasoning to its logical (and dangerous) conclusion when he sates, "To those who look at the rich material provided by history...it will become clear that there is only one principle that can be defended under all circumstances and in all stages of human development. It is the principle: *anything goes*."[5]

Undeniably, the arguments of Feyeraband and his postmodern colleagues seem persuasive; hence the reticence of so many Americans to affirm the existence of moral absolutes. But just here we would do well to remember once again the bitter fruits of Kahn's folly, and therefore to pause for a closer look beneath the surface of things. Moreover, as soon as we do, we begin to see immediately that, despite appearances, there are actually a great many signs pointing in an altogether different direction; signs pointing clearly and powerfully to the objective existence of the moral order, and the objective existence of a god who supports it. Let us survey a few of them now.

Signs of an Objective Moral Order

The first sign is our innate personal knowledge. By this I mean an inescapable inward awareness that the OMO does indeed exist, As one writer put it, there are certain things we "cannot not know"—and I would argue that the several elements of the OMO are definitely among them.[6]

A homespun parable will illustrate my point here. Suppose that a postmodern philosopher goes to the college business office and asks for his paycheck. To his amazement, the secretary tells him that the school administration has decided to donate his wages to The Society for Transcendentalism in Ethics. Would the professor say, "Well, stealing and breaking contracts are not right for me; but if they're right for you, then I guess it's OK for you to keep my check." Not likely. Rather, he will say that this is wrong, and that the administration had better right the wrong immediately by giving him his wages. Moreover, if he cannot persuade his employers of the righteousness of his cause, he will quite likely seek out a lawyer or a judge to *force* the righteousness of his cause upon them. Thus, at his podium our philosophy professor may deny the OMO, but in the rough and tumble of everyday life he knows it exists and acts accordingly.

Secondly, we have *the judicial sentiment.* The judicial sentiment may be defined as our innate tendency to judge and pass sentence upon ourselves and others (alas, it almost never happens in that order). I have in my files a cartoon that illustrates this tendency perfectly. The scene is hell. Amidst the flames, an elevator door stands open. Written over the door are the words, "New Arrivals." Coming through the door, with terror in their eyes, are the souls of Odai and Qusai Hussein, the depraved sons of Saddam Hussein. Two devils, with pitchforks at the ready, are welcoming them. One says to the other, "Well, whaddaya know, they've found a couple of weapons of mass destruction after all!"

This cartoon perfectly manifests the judicial sentiment. Furthermore, it shows that the judicial sentiment perfectly manifests our innate knowledge of the OMO. The cartoonist understands that these two wicked men egregiously broke the objective moral law. He also understands that they deserve to be punished, and that since punishment was not meted out in this life, it certainly will be in the next. We see, then, that the judicial sentiment—so deeply rooted in the human psyche—is spawned and guided by the OMO. Therefore, it stands as further testimony to the fact that the OMO really exists.[7]

Thirdly, we have the sign of *basic cross-cultural agreement.* The idea here is quite simple: though some differences do indeed exist, most people around the world agree on the contents of the moral law, our obligation to obey it, and the necessary connection between our actions and their moral consequences. Consider, for example, William Bennett's masterpiece, *The Book of Virtues.* This anthology extols the values—and the benefits—of self-discipline, compassion, responsibility, friendship, hard work, courage, perseverance, honesty, loyalty, and faith. But the stories illustrating these virtues come from all over the world: Europe, Africa, India, Asia, and the Middle East. Moreover, they have spoken powerfully to readers all over the world. It certainly appears, then, that the spiritual antennae of all peoples are picking up the same signals, presumably because those signals emanate from the same objectively real moral transmitter.

Fourthly, there is the richly significant phenomenon of *altruism and self-sacrifice*. Think, for example, of the religious order established by Mother Theresa, comprised of single women devoted exclusively to the care of the poorest of the poor. Or think of the villagers of Le Chambon Sur Ligne, who, at great risk to their own families, faithfully sheltered and evacuated over 5000 Jews during the Nazi Occupation of France. Now on naturalistic premises, actions like these are inexplicable, since they run contrary to what is allegedly the bedrock motive of the human organism: survival. Most of us would agree, however, that the will to survive, though powerful, can be trumped by something even more powerful: *a will to do the right thing*. In other words, altruism and self-sacrifice reveal that the human conscience is (or can be) attuned to something higher and more vital than biological life itself. That something is the OMO, a transcendent spiritual reality that can exist only in a transcendent spiritual being. So here again we glimpse the hand of the unknown god. And in passing, we do well to observe from the noblest monuments of human courage and sacrifice that this god is apparently not above sorely testing his human children. He wants to see if they will faithfully do the right thing, even at the risk of their own necks.

Finally, we have the evidence of *the urge to make amends*. This urge lies behind a whole class of behaviors manifesting a person's desire to be reconciled to the OMO after having broken one or more of its laws. Think, for example, of a murderer who, after many years in hiding, finally turns himself in to the police and confesses his crime. Think of the "conscience fund" at the IRS, filled with money anonymously sent in by guilt-ridden tax evaders. Think of Lord Jim, the sea captain in Joseph Conrad's famous novel, who spent his whole life trying to recover the integrity he lost by abandoning his passenger-laden ship during a violent storm on the high seas. Think of people who apologize, send gifts, offer animal sacrifices, or recite penitential prayers. Not only do these examples show that the OMO exists, but they also show that fallible mankind is often painfully burdened by its lofty demands and its dire warnings. Only the unknown god knows how much human energy and activity is devoted to our reconciling ourselves to this order once again.

The Problem of Cross-cultural Differences

But, asks the postmodernist, what about all the cross-cultural differences? Doesn't the fact that people can't agree on the exact contents of the moral law show that there is no such law at all? Well, as a matter of fact, it does not. Why? Because, as we have just seen, there are many lines of good evidence that positively prevent us from reaching such a conclusion. It appears, then, that an objective moral law does indeed exist, *but that for some reason mankind's subjective apprehension of the law has been weakened*. On this view, the world's various cultures are indeed aiming their consciences at the same moral law, rather like the world's various astronomers who are aiming their telescopes at the same stars. But just as one astronomer may see certain stars more clearly, so one culture may see certain laws more clearly. Or again, just as some astronomers may have a clearer picture of the heavens as a whole, so too may some cultures (at least at certain times in their history) have a better understanding of the moral law as a whole. Doubtless no culture sees it perfectly, but neither is any culture in total darkness.

Now among the myriad modern celebrants of diversity, this line of reasoning will no doubt seem presumptuous and arrogant. And given the lamentable human tendency to pride, it certainly could be. But is it *necessarily* so? Please think carefully before you answer. If you answer yes, you have immediately endorsed the philosophy that *anything goes*. You have disqualified yourself from all moral argumentation, from all fighting for the values that you hold dear, and from all striving to create a better world through reasoned moral discourse. For whether we wish to admit it or not, all moral struggle proceeds on the twin assumptions that absolute values exist, and that *we ourselves perceive those values more clearly than our opponents*. Again, this may seem arrogant, and can be. But it is precisely this kind of spiritual confidence that eventually produces any widespread shift in moral perspective, thereby enabling a culture finally to prevail against such institutionalized evils as polygamy, widow burning, child prostitution, female circumcision, the caste system, abortion, infanticide, slavery, ethnic cleansing, apartheid, and more.

But if all this is so, the question remains as to *why* our conscience has been weakened. Unfortunately, the answer here is not self-evident to the unaided human mind. It is clear enough from history and experience that conscience becomes increasingly darkened as people increasingly give themselves over to evil. But to know exactly how the fatal flaw entered the race lies beyond the reach of the naked intellect. If the unknown god really does exist, perhaps he has already told us, or perhaps someday he will. But whether or not we know that answer, we can still know that the OMO is real. Yes, some moral confusion exists. Yes, some personal and cultural differences in morality exist. Yes, the human conscience can be deceived, burdened, diseased, and manipulated—even by religious men and religious cultures. But if mankind's shared moral consciousness means anything, it means that we cannot explain these phenomena by saying that a world in *some* moral confusion is really a world in *complete* moral chaos. Our innate knowledge of the reality of the OMO simply will not permit it.

The Seeker and the Objective Moral Order

Let us conclude this leg of our journey by considering some of the ways in which the OMO should be of great interest to a seeker.

To begin with, the OMO reveals that there really is an unknown god. As we have seen, without him, absolute moral laws could not exist or be known. Without him, moral obligation could not exist or be known. Without him, moral cause and effect could not exist or be known. Self-evidently, the elements of the OMO are transcendent and spiritual. Just as self-evidently, they must exist in the mind of a transcendent spiritual being. You cannot have one without the other. Thus, the innate and undeniable knowledge of the OMO constitutes an innate and undeniable proof for the existence of god.

Next, the OMO tells us (more about) what this god is like and how he relates to man. For example, it tells us that he is good. It tells us that he is omniscient and omnipresent. It tells us that he acts in us, and that we live in him. It tells us that he is the moral governor of men and nations, a holy and sovereign lawgiver and judge. It tells us that he is a respecter of our choices, and a rewarder of all who choose well. It also tells us that there must be an afterlife, a future time and place where the unknown god will administer all the justice that he did not administer in the present life.

Finally, the OMO shows us yet again that the unknown god is a god of order. Just as he created and now sustains the natural order, so too he created and now sustains the moral order. Though the one is physical and the other spiritual, both are big, complex, powerful, beautiful, and compellingly real. Therefore, in contemplating these orders, seekers will naturally find themselves concluding that, in all likelihood, he has created a probationary order as well.

For all these reasons, then, conscience provides a very big hint of a heavenly hope.

At the Crossroads

We began our journey by considering a fresh perspective on the meaning of life. Probing various aspects of the human condition, we found that life, religiously and philosophically considered, looks more like a test than a mess—and that if we genuinely believe it to be so, our own lives can be richly filled with new meaning, adventure, and hope.

HINTS OF A HEAVENLY HOPE: CONSCIENCE

Eager to see if there was further evidence for the test perspective, we devoted a second stage of our journey to examining two more hints of a heavenly hope: nature and conscience. Looking at nature, we observed its dependency, order, and man-centeredness. In these characteristics we saw the presence and activity of a god of power, wisdom, artistry, and goodness. Looking at conscience, we discovered an objective moral order comprised of moral law, moral obligation, and a further law of moral cause and effect. In these we saw the presence and activity of a god of rulership, holiness, and justice. Moreover, in both realms we saw a god who certainly seems to enjoy creating orders! Here, then, is further encouragement for the seeker—further evidence that the god of the natural and moral orders has created a probationary order as well.[8]

Now in view of all this, it seems only fitting to pause here and ask: How does the falcon look to you now? Is she a foe or is she a friend? In other words, having journeyed thus far, do you still see life as a mess (if ever you did), or do you now see it as a test, or at least as possibly being a test?

Needless to say, I am hoping for the latter. And if the latter, I am hoping you are as enthused about it as I am. Why? Because now a new and profoundly promising road has appeared before you, beckoning you to set out upon it. It will, however, undoubtedly be a difficult road, for again, a test is not a test without some difficulty. Therefore, at this stage of the journey you have actually reached a crossroads, and at this crossroads three important decisions now face you.

First, you must *decide whether or not to seek*. This decision comes with the territory. In other words, once you believe that life is (or may well be) a test, there really is no escaping a decision as to whether or not you are going try to pass it. It may seem unnecessary to stress this point, but experience proves otherwise. Many people know—or at least strongly suspect—that a supreme being exists, that his truth is available to them, and that they should seek both him and it. Yet for various reasons they elect to keep him at arms length, dismiss or delay the search, and remain safely (if indeed it is safe) in the camp of the agnostic. Hopefully, you are not among them. Hopefully, after resting awhile here at the crossroads, you will elect to set out again. Hopefully, you already feel that you could not possibly do otherwise. For if you do feel that way, it means that something rare and wonderful has happened: It means a seeker after god has been born, and that a great and glorious journey is about to begin.

Next, you must *decide to gear up*. This decision also follows from your newfound faith in the test perspective. For if you truly believe that life is a test, then you also believe that your spiritual and intellectual faculties are not mere accidents of nature, but rather divinely supplied equipment for the journey ahead. More specifically, you see that the unknown god has given you *intuition, reason, conscience,* and *an inclination to hope for the best*. You see that these are precious tools, and that the tools, if welcomed and properly used, will doubtless ensure good success in your journey. Therefore, you also see that it only makes sense eagerly to take them up, strap them on, and get ready to put them to work.

Finally, you must *decide to set out in search of "god's appointed Teacher."* Once again, this decision flows naturally and logically from the test perspective. For if you know that an unknown god is testing you concerning your love of the truth—and that he has richly equipped you to find it—then you also know that his truth must be "out there" somewhere. In other words, you know that the unknown god *must have appointed some kind of Teacher through whom he is pleased to reveal his truth to all who seek.* For the moment you do not know who or what that Teacher is: an individual person, a group of persons, an institution, an intellectual discipline, a holy book, a mystical experience, whatever. You do know, however, that if life really is a test, then some such Teacher must exist. This means, then, that the next practical step in your test is to begin seeking him out, and to trust that the unknown god will indeed help you to find him.

So, the way ahead is now clear, and the falcon is urging us on. Shall we follow?

ONE MAN'S JOURNEY:
A SEEKER IS BORN

God did this so that men might seek Him,
in hopes that they would reach out for Him and find Him,
though He is not far from each one of us,
for in Him we live and move and have our being.
—Acts 17:27

IF I HAD to assign it a time and a place, I would say my test began on a cold winter evening of 1968, in a suburb of Paris, at the top of the Metro stairwell. That night, for the first time in my life, the world began to look strange.

Prior to that, my spiritual life was relatively uneventful. My brother and I had been raised in a nominally Christian home in Northern California. In our tender years, we periodically attended Sunday School at a nearby Presbyterian Church. There I came into contact with the fundamentals of the Christian faith, sowing my youthful imagination with memorable pictures of Adam and Eve, David and Goliath, Daniel in the lion's den, and Jesus with the little children. Occasionally, nearly always in seasons of duress, I would venture a brief prayer to God. Also, from time to time my brother and I would engage in lively discussions with the children of our devout Catholic neighbors. They would assure us that we Protestants were going to hell, or that the end of the world was at hand. Then, after a few moments of vigorous debate in which much heat was substituted for little light, we would all go out to play.

The problem, however, was that all this religious dabbling was done in a corner, leaving me with the distinct impression that in "real life" spiritual matters were relatively unimportant. My otherwise devoted parents did not pray with us, teach us from the Bible, or discuss ultimate questions. Nor did our other relatives. Nor did our public school teachers. Nor did the surrounding culture, mediated to us by books, magazines (e.g., *National Geographic*), and television (e.g., Walt Disney). So far as I could tell, nearly every authority figure in the world presupposed the truth of cosmic evolution, viewed the Bible as a book of useful myths, and regarded God (if he existed at all) as a practical irrelevancy. Having, then, been raised in an atmosphere of practical atheism, I graduated from high school and set out for college as a practical atheist.

And in 1965, millions like me were doing the same.

Playing at Philosophy

Spiritually speaking, my first two years at the University of California at Santa Cruz (UCSC) were only slightly more eventful. Though the motives behind it were badly mixed, my early decision to become a philosophy major did indeed reflect a measure of genuine enthusiasm for grappling with the big issues of life. Also, in retrospect I see that my philosophical bent, though faint, was usually towards more spiritually minded thinkers: Parmenides, Heraclitus, Plato, Anselm, Aquinas, Spinoza, Leibniz, Berkeley, Schopenhauer, and others. Atheistic philosophers, with one or two notable exceptions, left me cold.

But again, such pinpricks of light were only tiny marks on a large and otherwise darkened canvas. Truth to tell, my real attraction was not nearly so much to philosophy as it was to my first philosophy professor. In every way—in beard, brow, attire, demeanor, gait, vocabulary, sense of humor, and perennial cigar—he fascinated me. Under his spell, I had but one desire: to be like him. Omniscient like him, authoritative like him, funny like him, and impressive like him. I also hoped one day to have a prestigious job like him. In short, throughout my first two years in college I was a philosophy major, but not a philosopher. I had little or no love of wisdom, only of being thought wise.

I indulged this two-year charade amidst the rise of the counterculture, a movement that in time would affect me powerfully. It originated on campuses like my own, which enthusiastically played host to a wide variety of popular new ideologies: Neo-Darwinism, Marxism, Freudianism, Jungianism, existentialism, and various expressions of Eastern mysticism. Overshadowed by their growing presence, the old paradigm upon which our nation had been built—an easy-going partnership between sober biblical theism and optimistic Enlightenment rationalism—seemed ready to pass away.

It was during my freshman year that I first became aware of pantheistic mysticism. I heard about it from some of my fellow students who were experimenting with a powerful new drug called LSD. Claiming to have had religious experiences while high on this drug, they were now asserting that everything is one, everything is mind, everything is god. Pilgrims to the Haight-Ashbury district of San Francisco—then much in the news—were doing and saying the same. So were the Beatles, who soon would introduce us to their guru, Maharishi Mahesh Yogi, and to the mysteries of Transcendental Meditation. And then there were the pariah's of Harvard—Timothy Leary and Richard Alpert (alias Ram Das)—who, as prophets of the modern revival of pantheism, were urging students to "tune in, turn on, and drop out." Suddenly it seemed that young people everywhere were pursuing an abiding experience of god-consciousness, and also envisioning a whole new social order built upon it.

As the pantheistic chorus grew louder, I became more and more curious. In particular, I was strongly tempted to try the readily available LSD. However, for reasons discussed earlier, I finally decided against doing so and focused instead on my philosophizing. Still, all the talk of god and personal religious experience had quietly deposited a seed of spiritual hunger in the lowermost regions of my soul. In due season it would grow, rise, and powerfully burst into the light of day.

A Womb of Solitude

I spent the majority of my junior year in Paris. My friend, Mike, and I arrived in the summer of 1967, but Mike soon became seriously ill and had to return home. All summer long I lived by myself in a boarding house in Vincennes. For some reason I did not have the inner resources to venture out, explore the city, and take in the sights. Instead, the core of my day-to-day existence became a long trip on the Metro to the American Express office, where I hoped to find a letter from my girlfriend waiting for me. I did make a few acquaintances at a nearby youth hostel, but in the end found the linguistic and cultural barriers too high to create any soul-sustaining friendships. Nor did it help that at that time we Americans were largely *persona non grata*, despised for our current adventure in Vietnam, which, according to many, was darkly motivated by capitalist and imperialist greed. To court friendship with the French was to risk vilification and rejection. Better, then, to withdraw: into my room, into my books, into myself. I was lonelier than I had ever been.

This voluntary solitude was indeed painful, yet today I regard it as the pain of spiritual birth. During those difficult three months, something good was slowly forming inside me. Living by myself and within myself, I began to discover the thrill of *being* myself. I began to realize, for example, that I was drawn to certain kinds of authors, repelled by others, and curious to understand my reactions to both. I began to take honest stock of what I really knew (which turned out to be very little) and what I didn't know (which turned out to be just about everything). Yet I also felt that in all probability I could find out the truth about life as well as anyone else, if only I would carefully think matters through for myself. At this time I also began writing: poems, stories, letters, and essays. I even wrote a short story about my philosophy professor. Alas, he committed suicide. But when I had thus brought his (fictional) tale to an end, I was free at last from his spell: I could see him as a mere mortal, groping for the meaning of life, just like me.

School started in September, and for the next six months I studied French language, history, literature, and philosophy at the Institut Catholique. The discipline did me good, supplying goals to reach and work to do. Since the program was designed for foreigners, I was also able to make some English-speaking friends. There was even a romance with a bright and free-spirited American girl, one that in time would confront me yet again with the dismaying depths of my own spiritual poverty. But for the moment, things were going better. I was not so lonely and not so depressed. More than that, it appeared that something was awakening in my heart. I was actually getting interested in philosophy, and even feeling tiny wisps of confidence that I might be able to discover some enduring truth upon which to build my life.

It was right around this time that the world began to look strange. As a rule it happened at night, after my long ride home from school on the train. Emerging from the glare of the Metro into the palely lit streets of Vincennes, I now found myself repeatedly brought to a wondering halt. For there, silhouetted against the blackened sky—silent and enfolded in winter mists—stood a host of *things* (sky, trees, lamps, stores, cars, etc.), and also that mysterious fullness of things that we call *the world*. The strangeness was not in the way these things looked, but rather in the simple fact that they were there at all. The natural state of affairs, it suddenly seemed to me, was that there should be nothing. Yet here—spread out before my wondering gaze—was something, and something most impressive! How did it all get here? Who or what was keeping it here? Why was it here? Yes, the sheer existence of the universe was now speaking to me, but only in a whisper, only in a language that I could not yet understand. I remembered the dictum of Martin Heidegger, who said that true metaphysical inquiry begins when, with genuine philosophical concern, we ask the question,

"Why should there be something rather than nothing?" At last I was starting to realize what he meant.

With questions like these occupying my thoughts, I turned to the philosopher who seemed best able to address them: the existentialist Jean-Paul Sartre. Earlier at UCSC, I had read Sartre's *Nausea*, a novel in which he described experiences rather like my own. So now, looking for further insight, I opened up his 800-page magnum opus, *Being and Nothingness*. I decided to read it from cover to cover, every morning before school, for at least half an hour, in a French café—with my girlfriend sitting beside me reading her Simone de Beauvoir. I don't know whether the angels laughed or cried.

As hard as I tried to understand what he said, the journey with Sartre left me hungry and frustrated. Today, with the benefit of hindsight, I can see why. Something deep inside me was looking for the spiritual, the mystical. Sartre, on the other hand, was actually giving me brute atheism, and unintelligible atheism at that. But because his atheism sounded spiritual and mystical, I eagerly read on.

As the months passed, I again grew homesick. With rare exceptions, I found that I did not like the French or things French. My studies seemed irrelevant to my true interests. I was lonely in my boarding house. And in more ways than one, I was again failing morally. Against this gloomy backdrop, the friends, family, and familiarity of California seemed to beckon. At last I reached a decision: I would leave Paris early, return to Santa Cruz, and resume my studies for the third quarter of my junior year.

However, before I left I made some heartfelt resolutions. I would exercise every day. I would continue reading *Being and Nothingness*. I would abstain from sexual intimacy. I would spend quality time in solitude. I would keep up my writing. In short, I would do all I thought necessary to maintain the philosophical spirit and to discover philosophical truth.

Did I keep these resolutions? If only I could say I did. But in a way, even that did not matter. For during those nine lonely months in Paris, a new life had been conceived and a new philosopher born. He was not an especially intelligent one, still less a moral one. But for all that, he was a real one. And with his birth, the test of life would now begin.

Out of the Womb, into the World

When I returned to California in the spring of 1968, the nation was in a tumult. The shadow of Vietnam lay heavily upon all things. Campus protests had grown in size, number, and stridency. Ever-increasingly, young Americans were lifting up their voices against the "establishment," decrying its traditional faith, its capitalist economy, and its current self-understanding as the bulwark of freedom and democracy in a world menaced by godless Communism. Some of these voices spoke up in the name of Marx and outward political revolution. Others called us to mysticism and inward spiritual revolution. But all railed against the detested status quo. All agreed that now was the time for a true radicalism; for getting down to the very root of things, and for building a whole new world order upon what we found waiting for us there.

By and large, I remained aloof to all of this, electing instead to focus on my studies in philosophy. Moreover, I did so with considerable anxiety. I had slightly more than a year until graduation; slightly more than a year to discover some hard truth, fashion a viable personal philosophy, and settle upon a career. In short, I had to get a life, and I had to get one quickly.

But it was not to be. Indeed, as the months slipped by, it seemed that I was progressing backwards. One by one, my resolutions fell by the wayside. Yet again I succumbed to various moral failures. Worst of all, I became increasingly disillusioned with philosophy. By now I had given up on Sartre, over whose indecipherable words I clearly discerned a pall of metaphysical gloom. On the rebound from his existential mysticism, I turned to the later writings of Ludwig Wittgenstein, a linguistic anti-philosopher who did not even try to solve the questions of life, but instead attempted to *dissolve* them—to expose them as mental *cul de sacs* into which we naively drive ourselves by the misuse of language. Yet in time I fled this labyrinth as well, for there too I saw no hope of discovering any real answers to the real questions that really burned in my heart.

Finally, in a gesture of near intellectual despair, I decided to write a senior thesis defending philosophical relativism and determinism. My goal was to show that individual philosophies are never expressions of (unattainable) objective truth, but rather mere ideological reflections of the historical situation in which they arose. However, as the sheer pain of working on my thesis abundantly revealed, this flirtation with Marxism and postmodern skepticism was simply one more exercise in futility. Happily, I was soon able to see it, and honest enough to admit it. So I abandoned the thesis, and along with that any hopes of arriving at a personal philosophy before graduation day. I would have to take the senior exam, not telling my professors what I myself thought about the questions of life, but rather what other men thought, and what I now thought about what they thought. I did so with a bitter and unsparing anger, directed largely against Sartre. I also did so wondering right out loud whether modern philosophy might not make better headway in its vocation if it gave a little more thought to god. I aced the test.

ONE MAN'S JOURNEY: A SEEKER IS BORN

On graduation day I was all smiles but sick at heart. I had worked my way through the system, earned a bachelor's degree, graduated with honors, and seemed destined to go on to post-graduate study in law, education, or more philosophy. I had completed the charade, and in the eyes of the world was now on the road to success. But my heart kept reminding me of the terrible truth: four years and thousands of dollars later, I was graduating without a single conviction concerning a single higher-order question of life. In reality, I was a total philosophical failure. So now just one question remained: would I keep up the charade or would I *admit* that I was a philosophical failure and try to do something about it? As I exited the gates of UCSC once and for all, the terms of the test were becoming crystal clear.

A Seeker is Born

After my graduation, I remained in Santa Cruz. I took a job in a pizza parlor, and lived with my boss and his wife. I liked it. The rhythm of work, recreation, rest, and reflection seemed solid, even fulfilling. We made an excellent pizza, and it was a pleasure to see people enjoy it amidst music, family, and friends.

I knew, however, that this could not be my life's work. I had to decide upon a direction, a career, a vehicle of service to others. As I mulled my options, the counterculture continued to blossom. A fragrance of things eastern and mystical increasingly filled the air. Communes were springing up around the country. So too were natural food stores and New Age bookshops. Hindu gurus and Buddhist priests were arriving from distant shores. Multitudes of young people were having religious experiences and finding new meaning for their lives. Once again these things caught my eye. Little did I know that still another birth was about to occur.

It came one evening in the fall of 1969, at the home of my boss. Somehow we found ourselves watching a documentary about abstract artist Peter Max, one of the heroes of the counterculture. His colorful posters had become an advertisement for the "new consciousness" that many believed was the true hope and ultimate destiny of mankind.

Max himself had first experienced this consciousness while using psychedelic drugs, especially LSD. But he used them no more. Now, according to the documentary, he had set aside drugs in favor of a better way, a way that would produce a permanent expansion of consciousness. It was the way of yoga (Sanskrit for "union"), a mix of ancient physical and spiritual practices designed to lead the soul into a deep and abiding awareness of its own divine nature.

Max himself explained it all to us as we watched him interacting with his guru, Swami Satchidananda. Satchidananda had just established an Ashram (meditation center) here in the United States. The long-haired, bearded guru—dressed in a flowing white robe and walking barefoot in the sand—reminded me of the pictures of Jesus I had seen as a child. When he spoke, he seemed to exude an aura of peace, childlike enthusiasm, and confident authority. Undeniably, he looked like a man who knew god. Max, who followed him like a puppy, certainly thought so. As we watched, I found it hard not to envy the young painter. Not only had he found a faith and a direction for his life, but also a trustworthy teacher to help him along the way.

Did it happen gradually or instantaneously? I do not quite remember. I do know, however, that this documentary precipitated a fundamental change in my own perspective. Suddenly the disparate spiritual experiences of my life congealed into a single meaning. My childhood musings about God and the Bible, my enthusiasm for spiritually minded philosophers, my curiosity about LSD, my strange experiences in Paris, my inscrutable hunger for something more than this world (or philosophy) could satisfy—all these, like the pieces of a broken mirror, somehow arose, assembled themselves, and became a looking-glass. To my amazement, when I looked into that glass I saw not only myself, but also someone else standing behind me. He had been there—and been at work—all along.

In seeing him, the practical atheist died once for all. And there, in the place of that death, a seeker after god was born.

PART 2

IN SEARCH OF THE TEACHER

CHAPTER 4

IN SEARCH OF THE TEACHER

THE CLASSIC FILM *Fiddler on the Roof* contains a humorous vignette that is much to our purpose as we embark upon part two of our journey to the meaning of life.

The movie opens with the camera feasting on scenes from daily life in the little Russian Jewish village of Anatevya. Soon it rests upon the town's aged rabbi, who, like a mother duck with her ducklings, is ambling through the streets, surrounded by a cloud of eager and talkative students from the *yeshiva* (i.e., the village religious school). Suddenly, one of the students cries out, "Rabbi, is there a blessing for the Czar?" Thoughtfully, the rabbi stops, strokes his beard, raises a bony finger to the sky, and answers, "A blessing for the Czar? Why yes, there is. 'May the Lord bless the Czar. And may the Lord keep the Czar—far from us.'"

The scene is archetypal, capturing as it does the age-old relationship between teacher and student, wise and callow, full and hungry. More than this, it depicts certain fundamental truths about the human condition that we have already encountered on our journey to life's meaning: we all have a heart full of questions; we know we don't know the answers; and we know there is a god who does. Accordingly, at least some folks would very much like to find a Teacher sent by god who can reveal them to us, if indeed such a Teacher exists.

I myself have been among them. As I will relate in more detail later, during the first four years of my search for spiritual reality I attached myself to many different spiritual teachers: a Tibetan Buddhist lama, a Hindu guru, a Zen roshi, and, indirectly, a host of other religious leaders who had written books for the likes of me. As all this spiritual flitting about clearly indicates, I had some trouble finding a person with whom I could settle down. Nevertheless, one thing never changed: the impulse to have a teacher.

I knew I needed spiritual answers, I knew I needed spiritual experience, and I knew I could generate neither by myself. Therefore, I felt that I *must* keep on seeking until I found that certain, trustworthy spiritual someone who could show me the way.

Attuned to a Teacher

Having given myself to it so many times, I believe I understand the impulse to seek a spiritual teacher fairly well. It now seems to me that there at least three reasons why people go in search of one: because they *need to*, because they are *inclined to*, and because they are *meant to*. Let me briefly explain.

First, we *need* to seek a teacher because, as we saw earlier, all of us have existentially urgent questions burning in our hearts, and because the answers to those questions are not innate: they do not lie within us. Therefore, the stubborn fact that we cannot teach ourselves spiritual truth clearly requires us to look *outside of ourselves* for someone who can.

Beyond this, we are positively *inclined* to seek a teacher. That is, we all have a built-in tendency to search for a trustworthy spiritual authority. Little children, for example, instinctively turn to their father and mother for answers to the questions of life. Later, some of them will turn to priests, pastors, rabbis, gurus, lamas, roshis, or imams. If they were not raised in a particular faith, they may seek spiritual guidance from a respected professor, or from the writings of popular philosophers and religious leaders. It appears, then, from both history and personal experience, that mankind is indeed "attuned to a teacher." But this begs the question: if we really are attuned to finding a teacher, *who did the tuning, and why?*

This brings us to our final point, namely, that we are *meant* to seek a teacher. Such a conclusion flows logically both from our need of a teacher and from our inclination to find one, for it is impossible that these twin (spiritual) facts of life are mere accidents of nature. Rather, they must be purposeful. Indeed, they must be part of a distinctly *divine* plan, the work of an unknown god who both requires and beckons us to seek out a teacher. Note carefully, however, that any old teacher will not do. Rather, we are clearly meant to find one very special teacher: *the Teacher that god himself has appointed to reveal to all mankind the coveted answers to the questions of life.* Hereafter, let us call this special repository of divine revelation "god's appointed Teacher," or simply "the Teacher."

Observe how all that we have discussed so far fits in perfectly with the test perspective. As we have seen, this perspective declares that the unknown god is testing his human creatures concerning their love of spiritual truth.

But exactly how are they supposed to find it? The need of a teacher, along with the inclination to find one, show us how: *we are meant to find his truth by seeking out his appointed Teacher.* Moreover, because there will doubtless be some difficulty in finding this Teacher, our search for him turns out to be an essential ingredient of the test. Therefore, sustained by a strong desire for trustworthy answers to the questions of life, the earnest seeker will, if necessary, patiently sift through entire truckloads of false teachers until—god willing—he finds the true. Only thus shall he pass the test of life; only thus shall he justly receive its exceedingly great reward.

Now let us assume for the moment what is likely the case, that the unknown god has *already* sent or situated his chosen Teacher into the world. On this premise, the question immediately arises: who (or what) is this Teacher, and how can we find him?

Our purpose in the present chapter is to address these two crucial questions. But before embarking on what I take to be the most fruitful road to our destination, let us look briefly at two dead ends that have tempted many a seeking soul, yet have consistently proven to disappoint.

Two Dead Ends

In our search for further hints of a heavenly hope, we discovered that the unknown god reveals himself through nature and conscience, and that in these two arenas we can learn quite a bit about his character. It is important to understand, however, that neither nature nor conscience can be construed as god's appointed Teacher. Why? Because neither can do what the Teacher is supposed to do: reveal to us the *whole* truth about *all* the questions of life, thereby enabling us to possess and enjoy the one true worldview. In other words, *relative to our actually passing the test of life,* the natural order, the moral order, and even the richly meaningful probationary order are all dead ends.

Nor are they the *only* dead ends. Indeed, there are two more in particular that we must now examine with special care, since they have distracted so many eager seekers from far more fruitful paths, thereby devouring too much of their precious time and energy. I refer to two of this world's most popular spiritual *cul de sacs:* natural science and philosophy.

Natural Science

In our modern era of technological accomplishment, it is tempting for seekers to think that natural science is god's appointed Teacher. After all, if scientists can heal bodies, design computers, or send men to the moon, surely they can figure out the answers to the questions of life.

Or can they? Well, as a matter of fact, they cannot, as a little careful reflection will soon make clear. This is because natural science, by definition, confines itself to the study of nature, the *physical* side of reality. Its interest lies in discovering all that may be known about the *material* world: sun, moon, and stars; animal, mineral, and vegetable; earth, air, fire, and water; electron, proton, and neutron. Furthermore, the tools it uses—empirical observation, quantitative measurement, and the development of experimentally verifiable hypotheses about the laws that govern the behavior of such objects—are appropriate only for the study of presently observable physical things.

The questions of life, on the other hand, have to do with things that are *not* observable: things that are past, things that are future, and (if they really do exist) things that are *spiritual*. To better understand this point, consider the following questions. Can scientists devise a test by which to determine the ultimate nature of the so-called physical world: whether it is, in fact, matter or mind? Can they actually observe the origin of the universe, or experimentally create a universe so as to be able to make truly scientific statements about how ours began? Can they tell us with certainty how evil, suffering, and death entered the world? Can they tell us if, when, and how these things will be eradicated? With what kind of instrument shall scientists discover the meaning of life, or the moral laws by which we all should live? What kind of scope will allow them to scope out the afterlife, or to behold the end of the cosmos? And so on.

In all these questions, we see quite clearly that life's "ultimate issues" lie completely beyond the focus, tools, calling, and competency of natural science. And because this is so, it is evident that the proper posture of the natural scientist towards the questions of life must be one of deference and humility. He must say, "Such matters are beyond what we, *as scientists*, can study and know. If you desire certainty about them, you must look to disciplines other than ours."

Happily, many scientists do indeed adopt this very posture. Seekers should realize, however, that others do not. Instead, they illegitimately take to themselves the mantle of god's appointed Teacher and presume to make dogmatic pronouncements about religious and philosophical questions. They assert, for example, that the space-time-energy/matter continuum is all that exists; that the physical universe, in one form or another, is eternal; that cosmic evolution is a scientifically established fact; that the soul—understood as an immaterial entity which survives death—is simply an illusion; that the universe will one day become a lifeless dustbin; and so on.

But how exactly do these physical scientists reach such spiritual conclusions? Well, it is certainly not through the application of scientific method, for scientific method, as we have just seen, can supply no answers at all to the questions of life. The truth, then, is that these scientists reach their conclusions because they *assume* them to be true; because they have committed themselves beforehand to a naturalistic (and therefore to an atheistic) worldview; and because such conclusions flow logically from that worldview. Thus, whether intentionally or unintentionally, these men seek to lend the prestige of natural science to the axioms and corollaries of their own naturalistic philosophy.

This kind of philosophical *hubris* and overreach also appears when scientists try to tell us that scientific method *alone* can give us true knowledge. Today, this view is called *scientism*. When I first encountered it as a college student, it was called *logical positivism*. Seeking to bring the rigors of the scientific method to bear on the perennial questions of philosophy, the logical positivists proposed that a statement is meaningful and true only if it can be verified *empirically*, that is, by direct or indirect sensory experience.[1] Needless to say, such a narrow definition of valid knowledge immediately puts the great themes of metaphysics, theology, and ethics completely beyond the pale. It means that for millennia philosophers and theologians have been talking non-sense about non-entities, or at least about entities that cannot be known at all. Thus, the logical positivists presumed to "solve" the questions of life by *dissolving* them—by turning them into so much sound and fury, signifying nothing.

Even as a humble undergraduate, I perceived the arrogance and illegitimacy of this move. Yes, within its proper sphere scientific method yields true (or at least useful) knowledge and impressive results. But does this give scientific method a monopoly on true knowledge? Surely not. The fallacy of logical positivism—and of its birth mother, philosophical naturalism—is arbitrarily to identify nature with the whole of reality, scientific knowledge with the whole of knowledge, and empirical evidence with the whole of verification. But what if the poet was right? What if there really are more things in heaven and on earth than are dreamt of in our naturalistic philosophies? What if there really are spiritual things? What if intuitive, historical, or divinely revealed knowledge can put us in touch with them? What if we can see with the eyes of our mind certain things that we cannot see with the eyes of our head?[2]

Summing up on this matter, seekers would indeed be foolish and ungrateful to belittle the power and fruitfulness of the scientific method.

They must not, however, let its impressive accomplishments—or the imperialistic pretensions of some of its spokesmen—bewitch them into thinking that it gives access to all truth, or that it rules out other kinds of access to truth. Seeing natural science for what it is—a good but limited gift from the unknown god—they will gladly thank him for it, even as they pass it by in their continuing search for his appointed Teacher.

Philosophy

But what of philosophy? Surely in this time-honored discipline we have an excellent candidate for the Teacher. After all, what is philosophy supposed to do if not supply solid answers to the ultimate questions of life? Yet amazingly enough, it cannot. Try to imagine, then, the impact of this sad fact on a young philosophy major when at last he realized that it was so.

How well I remember my first class in Philosophy 101. Our professor—a paunchy, middle-aged man with a beard that glowed like hot copper—exuded passion, wit, and a veritable Niagara of exotic words and ideas. In all my born days I had never heard the likes of it. "This is the life for me," I cried as I left class that day: "…discovering the truth about things, fighting for it, helping others find it, impressing them with it, and getting paid for it to boot!" Not that I understood a word of what my professor had said. But all that would come in due time.

And how well I remember that late spring evening four years later when, with graduation looming, I sat alone in my living room with a copy of L. Wittgenstein's *Philosophical Investigations* in my taut and trembling hands. I was trying to make sense not only of his words, but also of my own life and future. I had embarked on the study of philosophy with such high hopes. Yet now, to my alarm and dismay, I found that I did not have a single solid answer to a single question of life! In a peculiarly satisfying fit of rage, I tore up the book and threw it piece-meal across the room. It—and I—would never be the same again.

Interestingly, not a few professional philosophers have reached the same melancholy conclusion about philosophy that I did.

"Philosophy is doubt," asserted the skeptical Montaigne.

Henri Bergson agreed, declaring that, "Intelligence is characterized by a natural incomprehension of life."

R. D. Hitchcock concluded, "A modest confession of ignorance is the ripest and last attainment of philosophy."

John Seldon, adopting the same minimalist approach, opines, "Philosophy is nothing but discretion."

IN SEARCH OF THE TEACHER

A story is told of the pessimistic German philosopher Arthur Schopenhauer, who, while visiting a greenhouse in Dresden, became so absorbed in contemplating a plant that his peculiar behavior elicited the concern of an attendant. "Who are you?" the attendant asked suspiciously. Schopenhauer replied, "Sir, if you could only answer that question for me, I'd be eternally grateful."

Similarly, someone once asked English philosopher Bertrand Russell if he would be willing to die for his beliefs. "Of course not," he replied. "After all, I may be wrong."[3]

Now all of this would be funny if it weren't so sad. How is it possible that the one discipline charged with discovering the answers to the questions of life should fail so completely in its mission? Are the postmodernists right after all? Is the greatest discovery of the "lovers of wisdom" that wisdom is not discoverable at all?

The test perspective, as we have already seen, supplies solid answers to these urgent questions. It teaches us that man is indeed imbued with the philosophical spirit: sooner or later we all want to know the truth about the questions of life. But it also teaches us that the answers are not innate. In other words, they are simply not accessible by means of introspection or logic. And this is just as true for philosophers as it is for the rest of us. All people—philosophers included—need a Teacher sent by god.

The history of Western philosophy only confirms these important conclusions. And yet, by surveying it for just a moment, we find that it does indeed supply a hint of a more fruitful road to travel.

Think of this history as a sandwich.

The bottom layer is the age of Greco-Roman philosophy (ca. 500 B.C. to 300 A.D.). It began when certain Greek philosophers cast off traditional mythological responses to the questions of life and sought to find answers through the use of unaided reason. Not surprisingly, as the years unfolded some of them turned to naturalism, others to pantheism, and still others to speculative theism. In the end, however, they could not agree. Accordingly, as this period drew to a close, Greco-Roman philosophy was in a shambles, characterized by uncertainty, skepticism, mysticism, and despair. The world was ripe for a new way of doing philosophy, a way that would not only revive the philosophical spirit, but also satisfy it at last.

The middle layer of the sandwich is medieval Christian philosophy (ca. 300 A.D. to 1600 A.D.). During this era most people believed that a new way had indeed come. Philosophy thrived. Yes, there were differences of opinion as, for example, between traditional Catholics and various reformers. Nevertheless, nearly all Christendom was united by a common philosophical culture. That culture was based on a common faith. All believed that God had revealed the answers to the questions of life by speaking to mankind through Christ and the Bible. For Christians, these two repositories of truth were his appointed Teacher. Men may have disagreed about how to interpret the words of the Teacher, but they did not disagree that the words had come from the one true God. Accordingly, this lengthy middle period of Western philosophy was marked by creativity, contention, and even occasional confusion. But it was never marked by skepticism or despair. Because they had found a trusted spiritual Teacher, philosophers—and the philosophical spirit—were alive and well.

The top layer of the sandwich is modern philosophy (ca. 1600 A.D. to the present). Because of fresh discoveries in astronomy, a revival of interest in ancient Greco-Roman culture, and certain abuses in the Roman Catholic Church, this period began with a loss of confidence in the Bible. Indeed, the battle cry of the so-called Enlightenment was "Reason, not Revelation!" Men felt that in casting off divine revelation they were actually casting off superstitions that had trammeled the mind and hindered its search for truth. Like the Greeks and Romans of old, they therefore decided to turn away from the ancient (Hebrew) myths and turn instead to science, logic, intuition, and introspection. Here alone was the way to discover whatever answers we might need—including the answers to the questions of life.

Looking back on some four hundred years of recent intellectual history, 21st century man is now able to see clearly what the *philosophes* of the Enlightenment could not: their "new" way of contemplating reality was actually an old way, and a counsel of despair as well. In taking the same path as the Greeks and Romans, they arrived at the same destination. Just as before, some turned to naturalism, others to pantheism, and still others to speculative theism. In the end, however, they could not agree. And so, beginning in the 1950's, many philosophers finally gave up on the "modern" quest for truth, the quest for truth apart from divine revelation. Note carefully, however, that most of them did not turn back to revelation. Instead, they inaugurated the so-called *post*-modern era, an era in which philosophy now courts its own destruction by abandoning the idea of truth itself. Postmodernists themselves hail this as a great discovery. History shows, however, that it is simply the age of modern philosophy ending like the age of ancient philosophy: in a shambles characterized by uncertainty, skepticism, mysticism, and despair. Among some, at least, it is also characterized by a desperate longing for a new and life-giving way of doing philosophy.

How vividly I remember seeing the truth of all this unveiled in the life of my own philosophy professor. The telling event happened one evening during my freshman year, when our college hosted the late Rabbi Abraham

MODERN PHILOSOPHY

TURNED FROM:	Revelation	
TURNED TO:	Reason	(Rationalism)
	Sensation	(Empiricism)
	Emotion	(Romanticism)
TURNED UP WITH:	Speculative Theism	(Rousseau, Leibniz, Paine, Voltaire, Kant, etc.)
	Pantheism	(Spinoza, Berkeley, Hegel, Schopenhauer, etc.)
	Naturalism	(Darwin, Marx, Huxley, Russell, Freud, Dewey, etc.)
	Skepticism	(Montaigne, Hume, Nietzsche, Rorty, etc.)
TROUBLED BY:	Uncertainty	
	Speculation	
	Recycling	
	Despair	

The era of modern western philosophy began in the 16th century with the Copernican Revolution and the rise of the Enlightenment. As the chart indicates, the turn from biblical revelation meant that philosophers now had to search for truth by turning within (to reason or emotion) or turning without (to sensation or empirical observation). The result was a continual recycling of the three basic worldviews: speculative theism, pantheism, and naturalism. In our day, this pattern has become so evident that some philosophers (i.e., postmodernists) have abandoned the quest for absolute truth altogether. Meanwhile, others are turning back to the Bible, finding that it does indeed display the marks of a trustworthy divine revelation. Not least among these marks is the fact that the Bible is a philosopher's paradise, supplying as it does reasonable answers to all the questions life, answers that appear to be the building blocks of the one true worldview.

Heschel as our guest speaker. This wise and good-humored man charmed us all with his spirited reflections about the meaning of life— reflections deeply rooted in the sacred scriptures of Orthodox Judaism.

Towards the end of the meeting, however, a very different note was struck when my philosophy professor, obviously quite agitated, posed a question to Rabbi Heschel: "How could God threaten Adam with the penalty of death when Adam had no idea at all what death was?"

Now up to this point the evening had not been particularly controversial in tone. Suddenly, it was—and urgently so for a man whom I thought to be quite secure in his own (pantheistic) worldview. What Rabbi Heschel replied I do not remember, and why my professor was so distressed I did not understand. Today, however, I understand very well. Despite his apparent philosophical confidence, my professor did not know what would happen to him when he died. Moreover, he was clearly wrestling with the possibility that the Jewish scriptures *did* know, and that they were bringing to mankind certain revealed truths that philosophy, left to itself, could never discover.

This anecdote puts flesh and blood on what the history of Western philosophy teaches, and on what the test perspective positively affirms: the answers to the questions of life are not innate, so that all men—philosophers included—need a Teacher sent from god. This means, of course, that in their quest for answers, seekers cannot turn to philosophy—*or at least not to any philosophy that spurns divine revelation*. Rather, they must acknowledge the truth of G. K. Chesterton's words, who said that the mind is like a mouth: it is meant to bite down on something hard. That something is divine revelation. Revelation is the philosopher's true food. Just as the natural scientist was meant to feast on nature, so the philosopher was meant to feast on revelation. He can try to bite down on the world of nature, or on the contents of his own mind and emotions, but it will only hurt his teeth. What's more, if he continues to do so, he will starve. Here, then, is the philosopher's true wisdom: feast on revelation and live.

The Good, Rough Road of Revelation

A seeker's journeys into all these spiritual *cul de sacs* can be deeply frustrating, but they need not be in vain. All that is necessary to make them profitable is for him to learn the lesson they teach: in his search for god's appointed Teacher, he cannot avoid traveling *the good, rough road of revelation*. In other words, however daunting it may seem, the seeker must now begin to look for the person, or group of persons, through whom the unknown god may have been pleased to reveal his religious and philosophical truth to the world.

Concerning this final stage in our search for the Teacher, there is both good news and bad. The good news is that the world is chock-full of purported divine revelation. Basically, this revelation may be divided into two categories: theistic and pantheistic. Let us spend a few moments getting acquainted with each.

Theistic Revelation

As defined by the vast majority of its adherents, theistic revelation is trustworthy religious and philosophical knowledge that is said to have come to us from the one true god, a god properly understood as *an infinite personal spirit* who upholds and governs his creation while remaining metaphysically separate from it.[4] Recognizing our spiritual need, this god graciously reveals some portion of his truth to certain chosen individuals, usually referred to as prophets or apostles. These in turn pass the truth along to the rest of us, whether orally or in sacred writings.

Though they use different names to further identify him—and though they understand his nature differently—almost all theists refer to this god as "God," a divine name that first appears in the Hebrew scriptures (Heb., *El*, *Elohim*). It is only fitting, then, that we begin our survey of theistic revelation with a look at the sacred writings of ancient Israel.

ORTHODOX JUDAISM

Orthodox Judaism, which dates from the destruction of Jerusalem in 70 AD, teaches that God's revelation is found in *the Law, the Prophets,* and *the Writings;* that is, in the 39 books of the Christian Old Testament. The Reformed and Conservative branches of Judaism, which arose after the Enlightenment, question the historicity of these Scriptures, and hold to a weaker view of their divine inspiration.

Orthodox Judaism places great emphasis on the *Torah,* also called the *Law* (Genesis through Deuteronomy). Written by Moses in about 1500 B.C., it opens with Genesis, the book of beginnings. It tells of the Creation (the beginning of the universe), the Probation and Fall of man (the beginning of evil, suffering, and death), the Flood, the Dispersion of Noah's descendants at the tower of Babel (the beginning of the nations), and the call of Abraham (the beginning of God's covenant family). Subsequent books record how God rescued Israel from captivity in Egypt, gave them his Law at Mt. Sinai, and taught them how to live and worship before him in their new homeland according to his manifold ordinances.

In *the Prophets* we read of the history of Israel from the time of the conquest of Canaan until their return from captivity in Babylon (ca. 1400 BC to 400 BC). There we also see how God, throughout this tumultuous period, repeatedly spoke to Israel and their neighbors, indicting them for their transgressions, warning of coming judgment, but also promising a latter-day restoration of his believing people and their (sin-cursed) world in the days his Messiah: a Spirit-anointed Prophet, Priest, and King who would arise out of the royal line of David in order to bring in the eternal Kingdom of God.

The *Writings* give us still more of Israel's history, but also include various songs, poems, and proverbs designed to govern their worship and deepen their personal relationship with the LORD.

Orthodox Jews read their Scriptures through the lens of the *Talmud*. This large body of Jewish teaching includes the *Mishnah* (a collection of legal rulings complied around 200 AD) and the *Gemara*, (a commentary on the Mishnah dating back to 550 AD). While not on a par with Scripture, these are held to give the sense and proper application of the sacred writings.

The Orthodox trust that through a strict adherence to the Torah, they will be welcomed into the Messiah's Kingdom when he appears, and that in the end they will attain to the resurrection of the dead and life in the eternal World to Come.

Orthodox Christianity

Orthodox (i.e., Bible believing) Christians refer to the Hebrew scriptures as the *Old Testament* (OT). They confess that the OT revelations were indeed divinely inspired, but also that God has enlarged and completed his revelation to mankind through his Son, Jesus Christ. Christians call this latter-day revelation the *New Testament* (NT), since their Teacher and Lord said that he had come into the world to inaugurate a New Covenant (or testament) that fulfills, illumines, and supercedes the Old. Thus, Christians believe that the two collections of sacred writings perfectly complement one another so as to produce a single completed book of divine revelation, *the* Book, the Bible (Greek: *biblios*).

The NT begins with the four *Gospels*. These are short biographies of the birth, life, death, and resurrection of Jesus of Nazareth, who is represented as the Son of God, Israel's Messiah, and the bringer of divine truth and salvation to all nations. Next comes the book of the *Acts* of the apostles, a brief history of the expansion of the Christian church from Jerusalem all the way to Rome. Then come the *Epistles*. These are letters written by various church leaders, designed to explain to new Christian converts what God has done for mankind in Christ, and how this is to be implemented and reflected in their daily lives. Finally, there is the *Revelation*, a lengthy prophecy given by God, through Christ, to the aged apostle John. It contains a series of highly symbolic visions designed to comfort the persecuted followers of Jesus with assurances of his love, his divine sovereignty over history, and his soon-coming return to raise the dead, judge the world, and bring in the eternal Kingdom of God.

ISLAM

Orthodox Muslims say that they respect the Old and New Testaments in their original forms, but argue that the revelation found in the extant versions of those scriptures has been contaminated by human error. Accordingly, they claim that God, through several visitations of the angel Gabriel, gave a perfect and definitive revelation through his prophet Mohammed. He, in turn, verbally passed along this new truth to his followers for some 20 years. Then, shortly after his death, his followers assembled the new revelations into a volume of 114 chapters called the Qur'an (i.e., the Reciting). Also, they compiled the *Sunna* and the *Hadith*. These included further collections of the sayings of Mohammed, stories about him and his followers, and special instruction designed to illuminate the meaning and precepts of the Qur'an. Though the Muslim scriptures purport to contain a definitive revelation from the God of Abraham, Moses, and Jesus, all parties in the ensuing religious debates agree that its teachings differ significantly from those of orthodox Judaism and Christianity.

In addition to the "big three" of theism, there are other faiths that claim to be based on special revelation from God, (e.g., B'haism and Mormonism). Like Islam, they typically acknowledge the value of the Old and New Testaments, but claim to go beyond them with a fuller, more accurate, and/or definitive revelation from above.[5]

Pantheistic Revelation

As a rule, the classic pantheistic faiths of the Far East—Hinduism, Taoism, and Buddhism—are not referred to as "revealed religion." This is because they do not understand god as a *personal* spiritual being who is different from his creation, and who could therefore reveal himself or his truth in a face to face encounter with his human creatures. Thus, in the Hindu *Upanishads* (ca. 800 B.C.) we never find the expression, "Thus says

Brahman." Similarly, in the *Tao Te Ching* (ca. 500 B.C.) we never read of the Tao (the god of Taoism) appearing in a vision, performing a miracle, or communing with his servants. And again, in Buddhist scriptures such as the *Diamond* or *Heart Sutras* (ca. 400 B.C.) we encounter an ultimate reality that is not only impersonal, but altogether beyond the reach of thought or language. The late Zen master Sunryu Suzuki Roshi, one of my teachers, ventured to call this reality Big Mind. But if someone had asked him whether Big Mind could tell us about himself or reveal his plans for the future of the universe, he would have laughed out loud. For the pantheist, spirituality is not *relating* to a transcendent personal god through the medium of (revealed) words, thoughts, dreams, visions, etc. Rather, it is *becoming* (one with) an immanent impersonal Mind, of which all "things" are a manifestation. The pantheist does not want to commune with god on the ground of his revelation to us; rather, he wants to become god himself!

And yet in spite of all this, there is indeed a sense in which we may still speak of the pantheistic scriptures as revelation. This is because the authors of those scriptures no doubt believed they had experienced the ultimate spiritual reality and were therefore eager to reveal it to others. Moreover, it is certain that their modern followers assume this very thing. In particular, Hindus, Taoists, and Buddhists regard the authors of their sacred books as men who attained enlightenment, and who thereafter "came down" from their exalted state of god-consciousness so as to show the rest of us the way. Thus, unlike theistic revelation, pantheistic revelation does not come *from* god, *through* men, unto other men; rather, it comes from men who have (supposedly) *become* god, unto other men who are trying to do the same.

As opposed to most theists, pantheists do not usually view revelation as a thing of the past. Rather, they regard the "canon" of pantheistic scripture as open and growing. Earnest Hindus, for example, will highly revere the ancient *Upanishads* and the *Bhagavad-Gita*, but will often turn with equal zeal to the words of modern gurus such as Sri Ramakrishna, Sri Aurobindo, or Swami Vivekananda. Similarly, most contemporary Buddhists will reverently study the sacred literature of their particular sects, yet pay no less attention to the teachings of their own priests, *lamas,* and *roshis.*

The same openness to fresh revelation is also found among modern New Age pantheists. These folks are spiritual eclectics. As a rule, they base their worldview on Hinduism or Buddhism, but also look to science (e.g., cosmic evolution, "deep" ecology, quantum physics, etc.) and various occult practices for further spiritual light. Importantly, not a few New Agers eagerly consult the words of so-called *channelers* or spiritists. They believe that books like *A Course in Miracles*, channeled by the late American psychologist Helen Shucman, contain trustworthy revelations from highly evolved spirit beings living in dimensions beyond our own.

So again, down the rough road of revelation there is good news, for there is plenty of (purported) revelation in the world.

The Bad News

But there is bad news as well, and it is this: the various revelations, all allegedly from god, frequently contradict one another, with the result that the *good* road of revelation is nevertheless *rough*. This becomes especially clear when we compare theistic and pantheistic revelation. These two worldviews give fundamentally different answers to each and every question of life. Also, despite some notable similarities, there are sharp differences between the several theistic religions, and between the various pantheistic religions, as well.

Let us consider a few examples of such doctrinal disagreement. Judaism and Islam teach that the ultimate reality is a single divine Person; Christianity teaches that it is a single divine being comprised of three distinct Persons, a three-in-one god, a trinity. Again, Judaism and Islam teach that salvation from sin and judgment is a reward to be earned by (different kinds of) good works. Christianity, however, teaches that salvation is a gift to be received through faith in Christ. Hindus believe that Brahman ordained the caste system, and that people in the higher castes are closer to salvation than those in the lower; Buddhists believe neither. Hindus and Buddhists hold that the (phenomenal) worlds sprang into being when Big Mind suddenly "fell" into a multitude of little minds or sentient beings. New Agers, however, argue that sentient beings slowly became conscious over long ages of evolutionary time. Also, classical pantheists teach that "salvation" involves the dissolution of the ego in the ocean of Big Mind. New Agers, however, generally look for a massive expansion and divinization of the ego. For them, the goal of evolution is a "collective divine consciousness" in which all (formerly) individual human persons are mystically united into a single divine Person with unlimited power to manifest the world of his best dreams.[6]

These illustrations only scratch the surface of the world's religious diversity, a diversity that can quickly cool a seeker's enthusiasm for the good road of revelation. Indeed, we can almost hear him crying out, "Surely all of this is beyond me! How can I possibly sort through all of these different revelations? How am I supposed to recognize the one that is true, if and when I happen to find it? What if *all* of god's truth is in one of them? What if *some* of his truth is in all of them? And what if *none* of his truth is in any of them? With all these possibilities, how can an average person like me ever hope to find the way?"

Such a reaction is completely understandable. Nevertheless, for those who have embraced the test perspective, panic is definitely against the rules. Why? Because the test perspective has already taught them to anticipate precisely this kind of trouble: again, a test is not a test unless it involves some difficulty. Yet the same perspective also offers much encouragement. For example, it implies that the divine Tester is on our side, that he wants us to pass his test. Furthermore, since he is on our side, it is only reasonable to assume that he has *already* given us at least some revelation, and that he has also taken positive steps to make it readily identifiable to anyone who really wants to find it, no matter how "average" he may seem to be. That the road of revelation is rough is part of the Tester's plan. But that the road is good is also part of his plan. Seekers must, then, confidently lift up their heads and begin to walk it.

Why the Road is Rough

One excellent way to begin walking down this road is to pause for a moment to consider *why* it is rough. Insight on this matter may not disclose the exact identity of god's appointed Teacher, but it could definitely prove useful in helping us to find him; in helping us to walk the road wisely, safely, and fruitfully. Let us therefore devote a few moments to exploring this important question.

We begin by noting the obvious: the road of revelation is rough because human beings are *fallible*. As a wise proverb declares, we all make mistakes. But if we all make mistakes in math, science, history, and philosophy, why not also in religion? Surely it is possible for sincere people to *think* they have received a revelation from god, when in fact their experience is the product of their own spiritual longing, overactive imagination, psychological disease, or mistaken perception. It is worth noting also that the delusions of one person can quickly spread to others as the founder of a new religious movement, through sincere but misplaced zeal, begins to win converts to his own error. Here, then, is yet another manifestation of human fallibility: the tendency of people who lack spiritual confidence to attach themselves to leaders and movements that do not. What do the repeated horror stories about deadly religious cults teach us, if not that error can all too quickly snowball when fallible people mistake what is popular, persuasive, and passionately proclaimed for a true revelation from god?

Secondly, painful experience also teaches that false revelation may be traceable to human *duplicity*. If seekers do not know it already, soon enough they will: there really are such things as "wolves in sheep's clothing." There really are evil people who lust for adulation, power, money, and illicit sex—and who know how to get them from gullible souls who are famished for a little truth and comfort from the unknown god. Donning the garb of the prophet, priest, evangelist, guru, imam, psychic, or spiritist, these religious hucksters declare themselves ready, willing, and able to impart their heavenly treasures—at a price. Almost always, the cost to those who pay it is unspeakably high.

Finally, and perhaps most troublingly, we must consider the possibility that at least some of the world's religious "messiness" is due to the secret activity of evil spirits, spirits that would harm seekers by using false revelation to keep them from the healing power of the true. This notion is, of course, scandalous to many in the West who have learned to rank belief in evil spirits as irrational superstition. However, thoughtful seekers should pause to examine their skepticism about evil spirits (if indeed they are skeptical), making sure that it is actually rooted in rationality, and not simply in the naturalistic presuppositions that have dominated Western science, philosophy, and psychology in recent generations.

Since this issue is important, let us briefly consider the case of the influential Viennese psychologist, Sigmund Freud. Early in his life, Freud embraced Darwinian naturalistic evolution. As we have seen, this atheistic worldview presupposes that eternal matter alone exists. Accordingly, Freud theorized that belief in spiritual beings—gods, angels, demons, fairies, etc.—is irrational and superstitious; that it originated long ago in the primitive stages of human development; that it reflects a child-like personification of the forces of nature; and that it involves deep-seated feelings of fear, helplessness, and longing for security that are embedded in the psyche of the human animal. In short, Freud neatly reduced the spiritual to the psychological, and the psychological to the material. Western seekers will do well to remember that he was definitely not alone in advocating such views.[7]

In considering Freud's story, we see clearly that "superstition" and "irrationality" are relative terms. This is because their meaning is dependent upon the worldview of the one who uses them, upon his assumptions about the answers to the questions of life. As we have just seen, Freud accepted naturalistic presuppositions. Therefore, he found it irrational to believe in spirits, whether good or evil. And given Freud's assumptions, he was reasonable to do so: how could he believe in spirits that he already "knew" (i.e., assumed) did not exist?

The seeker, however, cannot accept Freud's presuppositions—nor any religious, scientific, philosophical, or psychological theory built upon them. Why? Because, unlike Freud, *he is a seeker.* As such, his goal is not to build some kind of theory based upon his own set of presuppositions, but rather to determine which set of presuppositions—naturalistic, pantheistic, or theistic—is true. Now if, at the end of his journey, he determines that naturalism is true, then yes: evil spirits do not exist, it is irrational to say they do, and belief in them must be a product of the human brain. However, if theism or pantheism is true, then evil spirits may very well exist, it would be irrational to say they don't, *and philosophical naturalism itself may be a product of the demonic mind!* Note also that a seeker who has been won to the test perspective *already* believes that there is some kind of god, and therefore that naturalism is false. But if naturalism is false, and theism or pantheism is true, then evil spirits may well exist, since all theistic and pantheistic religions teach that they do. Accordingly, in his evaluation of different world religions he will not rule out the possibility that at least some so-called revelations may actually come from, or be contaminated by, evil spirits.

Importantly, there is not a little evidence to indicate that this is precisely the case. We know, for example, that the sacred writings of nearly every theistic and pantheistic religion warn against the deceptions and temptations of evil spirits. And this is to say nothing of the countless tribes around the world whose animistic beliefs require them more or less continually to placate and/or exorcise the evil spirits that would bring them harm. The sobering truth, then, is that the vast majority of mankind, past and present, have taken evil spirits seriously. To this very day orthodox Jews speak of Satan and demons. So do Christians, who further describe these malevolent beings as invisible inhabitants of the air, as the hidden rulers of a spiritually darkened world that is alienated from God. And there is more. Muslims speak of the *jinn,* Hindus of the *asuras,* Buddhists of the *pretas* and *narakas.* Even New Agers, famous for their enthusiasm about messages channeled from "ascended masters" living in the astral realms, now admit that at least some of these "entities" are not only untrustworthy, but dangerous.[8] This is impressive evidence. Is it reasonable, then, for a Western seeker to dismiss it out of hand and to deny the existence and activity of evil spirits altogether?

In conclusion, we have seen that human fallibility, human duplicity, and possibly even demonic deception have made the good road of revelation rough, littering it with spiritual chaff and fools gold. How such dark powers entered the world we do not know, though it is not impossible that a trustworthy revelation from god will supply the answer, since mankind has always wondered about the third great question of life, "What (if anything) went wrong?" But even if we do not (yet) know what *went* wrong, we at

IN SEARCH OF THE TEACHER

least have a pretty good idea of what *is* wrong. And for seekers determined to walk the good rough road of revelation, that is useful information indeed. As we are about to see, it teaches them how to walk that road wisely, safely, and profitably.

Be Bold, Be Wise, Beware

Our search for god's appointed Teacher has led us onto the good rough road of revelation. It is good because truth is likely to be found at its end. But it is rough because it is littered with an abundance of false revelation, revelation that could consume precious time by taking seekers down fruitless and even dangerous byways. How, then, shall they best proceed?

Happily, the test perspective again comes to our aid, helping us to answer this crucial question. It does so by enabling us to make some very useful assumptions, and also to derive from them some very practical guidelines. Let us now look briefly at several of the most important.

First, the test perspective teaches us to assume that *god's true revelation is surrounded by a manageable amount of error*. Already we have discussed this heartening implication, showing that it flows logically from the premise that the unknown god *wants* people to pass his test, and that he has therefore arranged things so that any sincere person can. Furthermore, we have seen that there are only two worldviews that acknowledge a spiritual ultimate reality, and that the religions falling into these two categories are relatively few and easy to distinguish. Knowing this, seekers have every right to *be bold*. They can confidently strike out in search of the Teacher, knowing that their options are manageably few, and that the divine Tester will gladly help them find the one that is true.

Secondly, the test perspective teaches us to assume that *god has equipped us to find his revelation*. We have already discussed this point as well, showing that the unknown god has *created* us to take his test, and has therefore fitted us with certain "truth detectors" so that we may pass it. Having pondered them at some length, I have concluded that the four most important are *intuition* (i.e., spiritual common sense), *reason* (i.e., logic, the laws of sound thought), *conscience* (i.e., moral intuition), and *an inclination to hope for the best*. Later we will examine these faculties more closely. Here, however, we need only to draw from them our second practical admonition: *be wise!* In other words, as you go in search of the Teacher, *be wise by listening to your heart, using your head, heeding your conscience, and hearkening to the voice of hope*. The test perspective teaches us that god's truth will ring true in all the faculties he has designed for apprehending truth. We are wise to seek accordingly.

The Way of Mysticism

Thirdly, the test perspective *warns against a turn to mysticism*. The reason for this is clear from the very nature of mysticism. In his search for spiritual truth, what is the mystic really doing? *He is seeking to bypass (the use of) his god-given faculties in favor of an immediate mystical experience of the ultimate reality.* When seekers won to the test perspective understand this, they will naturally be wary. Why? First, because mysticism *does not appear to be a god-approved avenue to truth;* and second, because *it may well be a demonically appointed avenue to big trouble.* Since these points are so important, I want to pause for a moment to examine them more closely.

When the mystic confronts the world's religious diversity, it does *not* lead him to the three possible conclusions that most folks would find most reasonable: 1) one of these revelations *probably* is true, 2) some of them *must* be false, or 3) all of them *may* be false. Instead, the mystic draws a very different set of conclusions: 1) the world's religions only *appear* to be contradicting one another; 2) they all are "really" saying the same thing; and therefore 3) it doesn't much matter which religion we practice, so long as we practice it sincerely. In short, since all roads lead to Rome, one road is pretty much as good as another.

If this viewpoint seems attractive, it is because there is an element of truth in it. All religions—to the extent that they acknowledge a spiritual ultimate reality—seek to understand and relate to that reality. They have caught a glimpse of the unknown god and are attempting to establish a closer connection with him. But even if all religions share this goal, it does not follow that they all succeed equally well in achieving it. For example, one religion may tell us the true name of the unknown god (assuming he has a name), while another may tell us that he has no name, or that he has many. One religion may describe him as he truly is, while another may describe him as it thinks he is, or as it wants him to be. One religion may enable seekers to establish a lasting connection with the (formerly) unknown god, while another may promise to do so, yet continually leave them in shadow. In sum, one religion may actually be a dependable revelation in which a personal god reaches down to man, while another may be an undependable speculation in which man—peering through the semi-darkness of nature and conscience—falteringly reaches up to god. The result is that all religions may be one in aspiration but not in attainment. But by believing otherwise, the mystic cannot find the one that is true.

Observe also that the mystic's understanding of religious diversity is always based on a pre-existing religious commitment, and that this commitment is usually pantheistic. How does the mystic "know" that all religions are really saying the same thing? It is because he "knows" that pantheism is true; that just as there is one Big Mind back of all (seemingly different) things, so too there is one Big Mind back of all (seemingly different) religions. And why does the mystic smile condescendingly at seekers who carefully compare and contrast the teachings of different religions, hoping to find the one that is true? It is because he already "knows" that such comparing and contrasting is futile; that the discriminating intellect is actually an enemy; that intuition, reason, language, and even conscience all tend to *divide* reality into (the illusion of) multiplicity, whereas the true spirit of religion tends to *dissolve* all things back into (the reality) of oneness.

Here, by the way, is the philosophical basis and rationale for all forms of Eastern meditation. On the assumption that the various faculties of the human personality are actually impediments to religious experience, the meditator embarks upon spiritual practices specifically designed to bypass—if not destroy—them altogether. His goal is to attain a state of consciousness beyond common sense, beyond reason, beyond language, beyond all knowledge of good and evil, beyond hope, and beyond personality itself. His goal is to become one with everything. But what if his assumptions are wrong and his goal is unreachable? What if he is not *meant* to become one with everything? What if he is meant to *relate* to god "dualistically," person to person, through words, in prayer and intellectual meditation? And what might be the consequences of his pursuing his own way instead of god's?

My point here—most emphatically made as a result of bitter personal experience—is that the wise seeker will not, because he cannot, walk in the way of the mystic. Why? *Because he has not made the distinctly pantheistic commitment of the mystic.* How could he, seeing that *as* a seeker he is not sure that pantheistic revelations are true? Accordingly, he cannot agree that all religions are "really" expressions of the one "perennial philosophy," pantheism. Indeed, he finds it interesting and important that we must do great violence to the actual tenets of the theistic religions in order to pull pantheistic rabbits out of theistic hats. Reason, joined with careful study, persuades him that on nearly every question of life the theistic and pantheistic answers stand opposed. And he has learned from the test perspective to listen hard to the voice of reason. He knows it is important equipment from the unknown god, vital in his search for truth. How then can he follow the mystic by casting aside reason—and all the rest of his discriminating faculties—as useless obstacles in the pursuit of spiritual reality? How then, through Eastern meditation, can he seek a mystical experience that may not even be possible? And how can he experiment with such meditation, knowing that it might be contrary to the will of a personal god, and therefore quite injurious to his own soul?

The Way of Spiritism

Just as seekers must beware of irrational mysticism, so too must they beware of its kissing cousin, spiritism. Now it is obviously true that a trustworthy divine revelation will come to us from some kind of spirit. For example, on theistic premises, it could come to us directly from the spirit we call god, or indirectly through an angelic spirit whom god desires to use as a messenger of his truth. On pantheistic premises, it could come to us from an enlightened human spirit, or possibly from other kinds of (enlightened) spirits living on other planes (of consciousness). In short, it belongs essentially to the rough road of revelation that seekers be open to communication from spirits, whether divine, angelic, or human.

However, such openness must be thoroughly tempered with reason, and even wariness. We have already seen why: virtually all world religions acknowledge the existence of evil spirits and warn against their deceptive activity. If a seeker is wise, he will therefore adjust his search accordingly. Before embracing a given revelation, he will make every possible effort to ascertain its true source, and will take every possible precaution against being deceived.

Practically speaking, what does this mean?

It means, first of all, that *he will not simply take a religious leader at his word when he claims to have received a divine revelation*. Such a claim may be true. On the other hand, because the spirit behind the revelation may be evil, the claim may also be false. Jesus, Mohammed, and Joseph Smith all claimed to have received divine revelations. Yet at many points their teachings contradict one another. Good logic therefore requires that at least some of these revelations are false, and clear thinking suggests that evil spirits may have been behind the ones that are false. Similarly, the Jesus who, by their own confession, inspired Peter, Paul, and John to write the New Testament, differs dramatically from the Jesus who, by her own confession, inspired spiritist Helen Schucman to write *A Course in Miracles*. The former give us a theistic worldview, the latter a pantheistic—and one whose evolutionary premises differ from classical Hinduism and Buddhism, as well. Now if all these teachers really were inspired by spirits other than their own, at least some of the spirits must have erred or lied. The implication is clear: seekers will have to look before they leap. Before receiving any revelation as true, they will have to *see* that it is true by finding compelling evidence to *show* that is true.

The possible existence of evil spirits also means that *a seeker will question revelations that come directly to him*. Experience indicates that this is not likely to happen to most of us, but also that it cannot be ruled out. Mohammed did not expect a visitation from an angel, but he received one—and when he did, he wisely considered the possibility that his experience was demonic. Helen Schucman, the psychologist mentioned above, did not expect a spiritual visitation, but one day heard a voice in her head, saying, "This is a course in miracles: please take notes." At the urging of a friend, she did so, and thus became a "channel" for a spirit that identified itself as Jesus. But just like Mohammed, she too had her doubts. Indeed, her biographer, Robert Skutch, tells us that she resented the voice, objected to taking down the material, was extremely fearful of the content, and had to overcome great personal resistance, especially in the beginning stages, in order to continue.[9] Such inner turmoil made Helen wonder—and should make all seekers wonder—whether or not these revelations were from a benign source. The path of wisdom would have been for her to find out at the beginning before receiving any more at all.

This leads us to a third and final warning, namely, that *seekers should not seek truth from the mouth of spiritists or mediums*, that is, from people who intentionally try to receive revelations from spirits other than god himself. For many reasons, this admonition makes good sense. If a seeker desires truth from god, why should he go to a medium? Why not simply seek it by himself, and why not seek it from god himself—a path commended not only by most theists, but also by most Hindu and Buddhist leaders. Furthermore, seekers should realize that the Jewish and Christian scriptures explicitly forbid consulting with mediums (Deut. 18: 9-14, Gal. 5:19-21). The god who speaks there calls himself "jealous": he will not abide that his human creatures should seek spiritual truth from an angel or a departed human spirit. Rather, they are to seek it from him and from his own written words (Isaiah 8:19-20). True, a seeker does not know if this particular god *is* god. But until he does, he would be foolish indeed to ignore such solemn warnings against spiritism of any kind.

Begin!

The test perspective has geared us up for a walk down the rough road of revelation, teaching us to be bold, be wise, and beware. But can it aim us in the right direction? Can it at least supply us with a hint of where we might best begin our search for god's appointed Teacher?

I believe it can. And once again, we find that it does so by enabling us to make a number of reasonable and useful assumptions. Here are my four favorites.

First, *a seeker may reasonably assume that the Teacher's identity will not clobber him over the head.* This assumption makes excellent sense, for if the unknown god made finding his Teacher too easy, the test would not be a test. Accordingly, the seeker should prepare himself for a stiff climb, understanding that a significant amount of effort may well be required of him. In particular, he should prepare himself to probe deeply into all credible revelations: deep enough to get past superficial similarities, deep enough to understand doctrinal distinctives, and deep enough to uncover any god-given evidences by which seekers are meant to receive assurance that this or that one is indeed the Teacher appointed by god.

Next, *a seeker may also assume that the Teacher's identity will not be too obscure.* This too makes sense. After all, the divine Tester is on our side. If he has sent us a Teacher, it is because he wants us to find him. Yes, the true Teacher may superficially resemble other teachers, just as wheat superficially resembles chaff, or gold resembles pyrite. But we should assume that in the end anyone who really wants to find him, can— even the simplest among us.

This assumption has several practical ramifications. It means that the Teacher is likely to be a public person rather than a private, a herald rather than a hermit. He will not disclose his message in some remote cave, but will likely shout it from the rooftops. Also, it means that he will offer the kind of credentials average people can respect; that he will use the kind of words average people can understand; and that he will make the kinds of demands with which average people can comply. Indeed, the thought of the divine Tester's goodness invites us to suppose that he will take special steps to make his appointed Teacher(s) evident to people of every kind, including those of humble intellectual ability and/or limited education. After all, it is not intelligence or knowledge that god is testing, but simply one's love of the truth.

This brings us to a third assumption, namely, that *the unknown god will likely direct us to his Teacher by means of supernatural signs.*

In order to understand this point, think for a moment about road signs. As a rule, they are big, bold, and bright. Were they designed to grab your car and take it to your destination? No, that you must do yourself. But they *were* designed to grab your attention, and thus to help you get yourself to your destination, both by pointing out the right route and steering you away from the wrong. You have a big part to play in reaching your destination, but happily it is also a simple one: all you have to do is follow the signs.

Keeping this humble illustration in mind, we may well ask: Is it reasonable to think that the heavenly Tester, desiring to grab a seeker's attention and direct him to his Teacher, might use a few signs of his own? Indeed, is it possible that the unknown god may have posted a sufficiently large number of bold-print signs all along the highway of man's religious history, so that anyone, great or small, smart or simple, could follow them to his Teacher, if only he were willing to do so?

If you answered "yes" to these questions, then another will likely have suggested itself as well: What *kind* of signs would the unknown god be most likely to use? The answer here, I think, is self-evident: he would use the unusual, even the miraculous. In the language of the theologians, he would use the supernatural—that which is not according to the ordinary course of nature—since the *extraordinary* is so perfectly suited to grabbing our attention, signaling god's presence, unveiling his will, and getting us to walk in the direction that is pleasing to him.

Observe also how the supernatural is so well adapted to putting men to the test. A reported miracle could be a lie. An observed miracle could be divine, but it could also be fraudulent or even demonic. Thus, to find out the truth about the miracle, folks will have to investigate, they will have to seek. In other words, by its very appearance in a messy world, a god-given miracle would have the effect of separating the spiritually lazy or recalcitrant from the spiritually diligent and openhearted. The former will likely shrug off the miracle as fraud or superstition, while the latter, *after careful investigation,* will finally come to see it as the handiwork of heaven, *and the person(s) it points to as the Teacher come from god!*

It appears, then, that seekers won to the test perspective have many good reasons for expecting guidance from supernatural signs. They understand that the probationary order points to an infinite personal god. They understand that the natural and moral orders do, as well. They understand that this is precisely the kind of god who *could* use the supernatural to direct us to his Teacher. And they understand that a display of the supernatural *would* immediately signal his presence, aim them in the right direction, and put their love of the truth to the test. Understanding all this, they therefore have at their disposal an excellent way to begin their search: *they should keep their eyes open for a teacher who is surrounded by supernatural signs.*

Finally, *a seeker may reasonably assume that if the Teacher has already come into the world, he will be surrounded by a large number of spiritually satisfied disciples who have followed the signs to his feet.* How indeed could things be otherwise? If this really is god's appointed Teacher, he will surely have brought to mankind all the truths and all the spiritual experiences for which the unknown god has prepared the human heart. And if seekers have truly found such things at this one's feet, why would they want to leave in search of another? They are seekers no more, but finders—finders who have come home. So then, those who have not yet come home do well to keep their eyes out for those who have.

A Concluding Challenge

On the present leg of our journey we have begun a search for god's appointed Teacher. So far, we have found that natural science and philosophy are dead ends. But we also found that those dead ends direct us the good rough road of revelation. We then saw how the test perspective encourages us to travel that road boldly, yet with wisdom and wariness. Finally, we saw how the same perspective grants us precious hints about the best way to begin the next stage of the journey—how it supplies a number of specific criteria which can help us find and identify the Teacher sent by god.

And now, in an effort to put those criteria to work, let me invite you to pause for a moment and ask yourself the following important question: Among all the world's religious teachers that you are familiar with, who best fulfills the several criteria we have just discussed? Who, above all others, had a notably public ministry, connected well with the common man, was surrounded by supernatural signs, gained a large, committed, and spiritually satisfied following, and claimed that he was bringing to the whole world god's own answers to the questions of life?

Think about it carefully, write down your top two or three choices, and then please follow the falcon once again: she has some thoughts on this matter that she would very much like you to hear.

CHAPTER 5

WINDOW ON A WORLD OF SIGNS

BY AND LARGE rumors have a bad reputation, being, for the most part, as inaccurate as they are injurious. Nevertheless, we must admit that sometimes rumors are true, and that occasionally they are of great importance. Indeed, in a world such as ours, it is not inconceivable that the unknown god himself might start a few rumors. He knows people talk. He also knows that there is nothing quite like a miracle—a supernatural sign—to get them talking, and possibly even moving towards the Teacher whom he has sent.

These reflections on rumors bring me to another question: When you made your short list of the world's best candidates for the office of god's appointed Teacher, was Jesus of Nazareth on it? I'd be surprised if he wasn't: except in the case of those who have never heard his name, Jesus is on just about *everybody's* short list. The reason, of course, is his reputation—a reputation that has been gossiped and rumored for centuries all over the world. Jesus is known for his wisdom. He is known for his virtue. He is known for his lovingkindness. He is also known for his miraculous signs—signs so abundant, so powerful, and so unique that they immediately put him in a class by himself. This is why Christian philosopher Os Guinness calls Jesus "the world's greatest magnet for seekers." With credentials like these, it is simply impossible for an alert seeker to avoid a rendezvous with this extraordinary man.

Here, then, is an extraordinarily reasonable place for the seeker to begin his search for god's appointed Teacher: Jesus of Nazareth. And here also is a reasonable place for him to begin his investigation of Jesus: *by checking out the supernatural signs associated with his name.* Why? Because once having determined that the signs surrounding Jesus are indeed credible, a seeker can feel quite confident that he is—or may well be—god's appointed

Teacher. That conviction will, in turn, give a seeker something else that he will very much need: a desire and a determination to study—at length, in-depth, and without flinching—all of Jesus' answers to the questions of life. In short, by certifying Jesus' signs, the seeker will likely find himself powerfully motivated to examine his teachings so as to determine, once and for all, if he really is the Teacher sent by god.

But how, a seeker may ask, *can I best examine the supernatural signs associated with Jesus' name?* Well, chances are he already knows the answer to that question, even as I myself did so many years ago. Moreover, it is the answer that Christians everywhere will always give to any seeker who asks it: *You must look for them in the Bible.* That's because the Bible contains a detailed record of the signs. It is, as it were, a window: a window on a great many things, including—not least of all—a *wide and wondrous world of signs*.

Stepping Up

In chapter 6 we will take a long look through this window and begin to check out the signs. Here, however, I want to pave the way by offering some further introductory comments about the window itself: the Bible. If this turn in the road seems like a digression, please bear with me: Unless I am greatly mistaken, the following discussion will much enhance your appreciation of the biblical signs, all the more so if you are a newcomer to the study of "The Book."

A Controversial Book

Let us begin by acknowledging a hard but richly significant fact of life: *the Bible is a controversial book*. Some folks love it, revering it as the very word of God. Others loathe it, rejecting it as the word of mere men: primitive men, deluded men, dishonest men, patriarchically oppressive men, and (for one or more of these reasons) dangerous men. Still others, whose numbers are legion, find themselves suspended somewhere between these two poles, not really knowing what to think. Though they are curious about the Bible, they observe a cloud of controversy—filled with unanswered questions—swirling all around it. It is a cloud that intimidates them, tempting them simply to turn and run away.

Here is a big handful of those troubling questions.

Are the original Hebrew and Greek manuscripts really inspired by God? Do we still have them? If not, are the copies that we possess reliable? Have any important books been left out, possibly even suppressed by biased religious authorities? What about the *contents* of the Bible? For example, how can we square the creation narrative with the Big Bang and cosmic evolution? Can anyone today seriously believe in a literal Adam and Eve, Noah and the ark, or Jonah and the whale? Hasn't science ruled out miracles? Aren't the biblical miracle-stories just legends? Why would a good and loving God command Joshua to exterminate the inhabitants of Canaan wholesale: men, women, children, and even livestock? How could he sanction slavery, which he apparently does in both the Old and New Testaments? How could he condemn multitudes to eternal torment in hell? And what about the terrible abuses perpetrated in the name of the Bible: forced conversions, crusades, inquisitions, anti-semitism, racism, oppression of women and children, and cults and quackery of all kinds?

Yes, the cloud of controversy swirling around the Bible is thick indeed, and it is hardly surprising that folks should be put off by it. If, however, a seeker has been won to the test perspective, *he now knows that he must not allow himself to be thus intimidated*. After all, what if the Bible, despite all the controversy surrounding it, really is what its defenders claim it to be: a book inspired by the one true God? And what if the controversy actually demonstrates one of the Bible's central teachings about man: that he is a fallen being with an innate aversion to the one true God, and therefore to his inspired words? In view of these very real possibilities, a seeker's proper course may not be easy, but at least it is clear: *above all else, and before all else, he must read this book for himself, trying to discover what it is about the book that persuades so many people to view it as the very word of the one true God.* Only then will he be ready to plunge into the cloud of questions listed above. Only then can he intelligently grapple with the arguments on both sides of the great debate. Only then can he decide which view of the Bible is the most reasonable to believe.

Let us therefore step up to the biblical window for a closer look. As we do, our present purpose is two-fold: 1) to acquire a feel for the Bible as a whole, and 2) to point out exactly what it is about the Bible that has persuaded so many to people to revere it as the word of God. Our approach in this will be to focus on two richly significant characteristics of the Bible: its *diversity* and its *unity*. On the lookout for both, let us turn to the window now.[1]

The Diversity of the Bible

As we saw earlier, the Bible is actually a book of books, 66 of them: 39 OT books and 27 NT books. In this simple fact, we see immediately that the Bible is characterized by a certain diversity. And this is far from the only instance of such diversity. For consider:

The Bible was written in a diversity of *places*: on three separate continents (Asia, Africa, and Europe), in city and country, palace and prison, at home and abroad.

It was written in a diversity of *languages:* Hebrew, Aramaic, and Greek.

It was written in a diversity of *literary genres*, including historical narrative, law, poetry, drama, proverb, prophecy, epistle, and apocalyptic vision.

Very importantly, it was written by a diversity of *authors*—about 40 of them—over the space of some 1600 years (ca. 1500 BC to ca. 90 AD). These authors were not just priests or theologians, but men from many walks of life. Among them were kings, peasants, fishermen, poets, statesmen, a herdsman, a military general, a cupbearer, a (Gentile) doctor, and even a tax collector! Furthermore, many of them were opposed by the spiritual leaders of their day, some were regarded as heretics, and not a few were killed for their faith. Clearly, the Bible is neither the handiwork of an isolated visionary nor of a close-knit religious cult.

Finally, we observe that in its various literary forms the Bible references an enormous diversity of *persons, places, things, events, institutions, and doctrines*. This is especially true of its historical narrative, which can only be described as epic—even cosmic—in scope.

Summing up then, we find that the Bible is characterized by a multi-layered diversity, a diversity so varied and so rich that it makes the second characteristic of the Bible—its *unity*—all the more astonishing.

The Unity of the Bible

In addition to its striking diversity, the Bible also displays a rich, multi-layered unity. We can get a feel for this unity—and its many different layers—by examining closely the following thesis statement: *The Bible is one story, about one god, administering one plan of salvation, centered around one divine Person, who is attested by one large and diverse body of signs, and worshiped by one people, according to one comprehensive worldview*. In the paragraphs ahead I will briefly expand on each element of this statement, and then point out some of the main implications of the Bible's unity for seekers. If the following descriptions seem frustratingly brief, please remember that we will discuss a number of these important themes in greater depth later on in our journey.

One Story

As we saw earlier, the Bible tells a single story. This story has a beginning, middle, and end. In essence, it tells of 1) the *creation* of the universe, life, and man; 2) their *fall* into sin, suffering, sickness, death, and divine condemnation, all through the disobedience of the first man, Adam; and 3) their *rescue* and *restoration* (i.e., *redemption*) by their triune creator turned redeemer.[2] Here, then, is the infrastructure of the biblical epic: the one story of the creation, fall, and redemption of the universe.

Because of this underlying structure, the Bible displays a fundamental *literary unity*, one in which many readers discern the hand of a single divine author. Note carefully, however, that the one story powerfully resists being received as a *mere* story, that is, as myth or legend. This is because the story is so meticulously embedded in detailed historical narrative. In other words, it forcefully presents itself as the kind of story we call *history*.[3] Indeed, the Bible presents itself as *the* story *par excellence*, the one true cosmic history from which all lesser stories—be they history or fiction—derive whatever truth, beauty, or meaning they may contain. Needless to say, a story like this will be of the highest possible interest to seekers, since it definitely touches on the questions of life!

About One God

In the one story, one character towers above all: God. In the OT, he is called *Elohim*, the majestic creator and sustainer of the universe. He is also called *Yahweh*, the covenant-keeping LORD of his people Israel. Very importantly, part of the drama of the biblical story is that over time we learn more and more about this god: his names, attributes, purposes, plans, prerogatives, mighty works, and mysterious ways. Then, as the story nears its climax, something of extraordinary interest finally comes to light: the one God is actually a trinity of persons: Father, Son, and Holy Spirit.[4] Nevertheless, even in the NT, the message of the Bible remains the same: "Hear O Israel, the LORD is our God, the LORD is one; there is no one else besides Him" (Deut. 6:4, 4:35, Mark 12:32, James 2:18). In other words, unlike the ancient pagan scriptures, with their elaborate theogonies (i.e., stories of the birth of the gods) and vast pantheons, the Bible displays a consistent *theological unity*. This is, of course, one of its main attractions, for intuitively we all feel that there is, and can be, only one god. And because we feel this way, we are not surprised to learn from God's book that a central part of his mission in history is to expose and dethrone every other so-called god, so that "...in that day there will be one LORD, and His name (i.e., Father, Son, and Holy Spirit) the only name" (Zech. 14:9, John 4:22-24, 1 Cor. 8:5, Phil. 2:8-11).

Administering One Plan of Salvation

Fundamentally, the Bible is a history book: a history of the creation, fall, and redemption of the universe. But since the vast majority of that history deals with God's redemptive acts, theologians frequently speak of the Bible as a book of *salvation history*. As we read about salvation history—especially in the part of the Bible that we call the New Testament—it becomes clear that God is always acting according to a plan. The plan—sometimes referred to as *the eternal covenant*—was formulated before the creation of the world. Throughout OT times God administered the plan by way of promise and preparation. In NT times, he administers it by way of Christ's redeeming life, death, and a resurrection; by a subsequent global proclamation of this good news; and finally by a grand consummation at the end of the age. What all this means is that the Bible is best understood as *a history of the administration of a single divine plan for the redemption of the universe*. Here is a rich, complex, and profoundly important idea, one that we will delve into later on. Yet even in these few introductory remarks, the alert seeker will catch a glimpse of what is sometimes called *the soteriological unity* of the Bible—a unity based upon God's one plan of salvation (Greek: *soteria*), administered in many different ways throughout the long course of salvation history.

Centered Around One (Divine) Person

The whole Bible—but especially the NT—declares that God's plan of salvation is centered around one person: the Messiah (Hebrew: *meshiach*). This word is not a name, but a title, a title that means *The Anointed One*. It was first used by certain OT prophets to declare that God, in days ahead, would raise up a man of his choosing and specially anoint him with the Holy Spirit, thereby enabling him to accomplish his (God's) eternal plan for the redemption of the world (Isaiah 42:1f, 61:1f).

As to his *nature*, the Bible teaches that the Messiah is both human and divine. He is, in the picturesque language of the early Greek theologians, the *theanthropos*, the God-Man. In particular, he is at once the human son of David (an ancient prototype of the Messiah as king) and the divine Son of God. Here, in the mystery of the Incarnation, we have one of the great themes of NT theology. Over and again, Christ's apostles marvel that God the Father has sent his divine Son into the world through the womb of a virgin, so that her human offspring, Jesus of Nazareth, might live, die, and rise again to redeem the universe.[5]

Concerning his *work*, the Bible portrays the Messiah as a world redeemer who accomplishes his mission by occupying three offices familiar to Israelites of OT times: prophet, priest and king. As a *prophet*, he brings God's truth not only to Israel, but also to all nations, thus redeeming them from ignorance and error (Deut. 18:15-19, Isaiah 2:1-4, 9:2, 49:6). As a *priest*, he offers himself as an atoning sacrifice for the sins of his people, thus redeeming all who trust in him from divine condemnation and retribution (Psalm 110, Isaiah 53, Zech. 6:12-13). And as a *king*, he rules from heaven in God's stead over the faithful of all nations, thus redeeming them from their sinful rebellion and autonomy (Psalms 2 and 110, Isaiah 9, Daniel 7:9-14). One day, the King will descend from heaven in power and glory to redeem the material universe itself.

For the NT writers, the person and work of the Messiah are the central themes of all divine revelation. For them, the primary characteristic of the so-called *Old Testament* books is that they look forward to the Messiah's coming. The primary characteristic of the *New Testament* books is that they celebrate his arrival in the person of Jesus of Nazareth, even as they continue to look forward to his return at the end of the age, when he will consummate God's redemptive plan by raising the dead, judging the world in righteousness, and eternally perfecting the cosmos. Thus, for the NT writers, the whole Bible displays an amazing *christological unity*. If, then, there is one plan at the heart of salvation history, there is also one Person at the heart of that plan: the God-Man, Jesus Christ (Phil. 2:1-11, 3:17-21, Col. 1:9-23).

Attested by One (Large and Diverse) Body of Signs

Now that Christ has come into the world, says the NT, the Father has a two-fold purpose towards sinful mankind: he is testing their love of the truth, and he is drawing a people to his Son so that they may experience the manifold blessings of salvation (John 3:16-21, 6:44). He accomplishes this through the proclamation of "the gospel," that is, by sending preachers out into the world to herald the good news about the redemption offered in Christ. But that is not all. For when the preachers preach, they must also point their hearers to a large and diverse body of signs, signs that attest to the truth of what they (the preachers) are saying. Though these signs are quite diverse, they all have a common nature and a common purpose: they are *supernatural* phenomena, designed by God to catch the attention of men, move them to spiritual inquiry, awaken and sustain faith, *and thereafter supply a body of compelling evidence by which they may demonstrate the reasonableness of their faith to others*. As we are about to see, the Bible opens a very large window onto these signs, revealing that God has posted them all along the highway of salvation history. Here, then, amongst the

Messianic signs, we discover what might be called the *evidential unity* of the Bible. The one (large and diverse) body of Christ-centered signs constitutes God's chosen vehicle of proof or evidence that Jesus is indeed his appointed prophet, priest, and king to the world.

And Worshiped by One People

The NT introduces us to a community of "saints," people gathered together by the Father for the worship of his Son, and (mysteriously enough) a people gathered together by the Son for the worship of the Father! This community is diverse, being comprised of Jew and Gentile, male and female, rich and poor, slave and free, good and (formerly) evil. Nevertheless, because of their God-given faith and love towards Christ, they are one. The Bible highlights this unity through many striking images: they are a seed, a people, a nation, a race, a priesthood, a congregation, a bride, a body, a temple, a flock, and a new man (1 Pet. 2:9-10). Jesus referred to this community as his Church: the company of those who are divinely *called out* of Adam's darkened world-system, and *called into* God's marvelous light, where they worship in spirit, truth, gratitude, hope, and joy. Importantly, they are precisely the kind of community seekers are looking for: a community of (former) seekers who have now become finders, and who are intent on telling the whole world why.

According to One Worldview

Jesus and his Church invite all men to join God's new spiritual community, and to worship him *according to the one true worldview*. They do so on the premise that God, in Christ, has now fully revealed the answers to all the questions of life. Students of the NT will not regard this as an extravagant claim, for there we do indeed find a comprehensive set of answers—answers that are, in the eyes of many, outstandingly intuitive, reasonable, hopeful, and morally sound. Moreover, these answers aim not only to satisfy man's philosophical curiosity, but also to address his existential longings and anxieties, promising spiritual peace and healing to all who will embrace them. In short, the Bible gives the seeker exactly what he is looking for: a comprehensive and fully satisfying worldview. Through it he can see things past, present, and future; things above, upon, and beneath; things without and within; things human, angelic, and divine. Here the seeker is bidden to a most high mountain, from which at last he is able to look out upon reality as a whole. In Part 3 of our journey we will explore this, the *philosophical unity* of the Bible, in greater depth. Readers should understand, however, that in the eyes of many the depths themselves are too deep for anyone to plumb; that the biblical worldview requires at least a lifetime—and perhaps even an eternity—to take in.

Reflections on the Book of Books

Our purpose in surveying the unity of the Bible has been to pave the way for a closer look at the one body of signs. However, before stepping up to that particular window, I want to offer a few concluding comments about the Book as a whole that should be of special interest to seekers.

First, seekers should realize that the multi-layered, Christ-centered unity of the Bible makes it *historically unique*. That is, no other body of scripture—whether theistic or pantheistic—gives us anything remotely like it. Hinduism reveres a collection of sacred writings that often fascinate but fail to display any underlying historical, literary, theological, or evidential unity. The same is true of Buddhism. At best, these twin pillars of classical pantheism offer us a bare philosophical unity—bare because their answers to the questions of life, though similar, are nevertheless fragmentary and sometimes even contradictory.

For different reasons, the same is true of Mohammed's *Qur'an*. Despite its lofty pretensions to being the full flower of divine revelation, we cannot read it long before seeing that its god, its story, and its worldview differ substantially from those of the Bible. In other words, there is no organic relation between the Bible and the Qur'an. Moreover, while the OT scriptures demonstrably anticipate and profile a Messiah exactly like Jesus, they make no reference whatsoever to a Messianic successor in the image of Mohammed. Mohammed's book is one book, written by one author, to whom no previous authors ever pointed. Therefore it displays no evidential unity at all. The result is that Islam invites the seeker to do something quite irrational: to take Mohammed's word simply because he *says* it is true, and not because there is a body of solid evidence *showing* that it is true.[6]

We find, then, that the study of different scriptural traditions only serves to highlight the multi-dimensional unity and historical uniqueness of the Bible. This is another important fact of religious life that seekers do well to consider with care.

Secondly, in the eyes of many, the unity of the Bible is so patently supernatural that it compels them to view it as a book *inspired by God*. How, they ask, could some forty different authors, spread out over some 1600 years, come up with a book that displays such a complex, multi-layered unity? For these readers, only one answer makes sense: in writing their portions of the book, *each of the different human authors must have been inspired by one divine Author*. The unity of the Bible must be *his* handiwork, far beyond the purpose, plan, or power of any of its human contributors. Also, they reach this conclusion still more decisively when they see how often the biblical authors explicitly *tell* us that God inspired them to write as they did (Ex. 34:27, Jer. 30:2, Rev. 1:11). Here, then, is why Christians do not hesitate to speak of the Bible as the Word of God. They see from its unity, and learn from its own teachings, that one divine Author has inspired many human authors, so as to give mankind one divine Word—*one completed revelation*—by which all may know the answers to the questions of life and enter into relationship with him.[7]

Finally, seekers should understand that the unity of the Bible, so compellingly supernatural, supplies the evidential basis for almost everything else that Christians believe about their Book.

For example, the Bible's unity clearly entails its *divine inspiration:* how else, apart from such inspiration, could its several authors have produced such many-faceted oneness (2 Tim. 3:16-17)?

But if the Bible is inspired, then it must also be *inerrant* in all it affirms, for how could a book inspired by the God of truth be in error (Num. 23:19, John 17:17)?

But if this book is inerrant, then it must also *be complete*—for both Christ and his apostles (inerrantly) taught that through them, and them alone, God was finalizing his revelation to the whole human race and sending it forth into the nations (Mt. 28:18f, Eph. 2:19-20, Jude 1:3, Rev. 22:18-19).

And if it is inspired, inerrant, and complete, then it must be many other things besides: *trustworthy* (Mt. 7:24-28), *authoritative* (Mt. 7:29), and *infallible*—unable to fail in all that it has been sent forth by God to accomplish (Isaiah 55:11, Col. 1:3-6).

Moreover, if God has gone to all the trouble of giving us such a revelation, how shall he not make sure that the manuscripts by which he communicates his revelation are *recognized* for what they are (Luke 24:45, 1 Thess. 2:13) and lovingly *preserved*, without corruption, for future generations (Mt. 24:36)?

We see, then, that Christians have built quite an edifice of faith upon the unity of the Bible! *One wonders, however, if seekers are not meant to do the same.* For is this not exactly what they have been looking for: a book that purports to tell us the story of the whole universe; to answer all the questions of life; to banish every fear, satisfy every hunger, and bestow upon all who welcome its message the gift of eternal redemption? Such claims are like neon signs, flashing beside the highway of life, crying out to seekers everywhere, "Turn in here, turn in here!"

Yet as inviting as all this is, there is something more inviting still: *the mysterious person who dwells at the center of all these claims, Jesus of Nazareth*. Why? Because the Bible heralds him as God's Messiah; and if as God's Messiah, then also as God's supreme prophet; and if as God's supreme prophet, *then also as God's appointed Teacher to the whole human race—the very one that seekers are looking for!*

Yes, Jesus is definitely a teacher with whom seekers will want to get better acquainted! Accordingly, their first inclination will likely be to step up to the Bible window at the place where they can see Jesus best. Moreover, as they do, they will no doubt be especially eager to learn all they can about the supernatural signs that commend him to so many as God's appointed Teacher. For again, if those signs should prove compelling, would they not create a reasonable presumption that Jesus is indeed the Teacher, and that his answers to the questions of life are trustworthy and true?

Join me, then, in doing this very thing. Let us draw near to the four panes of the Bible window through which we see Jesus best—the four gospels—, and let us take our fill. But brace yourself! When you do, you will soon find exactly what I found so many years ago: You are looking out upon a wide and altogether wonderful world signs!

CHAPTER 6

FIRST LOOK

HOW WELL I remember my first look through the gospel window. It was a very special moment in my journey through life, full of intellectual curiosity and spiritual hope. It was also a very personal moment. I was alone: alone with the unknown god, and alone with a book that multitudes down through the centuries had revered as his very Word. Moreover, in coming to this book, I found that I *wanted* to be alone: if this really was his Word, it only seemed right that he himself should be the one to show that to me.

I would take that experience—that solitary first reading of the gospels—from no one. Indeed, if our journey thus far has stirred in you a desire to lay aside *The Test* so as to read one or more of the gospels for yourself, I would heartily encourage you to do so. If we are meant to walk together again, we certainly will; and when the right time comes for it, you will certainly know.

If and when that time does come, it may be because you want further help in understanding some of the signs you have just encountered in your first look at Jesus' life. The next three chapters—in which I offer a systematic overview of the Messianic signs—are designed to supply just that kind of assistance.

Such an overview can be quite useful for all biblical readers. It helps them to identify the different signs when they come upon them. It helps them to understand their meaning. It enables them to see at a glance their abundance, diversity, and supernatural character. It helps them to see them as a whole, as a unitary body of evidence. And most importantly, it impresses upon them how marvelously the signs converge in one person—Jesus of Nazareth—, and how this tends to engender a deep confidence that he is indeed the Teacher come from God.

In the pages ahead, I will therefore offer a fairly exhaustive survey of the biblical signs pointing to Jesus. Since they are posted so plentifully along the highway of salvation history, I have divided them into three broad categories: 1) signs appearing *at* the coming of Jesus, 2) signs appearing *before* the coming of Jesus, and 3) signs appearing *after* the coming of Jesus. As we are about to see, they are not only quite numerous, but also deeply thought-provoking.

A Miracle Advisory

The present chapter is devoted to our first look through the Bible window. In it, we will examine the signs that occurred at the time of Jesus' coming; that is, the signs associated with the course of his earthly life and ministry. Relative to those that appeared at other stages of salvation history, these signs are *extraordinarily* abundant, diverse, and supernatural. Indeed, this is so true that some first-time readers have greeted them with skepticism, insisting that they must be legendary, the product of the overactive imagination of the early Christians. Thus, before taking our first look at the signs, I want here to issue a brief "miracle advisory."

In the discussion ahead, you will encounter the supernatural—the hand of the God of the Bible temporarily upending the ordinary course of human experience and setting aside the ordinary "laws" of cause and effect. If you have already caught a glimpse of the unknown god, this should not be too threatening. Indeed, it may be that you will view this unusual experience as a welcome opportunity: *an opportunity to see if the unknown god and the God of the Bible are one and the same; and to see if Jesus is his appointed Teacher, as* well.

If you are such a person, you will doubtless want to walk through the amazing world of the gospels in a way that is especially appropriate for seekers: openly, critically, and confidently. You will walk openly because you now believe that a personal god exists, and that he and the God of the Bible may be one. You will walk critically because the critics may be right: these astonishing stories may be legends after all. And you will walk confidently, because you know that if the signs really are the handiwork of the unknown god, then he will supply both the evidence and the insight to assure you that such is the case.

Again, my purpose in this chapter is to introduce and briefly discuss the signs associated with Jesus' (first) coming. In chapter 7 we will pause to consider the proper criteria for determining whether these signs—and the biblical Jesus who performed them—are history or legend. In chapter 8 we will complete our survey by looking at the signs given before and after Jesus' coming.

Signs at the (First) Coming of Jesus

Gazing through the window of the gospels, we see almost immediately that from his birth onwards, Jesus' life was literally enveloped in the supernatural. Though they are too numerous even to count, the signs we encounter in the gospels fall readily into seven broad categories. As much as possible, I have tried to arrange them chronologically, beginning with signs surrounding Jesus' birth, and concluding with signs surrounding his death and resurrection. Space does not permit me to write out all the relevant biblical texts. I do hope, however, that readers will follow each biblical reference, cited parenthetically, to its source in the gospels. To behold these jewels in the crown of their biblical context is always to see them at their best.

Signs Surrounding Jesus' Birth

Newcomers to the gospels cannot fail to be impressed with the abundance and diversity of signs that cluster around Jesus' birth. These include several angelic annunciations, Jesus' birth to a virgin, a revival of the Spirit of prophecy, and the mysterious journey of the *magi* to the birthplace of the newborn King. The message here is unmistakable: *this birth is important*. Matthew and Luke send the message quite forcefully. Concerning the baby Jesus, these gospel writers desire their readers to ask, "What kind of child will this be?" (Luke 1:66). Let us therefore look briefly at each of these four fascinating signs.

1. Angelic Annunciations

The Bible declares that we humans are not alone in the cosmos, but that we share it with a host of purely spiritual beings: God, the holy angels, and the fallen angels, who are also called demons. The holy angels live in heaven—a place above, possibly in or just beyond the expanse of space, but more likely another kind of space (i.e., what we could call another dimension) running parallel to our own. There, they worship God; and *from* there they are sometimes sent as his messengers to people in the earth below (Luke 1:19, 26). According to Matthew and Luke, the angels were especially busy at time of Jesus' birth, being commissioned on four separate occasions to help God's earthly children prepare for, and celebrate, the birth of his Messianic Son.

In the first, the archangel Gabriel appears to a humble priest named Zacharias, declaring that his wife Elizabeth—who had been barren for many years—will soon give birth to a prophet named John. But John will be no ordinary prophet. Rather, he will be "great in the sight of the Lord." Indeed, "He will go before Him in the power of the Spirit." Here, then, in Gabriel's enigmatic words, we find the *reason* for John's greatness: he will be great because he will go before the Messiah (as his herald), and also because the Messiah will *be* the Lord himself, bringing into the world the age-old hope of Israel, the Kingdom of God (Luke 1: 5-25; Mt. 11:1-19)!

In a second visitation, Gabriel appears again, this time to a virgin named Mary. Humbly, believingly, and gladly, she receives the news that soon she will be with child by the Holy Spirit, and that the holy offspring to come will not only be Israel's Messiah, but the very Son of God (Luke 1: 26-28).

In yet a third visitation, Gabriel comes to Joseph, Mary's betrothed husband. Assuring him that Mary's conception is not of man but by the Holy Spirit, Gabriel instructs him to call the child *Jesus*, which in Hebrew means, "Yahweh saves." Importantly, Gabriel also supplies the rationale for this name, thereby spotlighting the Messiah's core mission, namely, that "He will save his people from their sins" (Matthew 1:18-25, Mark 10:45).

Finally, there is a joyful annunciation—not by one, but by a great multitude of angels—to a group of shepherds watching over their flocks on the night of Jesus' birth:

> Do not be afraid, for behold, I bring you good news of great joy which will be to all peoples. For there is born to you this day, in the city of David, a savior, who is Christ the Lord…Glory to God in the highest, and on earth, peace to men on whom his favor rests!
> —Luke 2: 8-20, NIV

Importantly, Luke relates that the shepherds did exactly as the angels urged: they sought out the savior of whom heaven's host had so passionately sung (Luke 2:15-20). The visitation was a sign; and the sign, in this case, had its intended effect.

In a moment we will look at other angelic visitations, and comment on their significance for seekers. From these four, however, we may already draw an obvious conclusion: on the day of Jesus' nativity, heaven drew *especially* near to earth, and the messengers of heaven—the holy angels—were busier than ever before!

2. The Virgin Birth

Centuries before Jesus' nativity, the prophet Isaiah spoke these words of encouragement to fearful king Ahaz: "The Lord himself will give you a sign: behold, the virgin shall conceive and bear a son, and shall call his name

Immanuel" (Isaiah 7:13-14). Though this prophecy had a near fulfillment in the days of Isaiah, the gospel writers found its larger fulfillment in the birth of their Master (Mt. 1:23). Jesus, they said, was no ordinary man, still less a sinful one. Rather, he was the divine Son of God, conceived by the Holy Spirit in the womb of a virgin, and therefore born into the world as *Immanuel:* God with us in human flesh. Only thus, said the apostles, could he accomplish his redemptive mission. Only thus could our fallen world have exactly what it needs: a perfectly holy human savior, a sinless substitute for sinful men (Heb. 2:14-15, 7:26). Note carefully, however, that this high purpose does not exhaust the rationale for the virgin birth. It was also meant, as Isaiah had said, for a sign. It was meant to be rumored abroad, to astonish, and to get folks thinking about the man thus born. Above all, it was meant to get them moving towards him.[1]

3. Revival of the Prophetic Spirit

According to Luke, the birth of Jesus was attended by a revival of the prophetic Spirit, dormant since the days Malachi, but now, after four long centuries, stirring once again.

Before Jesus' nativity, we meet this Spirit in Zacharias who, at the birth of his son John, was moved to prophesy about his mission as the forerunner of the Messiah (Luke 1: 67-80). Then we meet it in Elizabeth, Zacharias' wife and the relative of Mary, who prophetically pronounced a divine blessing upon her younger cousin (Luke 1: 39-40). Finally, we meet it in Mary herself, who, having caught a glimpse of the Kingdom to be ushered in by her son, was moved to rejoice in God her savior, the redeemer of all the humble and spiritually hungry of the earth (Luke 1:45-56).

After Jesus' birth, we again find the Spirit of prophecy at work, this time in two aged saints who had long waited for the Hope of Israel (i.e., the Messiah). Simeon, present at Jesus' circumcision, sees that this child is the expected One, and therefore speaks grateful words of praise to God, as well as ominous words of warning to the child's mother (Luke 2: 25-35). Anna, Simeon's contemporary, also realizes that Jesus is the Messiah, and therefore speaks of him prophetically to other likeminded Jews who have been eagerly waiting for him to appear (Luke 2: 36-38).

In these fascinating accounts we therefore find that at the birth of Jesus the Spirit of prophecy placed men and women in the company of the angels, opening their eyes to behold something of God's plan of salvation, and also opening their mouths to speak of what they saw. Moreover, like the angels, these gospel prophets were clearly intended to function as signs, moving people to ask, "What kind of child will this be, what will he grow up to do, and what might he have to teach us about God and the questions of life?"

4. The Journey of the Magi

Here, in a narrative especially encouraging to Gentile seekers, we find sign upon sign. Matthew alone relates the story, telling us how certain "wise men"—most likely Zoroastrian priests living in Persia—saw an unusual star in the West. Perhaps being knowledgeable of the Jewish prophetic scriptures (see Num. 24:17), they concluded that this was a sign heralding the birth of Israel's long-awaited Messiah. Wanting to see him for themselves, they decided to follow the star, which (supernaturally enough) led them first to Herod's court in Jerusalem, and then to Bethlehem of Judea, the birthplace of Jesus. There they found and worshiped the child, offering gifts fit for a king: gold, frankincense, and myrrh (Mt. 2:1-12).

Again, this story provides sign upon sign. The star was a sign to the *magi*: this unusual heavenly body signaled heaven's blessing on the one over whom it so supernaturally shone. The *magi* were a sign to the Jews: they were the first of that great company of Gentiles who, as Isaiah had prophesied, would resort to the root of Jesse, to Israel's Messianic king (Isaiah 11:10). And now, having been memorialized by Matthew in his gospel, the *magi* serve as a sign to seekers everywhere, vividly portraying the character of *true wisdom*. Wisdom is to take note of every sign that appears in the firmament of one's life; wisdom is to follow those signs to the babe of Bethlehem; wisdom is to find out if he really is heaven's king; and wisdom is to worship him, if he is.

John the Baptizer

John the Baptizer, Zacharias' miracle son, was also a sign, especially to the Jews of his own day. When he came of age, John was drawn to live in the Judean wilderness. There, like Elijah of old, he dressed in garments of camel's hair and ate locusts and wild honey. And there, says Luke, the word of God came to him (Luke 3:2). When it did, John immediately began to preach, calling wayward Israel to a baptism of repentance, and also to faith in the coming One who would soon bring in the Kingdom of God. Thus, John became a prophet—not like Zacharias and the others who only prophesied on occasion—but like Elijah, who actually filled Israel's prophetic office. The nation had not had such a prophet since the days of Malachi. Now it did.

But even this was not all. As Jesus himself said, John was indeed a prophet, but also *more* than a prophet: he was the chosen forerunner and herald of the Messiah, predicted long before by Isaiah and Malachi (Isaiah 40:3, Mal. 4:5, Mt. 17:10f). Here, then, is why John is one of God's outstanding signs. Though he wrote no book and performed no miracle, he did point—and pointed as no one had ever pointed before—to the *presence* of the Messiah (John 1:26), to the *deity* of the Messiah (John 1:34), to the *atoning sacrifice* of the Messiah (John 1:29), to *divine judgment* at the hand of the Messiah (Mt. 3:12), and to a *Kingdom* soon to be ushered in by the Messiah (Mt. 3:12). Thus did John direct all Israel—and all who read or hear about his ministry—to Jesus of Nazareth, bidding them to see him as the Son of God, the Lamb of God, the Judge of the world, and the King of the world to come.

Angelic Visitations

In OT times, on rare and momentous occasions, angels appeared to God's ancient people.[2] Importantly, the relative paucity of such visitations serves to highlight the abundance—and rich significance—of those that occurred in Jesus' day. Many of these, as we just saw, took place at the time of his birth. There were, however, a number of others as well.

On the dark side, there was a visitation by Satan himself, the ruler of all the fallen angels. During Jesus' probation in the wilderness, Satan tried to thwart his mission by getting him to disobey his Father's will (Mt. 4:1-11). Here we should also mention Jesus' frequent contests with demons, minions of Satan that Jesus cast out of their oppressed human subjects. Observe that before obediently leaving their victims at Jesus' command, these malevolent spirits typically shrank in terror at his approach, confessing him to be both the Son of God and their eternal judge (Mark 1:21-29, 5:1-20, Luke 8:26-39).

Holy angels repeatedly arrived on the scene towards the end of Jesus' life. During his agony of soul in the garden of Gethsemane, one of them was sent to comfort and strengthen him for the terrible ordeal just ahead (Luke 22:43). Then, on the first Easter, angels again descended from heaven, this time to roll away the stone from Jesus' tomb, send the Roman guards into a dead faint, and announce the glad tidings of their Master's resurrection to his sorrowing disciples (Mt. 28:1f, John 20-21). Similarly, on the day of Jesus' ascension into heaven, angels again appeared to instruct and comfort his anxious followers (Acts 1:9-11). And even after his departure, the heavenly messengers periodically visited the saints in order to further the cause of the gospel (Acts 5:19, 8:26, 10:7, 12:7, 27:23).

These accounts are not only fascinating, but also richly significant. Obviously, they put the Bible on record as affirming the existence of angels, both good and evil. But more than this, they do so in a way that again shines the biblical spotlight on Jesus. In other words, these visitations are a sign: a sign that the man thus born is not *of* the angels, but *over* the angels as their divine creator, king, and judge (Eph. 1:21, Col. 2:10, Heb. 1-2). Presumably, such a man would have a good deal to tell us about the questions of life.

Theophany

A theophany may be defined as a display of God's presence in which he discloses himself to one or more of man's five senses. This mysterious accommodation of the infinite to the finite occurred periodically in OT times.[3] During Jesus' life, God granted at least two such theophanies, theophanies carefully recorded by the gospel writers and clearly prized as signs of the highest order.

The first took place at Jesus' baptism. Matthew describes it as follows:

> When he had been baptized, Jesus came up immediately from the water; and behold, the heavens opened to him, and he saw the Spirit of God descending like a dove and alighting upon him. And suddenly a voice came from heaven, saying, 'This is My beloved Son, in whom I am well pleased.'
>
> —Mt. 3:13-17

The record of this theophany comes down to us from John the Baptizer, who saw the event himself and who spoke of it to his disciples (John 1:29-34). Encountering it for the first time, newcomers to the Bible may not fully understand all that God meant when he called Jesus his beloved Son. But this much is clear: such words imply a relationship that was extraordinarily intimate—indeed, altogether unique. Therefore, this theophany powerfully signals that Jesus is a unique and peculiarly trustworthy vessel of God's truth.

Interestingly, we find God himself drawing this very conclusion in a second and even more impressive theophany. Here is Luke's extended version of that amazing event:

> Now it came to pass about eight days after these sayings that he took Peter, John, and James and went up on the mountain to pray.
> As he prayed, the appearance of his face was altered, and his robe became white and glistening. And behold, two men talked with him, who

> were Moses and Elijah, who appeared in glory and spoke of his decease that he was about to accomplish in Jerusalem.
>
> But Peter and those with him were heavy with sleep; and when they were fully awake, they saw his glory and the two men who stood with him.
>
> Then it happened, as they were parting from him, that Peter said to Jesus, "Master, it is good for us to be here. Let us make three tabernacles: one for You, one for Moses, and one for Elijah," not knowing what he was saying.
>
> While he was saying this, a cloud came and overshadowed them; and they were fearful as they entered the cloud. And a voice came out of the cloud, saying, "This is my Son, my chosen one. Listen to him!"
>
> When the voice had ceased, Jesus was found alone. But they kept quiet, and told no one in those days any of the things they had seen.
> —Luke 9: 27-36

Now it is safe to say that an experience like this would definitely be an attention-getter! True, the three Jewish disciples were not completely unprepared for it, since from their youth they had heard of Moses and Elijah. Moreover, they had also heard about the *Shekinah*, or visible cloud of God's manifest presence that had appeared from time to time throughout Israel's history (Ex. 13:21, 2 Chron. 7:1). Nevertheless, much of what they now beheld was unprecedented: the transfiguration of Jesus, the appearance of two long-departed saints, and the voice of God himself, mysteriously identifying Jesus as his Son and Chosen One. Small wonder, then, that a record of this event finds its way into all three synoptic gospels, and that Peter, only months before his death, was still speaking of it with reverence and awe (2 Pet. 1:16-18).

A passage like this clearly invites a great deal of commentary. Here, however, only two brief remarks need be made.

First, this theophany, like the one that preceded it, is plainly designed to highlight the unique relationship between God and Jesus. Its uniqueness appears not only in the fact that God speaks of Jesus as his Son, but also in the fact that he singles him out as his Son *over and against Moses and Elijah*, who were arguably Israel's two most famous spiritual leaders. To be sure, God loves and honors them both; yet he does not call them sons. Therefore, to the One speaking from the cloud, Jesus is unique—something that he clearly wanted the awestruck disciples to understand.

Secondly, this theophany dramatically underscores Jesus' authority as a revealer of divine truth. Here, the exchange with Peter is decisive. In suggesting that separate tents be pitched for each of the three men, Peter is evidently operating on the premise that all three are roughly equal in spiritual stature. The voice from the cloud soon disabuses him of that idea.

Jesus alone is his beloved Son. Jesus alone is his chosen one. Jesus alone is the teacher that Peter and the disciples are to listen to. Hitherto, they have lived under the Law (represented by Moses) and the Prophets (represented by Elijah). Henceforth, they are to live under Jesus, the ultimate lawgiver and the ultimate prophet. From now on, his word is supreme.

Such an account will give seekers of a trustworthy religious teacher pause. It specifically identifies Jesus as a teacher sent from God. It identifies him as a unique teacher, an extraordinarily authoritative teacher, and—in the eyes of men like the aged Peter—a divine teacher. Therefore, one may well ask: if the unknown god desired personally to single out a supreme teacher for the human race, would it be possible for him do so in a manner more pointed or more powerful than this?

Miracles

We come now to the most fascinating and controversial category of signs surrounding Jesus' earthly ministry, his miracles. Since these are of special interest and importance to seekers, we will examine them in some depth.

The NT writers use three different Greek words to describe what we today would call a miracle: sign (*semeion*), wonder (*teras*), and act of power (*dunamis*) (Acts 2:22). Bearing this in mind, we may therefore biblically define a miracle as *an extraordinary and powerful act of God that captures people's attention, amazes them, and causes them to wonder about the significance of what has happened*. The Bible reveals that God performed miracles all throughout OT history. Indeed, it indicates that he will continue to do so, even until the end of the age (Mark 16:14-18, 1 Cor. 12-13). However, in the gospels the situation is unique. There, God performs miracles of *extraordinary* power, and does so with *extraordinary* frequency, all with a view to spotlighting the *extraordinary* man through whom he performed them: Jesus of Nazareth. Moreover, the NT assures us that these miracles definitely produced the intended effect (Mt, 15:31, Mark 1:27, 2:12, 4:41). Let us look at them more closely now.

Jesus' miracles fall into at least six different categories. Most abundant of all were his *physical healings*, variously performed upon the blind, deaf, mute, lame, palsied, leprous, and others. Not surprisingly, the healer from Nazareth never failed to draw a crowd (Mt. 4:24, 8:16, 15:31).

Also quite numerous were Jesus' *exorcisms*, performed upon people who, for reasons unexplained, had fallen under the power of the demonic. Notably, Jesus is the first Jewish prophet on scriptural record to cast out demons (Mt. 8:16, 15:21-28, Mark 5:1-15).

FIRST LOOK

Next there are Jesus' miraculous *works of power over nature*. Examples here include his turning water into wine (John 2:1-12), calming a fierce storm on the Sea of Galilee (Mark 4:37-41), and feeding multitudes with a few loaves and fish (Mark 6:35-44).

Less frequent, but even more impressive, were his several *resuscitations* of people who had died, the case of his friend Lazarus being the most dramatic and memorable of all (Mt. 9:18-19, 23-25, John 11:1f). This particular miracle should be distinguished from a *resurrection,* which is biblically exemplified only in the case of Jesus, and is always unto eternal life.

Finally, we have the miracle of Jesus' *clairvoyance* and *predictive prophecies*. Here we think of Jesus seeing (the distant) Nathaniel beneath a fig tree (John 1:48, Mt. 17:24-27); or of his knowing the inmost thoughts of both friend and foe (Mt. 9:4, John 16:30); or of his prophesying the coming destruction of Jerusalem (Luke 21); or of his repeatedly attempting to forewarn the disciples concerning the exact details of his coming death and resurrection (Mark 10:32f).

From the prominence of the miraculous in all four gospels, we see clearly that the evangelists wanted people everywhere—both Jew and Gentile—to learn about Jesus' miracles, understand them, and respond to them appropriately. Unabashedly, they were spiritual "gossips," hoping that such amazing rumors about their Master would elicit Christian faith in all who heard. But what, precisely, did the evangelists *most* want seekers to understand about these signs? Here are six biblically based affirmations that I think would top their list.

First, *Jesus' miracles were acts of God.* That is, they were acts of the miracle-working God of Israel; the God of Abraham, Isaac, and Jacob; the God of Moses, Elijah, and Elisha. As such, they were designed to do what all God's miracles had done down through the years: bring glory to his name and identify him as the one true God (Mark 12:28-36, John 17:4). Unfailingly, Jesus ascribed his miracles to this very God, confessing that they were "the works of God" (John 9:3) accomplished by "the finger of God" (Luke 11:20). Similarly, these works were "from the Father" (John 10:32, 5:20, 36) and done in the Father's name, (John 10:25). Moreover, despite allegations to the contrary, Jesus and the evangelists explicitly denied that these miracles were the product of magic, sorcery, psychic powers, or demonic energies (Mt. 12:22-30, Acts 8:14-25). Rather, they were indeed the handiwork of the living God, working in and through his divine Son (John 8:49, Acts 2:22).

Secondly, *Jesus' miracles were historically unprecedented.* True, certain OT prophets did some of the same things that Jesus did. What is unprecedented, however, is the *scale* upon which he did them. For example, more than once we read that Jesus healed *all* who came to him (Mt. 12:15, Luke 6:19). Indeed, for many Jews it was the abundance of his miracles that gave them their Messianic significance: "When the Messiah comes, will he do more signs than these which this man has done (John 7:31)?" As for the apostle John, he wondered if the world itself could contain a written record of all the miracles that his Master had performed (John 21:25)!

Observe also that Jesus' miracles impressed his contemporaries with their unprecedented power: power to cast out legions of demons, power to heal a man born blind, power to walk on water, power to calm an angry sea, power to raise a man *long* dead, etc. Astonished by such wonders, Jesus' contemporaries freely confessed, "We have never seen anything like this (Mark 2:12, John 9:32)!" And seekers should note well that the world has never seen—or heard—anything like it since. Jesus' miracles were historically unprecedented *and remain historically unparalleled*. Miracle-wise, he is in a class by himself.

Thirdly, Jesus' miracles were MEANT to be rumored everywhere. We see this both from what Jesus did and what he said. What he did was to perform his miracles publicly: in synagogues, on open roads, among crowds, in towns and cities, and in the temple precincts themselves. This entailed, of course, that news of them would spread like wildfire, something Jesus no doubt desired and something that definitely occurred (Mt. 4:24, Luke 4:37). Moreover, on more than one occasion he specifically commanded the beneficiaries of his miracles to tell their friends and loved ones (Mark 5:19, Luke 17:4, cf. John 4:27f). True, Jesus showed himself mindful of the down side of such signs: that people might relate to them as ends in themselves (John 4:48, 6:26), or that public enthusiasm for the One who performed them might lead to a premature confrontation with the Jewish or Roman authorities (Mark 7:36, Luke 8:56). Yet for all that, he was far from downplaying his signs, or from doing what he did "in a corner" (Acts 26:26). He wanted people to see, to hear, and to marvel (John 5:20). And not Jewish people only, for he both anticipated and prepared for the day when rumors of his miracles would overflow the borders of Israel and pour forth into the nations (Mt. 24:14, 26:13, Luke 7:22, John 20:29, Acts 1:8). Thus, when seekers hear of Jesus' miracles, they do well to consider that such hearing is according to Jesus' plan; and that Jesus' plan, according to Jesus' words, was according to God's plan (John 5:20, Acts 2:22)!

Fourthly, *Jesus' miracles were also meant to identify him as a true prophet and teacher*. The Jews of Jesus' day understood this connection very well. These were folks who had heard about Israel's miracle-working prophets from their childhood, folks whom God himself had taught to look for miracles as one of the marks of a true prophet (Deut. 18:15-22). Not surprisingly then, many of them, upon seeing Jesus' miracles, came to honor him as a prophet (Mt. 14:5, Luke 7:16, John 9:17). Moreover, this was an honor that Jesus openly embraced (Mt. 13:57, Luke 13:39).

Trouble arose, however, when the signs began to do their appointed work of *calling attention to the prophet's message*. For when Jesus' persisted in identifying himself as the Son of God—and in summoning people to faith in him—many found his message incomprehensible, and even blasphemous (John 10:33). Later, we will discuss this dire development. Here, however, I would stress yet again that the gospels were written not just for Jews, but for Gentiles as well; and that the evangelists wanted seekers everywhere to view Jesus' miracles as a divine endorsement of his prophetic ministry (John 5:36, 14:11). In other words, they wanted the miracles *to identify Jesus as a teacher come from God* (John 3:2). Common sense would, of course, lead most seekers to assume that this was indeed one of the main purposes of the miracles. So too would the test perspective. Here, however, we find that the gospels say it outright, thus inviting seekers everywhere to identify the unknown god as Israel's God, and Jesus of Nazareth as his appointed Teacher.

Fifthly, *Jesus' miracles were meant to inspire hope*. Now it is clear from the gospels that his miracles *did* inspire hope, since multitudes of hurting people flocked to him for his healing touch (Mt. 4:23-25). Similarly, it is clear that Jesus' miracles *will* inspire hope wherever they are rumored, since they triumphantly confront some of the most fearsome enemies of the family of man. What Jesus wanted people to understand, however, is that his miracles were *meant* to inspire hope; that this was one of God's primary purposes in having him perform them. Note carefully, however, that the hope Jesus had in mind was not of a temporary deliverance from this or that enemy, be it physical or spiritual. Rather, it is was hope of an *eternal* deliverance from *every* such enemy; of life in a whole new world from which every consequence of man's sin has been forever banished. Following the OT prophets, Jesus called this world *the Kingdom of God*. Later we will discuss it in depth. Here, however, I would emphasize that throughout his entire ministry, Jesus explicitly interpreted his miracles as a sign that God's Kingdom—his long-awaited redemptive reign—was now breaking into our fallen world; and that when, in days ahead, it finally arrives in its fullness, God's people will be *rescued* from every enemy, and *restored* to complete wholeness by his glorious power (Mt. 4:23-5, 9:35, 10:5-8, 11:1-19, 12:28, etc.). In short, one of the main purposes of Jesus' miracles was to inspire hope in a coming Kingdom of God, and also a fierce determination to do everything necessary to enter it (Mt. 11:12 NIV, Luke 16:16)!

In all these considerations we see that it is not just the *fact* of Jesus' miracles, but their distinctive *character* that makes them so interesting to seekers. If the evangelists had told us that Jesus made feathers stand on end, or turned himself into a bird, or jumped unscathed off a high building (Mt. 4:5-7), the miracles would only excite incredulity, if not open scorn.[4] But because they tell us that he healed the sick, cleansed the lepers, cast out demons, and raised the dead, they excite us not only to curiosity, but to hope as well. Such miracles speak to the deepest spiritual needs of people everywhere, spotlighting a Teacher who promises not only to give us the truth, but also to heal our deepest wounds, once for all. Small wonder, then, that multitudes of hurting seekers throng to Jesus even to this very day!

Finally, *Jesus' miracles produce crisis and division among all who encounter them.* We first meet this in the gospels themselves, where the crisis that Jesus' signs produced was of a distinctly Jewish nature. Israel was a nation miraculously conceived. Miracles had graced her entire history. Moreover, God had actually taught his people to expect miracles from their prophets. For all these reasons, Jesus' contemporaries were actually quite open to supernatural signs (Mt. 12:38, John 6:30).

There was, however, a caveat, well known throughout the land. The people were not to receive miracle-workers uncritically, since God himself had forewarned that he would periodically test them by allowing *false* prophets to arise in their midst—men who could even perform (demonically inspired) miracles. Accordingly, loyal Israelites were first to test a prophet by examining his teaching. If it conformed to the law of the LORD, good: they could welcome him as a true prophet. But if not, he is a false prophet and must be put to death (Deut. 13:1-5). The crisis, then, for the Jews of Jesus' day, was not to determine whether Jesus had performed miracles: all agreed that he had (Mt. 14:1-2, John 11:47). The crisis was to determine the *source* of the miracles, whether they were from God or Satan.

The gospels tell us that this crisis led to a profound division throughout Israel (John 7:43, 9:16). Most of the people thought Jesus was a true prophet, even the Messiah, though in the end many turned against him. However, most of the religious leaders—the ones responsible for determining his true identity—thought he was a false prophet. In their ears, his enigmatic words rang false, heretical, and even blasphemous (Mt. 26:65, John 10:33). Accordingly, they ascribed his miracles to Beelzebul, the prince of the demons (Mt. 12:24f). However, some leaders were not so sure. How could demons cast out demons (Mark 3:23)? And why would evil spirits do so much good for so many people? One of these dissenters from the consensus view—a ruler named Nicodemus—actually came to Jesus by night, confessing, "Rabbi, we know that you are a teacher come from God; for no one can do these signs that you do unless God is with him" (John 3: 2). In his case, the signs had done all that Jesus intended: they had persuaded Nicodemus (and a few others in the Sanhedrin) that he was indeed a prophet, and they had brought him to him to receive the truth of God. To read the rest of the story is to know that Jesus did not let Nicodemus down.

As in days of old, so today: seekers who hear the rumors of Jesus' miracles cannot escape this kind of crisis and division. Indeed, their crisis may be even *more* acute than that of the Jews. First, they must become convinced that there really was a Jesus, and if so, that he really did perform miracles. Then they must go on to determine the true source of the miracles—whether they were from God (as Jesus said), from psychic powers (as modern pantheistic interpreters say), or from the devil (as the ancient Jewish leaders said). Needless to say, a challenge like this will lead to much division, much difference of opinion. Again, seekers should understand that the gospels predict this very thing (Luke 12:51). But since the challenge looks so very much like a test, they should also understand the importance of taking it up heartily, as indefatigable lovers of the truth.

Because the historicity of Jesus and his miracles is a matter of such importance for modern seekers, we will devote chapter 7 to discussing this question from a number of angles. Here, however, I would close with one final observation. As we saw earlier, the test perspective positively encourages the assumption than the unknown god may well direct seekers to his appointed Teacher through the use of supernatural signs, signs consistent with his goodness and his good will towards all mankind. Therefore, it cannot be without interest that all four gospels find the God of Israel doing this very thing: granting historically unprecedented and unparalleled miracles, miracles that are meant to attract people to the Messiah, serve as his credentials, inspire hope, and produce a spiritual crisis that probingly tests their love of the truth. Surely we all do well, then, to follow in the footsteps of master Nicodemus, thinking long and hard about what these signs might mean.

The Resurrection

We come now to what is arguably the single most important Messianic sign; a sign that the evangelists reckoned as God's supreme *imprimatur* upon all that their Master said and did; a sign explicitly held to identify Jesus of Nazareth as the divine Son of God, and also as his appointed prophet, priest, and king to a new humanity. That sign is Jesus' resurrection from the dead.

In the paragraphs ahead, I will focus my attention primarily upon the resurrection as an historical fact, and also upon its immediate significance for seekers. It must be understood, however, that this emphasis touches only on the topmost layers of its meaning. The deeper meaning flows from its intimate connection with Jesus' death. This is clear from all four gospels, which, aptly enough, have been described as passion narratives with long introductions and short conclusions. In other words, Christ's death is the center of gravity of the gospels in general, and of the resurrection in particular. Here, then, we locate the source of its deepest meaning. The resurrection points backwards to one who died; to one who died an atoning death; to one who died an atoning death predicted by the prophets and prepared for by the eternal God; to one whose atoning death proved acceptable to God; and to one whose atoning death guarantees a future resurrection of God's people. In sum, the sign of the resurrection was not intended simply to focus attention on the one who rose; it was intended to focus attention on *why the one who rose had to die*.[5]

Turning, then, to the biblical narratives themselves, we observe first that the sign of the resurrection is better described as the sign of the risen Jesus. This is because, according to the evangelists, no disciple actually saw Jesus rise from the dead. There were, however, many eyewitnesses of the risen Christ—disciples who therefore rejoiced to see and know that their Master had risen indeed.

The gospel emphasis upon the many eyewitnesses of the risen Christ is plain from Matthew's narrative, which I will cite at some length:

> Now after the Sabbath, as the first day of the week began to dawn, Mary Magdalene and the other Mary came to see the tomb. And behold, there was a great earthquake, for an angel of the Lord descended from heaven, and came and rolled back the stone from the door and sat on it. His countenance was like lightning, and his clothing as white as snow. And the guards shook for fear of him, and became like dead men.
>
> But the angel answered and said to the women, "Do not be afraid, for I know that you seek Jesus who was crucified. He is not here, for He is risen, as He said. Come, see the place where the Lord lay. And go quickly and tell His disciples that He is risen from the dead; and indeed, He is going before you into Galilee: there you will see Him. Behold, I have told you."
>
> So they departed quickly from the tomb with fear and great joy, and ran to bring His disciples word.
>
> —Mt. 28:1-8

Here, in fascinating detail, is just the beginning of an extensive NT testimony concerning the risen Christ. Indeed, on some ten different occasions, spread out over a period of forty days, he would appear to many different people, in many different places, and in many different ways. The NT data is impressive, and well worth surveying.

FIRST LOOK

As Matthew just told us, on the morning of his resurrection, Jesus first revealed himself to several women at the tomb (Mt. 28:1-10). Shortly thereafter he appeared privately to Mary Magdalene, and then again to Peter (John 20:11-18, Luke 24:34). Later in the same day, he walked and talked *incognito* with two disciples going to the village of Emmaus; then, during a subsequent meal at their home, he somehow disclosed his identity and promptly disappeared (Luke 24:13-32)! Next, he manifested himself indoors to his eleven fearful apostles (Luke 24:36-43). Not long after that, he paid them a second visit, this time directing some penetrating words to poor "doubting Thomas," an apostle who had refused to believe the eyewitness testimony of his brethren (John 20:26-31). Some time after this, he appeared to an unspecified number of disciples by the Sea of Galilee, where he ate breakfast with them, and also encouraged the faltering apostle Peter (John 21:1-23). A little later, still in Galilee, Jesus appeared to his eleven apostles on a designated mountain, and also to some 500 disciples at one time (Mt. 28:18f, 1 Cor. 15:7). Then, as the hour of his departure drew near, he again appeared in Jerusalem, first to James and then to the rest of the apostles (1 Cor. 15:7). His last appearance was to an undisclosed number of disciples standing on the Mount of Olives just outside Jerusalem: having given them final promises and instructions, he ascended bodily into the sky, into a cloud, out of their sight, and into heaven (Luke 24:44-9. Acts 1:9-11).[6]

Earlier I mentioned that Jesus of Nazareth is commonly regarded as "the worlds greatest magnet for seekers." As we have seen, a major component of his attractive power is the many signs associated with his name. But if the resurrection were the *only* sign commending him to seekers, he would still win that title hands down. Here are four important reasons why.

First, Jesus' resurrection was *unprecedented*. Yes, a few OT characters were temporarily resuscitated, and one or two were even carried alive into heaven.[7] But no one—not even those resuscitated by Jesus himself—died, rose again, and ascended into heaven above, there to live with God forever.

Secondly, Jesus' resurrection is *unparalleled*. In all world religion there is no evidence for—or even a claim of—such a resurrection. Of the founders of the world's two great theistic religions—Moses and Mohammed—it is written that they died and were buried (Deut. 34:6).[8] Among classical pantheists (Hindus, Taoists, Buddhists) it is indeed sometimes claimed that a given leader, through enlightenment, transcended the cycle of reincarnation, but never that he rose bodily to eternal life. Mind Scientists (e.g., Mary Baker Eddy, Emmet Fox, etc.), as well as some New Age teachers, have interpreted Jesus' resurrection as the supreme demonstration of his grasp of "metaphysical" (i.e., pantheistic) truth. Yet none of them has ever confirmed that theory by rising from the dead himself. In short, if Jesus really did rise, then in religion's age-old battle with the mystery of death, he is the last man standing—and also the best man to interpret the meaning of what he did.

Thirdly, the sign of the resurrection *thrills suffering and fearful humanity with hope*. Obviously, it supplies hope for life after death. Moreover, it supplies hope for life after death *in heaven with God,* the stated destination of the risen and ascended Christ (John 14:3, 20:17). But perhaps most importantly, it supplies hope of a personal relationship with Jesus. Why? Because if Jesus really rose from the dead, then he is alive today. But if he is alive today, then why could he not do for us now what he did for others before he died: come to us, teach us, forgive us, touch us, heal us, supply our needs, and possibly even raise *us* from the dead? If, in days past, he brought so great a message of salvation to Israel, why could he not now bring one to all nations? Yes, what a world of possibilities suddenly opens up to our imaginations once a man rises from the dead!

Finally, the sign of the resurrection *definitively singles out Jesus as the world's best candidate for the office of god's appointed Teacher*. Already, throughout the whole course of his earthly life, he had shown himself to be on extraordinarily good terms with God, performing more and mightier miracles than any prophet before him. Now, however, through the unprecedented and unparalleled miracle of his own resurrection, he is lifted up into a class of one. Accordingly, seekers may well ask: if an unknown god desired to use miraculous signs to direct us to his appointed Teacher, what more could he do to point the way than raise him from the dead?

The Resurrection and the Defense of the Gospel

Because of its extraordinary power, hopefulness, and uniqueness, Jesus' disciples made his resurrection the centerpiece of their defense of the gospel. In other words, whenever they proclaimed that Jesus was (and is) the divine redeemer of a new and eternal humanity, they substantiated these radical claims by pointing to his resurrection. The apostle Paul, for example, told the skeptical Athenians that God "…has appointed a day on which He will judge the world in righteousness by the Man whom He has ordained, having given assurance of this to all men by raising Him from the dead" (Acts 17:31). Similarly, he wrote to the Roman Christians that God himself, through the powerful work of the Holy Spirit, had publicly declared Jesus of Nazareth to be his divine Son through his (Christ's) resurrection from the dead (Rom. 1:4). In preaching Christ, the apostles could have appealed to many other signs, and did. But as so many NT passages show, they liked the resurrection best (Acts 2:32, 3:15, 4:33, 10:40, 17:18, 32).

FIRST LOOK

But what of the resurrection itself? How were the disciples to substantiate *that*? Reports of dead men rising from the grave would certainly be met with incredulity, if not open scorn (Acts 17:32). What evidence could they give to confirm its truth?

Interestingly, Luke's gospel shows that the risen Jesus himself fully anticipated this problem, and gave its solution. Suddenly appearing to the eleven apostles in hiding, he showed them his hands and feet, invited them to touch him, and even ate with them. Having thus persuaded them of his bodily presence, he then explained its significance, and also told them what they must do next:

> Then he said to them, "This is what I told you while I was still with you—*how everything must be fulfilled that is written about me in the Law of Moses, the Prophets and the Psalms*. Then he opened their minds so they could understand the Scriptures.
>
> And he told them, "This is what is written—that the Messiah must suffer and rise from the dead on the third day; and that repentance and forgiveness of sins should be preached in his name to all nations, beginning at Jerusalem. *You are witnesses of these things.* Behold, I am sending the promise of My Father upon you, but wait in the city until you are clothed with power from on high.
>
> —Luke 24:44-49

These rich words are notable both for their explicit and implicit meaning. Explicitly, Jesus is telling them that his life, death, and resurrection were all part of God's redemptive plan, a plan foreshadowed and foretold throughout the OT. But, says Jesus, the unfolding of this plan does not stop with his resurrection and ascension. Rather, it is meant to continue through the disciple's preaching. They are to tell people everywhere about the crucified and risen Messiah, so that all who repent and call upon his name may receive forgiveness of sins, and many other blessings besides. Thus shall God's redemptive plan progress, even until Jesus' return at the end of the age (Mt. 24:14, 28:20, John 14:3, Acts 1:10-11)

What concerns us here, however, is what Jesus tells them implicitly. How are men to be brought to faith in the risen Messiah? Jesus points the way by mentioning three lines of evidence, strongly implying that the disciples should intentionally use them all in their preaching, and that they will certainly do so with good results.

The *first* is *Jesus' own predictions of his death and resurrection.* "This is what I told you when I was still with you," said Jesus of the amazing events that had just transpired. The implication, then, is that in preaching the good news the disciples should tell others about their Master's miraculous foreknowledge of his own crucifixion, resurrection, and return to heaven.

This they were faithful to do. Mark, for example, poignantly relates the story of Jesus' last journey to Jerusalem, during which the unsuspecting disciples were troubled with premonitions of what was about to take place:

> Now they were on the road, going up to Jerusalem, and Jesus was going before them; and they were amazed. And as they followed, they were afraid. Then he took the twelve aside again and began to tell them the things that would happen to him.
> "Behold, we are going up to Jerusalem, and the son of man will be betrayed to the chief priests and to the scribes; and they will condemn him to death and deliver him to the Gentiles; and they will mock him, and scourge him, and spit on him, and kill him.
> And the third day, he will rise again".
>
> —Mark 10:32-34

Many similar texts from the gospels could be cited, all showing the evangelist's eagerness to confirm the truth of Jesus' resurrection by transcribing his own predictions of this extraordinary event (Mt. 16:21-23, 17:22-23, 20:17-19, John 2:19-22, 16:16-24).

The second line of evidence is *the Law of Moses, the Prophets, and the Psalms*. Here, Jesus has in mind the entire OT, especially the various *types* and *prophecies* that looked forward to his death and resurrection. Later we will investigate these two phenomena in some depth. Here, however, a few introductory words will suffice to show how the apostles were again faithful to their Master's lead.

A biblical *type* (Greek, *tupos: form, symbol*) may be defined as any OT person, place, thing, event, or institution that symbolically points ahead to the person and work of Christ. Importantly, Jesus himself periodically directed the disciple's attention to OT types of his imminent resurrection. For example, on one such occasion, certain religious leaders, skeptical about his claims, demanded that he produce a miraculous a sign to vindicate his teaching. He responded by saying:

> An evil and adulterous generation seeks after a sign, and no sign will be given to it except the sign of the prophet Jonah. For as Jonah was three days and three nights in the belly of the great fish, even so will the son of man be three days and three nights in the heart of the earth.
>
> —Mt.12: 39

Here, Jesus reads the OT typologically. Jonah's three-day ordeal in the belly of the great fish prefigures his own death and three-day burial. Similarly, Jonah's being vomited up onto dry land—thereafter to preach judgment, repentance, and mercy to the people of Nineveh—prefigures his own resurrection and subsequent ministry to Israel and the nations through the agency of his followers. By appealing to this OT type, Jesus desires his disciples—and seekers as well—to see that his death and resurrection were all part of God's ancient redemptive plan and promise.

Guided by Jesus, the disciples also found many OT *prophecies* of their Master's resurrection. One of their favorites appears in Psalm 16. There, king David wrote:

> For You will not leave my soul in Hades, nor will You allow Your Holy One to see corruption. You have made known to me the ways of life; You will make me full of joy in Your presence.
> —Psalm 16:10

Alive to the evangelistic power of this ancient text, the apostle Peter cited it in his sermon to the Jews in Jerusalem on the day of Pentecost, just ten days after Jesus' ascent into heaven. After quoting the psalm, he goes on to interpret it as follows:

> Men and brethren, let me speak freely to you of the patriarch David, that he is both dead and buried, and his tomb is with us to this day. Therefore, being a prophet, and knowing that God had sworn with an oath to him that of the fruit of his body, according to the flesh, he would raise up the Messiah, he, foreseeing this, spoke concerning the resurrection of the Messiah, that his soul was not left in *Hades*, nor did his flesh see corruption. This Jesus God has raised up, of which we are all witnesses.
> —Acts 2: 29-32

Here, in an effort to bring his Jewish brothers to the faith, Peter uses OT prophecy as an evidence for Jesus' resurrection. A study of the NT will show that the apostles did so often, not only in their public preaching, but also in their ministry to the churches.[9]

Peter's concluding words bring us to the third and most important line of evidence for the resurrection, *the eyewitness accounts of the disciples.* When Jesus appeared to the eleven, he said, "You are witnesses of these things." Several weeks later, immediately prior to his ascension, he spelled out the practical implications of this fact: "But you shall receive power when the Holy Spirit has come upon you; *and you shall be witnesses to Me in Jerusalem, and in all Judea and Samaria, and to the end of the earth*" (Acts 1:8). They were the privileged witnesses of Christ's life, death, and resurrection, so that they could *bear* witness of what they had seen to the world (Acts 4:20).

Again, we know from the NT that the disciples got the point and took it to heart. We see this both in their writing and in their preaching. Concerning the former, we find that all four of the gospels, through their minute attention to historical detail, plainly purport to give us eyewitness accounts of the resurrection. John explicitly declares that he was one such eyewitness (John 20:35, 21:34). Luke, in his prologue, assures us that his gospel—including the resurrection narrative—is based on eyewitness testimony (Luke 1:1-4). Paul, in his letter to the Corinthians, declares himself—along with all the other apostles—an eyewitness of the risen Christ (1 Cor. 9:1, 15:7). Peter, in his second letter to the churches, says the same (2 Peter 1:16). John, in his letter to the Ephesians, declares that he has not only seen, but also *handled* the risen Lord (1 John 1:1-4)! In sum, the NT documents find the apostles (and their intimate colleagues in ministry) at great pains to supply a large body of detailed eyewitness testimony to Jesus' resurrection. They wanted all men to see that their narratives were accurately recorded history, not myth, legend, or any other kind of "cleverly devised fable" (2 Pet. 3:16).

The apostles also gave eyewitness testimony to the resurrection in their preaching. Peter, for example, did so when he preached to the household of Cornelius, a Roman centurion. Having first proclaimed Jesus as Israel's Messiah and the divine "Lord of all," he then verifies his testimony by giving a brief sketch of Jesus' miraculous ministry. He concludes by saying:

> And we are witnesses of all the things that He did, both in the land of the Jews and in Jerusalem, whom they killed by hanging on a tree. Him God raised up on the third day, and showed Him openly, not to all the people, *but to witnesses chosen before by God*, even to us who ate and drank with Him after He arose from the dead.
> And He commanded us to preach to the people, and to testify that it is He who was ordained by God to be the Judge of the living and the dead. To Him all the prophets bear witness that, through His name, whoever believes in Him will receive remission of sins."
> —Acts 10:34-43

Observe how Peter here obeys Jesus' instructions to the letter. In a few brief strokes he first sets forth the course of Jesus' life and its redemptive significance. Then, in order to build a bridge for faith, he cites two of the three lines of evidence we have just discussed: the OT prophets and the disciple's first-hand experience of his death and resurrection. Importantly, Luke goes on to relate that God honored Peter's testimony by powerfully visiting Cornelius' household with his faith-creating Holy Spirit (Acts 10:44-48).

Why a Chosen Few?

In bringing our discussion of Christ's resurrection to a close, I want to address an important question that has arisen in the mind of many a seeker: Why would God *openly* show the risen Christ, not to all the Israelites, but only to a select group of eyewitnesses whom he had chosen beforehand? Indeed, why would he not send the risen Christ at least *once* to all men and women, so that they might believe in him? Why would he settle upon the far more cumbersome device of confirming the truth of the gospel through the eyewitness testimony of a privileged few who had seen the risen Lord with their own eyes?

To the best of my knowledge, the Bible does not address these questions specifically. Thus, the best answer may simply be, "It pleased God to do it that way." Nevertheless, a few closely related points are worthy of consideration.

To begin with, the Bible assures us that seeing a miracle first-hand does not necessarily result in faith. Jesus himself said that certain people would not be persuaded to turn to God even if their departed loved ones rose from the dead to plead with them about their spiritual condition (Luke 16:31). Indeed, it is written that some of Christ's own disciples worshiped the risen Lord with doubting hearts (Mt. 28:17)! All this harmonizes well with the biblical teaching that faith—in the end—is a gift of God (John 6:44-45, Eph. 2:8, Phil. 2:13, 2 Peter 1:1). What then does it matter whether faith comes through seeing the risen Christ with one's eyes, or through hearing someone else's eyewitness testimony about his resurrection (Rom. 10:17)?

But secondly, the method of preaching the resurrection—along with an appeal to the supporting evidence of types, prophecies, and eyewitness testimony—does indeed seem better suited for testing one's love of the truth. For if God desired to test a man's love of the truth about the resurrection, he could hardly do worse than send the risen Christ himself: such an experience would not stimulate a search for truth, but rather overwhelm him with the truth itself! Far better, then, to send him a preacher who proclaims the resurrection, sets forth the evidence to support it, and then lets his friend weigh the matter personally. This is, of course, the challenge that faces everyone who hears about the risen Jesus. He can simply dismiss this rumor as a "cleverly devised fable," or he can delve into the evidence—sifting, sorting, and evaluating it—until he finds out the truth for himself.

Interestingly, Jesus has some special words of commendation for people who are willing to walk this challenging path. We find them near the end of John's gospel, where we learn that the apostle Thomas, who was not present when Jesus first appeared to the others, refused to believe their eyewitness testimony about his resurrection. Said Thomas, "Unless I see in his hands the print of the nails, and put my finger into the print of the nails, and put my hand into his side, I will not believe" (John 20:25).

Eight days later, Jesus again appeared. This time Thomas was present, and this time he not only believed, but also worshiped, crying out, "My Lord and my God!" Seekers should listen carefully to Jesus' final words to the wavering apostle: "Thomas, because you have seen Me, you have believed. Blessed are those who have not seen and yet have believed" (John 20:29).

What does this mean, if not that the miracle of faith and assurance concerning Christ's resurrection is equally available to both groups: to those who have seen the risen Lord with their own eyes, but also to those *who have received and open-mindedly investigated the testimony of those who so saw?* Yes, both are blessed—enabled by heaven itself to cross over from doubt to perfect certainty. But, says Jesus, the better blessing is upon him who searched; upon him who so wrestled with the words of men that in the end he found the truth of God (John 17:20-21). Therefore, seekers struggling with the amazing NT story of Jesus' resurrection from the dead may surely take heart.

The Ascension

As with Jesus' resurrection, so with his ascension: it was, according to the NT authors, prefigured and prophesied in the OT (Gen. 5:24, 2 Kings 2:11f, Psalm 24, 110), predicted by Jesus himself (John 6:62), and later interpreted by his inspired apostles (Acts 2:34f, Eph. 4:7f, Heb. 9:24). Here, however, a simple description of this most supernatural event will suffice to display it as yet another unique and an important sign for seekers everywhere.

> Now when he had spoken these things, while they watched, He was taken up, and a cloud received Him out of their sight. And while they looked steadfastly toward heaven as He went up, behold two men stood by them in white apparel, who also said, "Men of Galilee, why do you stand gazing up into heaven? This same Jesus, who was taken up from you into heaven, will so come in like manner as you saw Him go into heaven."
> —Acts 1:9-11

Standing as it does here, with little or no theological explanation, this passage will raise many questions in a seeker's mind, just as the event itself did among the disciples who saw it. By whom or what was Jesus "taken up?" What was the nature of the cloud that received him? Was it the same cloud that appeared at his transfiguration (Luke 9:34)? Was the same divine Person behind both events? Where did Jesus finally go? What is he doing now? And what will he do when, as the angels predicted, he returns "in like manner?"

Clearly, the answers to such questions will shed important light on the nature of God, heaven, the afterlife, salvation, and more. In other words, Jesus' ascension touches implicitly upon many of the questions of life. Because it does, it too serves as a powerful sign, directing seekers to the risen and ascended Christ for answers that he alone can supply.

Conclusion

In our first look through the Bible window, we have concentrated upon signs associated with Jesus' (first) coming: signs surrounding his nativity, the virgin birth, angelic visitations, a revival of the prophetic Spirit, the advent of John the Baptizer, miracles, the resurrection, and the ascension. It is certainly an impressive list—and one which, amazingly enough, is still incomplete! We cannot, however, examine the rest of the signs until we have looked a little more at these. In particular, we must now address a question that will surely have been in the seeker's mind from the very beginning: how can I find out for sure whether all these signs, biblically associated with Jesus' coming, really happened—whether they are history or legend?

It is a perfectly reasonable question. Indeed, it is a question so reasonable that, as we are about to see, the unknown god has not only anticipated it completely, but also answered it in spades.

CHAPTER 7

THE GREAT DEBATE

WHEN I FIRST looked through the Bible window, the signs did not offend me in the least. As a young pantheist, I had faith in Big Mind, the spiritual fountainhead of all the phenomena that we call "things" and "events." I believed in "ascended masters," highly evolved sentient beings who now lived on other spiritual planes, and who occasionally visited our own. I also believed in *avatars*, true human beings who were so fully enlightened that they could "tap into" their divine nature at will and perform various kinds of miracles. Yes, I mistakenly brought my pantheistic bias to the NT, and so missed (or dismissed) the theistic worldview of its authors. But precisely because of this bias, it never occurred to me that the biblical signs might not be solid history, or that the supernaturalism of the Bible might be mere legend.

Little did I realize, back in those heady days of spiritual discovery, that the world was filled with folks who definitely did *not* share my enthusiasm for the miraculous; folks for whom supernatural signs were not just incredible, but preposterous. A brief anecdote will reveal the radically bifurcated intellectual world that I then inhabited.

Right around the time I was drinking in the biblical miracles, Christian evangelist Josh McDowell was defending his faith on college campuses all across America. On one such visit, he was speaking to a philosophy class, meticulously making the case for Jesus' resurrection. Suddenly, in the very middle of his presentation, the professor exclaimed out loud, "This is ridiculous! We all *know* there has to be some other explanation for the empty tomb."[1] Apparently it had never occurred to the man that the biblical signs might actually be solid history, or that the supernaturalism of the NT might be anything *but* legend!

127

Here, then, is an apt doorway to our theme in the present chapter: the Great Debate about the historicity of Jesus of Nazareth. Arguably, it is the single most important theological controversy of the last 200 years, since participants on all sides agree that the truth and survival of Christianity itself hangs in the balance.

In a moment, we will jump into this debate. But first, let us take a moment to get acquainted with the contestants. Though spokesmen from many different quarters have lifted up their voices on these matters, most scholars would agree that the controversy features two main opponents.

At one podium, we have the *theological liberals*. Like the philosophy professor I just mentioned, these folks believe that the biblical Jesus (or what they sometimes call "the Jesus of faith") is one thing, and "the historical Jesus" another. *Quite* another. For liberals, the historical Jesus was a man of whom we now know very little, except that he did not really perform miracles or rise from the dead. As for the Jesus of faith, he is largely a religious myth, the creation of the enflamed religious imagination of his devoted but deluded (or possibly even deceptive) followers. Says liberal NT theologian Rudolph Bultmann:

> I do indeed think that we can now know almost nothing concerning the life and personality of Jesus, since the early Christian sources show no interest in either; moreover, they are fragmentary and legendary, and other sources about Jesus do not exist.[2]

In other words, for Bultmann and his liberal followers, the historical Jesus has been forever lost to history, while the biblical Jesus survives as a testimony, not so much to a man, but to the myth-making powers of generations of his devoted disciples.

This brings us to the other podium, where we meet the *theological conservatives*. These folks argue that the historical Jesus and the biblical Jesus are one. For them, Jesus of Nazareth said, did, and experienced exactly what the NT records—the supernatural included. As Pierre Benoit puts it, "The preachers of the new faith may not have wanted to narrate *everything* about Jesus, but they certainly did not want to relate anything that was not real."[3] Believing, then, that the gospel preachers spoke and wrote truly, theological conservatives conclude that the unknown god and the triune God of the Bible are one and the same, and that Jesus of Nazareth is indeed the divine Messiah and the appointed spiritual Teacher of the whole human race. Accordingly, conservatives cannot urge us strongly enough to listen hard to what he had to say!

But what of seekers? Where exactly do *they* fit into the Great Debate? The answer, I would suggest, is that they fit right in the middle, inhabiting a kind of no man's land between the liberal and conservative camps. For on the one hand, they already believe in an unknown god, and even acknowledge that he just might use supernatural signs to direct us to his Teacher. Therefore, they are certainly not theological liberals, and so cannot simply dismiss the NT Jesus as mere legend. On the other hand, they are not theological conservatives, either. For even if they do believe that the unknown god *might* bear supernatural witness to his Teacher, that in itself is no guarantee that he actually has done so in the case of Jesus of Nazareth. In other words, theism may well be true, while the NT Jesus turns out to be a legend after all. How, then, is a seeker to proceed? How is he to know which side in the Great Debate is right?

The Primacy of Presuppositions

Many have been the responses to these crucial questions, but surely the first and foremost is: *Be aware of the philosophical presuppositions that are at work in this contest.* This point cannot be overemphasized. In the Great Debate, all participants come to the NT with certain presuppositions, with certain more or less non-negotiable assumptions about the way reality really is. The liberal has one set of presuppositions, the conservative another, and the seeker another still. Therefore, in his search for the truth, and in his evaluation of the Great Debate, nothing could be more important for a seeker than to become aware of *all* of the presuppositions involved. Why? Because the conclusions people reach about the NT Jesus will *always* be influenced by the presuppositions that they bring to their investigation.

Since these matters are so fundamental, let us take a few moments to examine them more closely.

Liberal Presuppositions

Broadly speaking, theological liberals bring *naturalistic assumptions* to the New Testament and to the Bible as a whole. That is, they presuppose either that there is no god, or that if there is, he is a god who cannot or will not act supernaturally in history. Accordingly, they find it unreasonable even to consider the possibility that the supernaturalism of the NT is historically true.

Since this is a serious charge, I will illustrate the point by again citing Rudolph Bultmann, arguably the 20th century's most famous liberal NT theologian. As you read his views on the task of NT scholarship, bear in mind that a great many theologians, philosophers, and historians consciously or pre-consciously share his perspective:

> The historical method includes the *presupposition* that history is a unity, in the sense of a closed continuum of effects in which individual events are connected by the succession of cause and effect...This closedness means that the continuum of historical happenings *cannot* be rent by the interference of supernatural, transcendent powers, and that therefore there is no "miracle" in this sense of the word. Such a miracle would be an event whose cause did not lie within history...It is in accordance with such a method as this that the science of history goes to work on all historical documents. And there cannot be any exceptions in the case of biblical texts if the latter are at all to be understood historically...(Therefore) an historical fact which involves a resurrection from the dead is utterly inconceivable.[4]

If nothing else is clear from these words, this much is: Mr. Bultmann is definitely *not* approaching the NT as a believer, or even as a seeker. He has already made up his mind. He has committed himself. He is a true believer in a worldview that *by definition* rules out the supernatural, and that limits real history to events that have purely natural causes. Once we see this clearly—once we understand Mr. Bultmann's naturalistic presuppositions—it is easy for us to see why he regards the *supernaturalist's* view of history as unreasonable, incredible, and absurd.

Historians like Bultmann are, of course, free to embrace philosophical naturalism, but they still have to reckon with the NT. After all, this body of religious texts is a real historical phenomenon. How then do they explain its origin? Well, as a rule, they almost always begin by acknowledging that a man named Jesus actually existed, for surely *someone* must have appeared in history to serve as the grain of sand around which the pearl of the Jesus legend would grow. But because liberals already "know," for example, that dead men don't rise, they also "know" that something else *must* have happened to generate the legend of Jesus' resurrection. Here, then, is where their *naturalistic speculations* come into play. Perhaps, they suggest, Jesus only fainted on the cross, awoke in the tomb, rolled away the stone, and returned to his disciples. Or perhaps the disciples stole his body, and then, out of misguided love for their Master, conspired to say that he rose from the dead. Or perhaps, in their grief and exhaustion, they simply hallucinated a risen Jesus. And so forth. The exact nature of the explanation is not really so important. The important thing is that some kind of natural explanation *must* be the case, since we already "know" that the supernatural explanation of the NT is not.[5]

Conservative Presuppositions

Leaving aside for the moment the question of how they arrived at them, it is clear that theological conservatives bring *theistic assumptions* to the NT documents. That is, they presuppose that there is indeed an infinite personal God, a divine creator and ruler of the world. Moreover, standing on this metaphysical ground, they see that the so-called "laws of nature" and "the law of cause and effect" are really only *divine norms*. That is, they reflect the way God normally works in his world. If, however, they are *only* norms and not ironclad laws, then clearly God is at liberty to set them aside if and when he so desires. Thus, conservatives do not find it unreasonable to view the NT as a historically viable record of the one true God doing this very thing. To use the earlier example, they readily admit that as a general rule dead men do not rise and ascend into the sky. It is not the norm. But, they ask, who is to say that the infinite personal God cannot break his own rule? Indeed, having examined the various lines of evidence—both biblical and extra-biblical—theological conservatives are fully convinced that he *has* broken his rule, and that "the unknown god" and the triune God of the Bible must therefore be seen as one.

The Seeker's Presuppositions

From these brief observations, we see how important it is for a seeker to be aware of the presuppositions that guide a given theologian's thinking. However, it is just as important for a seeker to be aware of his *own* presuppositions. Such self-understanding can only help him in his journey to truth, whereas ignorance of his personal assumptions will obviously tend to hinder him in his way.

Let us therefore briefly consider the case of a seeker who has been won to the test perspective. What will his presuppositions be?

To begin with, he will definitely presuppose the existence of an unknown god, an infinite personal spirit. Accordingly, he will also presuppose that the NT *could* be telling us the truth when it says that the unknown god has sent us a very special Teacher, surrounded him with supernatural signs, and inspired certain of his disciples to preserve, in writing, a trustworthy record of his life for the benefit of future generations. Presuppositions like these will encourage this seeker to approach the NT *openly*—with a mind alive to the possibility that the NT is indeed (part of) God's book, and that Jesus of Nazareth is his specially appointed and supernaturally attested Teacher.

On the other hand, the same seeker also presupposes that the unknown god is testing us; that he has placed us in a world where truth exists alongside error, lies, and possibly even demonic deceptions; and that he expects us to try to distinguish carefully between the two. Guided by these presuppositions, he will therefore approach the NT *guardedly* rather than *gullibly*. In other words, he will not let his desire to believe in *something* cause him to believe in *anything*. He will not let his *feelings* about this teacher get in the way of determining the *facts* about this teacher. In short, out of his love for the truth, this seeker will come to the NT with all his critical faculties on the alert, trying to find out whether it is true history or mere legend.

Finally, such a seeker will presuppose that the unknown god is on his side, that he wants him to pass his test, and that he has taken positive steps to help him do so. Therefore, he will come to the Great Debate *confidently*, trusting that if the biblical Jesus is the real Jesus, the unknown god will supply us with all the evidence that we need to ascertain that fact. In such a situation, both god and the seeker have roles to play. The seeker's part is simply to examine and evaluate the evidence. God's part is to supply the evidence, and then to use it to bring the seeker to an inward assurance of the truth: *to enable him, once for all, with full inward conviction, to see the Jesus story for what it really is, whether historical fact or historical fiction.*

The Seeker's Strategy

Having carefully examined his own presuppositions, and having adopted a spiritual posture based upon them, the seeker is now ready to plunge into the Great Debate. More particularly, he is now ready to develop a strategy for evaluating the historicity of the NT documents. But where should he begin? How exactly shall he proceed in determining whether or not this, or any other instance of sacred literature, is the real historical deal?

As we have just seen, the answer here is really quite simple. Indeed, it comes down to a single word: evidence. The seeker's basic strategy is simply to examine all the various lines of evidence for (or against) the historicity of the NT in general, and the gospels in particular.

In just a moment, we will look at a number of them. Here, however, I want to begin by reminding my readers of one line of evidence that we have already touched on: the *unity* of the Bible. As we learned earlier, this term is used to express the idea that the entire Bible, and not just the NT, is a profoundly Christ-centered book; that Jesus of Nazareth is not just the central theme of the New Testament, but of the Old as well.

How do we know this to be the case? As we shall see in chapter 8, it is because OT Messianic types and prophecies can be used *to construct a complete and highly detailed narrative of Jesus' entire life—the supernatural included*. Admittedly, we need the NT itself in order to see these types and prophecies clearly. But once having seen them—and once having seen them in their astonishing abundance, subtlety, and specificity—we realize immediately that they could not possibly be accidental, that they do indeed point to Jesus of Nazareth, and *that they therefore constitute an especially powerful line of evidence corroborating the NT portrait of his life.* Yes, the NT authors supply other kinds of proof for the historicity of Jesus, yet it is quite clear from their writings that these OT proofs are among their favorites (Luke 24:27, 44-45, John 5:39, 45-47)!

But beyond the careful study of OT types and prophecies, how else can seekers determine the historicity of the NT Jesus? The answer here is contained in the very nature of the NT. For when we remember that the NT purports to be a collection of *historical* documents—documents that contain the *eyewitness testimony* of Jesus' disciples—an exciting investigative strategy suddenly comes into view.

This strategy is essentially three-fold. First, we must isolate the criteria that historians use to evaluate the trustworthiness of historical documents. Next, we must isolate the criteria that judges and lawyers use to evaluate the testimony of eyewitnesses. And finally, we must apply all of these criteria to the NT. If the NT meets them, we may reasonably conclude that it is telling us the truth. If not, we may reasonably dismiss it as giving us mere legend.

This approach fits nicely into the test perspective. For if the unknown god has indeed sent Jesus to be our Teacher, and if he has moved Jesus' disciples to record his life in the gospels, then surely those writings will meet the traditional criteria of trustworthy history and testimony. Why? Because god certainly knows what the criteria are (indeed, it is safe to say he created them himself); because he knows that reasonable people will expect his book(s) to fulfill them; and because he wants such people to pass the test of life. Therefore, he will most certainly *cause* his book(s) to meet the various criteria. The seeker's part is simply to make sure that, in this or that particular case, he has actually done so.

But what are these criteria? For help here, we can do no better than to turn to the historians, lawyers, and judges themselves. In doing so, we discover that these professionals actually use a great many criteria for verifying the trustworthiness of a given testimony. When, however, we have fully isolated them, we will find ourselves fully equipped for the next step in our spiritual search. Henceforth, we are in a position to apply these criteria to the gospels, in order to see if these narratives of Jesus' life qualify as reliable history.

In preparation for doing this very thing, let me now introduce three reasonable assumptions about how the unknown god would likely substantiate the trustworthiness of the NT writings to thoughtful seekers.

First, he would see to it that we have reliable manuscripts of the story of Jesus' life, work, and teachings. This does not necessarily mean that he would preserve the original manuscripts themselves. It does mean, however, that he would do something almost as good: he would carefully superintend the duplicating process, thereby protecting the scribes from error and their copies from corruption, so that the extant manuscripts would be, in essence, identical with the originals. This fundamental requirement for the trustworthiness of any ancient document—what might be called the *manuscript test*—is very practical. In the case of the NT, it means that we cannot be satisfied with a small handful of manuscripts copied hundreds of years after Jesus (supposedly) lived. For an astute historian, that kind of manuscript evidence—or lack thereof—would cast a dark shadow over the Jesus story, making it historically dubious at best, and legendary at worst.

Secondly, he would see to it that the testimony contained in the NT documents met the highest standards of historical writing and legal acceptability. In a moment, we will see just how many separate criteria this *historiographic test* involves, and how challenging it is to meet them. The bottom line here is that the NT documents must so thoroughly bear the marks of good historical writing and valid testimony that they can stand up in a court of law or in a council of philosophically open-minded historians.

Finally, he would see to it that the life and teachings of Jesus—as well as the documents that described them—contained nothing that was inconsistent with his (i.e., god's) character or scandalous to our god-given faculties. This assumption is based upon all we have learned about the unknown god from the natural, moral, and probationary orders. As we shall see later in our journey, it entails many things, but especially that the person, work, and words of his Teacher should consistently strike us as reasonable, right, and hopeful. Thus, when putting the NT Jesus to *the spiritual test*, seekers will ask if this portrait of God's Teacher resonates with our deepest spiritual and intellectual intuitions about the divine. And again, these criteria are especially useful in helping us evaluate the New Testament's supernaturalism, which, in order to avoid consignment to the ash heap of the legendary, must strike us as plausible, purposeful, benevolent, and hopeful.

Here, then, are three valuable tests that seekers may bring to the Great Debate about the NT Jesus: the manuscript test, the historiographic test, and the spiritual test. If the unknown god wants us fully to trust the four gospels—and the supernaturally attested Teacher they so highly exalt—we may reasonably expect that he will enable them to pass all three with flying colors.

It is time now to see if they do.

The Manuscript Test

As with all the literary works of antiquity, so with the NT: we no longer possess the original manuscripts. Having been written on fragile paper or parchment, these documents perished with much using. We do, however, have copies, and lots of them. Thus, for seekers, the question is: Are the copies trustworthy? In other words, are they essentially the same as the originals?

In order to answer this kind of question, critics of ancient documents ask themselves three further questions: are the copies old, are they numerous, and do they agree? A "yes" answer to all three assures us that the extant copies (i.e., the copies that we have in our hands) are indeed trustworthy. Let us therefore examine the NT documents in light of these simple but important standards.

As to their age (i.e., the time gap between the originals and the oldest copies), all contestants in the Great Debate agree that the NT documents are, far and away, the best of antiquity. Today we possess fragments of certain NT books copied around 100 A.D.. We possess whole books (e.g., gospels, epistles, etc.) copied around 200 A.D.. With copies of books written between 100 and 350 A.D., we are able to assemble the entire NT. There is, then, a relatively small temporal gap between the original NT manuscripts and our oldest extant copies.

On this score, it is instructive to compare the NT documents with others of comparable antiquity. Homer's *Iliad,* for example, was written ca. 800 B.C.; our oldest copy dates to about 400 B.C.. The *History* of Herodotus was written ca. 450 B.C.; our oldest copy dates to 900 A.D.. Caesar's *Gallic Wars* were written ca. 75 B.C.; our oldest copy goes back to ca. 900 A.D.. Zoroaster lived and taught ca. 1000 B.C.; his sayings were not inscripturated until about 300 A.D.. Similarly, Gotama lived and taught ca. 600 B.C.; his biography was not written until the first century A.D.. Again, these contrasts show us that there is but the tiniest temporal gulf between the NT originals and our oldest extant copies. In the eyes of many, this situation is so unusual as to betray the purposeful hand of providence.

As to their abundance, all parties in the Great Debate again agree that the NT manuscripts stand in a class by themselves. Today we possess 5,686 Greek manuscripts or manuscript portions, copied by hand between the first and 16th centuries. Many of these, such as the papyri (109 of them, written on parchment) and the uncials (307 of them, written in capital letters) are very old. Again, this situation is unprecedented and unparalleled in antiquity. Of Homer's *Iliad,* we have 643 extant copies; of Plato's dialogues, seven; of Thucydides' and Herodotus' histories, eight. Yet no classical scholar would question the trustworthiness of any of these manuscripts. How much less, then, should we question the testimony of some 5,700 harmonious NT manuscripts?

This brings us to our third question: are the extant manuscripts accurate copies of the originals? Now it is clear that there is one easy way to find out: all we need to do is see if the copies agree. If, for example, we have only two copies of a given manuscript, and there is a 30-40% difference in content between them, then we know that at least one is seriously corrupted, and perhaps both. If, on the other hand, we have thousands of copies, and they show a 99% agreement, then we can be sure that *all* are quite faithful to the originals, and that between them *we have the originals themselves.*

Such is the case with the NT. Yes, there are slight differences between individual manuscripts: occasional word inversions, diverse spellings, a phrase omitted here or added there, even one or two paragraphs whose authenticity is in doubt. With so many extant manuscripts, such variants are to be expected, for despite the most stringent safeguards, fallible human beings, copying documents by hand, will occasionally make mistakes. However, in the case of the NT, few such mistakes were made—remarkably few. For again, the manuscripts agree over 99% of the time. Furthermore, careful comparison of all the manuscripts usually enables scholars to identify the correct reading with confidence. Again, this means that we not only have trustworthy copies of the original but, in effect, the originals themselves.[6] Such agreement is astonishing, almost to the point of being miraculous. But if it is almost miraculous, are we not again seeing the hand of God at work in history, carefully preserving his inspired scriptures for future generations?[7]

Christian philosopher Ravi Zacharias sums up the manuscript evidence as follows:

> In real terms, the New Testament is easily the best attested ancient writing in terms of the sheer number of documents, the time span between the events and the document, and the variety of documents available to sustain or contradict it. There is nothing in ancient manuscript evidence to match such textual availability and integrity.[8]

The NT Canon

We come now to the second part of the manuscript test. Yes, it is comforting to know that the NT manuscripts are so very old, numerous, and harmonious. But to feel sure that they give us an accurate picture of Jesus, we must also know that the traditional gospels (and the traditional NT) do not leave out any other books—books that might supplement, or possibly even challenge, the portrait given in the Christian Bible. In other words, thoughtful seekers will want to know if the four "canonical gospels"—the four gospels consistently approved by Christian leaders down through the centuries—are the *only* historically reliable gospels, the *only* documents that open a true window onto Jesus' life and teachings.

This is a live issue. Today, many people are claiming, for example, that the so-called Gnostic gospels give us a truer picture of Jesus' life and teachings than the canonical. "Scholars" and novelists of this persuasion therefore tell us that the historical Jesus was a mystic, a feminist, a mere man, possibly even a husband and a father! Tellingly, their opinions vary widely, but all in this camp agree on one thing: Jesus was certainly *not* the incarnate Son of God who died for his people's sins and rose again on the third day. *That* Jesus, we are told, is a myth and a legend, the fabrication of cunning Church leaders who violently suppressed the true (Gnostic) Christians, the true (Gnostic) gospels, and the true story and message of the true (Gnostic) Jesus—all in order to advance their own patriarchal interests. As fiction writer Dan Brown, of *Da Vinci Code* fame, sums up the situation, "It was all about power." And powerful the patriarchs must have been, since their ecclesiastical coup has allegedly succeeded in fooling and dominating Western Civilization for two millennia!

Needless to say, these are radical claims, and quite attractive to those who seek new and "broader" versions of the Christian faith. The important question, however, is whether or not the claims are true. Happily, the facts of the matter are readily available to all who want to find them. One need only spend a little time studying the well-documented history of the NT canon, a history about which responsible scholars on *both* sides of the Great Debate fundamentally agree. A brief overview of the evidence will suffice to show why the traditional NT canon has rightly held sway for some 2000 years.

The proper historical focus of such a survey is the time span between the creation of the original NT documents (ca. 50-90 A.D.) and the Synod of Hippo (393 A.D.), where the 27 books of the NT were *officially* ratified as genuine and authoritative.[9] At the very beginning of this period, says the NT, the apostles themselves taught the new converts orally (Acts 2:42, 5:42). Soon, however, various circumstances pressured them to communicate in writing. For example, theological and moral aberration in some of the infant congregations elicited letters of instruction, censure, encouragement, and exhortation (Gal. 1:6, 1 Cor 7:1, Col. 2:8, 2 John 1:7). Moreover, as it became clear that Christ was delaying his return, the apostles also began to feel the necessity of preserving the genuine gospel traditions in writing for future generations (Luke 1:1f, 2 Pet. 1:12-15). Very importantly, in the midst such ministerial duties, they realized that the living Christ was empowering *them, and them alone, to write NT scripture* (Mark 13:31, 1 Thess. 2:13, 2 Pet. 3:16). In other words, they saw that through his apostolic vessels, the heavenly Prophet himself was fulfilling his promise to lay the doctrinal foundation of his Church (Mt. 16:13-20, Eph. 2:19-22). This is why the apostles so strenuously insisted that all Christians—both leaders and laity—must receive their oral and written teachings as the all-sufficient rule for faith and practice (1 Cor. 4:6, 14:36-38, 2 Thess. 2:15, 1 John 4:6, 2 John 1:9).

Subsequent history vindicated the wisdom of the apostles' actions. In the years following their death, a multitude of spurious gospels, Acts of the apostles, epistles, and apocalypses appeared on the scene—books that modern scholars refer to as *the NT pseudepigrapha*. Many of these writings were promulgated by the Gnostics—Greco-Roman cultists who generally espoused their own peculiar mixture of Platonism, mysticism, feminism, asceticism, and sexual libertinism. Others were indeed the stuff of legend: fanciful embellishments of the story of Jesus and other famous gospel figures. From the very beginning, Church leaders rejected all such writings as spurious. This was not a complicated or difficult process. To determine the divine inspiration and authority of a given book, they had only to examine it in the light of four familiar, common sense criteria.

The first and most important of these was *apostolicity*. That is, in order to be included in the NT canon, a book had to have been written by an apostle, or by someone who had the approval of an apostle. Examples of the latter are Luke, the colleague of Paul, and Mark, the colleague of Peter.

The second criterion was early and widespread *usage* in the churches. Ultimately based on apostolicity, this criterion cut down whole forests of competitors, entailing as it did the rejection of any document appearing after the end of the first century.

The third standard was *doctrinal integrity*. Here, church leaders demanded that all the scriptures be "perfectly joined together in the same mind and the same judgment" (1 Cor. 1:10). That is, all *bona fide* scripture must tell the same story about Jesus Christ, and must assign to it the same redemptive meaning as articulated by the apostles.

The fourth and final standard was *the approbation of the Holy Spirit*. When he was on earth, Jesus had told his disciples that he would send them the Spirit of Truth, who would guide them into all truth (John 16:13). Having now received this Spirit, ancient Church leaders listened together for his inward testimony concerning the genuineness of any writing purporting to be from God (Acts 15:28).[10]

Using these four criteria, Church leaders effectually settled upon the extent of the NT canon *long before the Council of Hippo*, and were therefore easily able to recognize and reject counterfeits. We learn this important fact primarily from the voluminous writings of the so-called Church fathers, early Christian leaders who served from the second through the fourth centuries. A representative sampling includes Justin Martyr (A.D. 100-165), Irenaeus of Lyons (flourished, A.D. 175-195), Clement of Alexandria (A.D. 150-212), Origen (A.D. 185-253), Tertullian (A.D. 160-220), Hippolytus (A.D. 170-235), and Eusebius of Caesarea, (A.D. 265-339).

Their united testimony about the canonical gospels is most impressive. Together, these seven men cite or allude to the traditional four gospels some 19,000 times. Irenaeus reckons that God purposely gave us *exactly* four, thereby signaling that the one gospel message should reach the four corners of the earth. Needless to say, for Irenaeus the four-fold gospel canon was definitely closed![11] Importantly, these seven fathers also quote or allude to the traditional 27 NT books some 36,000 times. This is why scholars have repeatedly noted that we can reconstruct virtually the entire NT from scriptural citations or allusions found in the patristic writings.[12] Note also that in referencing the 27 canonical books, the fathers explicitly speak of them as sacred *scripture,* and cite apostolic authorship as their prime reason for doing so. Where they refer to non-canonical writings, it is almost always to repudiate them as spurious and/or heretical.

It is true that church leaders occasionally expressed reservations about a few of the NT books (e.g., Hebrews, James, Jude, 2 Peter, 2 and 3 John, and the Revelation). In some cases, the authorship of the book was in doubt (e.g., Hebrews, 2 Peter). In others, its doctrinal integrity was at issue (e.g., James, Jude, the Revelation). But such doubts were not widespread, nor did they ever stop these books from being used as scripture in most congregations. It is hardly surprising, then, that prayerful study and lively debate soon led church leaders to concur in the genuineness of all 27 books. Again, this shows that the early Church had, in effect, settled on the parameters of the NT canon centuries before the Council of Hippo. Feeling the need to ratify those parameters once for all, the Council simply applied its official seal.[13]

Saying "No" to Gnosticism

Having now surveyed the process of canonization, we can readily see why the fathers rejected the Gnostic gospels. Above all, these gospels were not apostolic. Having been written in the second and third centuries, they could not possibly have been authored by Christ's apostles or their associates. Moreover, they had no history of usage in the older and much larger orthodox Christian congregations. Rather, they enjoyed only limited and highly localized use in small sects that Christian leaders consistently dismissed as heretical.

Also, these gospels were manifestly unorthodox, and this for several reasons.

First, they were not gospels at all, since they made little or no effort to describe the life of Jesus, or to ground it in detailed, verifiable history. Rather, they were more in the nature of Socratic dialogues, with the Gnostics placing "wise" sayings in the mouth of Jesus in an effort to give credibility to their own doctrines and to win the orthodox disciples of Jesus to their cause (1 John 2:19).

Secondly, their teachings were at odds with every major tenet of Christian theism. The Gnostics denied the biblical doctrine of the Trinity, creation *ex nihilo*, the fall of man into sin, the incarnation of the Son of God, his atoning death, his bodily resurrection, and his coming again in glory to raise the dead and judge the world in righteousness. Instead, the Gnostic Jesus preached "salvation" by means of religious ritual and mystical experience, culminating in the absorption of the disembodied soul into the light of heaven above. Most emphatically, this was not the doctrine of the biblical Jesus. Therefore, Jesus' true apostles—reacting to the proto-Gnostic heresies in their own day—were at considerable pains to say so.[14]

Finally, the Gnostics did not even agree among themselves. In other words, their gospels do not give us one alternative to the biblical Jesus, but many. For example, *The Gospel of Mary* and *The Sophia Of Jesus Christ* cast women in a very favorable light, even seeing in Mary Magdalene a kind of spiritual consort to Jesus. Yet *The Gospel of Thomas* has Jesus acknowledging that women do not deserve eternal life, and promising Peter that he will so guide Mary as to make her into a male, "...for every female who makes herself male will enter the Kingdom of Heaven."[15] Some Gnostics apparently practiced ritual sexual intercourse, while others propounded a strict asceticism. Some taught that Jesus was a mere man, and that the Christ was a spiritual entity that descended upon him at his baptism; others taught that Jesus was not a man at all, but a purely spiritual apparition (a view called *docetism*). So again, the Gnostic gospels do not give us a single theology or a single Jesus. They do not speak with a united voice, whereas the canonical gospels do.

We see, then, why the Church fathers so easily and so vigorously rejected these writings. Despite their alluring titles, the Gnostic gospels fooled no one, since their late dates, limited usage, and unorthodox contents all proved them to be non-apostolic and therefore spurious. Having long had the real scriptures in their hands and in their hearts, these pastors could easily recognize and reject the false.

Our brief survey of the evidence therefore enables us to see that the four traditional gospels—and all the rest of the traditional NT books—pass the manuscript test with flying colors. The extant copies are old, numerous, and virtually identical. Moreover, because the pseudepigraphical gospels are none of the above, they have no right to be numbered among the canonical, or even to stand as a coherent canon by themselves. So far, then, we have no good reason to doubt that the traditional gospels open a clear and reliable window onto the historical Jesus.

The Historiographic Test

We come now to the second test by which one may establish the trustworthiness of an historical document: *the historiographic test*. That's a big word, but the underlying question it raises is really quite simple: Do the documents under discussion—in this case the four gospels—meet the traditional standards of trustworthy historical writing? Would they win the approval of a sharp, fair-minded judge or historian?

To answer these questions, we need to know the criteria by which sharp, fair-minded historians judge historical documents. Once we are clear on these, we can proceed to the step that most concerns us: applying the criteria to the gospels in order to determine their historical reliability.

Again, establishing these criteria is both a reasonable and important priority for seekers. Obviously, the unknown god knows that many people are skeptical about miracles. Assuming, then, that Jesus is his miracle-working Teacher, we may reasonably expect this god to overcome our skepticism by working meticulously to ensure the historical credibility of the documents that tell Jesus' story. Accordingly, the inspired record of the life of god's appointed Teacher should be an historian's delight, meeting and exceeding every criterion of good historiography. Only thus shall the specter of the legendary be banished once for all.

Now in preparing to isolate these criteria and apply them to the gospels, we need first to be clear about the *purpose* of any historical document. Fortunately, this is no big mystery: its purpose is to tell us what happened.

To say the same thing in legal jargon, its purpose is to *testify* about what took place. Significantly enough, we find that the gospel writers repeatedly use this very word in describing their work. As if to underscore the urgency of their message—and as if to invite readers to *judge* that message scrupulously—they tell us over and again that they are bringing us *eyewitness testimony* about the life of Jesus of Nazareth. Clearly, they want us to receive their books as history. Just as clearly, they expect us to judge their books according to traditional standards of good historiography. Therefore, being well acquainted with "cleverly devised fables," they are at great pains to make sure readers will not place their own narratives of Jesus' life and teachings in that despised category.

Let us respond, then, to their open invitation. Let us look briefly at seven basic criteria for good evidence and good historical writing—seven criteria for trustworthy historical testimony—and see how the gospels measure up to each one.

Quality

Trustworthy historical testimony must be of the highest quality. The highest quality testimony is, of course, *eyewitness* testimony. And this is just the kind of testimony that Church history—along with some of the evangelists themselves—tells us we have in the four gospels (Luke 1:2, Acts 2:32, 3:15, 13:31, 2 Pet. 1:16). Old and reliable tradition identifies the author of the first gospel as Matthew, a disciple of Jesus and an eyewitness of his entire ministry (Mt. 9:9). Mark, according to equally strong tradition, was a close associate of the apostle Peter, whose first-hand testimony about Jesus is reported in Mark's gospel (1 Peter 5:13, 2 Peter 1:15-16). Though Luke was not an eyewitness of Jesus' life, he shows himself the quintessential historian by declaring in his prologue that he has personally sought out and carefully arranged the eyewitness testimony of those who were (Luke 1:1-4). Like Matthew, John was one of the twelve; indeed, he was a member of Christ's inner circle of three (Matt. 17:1, Mark 5:37). His gospel abounds with assurances that what is written there is altogether trustworthy, and the reason given for this trustworthiness is that he himself has seen and heard these things firsthand (John 1:14, 19:35, 20:31, 21:24; cf. I John 1:1-4). Moreover, beyond the gospels we have the later writings of Peter and Paul, both of whom relate eyewitness testimony about their personal experiences with Jesus (2 Pet. 1:16, 1 Cor. 9:1).

We see, then, that the NT testimony about Jesus is indeed of the highest quality, since it is, by and large, firsthand testimony—*just the kind of testimony that carries the greatest weight in a court of law.* That the gospel writers explicitly describe it as such, and urge us to receive it as such, is all the more impressive, lending a palpable aura of historicity to these documents—an aura conspicuously absent from the world's myths and legends.

Quantity

In a court of law the testimony of a single eyewitness is weighty, but the concurring testimony of two or more is nearly always conclusive. Thus, judges, lawyers, jurors, and all good historians agree with what common sense and everyday experience teach: the *quantity* of testimony concerning a given event is nearly as important as its quality. Interestingly, the Bible confirms common sense, expressly prescribing that, "By the mouth of two or three witnesses every matter must be decided" (Deut. 19:15, Mt. 18:16, 2 Cor. 13:1).

The Bible's testimony about Jesus not only meets this requirement, but lavishly exceeds it. As we just saw, Matthew and John were themselves eyewitnesses of Jesus' life. Mark gives us the eyewitness testimony of Peter, and perhaps some of his own as well (Mark 16:5). Luke, an "investigator" of Jesus' life, gives us the eyewitness testimony of the people he interviewed. Doubtless this included Paul, some of Jesus' other apostles, Mary the mother of Jesus, and some of the disciples who followed Jesus early on, etc. (Luke 1:1-4, NAS). And again, the writings of Peter and Paul not only contain their own eyewitness testimony about Jesus, but also clearly assume the truth of what is written in the four canonical gospels (2 Pet. 1:12f, 1 Cor. 15:1f, Heb. 2:1-4). We have, then, within the pages of the NT itself, an impressive quantity of the best quality evidence. And as we shall see momentarily, there is still more testimony to be found outside the NT. No fair-minded historian could ask for more.

Independence and Harmony

These two criteria are closely related. Judges and historians are very pleased to receive testimony from two or more eyewitnesses. If, however, they are to deem it trustworthy, the witnesses must be independent. That is, there must be no sign of collusion between them. Only then will the harmony of their testimony tend to its credibility; only then will the testimony of the second and third witnesses reinforce the testimony of the first.

As to independence of testimony, the four gospels excel. Indeed, John's gospel is so independent from the other three that scholars have put it in a category all by itself. Yet even among the quite similar "synoptic gospels" (i.e., Matthew, Mark, and Luke) there are striking differences in contents, style, vocabulary, theological emphasis, and intended audience. Indeed, this is so true that despite 200 years of concerted effort, NT scholars are still unable to agree as to which one of the three synoptic gospels, if any, served as a prototype for the other two.[16] In short, there is no evidence of collusion or imitation on the part of the gospel authors. They are independent witnesses of Jesus' life and teachings.

All the more impressive, then, is the harmony of the four gospels. Yes, there are important differences among them. Yet with respect to the basic course of Jesus' life and the essential contents of his teaching, they are all in one accord. To be specific: all four evangelists testify about a Jesus who declared his own divinity, claimed divine prerogatives, performed numerous and powerful miracles, preached the Kingdom of God, taught "the mysteries" (i.e., new truths) of the Kingdom to his disciples, purposely surrendered himself to the authorities for crucifixion, died, was buried, and rose from the dead on the third day. And all the other NT writers did the same. Such harmony is impressive indeed, all the more so when we compare it with the historical and theological disharmony of the extra-canonical gospels.

Here, however, we must linger a moment to discuss a favorite theme of the liberal critics of the gospels: apparent discrepancies in gospel accounts of the same event. These are fairly numerous. Matthew, for example, tells us that there were two demoniacs at Gadara (Mt. 8:28-34); Mark and Luke mention only one (Mark 5:1-17, Luke 8:26-37). Matthew and Mark state that two blind men were healed as Jesus left Jericho (Mt. 20:29-34); Luke that one was healed as Jesus entered Jericho (Mark 10:46ff). Matthew seems to say that the centurion himself came to Jesus, seeking healing for his servant (Mt. 8:5-13); Luke tells us that the elders of Israel went in the centurion's place (Luke 7:2-10). Matthew states that Judas died by hanging himself (Mt. 27:5); Luke writes that he fell and his body burst open (Acts 1:18). Luke's version of Jesus' Sermon on the Mount differs significantly from Matthew's, (Mt. 5-7, Luke 6). Similarly, Matthew's genealogy of Jesus differs sharply from Luke's (Mt.1, Luke 3). What are we to make of such things?

Liberals argue that these kinds of discrepancies are the telltale signs of a process of legendary formation; that each of the canonical gospels is actually a collection of oral traditions that circulated and "evolved" over time; that for this reason we have lost sight of the nugget of historical truth lying at the core of the traditions; and that for this reason we are wise to regard the entire edifice of gospel supernaturalism as legend.

In the pages ahead we will probe this radical thesis from several different angles. Here, however, it suffices to say that, in the minds of conservatives, liberals are making a theological mountain out of a literary molehill. To begin with, they point out that in all essentials—including the distinctive NT supernaturalism—the four gospels agree. Thus, to use the cases just cited, all three synoptic evangelists agree that demons were cast out, that blind men received their sight, and that the centurion's servant was miraculously healed from a distance. In other words, no matter where we look—even into the midst of the alleged discrepancies—there is no escaping the supernatural "Jesus of faith." On what basis, then, can liberals justly dismiss him as legend?

Furthermore, conservatives do not concede that the differing accounts are really discrepant or contradictory. Most fundamentally, this position flows from their faith in the divine inspiration of the four gospels, a faith that logically entails the Bible's inerrancy.[17] But it also flows from common sense. Before concluding that the evangelists actually contradict one another, say the conservatives, why not give them the benefit of the doubt? Why not look for a far less radical solution? For example, why not consider the possibility that the different accounts simply supplement one another, or that they may actually describe different, though similar, events. Surely it is more reasonable to say that there were two demonized men at Gadara, but one who especially commanded Jesus' attention, than it is to say that the whole story is a legend. Or again, surely it easier to surmise that Jesus healed one blind man while entering Jericho, and two others while leaving, than it is to surmise that no healing happened at all.[18]

Finally, conservatives further respond by arguing that apparent discrepancies in the gospels actually lend *greater* weight, rather than less, to their historical credibility. For what if all the accounts were identical? Then skeptics would doubtless charge the evangelists with collusion, and rightly so. On the other hand, what if the accounts were profoundly discrepant? What if the evangelists *never* told the same story; or what if they did, but egregiously contradicted themselves on its fundamentals? Then again the skeptics would rightfully dismiss their historicity. It appears, then, that there are just enough differences between the testimony of the four evangelists to identify them as *independent and harmonious witnesses*. Indeed, so subtly do the four gospels walk the narrow band of ground between collusion and contradiction, that many scholars simply shake their heads in amazement, seeing the hand of God itself in the richly nuanced shape of these writings. How good and wise of him, they say, to give us exactly the kind of independent and harmonious testimony we need in order to believe that the gospels are not legend, but true history.

Integrity

Trustworthy witnesses are people of integrity, people who display soundness of mind and character. Let us inquire for a moment to see if the NT authors meet this important two-fold criterion.

As for soundness of mind, it is true that Jesus' disciples were sometimes accused of being mad (Acts 26:24), a charge leveled even against their Master (Mark 3:21, John 10:20). They themselves, however, considered their faith to be quite reasonable. Indeed, they reckoned it a species of madness *not* to embrace it (Acts 26:25f, 2 Thess. 3:2). These opposing perspectives on the Christian faith were, of course, rooted in opposing presuppositions and worldviews. A seeker must, then, first determine which worldview is true before he can know which part of the world was (and is) mad. Meanwhile, he will want simply to listen to the NT writers for himself, honestly asking whether madmen could have written the kind of words they wrote, or lived the kind of purposeful, consistent, and self-sacrificial lives they lived.

As to soundness of character, we do well to remember how emphatically the Teacher of the four gospel writers elevated the love of truth as a cardinal spiritual virtue, and how thoroughly he condemned lying as a work the devil himself (John 4:23-24, 8:32, 18:37; Mt. 19:18, John 8:44-6). Importantly, the NT shows us over and again that the disciples fully embraced this ethic, both in their ecclesiastical judgments and in their official teachings (Acts 5:1f, Col. 3:9, James 3:14, 1 John 1:6, Rev. 22:15). How likely is it, then, that their gospels were pious frauds, or that they wrote them with a careless disregard for the facts? And if indeed they were well-intentioned liars, how likely is it that they would have maintained their lies in the face of continuous ostracism and persecution, even unto death as martyrs? Jesus' followers had many opportunities—and many good reasons—to confess that they had fabricated the divine, miracle-working, risen Jesus of faith. Both biblical and extra-biblical church history reveals that they never did. Hard as it is, then, to believe that the apostles were lunatics, it is harder still to believe them liars. Everything we know about them commends them to us as men of integrity, sound in mind and sound in character, even to the death.[19]

Corroboration

In addition to direct eyewitness testimony, judges and historians look for corroboration: other kinds of evidence that indirectly support the first-hand testimony given. Here I will touch on two lines of evidence that corroborate the testimony of the evangelists: ancient non-christian testimony about Jesus

THE GREAT DEBATE

and his followers, and the more general testimony of secular history and archeology concerning events and conditions in Israel at the time of Christ.

Confirmations of NT history appear in the writings of both orthodox Jews and non-christian Gentiles. The Jewish historian Josephus (fl. A.D. 93), for example, wrote of John the Baptizer, describing him as a good man who summoned the people to express their piety through water baptism, and who was slain by evil king Herod. Though probably not as a believer, Josephus also wrote of Jesus, giving a thoroughly biblical sketch of his life, death, and resurrection. He described Jesus as "...one who wrought surprising feats, and (who was) a teacher of such people as accept the truth gladly." He also recounts the death of the apostle James by stoning, specifically mentioning him as the brother of Jesus.

Further corroboration is found in the *Mishnah*, a body of Jewish teaching compiled around 200 A.D.. Like Josephus, the *Mishnah* acknowledges that Jesus was a popular teacher, healer, and worker of miracles. However, unlike Josephus it goes on to ascribe his powers to sorcery, and condemns him as a false Messiah, justly sentenced to death.

Still more corroboration appears in the writings of Gentile authors. For example, in relating how Nero blamed the despised Christians for the great fire of Rome, the Roman historian Tacitus alludes to Jesus' death and resurrection. Again, Seutonius, an imperial secretary, confirms the testimony of Luke in Acts 18:2, that Claudius expelled the Jews from Rome, apparently as a result of controversy with Christians about the person and work of the Messiah. Or again, Pliny the Younger, a Roman administrator, wrote a letter to the emperor Trajan in which he describes in some detail the worship of the early Christians. In all of these late first century writings, we clearly see an outline of the NT Jesus of faith, and also how extensively believers worshiped him *as the divine Son of God* throughout the Roman Empire of the day.[20]

This is but a sampling of the extant extra-biblical testimony about Jesus. Further study would show that it supplies a remarkably detailed portrait of Jesus and the early Church, one that harmonizes perfectly with the NT records. Indeed, when asked what we could learn about Jesus strictly from the oldest extra-biblical writings in our possession, NT scholar Edwin Yamauchi responded:

> We could know that, first, Jesus was a Jewish teacher; second, many people believed that he performed healings and exorcisms; third, some people believed he was the Messiah; fourth, he was rejected by the Jewish leaders; fifth, he was crucified under Pontius Pilate in the reign of Tiberius; sixth, despite this shameful death, his followers, who believed that he was

still alive, spread beyond Palestine so that there were multitudes of them in Rome by A.D. 64; and seventh, all kinds of people from the cities and countryside, men and women, slave and free, worshiped him as God.[21]

This brings us to our second line of corroborating evidence, secular history and archeology concerning NT times. In broaching this topic, it is important to note at the outset that the NT—and the Bible as a whole—implicitly *invite* us to seek out historical and archeological confirmation for their assertions. This is because the gospels and the book of Acts read like history. Indeed, it is so important to the NT authors that we receive their accounts as history, that they purposely and prolifically tether their narratives to historically verifiable people, places, things, and events. For example, no one can read Luke's introduction to the ministry of John the Baptizer and think him a Homer or an Aesop (Luke 3:1-2). The evangelists do not write to create or purvey legend, but rather to safeguard against it (Luke 1:1-2).

Receiving, then, the implicit challenge of the NT documents, scholars have gone in search of historical and archeological verification. They have not come back empty-handed. They have found, for example, Herod's temple (Luke 1:9); Herod's winter palace in Jericho (Mt. 2:4); the possible site of Herod's tomb near Bethlehem (Mt. 2:19); the synagogue in Capernaum (Mark 1:21); the pool of Siloam (John 9:7); the pool of Bethesda (John 5:2); a Pilate inscription in Caesarea, identifying him as prefect of Judea (Luke 3:1); Peter's house (Mt. 8:14); and Jacob's well (John 4:4-6). And all this is to say nothing of dozens of other discoveries verifying specific historical details found in the book of Acts and the epistles.[22]

In this connection, we must not fail to note the special role that Luke's writings have had in winning respect for the overall historicity of the NT. His vivid and detailed descriptions of things religious, political, military, nautical, and geographical have been repeatedly confirmed by archeological research. Indeed, this is so true that scholars all across the theological spectrum reckon him to be one of the great historians of antiquity. Says classics professor E. M. Blaiklock, "Luke is a consummate historian, to be ranked in his own right with the great writers of the Greeks." Similarly, converted skeptic William Ramsey describes Luke as "...a historian of the first rank; (his) history is unsurpassed in respect of its trustworthiness."[23]

We conclude, then, that the testimony of the NT in general—and of the gospels in particular—finds substantial corroboration in extra-biblical history and archeology. Can legends do the same?

THE GREAT DEBATE

Preponderance

According to this criterion, the bulk of historical testimony must weigh heavily in favor of a particular version of a given event. In other words, because of the quality and quantity of evidence in its favor, one version of a particular event clearly stands out as superior to all others. Now on this score, the NT version of Jesus wins hands down, since, as have just seen, there is an abundance of high quality testimony favoring it, *and no historical evidence at all for any other!* The closest thing to an alternative Jesus we have is the Jesus of the Gnostics. But we have already seen that the Gnostic sects actually give us *many* different portraits of Jesus. And again, the Gnostic gospels are late, a-historical, non-apostolic, theologically unorthodox, and far outside the mainstream of early Christian understanding. There is, then, no sound historical evidence for any other Jesus besides the one we meet in the NT.

For students of the Great Debate, this crucial historical fact is decisive. All contestants in the Debate agree that Jesus was a real person. Conservatives argue that the NT describes him perfectly. Liberals are, of course, at liberty to disagree. But if they hope to win seekers to their position, *they are under a positive obligation to show us, from history, what kind of person Jesus really was.* But they cannot. For again, none of Jesus' contemporaries—let alone his disciples—left us with a single trustworthy document depicting a Jesus other than the one we meet in the NT. Nor is there corroborating evidence for any such Jesus.

For all these reasons, theological liberals are on a collision course with the historians. The liberal may say, "Look, we *know* that miracles don't happen and that dead men don't rise, so the real Jesus *must* have been different." And then, seizing upon preferred scraps of "evidence" from the gospels, he may go on to construct a more plausible and pleasing Jesus—say a feminist, or a socialist, or a misguided apocalyptic prophet. But the objective historian will reply, "I am not interested in your philosophical presuppositions, nor in your speculations. I am interested in your evidence. There is a lot of good evidence for the Jesus of the NT. Please show me your evidence for a different Jesus and I will gladly weigh the two in the balance." That historian (may his tribe increase) will have a very long wait, for there is none. There is an *absolute* preponderance of historical evidence favoring the NT Jesus, supernatural and all.

Summing up, we have seen that the canonical gospels pass the historiographic test handily. Their eyewitness testimony is of the very best quality. It is supplied in unexpected abundance. It is both strikingly independent and impressively harmonious. The witnesses themselves are people of integrity, displaying both soundness of mind and nobility of character. Their testimony is corroborated by Jew and Gentile, friend and foe, history and archeology. And quite decisively, there is no credible testimony of any other kind. Therefore, seekers may well ask, "If an unknown god wanted to use historical documents to bear witness to his Teacher, what more or what different could he have done to show their trustworthiness than we see in the case of the four canonical gospels?"

The Spiritual Test

We come now to a third and final test that wise seekers will bring to the gospels: the spiritual test. Here the seeker listens carefully to his deepest spiritual and ethical intuitions about a given teacher. In doing so, he consciously asks himself whether the life and doctrine of this teacher is consistent with what he already knows about the unknown god from nature, conscience, and the probationary order. More particularly, he asks whether a god so manifestly personal, powerful, wise, benevolent, and holy would be likely to send us a teacher such as this. It is true, of course, that this test is not infallible, since human intuitions and judgments are not infallible. On the other hand, it is still quite valuable. Indeed, I would argue that it is both indispensable and inevitable, since, as we saw earlier, spiritual and ethical intuitions appear to be god-given equipment in the seeker's search for truth. Therefore, seekers should indeed administer this test with all due caution, yet also with all due confidence, realizing that in their deepest intuitions about a given teacher they may well be hearing the voice of the unknown god himself!

Later in our journey we will apply the spiritual test to Jesus' teachings. Here, however, we must focus our attention on the aspect of his life that strikes some people as legendary: its supernaturalism. Having already surveyed this supernaturalism in considerable detail, I would now invite seekers to test it by bringing the following questions to the miracle-working Christ of the gospels.

First, is the supernaturalism that we find there intuitive? That is, does it win the assent of what might be called your "spiritual common sense?" In particular, do the supernatural elements of Jesus' life strike you as plausible, purposeful, and even beautiful? Could or would the unknown god perform such miracles through this man, or any man? Or, to the contrary, does the overall picture seem so counter-intuitive—so far-fetched, pointless, and bizarre—that you cannot help but dismiss it out of hand?

Secondly, is this supernaturalism right? That is, does it win the assent of your distinctly ethical intuitions? Think, for example, of how Merlin transformed King Uther into the likeness of the Duke of Cornwall, so that Uther could sleep with the Duke's wife and conceive Arthur. Does this story strike as you as history or legend? If as legend, why? Keeping your answer in mind, think now of how Jesus healed the sick, cast out evil spirits, fed the hungry, and raised the dead. Do these stories seem fundamentally different than the one about Merlin? If so, why?

And thirdly, does NT supernaturalism give you hope? Do Jesus' miracles, after eliciting nothing but your incredulity and scorn, return you to a dreary world whose farthest horizon is old age, sickness, and death. Or, to the contrary, do they somehow communicate the love, goodness, and concern of the unknown god—so much so that they fan into flame your smoldering dreams of a better life in a better world? If a man turns stones into doves, or inflates himself into a giant, you will doubtless think him a legend. But if he turns cripples into dancers, or sinners into saints, likely as not you will find yourself thinking—and even hoping—that he may well be a lord.

Turning the Tables

In the Great Debate about Jesus, it is the liberals who are usually on the attack, seeking to discredit the historicity of the NT Christ. Lately, however, conservatives have been turning the tables on them, showing why the liberal hypothesis of a legendary Jesus is not just historically implausible, but incredible. I have already discussed a number of their main arguments. Let us now conclude this leg of our journey by examining two more.

The Jesus Legend is Too Young

First, the NT Jesus appears on the scene far too early to be a legend. By their very nature, legends develop slowly, at least over a couple of generations, and sometimes over centuries. Traditions about the supernatural Jesus are, however, nearly contemporaneous with the man himself.

To illustrate this point, let us consider the NT tradition of Jesus' resurrection. Scholars all across the spectrum admit that Paul's first letter to the Corinthians was written about 55-57 A.D., slightly more than twenty years after Jesus' death. Yet this letter contains a ringing affirmation of the resurrection, giving a short but detailed list of certain people who had seen the risen Christ themselves. Indeed, *some of those persons were still alive even as Paul wrote* (1 Cor. 15:1f)! And if, as some scholars believe, Paul's words in this letter were actually part of a creed used in the worship of the nascent Church, then this particular formulation of the resurrection tradition could go back as far as 35-38 A.D.! An early legend, indeed![24]

Similarly, most scholars agree that Luke wrote the book of Acts around 63 A.D.. This respected history of the infant Church contains numerous accounts of the earliest apostolic preaching, which occurred first in Jerusalem and then in Gentile regions beyond. In all of them, the miracle-working, crucified, and risen Jesus is consistently proclaimed as Israel's Messiah and the Savior and Judge of the whole world (Acts 2, 10, 17). How could such "legends" have arisen so quickly? And if they were legends, how could they fail to be disputed by the living witnesses of the real, historical Jesus who knew better?

The Jesus Legend is Historically Implausible

Questions like these bring us to a second criticism of the liberal position, namely, that naturalistic theories about the origin of the Jesus legend are both historically implausible and psychologically incredible.

Consider, for example, the conspiracy theory of Jesus' resurrection. According to this view, the historical Jesus was indeed crucified, after which his dead body was either devoured by wild animals, thrown into a common grave, or placed in a tomb and later stolen by the disciples. In any case, the disciples—presumably moved by misguided devotion to their deceased Master—quickly conspired to propagate the claim that Jesus rose from the dead (just as he had said he would), and that he was indeed Israel's Messiah (just as he had claimed he was).

Conservatives argue that this hypothesis is actually more difficult to believe than the NT itself. Their reasons are many.

It is true, they concede, that the corpses of crucified men were sometimes placed in a common grave or eaten by animals. There is, however, no shred of historical evidence to the effect that this is what happened to Jesus' body. It is, of course, true that some of the Jewish leaders *believed* his disciples had stolen their Master's body (Mt. 28:11-15). But here again, we have no historical evidence that such was the case. Moreover, proponents of the conspiracy theory must somehow explain the origin of the early and detailed traditions connected with Jesus' burial: how Joseph of Arimathea asked Pilate for his body, took it down from the cross, wrapped it in cloths and spices, deposited it in his own unused sepulcher, and rolled a stone across the entrance, whereupon it was later sealed by Roman guards stationed at the tomb to guard it against theft. Did the disciples simply invent these traditions? If so, why is there no historical record of anyone—whether friend or foe—denying them?

To such glaring historical implausibility, the conspiracy theory adds immense psychological implausibility, as well. It does so by affirming that Jesus' numerous disciples would all conspire to build a whole new Jewish sect on a foundation of outright lies—and that multitudes of people were gullible enough for the lies to succeed.

Such affirmations definitely raise some troubling questions, questions that reveal how psychologically bizarre this theory really is. Here are a few.

How likely is it that Jesus' disciples, having unexpectedly lost their Master to a hostile mob, would have the courage, wit, or time to perpetrate an elaborate hoax about his rising again on the third day?

If they were devout Jews, why would they dedicate the rest of their lives to proclaiming a false Messiah, rather than simply admitting their error and joining the rest of Israel to wait for the true one?

If they were men of character who really loved their teacher, why would they desecrate his grave in order to erect a lie in his name? And if some of them were *not* men of character—if they were willing to lie for some imaginary personal gain—is it likely that *all* of them were?

In the face of the ostracism, beatings, and death that constantly dogged them, why would the conspirators persist in this hoax to the very end of their miserable lives, thereafter to meet the Holy One of Israel in judgment? Would there not be one—whether to ease his conscience or to save his own skin—who would be willing to expose the deception for what it was? And why is there no historical record of any individual or group doing this very thing?

How many original conspirators were there: just a few, or the hundreds of professing eyewitnesses mentioned by Paul? If just a few, how could they get the hundreds to lie? If hundreds, how could so many agree to lie, and continue to do so in the face of so much rejection and persecution?

How was Paul, a notorious opponent of new faith, won to the conspiracy? And how was James, the brother of Jesus and a complete skeptic (John 7:5)?

Finally, how could a lie so quickly overcome widespread disappointment, bitterness, and natural skepticism, that just eight weeks after his death, thousands in Jerusalem believed that Jesus had risen from the dead (Acts 2:41, 4:4)?

Yes, it is one thing to claim that the NT Jesus is a legend, but quite another to supply a plausible explanation of how the legend arose. Perhaps, then, in light of all the historical and psychological evidence we have just considered, the most reasonable conclusion is that he is not a legend at all.

Conclusion

On this leg of our journey our goal has been to plunge into the Great Debate about Jesus of Nazareth; to decide which of the two main views about the supernatural Jesus of the NT is most reasonable; to decide whether he is history or legend. To this end, we adopted a strategy consistent with our identity as seekers: we assumed that the NT Jesus *could* be god's supernaturally attested Teacher, but also that the unknown god would want us to check out this thesis by carefully and critically examining the documents that reveal him to us. We also assumed that if the unknown god really were revealing his Teacher in the NT, then he would surely be at pains to demonstrate the trustworthiness of those documents. Turning to judges and historians for guidance, we concluded that he would likely do so by enabling the NT documents to pass three important tests: the manuscript test, the historiographic test, and the spiritual test. In applying these tests, we found that the NT does indeed pass all three, and not merely acceptably, but exceedingly abundantly beyond all we could think or ask for (Eph. 3:20).

We conclude, then, that for seekers open to the supernatural and willing to be guided by the traditional canons of historical investigation, it is more than reasonable to believe that the supernatural Jesus of the NT is indeed the real historical deal.

CHAPTER 8

SECOND LOOK

AS I JOURNEYED with Jesus through Matthew's gospel, I was deeply impressed by the miraculous signs that surrounded his ministry. Soon enough, however, I began to realize something important: these signs were *not* occurring in a temporal vacuum. To the contrary, they were simply the most outstanding episode in a long history of divine activity and supernatural intervention. I saw this fact in the words of every major actor in the drama unfolding before my eyes: Zacharias, John the baptizer, Jesus, the disciples, and the gospel writers who gave us their story. To a man, they testified that God was not only granting supernatural signs in Jesus' day, but also that he had granted them *prior* to his coming, and that he would indeed grant still more *after* his coming, even to the end of the age. Thus, through the window of the NT, I began to see that the God of Israel had purposed to sow Messianic signs, like so many precious gems, *all along the highway of salvation history*. At no time—past, present, or future—does he leave himself or his Son without a supernatural witness (Acts 14:17).

We must, then, take a second look at the Messianic signs, this time focusing our attention upon the signs given before and after Jesus' earthly ministry. Having surveyed them briefly, we will then be fully acquainted with *the one body of God-given evidences* identifying Jesus of Nazareth as God's appointed Teacher—and as much more besides.

Signs Prior to Jesus' Coming

The signs prior to Jesus' coming fall into three main categories: christophanies, Messianic types, and Messianic prophecies. They appear throughout the *entire* OT. This fact is extremely important, so much so that it behooves us to say a few preliminary words about Jesus' understanding of the Jewish scriptures. As we shall see, it is an understanding that he effectively bequeathed not only to his apostles, but also, through them, to his entire Church.

Three key points may be made.

First, Jesus regarded the thirty-nine books of the Old Testament—what the Jews of his day called the Law, the Prophets, and the Writings—as "the Word of God" (Mt. 15:3-6). In other words, he saw these writings—which he himself referred to as "the scriptures"—as being divinely inspired, and therefore altogether true, trustworthy, and authoritative for the people of God (Mt. 21:42, 22:29, John 10:35).

But secondly, Jesus also regarded these scriptures as being incomplete. Why? Because for him they were, at their very heart, *forward-looking revelations awaiting latter-day fulfillment*. To be specific, he viewed the Law and the Prophets—which spanned some 3,600 years of human history, from the creation of the cosmos to the prophecies of Malachi—as the inspired record of a long, God-ordained *era of promise and preparation*. Accordingly, the main purpose of these writings was to supply a record of what God had said and done all throughout that era in order to prepare for the redemption of the world. Thus, whether meditating upon the words of the prophets, or upon the long, meandering course of OT history, Jesus saw in all of it a veiled and richly symbolic disclosure of the person and work of God's redeemer, the Messiah. But now, said Jesus as he embarked upon his ministry to the Jews, the era of promise and preparation is over. Now the mysterious, forward-looking revelations are being fulfilled (Mt. 26:54, Mark 1:15, Luke 4:21). Now the Messianic redeemer—as well as the rich fruits of his redemptive work—are entering into the world! Here, then, is the true meaning of Jesus' enigmatic words to his disciples: "Do not think that I have come to destroy the Law and the Prophets. I have not come to destroy, but to fulfill" (Mt. 5:17). He had not come to destroy the Jewish scriptures, but rather to *fulfill, supplant,* and *illumine* them through a supreme and final revelation of God's redemptive truth (Mt. 9:14-17, Heb. 8:13).

Needless to say, for the Jews of Jesus' day, this was a radically new perspective on the Word of God. By introducing this new motif of promise and fulfillment, Jesus was actually introducing a whole new method of scriptural interpretation. Henceforth, he implied, men must view the ancient Jewish scriptures as the inspired record of life under an "old covenant" (i.e., agreement), an old covenant that was secretly foreshadowing and preparing the way for a new (Jer. 31:31f, Mt. 9:17, Luke 22:20, Heb. 8:8-12). In other words, they must now interpret the old covenant *Christo-centrically*. That is, they must interpret it as mystically and symbolically looking ahead to the person and work of the One who would introduce the new covenant: the divine-human Messiah, the Lord Jesus Christ (Luke 24:44-49, Heb. 8). Thus, Jesus challenges readers of the OT to ask themselves, "What is the hidden, Messianic significance of these stories? What do they teach us about the person and work of the Christ, who, in the days of the prophets, was still to come, but who, in these last days, has now appeared and begun to fulfill them all" (Heb. 1:1-2)?

All of this brings us to our third and final point, namely that Jesus saw the OT as *a now-completed book of signs*, a book by which God would henceforth identify him (Jesus) to seekers everywhere as the promised Messiah: the divine-human prophet, priest, and king, anointed by God to redeem the world.

We vividly see this new perspective on the scriptures in one of Jesus' dialogues with the Jewish rulers. Speaking of the various signs by which the Father was pleased to bear witness to His Son, Jesus specifically mentions the OT writings, saying, "You search the Scriptures, for in them you think you have eternal life; *and these are they which testify of Me*" (John 5: 39). Truly, this is a radical statement. Here, Jesus is saying that the entire Old Testament has a single, secret, underlying, and unifying theme: himself! Shortly after his resurrection, he spelled this out in no uncertain terms, declaring to his astonished disciples, "This is what I told you while I was still with you: everything must be fulfilled that is written about me in the Law of Moses, the Prophets, and the Psalms" (Luke 24: 44).

Again, in all such statements Jesus' premise is unmistakable: He himself is the living heart of the entire body of OT revelation. But if this is so, then it is clear that the OT immediately becomes a vast treasury of Messianic signs. And interestingly enough, this has indeed been the faith of the Christian Church in every generation. Whether pointing to OT christophanies, Messianic types, or Messianic prophecies, Christians urge people to see them as yet another way in which God is pleased to direct seekers to his redeemer, open their hearts to his message, and establish them in a life of confident, ongoing faith in him.

Was Jesus correct in this radically new interpretation of the Jewish Scriptures? Were his apostles correct in following him in it? Is the Church correct, which has proclaimed and defended it for centuries? The only way for a seeker to find out is to examine and evaluate these signs for himself.

Let us embark, then, upon a brief survey of the three main categories of OT Messianic signs. Hopefully, this will go far towards enabling each reader to draw some solid conclusions of his own.

Christophany

A christophany may be defined as an appearance of the Son of God in Old Testament times. The OT does not, of course, identify this Person in explicitly trinitarian language: that kind of identification had to await the NT era, when God, through Christ, was pleased to unveil the mystery of the Holy Trinity once for all. Instead, the OT typically refers to him as *the Angel of God,* or *the Angel of the LORD*. Nevertheless, one need only examine the relevant texts themselves to see that they are not talking about a true angel (i.e., a *created* spirit being). No, they are clearly talking about a *divine* Person who, *like* the angels, briefly serves as Yahweh's messenger to his people, whether to inform them, guide them, or deliver them from their foes.

Such christophanies were fairly numerous, and occurred all throughout the era of preparation. We read, for example, how the Angel of the Lord appeared to Sarai's maid-servant, Hagar, supplying both her and her child with water, guidance, and words of encouragement (Gen. 16:7-13). Later he came to Abraham on Mt. Moriah, where, among other things, he delivered Isaac from death, and richly blessed his daringly obedient father (Gen. 22:11-15). Still later he visited Jacob, with whom he wrestled at night until the determined patriarch finally prevailed and won a blessing for himself and all Israel (Gen. 32:22f). Next he appeared to Moses and the Israelites in the wilderness, where he took up watchful residence in a pillar of cloud by day and a pillar of fire by night (Ex. 14:19-20, 23:20-23). After that he appeared to Joshua at the walls of Jericho, where he identified himself as the Commander of the LORD'S Army (Josh. 5:13-15). Similarly, on the eve of a great deliverance from the Midianite oppressor, he arrived to charge and comfort the fearful Gideon (Judges 6:11-24). Finally—and none too soon—he appeared in a furnace of fire to Shadrach, Meshach, and Abed-Nego, where, to the astonishment of king Nebuchadnezzar, he looked like a son of the very gods (Dan. 3:19-25)!

Once again, in nearly every one of these OT stories, it is evident that the Angel of the LORD is, in fact, a *divine* person. He is, as it were, an extension of Yahweh himself. This fact shines through with special brilliance in the following narrative of Moses' first encounter with the God of Israel.

> Now Moses kept the flock of Jethro his father-in-law, the priest of Midian. And he led the flock to the back of the desert, and came to Horeb, the mountain of God.
>
> And the Angel of the Lord appeared to him in a flame of fire from the midst of a bush. So he looked, and behold, the bush burned with fire, but

> the bush was not consumed. Then Moses said, "I will now turn aside and see this great sight, why the bush does not burn."
>
> So when the LORD saw that he turned aside to look, God called to him from the midst of the bush and said, "Moses, Moses!"
>
> And he said, "Here I am."
>
> Then He said, "Do not draw near this place. Take your sandals off your feet, for the place where you are standing is holy ground. Moreover, He said, "I am the God of your father—the God of Abraham, the God of Isaac, and the God of Jacob".
>
> —Ex. 3:1-6

As we learn at the outset of this text, the person in the burning bush is the Angel of the LORD. But for many reasons, it is quite clear that this "angel" is actually the LORD himself. We see, for example, that he warns Moses against too near an approach. Next, he commands him to take off his sandals. Finally, he tells him that the ground whereon he stands is holy. These are not the prerogatives of an angel, but of the holy God alone. Of special importance is the fact that the Person in the bush explicitly identifies himself as Yahweh, the covenant-keeping God of Abraham, Isaac, and Jacob. Here, then, is a great mystery: the Person in the bush is indeed a Messenger of the LORD, yet he is not an angelic creation of the LORD. Somehow, he is subordinate to the LORD, yet none other than the LORD himself. In short, while there is apparently only one divine Person in the bush, it appears that there are (at least) two divine Persons in the LORD!

None of this surprises trinitarian interpreters, who have learned from the NT to identify the Angel of the LORD as the eternal Son of the Father. In other words, they see this passage as narrating a christophany. Moreover, by identifying it as such, they feel they can now understand the symbolism of the burning bush, a symbolism that anticipates the incarnation of the Son of God. On this view, the bush represents Christ's humanity. It symbolizes his flesh, the physical side of his being, the part that springs out of the earth (Gen. 2:7, 1 Cor. 15:45). The fire, on the other hand, represents his divine glory, which, being infused into his flesh, radiates both light and warmth to all who behold it. Interestingly, the apostle John tells us that he himself beheld this glory in the person of Jesus of Nazareth—and that he, like Moses, therefore turned aside to look and to follow (John 1:14). The same was true of Peter, James, and Paul (Mt. 17:1, Acts 9:1-6, 2 Cor. 4:6). Indeed, the NT assures us that this kind of thing is happening even today: Through the mystery of preaching, heavenly light is seen to emanate from the Man from Nazareth, thus catching the eye of many a weary seeker wandering through the wilderness of this world (2 Cor. 3:18, Heb. 7:25, Rev. 1:12-17).[1]

Please take a few moments to reflect upon the many christophanies mentioned in this section. Do they unveil a mysterious duality within the godhead? Do they present us with subtle and beautiful pictures of a coming God-Man? Do they seem to point ahead to the NT Jesus? If so, then surely they are signs, gifts of God intended to invite seekers of a trustworthy divine revelation to come, sit, and listen awhile at Jesus' feet.

OT Messianic Types

As we saw earlier, the NT defines a "type" as any OT person, place, object, event, or institution that, in a veiled manner, points ahead to the person and work of Jesus of Nazareth. More particularly, the purpose of the types is to help us identify Jesus as God's promised divine-human Messiah, and to illuminate his work as the prophet, priest, and king of his people. In short, a type is a concrete, historical symbol; it is, as Paul expressed it, "...a shadow of things to come, whose substance (Greek: 'body') is of Christ" (Col. 2:16-17).

OT "typology" is rough terrain. Some OT types are quite clear and compelling; others, however, are subtler, sometimes even generating debate over whether they are types at all. Some are explicitly cited and interpreted by various NT personalities, including Jesus himself; others must be discovered and interpreted by the reader alone. Some scholars argue that there are relatively few OT types; others, say there are hundreds. So again, OT typology is rough terrain. As we are about to see, however, it is difficult indeed to argue that there is no ground beneath our feet at all!

In what follows, I will take a more conservative approach, largely confining myself to a survey of clearer types that enjoy the sanction of the NT writers themselves. In the end, however, it will be for each reader to distinguish between what he *thinks* he sees in the way of a type, and what he *knows* in his heart is really there.

Please note that I have included a number of scripture references at the end of my discussion of each type. These are supplied so that you may study the types more closely in their full biblical context.

1. Adam

In his letters to the Romans and the Corinthians, the apostle Paul states that Adam is a type of Jesus. This is true in several important respects. Just as Adam was the father of an earthly race, so Jesus is the father of a heavenly (i.e., a race of believers who have God's heavenly Spirit living within them). Just as Adam represented his children during his brief probation in the Garden of Eden, so Jesus represented his people during his own lengthy probation in Israel, where he, unlike Adam, lived blamelessly according to the word of God. Finally, just as Adam's disobedience brought evil consequences upon man and nature, so Jesus' obedience brought good consequences upon the same. There was, however, this important difference: Jesus' good work not only bestows its good fruit upon those who believe in him, but it also overrules and eliminates the bad fruit that Adam's evil work placed upon them through his fall.

(Rom. 5:12-21, 1 Cor. 15:35-49)

2. THE TREE OF LIFE

The NT indicates that the Tree of Life in the Garden of Eden was a rich type. In essence, it represented eternal life—the *kind* of life ever lived and enjoyed by the Father, Son, and Holy Spirit; a life offered to Adam and his family in the time of his innocence. More particularly, the *fruit* of this tree seems to represent Christ, whom one commentator shrewdly identified as the "receivable" person of the Holy Trinity (John 1:12). Also, the Tree of Life typifies the cross of Christ, whereupon Jesus died so that his believing disciples could enjoy eternal life with God, at first by faith, and later, in the age to come, by sight.

(Gen. 2:9, Gal. 1:1-5, 3:13, Rev. 2:7).

3. THE FIRST SACRIFICE

In Genesis we learn that immediately after the fall of Adam and Eve, the LORD God made tunics of skin and clothed them with them. In this mysterious act we find a type of the work of God through Christ. Just as God killed an animal in order to physically clothe the naked pair, so too, by the hidden workings of his providence, he brought about the sacrificial death of his Son, the Lamb of God, in order spiritually to clothe believers in Jesus. Formerly, they stood "naked" in the sight of God: open to his view, exposed to his wrath, and therefore inclined to flee, hide, and cover themselves. Now, however, having believed in Jesus, they stand "clothed" in the sight of God: forgiven of their sins, clothed with the righteousness of Christ, and therefore inclined to run *to* God, who, in thus saving them, has become a loving Father rather than a dreaded Judge.

(Gen. 3:21, Mt. 22:1-14, John 1:29, Acts 4:27-28, Rev. 3:5,18; 4:4; 7:9; 19:14).

4. Noah and the Ark

According to the NT, the familiar OT story of Noah and the ark abounds with types of Jesus and his redemptive work. Noah, whose name means "comfort" or "rest," is himself a type of Christ, the one who gives his people eternal comfort and rest through redemption. Accordingly, Noah received instructions from God to build an ark of salvation for his family, thereby depicting Christ, who in eternity past received the same. The global Flood is also a type, since, as Peter affirms, the waters of judgment in Noah's day typify the fires of judgment that will engulf the universe at the end of the age. The ark itself is also a type since, like Noah, Jesus built a vessel of salvation—his own perfect life and sacrificial death—by which sinful men can be saved from eternal punishment. Here, then, is a complex type that picturesquely preaches the good news about Jesus Christ: by coming to him—by getting on board "in Christ"—the believer is henceforth safe from the wrath to come, and looks forward to a whole new life in a whole new world purged of sin and filled with the glory of God.

(Gen. 6-9, Luke 17: 26-27; John 10:18, 1 Pet. 3:18-22)

5. The Exodus Event

The exodus—along with many of the events associated with it—is probably the most frequently cited type in the Bible. It includes three basic elements: Israel's exodus from Egypt at the hand of Moses, their 40-year sojourn in the wilderness of Sinai, and their entrance into Canaan, the land promised to them by God. Both explicitly and implicitly, the NT refers to all three, exploring their spiritual significance for believers in Jesus. Egypt, for example, represents the fallen world-system as a place of bondage to sin, from which Christians have been spiritually delivered through God-given faith in Christ. On this view, the Pharaoh who oppressed Israel represents Satan, who, according to the NT, is "the ruler of this world." The Wilderness of Sinai once again represents the evil world-system, this time as a place of testing, hardship, and persecution, in which God graces His pilgrim people with his presence, provision, and protection. Canaan represents heaven, or rather the new heavens and the new earth that God will create on the Last Day. Again, the NT repeatedly cites or alludes to the exodus event in order to encourage Christ's disciples to faithfully follow their heavenly Leader through the wilderness of this world, lest they, through the deceitfulness of sin, become like the multitudes of Israelites who rebelled against Moses, and so failed to enter the Promised Land.

(Exodus to Joshua; Mt. 2:14-15, 4:1-11, Acts 7, Rom. 4:13, 1 Cor. 10:1-11, Heb. 3:7-19, 11:23-40, Rev. 12:1ff, 20:7-10).

6. Moses

Moses is one of the Bible's most impressive types of Jesus Christ. We see this in the fact that their lives ran parallel at so many points. Both were first-born sons. Both were persecuted by wicked rulers at their birth. Both were hidden in obscurity for many years, then called by God and empowered by him to do miracles. Both wrought deliverance for their people; both led them through the wilderness. Both were prophets, priests, and lawgivers. Very importantly, both mediated and articulated a covenant for the people of God, so that both became founders of a new nation—the former of a physical nation, the latter of a spiritual. Both were spoken against by many, believed by some, and faithfully loved by a loyal few.
(Acts 7:17-43, 1 Corinthians 10:1-4, Hebrews 3:1f).

7. The Passover

The Passover is at once a watershed moment in the history of Israel and the first of that nation's several annual feasts. According to the NT, it positively drips with typological significance.

The event itself occurred at the very end of Israel's slavery in Egypt, a condition picturing the bondage of God's people to sin, Satan, and the peril of God's wrath (John 8:31-36).

Through Moses, God warned the Egyptians of a final judgment against the first-born sons of the land. Through Jesus, he warns all humanity of a final judgment against the sons of Adam at the end of the present evil age (Mt. 11:20-24).

Through Moses, God declared that he would execute local judgment by the hand of his angel. Through Jesus, he declares that he will execute universal judgment at the hand of his Christ (Mt. 25:31-46, John 5:22).

Through Moses, God brought mercy to his people, commanding the heads of each family to sacrifice an unblemished male lamb for the deliverance of their first-born sons. Through Jesus, he brings a greater mercy, commanding Christ, the sinless head of his people, to sacrifice himself for the deliverance his Church, the "first-born" (i.e., privileged, chosen) sons of God (John 8:46, 10:18, Heb. 12:23).

Concerning the Passover lamb, God commanded that it should be slain, but none of its bones broken. Concerning Jesus, God ordained that he too should be slain, and none of his bones broken (John 1:29, 19: 31-37).

God instructed his OT people personally to put the lamb's blood on the doorposts and lintels of their homes. Similarly, Jesus instructs all men personally to put their trust in him, thereby appropriating for themselves the merits—and blessings—of his bloody sacrifice (John 3:16, 6:54).

When the angel of death went through Egypt, he passed over every home where he saw the blood applied. According to Jesus, he and his Father have *already* passed over all who trust in Christ's atoning sacrifice—and will do so again at the Judgment on the Last Day (John 5: 24).

God commanded the Israelites to eat the flesh of the Passover lambs. Jesus commanded his followers to "eat his flesh and drink his blood" (John 6:53-59). Again, this means that he commanded them personally to appropriate, by faith, all the spiritual benefits of his substitutionary death.

Through Moses, God ordained that deliverance from Egypt should mark the birth of a physical nation, and that the birth should be commemorated annually by the feast of the Passover. Through Jesus, he ordained that deliverance from the power and penalty of sin should mark the birth of a spiritual nation, and that the birth should be commemorated regularly by the feast of the Lord's Supper (Luke 22:19, 1 Cor. 11: 23-26, 1 Pet. 2:9-10).

The gospels reveal that Jesus went to great lengths to associate himself and his work with the Passover. His final outreach to Israel came during the Passover week. His final meal with his disciples was at sunset on Passover eve. In instituting the second of only two sacraments for his Church, he appropriated two key elements of the Passover: the taking of bread and the drinking of wine. The betrayal, arrest, and trial that led to his death occurred on the night of the Passover. From all this, we conclude that Christ and his apostles earnestly desired seekers to ponder what is surely the single most important type of the Bible: the Passover. Why? Because this event, commemorated and celebrated by Israel for some 1,500 years, so powerfully pictures the single most important work that Jesus came to do.

(Ex. 11-12, Mt. 26:1-29, Mark 10:45, 1 Cor. 5: 7)

8. The Tabernacle

Immediately following the exodus, Moses led the Israelites into the wilderness of Sinai. There they met with God and received from him the (Mosaic) Law, the constitution by which the new nation would henceforth live. This Law consisted of two main elements: laws governing conduct (i.e., a moral law), and laws governing worship (i.e., a ceremonial law). These two elements were closely related. Because the people could not rise to the lofty standards of his moral law, God graciously gave them a ceremonial law as well. Those who diligently attended to the latter secured for themselves the forgiveness of sins, thereby making it possible for the Holy One of Israel to dwell in the midst of a grateful and worshipful nation.

The ceremonial law was complex, mysterious, and laden with types pointing to the person and work of Christ. Though we cannot pause to examine each element in detail, a few words of general explanation will serve to point the way.

The ceremonial Law centered upon the *tabernacle*. This was a large tent, divided into two parts: the Holy Place and the Holiest Place of All. Outside the tent there was an altar where animals were sacrificed; also, there was a laver, where the priests, before serving in the tabernacle, could purify themselves through various washings. Inside the Holy Place there were several items of furniture: a table, regularly furbished with twelve loaves of fresh bread; a single golden candlestick to illumine the priest's way; and a small altar for burning incense. The priests regularly entered the Holy Place to maintain all three.

Inside the Holiest Place of All there was a gold-covered box called the Ark of the Covenant. Inside the Ark there were two tablets, upon which were written the Ten Commandments. Resting upon the Ark was an ornate lid, overspread by the wings of two golden angels attached to either side of the Ark. This lid was called the Mercy Seat. Only the High Priest could enter the Holiest Place of All, and that but once a year, on the Day of Atonement, Israel's most solemn feast. When he did, he would place sacrificial blood on the Mercy Seat, thereby securing forgiveness for the sins of the people committed in ignorance throughout the previous year.

The typological significance of the Tabernacle worship is worked out in considerable detail by the anonymous author of the letter to the Hebrews. There the writer explains that in and of itself Israel's ceremonial law did not secure forgiveness of sin. How could mortal, sinful priests—repeatedly offering mere animal sacrifices—ever truly atone for Israel's many violations of the moral Law? No, the efficacy of these sacrifices actually derived from the sacrifice of the promised One who has now come and fulfilled them: Jesus, the Messiah. He alone was anointed by God to be both the eternal High Priest of his people and the perfect (i.e., human) sacrifice for their sins. Because of his perfection, he (unlike the priests of old) was able to enter once for all into the *true* Holiest Place (i.e., heaven), approach the *true* ark (i.e., the throne of God), and there deposit the blood that *truly* secures eternal forgiveness for God's people. In other words, in virtue of his very presence in heaven, he eternally presents to the Father the infinite merits of his bloody sacrifice.

Moreover, through spiritual rebirth and the faith that it engenders, all who believe in Christ may now follow him into that Holy Place. They may know God and worship in his very presence—uninterruptedly—both in this life and the next. What all this means, says the author, is that the ancient ceremonial law has now been fulfilled and therefore rendered obsolete. What the old covenant of Moses could not do, the new covenant in Christ has done, once for all. Now all of God's people may experience spiritual rebirth, forgiveness of sin, and unending access to God through simple faith in Jesus Christ. Whether for Jew or Gentile, the true High Priest and sacrifice for the people of God has opened the way.

(Ex. 25-30, Heb. 4:14-16; 6:19-20; 9:1-28)

9. The Manna from Heaven

Israel's forty-year sojourn in the wilderness saw many unusual events typifying the person and work of Jesus. One of the most memorable was God's miraculous provision of a heavenly food called *manna*. The story is found in Exodus. The people had just escaped from Egypt. As they began their journey through the wilderness, they grew hungry and complained to Moses about the lack of food. Overhearing their murmurings, God told Moses that he would rain down bread from heaven upon them. This bread appeared in the form of white, edible flakes that remained on the ground after the evaporation of the morning dew. In order to cultivate in Israel a sense of their continual dependency upon God, God told the people to gather their portion of manna each morning, saving none for the next day. They could, however, gather two portions on the morning prior to the Sabbath, and so rest on the Sabbath itself. This weekly routine continued for some forty years. On the day they entered Canaan, the manna ceased.

In a lengthy discourse to his Jewish kinsmen, Jesus repeatedly referred to the manna as a powerful type of himself and his mission. Here are a few of his own words:

> Truly, truly, I say to you, Moses did not give you the bread from heaven, but my Father gives you the true bread from heaven. For the bread of God is he who comes down from heaven and gives life to the world...Your fathers ate the manna in the wilderness, and are dead. This is the bread which came down from heaven. If anyone eats of this bread, he will live forever; and the bread that I shall give is my flesh, which I shall give for the life of the world.
>
> —John 6: 32-33, 49-51

In speaking thus, Jesus shows that he regards himself as *the true bread*—the divine reality that has now arrived to fulfill and illuminate the ancient shadow (Col. 2:17). Therefore, just as God formerly gave manna to the Israelites, so now he gives Jesus to the whole world. Just as he "rained down manna from heaven," so now he has sent his Son down from heaven (and his Son's Spirit, as well). Just as he gave manna for the physical life of his people, so now he has given Jesus' flesh (i.e., in sacrificial death) for the spiritual life of his people. Just as the Israelites had to gather the manna every day in order to live physically, so now Jesus' followers, through intimate personal communion with him, must "eat of this bread" every day in order to live spiritually. And just as the typical bread enabled ancient Israel to make their pilgrimage through the wilderness of Sinai, so now the true bread enables Jesus' Church to make her pilgrimage through the wilderness of this fallen world. Every day they may receive it, enjoy it, and grow by it; every day they must. Only thus shall they experience the forgiveness of their sins; only thus shall they experience eternal life; only thus shall they enter the Promised Land. When at last they do, the manna will cease to be received on earth by faith. But it will never cease to be received in heaven by sight.

(Exodus 16, John 6, Revelation 12)

10. The Water from the Rock

After complaining about a lack of food, the Israelites now began to complain about a lack of water. Once again God intervened, telling Moses to gather the elders of Israel, take them to a certain rock in Horeb, and there strike the rock with his rod. When he did so, water gushed out of the rock, and the people and the animals began to drink.

Very significantly, this miraculous provision occurred on at least one other occasion, when the people were again complaining about a lack of water. This time, however, God told Moses to *speak* to the rock—a command that Moses, out of anger towards his disgruntled kinsmen, disobeyed by striking the rock a second time. This proved a very costly mistake, since God immediately declared that Moses would not be allowed to enter the Promised Land because of his sin.

According to the apostle Paul, these mysterious events typify the things of Jesus Christ. Jesus is the rock, stricken by God, so that out of him the life-giving water of the Spirit may flow to all who are willing to drink (Isaiah 53:4). Furthermore, this spiritual drinking is not a one-time event. For just as the rock "followed" the Israelites in the wilderness of Sinai, so now Jesus follows his children in their walk through the wilderness of this world. Any time they need or wish, they may speak to the once-stricken rock and receive spiritual refreshment for the next leg of the journey.

A Christo-centric interpretation of the stricken rock also illuminates the severity of God's discipline towards Moses. God designed the striking of the rock to be a "once for all" event. Thereafter, Moses was simply to speak to the rock in order to get the water he needed. Analogously, in the NT we learn that God designed the striking of Jesus on the cross to be a once for all event. Now that Christ has died, no further sacrifices are needed. Henceforth, God's people are simply to speak to Jesus in order to receive the spiritual drink they need. Viewed in this light, Moses' angry gesture seems to mar a richly significant type, a type meant to underscore the once-for-all character of Jesus' sacrificial death. The ensuing discipline, however, not only preserves the type from such a fate, but also effectively underlines its rich significance for the saints of all ages.

(Ex. 17, Num. 20, John 7:37-38, 1 Cor. 10:1-5, Rev. 12)

11. The Bronze Serpent

Yet again the people fell to complaining, but this time God had had enough. In a display of divine displeasure, he sent "fiery serpents" into their camp. When some of the people began to die from the snakebites, the rest ran to Moses and pleaded with him to intercede. Moses acquiesced and God in turn responded mercifully, commanding him to make a serpent out of bronze, attach it to a pole, and lift it up from the earth for all the people to see. Any penitent Israelite who looked upon the bronze serpent would immediately be healed.

As in the case of the manna, so here: Jesus himself personally appropriated this episode as a type, one that would soon be fulfilled in his own death and the events to follow. Here is how he speaks of it to Nicodemus, an open and inquiring Pharisee:

> And as Moses lifted up the serpent in the wilderness, even so must the Son of Man be lifted up, that whoever believes in him should not perish but have eternal life. For God so loved the world that he gave his only-begotten Son, that whoever believes in him should not perish, but have eternal life.
>
> —John 3:14-15

In these familiar words we see that Jesus regards the company of wounded Israelites as a type of the human race. Just as the Israelites were infected with the poison of the serpents, so too all mankind, through Adam's transgression, have been infected with the poison of sin. Indeed, they carry about in their members the very nature of Adam's tempter, Satan himself. Therefore, like the Israelites of old, they have been stricken unto death. Not only are they full of sin, but they also stand guilty before God, condemned by his Law and in danger of an eternity in hell.

Happily, the story does not end here. For just as God acted in mercy among the dying Israelites, so too, says Jesus, he now acts in mercy among dying humanity. Just as he then ordained that a bronze serpent should be lifted up on a pole for the physical healing of OT believers, so now he ordains that his only Son should be lifted up on a pole for the spiritual healing of NT believers. Soon the holy Son will take upon himself the Satanic standing and punishment (though by no means the Satanic nature) of his sinful people. He does this so that they, in turn, may take upon themselves the godly standing, reward, and nature of the holy Son.

The healing, however, is not complete until sinful man responds to what Jesus has done for him. Just as the bronze serpent had to be lifted up for the Israelites to see, so Jesus must be lifted up for his people to see—not only on the cross, but also in a global proclamation of the gospel. And just as the Israelites, in obedience to Moses' word, looked in faith towards the bronze serpent and were healed, so Jesus' people, in obedience to his word, must (and will) look in faith towards him and be healed. Here, then, is the "true" and ultimate healing: healing from the guilt, penalty, power, and presence of sin—all through a spiritual union with God that comes from gazing, in faith, upon his life-giving Christ.

(Num. 21: 4-9, John 8:44, 2 Cor. 5:21)

12. THE CLUSTER FROM CANAAN

Let us conclude this portion of our journey with a look at one of the subtlest of all OT Messianic types. After about a year in the wilderness, Moses brought the people to the border of the Promised Land. At God's command, he then sent a company of spies—one from each of the 12 tribes—into Canaan, there to check out the new homeland and to bring back some of the fruit that they found growing there. The narrative of their adventure concludes as follows:

> Then they (the spies) came to the Valley of Eschol, and there cut down a branch with one cluster of grapes; they carried it between two of them on a pole. They also brought some of the pomegranates and figs. The place was called the Valley of Eschol (i.e., cluster), because of the cluster which the men of Israel cut down there. And they returned from spying out the land after forty days.
> —Num. 13:1-2, 17-24

Though Moses' own generation could not enter the Promised Land because of their unbelief, their children did so eagerly, for they well remembered the cluster of grapes, and much desired the blessings it represented.

Indeed, as our passage reveals, they memorialized the valley in which their fathers found the cluster. This appears to be an act of providence, and also a sign that we are dealing with a Messianic type. On this view, the cluster of grapes represents Christ, the fruit of the Heavenly Vine (i.e., God the Father) who brings the new wine of spiritual life to his redeemed people. Whereas the typical cluster came from the earthly Canaan, the real cluster—Jesus—comes from the heavenly. Just as the former was cut down and suspended on a pole between two men, so Jesus was cut down and suspended on a pole between two men. Just as it was carried to Israel as a token of the goodness of the land, so the news about Jesus was carried first to Israel, and later to all nations, as a token of the goodness of heaven. Just as most of the Israelites scorned the cluster and therefore wandered in the wilderness of Sinai for many years, so most Jews have scorned the good news about the crucified Messiah's spiritual Kingdom, and have therefore wandered in the wilderness of this world for many years. But just as a subsequent generation of Israelites enthusiastically entered the earthly Promised Land, so too, according to NT promise, a subsequent generation of believing Jews (and Gentiles) will enter the heavenly Promised Land. Through faith in Jesus Christ, they will be grafted into the True Vine, to enjoy its sweetness and intoxicating power both now and forever.

(Mt. 9:14-17, John 15:1f, 19:17-24, Romans 11:11-29)

Conclusion

Many Christian commentators would argue that these twelve examples constitute only a sampling of the hundreds of Messianic types hidden away in the pages of the OT.[2] Moreover, they would argue that the striking correlation of the minute details of the types with the minute details of Jesus' life and work bespeaks the very hand of God, working both in history and scripture to supply a compelling body of signs: signs pointing to Jesus of Nazareth and identifying him to seekers everywhere as God's chosen prophet, priest, and king.

And yet the OT story in this regard is *still* not complete!

OT Messianic Prophecies

The second main category of OT signs contains what are commonly called *Messianic prophecies*. These are explicit OT predictions of a coming world redeemer who—occupying the offices of prophet, priest, and king—will introduce the Kingdom (i.e., *direct rule*) of God into the earth. According to some scholars, there are as many as 300 such prophecies, given through a number of different men, over a period of some 3,500 years. They appear with special frequency during the six turbulent centuries between king David (ca. 1000 B.C.) and the prophet Malachi (ca. 400 B.C.), centuries of moral failure during which the need for divine intervention was painfully clear to every godly Jew.

Messianic prophecies gave birth to a lively hope among the devout of Israel. Accordingly, when Jesus arrived on the scene, many Jews were looking for a divinely empowered king—a mighty leader like Moses or David—who would once again rescue Israel from their foreign oppressors (e.g., Rome), and then go on to universalize the worship of Yahweh in a supernaturally transformed world. As we shall see, Jesus himself had a very different view of the Messiah's person and work. Indeed, he believed that a central theme of his teaching ministry was to bring to light certain divine "mysteries"—previously concealed secrets—about the *true* nature of the Messiah and the *true* nature of his Kingdom. Nevertheless, both he and the NT writers were thoroughly convinced that this new understanding involved nothing different from what the OT seers had predicted so many years before.

The following survey of the most important Messianic prophecies reflects this new, Christian understanding of the Messianic mission.[3] My approach will be chronological, showing how the NT writers found the entire course and meaning of Jesus' life predicted in the OT. As in our study of Messianic types, so here: it will be for each seeker to decide for himself whether the stunning correspondence between the details of Messianic prophecy and the details of Jesus' life is, in the end, a work of God or man.

1. THE MESSIAH'S DIVINE NATURE AND ETERNAL PRE-EXISTENCE

Though this idea never became part of the traditional Jewish understanding of the Messiah, the OT frequently refers to the Messiah as a divine person. King David, for example, referred to him as "Lord" (Psalm 110:1). Solomon referred to him as God (Psalm 45:6). Isaiah called him "Immanuel," which means, "God with us;" and also "Mighty God" and "Everlasting Father" (Isaiah 7:14, 9: 6).[4] Jeremiah called him "the Lord our Righteousness" (Jer. 23:5-6).

Jesus pointedly applied the first of these prophecies to himself, implicitly challenging the hostile Jewish leaders to recognize that the Messiah is not only the human son of David, but also the (divine) Son of God (Mt. 22:41-46). He also affirmed his pre-existence by saying that he had come down from heaven (John 6:51, 58); and his divine nature by saying, "Before Abraham was, I am" (John 8;58, 10:30).

2. Seed of a Woman

In the Bible's first Messianic prophecy, God himself states that the coming redeemer will be the seed (i.e., the offspring) of a woman (Gen. 3:15). Jesus, according to the gospel writers, was born of the seed of a woman—but not of a man, since he was not conceived by a man, but by the Holy Spirit (Luke 1:34-35, Gal. 4:4).

3. Born of a Virgin

Isaiah, in a prophecy commonly understood to be Messianic, declares that the Messiah will be born of a virgin (Isaiah 7:14). Citing this passage, Matthew and Luke both record that Jesus was indeed born of a virgin, lest, being born through the union of a man and a woman, he inherit the sin and condemnation of Adam (Mt. 1:18, 24-25; Luke 1:26-35). Jesus' opponents, aware of the unusual circumstances surrounding his birth, publicly denounced him as an illegitimate son (John 8:41).

4. The Seed of Abraham

In Genesis we read that God told Abraham, "By your seed shall all the nations of the earth be blessed" (Gen. 22:18). The NT writers saw this as an important Messianic prophecy. In relating his (human) lineage, they showed that Jesus was indeed "of the seed of Abraham," and that through his redemptive work all nations shall indeed be blessed. Like Isaac, he was a child of promise: the promised redeemer, through whom all the blessings of redemption would come to every tribe, tongue, family, and nation (Mt. 1:1, Gal. 3:16, Rev. 5:9).

5. Of the Tribe of Judah

Upon his deathbed, the patriarch Joseph predicted that a ruler would emerge from the tribe of Judah, to whom "the peoples" (i.e., the Gentile nations) would obediently come (Gen. 49:8-10). Jesus came from the tribe of Judah, and through the preaching of the gospel people from many different nations have obediently come to him, and continue to do so to this very day (Luke 3:23, 33, Rom. 1:5, Rev. 5:9).

6. Of the House of David

In many places, the OT declares that the Messiah will arise from the family of king David. The seminal prophecy is found in 2 Samuel, where

God himself promised David that "...I will raise up your seed after you, who will come forth from you, and I will establish his Kingdom. He shall build a house for My name, and I will establish the throne of his Kingdom forever" (2 Sam. 7:12-13). After this, the floodgates were opened, with one prophet after another looking ahead to "David's" glorious, universal Kingdom (Isaiah 9, 16, 22, 55; Jer. 23, 30, 33; Ezek. 34, 37; Hosea 3, Amos 9, Zech. 12, 13).

Joseph and Mary, Jesus' earthly father and mother, were both descendants of David (Luke 1:32, 3:23, 31). He was born in Bethlehem, the city of David (Luke 2:4). During his public ministry, Jesus was often called "Son of David" (Mt. 20:30). On his last visit to Jerusalem, the people, believing him to be the Messiah, cried out, "Hosanna to the Son of David" (Mt. 21:9). In the Revelation, we find the risen Christ referring to himself as "...the root and offspring of David" (Rev. 22:16).

7. BORN IN BETHLEHEM

The prophet Micah predicted that the Messiah would be born in Bethlehem (Micah 5:2). Jesus, by a remarkable turn of events, was born, not in his parent's hometown of Nazareth, but in Bethlehem (Luke 2). Bethlehem means "house of bread." He who was born in Bethlehem called himself "the bread of God" (John 6:33).

8. ANOINTED BY THE SPIRIT

The prophet Isaiah declared that God would anoint the Messiah with the Spirit of Lord (Isaiah 61:1f, 11:2). At his water baptism, in the sight of John the Baptizer, the Holy Spirit descended upon Jesus in the form of a dove (Mt. 3:16-17). Thereafter, Jesus began his public ministry, in which, supported by the attestation of miraculous signs, he presented himself to Israel as her promised Messiah; as the One anointed by the Spirit of God to fill—and fulfill—the three great OT offices of Prophet, Priest, and King.

9. MINISTRY TO THE GALILEANS

Isaiah also predicted that the Messiah's light would first shine in "...the land of Zebulun and Naphtali...Galilee of the Gentiles" (Isaiah 9:1f). The NT affirms that this came to pass. Shortly after his baptism, Jesus withdrew from the Jewish heartland in order to begin his ministry in Galilee, a frontier province of Israel and a crossroads for many nations (Mt. 4:12-17). This was the region where he chose to live, where most of his miracles were done, and where most of his followers came from. Jesus attached great significance to these circumstances, seeing in them a foreshadowing of his rejection by Israel as a whole, but also of his acceptance by Jewish "outsiders" and their Gentile neighbors (Luke 4:16-30).

10. Good News to the Poor

Isaiah prophesied that the Messiah would bring good news to the poor, and that he would use his supernatural powers to heal the oppressed (Isaiah 61:1-3). In his hometown of Nazareth, Jesus publicly appropriated this prophecy to himself (Luke 4:18f). Later, when John the Baptizer sent messengers from prison to ascertain whether he was the promised Messiah, Jesus answered in the affirmative, again citing Isaiah's prophecies (Luke 7:22). Thereafter, he began to gain a following primarily among the poor and oppressed, as he extended forgiveness, healing, and the hope of eternal life to all. As the apostle Mark put it, "The common people heard him gladly" (Mark 12:37).

11. Riding on a Donkey

Zechariah predicted that the Messianic king would come to Israel riding on a donkey, a beast of burden (Zech. 9:9). On his last trip to Jerusalem, Jesus humbly rode a donkey into the city, knowing that he would soon serve his people by being burdened with their sins, as well as with the cross upon which he would pay for them (Mt. 26:37, Luke 12:15, 19:35-37, Phil. 2:8).

12. Betrayed by a Friend

David, the main OT type of the Messiah, was betrayed by a close friend who ate at his table and lifted up his heel against him (Psalm 41:9). Fulfilling this prophetic type, Jesus was betrayed by Judas, a close friend and disciple who betrayed him on the very night they sat at the table together to take the Passover meal (Mt. 26:50, John 13:18).

13. Sold for Thirty Pieces of Silver

Zechariah predicted that the Messiah would be sold for 30 pieces of silver (Zech. 11:12-13). Judas sold Jesus to the Pharisees for 30 pieces of silver, showing that neither he, nor they, nor the nation as a whole, set any value upon the divine redeemer whom God had sent to be Israel's glory (Mt. 26:15, Luke 2:32).

14. Forsaken by His Disciples

Zechariah predicted that God's sword would strike the Shepherd (i.e., the Messiah), and that all the sheep would be scattered (Zech. 13:7). On the night of his betrayal, Jesus told his disciples, "Behold, an hour is coming, and has now come, for you to be scattered, each to his own, and to leave me alone; and yet I am not alone, because the Father is with Me" (John 16:32, Mt. 26:31). Hours later, when Jesus was betrayed with a kiss into the hands of his enemies, his disciples forsook him and fled (Mt. 26:56). This prophecy also appears to have had a larger fulfillment, first in 70 A.D. and then in 135 A.D., when the Romans, seeking to extirpate armed Jewish resistance, effectively dispersed the Jewish people from their Judean homeland.

15. Mocked, Beaten, and Scourged

Numerous OT prophecies predicted that prior to his death the Messiah would be handed over to the Gentiles (Psalm 2:1f), mocked (Psalm 22:7-8), spit upon and scourged (Isaiah 50:6), bruised and wounded (Isaiah 53:5). Jesus himself predicted that all these things would come upon him, saying, "For (the Son of Man) will be delivered to the Gentiles and will be mocked and insulted and spit upon. They will scourge him and kill him. And the third day he will rise again" (Luke 18:32-33). At the hands of the Jewish rulers and Roman soldiers, all of this came to pass, just as he and the ancient prophets had said (Mt. 26:67, 27:26, Mark 15:19, Luke 23:11, John 18:22).

16. Pierced

Two prophets, David and Zechariah, foretold that the Messiah would be pierced (Psalm 22:16, Zech. 12:10). Jesus, when he was crucified, was pierced in his hands and feet (Luke 23:3). A little later, in order to ascertain his death, a Roman centurion pierced his side (John 19:34-37). The Bible teaches that God will enable his people to look in penitent sorrow upon the Messiah whom they pierced with their own sins, and that in so looking they will find the joy of his salvation (Zech. 12:10-13:1).

17. Numbered with Transgressors

Isaiah foretold that the Messiah would be "numbered with the transgressors" and "assigned to the grave of wicked men" (Isaiah 53:12, 9). Jesus, reckoned by the Jews as a blasphemer, and by the Romans as an insurrectionist, was indeed numbered among the transgressors. Therefore he was appointed to the kind of death reserved for wicked men (i.e., crucifixion), and breathed his last while suspended on a cross between two criminals (Mt. 9:3, Mark 15:28).

18. HIS GARMENTS DIVIDED

David prophesied that the enemies of the Messiah would divide his garments among themselves and gamble for his clothing (Psalm 22:18). At the foot of his cross, Roman soldiers divided Jesus' outer garments among themselves and then cast lots for his tunic (John 19:23- 24).

19. INTERCESSION FOR THE TRANSGRESSORS

Isaiah foretold that the Messiah would "...make intercession for the transgressors" (Isaiah 53:12). This was partly fulfilled when Jesus prayed for God's mercy upon the soldiers who crucified him; these men elicited his compassion because they neither understood who he was nor why he was dying (Luke 23:34). However, its larger fulfillment, according to the apostles, occurs in heaven, where Christ, serving as the High Priest of his people, continually intercedes for them, pleading the merits of his righteous life and atoning death for the forgiveness of their sins (Rom. 8:34, Heb. 9:24).

20. GALL AND VINEGAR TO DRINK

The Psalmist foretold that the enemies of the Messiah would offer him gall to eat (i.e., a bitter, poisonous herb) and vinegar to drink (Psalm 69:21). When Jesus was crucified, the Romans offered him poisonous myrrh, which he refused (Mt. 27:34). Towards the end of his passion he cried out in thirst, after which they offered him vinegar to drink (John 19:28-30).

21. THE MESSIAH'S FINAL WORDS

King David, regarded by the NT writers as both a type and a prophet of the coming Messiah, anticipated Jesus' cry of dereliction when he prayerfully wrote, "My God, My God, why have you forsaken me?" (Psalm 22:1). Jesus, moments before his death, uttered these very words, not as an expression of despair (Luke 23:43, John 16:32), but in order publicly to appropriate this Messianic psalm to himself. Accordingly, even at the moment of his death, he affirmed his faith in God, again quoting David, saying, "Father, into Your hands I commend my spirit" (Psalm 31:5, Luke 23:46).

22. Died of a Broken Heart

In the highly Messianic Psalm 22, David wrote, "I am poured out like water, and all my bones are out of joint; my heart is like wax—it has melted within me" (Psalm 22:14). Jesus, with bones out of joint, and too weak to raise himself up for air, finally died of suffocation, leading to heart failure. Therefore, when the Roman soldier pierced his side in order to ascertain his death, "water and blood" poured forth (John 19:34). The clear fluid from the membrane around his heart (which John called "water") gave evidence that it had in fact "melted" (i.e., failed) within him.[5]

23. Not a Bone Broken

In the same Messianic psalm, David intimated that none of the Messiah's bones would be broken (Psalm 22:17, cf. 34:20). When the Roman soldiers were commanded by Pilate to break the legs of the three crucified prisoners, they came to Jesus, found him already dead, and broke none of his bones. In this the apostle John saw a fulfillment of the ancient Mosaic law (and type), according to which the bones of the Passover lamb must not be broken (Num. 9:12, John 19:36).

24. Buried with the Rich

Though Isaiah had declared that the Messiah would be numbered with the transgressors, he also hinted at his later vindication by predicting that in his death he would be "…with the rich" (Isaiah 53:9). And so it came to pass. A wealthy Pharisee, Joseph of Arimathea, received Jesus' dead body from the Romans, wrapped it in linen saturated with costly oils and spices, and placed it in a brand new garden tomb. Jesus' death was indeed with the rich (John 19:38-42, Mt. 27:57-60).

25. His Resurrection

David declared concerning the Messiah that God would neither abandon his soul to Hades nor allow his flesh to see corruption (Psalm 16:8-10). Peter, having personally seen and spoken to the risen Jesus, affirmed that this prophecy had been fulfilled in his Master. Similarly, Isaiah predicted that after the suffering of his soul the Messiah would "see the light of life and be satisfied" (Isaiah 53:11, NIV). Jesus, according to all the NT writers, experienced great suffering of body and soul, but rose from the dead, saw the light of life, and was profoundly satisfied with the faith, hope, and joy that arose in the hearts of those to whom he showed himself alive

(Mt. 28:9, John 20:21, Acts 1:3, Heb.12:1-2). Also, God declared through the prophet Hosea that "on the third day" he would raise up a torn and stricken nation, so that they might live in his sight (Hosea 6:2). According to the apostle Paul, God fulfilled this promise when, on the third day, he raised Jesus from the dead, thereby securing, for a people torn and stricken by sin, new spiritual life in union with Christ, as well as the resurrection of their bodies, in glory, at the end of the age (Mt. 27:63, John 2:19, Rom. 6:1-14, 1 Cor. 15, Eph. 2:1-10).

26. His Ascension

The psalms, in several places, hint at the ascension of the Messiah and his triumphant entrance into heaven. For example, David sang, "Lift up your heads, O gates, and be lifted up you everlasting doors, that the King of glory may come in!" (Psalm 24: 7; Psalms 16:11, 68:18, 110:1). Jesus, in the sight of many witnesses, ascended on high and, according to his apostles, triumphantly entered heaven, there to appear in the presence of God for his people (Acts 1:9, 2:33-36, Eph. 4:8, Heb. 9:24, Rev. 5).

27. His Exaltation to God's Right Hand

The prophets looked for a day when God would highly exalt his Messiah, sitting him down at his own right hand, whence he would rule over the nations (Psalms 2, 110, Isaiah 52:13, Dan. 7:13-14). Adopting an earthly interpretation of these promises, the Jews of Jesus' day believed that the Messiah's reign would emanate from Jerusalem. Jesus, however, brought a most unexpected revelation, teaching that his reign would not emanate from earth, but from heaven—from "the Jerusalem above" (Gal. 4:26; Mt. 28:18f, Luke 19:12, 22:69; John 4:20-23). Thus, alluding to these very OT prophecies, he told the hostile Sanhedrin, "Hereafter, the Son of Man will sit on the right hand of the power of God" (Mt. 22:41-46). In this the disciples followed suit, repeatedly affirming that God had fulfilled the OT promises of a Messianic reign by exalting Jesus to his own right hand in heaven. From there, they taught, he now rules over the entire universe, serving God's far-flung people as their divine—and divinely anointed—prophet, priest, and king (Acts 2:34-35, 1 Cor. 15:25-28, Phil. 2:5-11, Heb. 1:3, 5:5-6, 9:24, Rev. 5, 6, 12, 20).

28. Prophet

The OT indicated that the Messiah would be a prophet, bringing the full light of God's truth, not only to Israel, but also to all nations

(Deut. 18:15, Isaiah 11:10, 49:5-6, 60:3). Jesus specifically called himself a prophet (Luke 4:24), and was so regarded by most Israelites (Mt. 21:11, Luke 7:6). He spoke as a prophet—that is, as one having authority from God (Mark 1:22)—and did so not only with Jews, but also (on occasion) with Gentiles (Mt. 4:25, John 4:1-26). Though he declared that his earthly mission was primarily to the lost sheep of the house of Israel (Mt. 15:24), he clearly believed that after his death his message would reach all nations (Mt. 22:1-14, John 12:20-26). After his resurrection, he therefore commanded his disciples to take the gospel to the uttermost parts of the earth, promising that as they did so, he himself would be with them in the person of the Holy Spirit (Mt. 28:16-20, Acts 1:7-8). Thus did Jesus identify himself as the promised Messianic prophet who, by means of his Spirit and his people, would continue to bring the light of God's truth to all nations until the day of his return (John 14:15-18). And such was the faith of those who followed him (Acts 3:22, 7: 37, 13:47-48).

29. Priest

In several places the OT prophets described the Messiah as a priest; that is, as one who mediates between a holy God and sinful men, offering gifts and sacrifices for sin. The Messiah, however, would be a priest unlike any Israel had ever known. David, for example, said that he would be a *royal* priest, sitting at God's own right hand, and ruling as a king in the midst of his enemies (Psalm 110:2). Similarly, Zechariah predicted that the Messiah would "...sit and rule upon his throne; so shall he be a priest upon his throne, and the counsel of peace (*i.e., harmony*) shall be between both offices" (Zech. 6:12-13, NIV). Furthermore, we learn from these same prophecies that the Messiah will be an *eternal* priest. Unlike the Levites of old, he will neither die nor be succeeded, but will be "a priest forever, according to the order of Melchizedek" (Psalm 110:4).[6]

As regards the Messiah's priesthood, the prophecy of Isaiah 53 is of special importance since it is saturated with priestly language and imagery. Here Isaiah declares that in fulfillment of God's plan the Messiah will offer the ultimate sacrifice—his own life—in order to provide atonement for the sins of his people.

> Surely he has borne our griefs and carried our sorrows; yet we esteemed him stricken, smitten by God and afflicted. But he was wounded for our transgressions, he was bruised for our iniquities; the punishment for our peace was upon him, and by his stripes we are healed. All we like

> sheep have gone astray; we have turned every one to his own way; and the LORD has laid on him the iniquity of us all.
> —Isaiah 53:4-6

After thus describing the Messiah's atoning work, the prophet goes on to affirm what we just learned from David and Zechariah, that God, as a consequence of the Messiah's obedience unto death, will exalt him as a king:

> By his knowledge My righteous servant shall justify many, for he shall bear their iniquities. Therefore I will divide him a portion with the great, and he shall divide the spoil with the strong, because he poured out his soul unto death, and was numbered with the transgressors, and bore the sin of many, and made intercession for the transgressors.
> —Isaiah 53:11-12

The NT is prolific concerning Jesus' priestly ministry. Though not from the tribe of Levi—and therefore unable to exercise priestly functions under the Law—Jesus nevertheless clearly thought of himself as a priest; indeed, as the royal Messianic priest foretold by the OT prophets (Mt. 22:41-46). Moreover, throughout his ministry he exercised priestly prerogatives, praying for sinners (Luke 22:32, 23:34) and assuring the penitent of God's mercy and forgiveness (Mt. 9:2, Luke 7:48, 24:43). He even defined his life's work in terms drawn directly from Isaiah, declaring that his mission from God was to give his life a ransom for many (Mark 10:45). This is why, on the eve of his death, Jesus consecrated himself in prayer to God, offering himself as a sacrifice for the sins of his people and—as Isaiah had foretold—making intercession for all who would afterward believe in him (John 17).

Following his resurrection, Jesus conferred priestly prerogatives on his disciples, authorizing them to assure repentant believers of the forgiveness of their sins (John 20:23). In this manner, says the apostle Peter, he constituted his entire Church as a royal priesthood (1 Peter 2:9). Then, bringing his priestly work to a climax, Jesus ascended into heaven, there to appear in the presence of God forever, making eternal intercession for his people on the basis of his own righteous life and atoning death (Rom. 8:33-34, Heb. 4:14-16, 7:25-28, 9:24, Rev. 5). This invisible reality would soon become central to the apostolic preaching of the gospel. Henceforth, the disciples would urge all men—whether Jew or Gentile—to look to Jesus as their eternal High Priest, declaring that he alone is able to confer upon them the forgiveness of sins, and along with that the privilege of entering personally, as a NT priest, into the very presence of God (1 Tim. 2:5, Heb. 10:19-22).

30. KING

As we have already seen, a great many OT prophecies describe the Messiah as a coming king, a descendant of David who would arise to deliver the faithful in Israel from their enemies, judge the wicked, and usher in the blessings of a universal reign of God (2 Sam. 7, Psalms 2, 72, 110, Isaiah 9, 11, Jer. 23, 33, Ezek. 34, 37, Dan. 7, etc.). Because these prophecies are so numerous and so detailed, there was no consensus in Jesus' day as to how the great end-time events would unfold. Most believed, however, that the Messiah would first deliver Israel from Rome, and then—while ruling from Jerusalem—somehow extend the faith and rule of Yahweh throughout the earth. At the end of these so-called "Days of the Messiah," Yahweh himself would intervene to raise the dead, judge his remaining enemies, and create new heavens and a new earth, the eternal home of the redeemed.

Living in the midst of such volatile expectations, Jesus generally avoided bold public proclamations about his Messianic identity, lest he should prematurely awaken Messianic fervor in Israel, call the attention of the Roman authorities to his work, and so cut short his total ministry (John 6:15). Nevertheless, even from the beginning, he unabashedly taught that he was indeed Israel's royal Messiah (Mt. 16:17, John 1:41, 49-50, 4:26). In particular, he called himself a king (Mt. 25:34, 27:16, John 18:37), received worship as a king (John 12:13), and died under the accusation of pretending to be a king (Mt. 27:37).

Though Jesus projected himself as Israel's Messianic king throughout his earthly ministry, he repeatedly taught that his reign would not actually begin until after his death, resurrection, and return to heaven (Luke 19:11-27). That reign, as we saw above, would emanate from heaven *via* the work of the Spirit (John 14:15-18). Its chief purpose, as revealed in Jesus' parting words to his disciples, would be to gather into one a people for his own possession by means of a global, Spirit-led proclamation of the gospel at the mouth of his followers (Mt. 28:18ff, John 10:16, Acts 1:1-11, Titus 2:11-15).

In the NT we see that prior to Jesus' ascension the disciples understood little or nothing of this revolutionary view of the Messiah's Kingdom. After Pentecost, they did. They understood that henceforth Messianic prophecy had been—and was continuing to be—fulfilled; that their Master had sat down at God's own right hand in heaven; that he now rules from there as King of the cosmos; that "the Days of the Messiah" have now begun, during which the Holy Spirit is being poured out, the gospel is going forth to the nations, and the Gentiles are being converted to faith in Israel's God.

Also, they understood that when those days were over, the heavenly King himself, just as Jesus had said, would return again in power and great glory to raise the dead, judge the world in righteousness, renew the universe, and thereby usher in the eternal Kingdom of God (Acts 2:30-36, 3:18-21).

All this and more filled the disciple's minds as they went forth to tell the whole world that "Jesus is Lord" (Acts 10:36, Phil. 2:11).

Prophecy and the Critics

Down through the centuries, defenders of the Christian faith have cited these and other prophecies as evidence of God's sovereignty over history, the divine inspiration of the Bible, the uniqueness of Jesus of Nazareth, and the truth and authority of his message. They argue that these prophecies are signs, encouraging seekers everywhere to see in Jesus God's appointed prophet, priest, and king; signs granted by the God of Israel so as to engender and sustain a reasonable faith in him.

Critics, however, have not always responded favorably. Some allege, for example, that Jesus took active steps consciously to fulfill OT Messianic prophecies. Believers answer by cheerfully admitting that in some cases this was undoubtedly true (e.g., the triumphal entry), while in others (e.g., the place of his birth, or the minutiae of his trial, death, and burial) such maneuvering would have been impossible.

Others argue that all these prophecies were coincidentally fulfilled in Jesus. Here, believers respond by saying that the probability of this is so small as to be incalculable, and that such an hypothesis (which offers no account of the phenomenon of biblical prophecy in the first place) requires vastly more faith than the Bible's own explanation: that God himself brought it all to pass by his providence.

Still others argue that the disciples, using OT prophecy as their guide, simply fabricated corresponding stories about Jesus in order to buttress their claims of his being the Messiah. Believers respond by saying that this thesis is incredible, since such duplicity on the part of the disciples would require equal portions of sheer genius, moral degeneracy, and suicidal pigheadedness. And this is to say nothing of the problem of how such bald-faced lies about Jesus' life could so quickly spread and take root in Israel with no word of protest, either from his (honest) friends or his (determined) foes.

In the midst of all this critical smoke the seeker must, of course, decide for himself. Thankfully, the question here is really quite simple: is fulfilled Messianic prophecy the handiwork of the unknown god, or is it not? And if it is not, whose in the world could it reasonably be?[7]

SECOND LOOK

A Biblical Challenge

Before concluding this section on OT Messianic signs, I would like to issue a biblical challenge. According to many interpreters, the following passage from Genesis may well be the most fertile Messianic soil in the entire OT. In particular, it is commonly held that God has planted here a dramatic christophany, numerous Messianic types, and several Messianic prophecies. Please take a few moments to read it carefully. Then, drawing upon your own knowledge of Jesus' life, and also upon what you have learned in our journey so far, see if you agree with the commentators. If you do, be sure to ask yourself what these amazing parallels and correspondences might mean in your own search for the truth of the unknown god.

The passage is found in Genesis 22:1-19.

> Now it came to pass after these things that God tested Abraham, and said to him, "Abraham!"
>
> And he said, "Here I am."
>
> And he said, "Take now your son, your only son Isaac, whom you love, and go to the land of Moriah, and offer him there as a burnt offering on one of the mountains of which I shall tell you."
>
> So Abraham rose early in the morning and saddled his donkey, and took two of his young men with him, and Isaac his son; and he split the wood for the burnt offering and arose and went to the place of which God had told him.
>
> Then on the third day Abraham lifted his eyes and saw the place afar off. And Abraham said to his young men, "Stay here with the donkey; the lad and I will go yonder and worship, and we will come back to you."
>
> So Abraham took the wood of the burnt offering and laid it on Isaac his son; and he took the fire in his hand, and a knife, and the two of them went together.
>
> But Isaac spoke to Abraham his father and said, "My Father!"
>
> And he said, "Here I am my son."
>
> And he said, "Look, the fire and the wood, but where is the lamb for a burnt offering?'"
>
> And Abraham said, "My son, God will provide for Himself the lamb for a burnt offering." And the two of them went together.
>
> Then they came to the place of which God had told him. And Abraham built an altar there and placed the wood in order; and he bound Isaac his son and laid him on the altar, upon the wood. And Abraham stretched out his hand and took the knife to slay his son.
>
> But the Angel of the LORD called to him from heaven and said, "Abraham, Abraham!"
>
> And he said to him, "Here I am."

And he said, "Do not lay your hand on the lad, or do anything to him; for now I know that you fear God, since you have not withheld your son, your only son, from Me."

Then Abraham lifted his eyes and looked, and there behind him was a ram caught in a thicket by its horns. So Abraham went and took the ram, and offered it up for a burnt offering instead of his son. And Abraham called the name of the place, The-LORD-Will-Provide; as it is said to this day, "In the Mount of the LORD it shall be provided."

Then the Angel of the LORD called to Abraham a second time out of heaven and said, "By Myself, I have sworn, says the LORD, because you have done this thing, and have not withheld your son, your only son, in blessing I will bless you, and in multiplying I will multiply your descendants as the stars of the heaven and as the sand which is on the seashore; and your descendants shall possess the gate of their enemies. In your seed all the nations of the earth shall be blessed, because you have obeyed My voice."

So Abraham returned to his young men, and they rose and went together to Beersheba, and Abraham dwelt at Beersheba.

Signs Following Jesus' Coming

We come now to the final category of Messianic signs, those that have followed Jesus' coming. Strictly speaking, this category is occupied by a single entity: Jesus' Church. He himself anticipated that it would become a sign. We see this in the words spoken to his disciples just prior to his ascension: "But you shall receive power when the Holy Spirit has come upon you; and you shall be my witnesses in Jerusalem, and in all Judea and Samaria, and to the end of the earth" (Acts 1:8). Using the language of the courtroom, Jesus here foretold that God himself was about to equip his people supernaturally, so that they could testify to the world of what they had seen concerning the person and work of Christ. In other words, Jesus followers—his Church—were also to become signs. Adding their voice to the other signs, they too would point seekers to Jesus of Nazareth, identifying him as God's chosen Teacher, Savior, and King.

A Broken Sign

Most Christians will freely admit that this particular sign, unlike the rest, is sometimes bent, even broken. Indeed, they will agree that some who name the name of Christ have manifested attitudes and actions that only serve to drive thoughtful people *away* from Jesus rather than to him. The litany of such transgressions is familiar. We hear, for example, of the Crusades, the Spanish Inquisition, the wars of religion in Europe or Ireland, witch trials in Europe and America, slave-holding among Christians, Christian anti-semitism, etc. And all this is to say nothing of money-grubbing televangelists, or of priests who sexually abuse the children of their parishioners. If such things are signs at all, they are signs that something is drastically wrong with the people who practice them.

Appropriately enough, defenders of the faith blush at this constellation of sins, sadly confessing that they are indeed ugly, injurious, and inexcusable. Nevertheless, they also urge seekers to consider several good reasons for not throwing the baby out with the bath water.

First, such behavior in no way reflects the teaching or life-style of Christ and his apostles. If, for example, Jesus had personally taken sword in hand to forcibly convert unbelievers, or killed those who resisted his message, or punished with torture and death those who defected from it, or hated this or that class of persons, or instructed his disciples to do so—then yes, the sins of the followers might legitimately be laid at the feet of their Master. But he did not. To the contrary, his word to his disciples was that they should love, serve, and pray for all men, including their enemies; that they should leave judgment in this life to the State, and in the next life to God; that they should simply keep sharing the good news with all people, turning away from those who will not believe so as to press on in their search for those who will (Mt. 5:43-48, 10:11-15, John 18:10-11, Rom. 13:1f). If, then, some professing Christians seem to have fallen short of this standard, is it fair to charge the giver of the standard with his follower's faults?

Secondly, such behavior, though reprehensible, is nevertheless relatively rare. For example, deaths traceable to the Crusades (1095-1291), the Spanish Inquisition (1478-1834), the European Wars of Religion (1562-1638), and all the witch trials of Europe and America, total far less than a million. But tragic as these were, they fade into insignificance when compared with the trail of blood and tears that follows the atheists. One thinks, for example, of the various Communist pogroms in modern Russia, China, and Cambodia, which, all told, left over 100 million dead. Could it be, then, that a fair and balanced survey of human history actually speaks up *in favor* of Christianity, teaching us that faith in God and Jesus has a vastly greater power to restrain evil than no faith at all?

Thirdly, Christian moral failure, though real, is sometimes greatly exaggerated. Such, I would argue, has been the case with the Crusades (1095-1291). Opponents of Christianity attempt to characterize these seven European campaigns into the Levant as acts of unprovoked aggression against Muslims and Jews, motivated by imperialistic ambition and economic greed, and guided by deliberate policies of atrocity and forced conversion. Now it is sadly true that the Crusades were indeed marred by a number of (unauthorized) attacks on Jews, and also by occasional military excesses, especially in the battle to liberate Jerusalem (though these pale in comparison to the numerous atrocities of their Muslim counterparts). However, there was no effort to colonize or exploit the newly formed crusader states, still less to force their populations to convert. Instead, the Crusades were fundamentally an act of solidarity and self-defense on the part of Christendom as a whole. Here, West arose to the aid of East in the face of centuries of Muslim expansion that had resulted in the loss of Christian lives, liberty, lands, and holy sites—and that now threatened to overwhelm Constantinople itself. It is, then, a great irony that so many today cast the Crusaders in the role the aggressor when, as a matter of historical fact, their resolute defense of the Byzantine empire likely had the effect of preserving Europe from complete Islamic domination for centuries to come.

Fourthly, Christian moral failure is often traceable more to misguided zeal than to unalloyed malice. Whether we think of the European wars of religion, the Salem witch trials, or even anti-semitism and the ugly support of slavery, careful historical study reveals that ignorance and misunderstanding of the scriptures were nearly always involved. Moreover, in each of these cases, it was Christians themselves who pointed out the underlying hermeneutical failures, and who challenged their erring brethren with a more accurate understanding of God's revealed truth. We learn, then, from the actual course of its history, that Christ's Church, though undeniably fallible, nevertheless seems to be indwelt by a principle of self-examination, repentance, and fresh insight into a truer, better way. In other words, while Christians do fail, they also make progress, casting off error and failure through the fresh discovery of life-giving biblical principles such as religious toleration, the separation (and cooperation) of Church and State, and the God-given right to life, liberty, and respect that belongs to all who are created in his image and likeness.

Fifthly, it is not necessarily the case that all who call themselves Christians actually have Christ's Spirit, reflect his character, or serve him in sincerity. As Jesus himself warned:

> Not everyone who says to me, 'Lord, Lord,' will enter the kingdom of heaven, but he who does the will of my Father in heaven...Beware of false prophets, who come to you in sheep's clothing, but inwardly they are ravenous wolves. You will know them by their fruits.
> —Mt. 7:21, 15-16

Very significantly, the apostle Peter anticipates not only the misdeeds of these "false prophets" who make merchandise of the people of God, but also the calumnies that they inevitably bring upon the true Church, asserting that "...many will follow their destructive ways, *because of whom the way of truth will be blasphemed*" (2 Pet. 2:2). Let seekers consider, then, that both Christ and his apostles foresaw the presence of bad apples in the ecclesiastical barrel—and that the presence of a few bad does not logically entail the absence of many good.

Finally, we learn from the NT that even sincere disciples are not immune to moral failure, since their emancipation from sinful passions and deeds is, according to Jesus' own teaching, progressive rather than instantaneous (John 15:1-2, Rev. 3:18-19). This is why the NT insists that even to the end believers must remain vigilant against the temptations of the world, the flesh, and the devil (Mt. 6:13, 26:41, Luke 22:31). Seekers cannot, therefore, justly expect moral perfection from all of Jesus' followers, only consistent moral aspiration and gradual improvement in the majority of those who call upon his name. Moreover, anyone who has personally felt the powerful downward drag of modern world culture will likely forbear in judging others too severely. After all, he himself may need the same forbearance in days to come (Mt. 7:1f, Gal. 6:1f)!

Fair-minded investigators of the faith will not quickly dismiss these responses to Christian moral failure as mere rationalizations; nor will they dismiss the other biblical signs because of the imperfections found in this one. Rather, they will ask themselves, "In spite of all the failures of real or nominal Christians, is there anything in the lives of the majority of Jesus' followers—past or present—that can justly be said to display the supernatural; anything that resembles Jesus himself; anything that looks like the hand of the unknown god working in the world through these people who dare to call themselves the children of the Lord?"[8]

A Supernatural Sign

In order to answer these particular questions, it will be necessary first to ask another: How, precisely, did Jesus *expect* his disciples to serve as signs? Once we know his expectations in this matter, we will have a standard. Having a standard, we can then look down the long corridor of Church history and see how well Christ's people have done in living up to it. Here, then, from my own reading of the NT, are some the most important ways in which Jesus expected his followers to be signs.

In Word

In Jesus' mind, all of his followers are "seers," earthly witnesses of heavenly realities. Moreover, they now have a commission to tell others about what they have seen. From the very beginning, this mandate was clear. Jesus told John's disciples, "Go and tell John the things you have seen and heard" (Luke 7:22). Just prior to his ascension, he made this the norm for all of his followers, telling them to bear witness to him in Judea, Samaria, and the uttermost parts of the earth (Acts 1:8). When he appeared to Saul on the road to Damascus, he said the same thing yet again: "Arise, stand on your feet. For I have appeared to you for this purpose, to make you a minister and a witness, both of the things which you have seen, and of the things which I will yet reveal to you" (Acts 26:12-18).

A study of Church history makes it clear that Christians do indeed behave as if they have seen and heard heavenly things, and also as if they are under orders to communicate those things with anyone willing to listen. Whether at home or in distant lands, whether in private conversation or in open air preaching, whether in churches, homes, schools, or hospitals, whether in print, over the radio, on TV, on tape, on records, in film, and even over the Internet—they are ever eager "to get out the word," to point people to Jesus Christ. Critics have sometimes ridiculed "poor, talkative Christianity." Yet however great or small their sin of loquaciousness, the question still remains: What is it about these Christians that compels them to talk so much? What, if anything, have they seen?

In Deed

It is written of Jesus that God anointed him with the Holy Spirit so that he "...went about doing good" (Acts 10: 38). Anyone familiar with the NT knows that he expected his disciples to do the same. Their works, however, were not to be mere imitations of his own. Rather, they were to be the natural outgrowth of a *supernatural* relationship with him. He would live in them, and they in him; for, said Jesus, "Apart from me you can do nothing" (John 15:1-8). It was, then, in anticipation of this new relationship that Jesus could make the astonishing promise, "The works that I do, you shall do also" (John 14:12). Through his disciples, the risen Christ would *continue* to go about doing good in all the world.

In Jesus' mind, this was how the deeds of his followers would become signs. However flawed, such works would still bear the stamp of heaven; they would be luminously supernatural, originating in the One who called himself "the light of the world" (John 9:5). Here is why Jesus could confidently say to his disciples:

You are the light of the world. A city that is set on a hill cannot be hidden...Let your light so shine before men, that they may see your good works and glorify your Father in heaven."

—Mt. 5:13-16

The disciples will become the light of the world because the light of the world is living in them and working through them. As he does, they will also become signs—luminous signs, directing all who live in the darkness of this world to the brightness of the City of God.

In the view of many, the history of the Christian Church may be read as a record of the fulfillment of these mysterious words. Let us consider just a few of the ways in which this might be so.

As Jesus went about teaching, so his disciples have always taught: in streets, homes, churches, schools, universities, and mission outposts around the world. This has been especially true since the days of the Reformation, when the Bible finally found its way into print, into the hands of the people, and into the very foundation of educational institutions worldwide.

As Jesus went about healing, so his disciples have always healed—occasionally through miracles granted in response to earnest prayer, but usually through hospitals, clinics, leprosaria, orphanages, unwed mother's homes, counseling centers, and simple words of wisdom and encouragement passed from friend to friend.

As Jesus went about supplying material needs, so his disciples have always supplied material needs—money, food, shelter, clothing, blankets, medicine, wells, equipment, seed, farm animals, etc. And along with these material gifts, they have sought to give a far greater spiritual gift: the gospel of the gift of eternal life in Christ.

As Jesus went about teaching submission to divine law, love of one's neighbor, and respect for every creature made in the image and likeness of God, so too have his disciples ever been in the vanguard of those who militate for social justice. By way of illustration, let us hear missiologist Herbert Kane extolling the dedication and effectiveness of 19th century Christian missionaries:

> The missionaries of the nineteenth century were a special breed of men and women. Single-handedly and with great courage they attacked the social evils of their time: child marriage, the immolation of widows, temple prostitution, and untouchability in India; footbinding, opium addiction, and the abandoning of babies in China; polygamy, the slave trade, and the destruction of twins in Africa. In all parts of the world they opened schools, hospitals, clinics, medical colleges, orphanages, and leprosaria. They gave succor and sustenance to the dregs of society

cast off by their own communities. At great risk to themselves and their families they fought famines, floods, pestilences, and plagues. They were the first to rescue unwanted babies, educate girls, and liberate women.

By precept and example they inculcated the ideas and ideals of Christianity: the sanctity of (human) life, the worth of the individual, the dignity of labor, social justice, personal integrity, and freedom of thought and speech, (all of) which have since been incorporated in the Universal Declaration of Human Rights, drawn up by the United Nations.[9]

Notably, 21st century Christians do not lag behind their forefathers in commitment and zeal, having dedicated themselves to the eradication of such modern evils as abortion, pornography, sexual trafficking, female circumcision, religious persecution, cloning, euthanasia, environmental destruction, and more. The so-called "culture wars" are not for nothing. In large part, they reflect the Church of Christ seeking to call Western Civilization back to the values that made it great: faith, family, and personal and societal righteousness, especially as these are defined and exemplified in the life and teachings of Christ.

When a seeker looks steadfastly at mankind's powerful, age-old bent towards selfishness and exploitation—and then at the Church's long history of compassion and self-sacrifice in behalf of the poor—the contrast is striking indeed. Likely as not, it will move him to ask, "What is the meaning of this long obedience in the same direction? Where do these people receive the wisdom and strength to keep on laboring for the physical and spiritual uplift of suffering humanity? Is this a natural or a supernatural phenomenon? Of what—or of whom—are the good works of Jesus' Church a sign?"

In Transformed Character

Jesus taught that all who come to him have experienced spiritual rebirth, a rebirth that transforms a sinner into a holy son or daughter of God (John 3:1-8). In a great many cases, the biographies of his people seem to vindicate this amazing claim—and along with it, the life-changing power of their Master. We consider a few here.

Peter, an impulsive and unstable fisherman, was transformed into a pillar of the Church. John, a "son of thunder" calling down fire on his enemies, was transformed into the apostle of love. Saul, a violent blasphemer and waster of the Church, was transformed into its greatest missionary. Augustine, a proud and reckless profligate, was transformed into a seraphic doctor. Francis, the disillusioned scion of a wealthy merchant, was transformed into a holy beggar who fed the world.

Such has been the case right up to our own time, not only among Christian notables, but among multitudes of everyday "saints" who declare that they have been delivered from destructive spiritual bondages and restored to lives of purpose, order, and dignity. Along these lines, the story is told of a certain agnostic who challenged Christian leader Harry Ironsides to a debate. Ironsides agreed, on the condition that the agnostic bring to the debate just one person who had been rescued from a life of degradation by agnosticism. Ironsides, for his part, agreed to bring 100 who had been powerfully transformed by the gospel of Christ. On further reflection, the agnostic withdrew his challenge.

By most men's reckoning, the transformative power of the gospel is at least intriguing, at most, miraculous. Thoughtful seekers will want to inquire just how it is that this miracle occurs.

In Perseverance

Jesus said, "I will build my Church, and the gates of Hades will not prevail against it" (Mt.16:18). In these cryptic words, he assured his followers of two great inevitabilities: conflict generated from beneath, and perseverance granted from above. 2000 years of Church history seem clearly to have confirmed his prediction.

In the Gospels and the book of Acts we learn that the early evangelists were imprisoned, beaten, run out of town, stoned, left for dead, lied about, mobbed, vilified, and killed. All of Jesus' apostles, with the possible exception of John, died as martyrs. Since then—and never more so than in our own day—his followers have been plundered, ostracized, kidnapped, raped, slandered, jailed, "re-educated," starved, tortured, and murdered. According to reliable sources, in the 20th century alone some 120 million Christians perished for their faith.[10]

Furthermore, Jesus' sobering prophecy spoke not only of enemies without, but of enemies within: "false christs," "false prophets," and "false brethren" who would arise to distort his message, thereby drawing people away from him to themselves (Mt. 24:24, Acts 20:30). The Church's longstanding history of doctrinal debates, councils, creeds, schisms, and opposing sects gives tangible meaning to these prescient words.

And yet despite all these varieties of conflict, the worldwide Christian Church not only continues, but continues to grow. How can people endure such protracted opposition, not merely stoically, but often with a song upon their lips? How can they keep on working and serving, with or without visible success or rewards, sometimes even unto death? To what hidden power does the perseverance of Jesus' Church point? Of what—or of whom—is it a sign?

In Growth

In one of his parables, Jesus taught that his Kingdom is like a mustard seed: once planted in the field of this world, it will grow to such great size that the birds of the air will be able to come and nest in its branches (Mt. 13:32).

This prediction also has come to pass. From the day in which Jesus' dead body was planted, seed-like, into the ground, the Church has grown steadily, so much so that there are now over two billion souls who claim allegiance to Christ. The New Testament has been translated into thousands of languages; churches have sprung up on every continent and in every country; missionaries continue to seek out all who have not yet heard the gospel. So here again history gives the seeker pause, inviting him to ask, "What secret power is behind this continuing expansion? Of what—or whom—is the growth of Jesus' Church a sign?"[11]

The Seeker and the Signs

For all open-minded readers of the Bible, the Messianic signs are at least thought provoking, and usually quite impressive. The last few chapters of our journey explain why. These signs are both numerous and diverse, falling readily into three broad categories. First, there are the signs that occurred *at* Jesus' coming: supernatural events surrounding his birth, angelic visitations and testimonies, theophanies, miracles, and Jesus' bodily resurrection from the dead. Then there are the signs that occurred *prior to* his coming: christophanies, Messianic types, and Messianic prophecies—a whole sky full of scriptural stars, shining brightly in the firmament of the OT! Finally, there are the signs that have occurred *after* his coming. Centering around his Church, these include his people's words, deeds, transformed character, perseverance in the face of suffering, and growth in numbers and influence around the world. Such an amazing constellation of signs can hardly fail to draw earnest seekers into the luminously supernatural world of the Bible.

As I mentioned earlier, when I myself first encountered the Messianic signs, I found them both fascinating and believable. I did not, however, even begin to appreciate the full measure of their abundance, meaning, or importance. Today, after many years reflection, I trust that I am beginning to do so. Therefore, permit me to bring this portion of our journey to a close by offering two personal observations, observations that should be of special interest to seekers.

First, I am now persuaded that *the Christian faith is altogether unique in commending its truthfulness to the world by means of signs*. Yes, all religions claim to be true. And yes, some even ascribe supernatural phenomena to their founders. But none—with the exception of Christianity—issues its truth-claims, cites a wide variety of supernatural evidences in their support, and then *explicitly challenges seekers to ascertain the truth by examining them both*. In short, Christianity alone explicitly puts us to a test.

It was Jesus himself who laid down this pattern. We think, for example, of how John the Baptizer, plagued with doubts about Jesus' identity, sent messengers from prison to ask, "Are you the Coming One, or should we look for another?" In reply, Jesus appealed both to his miracles and to several OT prophecies. Citing from Isaiah, he told the emissaries:

> Go and tell John the things that you hear and see: the blind receive their sight and the lame walk; the lepers are cleansed and the deaf hear; the dead are raised up and the poor have the gospel preached to them. And blessed is he who is not offended because of me."
> —Mt. 11:1-6, Isaiah 35:4-6, 61:1

Nor was this an isolated instance. Consider, for example, how Jesus challenged his Jewish opponents to search the OT scriptures, claiming, "… these are they which testify of Me" (John 5:39). In other words, he charged all Israel to see whether or not it was he himself—in a multitude of OT christophanies, types, and prophecies—who lay hidden at the very heart of the ancient oracles of God. Or again, this time urging his own disciples to faith, he said, "Believe Me that I am in the Father and the Father in Me, *or else believe Me for the sake of the works themselves*" (John 14:11). Here Jesus is pointing to his miracles, the supernatural works that the Father had given him to do. He exhorts his disciples to understand that these were not only designed to help the poor and needy, but also to serve as solid ground for a rational faith in the Father's Son.

In all such passages we therefore learn that the Teacher from Nazareth does not expect seekers simply to accept his words on his own say so, but in addition to this directs them to the one body of Messianic signs as the proper foundation for an intellectually satisfying faith in him, his teachings, and his God.

Jesus' disciples did the same. An excellent example of this is found in Peter's sermon on the day of Pentecost. Earnestly desiring to win his Jewish kinsmen to faith in Christ, he declared:

> Men of Israel, listen to these words: Jesus of Nazareth, *a man attested to you by God with miracles and wonders and signs which God performed through him in your midst*...this man you nailed to a cross by the hands of godless men and put to death. *But God raised him up again.*
> —Acts 2:21f

Here, Peter commends the truth of Christianity to the Jews on the basis of Jesus' miracles and resurrection. To read further is to learn that he next cites several OT predictions of these very events. In all of this, Peter was simply following in the foot-steps of his Master, who had himself held forth both his miracles and the OT scriptures as proofs that the Father had sent him into the world to be its authorized prophet, priest, and king (John 5:31f; Acts 10:34-33, 17:22). Not surprisingly, Christian preachers and teachers down through the centuries have followed suit. They have operated on the assumption that life is a test of our love of the truth, and that considering and following the signs granted by Israel's God is one of the best ways to discover what that truth is.

Again, this appeal to a large and varied body of supernatural signs is absolutely unique in all world religion. For example, we find nothing remotely like it in the three largest non-biblical religions: Hinduism, Buddhism, and Islam. None of them even attempts to boast of a rich, historical mosaic of types, prophecies, theophanies, and miracles—still less of a virgin birth, a transfiguration, or a physical resurrection from the dead. The Bible alone reveals such a body of signs, and the Bible alone challenges seekers to check it out.

This brings me to my second point, namely that *the biblical signs create a reasonable presumption that Jesus of Nazareth is indeed God's appointed Teacher.* This conclusion follows logically from the great abundance of the signs, their amazing diversity, their having been spread out over some 6000 years of human history, their appearance in highly credible historical documents, and, above all, their marvelous convergence in one man, Jesus of Nazareth.

I have stated that this phenomenon is unprecedented and unparalleled in religious history. But even more importantly, *it is altogether inexplicable without reference to the divine.* Such a confluence of supernatural signs lies completely beyond the capacity of mortal man even to imagine, let alone to fabricate. It must, therefore, be the handiwork of an infinitely intelligent and powerful supreme being. Like the Star of Bethlehem, shining with incomparable splendor in an otherwise darkened sky, the one body of biblical signs is manifestly a supernatural invitation from the unknown god. Through it, he is clearly inviting wise men of every time and place to come, sit, and listen to the Teacher from Nazareth.

When they do come, and when they do take their place at his feet, their purpose will be as simple as it is important: Now they must try to find out if this Jesus—who unabashedly called himself "The Teacher" of all mankind—has indeed brought us trustworthy answers to all the questions of life.

ONE MAN'S JOURNEY:
GOOD NEWS FROM A DISTANT LAND

*Like cold water to a weary soul
is good news from a distant land.*
—Proverbs 25:25

IT WAS A beautiful spring day in Berkeley, I was right where I felt I should be, my deepest desire was about to be fulfilled, and I was scared spitless. It was one thing to read about Tibetan lamas (priests) in books, but quite another to knock on one's door and ask to become his student! But as I reflected on the events of the past few months, I realized I had no other choice. I simply had invested too much in this moment to let fear rob me of my dream.

The journey to Berkeley had begun several months earlier, shortly after my watching the documentary about Peter Max and coming to a solid faith in the existence of god. I was all questions, all excitement, all hope. I was a newborn seeker of religious truth and spiritual experience. So I did what every newborn does: I cried out for someone to feed me. In other words, I started looking for a teacher, a trustworthy spiritual guide who could help me experience the mystical union with god that all the gurus were proclaiming.

Interestingly, I did not immediately seek out Swami Satchidananda's group. Instead, I made some new acquaintances and read some fascinating books that attracted me to Tibetan Buddhism. Eventually I heard about Lama Tarthang Tulku Rinpoche, a Tibetan Buddhist priest who had recently arrived from India to establish the Tibetan Nyingmapa Meditation Center in that haven of all things radical, Berkeley, California. Being radically interested in god, I headed out.

When at last I found the courage to knock on his door, it opened up into a whole new world. Rinpoche, as his students called him, warmly greeted me himself, introduced me to his wife and children, and then invited me to join him in the empty meditation hall. The polished wood floor of the cavernous Victorian living room was covered with mats: here the students sat in mediation and listened to his teaching. Ornate tapestries covered with boddhisattvas (enlightened men, now elevated to the status of demigods) hung from the walls. On the dais where we visited there were books of sacred scriptures, prayer wheels, and other accoutrements of Tibetan worship. What had I gotten myself into?!

The brief interview began. Rinpoche asked me to tell him the story of my interest in Tibetan Buddhism. After relating it to him, he grew silent, reached for a small container, shook it several times, and cast its contents onto the floor before us. Realizing that he was seeking to divine my suitability as a disciple, I waited nervously.

At length he got his answer and, to my relief and joy, agreed to accept me. He told me about the various gatherings for meditation and then gave me some translated Tibetan scriptures to read, along with a colorful, poster-size picture of Padmasambhava, one of the great Tibetan boddhisattvas. In order to advance to the next stage of my discipleship, I would have to complete 100,000 prostrations before this picture. I assured him that I would.

As I emerged from the darkened house into the light and warmth of the sun, my mind was spinning. What were the other students like? What kind of spiritual experiences had they had? What kind of experiences had Rinpoche had? How long would it take me to become enlightened? What would that be like? And what happens *after* someone is enlightened? But however many my questions, all were overshadowed by a single, joyful fact: like the Beatles, like Peter Max, and like thousands of other young American seekers on the road to the East, I had found my teacher.

Looking back on this episode, I cannot help but smile, since this epoch-making submission to my first "guru" produced a relationship that lasted scarcely more than six months. Indeed, lama Tulku was only one of several teachers to whom I would attach myself in the years ahead. Returning to Santa Cruz, I briefly joined with the followers of Swami Satchidananda. Then, following a weeklong retreat at a nearby monastery in Tassajara, I decided that the way of Zen Buddhism better suited my ever-evolving sensibilities. Accordingly, I joined the Santa Cruz Zen Center, placing myself under the tutelage of a winsome young Japanese priest by the name of Kobun Chino. But after that—despite a general adherence to Zen Buddhism—I would sit, figuratively speaking, at the feet of any number of modern pantheistic writers, including Kahil Gibran, Jiddu Krishnamurti,

Ram Das, Emmet Fox, and Joel Goldsmith. In short, my behavior in those days pretty much corresponded to my mood: I was always spiritually hungry, always spiritually restless, and always wondering if the spiritual grass was greener on the other side.

My New Worldview

Throughout this time I read widely in world religions, but almost always with a bias towards pantheism. To my amazement, I soon realized that "the perennial philosophy" (pantheism) had its defenders in nearly every land. From Tibet I received the *Tibetan Book of the Dead*, the *Tibetan Book of the Great Liberation*, and a variety of other Buddhist texts supplied by my first teacher. India gave me the *Upanishads*, the *Bhagavad-Gita*, the *Biography of Sri Ramakrishna*, and the philosophical writings of his most famous disciple, Swami Vivekananda. China supplied me with Lao Tze's spiritual classic, the *Tao Te Ching*, as well as the writings of his most famous disciple, Chuang Tze. From (or through) Japan came the *Mumonkan*, the Zen poetry of Basho, the philosophical works of D.T. Suzuki, and the deeply affecting sermons of the American émigré, Sunryu Suzuki Roshi. Europe gave me the mystical novels of Herman Hesse, especially his popular classic, *Siddhartha*. I even found pantheists springing up from American soil, and so devoured Thoreau's *Walden Pond*, the essays of Emerson (especially "The Transcendentalist" and "The Over-Soul"), and Walt Whitman's "Song of Myself." And there was, of course, the new generation of American mystics who had turned us on to all of the above, men like Alan Watts, Richard Alpert (alias Ram Das), Allen Ginsberg, and Gary Snyder. Needless to say, the ubiquity, power, and current popularity of these writings only reinforced my confidence in the truth of pantheism.

Immersed as I was in all this reading, a definite worldview began to take shape in my mind. Fundamentally, it was Hindu/Buddhist, though I did not hesitate to borrow freely from other schools of thought. In the end I concluded that the ultimate reality was Big Mind (or Brahman, the Tao, Gaia, etc.), whom I thought of as an infinite impersonal (or suprapersonal) Spirit. The universe, life, and man were all manifestations of this one Spirit, as were the several other spiritual planes of consciousness on which various kinds of sentient beings also lived. How it all began no one really knew, except perhaps the enlightened ones, who had obviously declined to describe the beginning in anything other than poetic idiom. I did, however, accept the truth of cosmic evolution, having imbibed that assumption from just about every intellectual authority figure I had ever met. As for evil, suffering, and death—I regarded these as painful illusions, the unwelcome byproducts of the dualistic consciousness that grips and actually constitutes each and every sentient being. Like consciousness itself, these enemies were wrought by Maya, a mysterious spiritual power that had somehow subjected Big Mind to a long and difficult cosmic dream. (Or was it that Big Mind had "intentionally" subjected himself to the dream?) The purpose of life, then, was to attain enlightenment: to escape one's painful bondage to dualistic consciousness by awakening to one's true identity as Big Mind. And how were sentient beings to accomplish this? All the gurus gave the same paradoxical answer: freedom and enlightenment for the (divine) self can only come through the dissolution of the (human) self. To experience salvation, the illusory man of salt must be dissolved in the ocean of Big Mind.

This worldview had practical implications. Above all, it meant that I must live selflessly, meditatively, and in spiritual detachment from the phenomenal world—ever ready for the gracious moment of mystical union with Big Mind. Happily, I believed that society had now arrived at a moment in cosmic history when enlightenment was coming to many. Indeed, it would soon come to all, since evolving mankind, amidst many birth-pangs, was now casting off the old paradigms, awakening to its divine nature, and entering a New Age of global unity, peace, and happiness. And if I myself should die before it all came to pass, not to fear: I would surely be reincarnated as a different person, and so rejoin my spiritual brothers and sisters once again for the next step in the great ascent towards the deification of the universe, life, and man.

Were there philosophical problems with this new worldview? Definitely. Did I have any doubts about it? Yes. Still, it hung together well enough, multitudes believed it (or something very like it), and there seemed to be no other worldviews around that were remotely competitive. Therefore, I embraced this one enthusiastically.

So now I knew the truth. Now I had a purpose. Now I had a spiritual family with whom to share that truth and pursue that purpose. How wonderful to realize that I was getting better, the world was getting better, and Paradise was drawing nearer every day! Yes, life was good.

Little did I know, however, that my good life was about to be turned completely upside down. The test that I thought I was so soon to pass had, in fact, only begun.

The Way of Devotion

It all started in the late fall of 1971. Ever the way-taster, I became interested in Bhakti Yoga, the Hindu path of union with god by means of an intense personal devotion to one of his alleged incarnations. My friend and business partner, Mike, had embraced this path fervently. Like the saffron-robed worshippers of Krishna that were appearing on street corners everywhere, he and his spiritual community were pursuing *samadhi* (god-consciousness) through enthusiastic devotion to their Indian teacher, a man they affectionately called Babbaji. They believed that Babba was a fully enlightened being, an "incarnation" of Big Mind himself. By worshiping him, they hoped to become enlightened as well.

As I said, I was attracted to this "way of devotion," but not, for some reason, to Babbaji or any of the other Indian gods and gurus. I was, however, drawn to Jesus of Nazareth. At that time, I knew very little about the details his life. Nor did I have among my close friends a single one his followers, someone who might have introduced me to his Master and told me more about his life and teachings. I did, however, remember a few basic facts from my childhood "training" in the faith. I knew, for example, that Jesus was a real, historical person. I knew that the biblical authors ascribed miracles to him—the most dramatic of all being his resurrection from the dead. I knew that they regarded him as divine, as the very Son of God. And I knew that just about everyone—pantheists included—honored him as a good, loving, wise, and profoundly important spiritual leader.

As I mulled all this, something quite unexpected happened: the rumors about Jesus suddenly struck me as "good news from a distant land," as a heavenly hint directing me to a way of devotion that I myself could readily embrace. After all, Jesus was a teacher with impeccable credentials, one I already knew about (at least a little), and one I already trusted. If, then, I was supposed to seek enlightenment by focusing upon a human incarnation of Big Mind, how could I do better than to choose the carpenter from Nazareth?

And so, on the strength of these few rumors from ancient Israel, I made a decision. I would dig out my deceased aunt Ethel's old King James Bible, open it up, sit down at Jesus' feet, and hear what he had to say about the nature of the ultimate reality, enlightenment, and all the other great questions of life.

The heavenly Tester was, I trust, well pleased.

A Gift of Tears

Forever etched in my memory are the simple circumstances of this life-changing season: the quiet, one-room cottage where I lived, the brown recliner in which I comfortably sat, and the beautiful old Bible—with its marvelous fragrance of India paper and aged leather—lying open in my lap. Then, as now, an atmosphere of destiny hovered over the whole scene. With an unfamiliar sense of reverence and anticipation, I began to read.

My journey into the biblical world started at the Gospel according to Matthew. It also started with my being a committed pantheist. This was, of course, a theological bias that would powerfully affect my reading. It did, however, have one advantage: it left me fully open to the supernatural. Accordingly, as I came daily to the Bible window and beheld the various supernatural signs surrounding Jesus' life, I had no problem whatsoever in believing them. I did not question, for example, his virgin birth, or the occasional appearance of angels, or the miracles he performed, or the amazing fulfillment of numerous Old Testament prophecies in the events of his life. To the contrary, I not only believed these things, but wanted to know how and why they had occurred. Like theists, pantheists too long to see and understand the hand of God at work in the world.

But all was not well. The more I read about Jesus' words and manner of life, the more the signs troubled me. Why? Because I now began to realize that all these supernatural phenomena were enlisted in the service of Jesus' worldview, and that his worldview was different from that of any of the lamas, gurus, or roshis I had been following. *Radically* different. Indeed, I soon realized that Jesus did not concur with a single one of their answers to the various questions of life. Moreover, far from being deferential to other spiritual teachers and traditions, he seemed both implicitly and explicitly to charge them with error and even deceit, all the while making bold, unmistakable claims to a unique spiritual authority based upon a unique spiritual relationship with God. The mood of the religious counterculture in Santa Cruz was inclusive, non-judgmental, and laissez-faire. Reading Matthew's Gospel, I saw quite clearly that Jesus of Nazareth was in another mood altogether.

I tried to reconcile all this with my pantheism—to discover a hidden, pantheistic sense for Jesus' words. I wondered, for example, if his teachings—seemingly premised on the existence of a personal god who is both transcendent and immanent, a god who remains metaphysically separate from his creation yet intimately related to it—were just an accommodation to the limitations of his Jewish audience; indeed, to the limitations of the entire human race in a more primitive stage of its spiritual evolution. After all, many modern pantheists had claimed this very thing—Gibran, Ramakrishna, Vivekananda, Yogananda, and others. In the end, however, I found it impossible to escape the impression of Jesus' uniqueness. He simply refused to be reckoned among the gurus. Thus, for the first time in his brief spiritual journey, this callow young seeker began to experience some serious religious and philosophical conflict.

And he was about to experience something more—something that would not only reinforce his sense of Jesus' uniqueness, but forever change the trajectory of his journey towards the truth about God. For now, having made my way through the story of Jesus' life; having tasted of his wisdom, kindness, and power; having gotten the gist of his worldview; and having beheld the many signs that worked together to confirm it, I came at last to the climax: the climax of Jesus' work on earth, and the climax of my first real encounter with it. In other words, I came to Matthew's account of the dramatic events of Holy Week: Jesus' triumphal entry into Jerusalem, his final season of public ministry, his terrible clash with the hostile religious authorities, his betrayal, his capture, his trial, his rejection by (most of) the Jewish nation, and his crucifixion, death, and burial at the hands of Rome.

Pondering all these things, I found myself in the grip of a strange double-consciousness. I had already read Jesus' own predictions of his imminent suffering, and knew perfectly well that they would all be fulfilled. Yet despite the inevitability of the outcome, I suddenly found myself both amazed and appalled that this good man, who had done so much for so many, should be treated so badly by the very ones he had come to serve.

Indeed, as I read on, it seemed to me that here I was gazing upon goodness itself—the very embodiment of innocence, kindness, mercy, and love. Yet now, for reasons that I could not even begin to understand, this perfect purity had fallen into the hands of stupid, ungrateful, selfish, and cruel men. I knew full well that he could easily have escaped from this pack of murderers, and just as easily have destroyed them all. Yet here he was, voluntarily surrendering himself to their will. Hundreds of years earlier, the prophet Isaiah had tersely captured the mystery and pathos of it all: "He was led as a lamb to the slaughter; and as a sheep before its shearers is silent, so he opened not his mouth" (Isaiah 53:7). As I read of Christ's passion, the heartbreaking reality behind Isaiah's words went straight through me. Seeing the Lamb of God in the hands of his slaughterers—shearing him of both life and dignity—my heart broke. If only I could have reached into my Bible and rescued him! But alas, I sat there helpless. All I could do was weep, moved by a strange, unbidden love that I deeply felt but could not even begin to fathom.

A Turn in the Road

This spiritual experience was a major turning point in my search for truth. It did not bring any new philosophical insights, nor did it transform me into a biblical theist. But it definitely changed me. From that day on, I knew God had touched me. Moreover, I knew *why* he had touched me:

so that I might further investigate Christ and Christianity. As a committed pantheist, I still hoped that Jesus would turn out to be a guru: the greatest of all, no doubt, but an ordinary man like me, nonetheless. Yet I could not honestly deny that his teachings powerfully resisted this self-serving interpretation. Was I mistaken then? Did the truth about God lay in another (theistic) direction altogether? I didn't know. All I knew was that a gift had been given and an invitation extended. I dared not turn away.

But what was I to do?

My decision came quickly. The following day I told my friend Mike what had happened. I asked if I might take a leave of absence from the bakery and set out in search of the truth about Christianity. Graciously, he sent me on my way. And since Roman Catholicism seemed to be the oldest and largest spokesman for that faith, I decided to begin my search there. I would contact a local Catholic priest, tell him about my experience, and ask him what it meant and what I was supposed to do next.

It was time to seek a teacher once again.

PART 3

THE TEACHER ON THE QUESTIONS OF LIFE

CHAPTER 9

WHAT IS THE ULTIMATE REALITY?

IN OUR JOURNEY to the meaning of life—and in our search for the one who can reveal it to us—we have passed through the foothills and now stand at the base of a great mountain. Christianity towers above us. Unlike other world religions, it has commended its truth to us by means of evidence, for unlike other world teachers, its founder, Jesus of Nazareth, is surrounded by a large, diverse, and noteworthy body of supernatural signs. Does this mean our journey is over?

No, it is does not. True, the signs are impressive. And yes, they certainly seem to be aiming us in the right direction. Yet they are not enough, in precisely the same way that signs directing us to our local bakery or grocery store are not enough. *They are not enough for the simple reason that spiritually hungry seekers cannot feed on signs, no matter how abundant or impressive they may be.* If, then, we want to find full satisfaction, we must *use* the signs; we must follow them to the spiritual destination—the spiritual food and drink—that we need, want, and are hoping to find at the end of our search.

Here, then, is our road map for Part 3 of the journey. In the chapters ahead we will let the one body of biblical signs do exactly what they were meant to do: bring us to the feet of Jesus so that we may inquire of him concerning the questions of life. In particular, we will see if Jesus 1) addresses all or most of the questions of life, 2) does so in a manner that is satisfying to intuition, intellect, conscience, and hope, and 3) thinks of himself as the one sent by God to do this very thing. If he really is god's appointed Teacher, it is certain that he will do all three of these things, and that he will do them well.

The Teacher on the Questions of Life

In just a moment we will resume our journey by hearing Jesus on the first and most important question of life: What is the ultimate reality? However, before setting out, a few preliminary remarks are in order.

First, in the chapters ahead I have tried to offer a *substantive sketch* of Jesus' answers to each of the questions of life. Hopefully, these surveys are short enough to keep the larger goal in sight (i.e., the biblical worldview as a whole), yet long enough to capture your imagination and provoke you to further study. To that end, I have parenthetically cited a great many biblical references, so that you may check out the texts upon which I have based my assertions. Also, in the notes at the end of each chapter I have tried to mention at least two of the better books on the theme under investigation. These should enable motivated seekers to explore the riches of Jesus' teaching in greater depth.

Secondly, in the discussion ahead you will find that I have cited not only Jesus' words, but also those of his apostles. I do so because Jesus himself regarded his apostle's teachings as extensions of his own. Exactly how this works will become clear in chapter 17, where we examine Jesus' claims to being the Teacher of all mankind, and the means by which he planned to fulfill that privileged role.

Finally, a few words about the propriety and method of evaluating Jesus' answers to the questions of life. Now at first glance it may seem presumptuous—and possibly even blasphemous—to do what I enthusiastically do at the end of each chapter in Part 3: *evaluate* Jesus' teachings. After all, how can mere mortals who are so prone to bias and error presume to sit in judgment on the words of a teacher with credentials like these? The answer, I would suggest, is that until we *know* he is the Teacher sent by god, we have no other choice. In other words, so long as we are seekers, we are compelled to keep on doing what seekers do: search for truth. And how can we actually *find* truth unless we hear and weigh what purported truth-tellers have to say? Yes, it is clear that the biblical signs create a rational presumption that Jesus is god's appointed Teacher: therefore, we should listen to him thoughtfully and humbly. But it is equally clear that the unknown god has also purposely equipped us to evaluate religious truth-claims: therefore, we should *use* that equipment, fearlessly applying it to Jesus' teaching. Moreover, if Jesus really is the Teacher, what could please god more than to see his seeking children doing that very thing? *Indeed, it is precisely in this process of active inquiry that the unknown god is most likely to draw near and turn seekers into finders; into men and women who have received personal, inward knowledge and assurance of the truth.*

This brings us to a very practical question: How, exactly, is one to evaluate Jesus' teachings—or those of any other religious leader? Here we find our answer by looking once again at the faculties with which the unknown god has equipped us. As we saw earlier, these include at least four "truth monitors:" intuition, reason, conscience, and the human inclination to hope for the best. Accordingly, we may say that the one true worldview—and the one true answer to any of the questions of life—must be:

1. *Intuitive*—This means that it must not offend, but rather win the assent of, our most basic intuitions about reality. Now it is certainly true that human intuitions may be flawed or weakened; indeed, the Bible insists that sin has so deeply weakened our minds that divine revelation itself strikes many people as utter (counter-intuitive) foolishness (1 Cor. 1:18-31, 2:14). Nevertheless, if we truly are creatures of an unknown god—living under a mandate to seek out his truth—then it would be strange indeed for a seeker *not* to listen to his intuitions, since they are not only given to him by god, but are integrally involved in every religious and philosophical judgment he is called upon to make. In short, while making all due allowance for human brokenness, we may nonetheless reasonably expect that in the end, and with god's help, true answers to the questions of life will indeed resonate with what might be called our "spiritual common sense."

2. *Reasonable*—This criterion is actually three-fold. It means that a trustworthy divine revelation must be a) *understandable*, b) *logical* (i.e., it cannot contradict itself, but must obey the laws of sound thought), and c) *supported with an abundance of good evidence*. All this does not, of course, rule out "mystery," in the sense of truth that is hidden from our sight or from complete understanding. It does, however, rule out mysticism, by which I mean any religion or philosophy that disparages our god-given faculties for apprehending and discussing truth (e.g., reason, logic, language, etc.) in favor of irrational spiritual experience.

3. *Right*—This means it must not violate our conscience, but rather commend itself to our distinctly ethical intuitions as being consistent with the good and holy god who created and sustains the objective moral order.

4. *Hopeful*—This means it must awaken hope, not only the hope of finding trustworthy answers to the questions of life, but also of

laying to rest the spiritual longings and anxieties associated with each one of them. In other words, a true revelation must not only affect us intellectually, but also existentially. It must offer us peace of mind, both for this life and the life to come.

This brings me to a final preliminary remark. Throughout Part 3 of our journey, I will conclude each chapter with a brief section entitled "Especially for Seekers." My purpose here is to give you a feel for the application of these four criteria in the evaluation of Jesus' teaching. In this process I will also address certain topics, questions, and objections that are typically of great interest to seekers, thus opening a small window onto some of the lively theological debates that surround the matter at hand.

And now, with these preliminaries in mind, let us head up the mountain and take our place at the feet of Jesus. We will begin at the beginning, listening to his words on the first and most fundamental question of life, the question of the ultimate reality.

On the Ultimate Reality

During the last week of his earthly ministry, as he taught the people who had gathered in Jerusalem for the Passover, Jesus was interrogated by a zealous young scribe who asked, "Teacher, what is the greatest commandment of all?" Mark records his reply as follows:

> Jesus answered, "The greatest of all the commandments is, 'Hear O Israel, the LORD your God, the LORD is one. And you shall love the LORD your God with all your heart, with all your soul, with all your mind and with all your strength.' This is the first commandment."
> —Mark 12:29-30

Here we find Jesus reciting the *shema*, the supreme creed and confession of Orthodox Judaism (Deut. 6:4). Here too we meet his understanding of the ultimate reality. For Jesus, the ultimate reality is *Yahweh Elohim*, the LORD God, the creator of the universe, the redeemer of his people Israel, and the king of a glorious new world to come.

Concerning this Supreme Being, Jesus taught things both old and new (Mt. 13:52). In other words, he affirmed the OT understanding of the ultimate reality, even as he himself sought to enlarge and complete it. As we begin our journey, let us therefore turn first to the ancient Jewish Scriptures, in order to see what the Hebrew prophets had to say about the nature of their god.

An Infinite Personal Spirit

In venturing onto OT ground, we immediately find ourselves in the presence of a god who may be concisely described as an *infinite personal spirit*. Each term in this basic definition merits close attention.

Beginning at the end, we observe first that the LORD God is a *spirit*. In other words, he is *a formless, immaterial substance, capable of interacting with matter.*[1] In the Bible we learn that there are four different kinds of spirits: divine, angelic, human, and animal. The first three are personal, the last impersonal. In the case of men and animals, their spirits normally indwell material bodies. God, however, is an infinite personal spirit without a body, and also the creator of every other kind of spirit that exists (Heb. 12:9). With all this in mind, Jesus tells the Samaritan woman, "God is spirit, and those who worship him must worship him in spirit and in truth (John 4:24, 3:8; Gen. 2:7, Deut. 4:15-18, Num. 16:22, Psalm 104:4).

Secondly, God is *personal*. Always and everywhere, he is referred to as a "he," but never as an "it." Like all persons, he has a name. Indeed, he has several names, each one supplying a special glimpse into this or that attribute of his divine nature (e.g., *El, Elohim, Yahweh, Adonai*, etc). Very importantly, in manifold ways God is like the human persons that he created specially in his own image and likeness: both possess self-consciousness, intelligence, imagination, emotion, will, conscience, creativity, gender, and more.[2] Such attributes are on display throughout the OT, where we meet an intensely personal god who sees, plans, acts, reacts, and speaks in history. Seekers should not fail to grasp the significance of this: God has made men *like* him, so that they may relate *to* him. His desire is for intimate personal relationship with human and angelic persons: mind to mind, heart to heart, face to face (Gen. 18:19, Ex. 33:11).

God's personhood is also seen in his moral perfections, or the various facets of his *ethical holiness* (Lev. 11:45, Isaiah 1:4, 5:24). These include his righteousness (Deut. 32:4), goodness (Ex. 33:19; Ps. 27:13, Mt. 19:17), and "loving-kindness," the latter being a special covenant-love that he graciously bestows upon his own people (Psalm 107:1, 145:9).

Such attributes govern the interactions of a sovereign creator with his human creatures, who therefore find him to be truthful, faithful, patient, jealous, zealous, angry, indignant, just, compassionate, pitiful, merciful, tender, kind, humble, and more. In the gospels, Jesus ascribes many of these moral perfections to his Father (Mt. 5:44-45, 19:17, John 3:16, 17:11, 17, 25, etc.). Jesus' disciples, awed by the beauty of their Master's own character, frequently ascribe them to him (John 1:14, Heb. 7:26, 1 Pet. 1:9).

Thirdly, God is *infinite*. This means that he is limited by nothing except the requirements of his own nature. God's infinity is especially visible in what theologians have called his "incommunicable attributes." These are attributes that he cannot and therefore will not pass along to his finite creatures. They include:

- His *self-existence*, or the fact that his existence is necessary and owed to none (Ex. 3:14, John 5:26, Acts 17:34). This is God's infinity with respect to his origin.

- His *immutability*, or the fact that he does not change in his nature, purposes, plans, or promises (Num. 23:19, Psalm 33:11, 107:25f, Isaiah 40:21-26, Malachi 3:6, James 1:17).[3] This is God's infinity with respect to his perfection or completeness.

- His *eternity*, or the fact that he is without beginning or end, but endures forever. This is God's infinity with respect to time (Gen. 1:1, Psalm 90:2, Isaiah 40:28, 57:15, John 8:58, 1 Tim. 1:17).

- His *omnipresence*, or the fact that there is no place where he is not, since all places, and all the things within them, are created and sustained by him. This is God's infinity with respect to space (Psalm 139:6-7, Isaiah 40:12ff, Jer. 23:23, Acts 17:24).

- His *omniscience*, or the fact that he knows all things about himself, his creation, and what will happen or would happen under a given set of circumstances. This is God's infinity with respect to his knowledge (Psalm 33:13, 139:1-6, 147:5, Isaiah 41:21-29, Dan. 2:20-22, Mt. 6:8, 11:12, 10:30, Rom. 11:33-36, Rev. 1:17-19).[4]

- His *omnipotence*, or the fact that all power belongs to him and ultimately comes from him; also, it includes the fact that nothing can hinder him from wielding his power except the demands of his own nature. This is God's infinity with respect to his ability to act (Gen. 17:1, Psalm 33:6-7, 62:11, 135:6, Jer. 10:12, 32:27, Mt. 19:26).[5]

- His *unity*, or the fact that, in virtue of all his other attributes, he is absolutely unique; that, being who he is, he alone is God (Deut. 6:4, 2 Sam. 7:22, Isaiah 40:25, 45:5-7, 1 Tim. 2:5).

Because God alone possesses these incommunicable attributes, he displays what theologians refer to as *ontological holiness*. This means that because of his radically unique nature, God is "wholly other," qualitatively *different* or *set apart* from his every creature. With such holiness in mind,

WHAT IS THE ULTIMATE REALITY?

God therefore asks his people, "'To whom will you liken Me, that I should be his equal?' says the Holy One" (Isaiah 40:25).

Similarly, the OT declares that God is *glorious*. The root meaning of the Hebrew word for "glory" is "heavy" or "weighty." Thus, God is glorious because, in each of his attributes, and in the sum total of his attributes, he infinitely "outweighs" or surpasses his finite creatures. Pierced by the unveiling of God's glory, Moses cries out, "Who is like you, O LORD, among the gods? Who is like You, glorious in holiness, awesome in praises, doing wonders" (Ex. 15:11)?

Intimately and Intricately Related to His Creation

The Bible reveals that the LORD God relates to his universe in a manner completely different from the gods of antiquity, gods that people typically viewed as emanations of some pre-existing eternal substance (e.g., fire, water, ice, etc.). On the one hand, he is said to be *transcendent*. This means that by his very nature he is "above," or qualitatively different from, the universe. Though he created the heavens and the earth, they are not extensions or emanations of his being (Ps. 33:13, 113:5, Isaiah 57:15).

On the other hand, God is also *immanent*. This means that he is intimately and intricately related to the whole world. Initially, he is its *creator* (Gen. 1:1, Ex. 20:11, Isaiah 45:12-18,1 Cor. 8:6). From creation until the end of the age, he is its sovereign *sustainer, judge, controller,* and *redeemer* (Psalm 104:27-30, Acts 17:27; Isaiah 26:8-9, Rom. 2:5-6, 8:20-22; Isaiah 45:7, Rom. 8:28; Ex. 6:6-8, Mark 10:45, John 3:16, Eph. 1:7). At the end of the age, he will become its *destroyer* and *re-creator* (Isaiah 24:17-20, 34:4, Joel 2:30-31, Zeph. 1:2f, 2 Pet. 3:10-13; Isaiah 65:17, Rom. 8:20-21, Rev. 21:5). Thus, at all times all things live and move and have their being in the sovereign God (Psalm 139, Isaiah 42:5, Dan. 5:23, Acts 17:28).

Believing all these things, Jesus was certainly no pantheist: someone who teaches that all is one, all is mind (or spirit), and all is god. Rather, he was a *monotheist*: someone who taught that the one true God is creator of all, over all, and related to all, but metaphysically different from all. As if to underscore both God's majestic transcendence and comforting immanence, Jesus reverently refers to his Father as the Great King and the Lord of heaven and earth (Psalm 48:2, Mt. 5:35, 11:25).

ATTRIBUTES OF GOD	
Incommunicable	**Communicable**
Self-existence	Spirituality
	Personality
Immutability	self-consciousness
	intelligence, wisdom
	emotion
Eternity	conscience
	freedom
	creativity
Omnipresence	Gender
	Ethical Holiness
Omniscience	goodness, kindness
	righteousness
	justice
Omnipotence	truthfulness
	Relationship
Ontological Holiness	communion
	hierarchy / sovereignty
	role
Unity	other-oriented love

Existing as an Eternal Communion of Three Divine Persons

Here, then, is a tiny OT glimpse of *Yahweh Elohim*, the LORD God of Israel. Like every orthodox Jew, Jesus passionately affirmed that he is the sole ultimate reality, the one true God. However, Jesus did not stop there. Instead, building upon the foundation of traditional Jewish monotheism, he sought to bring his countrymen a further—indeed, a final—revelation of the nature and purposes of God. In particular, he sought to disclose to them a truth hinted at in the Jewish Scriptures, but now being fully unveiled in his own prophetic ministry: *Yahweh Elohim* is indeed *a single divine being*, but is also a being comprised of *three distinct divine persons*: the Father, the Son, and the Holy Spirit. And as if this revelation were not controversial enough, Jesus then went on to tell his Jewish brethren that he himself was that very Son! It was a teaching that would cost him his life.

Because this additional revelation of the nature of God is so central to the Christian faith, let us examine it now with some care.

Observe first that in speaking of Father, Son, and Holy Spirit, Jesus regarded each as a *divine* person. This is particularly evident with respect to the Father, whom he identified with Israel's God and worshiped accordingly (Mt. 4:9-10, Luke 2:49).[6] Thus, he prayed to the Father (Mt. 11:25f, John 17:1f), received guidance from the Father (John 5:30), obeyed the Father (John 5:17), and always strove to please the Father (John 8:29). He also ascribed divine attributes to the Father, referring to him as the eternal creator (John 17:24), benevolent sustainer (Mt. 6:25f), righteous judge (Mark 11:25), and merciful redeemer of the world (Luke 15:11f).

But why did Jesus feel compelled to "manifest" a new name for God (John 17:6)? And why did he train his disciples to use that new name in their prayers to him (Mt. 6:9-15)? We discover the answer to this crucial question when we realize that Jesus' revelation of the Father entailed another revelation more controversial still: from all eternity the Father has had a Son. He is a Son who shares with him both his divine nature and prerogatives; a Son whom the Father has sent into the world in human form; a Son who has come to teach, redeem, and rule over God's people; a Son who stands before them now in the person of Jesus of Nazareth.

This astonishing claim to deity is seen in a number of important ways.

First, *Jesus took to himself divine names and titles*. For example, he most often referred to himself as "the Son of Man," a reference to the palpably divine-human Messiah portrayed in the book of Daniel (Dan. 7:13-14, Mt. 24:30-31). Alluding to other OT Messianic prophecies, he also called himself "the Son" (Psalm 2:12, 110, John 5:16-33). Similarly, on more than one occasion, he bluntly identified himself as "the Son of God" (Luke 22:70, John 5:25, 9:35-36), and permitted others to do so as well (Mt. 4:6, 14:33, John 1:49). Moreover, in tense exchanges with his opponents he even appropriated the traditional divine names, referring to himself as *Adonai* (Mt. 22:41-46) and *Yahweh* (John 8:58).

Secondly, *Jesus claimed and displayed divine attributes*. In calling himself "I AM" he not only took the divine Name, but also implicitly asserted his own eternity and self-existence (John 8:58, 17:5). In promising that he would be with his disciples to the end of the age, he asserted his (future) omnipresence (Mt. 28:20, John 14:23). By disclosing the secrets of his follower's hearts he seemed to display the divine omniscience (John 4:1-26, 16:17-30); by claiming to know all of his sheep of all times and places—and by promising to guide them into all truth—he directly asserted it (John 10:14, 16:13). By performing a wide variety of miracles, he seemed to display divine omnipotence (John 11, Mark 4); by predicting that he would one day take in hand the entire cosmos, he directly claimed it, and universal sovereignty as well (Mt. 11:27, 28:18ff; John 5:25). In asking his opponents, "Which of you convicts me of sin?" he explicitly professed to be perfectly good (John 8:46); in declaring that "There is none good but God," he therefore implicitly professed to *be* God (Mt.19:17).

Thirdly, *Jesus claimed and displayed divine prerogatives*. He taught, not as the scribes and Pharisees, but as one having (divine) authority (Mark 1:22). He forgave the penitent their sins, a privilege which the Pharisees properly ascribed to God alone (Mark 2:1-12, Luke 7:36-50). He demanded the absolute obedience of his followers, an obedience that Israel had been trained to give only to God (Mt. 11:25-30, Deut. 13:1f). Most impressively, he told the Jews that his Father had granted him to impart spiritual life, judge the world, raise the dead, and be honored even as he (the Father) is honored. Understanding his meaning perfectly, Jesus' opponents therefore sought to kill him, asserting that he, being a man, had (blasphemously) made himself equal with God (John 5:16-30). Finally, we observe that on more than one occasion Jesus' disciples actually referred to him as God and Lord, and worshiped him as such (Mt. 8:2, Luke 24:52, John 9:38, 20:28). He did not demur in the least.[7]

The third divine person is the Holy Spirit. Jesus' richest teaching on the Spirit was delivered towards the end of his life in a certain upper room in Jerusalem, where he sought to prepare his disciples for his imminent departure (John 13-16). Here, the Spirit is repeatedly referred to as "he" and "him," but never "it." Also, the Spirit is said to do the kinds of things persons do: help, live in a home, remind, guide, disclose, convict, etc., (cf. Eph. 4:30, Heb. 10:29, Mt. 12:31). Moreover, this person is clearly divine. By being called *the* Holy Spirit, he is placed on the same footing as *the* Father and *the* Son. Similarly, he has divine attributes. For example, like the Father he is pure spirit, since the world cannot see or know him (14:17). He is eternal, since he will live with the disciples forever (14:16). He is omnipresent, since he will simultaneously live in all Christ's people (14:17). He is omniscient, since he will teach them all things, guide them into all truth, and disclose events and realities yet to come (16:13). He is holy, for he will convict the world of sin (16:8). And he is omnipotent, since he will empower all of Christ's disciples of all times (16:7, Acts 1:8). As with the Son, so with the Holy Spirit: both clearly display the attributes and prerogatives of God.

Summing up, we conclude from Jesus' overall teaching that he was indeed a monotheist, but that he also regarded the Father, the Son, and the Holy Spirit as thoroughly and equally divine. Good logic therefore requires that the three divine persons constitute a single divine being. Importantly, Jesus affirmed this very thing. For example, he said, "I and My Father are one," but also that he is *in* the Father and the Father *in* him (John 10:30;

14:10-11). Thus, he clearly regards the two persons as distinct, yet also as "parts" of a single being. Similarly, he promised that the Spirit would soon arrive to indwell the disciples, and that when he did, he would bring with him the Father and the Son (John 14:15-18, 23-24)! Again, the persons are distinct, yet they are clearly represented as aspects or facets of a single divine being.

Here, then, in Jesus' own words, is the basis for the historic Christian view that God is a tri-unity, or a trinity: one divine being, ever living together as a "Holy Family" of three divine persons sharing a common essence. Nor is this view confined to Jesus' own teachings, but pervades, in yet fuller form, the entire New Testament, and is also much alluded to in the Old.[8] If, then, it is true that the Bible never explicitly uses the word "trinity," it is equally true that its understanding of the ultimate reality is trinitarian from beginning to end.

Relationships Within the Holy Family

Common as they are, the various kinds of human relationship are really quite mysterious. How is it that out of the great mass of humanity we find ourselves related in special ways to the persons we call father, mother, wife, children, friend, colleague, etc.? The answer, according to the NT, is that all such relationships are God's idea; indeed, that they are actually faint, earthly reflections of something higher and richer that continually shines in heaven. In other words, human relationships are patterned after life in the Holy Trinity, life in a *Holy Family*.[9] If, then, we want to glimpse the ultimate reality at its deepest and most mysterious level, we must look briefly at the main principles that govern the (prototypical) relationships in the Family above.

We begin by observing that the Holy Family lives within a *hierarchy*. This simply means that there is a definite authority structure within the Trinity: the Father is over the Son, and the Father and the Son are over the Spirit.[10, 11] Very importantly, it does not mean that the Son is less divine or less important than the Father. Nor does it mean that the Spirit is less divine or less important than the Father and the Son. Since all three Persons share the same essence and the same attributes, all three are equally divine and equally valuable. The NT is quite clear, however, that *with respect to authority* the three Persons do indeed differ; that there is a hierarchy of rulership within the Holy Family.

This is especially evident from the NT portrait of the Son's relationship to the Father. Throughout his days upon the earth, Jesus constantly presented himself as a "man under authority," explicitly stating that he did nothing on his own initiative, but only what he saw the Father doing (Mt. 8:9, Luke 2:49, John 5:19, 30, 8:28, 12:49, 14:10). Accordingly, towards the end of his life, in anticipation of his supreme act of obedience, he could say in prayer, "Father, I have glorified You on earth; I have accomplished the work that You gave me to do" (John 17:4). Observe carefully from Jesus' own words that this work was in the nature of a *commandment*, a commandment that the Father had given to the Son *before* he *sent* him into the world (John 6:38-40, 10:18, 14:31; Heb. 10:5-10). Such passages clearly reveal that the Son's obedience to the Father did not begin with the incarnation, as some assert, but that he lives in *eternal* submission to the Father (cf. 1 Cor. 3:21-23, 11:2-3, 15:20-28). And much the same can be said of the Holy Spirit: eternally proceeding from both the Father and the Son, he ever delights to promote their glory through perfect submission to their every command (John 15:26, 16:13-15, Acts 2:33, Rev. 5:6).

Secondly, the Holy Family is characterized by *role*, that is, by a definite division of labor. In this family, the Father is the *initiator*, the one who devises and spearheads the divine purposes, plans, and activities. Viewing him thus, Jesus often affirmed, "I can do nothing on my own initiative…I do not seek my own will, but the will of Him who sent me" (John 5:19, 30, 8:28, 42, 12:49, etc.). Observe also that in so speaking, he implicitly defines the role of the Son, which is that he should be the divine *mediator*, the one *through* whom the Father is pleased to do his work in the world. Thus, the Son is, as it were, a two-way door: he is the One through whom the Father comes down into the world, and he is the One through whom men go up to the Father and into his heaven (John 1:17, 10:9, 14:6; 1 Cor. 8:6, Col. 1:16, 1 Tim. 2:5, Heb. 1:1-2). As for the Spirit, he is primarily revealed as the *implementer*, the very "finger of God" whom Jesus saw as performing the "hands-on" work of creation, providence, and redemption (Gen. 1:2, Psalm 104:27-30, Luke 11:20, John 3:5, 6:63, 14:26,16:18).

Finally, the Bible reveals that life within the Holy Family is characterized by *other-oriented love*. There is a burning desire in the heart of each divine person to see the other two persons pleased and glorified. For example, Jesus taught that the Father so loves the Son that he has privileged him to impart spiritual life, judge the world, and raise the dead. Why? "So that all should honor the Son, just as they honor the Father" (John 5:19-30; Col. 1:9-18, Heb. 1:1-4). Or again, in teaching the disciples about his imminent death by crucifixion, Jesus explains that, "The world must know that I love the Father, and that I am doing exactly what (he) has commanded me" (John 14:31, NIV). Meanwhile, the Holy Spirit is portrayed as the most deferential person of the Trinity, being well content to deflect human attention away from himself and onto the Son, so that the Son may be glorified, and through him the Father as well (John 16:13-15, 17:1, Phil. 2:9-11). He does this, however, not because he is timid or in any way inferior, but simply because the exaltation of the other two Persons is his appointed and freely chosen labor of love.

Here, then, in Jesus' teaching about the Holy Family, we arrive at the very heart of the "new things" that he sought to reveal to Israel about the ultimate reality. In his mind, this was no mere addendum to Jewish theology. Rather, it was the opening of the flower, the delivery of the child, the climax of God's self-disclosure and personal unveiling to all mankind. Accordingly, this doctrine is rightly held to be one of the two or three cardinal characteristics of biblical theism, that which distinguishes Christianity from all other theistic religions (e.g., Judaism, Islam, B'hai, etc.) and also from the various Christian sects that deny the Holy Trinity (e.g., Unitarianism, Mormonism, Christian Science, Jehovah's Witnesses, etc.). In short, it is that doctrine which, at the greatest possible cost to its founder, makes Christianity unique.[12]

Summary

We have seen that for Jesus of Nazareth the ultimate reality is the infinite, tri-personal God of the Bible. This God has both communicable and incommunicable attributes. The former include spirituality, personality, gender, ethical holiness, and relationship. The latter include his self-existence, immutability, eternity, omnipresence, omniscience, omnipotence, unity, and ontological holiness. In addition, he may also be understood as a Holy Family, since the one God exists necessarily and from all eternity as three equally divine persons—Father, Son, and Holy Spirit—bound together in a unique relationship that is characterized by hierarchy, role, and other-oriented love. As to his relationship with the universe, the triune God is both transcendent and immanent, being metaphysically separate from his creation, yet intimately related to it as its absolutely sovereign sustainer, ruler, judge, redeemer, and—at the end—its destroyer and re-creator as well.

Again, it is clear from the NT that Jesus thought of himself as a special teacher who had come from the Father to bring mankind a definitive revelation of the one true God—the ultimate reality. But as we shall soon see, it is equally clear that he thought of himself as coming to do something even more important: to live, die, and rise again, so that all of his followers might not only learn *about* God, but also enter into an intimate personal relationship *with* God—both now and in the life to come. Thus, in the words of the apostle Paul, Jesus' teaching on the ultimate reality brings to poor, seeking humanity a hope that is "exceedingly abundantly beyond all that they could think or ask" (Eph. 3:20). It brings them the hope of knowing God.

Especially for Seekers

Having now surveyed Jesus' teaching about the ultimate reality, let us pause to look at certain of its features that should be of special interest to seekers.

To begin with, Jesus' theism accords very well with our most fundamental intuitions about the ultimate reality. As we saw earlier, man's experience of both himself and the world of nature involves an inescapable awareness that the universe is upheld not simply by a spiritual being, but by a *personal* spiritual being—someone who is infinite, wise, powerful, and good. This is why philosophical naturalists, in their unguarded moments, find themselves speaking of "Mother Nature," and why they regale us with myths about her evolutionary "ingenuity." This is also why pantheists speak of Big Mind as a "him" rather than an "it," and why the Hindu and Buddhist masses worship and pray to multitudes of personal gods, or to human incarnations thereof. We humans are, it seems, hard-wired to regard the ultimate reality as an *infinite personal spirit*. And since this is precisely how Jesus depicts that reality, his teaching is intuitive and easy to receive.

But what of Jesus' unique contribution to our understanding of the ultimate reality: his distinctly *trinitarian* theism? Is this also intuitive and reasonable? That his teaching at this point is unexpected, and even to an extent inscrutable, can hardly be denied. But is this necessarily to its detriment? C. S. Lewis did not think so, arguing that the very strangeness and unexpectedness of Jesus' trinitarianism militates *in favor* of its truthfulness. What mere mortal, asked Lewis, could dream up the idea of a Holy Trinity? And what mere mortal, even if he *could* dream it up, would try to promote it among his radically monotheistic peers? No, if a man wanted to invent a theistic religion, he would invariably posit a uni-personal god. But to posit a tri-personal god—well, that would seem to require no mere man, but a tri-personal god himself.

Again, all agree that Jesus' trinitarianism is mysterious. But the fact that a doctrine is overshadowed by mystery does not necessarily make it counter-intuitive or unreasonable. If, for example, Jesus had taught that God is both one person and three persons, then yes, his teaching would indeed be contradictory and irrational. As it is, however, he did not speak of a single person, but of a single God who exists eternally *as* (a fellowship of) *three persons*. Such a being is indeed unfamiliar and unprecedented, but certainly not inconceivable or scandalous to our sense of logic.

WHAT IS THE ULTIMATE REALITY?

Going further, theologians like to point out that our everyday experience actually brings us into regular contact with the essence of the trinitarian mystery: the phenomenon of *unity amidst diversity*. We find this everywhere. One thinks, for example, of atoms, cells, organs, organisms, ecosystems, our earth, the solar system, the stars, the galaxies, and the universe itself. Consider also the broad spectrum of human relationships: marriages, families, friendships, intentional communities, ethnic groups, etc. Each of these is a kind of system, a collection of component parts mysteriously bound together into a single functional unit. How and why do these systems hold together as one? Why are they so pervasive in nature? Could it be that they bear the very fingerprint of heaven? Could it be that they were designed to send us a message about the "unity in diversity" that characterizes their creator?

A "yes" answer to these questions seems even more reasonable when we consider all the "little trinities" with which we humans are involved. Think, for example, of space, how it is comprised of length, width, and depth. Think of time, how it is experienced as past, present, and future. Think of matter, which exists simultaneously in the universe in three different forms: gas, liquid, and solid. Think of all three—time, space, and matter—bound together in (our experience of) the one grand system that we call the universe. Finally, think of the unitary human self, a mysterious spiritual entity comprised of intellect, emotion, and will. Do these trinities in any way scandalize our intuition or violate our reason? Surely not. In fact, one could argue that such phenomena actually illuminate Jesus' teaching, and also support its truthfulness. Why? Because beneath the light of his teaching we can easily see how they may well serve as *signs*, signs woven by God into the very fabric of his creation so as to strengthen our faith in a triune creator and redeemer.

Secondly, we find that Jesus' view of the ultimate reality affirms our common sense impression of the relationship between the unknown god and the world. Like most folks, he was neither a monist nor a pantheist. Rather, he taught that God is metaphysically separate from, yet intricately related to, his various creations. Again, this understanding is quite intuitive. Indeed, this is why pantheistically oriented seekers often welcome Jesus' teaching, since it lifts from their shoulders the intolerable burden of having to think of themselves and their world as god himself.

Thirdly, Jesus' theology confirms our distinctly ethical intuitions about the ultimate reality. As we have seen, he consistently represents the triune God as holy and righteous. Furthermore, he portrays this God as the moral governor of the universe, as the author and sustainer of the objective moral order. Indeed, it is fair to say that of all God's attributes, Jesus seems most preoccupied with God's ethical holiness and judicial sovereignty, since they represent such a terrible menace to his rebellious and unholy human creatures. It is true that critics have often questioned the goodness of God, asking how he could permit natural and moral evil to enter his universe, or order the extermination of the Canaanites, or send people to an eternity in hell. These are serious questions of great concern to seekers, questions that we will address in the pages ahead. Here, however, we need only point out that Jesus himself had no qualms whatsoever about the divine integrity. His testimony concerning the triune Yahweh is well summed up in the words of the Psalmist: "You are good, and what you do is good" (Psalm 119:68 NIV, John 17:11). The spotless integrity of Jesus' own life has since persuaded multitudes that this testimony is true.

Fourthly, Jesus' teaching on the ultimate reality extends to seeking and suffering humanity a profound spiritual hope. As we saw above, this is because he came not only *to tell mankind about* the Holy Family, but—amazingly enough—*to adopt a people into it*, so that they might live in and with the Triune Family forever. This exalted hope pervades one of Jesus' longest and richest prayers, a prayer that includes these deeply spiritual words:

> I do not pray for these alone (i.e., the eleven apostles), but also for those who will believe in Me through their word, that they all may be one. Even as You, Father, are in Me, and I in You, that they also may be in us, that the world may believe that You sent Me...I in them, and You in Me, that they may be perfected in unity, and that the world may know that You have sent Me and have loved them, even as You have loved Me."
> —John 17:20-23

Fundamentally, this is a prayer for Christian unity, and also for its intended impact upon an unbelieving world. But notice the basis of the unity: *the mutual indwelling of the triune God and his people*. He is to live in them, and they in him, even as the several persons of the Trinity are already living in one another. Thus, Jesus envisions a day when believers in him will be *incorporated into the ultimate reality, into the very life and being of the Holy Family*. This incorporation is not absorption. Unlike the pantheist, Jesus anticipates neither the annihilation of the individual human personality, nor its deification. The human sons of God will never possess the infinite attributes or the unique prerogatives of the godhead. They will, however, be brought into a vital spiritual union with all three persons of the Trinity, and so come to experience what Jesus called "eternal life"—the *kind* of life lived by the Holy Family, and *that life lived forever* (Mark 10:30, John 3:15, 10:28, 17:2). Thus, Jesus' teaching about the ultimate reality speaks to the seeker's head and heart, offering full and lasting satisfaction to the deepest needs of both.

A Challenging Hope

This brings us to our final point, and to an important caveat. Though rich in hope, Jesus' teaching about the ultimate reality has often proved challenging for seekers to receive, and costly for them to embrace. The reason is located in the very premise and nature of his mission. The premise of his mission is that the whole world—apart from the faithful among Israel—lies in bondage to false or grossly distorted conceptions of the ultimate reality. Accordingly, the nature of his mission is that he should deliver the peoples of the world from their ignorance and error by means of a definitive revelation and proclamation of the one true God. In Jesus' mind, this is all to the good. But again, there is a down side. For if people are going to enter into fellowship with the one true God, it is clear that they must first surrender their attachment to the many false. Jesus well knew that such a transition could prove challenging indeed.

In order to put flesh and blood on this challenge, let us consider Jesus' well-known dialogue with the Samaritan woman (John 4). After realizing that he had supernatural knowledge of certain intimate details of her life, this spiritually hungry woman said to him:

> "Sir, I perceive that You are a prophet. Our fathers worshiped on this mountain, and you Jews say that in Jerusalem is the place where one ought to worship."
>
> Jesus said to her, "Woman, believe me, the hour is coming when you will neither on this mountain, nor in Jerusalem, worship the Father. You worship what you do not know; we know what we worship, for salvation is from the Jews. But the hour is coming, and now is, when the true worshipers will worship the Father in spirit and truth; for the Father is seeking such to worship Him. God is spirit, and those who worship Him must worship in spirit and truth."
>
> The woman said to Him, "I know that Messiah is coming. When He comes He will tell us all things."
>
> Jesus said to her, "I who speak to you am He."
>
> —John 4:19-24

Here we see that Jesus does not shrink from a direct confrontation with the woman's false concept of God. He knew very well what all his fellow Jews knew, that hundreds of years earlier the Assyrians had deported the Jewish population, brought in a host of foreigners from distant lands, and then reintroduced a few Jewish priests to provide a semblance of spiritual continuity. The result was Samaria—and with it, a distorted faith that departed significantly from Jewish orthodoxy.

In his dialogue with the woman, Jesus therefore speaks the truth in love. He tells her that her thinking about God is in error, her worship marred, and her hope misplaced. However, unlike his Jewish countrymen, he did not shun her. Nor, like many today, did he say, "Not to worry, we both worship the same God, just in different words and different ways." To the contrary, being fully convinced that his Father desired to be worshiped "in truth"—and being fully eager that she not miss this life-giving experience—he bluntly told her, "You do not know what you worship." This could mean, "You have no knowledge of the God whom you are trying to worship." Or it could mean, "You do not realize that what you are worshiping is not God at all, but a distortion and misrepresentation of the real." Perhaps he meant both.

Notice, however, that Jesus is not content simply to challenge her faith. Rather, he goes on to tell her where she can find the reality that she obviously longs for. First, he directs her to "the Jews." These alone, he says, know what they worship—not because they are especially smart or good—but simply because the gracious God has chosen to make himself known to them. Moreover, it is through them that "salvation" is now coming to the world: forgiveness of sins and an intimate personal knowledge of God. However, Jesus does not try to convert her to the Judaism of his day. Rather, he directs her first to the Father, and then to himself as his Messiah who is the way to the Father. In other words, he here unveils something of the new, trinitarian view of the ultimate reality that, if embraced from the heart, will enable this woman—and all Samaritans and all nations—to worship God "in spirit and in truth" (John 4:39-42).

Truly, this narrative speaks loudly to modern seekers. Here we see that Jesus does not tolerate religious confusion. He knows that his Father desires to be worshiped in truth, he knows that people need to worship in truth, and he knows that he himself loves all three: the Father, the people, and the truth. It is hardly surprising, then, that he feels compelled to confront error, declare truth, and challenge all people to forsake the former so as to follow the latter.

Both the Bible and history show that the cost of following Jesus into this new trinitarian universe can be very high, not only for seekers affiliated with other faiths, but also for seekers with no faith—seekers inclined by the religious diversity around them to embrace vague, mystical, and undemanding conceptions of the ultimate reality.

Because this point is so important, let us conclude our discussion by taking a moment to count the cost in some detail.

Counting the Cost

First, Jesus' teaching is costly because *it means the surrender of all religious agnosticism*. He does not take ignorance for an excuse; he does not permit us to say, "I do not know"—whether about God's existence, names, nature, or works. Rather, he insists that we *can* know, precisely because God has so richly revealed himself in order that we might. The only condition is that we are willing (John 7:17).

Secondly, this teaching is costly because *it means the surrender of irrationality and mysticism*. Here I have in mind the (usually pantheistic) kind of spirituality that places the knowledge of God more or less completely beyond intellect and verbal description. Those who say, for example, that the various world religions are really a kind of poetry by which men have tried to describe a single ineffable spiritual reality, are speaking as mystics. So too are those who assert that mankind is evolving towards a state of spiritual enlightenment, in which we shall finally recognize the unity of all faiths. Jesus will have none of this. His premise is that we live in a world where truth always exists beside error; that God has equipped us with various faculties (i.e., intellect, language, conscience, etc.) so as to distinguish truth from error; and that we must apply these faculties to the revelation he now brings us, in order to see if it is true. In short, Jesus' summons the mystic, not to deny his faculties, but to engage them in an honest search for "the one true truth" about the ultimate reality.

Thirdly, Jesus' teaching is costly because *it means an end to the peaceful coexistence of competing versions of the ultimate reality*. This conclusion again flows from his assumptions about the nature of the present world: in this world, truth about the ultimate reality exists, it is important to God that men hear it, and it is vital that they embrace it. Therefore—as Jesus' dialogue with the Samaritan woman makes clear—*it must be carried to all people and impressed upon them*. In other words, for Jesus, the presence of revealed truth in the world entails *proselytism:* loving proselytism, intelligent proselytism, proselytism that is always respectful of people's decisions—but proselytism nonetheless. His teaching implies, for example, that pantheists who desire to experience the ultimate reality must become theists. Similarly, it implies that non-trinitarian theists must become trinitarians. The completed revelation of the ultimate reality is not only to be pondered, embraced, and enjoyed: it is to be publicly professed, defended, and propagated (Mt 28:18ff). Such, for Jesus, are the unavoidable entailments of truth. Admittedly, they fall hard upon the ears of modern man, in whose case the (quite biblical) doctrine of religious toleration is often distorted to imply the truthfulness of all religions and the corresponding impropriety of trying to win a person from one to another. However, on this matter the seeker who would follow Jesus cannot remain a modern man.

Finally, Jesus' teaching is costly because *it means an end to religious sentimentalism*. Many today think that god, whoever he may be, does not much care what we think about him, so long as our intentions towards him are sincere. Jesus' dialogue with the Samaritan woman shows that he regards this as a false and sentimental understanding. Yes, the Father is pleased with religious sincerity (John 7:17). But, says Jesus, he is now actively seeking a people who will worship him in truth, actively confronting them with truth, and actively challenging them to turn from error to truth. Thus, while God is pleased with religious sincerity, he is not *satisfied* until religious sincerity expresses itself in a search for truth, and is vindicated by a person's actually finding it. This alone fulfills the purpose of God; and this alone will fulfill the deepest spiritual longings in man.

CHAPTER 10

WHAT IS THE ORIGIN OF THE UNIVERSE, LIFE, AND MAN?

ALWAYS AND EVERYWHERE, man is fascinated by the beginning. A little reflection on the matter reveals why: *There is a fantastically rich philosophical connection between "the beginning" and the other questions of life.*

To get a feel for this connection, consider the following thought experiment. Suppose that someone has just loaned you his state-of-the-art time machine and given you permission to take it on a single trip of your choosing. Bush league philosopher that you are, you have no desire to waste the spiritual potential of this rare opportunity, so you mull your options carefully. Finally, the decision comes: You will travel back through cosmic history in search of the origin of the universe, life, and man as we now know them. Why? Because you realize that such a journey, if successfully completed, will disclose many things of transcendent importance, things that will no doubt lift a bush league philosopher into the majors!

For example, assuming that you did indeed reach an absolute beginning, you could see for yourself *the nature of the ultimate reality:* whether it is the eternal "time/space/energy-matter continuum" of the modern naturalist (possibly compressed into a cosmic egg), or the impersonal Big Mind of the pantheists, or the infinite personal creator God of the theists. Similarly, you could discover *the metaphysical nature of the universe* (that is, it's exact relationship to the ultimate reality): whether it exists by way of a *transformation* of eternal matter, a *manifestation* of Big Mind, or a divine *creation* "out of nothing." Also, you could learn how order arose in the universe: whether instantaneously by some sort of divine creation, or gradually by some sort of evolution or progressive creation. You could see how evil, suffering, and death entered the universe. And you might even be able to learn something about its *purpose* (if there is a purpose), or about *the way we are intended to live in it* (if there is an intention), or about *its ultimate destiny* (if it has a destiny). Yes, the beginning is clearly a place rich with meaning, and (we sense) big with blessing. Therefore, with not a little existential urgency, we *all* would like to make our way back for a closer look.

Unhesitatingly, Jesus of Nazareth points the way. Yes, for seekers steeped in modern theories of cosmic evolution (CE) his answer may be difficult to receive, but there is no difficulty whatsoever in determining what it was: along with his Jewish contemporaries, Jesus believed and taught all that Moses had written about the beginning in the book of Genesis. But, as we shall soon see, he taught a good deal more besides.

Jesus' allegiance to OT cosmogony is reflected in many of his sayings. To cite but one, here is his response to a question from the Pharisees concerning marriage:

> And Jesus answered and said to them, "Because of the hardness of your heart he (Moses) wrote you this precept (i.e., a law permitting divorce). But from the beginning of the creation, 'God made them male and female. For this reason a man shall leave his father and mother and be joined to his wife, and the two shall become one flesh.' So then, they are no longer two, but one flesh. Therefore, what God has joined together, let no man separate."
>
> —Mark 10:5-9

Here we see that Jesus not only embraced the OT account of the beginning, but also drew important ethical conclusions from it. In the beginning God laid down more than the physical universe. He also laid down certain norms for men and women, from which they ought not to depart. With the natural order, he created a moral order as well.

Many such examples could be given, not only from Jesus' words, but also those of his apostles.[1] In studying them, we learn that the New Testament cosmogony (i.e., its account of cosmic origins) fully embraces the old, even as it supplements and enriches it with fresh revelations. Therefore, in order fully to understand Jesus' cosmogony, we must journey back to Genesis for a closer look at its OT foundations.

As we set out, let us first take note of an oft-neglected biblical fact: Genesis gives us both a narrow and a broad view of the beginning. The narrow view, found in Genesis 1-2, follows God through his six days of creation, bringing the reader to *the world as it was when God took his rest*. A good beginning. The broad view, found in Genesis 1-11, spans a considerably larger portion of cosmic history, some 1500 years. It speaks to us not only of the *creation* (Gen. 1-2), but also of a *curse* that subsequently fell upon nature

WHAT IS THE ORIGIN OF THE UNIVERSE, 229
LIFE, AND MAN?

as a result of Adam's sin (Gen. 3), a global *catastrophe* (i.e., the Flood) that completely restructured the original earth (Gen. 6-9), and a *confusion* (at the tower of Babel) that gave rise to the diverse languages and nations of the family of man (Gen. 10-11). All told, a bad beginning—but a beginning that is good for seekers to keep in mind, since it so thoroughly meets the criteria of a viable cosmogony by explaining the origin of the world *as we now know it*. Our strategy, then, will be to focus on the good beginning here

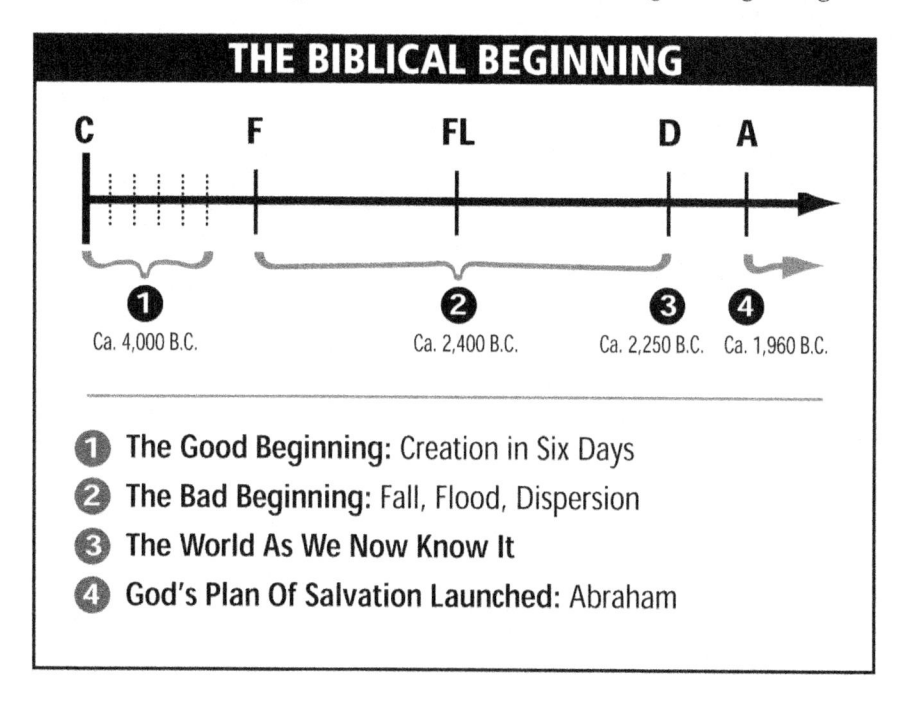

THE BIBLICAL BEGINNING

```
C        F        FL              D     A
|--------|--------|---------------|-----|---->
  \__①__/_____②_____/ \_③_/ \_④_
Ca. 4,000 B.C.   Ca. 2,400 B.C.   Ca. 2,250 B.C.  Ca. 1,960 B.C.
```

① **The Good Beginning:** Creation in Six Days
② **The Bad Beginning:** Fall, Flood, Dispersion
③ **The World As We Now Know It**
④ **God's Plan Of Salvation Launched:** Abraham

in chapter 10, and on the bad beginning in chapter 11. This approach will enable us to see the biblical cosmogony as a whole.

The Good Beginning

We may summarize the Genesis narrative of the good beginning as follows: *In the (good) beginning, God created the heavens, the earth, the sea, and all that is in them; he did so in a definite sequence, with a definite structure, and for a definite purpose; he also did so in six literal days, after which he saw that all he had made was very good, rested from his creative work, and blessed and sanctified the seventh day.*

Since there is a wealth of cosmological meaning buried in this short definition, let us pause to mine each element just a little.

In the beginning:

This important phrase, which first appears in Genesis 1:1 (and which is echoed in John 1:1), teaches us that the universe had a definite or "absolute" beginning. Unlike God, who exists "from everlasting to everlasting," the cosmos is not eternal. Or rather, it is not eternal in the same way that God is eternal, since God is without beginning or end, whereas the universe, in one form or another, is indeed without an end, yet with a definite beginning. The *kind* of beginning it had is explained in the remainder of the creation story.

God:

Here is the agent of creation: the infinite, personal God of the OT. In Genesis 1, he is God (Heb., *Elohim*), the powerful and majestic creator and sustainer of the universe. In Genesis 2:4ff, he is "the LORD God" (Heb., *Yahweh Elohim*), the One who, having created the world, now enters into personal relationship with the man who is to rule it along with his wife as helper. As we shall see momentarily, he is also the triune God, fully revealed only by Jesus and his apostles, but hinted at even here in Genesis 1, where the agent of creation is three-fold: God (1:1, John 1:1), the Word of God (1:3, 6, 9; John 1:1), and the Spirit of God (1:2).

Created:

This word (Heb., *bara*) describes the character of God's action during the six-day beginning. From Genesis we learn that it is essentially two-fold. On the one hand, God created by *drawing his creatures into existence* by word and deed. Here we think especially of the divine fiats, as, for example, when God said, "Let there be light," and there was light (Gen. 1:3, 14). This "bringing into being" is sometimes referred to as creation *ex nihilo;* that is, as creation "out of nothing." However, in strictness God's creation cannot be *ex nihilo*, since *ex nihilo nihil fit:* "Out of nothing, nothing comes." If, then, creation may be said to have come out of anything, it was out of the purpose, plan, and power of God.

On the other hand, God also created by *forming* or *fashioning* that which he had previously brought into being. Of special interest here is the creation of the man and the woman: the man was formed out of the dust of the ground (Gen. 2:7), and the woman was formed out of a rib extracted from the man (Gen. 2:22; cf. Eph. 5:22f). As the case of the woman reveals, it is not always easy to distinguish God's bringing into being from his fashioning. But this much is sure: The biblical cosmogony is altogether unique in world religion and philosophy. As opposed to pantheistic views, it

WHAT IS THE ORIGIN OF THE UNIVERSE, LIFE, AND MAN?

teaches that the physical universe is objectively real, external to God's being, and chronologically prior to any sentient creature's consciousness of it. In other words, it is a true creation, not an emanation or mere phenomenon appearing in someone's mind. As opposed to naturalistic views, it teaches that the universe had a true (or absolute) beginning. First, the universe was not; then—as the psalmist sang—"The LORD spoke, and it came to be; He commanded, and it stood firm" (Psalm 33:9).

The heavens, the earth, the seas, and all that is in them (Ex. 20:11):

Here are the objects of God's six-day creation, the cosmos as a whole. Broadly speaking, Genesis teaches that God first created three environments—the heavens, the seas, and the earth—and then bountifully filled them with light and life.

The heavens, as the "dual" Hebrew noun (Heb., *shamayim*) indicates, are two-fold. They include a near heaven (i.e., the atmospheric heaven, the air, Eph. 2:9, 6:12), and a far heaven (i.e., the expanse, "outer space"). However, it was during the creation week, and quite early in it, that God also created an invisible spiritual heaven, either invisibly embedded somewhere in the expanse of space, or situated just beyond its outer edge, or else existing as another dimension that enfolds or runs parallel to it (see below). The near heaven contains the birds of the air (Gen. 1:20, Mt. 6:26), while the far contains the luminaries: the sun, moon, and stars (Gen. 1:14-19). Both contain light separated from darkness (Gen. 1:4, 14, 18). The spiritual heaven is the proper abode of the angels, bodiless spirits who continually behold the glory of God (Isaiah 6:1f). The seas are home to teeming fish and giant sea creatures (Gen. 1:20-23). The earth abounds with vegetation, creeping things, cattle, beasts of the earth, and man (Gen. 1:9-31). Israel's singers marveled at all this richness: "O LORD, how manifold are thy works! In wisdom thou hast made them all: the earth is full of thy riches" (Psalm 104:24, KJV). The fullness of the universe is testimony to the fullness of God's wisdom, power, and goodness to all.

In passing, we do well to observe that the Bible refers to our universe as "*the* creation" (Mt.10:6, Rom. 8:19-21), "*the* creation of God" (Rev. 3:14), and "the *whole* creation" (Rom. 8:22). Such phrases entail that God limited his creative activity to one universe: ours. This rules out the existence of other (physical) universes, a favorite theme of modern speculative cosmology. Moreover, it very highly exalts the earth—which the Bible situates at the center of the cosmos—as the privileged object of God's eternal interest and concern.

In a definite sequence:

The good beginning is an orderly, three-staged event, suffused with purpose and rationality.

First, we have *the primordial creation*, in which God brings into being the rudiments of the universe. This occurs on day one of the six-day beginning. The relevant text here, Gen. 1:1-5, is mysterious and difficult to interpret. If, as some argue, verse 1 describes the first act of the primordial creation, then the primordial creation involves three basic elements. First, God creates "the heavens" (i.e., vacant space, and possibly the angelic realm as well). Then, in the midst of these heavens, he creates and suspends "the earth in the deep" (i.e., the unformed earth, covered by, or soluble in, the deep primeval waters), (Job 26:7). Then he creates a bank of light, apparently revolving in space around the earth in the deep, thereby dividing light from darkness and instituting astronomical time by means of the first day and the first night.

If, however, as others contend, verse 1 is simply a title and summary statement for the entire creation narrative (see Gen. 2:4), then we may read verse 2 as presenting something considerably more dramatic: *the primordial universe as a whole*, to be understood as an inconceivably "deep" (i.e., enormous) watery sphere, within which "the heavens" shall soon appear when God creates the expanse on the second day (Gen. 1:9)! On this view, "the face of the deep" (v. 2) is, in effect, the outer edge of the primordial universe, beyond which there is nothing at all—unless, perhaps, it be the spiritual heaven, centered around the throne of God (Isaiah 66:1, Rev. 4-5).

Whichever interpretation is best, this much is clear: in the primordial creation God brought into being a universe that was as yet "formless and empty"—and therefore waiting to be formed and filled. The Spirit of God, brooding over the waters like a mother eagle above her nest, is poised to do this very thing (Gen. 1:1; Deut. 32:11, Isaiah 31:5).

Stage two is *the forming of the universe*. This occurs during the second and third days of God's creative work, when he prepares four separate environments for their respective inhabitants (Gen. 1:6-12).

Thus, on day two God creates a firmament, or expanse, between the waters that are above and beneath it (Gen. 1:6-8). This he calls "heaven" (cf. Gen. 1:1). Significantly, there are a large number of OT texts that speak of God as "stretching out" the heavens (Job 37:18, Psalm 104:2, Isaiah 40:22, 42:5, 44:24, 48:13, 51:13, Jer. 10:12). Is it, then, that God opens up an immense womb of space in the midst of The Deep by pushing back the bulk of the primeval waters to a great distance, thereby creating not only the heavens, but also an outer boundary of ice for the resulting heavenly sphere? Or, more modestly, is it simply that he elevates a portion of the primeval waters

WHAT IS THE ORIGIN OF THE UNIVERSE, LIFE, AND MAN?

to a position a few miles above the surface of the earth, thereby creating the clouds—or possibly a canopy of water vapor—beneath which lies the newly created bank of air (Psalms 108:4, 148:4, Proverbs 8:27-28)?[2] By my lights, the first view, startling as it may be to modern sensibilities, stands truest to the biblical text. But whatever the final solution, it is clear enough that God's action on the second day puts the finishing touches on a two-fold environment that will soon house the heavenly bodies, the birds of the air, and all other things that draw the breath of life (Gen. 2:7).

In passing, we should note here that the Bible situates the creation of the holy angels very close to the beginning, presumably on the first or second day, depending upon the whereabouts of the spiritual heaven. That they were rapt observers of much of the creation is clear from God's own question to Job concerning the origin of the earth: "On what were its footings set, or who laid its cornerstone, while the morning stars sang together and the sons of God (i.e., the angels) shouted for joy" (Job 38:6-7)? From related passages, we learn that the angels *still* have not stopped praising him for his creative acts (Psalm 145:1f, Rev. 4:11).

On day three, two more environments attain their final form: the dry land emerges from the remaining waters and the seas pour into their newly carved basins. Henceforth, the seas are ready for fish, and the dry land—laden with edible vegetation—for creeping things, animals, and man (Gen. 1:9-13; 2 Peter 3:5, Psalm 104:7-9). Now that all the habitats have been formed, the inhabitants are free to appear.

Finally, we have the third stage of the good beginning, *the filling of the universe*. This takes place during the last three days of creation (Gen. 1:14-28). On the fourth day, God fills the expanse with the luminaries: the sun, moon, planets, and stars. These will serve man by giving him light, enabling him to reckon time, and—in their capacity as signs—speaking to him of the glory of God and the mysteries of redemption (Gen. 1:14-19; Psalm 19:1, Isaiah 37:7-8, Dan. 12:3, Mt. 2:2, Luke 21:25). On the fifth day, God begins to fill the seas with fish and giant sea creatures. So too does he begin to fill the air with birds that will wing their way across the face of the expanse (Gen. 1:20-23). On the sixth day, he begins to fill the dry land with creeping things, land animals, and—as lord over all—the crown of his creation: man (Gen. 1:31). At God's command, all these living creatures are to be fruitful and multiply, thereby filling up his creation and fulfilling his manifold purposes for the world (Gen. 1:22, 28).

Note carefully that the sequence of creation evinces something important about the purpose of the universe: it is designed to be a home for living things, and especially for man. The prophet Isaiah set it down this way:

*For thus says the LORD,
Who created the heavens,
Who is God,
Who formed the earth and made it,
Who did not create it to be empty,
Who formed it to be inhabited:
"I am the LORD, and there is no other."*

—Isaiah 45:18

THE SIX DAYS OF CREATION

Days of Forming (Habitats)	Days of Filling (Inhabitants)
Day 1 The Earth in the Deep Light & Darkness Day & Night	**Day 4** The Lights of Heaven: Sun, Moon, Stars
Day 2 The Expanse of Heaven: Sky, Air	**Day 5** Fish Birds
Day 3 Earth Seas Vegetation	**Day 6** Insects Land Animals Man

With a definite structure:

The biblical universe, fresh from the creator's hand, was highly structured both physically and spiritually. Acting in accordance with a pre-existing plan, God impressed specific forms, functions, motions, and relationships upon all things. In six days he brought into being "a fixed order," after which he began to preserve, animate, and direct that order to its appointed ends (Jer. 31:35-36, Psalm 148:1-6).

The creation story, as illumined by other biblical passages, abounds with examples of God-given structure:

The universe itself is (geocentrically) structured. Though interpretations differ, many glean from the Bible that the universe is a finite sphere, possibly bounded by unseen waters above, that rotates around an earth sitting immovable in its midst. This—the *geocentricity* of the biblical cosmos—is especially clear from Genesis 1, where, according to either reading of the primordial creation, we behold the formless earth resting in stillness at the absolute center of God's interest and creative activity (Gen. 1:1-5). Geocentricity is further underscored by the work of the fourth day, in which

WHAT IS THE ORIGIN OF THE UNIVERSE, LIFE, AND MAN?

God fills the heavens with "lights" that certainly appear—both in Scripture and real world experience—to revolve around a stationary earth, and that exist for the sole purpose of serving those who dwell upon it (Gen. 1:14-19). This view of the structure of the universe is, of course, scandalous to most modern scientists, governed as they are by Copernican and Relativistic assumptions. Nevertheless, seekers should realize that even today it has a growing number of skilled defenders, scholars who argue both from the Bible and science that cosmic geocentricity is, by far, the most reasonable option of all.[3]

The earth is structured. The earth is comprised of two main environments: the seas and the dry land (Gen. 1:9-13). These are separated by fixed boundaries (Job 38:8-11), and each is occupied by inhabitants specifically prepared for it (Gen. 1:20-31).

All physical things are structured. Sun, moon, and stars; seas and dry land; trees and vegetation; fish, birds, insects, animals, and men—each has its own unchanging structure direct from the creator's hand. The universe is a "fixed order," in part because all things in it have fixed forms and functions (Jer. 31:15, Isaiah 45:7). In the case of living beings we see this with special vividness: in several broad categories (e.g., trees, vegetation, water-dwellers, creeping things, beasts of the field, etc.) God created "each according to its kind" (Gen. 1:11, 21, 24). That is, all living beings, by creation, have received from God definite physical and behavioral structures, structures that cannot fundamentally change, since it is also ordained that these beings should reproduce "each according to its kind" (Gen. 1:11-12, 1 Cor. 15:39-41). Needless to say, this puts the biblical cosmology in direct opposition to modern views of cosmic and biological evolution.

Living things are structured according to a hierarchy of value. At the bottom of the hierarchy is vegetable life: grass, plants, and trees, largely serving to provide food and other necessities of life for animals and man. Next come the "living creatures" (Heb., *nephesh chayim*). These are distinct from vegetable life in that they have invisible souls or spirits (Heb., *nephesh, ruach*).[4] They include fish, birds, insects, and animals. And finally, ruling over all, is man. He too is a "living creature," but a supremely privileged one, since his soul is uniquely cast in the image and likeness of God (Gen. 1:27-28, Psalm 8:3f, Col. 3:10).

Observe from all of this that the Bible sees biological life *in conjunction* with matter, but never as *the product* of matter. In other words, biological life always involves the *natural* (i.e., the material) animated by the *supernatural* (i.e., the spiritual). In the case of men and animals, organic matter is indwelt by supernatural souls (or spirits, Luke 1:46-7). And in all cases, it is created, sustained, and vivified by the Spirit of the living God (Psalm 104:30, Job 12:10). With him is the fountain of life (Psalm 36:9). It is God alone who gives life, breath, and all things to those who live (Acts 17:25).

Man is (very intricately) structured. As the creation account reveals, man is an intricately structured physical being in whom God has placed an animating spirit (Gen. 2:7, James 2:26). Moreover, man's spirit is also intricately structured, being created in God's own image and likeness, and therefore endowed with self-consciousness, intellect, memory, emotion, will, conscience, gender, rulership, and (before the fall) perfect freedom and moral rectitude (Gen. 1:26-27). Marveling at this imprint of the divine upon a mere creature, the Psalmist exclaims that man is only "a little lower than God" (or the angels) and "fearfully and wonderfully made" (Psalm 8:5, 139:14).

Man's relationships are structured. God created Adam and Eve in and for different kinds of relationships. He related them to himself, each other, their offspring, the animals, and the rest of the world of nature. He also revealed the privileges and responsibilities peculiar to those relationships. Here we find the basis of much biblical morality. What is good is what is *normal:* it conforms to God's norm, or design, for the relationship. Jesus' words concerning marriage illustrate this important principle. Divorce, he said, is forbidden because God created the man to cleave to his wife and to become one flesh with her. Other biblical exhortations to marital love and faithfulness, as well as prohibitions against all forms of sexual deviance, have the same creational basis. Right and wrong, in the biblical universe, depend upon the structure of things, a structure laid down by God in the beginning.[5]

Summing up, we have seen that at its creation the entire cosmos, both as a whole and in each of its separate parts and relations, received a fundamentally unchanging structure from the hand of God. This was, by the way, the faith of most of the founders of modern Western science. Steeped as they were in the biblical worldview, these pioneers believed that God had created the universe according to a rational plan. That plan made their work possible and guaranteed its success. In uncovering the structures (or "laws") of nature, they were learning, as Kepler declared, "to think God's thoughts after him."[6] Naturalistic evolutionists, on the other hand, have no such basis for their scientific labors, believing that the cosmos has neither a rational creator nor any permanent structures. Here again we see how starkly the two worldviews are opposed.

WHAT IS THE ORIGIN OF THE UNIVERSE, LIFE, AND MAN?

For a definite purpose:

The stages and structure of the six-day creation reveal a God with a goal. Though Genesis does not exhaust the biblical revelation of God's purposes in creation, it tells us much. Broadly, we see that God created the universe—and especially the earth—for man. The biblical universe is profoundly anthropocentric.

To be specific, we see first that God intended the world to be man's *home*. It is his "proper abode," a lovingly prepared and lavishly endowed dwelling place created specially for him (Psalm 115:16, Jude 6).

The world is also given to man as his *domain*, for God has specially appointed him to rule as his vice-regent over the fish, the birds, the cattle, the creeping things, and all the earth. As the psalmist prayerfully phrased it, "Thou hast put all things under his feet" (Gen. 1:26, Psalm 8).

Similarly, God purposes that the world should become a kind of *workshop* in which his human children, co-laboring with their heavenly Father, fulfill a divine calling to "subdue" the earth. Sometimes referred to as "the dominion mandate," this calling means that mankind is charged and equipped to discover, harness, and bring forth all the hidden potentials of the natural world. The dominion mandate also involves the enlargement of the human family through reproduction, so that it can exercise a princely dominion and a loving stewardship over all the earth (Gen. 1:26-28, 2:8, 15, Acts 1:26-28). Observe from this that the Bible does not view a growing population as a burden upon the earth, but rather as an important key to its proper and fruitful development (Psalm 127:3-5, 128:1-6, Prov. 14:28).

Finally, it appears that the cosmos was also designed to be a kind of *theatre*, and this in a two-fold sense. On the one hand, it was to be a theatre in which men (and angels) could *behold the glory of God*. This means that in nature, in the marvels of his own being, and in his direct contacts with God, man would be able to grow in the knowledge of the many-faceted character of his creator. The apostle Paul affirms this purpose by declaring that in their experience of the physical world, all people behold something of God's glory—his eternity, power, goodness, and other "invisible attributes" of the divine nature (Acts 14:17, 17:25, Rom. 1:20-21). In short, God created the cosmos in order to bestow upon his human and angelic creatures the gift of the knowledge of himself. Interestingly, it appears that the angels also grow in their knowledge of God's purposes and glory, especially by scrutinizing what goes on among men in the earth below (Eph. 3:8-13, 1 Pet. 1:12).

On the other hand, the cosmos was also intended as a theatre in which men would *enhance the glory of God*. This does not mean, of course, that man could add anything to the perfections of the divine nature. But it does mean that he could bring honor—or dishonor—to his creator in the sight of others; that he could reflect well, or ill, on his maker, depending upon the way in which he responded to him. Not surprisingly, the Bible repeatedly exhorts people to take the high road of honoring God with our lives. Jesus, for example, commanded his followers to "Let your light so shine before men that they may see your good works and glorify your Father in Heaven" (Mt. 5:16). Similarly, the apostle Paul tersely exhorted the Corinthians, saying, "Glorify God in your bodies" (1 Cor. 6:20). Thus, one of God's high purposes in creation was to secure honor and pleasure for himself as his extended human (and angelic) family delighted in the knowledge of his glory and showed their gratitude through freely chosen acts of obedience and praise.[7]

We find, then, that God had many reasons for creating the cosmos. But before any of these purposes could be fulfilled, the original pair must pass a test.

In six literal days:

The Bible is quite emphatic that God created the universe in six literal (i.e., solar) days. This foundational fact is first revealed in Genesis, a book that patently falls into the category of historical narrative. Read in its entirety, we see immediately that it is intended as a history of beginnings, whether of the universe, life, man, sin, suffering, death, global defacement, diverse languages, separate nations, or God's plan of redemption. It is certainly not intended as myth or poetry.

The biblical evidence for recent creation abounds. In Genesis 1, a creation day is carefully defined in terms of "evening and morning," the writer apparently wishing to leave no doubt as to its length (Gen. 1:5, 8, 13, etc.). The literal view is further supported by the fact that whenever the OT uses the word "day" with a number (410 times), it is always a literal day (1:5, 8, 13, 19, etc.). Similarly, whenever it uses the word "day" with the word "evening" or "morning" (61 times) it is again a literal day. At Sinai, God confirmed the literal view when he unveiled to Israel the rationale for their Sabbath observances: "For in six days the LORD made the heavens and the earth, the sea and all that is in them, and rested on the seventh day; therefore the LORD blessed the Sabbath (Heb., *shabbat,* seventh) day and made it holy" (Ex. 20:11). The creation week serves as the proto-type of his people's workweek, and is therefore of equal duration.

As we have seen, Jesus himself espoused recent creation, declaring that male and female were present "from the beginning of the creation" (Mark 10:6). Similarly, the apostle Paul asserted that God has revealed himself to

WHAT IS THE ORIGIN OF THE UNIVERSE, LIFE, AND MAN?

mankind through nature "since the creation of the world" (Rom. 1:20). The apostle Peter, in his discourse on the end of the age, manifestly embraces the young earth cosmology of Genesis 1-11 (2 Pet. 3:1-13).[8] Importantly, a large majority of early Christian leaders (the so-called Church Fathers) explicitly identified the 6 days of creation as 24 hour periods; only three (Clement of Alexandria, Origen, and Augustine) interpreted them figuratively, yet these too still embraced recent creation, teaching that the world is only a few thousand years old. Down through the centuries the vast majority of Christians have followed suit. In modern times, some interpreters, pressured by alleged scientific evidence for an old earth and an old universe, have tried to explain the days of creation figuratively. But even these are honest enough to admit that extra-biblical considerations alone compel them to depart from the *prima facie* sense of the text. In short, all agree, friend and foe alike, that the Bible itself unequivocally teaches a recent creation.[9]

Seekers should understand that the doctrine of a recent 6 day creation is not a theological "fine point," but rather foundational to the entire biblical worldview. In other words, as compared with modern, non-literal interpretations of Genesis 1—interpretations expressly designed to accommodate billions of years—the traditional, common sense view stands *alone* in upholding the glory of God and the internal coherence of his revelation. Here are a few important reasons why.

First, it alone adequately magnifies God's power, since it concentrates his creative work in 6 short days rather than spreading it out over billions of years. It is precisely such concentrated power that the psalmist had in mind when he sang:

> *By the word of the LORD were the heavens made,*
> *Their starry host by the breath of His mouth.*
> *He gathers the waters of the sea into jars;*
> *He puts the deep in storehouses.*
> *Let all the earth fear the LORD;*
> *Let all the inhabitants of the world stand in awe of Him.*
> *For He spoke, and it came to be;*
> *He commanded and it stood firm.*
> —Psalm 33:6-9, NIV

Secondly, it alone is consistent with God's manifest purpose in creation: to provide a home, a domain, and a workshop for man (Is. 45:18). Why would God build a house, and then wait billions of years to create the people who were meant to occupy it?

Thirdly, it alone supports the destiny and dignity of man. For if God's original workweek is a prototype of man's, then man's implicit destiny is to work like God and rest like God, living and serving in nature as a co-creator with him. By denying the symmetry of the two workweeks, other views clearly belittle the glory of man.

Fourthly, it alone preserves the original goodness of the universe, as well as the goodness of the One who made it. For if God's creative activity produced all that theories of an ancient universe seek to accommodate (i.e., biological trial and error, violence, bloodshed, death, and extinction), how could he, or his creation, be good?

Fifthly, recent creation alone supports the cardinal biblical teaching as to how moral and natural evil really did enter the world: through the sin of the first Adam. In other words, by ruling out evolutionary schemes, it re-enforces the pervasive biblical assumption that natural evil (i.e., physical disintegration, suffering, and death) is a divine judgment on (man's) moral evil. Accordingly, it helps us to view both kinds of evil as enemies and interlopers in God's good creation, enemies that we ought to actively resist (rather than evolve out of), and from which only God can ultimately deliver us.

Finally, recent creation alone supports the equally cardinal biblical teaching as to how moral and natural evil will be expelled from the world: through the righteous life and atoning death of Jesus Christ, the last Adam (Rom. 5:12ff). This point—and the one just preceding it—are especially important, since they introduce us to *the very infrastructure of biblical redemption:* the idea that the Last Adam, Jesus Christ, *rescues* his people from all the physical and spiritual enemies to which the first Adam enslaved them by his sin; and the parallel idea that the Last Adam also *restores* his people to all the spiritual and physical blessings that the first Adam forfeited because of that same sin.

Later we shall explore these crucial themes in greater depth. However, even from the little we have said here it is evident that old earth cosmogonies of every kind tend strongly to *undermine* the biblical infrastructure of redemption. Why? Because they are expressly designed to accommodate billions of years of cosmic evolution; because cosmic evolution understands natural (and even moral) evil as an integral part of the evolutionary process; because this view *explicitly* contradicts biblical testimony to the effect that evil entered the world as a judgment upon the sin of the first Adam; and because this *implicitly* contradicts biblical testimony to the effect that God will purge the world of evil—whether in judicial wrath or redemptive mercy—through the Last Adam, Jesus Christ. In short, old earth cosmologies pave the way for cosmic evolution, and cosmic evolution—dispensing with the crucial biblical infrastructure of the two Adams—paves the way for evolutionary interpretations of sin and redemption.

WHAT IS THE ORIGIN OF THE UNIVERSE, LIFE, AND MAN? 241

Anyone who doubts this may turn to the writings of Catholic theologian Teilhard de Chardin, or to those of his disciples in the New Age movement. Though often casting their ideas in biblical language, these men want us to think of redemption as *an evolutionary destiny*. They would train the eye of faith, not on a transcendent personal God acting redemptively and supernaturally in history, but on an evolutionary process that mystically culminates in "god-consciousness," a universal awareness that all is god. In short, they believe that evolution, rather than Christ, will save us and bring us to Paradise. However, recent creation—immediately, obviously, and decisively—precludes every such view. Thus, along with related biblical doctrines, it effectively becomes a mighty sentinel standing guard over the integrity of traditional Christian cosmology and soteriology (i.e., doctrine of redemption).

In view of all these considerations, it is hardly surprising that many theological conservatives vigorously defend the doctrine of recent creation, often at great personal cost. They believe, correctly, that the entire biblical worldview—with its unified story of cosmic creation, fall, and redemption—rises or falls with the integrity of Genesis 1-11.

After which he saw that all he had made was very good:

Throughout the six days of creation God saw that his work was good; on the seventh day he saw that everything he had made was *very* good (Gen. 1:31). This recurring judgment, so manifestly exuding satisfaction, impresses upon its readers a vital cosmological truth: the world in which man now lives is not the world as it was in the beginning. Originally it was "good;" now it still is good, yet no longer completely good, being strangely mixed with evil. Originally it knew nothing of the moral evil, guilt, sickness, injury, death, toil, pain, and other disruptions of nature that came in with man's fall; now it does (Gen. 2-3). Accordingly, the biblical beginning fully supports a complex set of human intuitions: that the world is good, that it should be better, that something has gone wrong, and that perhaps things can be made right again. Similarly, this cosmogony supports our intuition that the creator is good, thus explicitly protecting him from charges that moral and natural evil sprang directly from his creative hand.

It is clear that the doctrine of the original goodness of the creation once again pits biblical cosmology against all forms of cosmic evolution (i.e., naturalistic, pantheistic, or theistic). As we saw above, cosmic evolution teaches that natural evil, in one form or another, has been present in the universe from the very beginning. Moreover, in the case of theistic evolution or progressive creation, it is God who put it there.[10] The Bible, on the other hand, teaches that all natural and moral evil is traceable to man's sin, not

God's creation (Rom. 5:12f, 8:18f). On this point, as on so many others, the two cosmologies are completely incompatible. For this reason, modern efforts to reconcile biblical creation with cosmic evolution have only resulted in casting doubt upon the clarity and trustworthiness of the scriptures, as well as upon the intellectual honesty of interpreters who thus compromise their biblical faith.

And rested from his creative work:

The divine rest does not mean that on the seventh day God stopped working in the universe (as Deism taught), only that he stopped creating (Gen. 2:1-3). In other words, he is no longer bringing new things into being or fashioning new things out of pre-existing materials. The universe is now filled. The forms, functions, natures, and motions of things are essentially fixed. Henceforth, God no longer creates, but is at work to sustain, animate, and direct all things to their appointed ends (Psalm 36:5f, 104).[11]

The declaration of God's creation-rest yet again opposes the Bible to evolution. The Bible states that creation was a brief once-for-all event that is now completed; evolution states that it is an ongoing process. Happily, we can easily test both views simply by looking at the world around us.

And blessed and sanctified the seventh day:

Though God created no physical objects on the seventh day, he did perform a final creative act: he blessed and sanctified the seventh day. This appears to mean that he impressed upon the inmost nature of his human children to set apart one day in seven to emulate him (Ex. 20:11). In other words, they were to rest (i.e., cease) from their work and to reflect with satisfaction upon all that God had enabled them to accomplish during the previous six days. Here, too, was a special opportunity for them to think about their creator, ponder his plans for the future, thank him for his many gifts, and in all of this to receive from him a special blessing. Thus, by sanctifying the seventh day, God instituted in man's very being a weekly rhythm of work and worship. As one thoughtful commentator put it, he "...oriented the whole created order toward the worship of God."[12]

Much later, after the fall of man, God would explicitly command his OT people Israel to observe the Sabbath (Ex. 20:8-11). Prior to the fall, however, no such command was necessary. Come the seventh day, it would only have seemed natural for Adam and Eve to join with all creation in gladly worshipping the LORD, the maker of heaven and earth (Psalm 146:1-7).

Heaven

Though Genesis 1-2 does not speak of it explicitly, other Bible passages indicate that in the beginning God brought into being a distinctly spiritual world. As a rule, it is called heaven (Gen. 28:12, 2 Chron. 28:11-19, Mt. 5:12, 45, 48). Ezekiel, however, refers to it as Eden (not to be confused with the earthly Eden), the Garden of God, and the Holy Mount (Ezek. 28:11-19). Jesus, apparently following Ezekiel, also calls it Paradise, a word of Persian origin meaning "a garden with a wall" (Luke 23:43, 2 Cor. 12:4, Rev. 2:7). The apostle Paul, contrasting it with the air and the sky above, calls it "the third heaven" (2 Cor. 12:2). As we are about to see, for humbling the human intellect there is nothing quite like pondering the precise nature and location of the spiritual heaven. Nevertheless, the four following biblical affirmations may prove helpful in dispelling confusion and taking us up to the edge of this great mystery.

A Creation

First, heaven is a *creation* of God. This is especially clear from the words of the writer to the Hebrews, who picturesquely describes it as "...a sanctuary and a tabernacle that the Lord pitched...not made with (human) hands, that is, not of this creation" (Heb. 8:2, 9:11). True, heaven is "not of this creation," (for it is a spiritual rather than a physical realm). Nevertheless, since the Lord "pitched" and "made" it, we cannot simply identify it with the (omnipresent) Spirit of God, or say that it is a (spiritual) state of mind. No, heaven had a true beginning at the hand of God; therefore it is a true creation.

An Abode

Secondly, heaven is an *abode*, or home. In the beginning, it was home only to the *holy angels*, a vast host of personal spiritual beings created early in the creation week, probably on the first or second day (Psalm 148:1-5, Job 38:1-11). God made different kinds of angels (e.g., *seraphim* and *cherubim*), and set them in different ranks, (e.g., angels and archangels). As to their purpose, God granted that the angels should behold, contemplate, and enthusiastically worship him in all his glory (Isaiah 6:1f, Rev. 4, 5). In doing so, they also perceived some kind of heavenly environment. In the very beginning, they rejoiced to watch God complete his creative handiwork for the sake of man (Job 38:1-11). Moreover, in days ahead it would be their joy actually to descend to the world below, serving as

God's heavenly messengers to his earthly people (Dan. 10:20, Luke 1:19, 26, Heb. 1:14). Thus, like the sun, moon, and stars, heaven itself was (and is) centered on the world of men!

All too soon, however, heaven underwent a change. When sin entered the world—and when God began to trump sin by administering the redemption that is in Christ—he opened heaven up to the spirits of the departed saints as well. Seeking to encourage wavering Christians with this very hope, the writer to the Hebrews gives us a glimpse not only of heaven's (enlarged) population, but also of its unspeakable joys:

> But you have come to Mount Zion, to the heavenly Jerusalem, to the city of the living God. You have come to thousands upon thousands of angels in joyful assembly, to the Church of the firstborn, whose names are written in Heaven. You have come to God, the Judge of all men, to the spirits of righteous men made perfect, to Jesus, the Mediator of the new covenant, and to the sprinkled blood that speaks a better word than the blood of Abel.
> —Heb.12:22-24, NIV

Here we have the very essence of the biblical picture of heaven as it exists today: heaven is the common abode of the holy angels and the perfected saints, joyfully worshiping God and Christ together in a city that lies mysteriously "above."

A True Place

This brings us to our third observation, namely that heaven is *a true place*. More particularly, it is a place *above the earth*. As the psalmist wrote, "He looked down from the height of His sanctuary; from heaven the LORD viewed the earth" (Psalm 102:19, 11:4). Angels are sent *down* from heaven to the Earth below (Dan. 10:11f, Luke 1:19, 26). So too was God's Son, who, after his resurrection, ascended into heaven bodily (Acts 1:9-11, John 6:62; cf.1 Kings 22:19f). Thus, the Bible repeatedly depicts heaven as a true place above, even as it likewise represents *Hades* as a true place beneath (Prov. 15:24, Ezek. 13:15f, John 8:23, 2 Peter 2:4).

The great question, however, is: *In what sense* is heaven a true place above? Or, to put the matter slightly differently, *where exactly IS heaven?* Responding to this challenging problem, biblical interpreters have offered three main views.

Some suggest that heaven is—or is in some portion of—space itself; that it is invisible to us simply because God has made its inhabitants invisible to us; that it could actually be quite near to us, with God's throne, for example,

WHAT IS THE ORIGIN OF THE UNIVERSE, LIFE, AND MAN?

being situated directly above the earthly Jerusalem, and with heaven's other citizens being spread out in a sheath around the whole Earth, or even filling the depths of space. Proponents of this view base their case on the fact that both Old and New Testaments use the same word (Heb., *shamayim;* Greek, *ouranoi*) to describe the spiritual and the physical heavens. They also remind us that if the angels seem to travel *through* our space, then surely it is reasonable to suppose that they also live *in* it (Dan. 6:22, Luke 1:19, Acts 12:11). Additionally, they point out that Christ (like Enoch and Elijah) now has a (glorified) physical body and must therefore still live in some kind of space. And since he was born into our kind of space, why should we think of him abandoning it for another? However, as we have seen, the Bible represents heaven as a true creation, and as a creation that is "not of this creation." This seems to mean that heaven is not part of the (finite) physical cosmos that God created in the beginning. But if not, how can it be basically identical with the expanse of space?

Another view—and one with a long and venerable history—declares that heaven lies *above* the firmament; that it is a kind of "hyper-space" situated just beyond the outer edge of our own (finite) physical universe. Scriptural support for this idea is considerable. God has set his glory *above* (or upon) the heavens (i.e., the expanse) (Psalm 8:1, 113:4). He is high above all nations, and his glory is *above* the heavens (Psalm 113:4). He has set his seat on high, and humbles Himself to regard the heavens (Psalm 113:5). In the Day of Judgment he will call to the heavens from *above* (Psalm 50:4). Because of his lofty transcendence, all creatures should praise the LORD: the angels who dwell "in the heights," the sun, the moon, the stars, and "the heavens of the heavens" (Psalm 148:1-4). Very suggestively, Ezekiel, in a majestic vision of spiritual things, beheld four glorious cherubs. Above them he saw "...the likeness of *an expanse,* like awesome crystal (or ice) to look upon." And *above* that he saw the throne of God, and Him who was seated upon it (Ezek. 1:22ff). Does this vision picture something of the structure of the universe and the whereabouts of heaven? It certainly appears to. And yet, intriguing as this view is, there seems to be a problem: It makes heaven quite remote from the Earth (unless—as could well be the case—the universe is much smaller than we presently think). However, many Bible passages seem to represent it as being quite near (see below).

A third group of interpreters agrees that heaven is indeed a place above, but argues that we ought to interpret such language figuratively; that we should not think of heaven in *physical* terms, but in *metaphysical;* that heaven is best conceived as *another dimension that is different from, yet closely related to, our own.* John Byl succinctly expresses this notion by saying: "The biblical description suggests that the spiritual heaven is a universe parallel to the physical universe." [13]

Mystics feel that their approach explains the biblical data as well or better than that of the common sense school. When, for example, the apostle declares that Christ "...ascended far above all the heavens," mystics interpret him as saying that Christ entered another *kind* of space; a space that *transcends* our space, but which is nevertheless closely related to it; a higher order space in which our space may, in some ineffable way, be embedded (Eph. 4:10; 1:9-23, Phil. 2:6-11). Or again, when angels suddenly appear to shepherds, or when Christ suddenly appears to his disciples, it is not necessarily that they have traveled vast distances through the skies, but rather that they have simply slipped into earth's space from heaven's—a space that, metaphysically speaking, is quite near to our own (Luke 2:13f, 24:31, 36, John 20:19-20). Also, mystics argue that their view does not compel us to think of the ascended Christ as being far away from us—e.g., beyond the outer edge of the universe. Moreover, this view may help us to understand why heaven seems so close to the saints on earth, before whose eyes it is, on occasion, mysteriously "opened up" (Gen. 28:18, 1 Kings 16:4, Mt. 3:16, John 1:32, Acts 7:55-6). For all these reasons, the mystical approach certainly seems plausible. Yet one wonders if it is not a bit too facile, seeing that we human speculators can make "other dimensions" do just about anything we want them to do!

Which of these three views is best? It is hard to say: All accommodate the biblical texts well enough, all have strengths and weaknesses. If I had to judge, I would choose the second as being truest to the Scriptures. And yet, in view of all the difficulties involved, the truth could well be that God did not intend to reveal the exact whereabouts of his heaven, only the fact that there really is such a place somewhere "up there." Thus, for a complete understanding of the place of heaven, seekers will likely have to wait until they enter it themselves, even as they make every effort on earth to be sure they do.

A Visionary World

As it is now being experienced, heaven appears to be *a visionary world*. Negatively stated, this means that "the furniture of heaven"—most of the things that the saints and angels perceive up there—are not physical in nature. That is, heaven's "things" are not like our earthly things, only made of a finer, more ethereal kind of matter. Rather, they are purely spiritual phenomena, since heaven is the place where God is pleased continually to manifest himself and his truth *by way of spiritual visions* to all his holy ones.

WHAT IS THE ORIGIN OF THE UNIVERSE, LIFE, AND MAN?

Strange as this conclusion may sound, the Scriptures themselves seem to drive us to it. For on the one hand, the Bible often gives us visions of heaven in which God appears to men and angels in a more or less human form: sitting on a throne, inhabiting a temple, etc. (Isaiah 6:1-3, 2 Chron. 18:18f, Ezek. 1, Rev. 4). On the other hand, it also insists that God is an infinite personal Spirit, that he has no form, and that he cannot be confined to a single place (Ex. 20:4, 1 Kings 8:27, Isaiah 66:1, 1 Tim. 6:16). Now unless the scriptures are at odds with themselves, there appears to be only one viable solution to these seeming contradictions: heaven is not a physical world like our own, but must rather be a *visionary world—a world in which the presence, glory, and truth of the infinite and invisible God are revealed to human and angelic spirits under earthly imagery by means of sustained spiritual visions.*[14]

This approach permits us to understand the biblical descriptions of heaven in a more spiritual manner. For example, it helps us to see that God (Christ now being excepted) does not really have a human form (as some interpreters erroneously assert that he does), but that in visions he is seen that way in order to reveal his metaphysical similarity to man. Similarly, God does not really sit on a throne, but in visions he is seen that way so as to represent his sovereignty over all creation. Or again, God does not really live in a temple, but in visions is seen that way in order to reveal his desire for the worship of his creatures in the chosen place of his dwelling (Eph. 2:22). Using the words of the apostle Paul, we may therefore say that in heaven, as upon the earth, "...the invisible things of Him are clearly seen, being understood by (visions) of the things that are made."[15]

By way of conclusion, let us note carefully an important implication of this view. If heaven is essentially a visionary world, *then heaven's place must always be with heaven's population, with those who experience the heavenly visions.* In other words, by its very nature, heaven is *a movable reality* within the cosmos. Thus, on the first day it was situated somewhere "above" the earth, for that is where the angels dwelt, beholding visions of God and God's truth. Today, according to the NT, it is still above the earth, for that is where the (holy) angels and the spirits of the departed saints now dwell, beholding visions of God, Christ, and *more* divine truth (Heb.12:22f). Some day, however, heaven will actually descend to the earth, for that is where the (resurrected) saints and the holy angels, according to divine promise, will continue to enjoy the beatific vision, only this time under a new sky and upon a new earth (Rev. 21:1-3). For believers in Jesus, it is a day of unfathomable mystery, yet also a day that is devoutly longed for—a day when heaven and earth shall at last and forever be one.

New Light on the Beginning

Just as Jesus enlarged Israel's understanding of the ultimate reality, so too he shed new light on the beginning. The light that he brought was as mind-boggling as it was radical: he taught that *he himself was the creator of the cosmos!* The NT revelation on this weighty theme comes in three distinct stages.

First, we have the instruction of Jesus himself. This came both in word and miraculous deed. Concerning the latter, we think of cases like the feeding of the 5000, in which he apparently created something out of nothing (Mt. 14:13-21, 15:32-39, John 6:1-14). At other times, he reminds us of the One who created by fashioning what he had just brought into being. Here we think of Jesus' first miracle, when he turned water into wine (John 2:1-12); and also of his many restorative healings (e.g., Mt. 9:27-31, Mark 1:40-41, John 11). Finally, there are the miracles in which Jesus demonstrated his power over nature. On this score, one episode is especially noteworthy. When Jesus calmed the raging Sea of Galilee with a single command, his incredulous disciples asked, "Who can this be?" The suspicion that Jesus was none other than the creator himself seems to have hovered, ghost-like, at the edge of their shaken minds (Mark 4:35-41, Mt. 14:33; cf. Psalm 107:23-32, Luke 5:1-11).

The gospels do not have Jesus straightforwardly identifying himself as the creator. Nevertheless, there are loud hints. By calling himself "I AM," he identified himself with *Yahweh*, the creator of the universe (John 8:58). Similarly, in his final prayer for the disciples, he stated that he existed with the Father "...before the creation of the world," (John 17:24). Such an utterance could hardly help but raise suspicions that he was putting himself on a par with the eternal One who made the world.

These hints exploded into positive affirmations after Jesus' apostles received the Holy Spirit on the day of Pentecost. Henceforth, they proclaimed the mystery of the Holy Trinity, and in doing so identified the pre-incarnate Christ as a divine agent of creation (John 1:1-3, 10, 16:12, Acts 2:1f). The epistles, in particular, give us text after text affirming that God the Father created the universe *through* him (Heb. 1:1), *by* him (Col. 1:16), and *for* him (Eph. 1:10, Col. 1:16, Heb. 1:1-4). Moreover, the apostles go on to add that the glorified Jesus Christ has now taken in hand the reins of divine providence: by the Spirit, the Son of God now holds all things together, even as he directs all things to the specific ends appointed by the Father (Col. 1:17, Heb. 1:3, Eph. 1:22-23, Rev. 5). Ravished by the sight of their exalted and glorified Master, these men boldly declared Jesus Christ as the divine Creator and King of the entire cosmos.

Finally, we have the words of the glorified Christ himself, spoken to John on the island of Patmos. Appearing in a vision to his awestruck apostle, he immediately identifies himself, saying, "I am the Alpha and the Omega...he who is and who was and who is to come, the Almighty" (Rev. 1:8). Later, he calls himself "The Beginning and the End," and "The First and the Last" (Rev. 1:17, 2:8, 22:13). Christ's use of these exalted titles is clearly designed to comfort his persecuted apostle. He reminds John (and all suffering Christians) that their Master is not only the omnipotent creator of the universe, but its omnipotent consummator as well. They are to trust that he who created in the beginning can be counted on to return, resurrect, and gloriously re-create in the end (Rev. 21:5).[16]

Especially for Seekers

Of all Jesus' answers to the questions of life, this one may be the most difficult for modern seekers to receive. The reason is clear: ever since the days of Copernicus and the so-called Enlightenment, Western intellectuals have increasingly abandoned theistic cosmology for one form or another of *cosmic evolution* (CE). Not surprisingly, young people raised and educated in this modern philosophical environment simply assume that CE is true—and that the older biblical cosmology must be a relic of man's intellectual infancy, a pleasant myth now overshadowed by the powerful advance of science. There are, however, a number of good reasons why seekers should question this familiar cultural consensus, and why they should take a careful second look at Jesus' teaching on this crucial theme. In bringing our chapter to a close, let us touch on a few now.

First, seekers should understand that here, as elsewhere, the majority does not necessarily rule. Suppose, for example, that from time to time the unknown god is pleased to allow the intelligentsia to fall into error, thereby setting the stage for a fresh test of our love of the truth concerning a given question of life. A backward glance suggests that intellectual history is actually quite full of such dramas. Perhaps, then, in our own day, god has ordained that the question of origins should be a point of especially rigorous testing. If so, it would be foolish indeed for seekers to accept uncritically the prevailing academic consensus about the beginning, especially since that consensus is actually quite fragile, and could at any moment give way to another view. In short, the seeker's only safe course is to examine *all* viable perspectives, in order to see which one best commends itself as the truth.

Secondly, seekers who are willing to do this very thing will find, often to their great amazement, that the biblical cosmogony has a lot going for it. Indeed, many would say that it has a lot *more* going for it than any of its competitors.

Consider, for example, some of the points at which Jesus' cosmology is highly intuitive. It offers us a distinctly *personal* creator, exactly the kind of god we see displayed in the natural and moral orders. It tells us that this god is both transcendent and immanent; that he is different from his creation, yet related to it. It tells us that his universe is not *monistic* (i.e., made of one substance), but *dualistic* (i.e., made of both spiritual and physical substances, the two sometimes being united in one creation). Also, it tells us that the universe has a definite purpose (i.e., to be a home for man and a theatre for the display and enjoyment of the glory of God), and that the particulars of its (six day) creation and its (geocentric) structure dramatically reflect that purpose. On these and other key points, Jesus' cosmogony clearly appeals to our "spiritual common sense"—and far more so than its naturalistic and pantheistic counterparts.

His cosmogony also accords very well with our distinctly ethical intuitions about the world and its creator. Above all, his teaching revolves around a *good* god who created a *good* world. True, the fall of man has marred the world's original goodness, but this further addition to the biblical cosmogony only serves to illumine the depth and complexity of our feelings about the world: that it *is* good, that it *should be* better, and that one day, with God's help, it *may well be perfect*.

Observe also that Jesus' teaching supplies a clear theological base for many of mankind's most cherished ethical norms. For example, it grounds our innate conviction about the sanctity of human life (Gen. 1:27, 9:6). It confirms our intuition that man is a purposeful being, with God-ordained work to do and goals to reach. It supports our feeling that mankind has a vocation to develop the earth, and that in fulfilling it we must carefully steward the world's natural resources, especially its animal life. It sharpens our sense for healthy sexual relations, explicitly teaching that it is not good for men and women to live alone; that heterosexual marriage is divinely ordained for companionship, procreation, and teamwork; that in marriage each partner has distinctive roles and responsibilities; and that husband and wife must be faithful to one another all their days. Thus, the biblical cosmogony not only speaks directly to our ethical intuitions, but also serves to train and strengthen them for wise and fruitful living.

Is Jesus' cosmology hopeful? Eminently. The modern naturalistic view of the beginning (i.e., the Big Bang) entails that the cosmos will one day perish through "heat death" and become a lifeless dustbin. Pantheistic views are nearly always based on the assumption of "eternal recurrence," the idea that the universe begins and ends, begins again and ends again, and so continues forever—entailing that man will struggle and suffer forever. But the biblical creation story, unlike both of these, gives us the richest conceivable hope. This is chiefly because it posits a good creator whose original purpose was to be a Father to his free creatures. Seeing, then, that he is also an almighty creator, we take hope, knowing that he who purposed man's joy in the beginning is doubtless well able to bring it to pass in the end. Thus, the biblical beginning is actually a whispered promise of redemption. A creator like this cannot fail. He will bring his errant children home, meet them in Paradise, and there walk with them again (Gen. 3:8, Rev. 21:1-5).

Summing up, we find that Jesus' cosmogony is quite intuitive, ethically sound, and full of hope. But again, the great question in our day is: *Is it reasonable?* Here, of course, is where the evolutionists balk. They are usually willing to admit that the biblical cosmogony is comprehensible, coherent, and even attractive. But they are not willing to admit that it is reasonable, in the sense of being supported by lots of good evidence. To the contrary, in their view, the evidence clearly favors their preferred model of "creation"—which is cosmic evolution.

Careful observers of "the culture wars" know, however, that in recent years biblical creationists have been giving the evolutionists a run for their money, setting forth an increasingly sophisticated case not only for the rationality of the traditional biblical cosmogony, but also for the *irrationality* of CE. Interestingly enough, many open-minded seekers are now quite willing to hear it. We must, therefore, in the paragraphs that remain, survey this argument *in very general terms*. Those interested in further exploring the details of the great debate about origins may follow my notes to a number of valuable books, articles, and websites devoted to this most fascinating and controversial theme.

The Case for Biblical Creation

The case for biblical creation is built upon a simple but profoundly important epistemological fact: man *cannot* observe the origin of the universe with his physical eyes, or with any instrument designed to extend his vision (e.g., telescope, microscope, etc.). Why? Because the beginning (if indeed there was one) happened before man came upon the historical scene. It lies hidden in the unobservable past, *and therefore beyond the reach of strict scientific confirmation*. This means that we may be able to develop different scientific *models* of the beginning, and that some of those models may be better than others. But *left to himself*, scientific man can never directly verify which, if any, model is true.

Nevertheless, say the creationists, all is not lost, for perhaps we can "see" the beginning in another way. Suppose, for example, that the unknown god has *not* left us to ourselves as mere scientific model-makers; suppose that he has actually given us a trustworthy divine revelation of the beginning. Under such happy circumstances, we could indeed look with confidence upon the origin of the universe, life, and man. True, we could only see it "by faith," and not by actual sight. But we could see it nonetheless (Heb. 11:3). This revelation would be for us *a god-given model*—a very special kind of spiritual and philosophical telescope through which we could not only look at the beginning, but also fruitfully ponder many of the puzzling phenomena that we observe today in the world around us, (e.g., the geocentric distribution of galaxies and quasars, the peculiarities of the fossilized geological column, the Second Law of Thermodynamics, the Law of Genetic Stasis, etc.). In other words, such a model would not only satisfy our spiritual and intellectual hunger to behold the beginning, but would also likely enhance the scientific study of man and nature as well.

Here, then—and not in the narrow realm of natural science alone—is the real battleground upon which the fierce debate about cosmic origins is being fought. "For," say the creationists, "the Bible does indeed give us a trustworthy divine revelation of the beginning. Moreover, it is quite reasonable for us to believe this revelation, since there is good evidence *from many different quarters* that strongly supports its truthfulness (e.g., from the realms of intuition, conscience, the biblical signs, science, history, etc.). Why, then, should we not consult this revelation in our search for cosmological truth?"

That question certainly seems reasonable enough, but the evolutionists have an answer. "Because," they say, "it is *unscientific* to consult divine revelation. To do so goes against the rules of good science. True scientists will therefore strictly confine themselves to man-made hypotheses—and in particular, to *hypotheses that make no appeal whatsoever to spiritual causes lying beyond the reach of direct observation.* Naturalistic cosmic evolution is one such theory. We think the evidence richly supports it—*and that any other kind of evidence does not qualify as evidence at all.*"

So again, we see that the creation-evolution debate is, at its heart, an epistemological debate. One side wants to admit knowledge and evidence of many kinds; the other will only admit knowledge and evidence of one kind. However, as we saw in chapter 4, there really is no good reason to define "science" so narrowly. Why not define "true scientists" in the broadest possible sense? Why not define them as "true knowers," people who will gladly receive knowledge and evidence from any quarter, just so long as that knowledge and evidence are reliable, and so further the cause of truth?[17]

Because this approach to the search for cosmological truth seems to me so reasonable, honest, and potentially fruitful, I will now offer a case for

WHAT IS THE ORIGIN OF THE UNIVERSE, LIFE, AND MAN?

biblical creation that allows the creationists fully to spread their wings. That is, I will present—in *very* general terms—their arguments and evidences from *all* realms, not just the scientific. Hopefully, at this stage of our journey, readers will not find it unreasonable or "unscientific" to do so.

The Realm of the Three Orders

The creationist argument begins by spotlighting the *natural, moral,* and *probationary orders*. As we have seen, in many different ways these orders evoke in us an inescapable awareness of an unknown god. Indeed, they tell us quite a bit about him, namely, that he is an infinite personal Spirit who is wise, powerful, and good. Therefore, the evidence revealed in these three orders automatically rules out all naturalistic and pantheistic cosmologies, since none of them posits such a god. On the other hand, the evidence from these realms rules in some kind of theistic cosmology, including the one we find in the Bible.

The Realm of the Biblical Signs

Next we have the large and diverse body of God-given *signs* demonstrating that Jesus of Nazareth is his appointed Teacher. Some of them are quite *supernatural*, such as OT Messianic types and prophecies, Jesus' miracles, his resurrection from the dead, and the transformative power of his Gospel. Others are more *providential*, such as the astonishing quantity, quality, and preservation of the biblical manuscripts. All these signs confirm that the unknown god and Israel's God are one, and that the Bible is his book. Appearing before, at, and after Jesus' coming, they constitute a massive treasury of indirect evidence favorable to the distinctly *biblical* cosmology. In other words, they lend the full weight of their authority to the cosmological teachings of Christ and the Bible.

The Realm of Scientific Evidence

Next we have a wide range of scientific evidences that, by exposing the great weakness of the evolutionary model, offer strong support for the creationist model. These evidences fall nicely into three broad categories.[18]

First, there is good evidence that *CE is not happening*. Looking around us we do not see, for example, energy/matter springing into existence anywhere in space. Notwithstanding claims to the contrary, we do not actually see stars or galaxies being born. We do not see "transitional animals" sporting useless, randomly generated appendages, appendages that would actually jeopardize their chances for survival rather than enhance them. Thus, in the words of evolutionist Stephen J. Gould, it appears that all throughout nature "the evolutionary clock has stopped." Indeed, it appears that the evolutionary clock is ticking backwards since, as time progresses, all things are actually *devolving*. For again, wherever we look—whether at the stars, the mountains, the animals, or the human genome—what we *really* see is decay. In obedience to the Second Law of Thermodynamics, all things are sliding towards disintegration and death. This is exactly what the biblical model, with its two-fold doctrine of creation and fall, predicts. And it is exactly the opposite of what the evolutionary model predicts.

Secondly, there is good evidence that *CE did not happen*. Broadly speaking, this evidence consists in the fact that all of the so-called "proofs" of CE have been discarded, are presently contested, or are better explained by the creationist model. Such "proofs" include galactic red shifts, the cosmic microwave background (CMB), the relative abundances of elements in stars, the fossilized geological column, homologous biological structures, so-called "microevolution," hominid fossils, and vestigial organs.

Also, diligent students of cosmology will encounter a growing body of observational evidence that powerfully undermines CE in general, and the standard Big Bang model in particular. This includes: 1) missing mass in the universe, needed to reconcile the Big Bang with cosmic evolution, 2) the "clumpy" distribution of matter in space, not predicted by the Big Bang model, 3) numerous physical obstacles to (a purely naturalistic) evolution of stars, galaxies, and the elements (e.g., Second Law of Thermodynamics, molecular pressure in nebulae, etc.), 4) various peculiarities of our so-called solar system (e.g., the non-uniform motion, spin, chemical composition, and angular momentum of the earth, the sun, the planets, and their several moons), 5) miscellaneous evidences for cosmic geocentricity (e.g., geocentric structure of the CMB, geocentric distribution of galaxies, quasars, etc.), and finally 6) the fact that *none* of the proposed mechanisms for biological evolution (i.e., spontaneous generation, random genetic mutations, and natural selection) is adequate for the task, or has *ever* been observed to accomplish it, even under ideal laboratory conditions.[19] Because of such troubling evidence, *hundreds* of researchers—representing the entire spectrum of scientific investigation and philosophical persuasion—are now publicly airing their doubts about one or another aspect of cosmic evolution.[20]

Finally, there is good reason to believe that *CE cannot happen*. This is so because CE—at least of the naturalistic variety—violates a large number of well-established natural laws. These include: 1) the Law of Cause and Effect, which posits that a given cause must be adequate to

WHAT IS THE ORIGIN OF THE UNIVERSE, LIFE, AND MAN?

produce a related effect, as the proposed causes of CE are not, 2) the Law of Universal Gravitation, which would certainly seem to rule out an explosion of the concentrated mass of the entire universe, 3) the Second Law of Thermodynamics, which declares that over time all physical systems lose structural complexity and integrity, rather than gain them, 4) the Law of Biogenesis, which declares that life cannot come from non-life, as CE says it did, 5) the laws of probability, which rule out the "random" creation of highly complex genetic material, cells, and organs, 6) the Law of Genetic Stasis which, following Mendel, states that living beings are genetically equipped to *adapt* to their environment in minor ways, but not to transcend the genetic boundaries of their own kind, and 7) the Law of Irreducible Complexity, which implies that the several elements of any biological system cannot have evolved piece-meal, since all of them must be up and running simultaneously for the system—and the creature that carries it—to function and survive.

Again, these and other natural laws completely rule out naturalistic cosmic evolution. It is, of course, possible that an omnipotent personal creator-god could have "gone against the grain" and supernaturally evolved a cosmos; hence the appeal of theistic evolution. But then one must ask: Why would this god work contrary to the very laws by which he decided to govern his world? Also, even if an infinite personal god *could* evolve a cosmos, there is certainly no good reason to believe that he has, and many to indicate that he has not. Furthermore, we have no credible revelation from any theistic religion to the effect that its god evolved the universe. We do, however, have a credible revelation from the God of the Bible, who says he created it in six literal days.

A Young Universe?

This brings us to yet another body of evidence unfavorable to CE: evidence suggesting that the universe, life, and man are actually quite young—so young that there has not been enough time for evolution to occur. Included in this category are: 1) (supposedly) old spiral galaxies that should long ago have wound themselves up into an amorphous mass of stars, but have not, 2) the paucity of supernova remnants in our Milky Way galaxy, of which there are just enough to indicate a galactic age of about 7000 years, 3) the changing temperature of the sun, which 1.5 billion years ago would not have allowed proto-life to evolve on earth, 4) dust particles near the sun, which should have been "blown" away by solar wind eons ago, 5) the scarcity of meteorites in the earth's allegedly ancient crust, 6) the decay of the earth's magnetic field, whose strength only 20,000 years ago would have signaled the presence of interior electrical currents powerful enough to destroy the earth altogether, 7) the scarcity of helium in the air, whose current volume points to an atmosphere that is thousands of years old, not billions, 8) the amounts of sodium, copper, gold, lead, mercury, and nickel in the oceans, which should be vastly larger if the oceans really are 3 billion years old, 9) the recent discovery of hemoglobin and soft tissues in dinosaur remains allegedly some 60 million years old, and 10) the present (low) level of world population, a level that correlates almost perfectly with the biblical post-flood scenario. Again, all of these phenomena, and many others like them, suggest that the universe, life, and man are really quite young. This not only rules out CE, but also adds further strength to the case for recent, biblical creation.

But what about the fossilized geological column, radiometric dating, and the light that reaches us from distant stars? Don't these prove an ancient world and universe?

As a matter of fact, reply the creationists, they do not, since the Bible enables us to explain them in (non-naturalistic) ways that are consistent with its own doctrine of recent creation. For example, the geological column may well have been laid down suddenly by the global Flood of Noah's day. Indeed, much scientific evidence suggests that this is *by far* the best option. Or again, rates of radioisotope decay may have been much faster in the past, perhaps due to some peculiarity of the creation week or to some special effect of the Flood. Or again, on the fourth day God may well have created cords of light binding the distant stars to the earth and one another; or he may have made the speed of light very fast at the beginning, and then, as time progressed, slowed it to a constant. In other words, while the Bible does not supply specific answers to these three fascinating problems, its cosmology definitely opens the way for fruitful thinking about plausible solutions. Therefore, so long as we are open to the biblical worldview, it is really quite easy to believe that there are reasonable explanations for them all.[21]

The Realm of Historical Evidence

The case for recent creation also includes a miscellany of historical evidences. For example, the biblical history of mankind shortly after the Flood and the events at Babel fits in perfectly with what we know from archeology about the age, location, and manner of life of the earliest civilizations. Furthermore, extensive research into ancient European

WHAT IS THE ORIGIN OF THE UNIVERSE, LIFE, AND MAN?

chronologies and genealogies tends strongly to confirm the accuracy of the biblical narrative (see Gen. 11).[22] Similarly, cultural anthropologists have supplied us with numerous legends from around the world—legends that mirror, to a greater or lesser degree, the biblical narratives of the creation, fall, flood, and dispersion of mankind.[23] This is particularly true of the story of the Deluge (Gen. 6-9), cited in over 200 Flood legends worldwide. Such legends are most reasonably seen as corrupted versions of the Genesis account, whose truthfulness is corroborated by the various evidences for the divine inspiration of the Bible.

Conclusion

Our brief evaluation has shown that Jesus' teaching on the origin of the universe, life, and man appeals richly to our spiritual common sense, ethical intuitions, and natural inclination to hope for the best. Moreover, in the eyes of creationists at least, it is not only reasonable, but far *more* reasonable than the next best option: one form or another of cosmic evolution. Perhaps, then, despite a sizable academic consensus to the contrary, the 45% of Americans who still believe in the traditional biblical cosmogony are not so foolish after all. But to the right-minded seeker, it is of relatively little importance whether a given cosmology is embraced by many or by few. His concern is simply to find out whether or not it is true. Therefore, with his eyes confidently fixed upon the heavenly Tester, he will keep on searching till he does.[24]

CHAPTER 11

WHAT, IF ANYTHING, WENT WRONG?

OFTEN, IF NOT always, man is on the rack. His consciousness is stretched, sometimes to the breaking point, between two powerful poles: between the good and the evil, the ideal and the real. We are sick when we ought to be healthy. We are at war when we ought to be at peace. We are foolish when we ought to be wise. We are cruel when we ought to be kind. We are held captive, when we ought to be free. As if through a fog, we somehow behold the beauty of the ideal—perfection of motive, thought, word, deed, form, and function—hovering just above us. But no sooner do we reach out for it, than it recedes from us—elusive, tantalizing, and painfully beyond our grasp. Finally, the volcano erupts, and a hot lava of rage pours forth from our lips: "What in the world is *wrong* with the world? Why can't things be as they *should* be?" The cry sounds like a question; in reality, it may well be a prayer.

Jesus of Nazareth answers the cry. Along with his apostles, he explicitly affirms what many of us feel: no, the world is not as it should be; and yes, something did indeed go wrong. To understand exactly what that something was, Jesus once again would have us return to Genesis, this time to its record of "the bad beginning." But he would not have us travel alone. Rather, we must take along both him and his apostles as guides. In other words, we must use the luminous revelations of the New Testament era to help us understand the dark mysteries of the Old.

The State of Man in the Garden of Eden

(Genesis 2, Romans 5, 8)

Like all orthodox Jews, Jesus followed the Hebrew scriptures in tracing evil, suffering, and death to the sin of Adam, the earthly father of the human race (John 8:44). Genesis 2 and 3 recount the whole terrible tale. Let us briefly survey it now.

In Genesis 2 we learn that the LORD God created Adam out of the dust of the ground and placed him in the Garden of Eden, to tend and enjoy it. In the midst of the garden, God had planted two special trees: the Tree of Life and the Tree of the Knowledge of Good and Evil. No special instructions were given concerning the former: Adam could eat of it any time he liked. Concerning the latter, however, God gave very strict instructions: "Of every tree of the garden you may freely eat; but of the tree of the knowledge of good and evil you shall not eat, for in the day that you eat of it you shall surely die" (Gen. 2:16-17). These pregnant words teach us several important facts about the state of Adam before his fall.

First, he was *innocent*. That is, Adam had no knowledge of good and evil. This does not mean that he was *experientially* ignorant of goodness, for everything he experienced in his short existence before the fall was good: God, the world, and himself (Gen. 1:31). It does mean, however, that he was *conceptually* ignorant of goodness: he had no *idea* of goodness, because he had no idea—or experience—of its opposite, evil. In evil, he was a babe (1 Cor. 14:20, Isaiah 7:15-16). And in this case, ignorance truly was bliss.

Secondly, he was *on probation*. In other words, God was pleased to test Adam's love for him by requiring him to obey a simple command concerning the Tree of the Knowledge of Good and Evil. How long the test was to last we do not know. Apparently, Adam himself did not know. Indeed, it is doubtful that he even knew he was on probation. But with the benefit of biblical hindsight we see clearly that he was, and that he might soon have passed his test if only he had remained loyal to God and eaten first from the Tree of Life (Gen. 3:22).[1]

Thirdly, we learn that Adam was *mutable*. This means that if he ate from either of the two trees he would immediately change, either for the better or the worse. The nature of the change is indicated by the names God gave to the two trees.

If, on the one hand, Adam were to eat of the Tree of the Knowledge of Good and Evil, he would change by coming to know good and evil. In part, this simply meant that he would awaken to the presence of evil in the cosmos, evil that had already entered with the fall of the angel Lucifer (see below). This kind of knowledge was not necessarily bad. God himself had it, and in due time might even have bestowed it, without injury, upon Adam and his children (Gen. 3:22, 1 Cor. 6:2).

There was, however, another way of knowing good and evil that was vastly more dangerous. By eating of this tree *he would come to know goodness as something that he had lost, and evil as something that he had become*. Why?

Because to eat would make him disobedient to God's commandment; it would make him a transgressor of God's law. But since God, under such circumstances, could not possibly dishonor himself by breaking his word, he would have to make good on his threat to put Adam to death. As events were soon to prove, this did not mean that God must immediately kill him physically. It did mean, however, that he must immediately withdraw his soul-sustaining power and presence in such a way that Adam would die spiritually. In other words, God's just departure from the sinning Adam would lead to a collapse of the latter's spiritual integrity, and to a resulting distortion, or pollution, of his inner life. Because of this he would come to know good and evil in a way that God can never know them: he would know evil *by knowing himself to be evil,* and goodness *by seeing it from afar, as a distant and elusive ideal.* Henceforth, goodness would be the *norm* for his existence (i.e., what he knows he *should* be and do), but a norm that now has flown away, and that cannot be retrieved by any human device. In short, if Adam were to eat of this tree, he would immediately find himself on the rack.

On the other hand, if Adam were to eat of the Tree of Life, he would change for the better: he would experience "life." Genesis reveals very little about this life, but the NT fills in the blanks. There we learn that the life God offered to Adam was nothing less than *eternal life.* Jesus himself defined this for us by saying, "This is eternal life, *that they might know You, the one true God, and Jesus Christ, whom You have sent*" (John 17:3). Thus, the NT implies that in Eden Adam did indeed have biological life, but that he did not yet have eternal life. Yes, life in that garden was glorious, but at the Tree of Life God offered Adam something more glorious still. He offered him eternal spiritual life: spiritual communion with the triune Holy Family, and that communion forever.[2]

This brings us to our final point, namely that throughout his probation Adam stood before God as the *representative of the entire human race.* He was, as it were, "our man in Eden." What he decided, he would decide for us all. What he gained, he would gain for us all. What he incurred, he would incur for us all. Moreover, his decision would impact not only his family, but his family's home: the world of nature, the whole creation. In other words, if he passed the test before him, he would, as it were, lift up all things—the very universe itself—into eternal life. On the other hand, if he failed, he would drag them down together into death and destruction.

It is true, of course, that Genesis does not explicitly teach that Adam was the "head" of the human race. Nor does it indicate that he was aware of his stupendously consequential role and responsibility. Nevertheless, from the aftermath of his sin we can see immediately that he was indeed our representative. Moreover, Jesus' apostles affirmed this very thing. Thus, we find the apostle Paul likening Adam and his transgression to a door: "Therefore, just as through one man sin entered the world, and death through sin, and thus death spread to all men, because all sinned..." (Romans 5:12).

How did all sin? Obviously not in person, since all persons were not yet born. Rather, all sinned "in Adam" and in God's sight, for in God's sight all were represented by Adam. Accordingly, the dreadful consequences of the sin of the head of the family—guilt, depravity, suffering, and death—fell not only upon him, but upon his children as well, and also upon the entire creation in which they lived.

Here then, in Genesis 3, we have our first encounter with the biblical understanding of God's dealings with mankind. It would be hard to exaggerate its importance. Fundamentally, God deals with mankind through representatives. There are two of them: the first man, Adam, and the last man, Jesus Christ. The first man ruined us, and that beyond anything he or his children could ever do to repair it. But rescue and restoration—even unto eternal life—are still possible. Indeed, they are inevitable, since God, in the fullness of time, will send another Adam—the last Adam—to do what the first failed to do, and to undo all the terrible consequences of what he has done. More on this later.

After placing Adam in Eden, God decided to create for him a companion and a helper, someone with whom he would now begin to be fruitful and multiply, thereby filling the earth and bringing forth the family of man. Accordingly, in an act full of Messianic symbolism, God put Adam to sleep, extracted a rib from his side, and from that rib fashioned a woman, "bone of his bone and flesh of his flesh" (Gen. 2:23, Eph. 5:22-33). Genesis 3 implies that Adam spoke to Eve about the forbidden tree, and that she was inclined to obey the divine warning that had come to her through her husband. Thus, for a short season at least, the probation in Eden did not seem too difficult. Soon, however, it would take them to the very brink. As never before, the original pair were about to be put to the test.

Temptation and Fall

(Gen. 3:1-6, Ezek. 28:11-19, Isaiah 14:12-15)

The biblical story of the fall of man actually begins in heaven, where, presumably on the first or second day, God created the angels. Among them was an angel of extraordinary wisdom, beauty, and rank—Lucifer, or "Day Star." Like Adam, Lucifer and the other angels were apparently on

WHAT, IF ANYTHING, WENT WRONG?

probation. The Bible says nothing about the nature of their test, only that Lucifer was the first to fail it, since shortly after his creation there came a dreadful moment when "unrighteousness was found in him" (Ezek. 28:15). This cryptic phrase marks the entrance of evil into the universe. Henceforth, the entire course of Lucifer's existence would be driven by a sinful two-fold animus: pride and hatred. In his pride, he would seek to supplant God by usurping both his worship and his sovereignty (Isaiah 14:12-15, Mt. 4:8-11). In his hatred, he would seek to wound God, primarily by using his formidable spiritual resources to injure his beloved creations (John 10:10). Thus did Lucifer become Satan (Heb., *adversary*), the adversary of God and the adversary of all that God loves, especially the race of men.

Moved by his new and evil nature, Satan immediately undertook to build a counterfeit kingdom of his own. His first prey were the other angels. The Bible indicates that he was personally active in tempting them, and that a sizable number quickly succumbed (Rev. 12:4). Through their sin, they too corrupted their original nature, transforming themselves into demons (Mark 5:1f). Some were immediately cast into *Hades*, a place of darkness and torment ordained by God for the punishment of his enemies (Luke 8:31, 2 Peter 2:4, Jude 6). Others, however, for wise reasons, were permitted by God to remain "in the heavenly places," where Satan, their overlord, arranged them into a hierarchy of evil rulers (Eph. 2:2, 6:10-12). Thus was the kingdom of Satan born, an alien "domain of darkness" in the previously perfect Kingdom of God (Mt. 12:25, Col. 1:13).

Satan's next target was Adam, whom he would tempt through his wife, whom he would tempt through a serpent. In a moment we will discuss this temptation. Here, however, let us pause to ask a common question: Why did God permit the temptation in the first place?

Answers here are many, but one thing is clear enough: God himself definitely desired to test Adam and Eve. Moreover, as we shall see later, their probation in Eden appears to set the pattern for God's dealings with mankind throughout all history. As the prophet wrote, the LORD is a God who tests the heart and the mind (Jer. 11:20). The Bible helps us to see why. Divine testing, when victoriously endured, contributes directly to the formation of godly character (James 1:2-8), earns a great and eternal reward (2 Cor. 4:17-18, 1 Peter 1:7), and brings pleasure and glory to God (Job 1:8, 2:3, John 21:19, 1 Peter 4:16). It seems that God considers such possible outcomes of testing to be worth any of the risks or sufferings involved. Therefore, for this and other reasons, he was pleased to put Adam and Eve to the test.

Unfortunately, we cannot linger here to explore the nuanced record of Adam's temptation and fall. Suffice it to say that in that hour, Satan did what came most naturally to him: he lied. Or, more precisely, he spoke numerous half-truths with an intent to deceive (John 8:44, 2 Cor. 11:14, Rev. 20:3, 8). His words to Eve involved an attack on both the word and character of God. First, he contradicted God's warning, saying that if she ate of the forbidden fruit she surely would *not* die. Then he impugned God's motives for issuing the warning, suggesting that he was selfishly, fearfully, and jealously withholding from them the best gift, the one that would make them like him: the knowledge of good and evil. In receiving the serpent's words, her heart was therefore filled with doubt about God's goodness, and also with illicit desires to free herself from his rule, become his equal, and make her way forward in life independently of him. Though the voice of conscience must loudly have warned against it, she ate.

Concerning Adam's fall, the Bible simply records that "She also gave to her husband with her, and he ate" (Gen. 3:6, NAS). Was Adam at her side throughout the temptation? So it would appear. In any case, the apostle Paul insists that Adam was not deceived (2 Cor. 11:3, 1 Tim. 2:14). Why, then, did he eat? Was it simply to please his wife, or at least not to displease her? Or did he want, like her, to know good and evil—especially since that knowledge, in her case, had seemingly produced no ill effects?[3] The Bible does not say. Yet this much is sure: because Adam was not deceived, he was all the more culpable, for he had nothing like Eve's excuse for disobeying, and was therefore exercising the purer form of rebellion against his creator and Lord.

Many people today regard the biblical story of the fall of man and nature as a myth. How, they ask incredulously, can anyone believe that God would attach such cosmically disastrous consequences to a man's eating a piece of fruit, forbidden or not?

The answer, of course, is that the consequences attach, not to Adam's eating a piece of fruit, but to the (nature of the) Being who commanded him not to do so. And those consequences seem even more appropriate when we consider how well he must have known that Being (Luke 12:48). For though Adam did indeed stand only at the beginning of his life's journey, he dwelt continually in God's presence. More than most (if not all) of his sinful progeny, he beheld God's glory: his sovereignty, holiness, goodness, and more. Such perfections would have registered profoundly upon his pure spirit. Moreover, those same perfections would have plainly and powerfully set before him the path of duty and blessing: He must, in all things, be obedient, content, and profoundly grateful. How was it, then, that amidst so great a blaze of light, he and his wife together elected to spurn the voice of conscience, reckon God a liar, impugn his motives, rebel against his rightful rule, and elevate themselves to a position of equality with him?

All too well do the words of the apostle seem to apply to the guilty pair, even as they explain the seriousness of eating a piece of forbidden fruit:

> Although they knew God, they did not honor him as God, nor were they thankful, but became futile in their thoughts, and their foolish hearts were darkened...(They) exchanged the truth of God for a lie, and served the creature rather than the Creator, who is blessed forever, Amen.
> —Rom. 1:21, 25

The Consequences of the Fall
(Genesis 3:7-24)

The remainder of Genesis 3 details the consequences of Adam's fall. When supplemented with NT teaching, we realize that they were nothing less than cosmic in proportion, extending up into heaven, out across the whole face of nature, down through the generations, and deep into the recesses of the human heart. To form a complete picture of them, let us remember again that the Bible likens Adam to a door (Rom 5:12). When he sinned, many dear friends went out the door, and many deadly enemies entered in. We will survey a few of the most important now.

Friends That Went Out

Adam's greatest loss was his easy *relationship with God*. If this was not yet full spiritual sonship, it was certainly friendship. When he sinned, that friendship was broken, God withdrew, and—in immediate fulfillment of his warning—Adam died, spiritually speaking (Gen. 2:17).

With this loss, there followed necessarily a loss of *original integrity*, both spiritual and physical. Henceforth, Adam's faculties, his body, his world, and his manifold relationships were weakened, twisted, broken, and polluted beyond any human repair (Gen. 3:7-8, 14-19).

With these two losses there came a third: the loss of *original freedom*. Freedom, in biblical perspective, is never autonomy or independence, but rather the simple ability to be what one was created to be. To be free is to live according to one's own God-given nature, without hindrance.[4] Therefore, when sin wrought its dreadful change in his nature, Adam was no longer free to be his normal godly self. Indeed, apart from divine grace, he was not even *inclined* to be his normal godly self (Rom. 8:7). In other words, instead of being a slave to God and righteousness, he had become a slave to sin (John 5:42, Rom. 6). And again, the freedom that Adam lost for himself, he lost for all humanity.

Finally, and very importantly, Adam lost *access to the Tree of Life* (Gen. 3:22-24). Again, this tree represented eternal life in union with the triune God. In his innocence, Adam might have "worked" so as to receive this life for himself and his posterity: he had only to eat of this tree and thereby live forever. However, having disobeyed, he came guilty and polluted with sin, with the result that God could no longer grant him access to the Tree of Life. To do so would be for him to break his word (i.e., the threat of death), compromise his justice, and stain his honor by joining himself to a rebel. No, some provision must first be made for Adam's sin, both to forgive it and to eradicate its manifold consequences. Only then could the family of man eat from the Tree of Life; only then could they regain all that was lost.

Enemies That Came In

While many precious friends were going out the door, many deadly enemies were coming in. Moreover, these enemies did not enter simply to harass the sons of Adam, but to take them captive and, if possible, drag them down to eternal destruction. Under four broad categories, I will here touch on the most important.

First, there were *interior spiritual enemies*, enemies that took hold of the spirit (or soul) of man. Chief among them was *sin*—biblically depicted as dark, powerful, and unnatural spiritual passions (or lusts) that bend every human faculty towards self: self-satisfaction, self-exaltation, and self-rule over against the rule of God and his law.[5] In other words, indwelling sin effectively ensnares the sovereign creator's very own image-bearers in a spirit of deep-seated, hostile rebellion against his rightful dominion over their lives (Luke 19:27, John 5:42, 8:42f, Rom. 8:7, James 4:4, 1 Pet. 4:17). The apostle Paul specifically traces this condition to Adam, who "sold" his posterity "under" sin, so that henceforth all his offspring would be born in sin's chains (Rom. 7:14, Psalm 51:5). It is, however, from the lips of Jesus—of whom it is written that he knew full well what lurks in man—that we receive the most piercing diagnosis of the human heart (John 2:25):

> For from within, out of the heart of men, proceed evil thoughts, adulteries, fornications, murders, thefts, covetousness, wickedness, deceit, licentiousness, an evil eye, blasphemy, pride, foolishness. All these evil things come from within and defile a man.
> —Mark 7:21-22

Another spiritual enemy is *guilt*. Biblically, true guilt (as opposed to psychological or man-made guilt) is a subjective awareness of an objective fact: one has fallen short of God's standard in who one is and what one has done. Unless a man's conscience is past feeling, his guilt typically involves fear (of divine punishment) and shame (1 Tim. 4:2, Eph. 4:19, 1 John 4:18). It can also produce desperate acts by which he hopes to get free from such feelings. So it was with Adam and Eve who, having sinned, immediately awoke to their guilt, felt ashamed of their nakedness (i.e., they knew that God could "see right through them"), tried to cover themselves with fig leaves, and instinctively fled at God's approach (Gen. 3:7-8). The Bible repeatedly confirms what their experience teaches: true guilt can be a formidable enemy indeed, capable of darkening the entire sky of one's existence, crushing the spirit, and even sickening the flesh (Psalm 5, Mark 2:1-12, Luke 7:36-50).

Secondly, there were *physical enemies*. When Adam sinned, God cursed the whole of nature, so that a host of physical evils entered the world. Genesis itself supplies some important examples. God cursed the serpent, so that henceforth, in all vulnerability, it would go upon its belly on the ground (Gen. 3:14). He cursed the cattle and the beasts of the field (i.e., the entire animal world), thereby introducing animal violence and a dreadful new economy of predation (Gen. 3:15, Lev. 26:22, Isaiah 11:6-9). He cursed Eve's body, so that she and her daughters would give birth in pain (Gen. 3:16). He cursed the ground (and the entire plant kingdom), so that henceforth it would yield its treasures reluctantly, barring the way with thorns and thistles (Gen. 3:17). And he cursed man's body, so that through death what had originally come from the ground would, contrary to God's plan, return to it again (3:19).

In short, the curse introduced the entire spectrum of what theologians call *natural evil:* birth defects, pain, fatigue, injury, sickness, old age, physical death, drought, famine, plague, pestilence, earthquake, storm, and more. Fallen man, according to the Bible, often reckons these manifestations of the curse to be a sign of God's indifference, cruelty, or non-existence (Prov. 19:3). However, as we shall see below, they are far better understood as "severe mercies," wisely and benevolently designed for our eternal good.

Next, there were *Satanic enemies*. When Adam sinned he effectively repudiated God's rule over his life, came out from under his protection, took on Satan's fallen nature, and unwittingly placed himself under Satan's spiritual influence (John 8:44). Moreover, what he did for himself, he did for the entire race: he "handed it over" into Satan's custody, thus incorporating the family of man into Satan's growing kingdom of darkness (Luke 4:5-7, Mt. 4:8-9, 12:26). Here, then, is the beginning of what the NT calls "the world," or "the world system." The world, in the dark sense of the word, is human society insofar as it is separated from God, going its way independently of him, and largely organized, energized, and directed by Satan and his demonic hosts. Jesus himself acknowledged these sobering realities, thrice calling Satan "the ruler of this world," (John 12:31, 14:30, 16:11).

Because this unseen ruler is also a deadly enemy, the NT writers are at pains to expose his purposes, plans, and procedures to all men (John 10:10). Again, Satan's purposes are to feed his pride by usurping the worship of God's creations, and also to wound God by destroying as many of those creations as he can (1 Pet. 5:8). His plan for accomplishing this is to set in place over the peoples of the earth a vast hierarchy of demonic "rulers and authorities" (Eph. 6:12). Moving about in the air, these invisible evil angels determine "the course of this world," secretly influencing the thoughts, passions, and deeds of men (Eph. 2:2).

In all of this, Satan's procedures are manifold. Sometimes he entices men and nations into gross sins that quickly engulf them in depravity (Rom. 1:18f), demon-possession (Mark 5:1f), and final destruction (Lev. 18). Other times he entangles them in idolatry, turning perverted forms of politics, religion, philosophy, culture, and commerce into false gods (1 Cor. 10:20, Eph. 2:2, Rev. 12, 13, 17). His strategy here is so to feed man's fallen nature—his self-centered lust for pleasure, power, fame, and fortune—that he (man) has neither time nor inclination to heed God's call, and so perishes in the end (Gal. 5:16, 2 Peter 1:4; Mt. 6:19-34, Luke 12: 13-21, 16:19f, Rom. 1:18-32). Furthermore, if any of God's loyal human servants should attempt to stand in his way by preaching and teaching God's truth, Satan will quickly flood their minds with temptations (Eph. 6:16), sow their assemblies with false teachers (Mt. 7:15, 2 Cor. 11:13-15, 1 John 2:19), and move unbelievers to oppose, slander, persecute, and even kill them (Mt. 10:25, 1 Pet. 5:8-10, Rev. 2:10, 12:1f).

While the modern mind often scoffs at the notion of Satanic enemies, the NT writers regard them with utmost seriousness. At any given time, the majority of mankind are their (unwitting) slaves (Rev. 12:9). The ungodly are ensnared by the devil, having been taken captive by him to do his will (2 Tim. 2:24-26). The fallen world is Satan's "domain," a prison-house of darkness (Col. 1:13). It lies in the hand and power of the evil one, so much so that he can summon entire empires onto the stage of history (1 John 5:19, Rev. 13:1). Satan is a "strong man" who holds the fallen sons of Adam as his helpless goods; they are unsuspecting slaves who could not possibly escape his prison-house, even if they wanted to. Their only hope, says Jesus, is that someone stronger than Satan should enter the prison-house: to open their eyes, change their hearts, and thereby set them free from an evil enemy whose sole intent is to steal, kill, and destroy (Mt. 12:22-30, John 10:10).

Finally, Adam's sin brought upon the world a dark trinity of *divine enemies: condemnation, wrath,* and *the peril of eternal punishment.* Though hidden in God, these are by far the most deadly and fearsome enemies of all.

Because Adam represented all, his sin brought *condemnation* upon all. This means that all stand (or at one time have stood) guilty before God as transgressors of his law, and therefore worthy of death in every form: spiritual, physical, and eternal (Rom. 5:12, 16, 18). Furthermore, this inherited condemnation can be aggravated by one's own sins, so that on the last day some people will be worthy of "greater condemnation" than others (Mark 12:40). Divine condemnation is a profoundly menacing enemy because fallen man can do nothing to defeat it. The divine standard for acceptance is complete moral perfection, embodied in the character of God, the Law of God, and the Christ of God (Mt. 5:48, Rom. 3:23; Psalm 19:7, Rom. 7:12f; Mt. 10:25, John 1:14, 8:46, Romans 8:29). Moreover, such perfection is not confined to deeds alone, but also includes attitudes, thoughts, and words (Mt. 5:21-30). Therefore, no sinner can attain it, no matter how good or how abundant his works (Rom. 3:19-20, 8:3-4). If ever he is to stand before God uncondemned, it is God himself who must find a way to forgive him and to clothe him with a perfect righteousness not his own.

Closely related to condemnation is divine *wrath.* This is not to be understood as an impersonal principle, like the *karma* of the Hindus and Buddhists, but rather as a true passion in a true person: God (Ex. 32:11, Deut. 29:28, 31:17, Psalm 5:5-6, 7:11-13). It does not cancel God's love, eliminate his generosity, or eclipse his pity for the wounded sons of Adam (Ex. 34:6, Psalm 103:14, Mt. 6:43, 9:36). Still, he cannot and will not look on impassively while men suppress his truth in unrighteousness and knowingly dishonor their creator and king (Rom. 1:18f). To the contrary, their defiance awakens his anger—an anger that grows with every willful sin, and that is "stored up" against the Day of Judgment when, in painful retributions, it will be fully and terribly unleashed (Rom. 2:1-16).[6] Jesus assures us that this wrath looms over individuals, cities, nations, and the whole world (Mt. 23:33, 11:20-24, Luke 13:1f, 21:23, 36; cf., John 3:36, Eph. 2:1-3). As with divine condemnation, there is nothing man can do to remove it. Unless God devises a means of placating himself, his wrath will fall on every sinful soul.

This brings us to the last and most fearsome divine enemy, *the peril of eternal punishment.* This consummate divine judgment is actually two-fold, involving eternal separation from every life-giving blessing of God, along with eternal subjection to his wrath under painful retributions throughout the age to come (2 Thess. 1:9). No biblical figure speaks of this enemy more often or more forcefully than Jesus of Nazareth. To give but one example, he warns his disciples, "Do not fear those who kill the body but cannot kill the soul. But rather fear Him who is able to destroy both soul and body

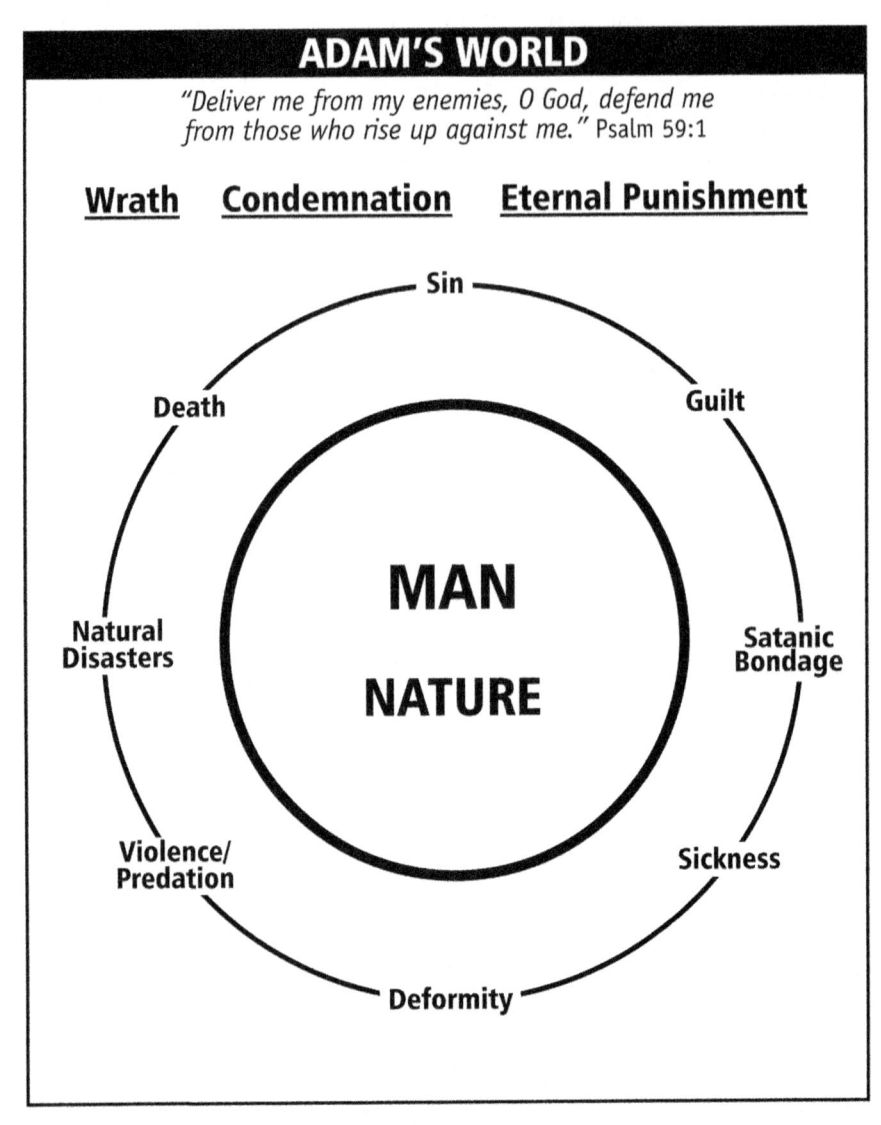

ADAM'S WORLD

"Deliver me from my enemies, O God, defend me from those who rise up against me." Psalm 59:1

Wrath   Condemnation   Eternal Punishment

- Sin -
- Death
- Guilt
- Natural Disasters
- Satanic Bondage
- Violence/Predation
- Sickness
- Deformity

MAN NATURE

in hell" (Mt. 10:28). Just as condemnation and wrath loom above, so too the peril of hell lurks beneath. For the moment—amongst the living, at least—these enemies stand strangely at bay. Yet they will not do so forever. If, then, God has made a way of escape, men must now do all they can to find it. They must find the appointed door through which they may safely "flee the wrath to come" (Mt. 3:7, 1 Thess. 1:10).

Conclusion

Our goal in this chapter has been to hear Jesus on the third question of life, "What went wrong?" His answer is: Adam's sin gave us "Adam's world." It is a world created and loved by God, yet alienated from him. Here, both man and nature have lost their original friendship with their maker, along with their original integrity, freedom, and access to the Tree of Life. Here, all people have been delivered into the hands of a host of deadly enemies: spiritual, physical, Satanic, and divine. Truly, Adam's world is a "domain of darkness," a dark prison-house from which none of his sons or daughters have the moral standing or spiritual power to deliver themselves.

Yet there is hope. For though God might instantly have destroyed the world when Adam sinned, he did not. In fact, instead of killing Adam, he actually sought him out and—in still another richly symbolic gesture— clothed both him and his wife (Gen. 3:9, 21). Somehow, Adam and Eve found mercy and grace. So too did Abel, Seth, Enoch, Noah, Abraham, Isaac, Jacob, Joseph, and many more. Thus, for reasons unexplained in the OT, Adam's sin did not prevent God from continuing to relate to Adam's race. To the contrary, he went on testing men individually, and he went on gathering to himself a willing people for his own possession. But how could he do this justly? Was not all such unmerited favor to sinners a violation of his word and a compromise of his standards? Or did he have in mind some kind of plan, a plan by which he might satisfy the demands of his own justice, yet also rescue a beloved people from their enemies and bring them safely back to the Tree of Life? In other words, were the OT saints somehow already benefiting from something great—something redemptive—that God was going to do one day up ahead?

To read the Old Testament is to learn that many prophets and wise men asked these very questions, and that they did indeed receive from God rich promises of just such a day. To read the New Testament is to learn from Jesus and his apostles that that day has dawned at last!

Especially for Seekers

It is commonly argued that the presence of evil, suffering, and death in the world is the Achilles heel of biblical religion. Critics charge, understandably enough, that it seems impossible to reconcile these dark facts of life with the sovereignty, omnipotence, and goodness of God. Accordingly, they contend that "the problem of evil" presents us with an insuperable barrier to a conscientious and reasonable faith in the God of the Hebrew scriptures.

Theologians respond by pointing out that the situation here is far more complex than it seems. As a rule, they admit that the Bible does not supply us with an exhaustive "theodicy," that is, a thorough explanation of the problem of evil. They argue, however, that it is both reasonable and right to exercise faith in what God *has* revealed on this matter, rather than to defect from him because of what he has not. Moreover, they go on to point out that the undeniable reality of evil is problematic for *all* worldviews; that some explain it better than others; and, indeed, that the Bible explains it best of all. In sum, they urge seekers to recognize that while the biblical theology of evil may be incomplete, it is nevertheless sufficiently intuitive, reasonable, hopeful, and right to enable us to make our way confidently through a land of shadow until, one day up ahead, we see more fully in a land of light.

But because these things are so important, let us consider them in further detail. We will do so by way of a careful evaluation of Jesus' overall teaching on the origin of evil, suffering, and death.

To begin with, we see that Jesus' doctrine rests squarely upon a number of fundamental human intuitions. For example, unlike naturalism (which cannot provide a credible explanation for our powerful and inescapable moral intuitions), it affirms that there is a god, that he is personal, that he is good, and that his creation—despite a mysterious invasion of evil—is also good. Unlike pantheism, it affirms that God is metaphysically separate from his creation, and especially from the evil we now find in it. Very importantly, it also affirms that evil entered the world, not as the result of a divine deed, but a human misdeed. In other words, unlike pantheistic worldviews, Jesus' cosmogony does exactly what our ethical intuitions require: it safeguards the holiness of the creator by tracing moral and natural evil back to the sin of the human creature. We conclude, then, that Jesus' cosmogony is not only intuitive, but also significantly more intuitive than naturalistic and pantheistic worldviews.

Nevertheless, the question remains: Is it reasonable for us to believe it? Here, Christians respond by directing the seeker's attention to several different lines of evidence.

First, there is the panoply of supernatural signs supporting the trustworthiness of Jesus' teaching, and that of the Bible as a whole. Just as these confirm the biblical revelation about the good beginning, so too they support its teaching about the bad.

Next, there is the testimony of human expectation, which, as we saw earlier, persistently looks for the good, and is just as persistently scandalized by the evil. Closely related to this habit of mind is the perennial human tendency towards idealism, even utopianism; a tendency that displays man's innate desire to bring heaven to earth, to make the ideal real in history and experience. In the naturalistic and pantheistic universes, these two proclivities make little or no sense. They are, however, richly illuminated by the biblical. In other words, they too confirm what Jesus and Genesis teach: that man was *made* for heaven on earth, that it was somehow forfeited in the past, but that (for those with a will to seek) it awaits us in a world to come.

Still another line of evidence favorable to the biblical teaching was introduced by the Christian philosopher, Blaise Pascal (1623-1662). Pascal argued that the biblical worldview alone can explain one of the most painful paradoxes of human existence: *that man is at once both good and evil, glorious and wretched, divine and depraved.* He speaks of it thus:

> What sort of freak then is man! How novel, how monstrous, how chaotic, how paradoxical! Judge of all things, feeble earthworm; repository of truth, sink of doubt and error; the glory and the refuse of the universe... Man's greatness and wretchedness are so evident that the true religion must necessarily teach us that there is in man some great principle of greatness and some great principle of wretchedness."[7]

If we follow Pascal, we must conclude that naturalism is not the true religion, since it cannot explain man's hunger for spiritual greatness, sometimes pursued even at the cost of one's own physical survival. Similarly, pantheism cannot be the true religion, since it does not explain why a sentient being (i.e., man) who is locked up in a phenomenal world of opposites should so naturally, persistently, and ardently desire a good world, rather than to transcend both good and bad through mystical experience. The true religion, then, must be found in the Bible, for it alone explains both man's greatness (he is cast in the image and likeness of God) and also his wretchedness (he has fallen from his god-likeness). In other words, the Bible alone explains why man is "on the rack," ever called upward to truth, goodness, and beauty; ever dragged downward into error, evil, and ugliness. He is on the rack because Adam put him there, bequeathing to his children "the knowledge of good and evil," so that henceforth they are haunted by a goodness that seems irrevocably lost, and gripped by an evil that will not let them go. This, says Pascal, is why man is both majestic and miserable—and ever hungry to hear good news of a way back to freedom, fulfillment, and Paradise.

The biblical cosmogony of evil is also supported by solid evidence for the existence of evil spirits. It appears in many quarters. As we have seen, nearly all world religions teach that evil spirits exist. Indeed, animistic cultures are almost wholly pre-occupied with them, ever seeking to please and/or placate their invisible enemies. Meanwhile, here in the West, spiritists and New Age channelers have lately conceded that some "astral entities" are neither truthful nor benign. Also, not a few Western psychiatrists now quietly admit that demonic oppression or possession may be the best explanation for some of the mental disorders they are called upon to treat. Finally, there is the disturbing phenomenon of radical sociopathology, as, for example, when a crazed individual commits a particularly ghoulish crime, or when whole tribes or nations go on sudden, genocidal rampages. How are we to explain these things? Is it not reasonable at least to wonder if such persons were not seized and driven by powers even more wicked than themselves? In sum, while we may not like the biblical teaching on Satan and evil spirits, we must admit that it goes far towards illuminating some of the darkest corners of our world. This is precisely what we would expect the one true worldview to do.

Finally, we have the testimony of missionaries and anthropologists living among tribal peoples who apparently still retain an historical memory of the fall. One such tribe is the Sulawesi of Indonesia. Their age-old story of "The Snake and the Man" parallels the biblical account at nearly every point. It speaks of a single creator god ("The One Who Formed Our Fingers"), a garden ("a beautiful place"), the original blessedness of the original pair ("their fire never went out and their flasks were always full"), forbidden fruit, a snake, a temptation, the man's disobedience, the pair's expulsion from the beautiful place, painful physical consequences ("the water, the firewood, and the food no longer came by themselves"), the withdrawal of God ("he is now above and very far away"), and eventual death—which Sulawesi rituals can sometimes briefly forestall, but never prevent. Though not as abundant as those of a global flood, extant legends of a fall powerfully confirm the biblical cosmogony, making it still more reasonable to believe.[8]

We find, then, that Jesus' answer to the question about "what went wrong" seems both intuitive and reasonable. But is it right? Does it satisfy the demands of our distinctly moral intuitions? We have just seen that it does, and that it does so better than the naturalistic and pantheistic alternatives. Nevertheless, because Jesus posits a holy, sovereign, loving, and just God, his teaching on evil does indeed raise a number of serious ethical questions. Let us therefore briefly address a few of the most important.

Is Representative Headship Just?

First, there is the question of how a just God can curse the whole world—the human race, the animals, and all the rest of nature—for one man's sin. More particularly, is it right that God should impute Adam's sin to all his children, so that all are born guilty and under condemnation, even though they themselves have not yet done anything wrong? This problem seems all the more acute when we remember that God himself assures us that, "The soul who sins is the one who will die. The son shall not bear the guilt of the father, nor the father bear the guilt of the son. The righteousness of the righteous shall be upon himself, and the wickedness of the wicked shall be upon himself" (Ezek. 18:20). Did God do to the family of Adam what he said he would never do to the families of Israel?

In response, we must begin by noting the obvious: because Adam—and Adam alone—stood as mankind's representative in Eden, his case is unique. To Ezekiel, God states the general rule: though children may groan under the consequences of their father's sins, their personal standing before God depends upon their personal responses to him (Ex. 20:5). The rule is: the sins of the fathers are not imputed to the children. However, in the case of Adam—the head of the entire human race—there is an exception to the rule.

Importantly, this exception actually appears to be a mercy. For suppose that each of Adam's children had to stand alone before God and take his own test, rather than come to him through a representative. In that case, if a man fell, he would have no hope of salvation or eternal life: he has failed the test, *and there is no provision for him to get back to God through a representative*. It appears, then, that God, foreseeing the many who would sin, elected to have all sin through a bad representative (the first Adam), so that under a system of headship he might be able to save a people through a good representative (the last Adam, Jesus Christ). Moreover, under a system of individual testing, a single sin would be sufficient to destroy a soul forever. But under a system of representative headship, many sins can be forgiven if a good head has somehow made provision for them all. Thus, far from being unjust, the pattern of representative headship laid down in Eden seems to reveal God establishing a very special kind of justice, one that allows him not only to be just towards sinners, but merciful as well (Rom. 3:26).

Observe also from the Bible that the God-ordained system of headship does not cancel God's individual dealings with man. Under easy circumstances, God tested Adam concerning the fruit of a particular tree. Under difficult circumstances, he has ever since tested Adam's children concerning their own obedience to his revealed will, however this may have been made known to them.[9] The Bible teaches, then, that God deals with all equally: all must take a test. Moreover, it is worth noting that Adam's children may well be in a better position to pass the test than he was, since they have known the pain of life in a fallen world—pain carefully designed and calibrated by God to move people towards him and his truth, so that they may learn how to live right and die well (Psalm 107, Amos 4:6-13, Heb. 12:3-11, Rev. 3:19). Perhaps, then, the sons of Adam should not be too quick to bemoan their sorrows, or to blame the sovereign One who, in wisdom and love, places those sorrows upon them.

Having said all this, we must not forget that the Bible also traces much of our suffering, not to Adam's sin or to God's curse, but simply to our own bad choices. "Do not be deceived," warned the apostle. "God is not mocked; whatsoever a man sows, that he will also reap" (Gal. 6:7, Prov. 22:8). Importantly, this affirmation sits well with moral intuition. It seems altogether fair and just to us that God should bring upon men exactly what they have brought upon God and their fellow man, whether it be good or evil.

Why Do the Innocent Suffer?

It is easy enough to understand the suffering of the wicked: In a world governed by a holy, just, and sovereign God, this is only to be expected. But, as Rabbi Kushner asks, "Why do bad things happen to good people?" What theological sense can we make of the fact that folks simply going about their own business so often fall victim to crime, abuse, oppression, genocide, disease, starvation, tragic accidents, and various natural calamities? Is it that God is not really in charge (as Rabbi Kushner concludes), or is it that he is not good after all?

The Bible does not dodge these serious and difficult questions. Indeed, as if to calm our fears on this very score, it repeatedly gives us the stories—and the anguished cries—of men and women like Job, Joseph, Jeremiah, Lazarus, Martha, and Mary: good people, yet great sufferers. Were they mystified by their pain? Were they scandalized by its apparent injustice? Were they shaken by God's seeming indifference to it? "Yes" to all of the above. Yet in the end they understood—and took refuge in the fact—that despite the inscrutability of his ways, a sovereign God was indeed in control; and that a purposeful, just, and compassionate God meant it for their good (Gen. 50:20, Rom. 8:28).

In their case we therefore discover the Bible's nuanced approach to the problem of the suffering of the innocent: While it does not seek *fully* to resolve the element of mystery, it nevertheless reveals enough to richly encourage the element of faith. In so doing, God gives saints and seekers alike good reason—and ample opportunity—to trust, please, and glorify their holy Creator and King.

Since this question weighs so heavily upon the minds of so many, let us survey some key biblical affirmations designed to bring light and comfort to all who wrestle with the problem of the suffering of the innocent poor.

First, *God is indeed sovereign over their suffering.* In other words, God is the one who ordains, permits, and controls it. This conclusion flows logically from the biblical declaration of God's absolute sovereignty over *all* events (more on this below). Moreover, it is the explicit teaching of scripture. Has calamity struck a city? Is someone born mute, deaf, blind, or otherwise handicapped? Are the saints suffering grievous persecution? The LORD himself has done it (Amos 3:6, Ex. 4:11, 1 Thess. 3:3). Yes, this affirmation raises difficult theological questions. But once we believe that God is good—and that he does not "willingly" (i.e., with malicious pleasure) afflict or grieve the children of men—his sovereignty can actually become a source of great comfort (Lam. 3:3). For which is worse: to puzzle why a good God would appoint us to this or that particular affliction, or to believe—and fear—that he is either unable or unwilling to control the affliction; that at any moment, when his eye is briefly turned away, some random disaster or wicked scheme might sneak across his desk in order to destroy us? Here, then, was Job's ultimate anguish, but also his ultimate solace: God is sovereign, *and* God is good. Believing this, he could therefore survey the utter wreckage of his life, and still ask, "Shall we indeed accept good from God, and not adversity? The LORD gave, and the LORD has taken away; blessed be the name of the LORD" (Job 1:21. 2:10, 38:11).

Secondly, *all suffering is traceable to man's sin.* As we have seen, it was Adam, not God, who brought the curse upon creation (a curse that has wise and benevolent purposes). Moreover, it is clear that a great deal of human suffering stems not from natural calamities, but from man's own freely chosen inhumanity to man. Is a child starving in Africa? Look for a wicked ruler who cares more about his power than his people. Is a promising high school student killed or crippled for life in a car wreck? Look for a drunk driver who hit her head on. Are little children criminally neglected or abused? Look for absentee dads, drug-addicted moms, or dead-beat boyfriends. Yes, the Bible represents God as sovereign over all such suffering (an intuitively known fact that makes us wonder why he did not step in to prevent it); but it also represents sinful man as being *responsible* for it, and as being responsible for doing something about it. Here then is a true truism: If we all would simply do as Jesus said—love God and love our neighbor—the world would be halfway to Paradise (Mt. 22:34-40).

Thirdly, *no one is "innocent."* It is true, of course, that relative to man's law many sufferers are innocent: Though they were minding their own business and committing no crime, disaster—for no *apparent* reason—suddenly struck (Psalms 7:4, 55:20). However, relative to God and his law, they are *not* innocent, for all people—even tiny babies—are born in sin (i.e., with a sin nature), commit sin, and lie under condemnation for sin (both their own and Adam's) (Psalm 51:5). Moreover, since all must one day stand before the judgment seat of Christ, all must receive salvation now, in this world, in order safely to enter the next (John 3:36, 5:24, 8:24, 2 Cor. 6:2).

This axiom of biblical faith, so often overlooked or rejected by modern critics, is indispensable for a right understanding of the suffering of the "innocent." For what if God, knowing a sinner's true condition before him—and looking ahead to the perils of the Judgment—determines that a measure of sorrow in this life is necessary in order to secure an infinitely greater measure of joy in the next? This is, of course, precisely the biblical view: *All* suffering is related to man's sin (whether ours or Adam's), with the result that *much* suffering—including the suffering of the "innocent" poor—is related to God's redeeming love for sinful mankind (Rom. 5:1-5, 12, 8:18-23; Acts 14:22).

This brings us to our fourth point, namely, that *God has wise and benevolent purposes in the suffering of the innocent poor.* By way of introduction here, observe carefully that the Bible does not view earthly suffering as *punishment* for sin: There is only one punishment for sin, and that is death (Gen. 2:17, Ezek. 18:20, Rom. 6:23). Instead, earthly suffering—in very large part—is best understood as *chastening* or *discipline*. That is, it has a redemptive purpose, being designed to promote repentance, faith, holiness of life, and other spiritual and temporal goods (Heb. 12:1-13).

God pursues these ends among different categories of people. In the case of the sufferers themselves, he wisely uses their pain—and his own goodness in the midst of it—to move them towards salvation. In order to understand this crucial point, let us consider a truly "hard case," the case of an unborn baby about to suffer a painful death at the hand of an abortionist. Surely no one in the world is more innocent, weak, vulnerable, and "poor" than she. Yet she is still a sinner, and therefore in need of a savior. Could it be, then, that in the brief season of her agony, God—in mercy, love, and grace—secretly works in her little heart so as to turn her to Christ? While she is yet in her mother's womb, could he mature her, teach her, convict her, and graciously draw her to the Savior—all in "the twinkling of an eye"? Though we cannot dogmatically affirm this scenario, a number of biblical texts suggest that something like it is quite probable (Psalm 22:10, 71:6, Isaiah 48:14-15, Mt. 19:14, Luke 1:44, 1 Cor. 15:50-57). And what is true for the unborn baby, may, in slightly different ways, be true for other "innocent" sufferers as well. In wisdom and love, God skillfully uses their pain to turn otherwise reluctant eyes upon Jesus, thereby creating in them a miraculous deposit of repentance, faith, and new spiritual life (Deut. 4:25-31, Judges 6:1-6, Psalms 32, 107, Zech. 12:10f, Mark 5:1-20, John 11:1-44).

The suffering of the innocent poor can serve other purposes as well. Suppose, for example, that a criminal, an oppressor, or an abusive parent has injured or killed an innocent person. Will not the victim's innocence—along with his evident pain and sorrow—magnify the perpetrator's sense of guilt? And might not this in due season move him to seek relief at the feet of the Savior (Mt. 27:3-10, 15-24, Mark 6:14-29, Luke 18:13, Acts 2:37-39)? Or perhaps the suffering of the innocent poor will induce a thoughtful seeker to contemplate the ultimate cause—and cure—of the world's grievous injustices (Psalm 73). Moreover, perhaps it will move him—and some of the saints as well—to try to rectify one or more of those injustices, and so to turn to God for the wisdom and help that they will surely need (Psalm 94, Prov. 24:11-12). Or again, perhaps such suffering will awaken in the rich and powerful a greater compassion for the poor (Luke 10:25f, 16:19f), a compassion that leads to sacrificial service on earth and rich rewards in heaven (Luke 7:7-14). Yes, on the face of it, the suffering of the innocent often seems appallingly senseless. Yet the Bible encourages us not to avert our eyes, but instead to look a little deeper, and so to discover the various ways in which a sovereign God can use temporary suffering to produce eternal good (2 Cor. 4:17).

Fifthly, *God deals justly with the innocent poor.* This theme pervades the scriptures. Over and again we see how God—who loves a just balance—is pleased to make the (believing) poor of this life unspeakably rich in the next, even as he makes the (unbelieving) rich of this world unspeakably poor in the world to come (1 Sam. 2, Psalm 17, Luke 1:46-56, 2 Thess. 1:3-12). Jesus himself said it this way:

> Blessed are you poor, for yours is the kingdom of God. Blessed are you who hunger now, for you shall be filled. Blessed are you who weep now, for you shall laugh... But woe to you who are rich, for you have received your consolation. Woe to you who are full, for you shall hunger. Woe to you who laugh now, for you shall mourn and weep...
> —Luke 20-26; Mt. 5:3f

No, this is not to say that salvation is based upon poverty, for salvation is always based upon faith in Christ (John 3:16, Rom. 3:28, Eph. 2:8). But it is to say that God often bestows such faith upon the poor (thus making them savingly "poor in spirit"), even as he often withholds it from the rich (thus leaving them in their sinful pride and self-righteousness), (Mt. 5:2, Luke 18:9-14, 1 Cor. 2:26-31, James 2:5-7). From such biblical affirmations of ultimate justice we may therefore reasonably conclude that the rich and powerful king Herod had his good things in this life, while the child martyrs of Bethlehem, whom he cruelly slew for Christ's sake, now have theirs in the next (Mt. 2:16-18, Luke 16:19f). This means that their suffering was not a blot on God's sovereignty or goodness, but instead a testimony to his inscrutable wisdom, justice, and sovereign grace.

Finally, *God is compassionate towards the innocent poor and actively involved in their suffering*. Repeatedly, the Bible affirms that the LORD is good to all; that he has compassion on all that he has made (Psalm 145:9; Ex. 34:6, Psalms 86:15, 103:13, 2 Cor. 1:3, James 5:11). In love and pity he freely and feelingly enters into the suffering of his creatures, especially those of his own people: "In all their affliction, he too was afflicted" (Isaiah 63:9). The divine empathy is most fully revealed in the divine Christ, of whom it is written that he had compassion on the sick, the hungry, the confused, and the bereaved (Mt. 9:36, 14:14, 20:34, Mark 8:2, Luke 7:13). Being himself a man of sorrows acquainted with grief, he could weep with those who weep; being himself familiar with temptation, persecution, and pain, he could (and can) be a compassionate High Priest, touched with the feeling of his people's infirmities (Isaiah 53:3, Luke 4:1-33, 22:39-46, John 11:35, Heb. 4:14-16).

Very importantly, God's compassion is not divorced from specific acts of kindness to those who suffer. For example, in wisdom, love, and mercy the sovereign Lord sets precise boundaries around each person's trial, saying to its proud waves, "This far you may come, and no farther" (Job 38:11, Mt. 24:22, 1 Cor. 10:13)! Also, when the trial has served its benevolent purpose, God is faithful to open up a way of escape (1 Cor. 10:13, James 1:4, 1 Peter 5:10). Thus, like the fourth Man who appeared in the fiery furnace alongside Shadrach, Meshach, and Abed-nego, God is not only *with* his people in their suffering, but also *working* to shield them and to bring them through it (Daniel 3, Isaiah 43:2).

Such promises are not to be interpreted naively. Suffering is real, and death may well be its terminus (Luke 21:16-19). But who knows what secret comforts the God of compassion is pleased to bestow upon his hurting children? With good reason, Christ himself could cry out, "My God, my God, why have you forsaken me?" (Mt. 27:46). Yet even he, at the nadir of his agony, could declare, "I am not alone; the Father is with me" (John 16:32). Might not this have been the experience of all the aborted babies; or of many, many prisoners in the Nazi death camps; or of many, many office workers in the Twin Towers (Psalm 34:17)? Who can tell what invisible transactions occur between sinful men and their Redeemer as they pass together through such dire straits? Dare we judge by appearance only, and not with righteous (i.e., biblically informed) judgment (John 7:24)?

I conclude by reiterating the point with which we began: While the Bible has not given us an exhaustive explanation of the suffering of the innocent poor, it has told us much. In essence, it reveals that sinful man is responsible for all such suffering, but that a good, just, wise, purposeful, compassionate, and deeply involved triune God holds it firmly in his all-controlling hands. Such a revelation puts all men—saints and seekers alike—to the test. Will they focus on the truth they *do* have, give God their allegiance, and trust him for what presently lies in shadow (1 Cor. 8:2, 13:8-12)? Or will they focus on the truth they *don't* have, trust him for nothing, and deny the very possibility of an explanation—or withhold their allegiance until he gives them one on demand?

Those inclined to the latter option would do well to read again the story of Job. This devout and righteous man was at a complete loss to understand why God had seemingly turned his back on him and his family. Amidst terrible trials—and being absolutely convinced of his own innocence—he had but one desire: to have his day in court with the Almighty. In the end, God granted him his petition. However, when the day arrived, there were no explanations. To the contrary, it was God who now questioned the questioner; it was God who put Job in the dock, altogether exposing the profound ignorance of his finite, sinful, and creaturely mind (Job 38-42).

What then was Job's response to the divine Interrogator, and to this direct confrontation with his glory—a glory overflowing with truth, justice, wisdom, goodness, and the sovereign prerogatives of an omnipotent Creator? Beholding in that radiant light the utter folly and cosmic impropriety of his judging God or calling him into account, he said:

> I am unworthy—how can I reply to you?
> I put my hand over my mouth.
> I spoke once, but I have no answer;
> Twice, but I will say no more...
> My ears had heard of you,
> But now my eyes have seen you.
> Therefore, I despise myself,
> And repent in dust and ashes.
> —Job 40:4-5, 42:5-6

If, as the Bible warns, every one of us is to have his own day in court before this great God, would it not be reasonable for those with unresolved questions about the suffering of the innocent poor to remember blessed Job's reply, and even now to do and say the same?

Why Are Nature and the Animals Burdened with the Painful Consequences of Man's Sin?

But what of the ugliness, violence, and agony found in nature? Why must the non-human orders suffer for Adam's sin? More particularly, why would a just and compassionate God place such heavy burdens on birds, fish, insects, and animals that not only *did not* sin, but *cannot* sin?

Here again, we may not have all the answers, but the Bible does bring a number of good ones to our attention.

First, the brokenness, ugliness, and opposition found in nature serve well to restrain the pantheistic impulse in man. Spending a spring morning in Yosemite, one might be tempted to worship nature as god; spending a summer afternoon in Death Valley, one will not be so tempted again. The curse on the whole creation keeps man from a perennial temptation and a most grievous sin: worshiping the creature rather than the creator (Rom. 1: 24-25).

Secondly, blights upon nature are designed to teach man important lessons about the character and consequences of sin. Disease, injury, drought, famine, pestilence, earthquake, whirlwind and more—all are used in Scripture to depict the ugliness and devastation that are visited on personal and national evil. In this vein, the Bible regularly draws upon darkness in the animal world to warn and instruct sinners. Vicious speech is likened to the poison of asps (Rom. 3:13, James 3:8); death to the sting of a scorpion (1 Cor. 15:55-56); quarrelsomeness and feuding to animals that bite and devour (Gal. 5:15); the divine Judge of the wicked to a lion who tears his prey (Psalm 50:22); and depraved men to brute beasts that are ready to be destroyed (by God) virtually at first sight (2 Pet. 2:12). In the beginning, God designed the natural world to be a mirror in which men might behold the glorious attributes of their maker. After the fall, it became a mirror in which they must now also behold, vividly and viscerally, the ravages of sin, and—in a severe mercy—glimpses of hell itself.[10]

Finally, the suffering of animal life must be kept in perspective. As with men, so with the animals: their suffering is relatively rare and usually brief. "The LORD is good to all and His tender mercies are over all His works" (Psalm 145:9). Moreover, the animal world not only retains much happiness, but much beauty and goodness as well, so that most animals can picture to the saints important truths about God, Christ, the Spirit, and sound character (Deut. 32:11, Isaiah 53:7, Psalm 42:1, Prov. 6:6,

30:28, Mt. 3:16, Rev. 4:7). And again, if a good man may be trusted to show mercy and kindness to the animals he owns, how much more may the good God be trusted to show mercy and kindness to the animals he has created, especially in the day when these descend into their own valley of tears (Psalm 34:18, Prov. 12:10, Luke 14:5f)?

Why Did God Permit the Fall?

At any point in the drama of Adam's probation, God could have stepped in so as to prevent the fall. He might have kept Lucifer from sinning in heaven; he might have kept Satan from entering the Garden; he might have stopped the serpent's mouth, or Eve's ears, or Adam's hand as it reached out for the forbidden fruit. Certainly the omniscient God understood the dreadful consequences of his own inaction: multiplied billions born into a sin-cursed world to suffer, die, and (in many cases) perish forever in hell. Yet he did not intervene. Why?

Down through the centuries, men and women of biblical faith have wrestled long and hard with this and other closely related questions. I will do so myself in the pages ahead. It is helpful to know, however, that in the end they almost always gravitate to one of two biblically based responses. Very importantly, these responses are rooted in two biblically based "paradigms," or ways of looking at the unfolding history of God's dealings with man. Let us briefly consider Adam's fall in the light of both.

The first perspective may be called *the paradigm of man's freedom on probation*. According to this paradigm, man, having been created in the image and likeness of God, is a rational free agent. As such, he has a unique opportunity—and responsibility—to use his freedom to love and glorify his creator through freely chosen acts of obedience. Notably, the choices he makes will result in reward or retribution at the hand of the sovereign God. But according to this paradigm, God does not express his sovereignty by *forcing* those choices upon man, by doing violence to his will. No, the decisions are truly man's, and with them comes a special opportunity to bless and glorify his maker, if only he will.[11]

As we have seen, the data of Genesis 2-3 conform very well to this paradigm. On this view, God intended purposely to test Adam as he did. Far from being surprised by Satan's malicious incursion into Eden, he wisely permitted and even ordained it so as to give Adam and Eve a precious opportunity freely to love him, honor him, and receive for themselves his most excellent gift of eternal life. Therefore, in order to preserve the integrity of the test, he did not step in to prevent the fall.

284 THE TEST

The second perspective may be called *the paradigm of God's absolute sovereignty over history.* This paradigm does not deny the existence of man's free agency, or the moral consequences of the decisions that men make. What it adds, however, is the baffling and sometimes unsettling notion that those decisions were predestined to occur! Indeed, according to this view, *all* the events of cosmic history—great or small, physical or spiritual, good or evil—are like the frames of a motion picture film, "shot" by God before the universe began, and now unfolding before our eyes as history itself.

Again, this paradigm can be quite disturbing, and it is easy to see why. If it is true, what becomes of our "freedom?" Moreover, what about the question now before us: Adam's fall, and all the evil, suffering, and death that flowed from it. If God not only permitted these things, but actually *decreed* them, is not he—the Holy One of Israel—the author of evil?

In addressing these daunting questions, we must begin at the beginning, and with a crucial question: Does the Bible really teach this paradigm? I believe it does. The apostle Paul, for example, tells us in his letter to the Ephesians that God "…works *all things* according to the counsel of His will" (Eph. 1:11). Read in its context, this phrase envisions God as "taking counsel" with himself before the creation of the world, wisely settling on the best possible plan for "all things" (i.e., the total panorama of cosmic history), and then working out that plan in the spheres of creation, fall, and redemption. Similarly, in his letter to the Romans, Paul writes, "And we know that God causes *all things* to work together for the good for those who love God" (Rom. 8:28). A little later, he again says much the same: "…for from Him, and through Him, and to Him are *all things*, to whom be the glory forever, Amen" (Rom. 11:36). These and other biblical passages reveal God as the sovereign controller of history, working all events—great or small, good or evil—in accordance with his eternal purpose and predetermined plan (Psalm 33:10-11, Prov. 19:21, Isaiah 46:8-11).

The conviction of such absolute predestination underlies the words of all God's ancient prophets. Looking ahead to the rise and fall of men and nations, seers like Isaiah, Jeremiah, and Daniel were given to behold the invisible hand of the LORD God of Israel, sovereignly working out in history his secret plans for the glory of his name and the good of his people (Isaiah 41:21—29, 43:8-13, 44:6-8, Jer. 25:12-13, Dan. 4:34-5, 9:24-27).

Interestingly, the NT expresses exactly the same conviction in the apostle John's majestic prophetic vision of the sovereign Christ (Rev. 4-5). In a vision granted by the Holy Spirit, John enters heaven. There he sees God, sitting on his throne with a scroll in his hand: it is a last will and testament, sealed with seven seals. Then he sees a seven-horned Lamb, as if slain, approaching the throne. All heaven rejoices to behold the Lamb taking the scroll and then breaking the seals so as to reveal its contents to God's people. The meaning? Under apocalyptic imagery we are here given to understand that the crucified, risen, and ascended Christ has now received "all authority in heaven and earth" (Mt. 28:18). In particular, the Father has given him absolute authority to unfold every remaining detail of cosmic history, and in so doing to bring his redemptive plan to its ultimate conclusion in a glorious new heaven and earth, the final inheritance of the saints (Rev. 21:1f).

Many other biblical passages flesh out what is implied by these prophetic texts. They teach explicitly that God, working according to his predetermined plan, is, *in one way or another,* the "first" or ultimate cause of everything that occurs. For example, God's sovereign hand is behind the motions of all *inanimate objects*, causing the rains to fall, the lightning to flash forth, the winds to blow, the vapors to ascend, the seas to roar, and the sun, moon and stars to move in their courses (Job 38:32, Psalm 135:7, Isaiah 40:25-26, Mt. 5:45). It is behind the behavior of *living creatures,* causing the hawks to fly, the eagles to mount up, the deer to calve, the whales to frolic, the sparrows to fall, and the locusts to appear in the land (Job 39:26-27, Psalm 29:9, 104:20, Mt. 10:29, 2 Chron. 7:13). It stands behind all *"chance events,"* causing randomly shot arrows to fly to their appointed mark, lots to fall in their appointed places, and hooks to catch their appointed fish (1 Kings 22:34, Prov. 16:33, Jonah 1:7, Mt. 17:27). It stands behind *natural (i.e., physical) good and evil,* forming light and darkness, creating peace and calamity, and making the mute, the deaf, the seeing, and the blind (Ex. 4:11, Isaiah 45:7, Amos 3:6, John 9:2-3). And finally, in ways that pass our comprehension, it also stands behind the freely chosen *words and deeds* of men and angels, whether these be good or evil (Gen. 50:20, 2 Sam. 24:1, Prov. 16:4, Ezek. 38:1f, Luke 22:22, 1 Peter 2:8). Thus, both explicitly and implicitly, the Bible teaches that by his decree God foreordained all that would come to pass, and that by the secret workings of his providence he is presently bringing that to pass. Inescapably, this includes all evil events, extending even to the fall of Satan and the original sin of Adam.

In just a moment we will address the troubling ethical implications of this conclusion by looking at some further biblical texts. Here, however, we must briefly pause to ask *why* God would decree an event that, along with its aftermath, seems so contrary to his character and pleasure.

The biblical answer, to be explored later, seems to be that God decreed Adam's fall *with a view to a greater good.* More particularly, he decreed it in order to set the stage for redemption in Christ, and he decreed redemption in Christ in order to secure the fullest possible manifestation of his glory, especially the glory of his sovereign mercy and grace. In other words, the

Bible invites us to examine God's decrees under the light of his ultimate purpose for the universe. That purpose, says the apostle, is that in the Kingdom to come his chosen people should forever be "to the praise of the glory of His grace" (Eph. 1:6, 12). Viewed from this perspective—from the perspective of the eternal worship of the saints—the fall can be seen as a lesser evil permitted with a view to a greater good. Yes, God foreknew the effects of the fall, many of which were repugnant to him. But he also foreknew that it would lead to his redemptive work in history; that this, in turn, would lead to the largest possible showing forth of his glory; and that this, in turn, would fill the eyes of his adoring saints forever, eliciting their songs of gratitude to all eternity (Eph. 3:20-21, Rev. 4-5, Rev. 15:1-8). Apparently such fervent, everlasting praise seemed good to God: good for his people and good for his glory. Therefore, despite all the evil foreseen, he created the world and permitted the fall.[12]

Having discussed the theological issues underlying the doctrine of the fall, let us now turn to their ethical implications. We have concluded from scripture that God decreed the fall. But in order to be faithful to the whole teaching of the Bible, we must carefully qualify this statement in several important ways.

First, the fact that God decreed the appearance of evil in his creation *does not mean that he approves of evil*. To the contrary, the Bible is quite emphatic that he hates it. Sin, as we have seen, is altogether alien to his holy character, contrary to his revealed will for his human children (i.e., to his "will of precept"), repugnant to his sensibilities, under his wrath, and liable to judgment.[13] As the prophet Habakkuk said, "Your eyes are too pure to approve of evil; you cannot look on wickedness with favor" (Hab. 1:13). It appears, then, that faithfulness to the scriptures requires us to confess that in the case of evil, God has decreed what he hates. That this seems ethically counterintuitive cannot be denied. However, the scandal is greatly mitigated when we remember that he had *good* reasons for doing so. Consider also that it would be far *more* counterintuitive to think of God as a sovereign creator and sustainer who had no control over evil, or as a holy and righteous judge who took pleasure in sin.

Secondly, if God is, in some sense, the "first cause" of the deeds of rational free agents, it is important to understand that he is not the first cause of evil deeds in the same way that he is the first cause of good deeds. In the case of good deeds, he himself is the active agent behind them. One thinks here of the way in which God inspired his prophets to speak and write, or enables his people to see and do what is right. However, in the case of evil deeds he is *not* the active agent, and therefore is neither responsible for them nor their author. Rather, he *permits* "secondary personal causes"—whether angelic or human—to perform their evil acts in accordance with their own judgments and desires. However, this permission is of a very special kind, since here God permits evil acts *in such a way as to make their occurrence certain*. Theologian W. D. Smith expressed the matter in this way:

> When it is known, certainly, that it will be done unless prevented, and there is a determination not to prevent it, it is rendered as certain as if it were decreed to be done by positive agency. In the one case, the event is rendered certain by agency put forth; and, in the other case, it is rendered equally certain by agency withheld. It is an unchangeable decree in both cases.[14]

This brings us to our third point: Because God is neither the author nor the agent of sin, the Bible insists upon laying *responsibility* for sin squarely at the feet of secondary personal causes: Satan, evil spirits, Adam, or Adam's sinful children. In other words, when assigning responsibility for sin, the biblical authors consistently resort to the paradigm of man's freedom under probation. Paul, for example, declares that "Through one *man* sin entered the world" (Rom. 5:12). Similarly, wise Solomon wrote, "God made man upright, but *they* have gone in search of many schemes" (Eccl. 7:29). Such thoughts are only an echo of the very words of God in the Garden, "What is this that *you* have done?" (Gen. 3:13). Thus, even if God decreed the *entrance* of sin into the world, he reckons Satan and Adam as its true authors, and therefore as the ones who are responsible for it. Similarly, if God has decreed the *presence* of sin in the world, he nevertheless holds Adam's fallen children accountable for it. As James wrote, "Let no one say when he is tempted, 'I am being tempted by God.' For God cannot be tempted by evil, and he Himself does not tempt anyone. Rather, each one is tempted when he is carried away by his own lust" (James 1:13-14). In this fallen world, says James, sinful acts emanate from sinful lusts. And sinful lusts repose in sinful man. Yes, if God is so pleased, he can graciously remove those lusts, or grant men self-control over them. But if they break forth, then the one from whom they break forth is, fittingly enough, the one who is held responsible for them (Mt. 7:17, Mark 7:21).

We find, then, that in discussing the great flow of human events, the Bible strikes a delicate balance between the two paradigms. This balance is seen quite vividly in the preaching and praying of the early Church. Peter, for example, declared that Jesus of Nazareth was delivered up to death "…by the pre-determined plan and foreknowledge of God" (Acts 2:23). Similarly, the praying disciples declared that those who rejected and killed Jesus were only doing what "…(God's) hand and (God's) purpose predestined to occur" (Acts 4:27-28). Clearly, these men regarded God as the "first cause" of the crucifixion. Yet that did not in the least stop them from placing full moral responsibility for the most heinous crime in history squarely at the feet of their Jewish brethren, and at the feet of their Gentile overlords, as well. Hear how vigorously Peter charges them: "*You* disowned the Holy and Righteous One...*you* asked for a murderer to be granted to you, but put to death the Prince of life...*you* nailed (him) to a cross by the hands of godless men" (Acts 2:23, 3:14). The apostle will not let them off the hook. True, everything they did was predestined to occur, *yet they knew better, they ought to have done otherwise, and they could have done otherwise, if only they had they wanted to*. Therefore, they were fully responsible for what happened, as indeed many of them were quick to confess (Acts 2:37f; cf. Gen. 50:20). Now what was true of the Jews in Jerusalem must certainly have been true of Adam in the Garden: though God foreordained his sin, Adam was the one responsible for it. Thus, if we wish to remain on biblical ground, we must conclude that Adam—and Adam alone—is the author of sin, suffering, and death in the world.

Do these two paradigms—the paradigm of God's absolute sovereignty and the paradigm of man's freedom and responsibility—seem irreconcilable to you? If so, you are not alone. When, however, this highest of biblical mysteries threatens to overwhelm, it will help to bear in mind one final observation: *The biblical writers make no philosophical attempt whatsoever to resolve the apparent contradiction between the two paradigms*. Nowhere do they try to probe the hidden nexus between heaven's decrees, God's providence, and man's free choices. Nowhere do they attempt to explain how a spotlessly holy God can foreordain all that occurs—whether good or evil—while man (and Satan) alone remains responsible for the evil. Apparently, they placed these profound mysteries in the category of "the secret things (that) belong to the Lord our God" (Deut. 29:29). In other words, they classed them among the hidden truths that now glorify God's inscrutability, and that also test man's willingness to humble himself before his Maker, and to trust implicitly in his wisdom, power, goodness, and justice (Gen. 18:25, Rom. 11:33f, 1 Cor. 13:9, 12, 13). Believing that both paradigms are vital for the spiritual health of God's people, the apostles proclaimed them both: fully, fairly, and faithfully. But again, they made no attempt to explain or reconcile them philosophically, *nor did they permit mere men to demand that God should do so* (Romans 9:14f). A fuller understanding of their hidden harmony may indeed be possible, but in order to see it we will simply have to wait for another, clearer day (1 Cor. 13:12).[15]

And now a concluding word especially for seekers.

In this notoriously difficult matter, I believe that the path of wisdom is *to follow the apostle's example*. In particular, seekers must never allow the biblical paradigm of God's sovereignty to confuse, offend, paralyze, or terrify them. Why? Because to do so would be to neglect the equally important paradigm of man's freedom under probation. In other words, they should remember that the biblical rule of action for our life is not the mystery of God's decrees (which we cannot see), but the revelation of his precepts (which we can see, especially in the pages of scripture). Practically speaking, this means that in his search for truth, a seeker should simply do what the Bible tells him to do. That is, he should let the biblical signs bring him to Jesus' feet. Then he should listen honestly and openly to what Jesus says. And then he should believe and do what Jesus says, if and when he sees that this is true and right.

Happily, any seeker who freely chooses this path can rest assured that the sovereign God has decreed good success. "For thus says the Lord: 'You will seek Me and you will find Me, when you search for Me with all your heart'" (Jer. 29:10,13).[16]

Hope and the Bad Beginning

Is Jesus' cosmogony of evil hopeful? Eminently. Unlike pantheism, it does not represent evil, suffering, and death as *essential* components of the phenomenal world, nor as manifestations of the being of god. Rather, it portrays evil as an alien presence in a fundamentally good universe, a presence that God hates, opposes, and judges. Sobering as this doctrine is, it nonetheless gives us hope. For if God is opposed to evil, then there is every reason to suppose he will one day act to eradicate it. True, he did not eradicate it in the beginning, nor has he yet (fully) done so. But this does not necessarily signal indifference to evil, only a postponement of his determination to judge and remove it. Moreover, as we shall soon see, this postponement was and is purposeful, since it has allowed him to fulfill his original purpose in creation by introducing a scheme of redemption. One day, however, according to all of God's prophets, he will indeed step in to eliminate evil, and will do so once for all.

Interestingly, the Bible first extends this redemptive hope in its narrative of the fall itself, and even indicates the manner in which God will bring it to pass. When he spoke words of judgment to the serpent, God said, "I will put enmity between you and the woman, and between your seed and her seed; he shall crush your head, and you shall bruise his heel" (Gen. 3:15). These pregnant words would be fulfilled at many levels and in many ways. According to the NT writers, the richest fulfillment is in Jesus Christ.

He is the ultimate Seed of the woman, whose heel was bruised by Satan at Calvary, but who will himself fatally crush his adversary's head at the end of time (Luke 1:39f, Gal. 4:4, Rom. 16:20, Rev. 12:1). This is a promise, not only of the destruction of Satan, but of the reversal and eradication of every consequence of his evil work. It gave Adam and Eve hope, and it continues to give multitudes of their children hope: hope of evil forever banished, hope of Paradise forever regained.

Final Thoughts for Seekers

Jesus' teaching on what went wrong contains much to enlighten and encourage seekers in their way. As we wrap up this leg of our journey, let us briefly consider three further points.

First, in the Bible's account of the fall we begin to see a biblical confirmation of the idea that life is a test. Here, God is revealed as one who tests his human creatures. And it is not only here. The pattern is first laid down in Eden, where he tests Adam and Eve concerning their obedience to his word. Then, after the fall, it continues, as he likewise tests Cain and Abel (Gen. 4), the "sons of God" and "the daughters of men" (Gen. 6-9), the family of man at Babel (Gen. 11), and Abraham and his seed (Gen 12ff). Later on we will see that Jesus' explicitly affirms what all of ancient biblical history implies: life is indeed a test of our love of God, truth, and righteousness.

Secondly, the biblical cosmogony of evil explains a phenomenon that is both puzzling and painful to seekers: *the phenomenon of religious and philosophical diversity*. As we saw earlier, some modern philosophers view this diversity as a human norm, and therefore urge us to accommodate ourselves to it by abandoning ideas of absolute truth and morality. But the Bible says just the opposite. It says that the norm is for all men "to speak the same thing, to be perfectly joined together in the same mind and the same judgment" (1 Cor. 1:10). More particularly, the norm is for all to worship the one true God—a norm towards which God is now working in history, and which will one day be fully attained (John 4:1-26, 17:3, Zech. 14:9). That mankind is now religiously and philosophically divided is therefore to be seen as a temporary aberration. And again, the Bible traces this aberration back to Eden, where, because of Adam's sin, man's understanding was darkened, his will inclined towards the suppression of divine truth, and his mind opened to intellectual infection by deceiving spirits. Yes, such news is sobering, but it is heartening as well, for it encourages seekers to believe what they already suspect: objective truth (surrounded by many lies and errors) really does exist; it is pleasing to the unknown god that we should seek it; and it is possible, under this god, to find it.

Finally, the biblical explanation of evil motivates seekers to inquire after the biblical solution to evil. This is because the story of the fall and its tragic aftermath has a mysterious capacity to raise our hopes. Reading it, we can hardly help but wonder: if God can curse his creation, perhaps he can heal it again. If evil, suffering, and death can come in through one man, perhaps they can go out through another. And if by one man's sin Paradise and the Tree of Life were lost, perhaps through another man's righteousness they can be regained.

Thus, in the biblical story of the fall, attentive seekers can hear a whispered promise of redemption. Hearing it, they will be inclined to turn yet again to Jesus, to see if he makes such a promise explicitly. When they do, they will not be disappointed. On the next leg of our journey, we will see why.

CHAPTER 12

WHAT, IF ANYTHING, CAN BE DONE?

AS NIGHT IS followed by day, so our encounters with evil, suffering, and death are followed by the fourth question of life: What, if anything, can be done? Again, this is the central theme of *soteriology*, the study of "salvation." Soteriology involves a number of other questions, as well. If something really can be done, how much? Do we dare to dream of a perfect world—a Paradise—one day up ahead? If so, who is to bring it in: god alone (if there is a god), man alone (if man really is alone), or god and man somehow working together? Also, exactly *how* shall it come in? And *when*? And when it does, *how long* will it last?

In our journey thus far, we have seen that these perennial questions are both mysterious and significant. This is because they arise out of a consciousness shared by people everywhere, a consciousness that the ideal somehow haunts or hovers over the real; that the ideal *ought to be* the real; and that some day it may actually *become* the real. But where does this provocative consciousness come from? Is the age-old dream of Paradise simply a fantasy of the human animal, a mere wish growing out of its desire for the peace and safety necessary to its survival? Or could it be something more, something spiritual, and something profoundly hopeful? Could it be a deposit from the unknown god; a whispered promise of a perfect world to come; a challenge not only to believe in such a world, but also to look strenuously for the door that might give access to it?

To all of these soul-stirring questions, Jesus of Nazareth replies in no uncertain terms. "Yes," he says, "something *can* be done about evil, suffering, and death. Indeed, something *has* been done, and something more *will* be done. A redeemed humanity is about to awaken from its dreams of Paradise into Paradise itself. Watch for it. Wait for it. It will happen at the coming of the Kingdom of God."

The Promise of the Kingdom

In the gospel according to Mark, the first words out of Jesus' mouth are these: "The time is fulfilled, and the Kingdom of God is at hand. Repent and believe the good news" (Mark 1:15). No doubt they fell sweetly upon the ears of all Israel. For centuries their prophets had promised a day when God would bring in his Kingdom. At that time he will send a Son, his Messiah, a Spirit-anointed King who will be both human and divine (Psalm 2, Isaiah 9:6-7). In his days, a universal transformation will occur, so that henceforth all nations will worship before the LORD, the God of Israel (Isaiah 2:1-4). His reign will be characterized by spiritual renewal (Isaiah 44:3, Joel 2:28-29), divine forgiveness of sin (Isaiah 53, 55, Jer. 33:14-18), personal and societal holiness (Isaiah 35:8), inward and outward healing (Isaiah 61:1-3), the banishment of Satan (Isaiah 27:1), victory over death, (Isaiah 25:6-8, Daniel 12:2), a fully restored universe (Isaiah 65:17, Ezek. 47:1-12), and a visible manifestation of the glory of God (Isaiah 40:5, Hab. 2:14). Bathed in God's very presence, all will live in peace, justice, wholeness, and eternal joy (Isaiah 11:6-9).

For centuries, Israel had waited for this Kingdom. And now, said Jesus to his astonished countrymen, it is "at hand"—very near, and drawing nearer by the moment. The people were to prepare themselves spiritually. The hope of the ages was upon them.

These rich promises enable us to define the biblical idea of the Kingdom of God with some precision. In them we see that the Kingdom promised in the OT, and proclaimed in the NT, is best understood as *the direct or unmediated reign of God*. Accordingly, the Kingdom may also be defined in a secondary sense as *the totality of the persons, places, and things living beneath God's reign*. In short, the Kingdom of God is his direct *reign*, and also the *realm* that dwells blessedly beneath it.

In this definition, the crucial word is *direct*. Yes, says the Bible, God is reigning even now over the present fallen world (Psalm 93:1, 97:1, Dan. 2:20-21, 4:34-37, Amos 3:6). But he is reigning *indirectly*, through a judicial curse and a resulting distortion of nature that he himself has placed upon all things. In the days of his Kingdom, however, the curse will be lifted, so that henceforth he will reign directly. The necessary fruit of such a reign is that everything beneath it will reflect God's own character and beauty. In other words, his subjects will be as perfectly whole as he is. As Jesus tersely put it, in the days of God's Kingdom, his will shall be done *on earth as it is in heaven* (Mt. 6:10).

Observe carefully two important implications of this understanding of the Kingdom, and how they both speak loudly to the fourth question of life, "What, if anything, can be done?"

On the one hand, a direct reign of God over his creation implies *rescue* (or deliverance) from every enemy introduced by the fall of Adam. This stands to reason, since God cannot reign directly over a person or situation while they are still under the power of sin, sickness, Satan, or death. Here, then, is why Jesus' proclamation of the Kingdom was such good news: amongst his hearers it raised hopes of deliverance from all such foes. Moreover, to read the gospels is to learn that Jesus not only *proclaimed* this kind of rescue, but actually *demonstrated* it. Here, indeed, is one of the deep meanings of his earthly ministry: by forgiving the guilty, healing the sick, raising the dead, and casting out evil spirits, Jesus gives, as it were, a sneak preview of the Kingdom of God. In all such mighty works we therefore catch a glimpse of a world to come in which both man and nature will be permanently freed from every spiritual and physical foe (Mt. 4:23-24, 12:28, Luke 1:73-75, 1 Cor. 15:25, Col. 1:13).

On the other hand, from the same miracles we learn that the presence of the Kingdom entails not only rescue, but also *restoration*. This too stands to reason: where God directly reigns, all things must return to the condition he originally intended for them. And this, in good measure, is precisely what they did beneath the healing touch of Jesus, who restored withered hands (Luke 6:10), blind eyes (Mark 8:5), leprous flesh (Luke 5:13), tormented minds (Mark 5:5), hardened hearts (Luke 19:8), and burdened consciences (Luke 7:36-50). Importantly, these restorations were not permanent, nor did they return their happy recipients to the wholeness that Adam and Eve knew in the Garden. Instead, they were designed to give a tantalizing glimpse of the *ultimate* restoration. Jesus called this "the regeneration," a term he used to depict a world not only restored to the original wholeness of Eden, but also lifted beyond that into the perfection of "glory" (Mt. 19:28). Interestingly, he gave his disciples a glimpse of this very thing at his own transfiguration. Here was yet another sneak preview of that happy day when "the Kingdom will have come with power;" when the children of God will "shine forth as the sun in the Kingdom of their Father" (Mark 9:1f, Mt. 13:43). Thus, the Kingdom of God involves a cosmic restoration to every blessing promised to Adam and his seed at the Tree of Life (Acts 3:21, Rev. 2:7).

We find, then, that in the OT God promised his people a Kingdom, and that in the NT he gives us an inspiring glimpse of it in Jesus' earthly ministry. This Kingdom is, in essence, God's direct reign over man and nature, a reign that entails divine *rescue* from every enemy (whether physical or spiritual) and divine *restoration* to the condition that God originally planned for his world.

Accordingly, if a Gentile seeker of OT times were to ask the God of the Bible, "What, if anything, can be done about evil, suffering, and death," he would likely have replied, "Much, indeed. What can be done—and what will be done—is that I will send my King, through whom I will again reign directly over my fallen creation. In his days, my people and my world will be *redeemed*. By this I mean that they will be *rescued* from every enemy and *restored* to every friend that I originally planned for them in the Garden of Eden. Therefore, in those days the real and the ideal will finally become one. And not just for awhile, but forever."

The Coming of the Kingdom

The central theme of Jesus' words and works was the Kingdom of God. But what exactly were his thoughts about the coming of the Kingdom? Did he think of it as being present in his earthly ministry? Was it still to come? And if it was still to come, would it come all at once, or in several stages? In other words, what was Jesus' view as to *when* the promised redemption of the universe, life, and man was to occur?

Here the NT responds bountifully. Indeed, one of its outstanding characteristics is that it supplies, at long last, *a complete revelation of the course of cosmic history*. Jesus initiated this revelation, and his apostles completed it (Mt. 13:11, Eph. 1:9). The result is that the NT sheds light on events that took place "before the foundation of the world," on events that will take place "at the end of the age," and on all the key (redemptive) events that must occur in between. In short, the NT supplies us with a clear picture of *salvation history,* a helpful theological phrase that may be defined as *the history of God's acts by which he redeems his people and his world; the acts by which he brings in the Kingdom of God.*

In order best to understand the coming of the Kingdom, it behooves us to take a brief journey through salvation history. Let us do so now, using the time-line below as our map, and asking Jesus and his apostles to be our guides. Please bear in mind that our purpose here is not to examine salvation history in detail, but simply to get acquainted with the basic biblical teaching as to how and when God's Kingdom is to appear in history.

Before the Foundation of the World

Many NT texts supply fascinating glimpses of the triune God acting redemptively in eternity past (Mt. 25:34, Eph. 1:3f, 3:11, 2 Tim. 1:9, Titus 1:2, 1 Pet. 1:20, Rev. 13:8, 17:8). In studying them, we realize that "before the foundation of the world" God formulated a detailed plan of salvation

SALVATION HISTORY

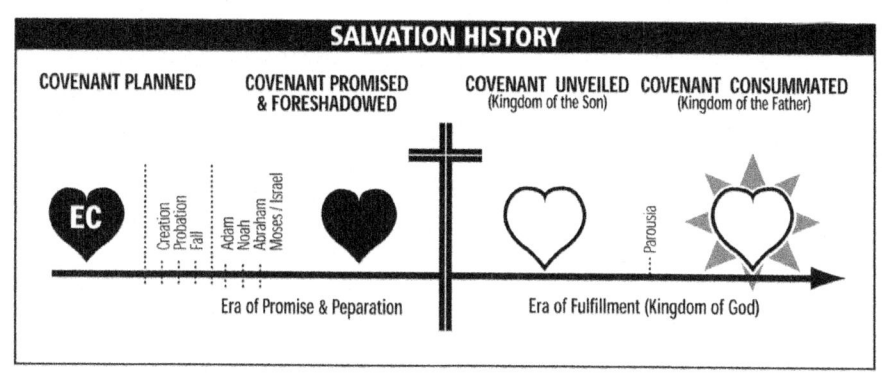

COVENANT PLANNED | **COVENANT PROMISED & FORESHADOWED** | **COVENANT UNVEILED** (Kingdom of the Son) | **COVENANT CONSUMMATED** (Kingdom of the Father)

Era of Promise & Peparation | *Era of Fulfillment (Kingdom of God)*

(Creation, Probation, Fall; Adam, Noah, Abraham, Moses/Israel; Parousia)

(Eph. 1:3). The writer to the Hebrews refers to this plan as "the eternal covenant" (Heb. 13:20). As we are about to see, the eternal covenant is a fabulously rich biblical theme. Indeed, in the eyes of many theologians, it is the conceptual key that opens up the true meaning of salvation history. On this view, salvation history is properly understood as *a progressive administration of the one eternal covenant, with a view to the final redemption of the universe, life, and man.*

But what exactly is meant by "the eternal covenant?" Based upon the overall teaching of the NT, we may define it as follows: *the eternal covenant is a redemptive arrangement, settled upon in eternity past, by which God the Father determined to redeem a chosen people out of Adam's fallen race, thereby fulfilling the totality of his purposes for his Son, his creation, and his own glory.*

Observe first from this definition that the eternal covenant is *one*. That is, there is, and always has been, but a single plan of salvation. Nevertheless, the NT invites us to contemplate this single plan from two different perspectives. Indeed, many would argue that, for all practical purposes, we must think of the one eternal covenant *as involving two separate but closely related sub-covenants*. The first of these is *the covenant of redemption*. This is a covenant between the Father and the Son, according to which the Son agrees to fulfill the Father's plan for the redemption of his people, even as the Father agrees to enable him to do so, and to reward him richly for his labors. The second sub-covenant is *the covenant of grace*. This is a covenant between the triune God and sinful men. Here, God graciously agrees to give to sinners the gift of eternal life upon condition of simple repentance and faith in Christ. Clearly, the two sub-covenants are related. Yet just as clearly, they differ. For example, God's Son entered the covenant of redemption in eternity past, whereas penitent sinners enter the covenant of grace all along the highway of salvation history. Also, the covenant of redemption highlights the sovereignty of the triune God in bestowing redemption, whereas the covenant of grace highlights man's responsibility

298 THE TEST

to receive the proffered gift during the days of his probation on earth. So again, there is only one arrangement for the salvation of sinners, yet two different perspectives through which we may contemplate it. To be aware of both perspectives—and to keep them in balance—leads us to the fullest possible appreciation of God's redemptive plan.

Having said this much by way of introduction, let us now look a bit more closely at the two covenants.

1. THE COVENANT OF REDEMPTION

Strictly speaking, the covenant of redemption is an agreement among all three persons of the Trinity, an agreement into which they entered "before the foundation of the world" (1 Peter 1:2). Nevertheless, in discussing this covenant the NT authors clearly emphasize the special arrangement between the Father and the Son. This will be our focus as well in the paragraphs ahead.

As we saw earlier, in formulating his plans for the world, God the Father purposed to honor his Son by making him Head over the entire creation, an event that would occur as soon as Adam had passed his probation in the Garden and eaten from the Tree of Life (John 5:23, Col. 1:16). However, foreseeing Adam's sin—and realizing that it threatened to frustrate his fundamental purpose—God was compelled to devise a further and distinctly redemptive plan. Through this plan, his original purposes for his Son would be fulfilled, and many other important purposes besides.

What exactly was the nature of his plan? The first and most important answer to this question is that it revolved around God's Son. More particularly, the Father required of his Son that "in the fullness of time" he would enter the world as a man, in order to become *another* Adam, a *better* Adam, and the *last* Adam (1 Cor. 15:45, Gal. 4:4f). In other words, God's plan was, as it were, to "start from scratch"—to create a new and better head for a new and better humanity. Very importantly, this new humanity would be a *chosen* people, whom God—in a sovereign expression of his love, mercy, and grace—would place under the headship of his Son (Eph. 1:3-6, Col. 1:13, 1 Peter 1:2). Through the Son, these people would find redemption. Or, to use the biblically favored metaphor of the Kingdom, through him they would experience all the blessings of God's direct reign: rescue from their every enemy, and restoration to the promise of eternal life (Rom. 5:12f).

To accomplish all this, the Father would, of necessity, require a perfect, two-fold obedience of his incarnate Son. The first would be an *active* obedience. Here the Son *must do what the first Adam failed to do*. That is, acting as a substitute on behalf of God's chosen people, he must successfully recapitulate the probation that the first Adam had failed on behalf of all. Through a perfect conformity to God's will and Law, the Son must win for his people the prize of eternal life (Rom. 5:12ff).

Let us pause a moment to observe how richly this idea illumines various facets of Jesus' earthly ministry. For example, it explains why Jesus said to John the Baptizer that he (Jesus) "must fulfill all righteousness" (Mt. 3:15). It explains why he was thrust into the wilderness to be tested by the devil, much as Adam was tested in the Garden of Eden, and Israel was tested in the wilderness of Sinai (Mt. 4:1f). It explains why he was "born of a woman, born under the Law," and why he scrupulously obeyed that Law in all particulars (Gal. 4:4; Mt. 5:19, 8:4, 26:18). In these and like passages, we see plainly that Jesus was a man on probation, a man who was actually retracing the steps of the first Adam. For man and nature to receive the eternal life forfeited in Eden, he must not fail the test.

The second obedience would be *passive*. Here the Son *must undo what the First Adam had done*. Strictly speaking, this obedience alone is the redemptive part of his mission, since here alone he pays his people's debt to the justice of God, thereby "purchasing" them back for his possession. Again, it will not be enough for the incarnate Son simply to earn eternal life for God's elect through his own perfect righteousness. Until their sins are forgiven—until they themselves are legally reconciled to the holy and sovereign Judge of all—they remain ineligible to receive the gift of life. Therefore, first and foremost, the Last Adam must passively represent his people in judgment.

The biblical teaching on this theme—the atonement for sin wrought by Christ upon the cross—is both solemn and nuanced. On the one hand, atonement requires that the Father lay his people's sins upon the head of his Son; that he "impute" them to his Son, or credit them to his account; in short, it requires that he make his Son to be the one true sacrificial lamb of God (Lev. 16:21-22, Isaiah 53:6, John 1:29). On the other hand, atonement also requires that the Son, having taken those sins upon himself, now endure the three divine enemies that ever loom over Adam's fallen race: wrath, condemnation, and the divinely declared penalty for sin, which is spiritual and physical death (Gen. 2:17, 2 Cor. 5:21, 1 Peter 3:18). Only thus—only through this great substitutionary legal transaction—can the Father be both just and the "justifier" of those who will one day put their trust in Christ (Rom. 3:21-26). And only thus can he finally bestow upon them the gift of eternal life beneath his glorious reign.

It is fitting to observe here that Jesus, both in word and deed, showed himself keenly—and sometimes painfully—aware of this dreadful aspect his mission. He has come to give his life a ransom for many (Mark 10:45). He will lay down his life for his friends, and give up his life for the sheep (John 15:13, 10:11). He must be lifted up from the earth, that he might draw all God's people to himself (John 12:32). Shrinking from the cruel death by which he will soon accomplish these things, he says, "I have a baptism to be baptized with, and how distressed I am until it is accomplished" (Mt. 20:22, 26:39, Luke 12:50, John 18:11)! Yes, this baptism is distressing, but no, its accomplishment is not in doubt. Therefore, as the final Passover draws near, Jesus fixes his eyes like flint upon the city of his imminent demise, fully intent on obeying the commandment he has received from his Father—and fully persuaded that in doing so he will redeem, once for all, the eternal people of God (Isaiah 50:7, Mark 10:32f, Luke 13:33, John 10:18, Heb. 12:2).

Here, then, is something of the costly obedience that the Father set before the Son in the covenant of redemption. And what reward did he offer him in exchange for it? As we shall see, the NT is not shy in replying. Among other things, his reward would include the privilege of being the appointed prophet, priest, and king of the people of God; of becoming the ruler of cosmic history subsequent to his ascension and coronation in heaven; of administering, from heaven, the redemption that he had purchased through his work on earth; of consummating that redemption by returning to the earth in glory, raising the dead, judging all men and all angels, and renewing and glorifying the whole creation. In short, his reward would be that he should bestow upon the Father's beloved children the life-giving gift of the knowledge of the glory of God, and that in doing so he should infinitely please and glorify the One who had planned this great work and sent him to it (John 5: 24-30, 17:3, Phil. 2:5-11, Heb. 1:1f, 12:1-3, Rev. 5). To read the NT is to learn that the Son very much liked the terms of this agreement, and that he did indeed take up the Father's command with holy obedience, zeal, and joy (John 4:34, 10:18, 12:49, 17:1-4, Heb. 10:5-7, 12:2).

2. THE COVENANT OF GRACE

We have seen that in formulating the covenant of redemption, the Father also had in view a *covenant of grace between God and men*. The agreement made with the Son in eternity past must be played out upon the stage of world history. The drama will begin in earnest when the Father sends his people (the Church) to proclaim the gospel of his Son, to make known the good news of his redemptive work to all nations. The purpose of this proclamation is that men should hear *the terms* of the eternal covenant.

They will learn, for example, that the *parties* in the covenant are God and sinful men; that the gracious *provision* of the covenant is the Lord Jesus Christ, the Son of God and the Last Adam, the One whose active and passive obedience make the covenant relationship possible; that the *promise* of the covenant is eternal life with God, both now and in the Kingdom to come; that the *proviso*, or condition of entry into the covenant, is not any combination of human works, but simple faith in the all-sufficient work of Christ; and that the *penalty* for all who disobediently spurn the covenant is eternal punishment. In thus making known the terms of this arrangement, *God will, in effect, be putting all who hear on probation*, testing their love of spiritual truth. And in thus testing all who hear, he will surely bring his elect to Christ, through whom they will enter at last into an eternal covenant relationship with himself.

Here, then, is a tiny glimpse of the triune God working redemptively "before the foundation of the world," formulating the eternal covenant by entering into a covenant of redemption with his Son, and by making plans for the historical manifestation of a covenant of grace. Moreover, it is clear from scripture that the Father also made elaborate plans for the *administration* of this covenant throughout salvation history. As we have seen, God decided that the goal of salvation history would be the deliverance of a chosen people from Adam's doomed world system, and the "heading up" of all things under the benevolent rule of his Son (Eph. 1:10, Col. 1:13). However, he also decided that there would be a number of historical steps involved in this "heading up." In other words, his plan would not be fulfilled instantaneously. Indeed, it would not even *begin* to be fulfilled until several thousand years after the fall! Rather, the fulfillment must first be prepared for. Then, when it finally comes, it must unfold progressively, in two great stages. Moreover, as it unfolds, it must do so in a very special manner: at the hand of the Messianic Son himself, who will minister redemptively to the world as its appointed prophet, priest, and king; who will, in the exercise of these three offices, keep on working in history until he brings to pass *all* that the Father purposed "before time began" (Titus 1:2; 1 Cor. 2:7, 2 Tim. 1:9).

But rather than discuss all these things here, let us do so as we meet them one by one in the remainder of our journey down the road of salvation history.

Creation, Probation, Fall

Once the divine playwright had settled upon the script, the drama of cosmic history began: God created the universe, put Adam on probation, and then, in consequence of his sin, banished him from the Garden of Eden and placed the world in subjection to a host of physical and spiritual enemies. The universe itself became a "domain of darkness," so that all creation groaned, crying out for rescue and restoration, for the blessedness of the reign of God.

Era of Promise and Preparation

Even in Eden God answered this cry. He did not, however, answer it by sending his Son. In other words, he did not immediately administer the covenant of grace—at least not as it was in and of itself. Instead, like a parent in anticipation of his first child, he inaugurated a lengthy *era of promise and preparation*. The OT gives us the record of this era, a record whose deepest meaning is seen only in the light of the events that would fulfill it: the actual appearing of the Messianic Son—the Last Adam—in history, who, as a result of his redemptive work, would bring in the manifold blessings of the Kingdom of God (Luke 24:27, Acts 3:24, 2 Cor. 3:7-18).

In order to understand these things better, let us look briefly at God's work throughout this era. Essentially, it was three-fold: he *prepared* for the appearing of Christ and the covenant, he *foreshadowed* it, and he explicitly *promised* it.

First, there was God's work of *preparation*. Arguably, this was the most important and fundamental work of all, for here he chose and preserved through many trials a special people by whom he would one day bring his Messiah into the world. This, by the way, is why the Bible is so full of genealogies. In telling us about Adam, Seth, Enoch, Noah, Shem, Abraham, Isaac, Jacob, Judah, Moses, David, and other OT stalwarts, it gives us a large and colorful portrait of the King's family tree—the human lineage of the divine-human redeemer.[1]

For a picture of the human cost involved in this work of preparation, we can do no better than to turn to one of the many visions granted to the apostle John on the island of Patmos. While suffering imprisonment there for his own proclamation of the word of God, he saw a great sign: "...a woman clothed with the sun, and the moon under her feet, and on her head a crown of twelve stars; and she was with child; and she cried out, being in labor and pain to give birth" (Rev. 12:1-2). The woman's child, to whom she did indeed give birth, is the redeemer. The woman herself is the people of God in general, and at this point in the vision, God's OT people in particular. God chose her, tested her, and disciplined her under many sore trials. Her pregnancy was very long, very hard, and very painful (Heb.

11:20-40). But God, in preparing to redeem the world, was faithful to bring both her and her labors to their appointed end.

Secondly, throughout this era God worked to *foreshadow* Christ and the things of the covenant. He did this by administering the covenant of grace at different times and in different ways throughout the 4000 years of history preceding the advent of his Son. Again, during this time he did not administer the covenant as it was in and of itself: he did not actually send the Last Adam to perform his redemptive work. Instead, as our timeline indicates, he administered the covenant *in a veiled manner.* He gave, as it were, sneak previews of the several elements of the covenant through various persons, places, things, and events of OT history. Here, then, is one of the great keys to understanding and enjoying the OT: seeing it as a divinely inspired record of *the veiled administrations of the eternal covenant.*

To get a feel for this, recall one of the points in our earlier discussion of OT Messianic types. After Adam and Eve sinned, God did something quite mysterious: he killed an animal, came to the guilty pair, and placed skins from the animal over their slumping shoulders so that they might not feel ashamed before him (Gen. 3:21). In the light of what we have now learned from the NT about God's plan of redemption, we can easily see what he was doing: *he was bringing them into the covenant of grace.* He was, however, doing so only in a veiled, typological manner. The result, for us, is a rich foreshadowing of the several elements of the covenant. Thus, Adam and Eve became a type of God's chosen people, the *parties* of the covenant. The innocent animal, killed in their place by God himself, became a type of Christ, the *provision* of the covenant. Under God's hand, the animals' skin now typified Christ's righteousness and the merits of his sacrifice, with which he covers the sin of his elect. The guilty pairs' willingness to receive the covering typified faith towards Christ, the *proviso* of the covenant. Because of such faith, God gladly received them into fellowship with himself: once again, he was their God and they were his people, living in peaceful fellowship with each other—the *promise* of the covenant (Gen. 17:8, Jer. 31:33, Ezek. 37:23, Rev. 21:3).[2]

Having already examined OT types at some length, we know that this kind of thing occurred all throughout the era of promise and preparation. It is especially prominent in God's dealings with Adam, Noah, Abraham, and (through Moses) Israel. In each of these cases, he administered the eternal covenant in a veiled manner, and therefore in such a way as to provide a rich body of OT types foreshadowing the things of Christ and the covenant. When, therefore, Jesus appeared on the scene, he and his followers could point to these types (as well as to various christophanies) as God-given proofs that Jesus was indeed God's Messiah, and that the

OT (with the New to interpret it) is his inspired Word (Acts 3:24, Rom. 16:25-27, 2 Tim. 3:14-17). It appears, then, that even among the saints of OT times, God was making careful preparations to help seekers of NT times take the test of life.[3]

Finally, God worked throughout the era of preparation to give his OT people hope. As we have seen, he did this by means of Messianic prophecies. With ever-increasing frequency, the OT prophets foresaw and foretold the things of Christ and the covenant. Above all, they spoke of the *provision* of the covenant: the divine Christ, who would serve his people as their appointed prophet, priest, and king (Isaiah 9:1f, Psalm 110:4, Daniel 7:13f). But they also spoke of the *proviso* of the covenant, which is faith in Christ (Psalm 2:12, Isaiah 53:1, Hab. 2:4), and of the *people* of the covenant, both Jew and Gentile, who would come to such faith (Isaiah 11:10, 60:1f). In dreadful terms, they spoke of the *penalty* reserved for those who would spurn the covenant (Isaiah 2:1f, 63:1f, Zeph. 1:2f, Zech. 14:1f), but also of the glorious *promise* of the covenant, the eternal Kingdom of God (Isaiah 11:1-9, 35:1f, 40:3). True, the prophets did not see all these things clearly: Christ and the covenant were, after all, still veiled (Mt. 13:17, 1 Peter 1:11). But they saw enough to be able to speak and write, and they spoke and wrote enough to give great hope to the saints of old.

Anyone familiar with OT history knows how much those saints needed hope. For again, the OT is much more than a collection of genealogies or a book of symbols and predictions. No, it is high drama, on whose blood-spattered pages we see nothing less than a cosmic clash between heaven and hell. On the one hand there is God, graciously preserving his line of faithful worshipers: chastening them, teaching them, moving them to cleave to him by means of precious promises of a coming king and a coming Kingdom. On the other hand there is Satan, working behind the scenes through manifold temptations and persecutions so as to destroy *all* of God's people, if perhaps he can destroy the *one* by whom he himself is destined to be destroyed (Gen. 3:15, 1 Chron. 21:1, Zech. 3:1, Mt. 2:16-23, Rev. 12:1-6).

Yes, the OT saints needed hope—and so did Jesus' disciples, who reflected often and with great profit upon the trials of their faithful predecessors (Rom. 15:4, 1 Cor. 10:11). For even in the era of fulfillment in which they were privileged to live, they too would endure excruciating spiritual warfare, and therefore need to draw often upon the inspiring example of the men and women of old. Yet the disciples themselves would never have dreamed of returning to the former times, to the times of shadow and longing. Why? Because now, in their own day, the truth is out. Now Christ and the covenant have been revealed. Now the King is living among his people. And now, in the era of fulfillment, he himself is leading them into battle. Indeed, he himself is their *strength* for the battle, filling their hearts with hope and assurance that through his great redemptive work the battle has already been won!

Era of Fulfillment

The era of fulfillment is the era in which God actually fulfills his redemptive plans—plans settled upon in eternity past, foreshadowed and foretold throughout the era of promise, and now manifested upon the stage of history. More particularly, it is the era in which he administers the eternal covenant *as it is in itself*, rather than typologically. As such, it is the era in which he sends his Son into the world to accomplish his redemptive work, and then raises him again to his own right hand in order to apply it to his people (Heb.1:1f). Accordingly, it is also the era in which God's people fully experience the promise of the covenant, the era in which they are indeed rescued from every enemy and restored to eternal life in fellowship with the triune God. In other words, it is the era in which the Kingdom of God has actually come.

As our time-line indicates, the era of fulfillment is divided into two basic stages. In a moment we will compare and contrast them carefully. Here, however, it suffices to note that the first stage is temporary, during which time the covenant is unveiled by Christ and then proclaimed by his Church in such a way that God's elect all over the world enter the covenant and *begin* to experience the blessings of the Kingdom *in the Kingdom of the Son* (Mt. 13:41, Col. 1:13) The second stage, which begins at Christ's return, is eternal. Here, the covenant is not simply unveiled, but consummated. Here, God's people enjoy *all* the blessings of the Kingdom *in the Kingdom of the Father* (Mt. 13:43, 26:29). More on this in just a moment.

The Days of the Messiah

The little we have said so far about the era of fulfillment makes it clear that in eternity past God planned for a *progressive* administration of the covenant, even in the days of his Son. The OT prophets, as we have already seen, predicted this very thing. Catching a glimpse of what the Jewish teachers of Jesus' generation called the "Days of the Messiah," they understood, if only sketchily, that the Messiah would appear in Israel, gather a faithful people to his side, undertake a global work of redemption of some duration, and then, following the Day of the LORD (i.e., the Day of Judgment), usher in the eternal Kingdom of God for believing Jews and Gentiles. Happily, Christ and his apostles richly fill in the missing details, making it possible for us to survey the Days of the Messiah and the progressive appearing of the Kingdom in all their fullness. With the help of the diagram below, let us do so now.

The Days of the Messiah begin with the incarnation of the Son of God and conclude with his return in glory at the end of the age. As we are about to see, it is during this lengthy period that the Father fully redeems the cosmos through his Messianic Son, thereby ushering in the Kingdom in its complete and eternal form. Our diagram shows that these days may be divided into two main phases: the days of the Messiah's *humiliation* and the days of his *exaltation* (Phil. 2:5-7). Let us look briefly at the various events that fill them both.

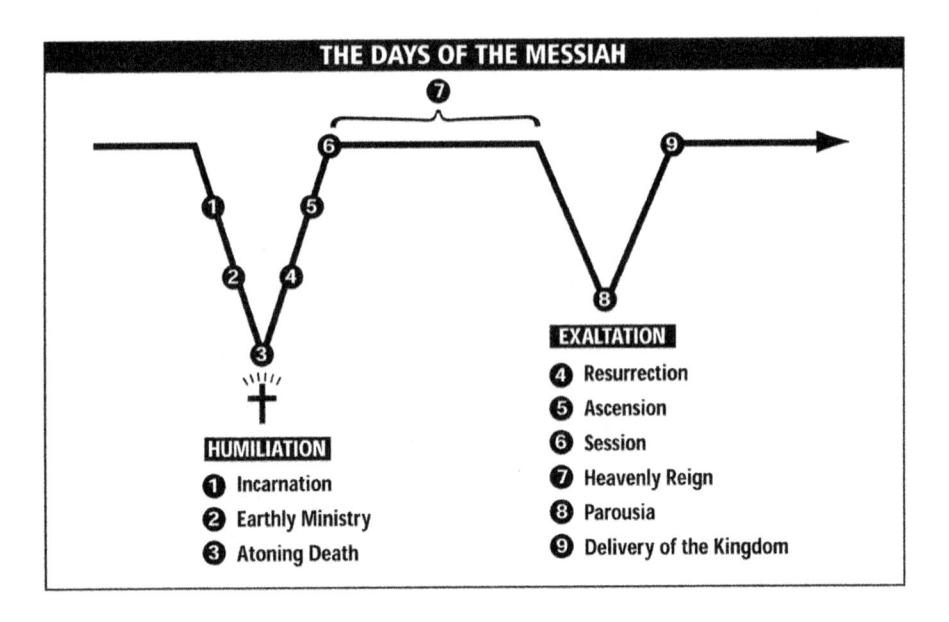

THE DAYS OF THE MESSIAH

HUMILIATION
1. Incarnation
2. Earthly Ministry
3. Atoning Death

EXALTATION
4. Resurrection
5. Ascension
6. Session
7. Heavenly Reign
8. Parousia
9. Delivery of the Kingdom

1. THE MESSIAH'S HUMILIATION

The humiliation of the Son of God began with his *incarnation*, when he laid aside his divine form, glory, and prerogatives in order to "tabernacle" in human flesh as a man, Jesus of Nazareth (John 1:14, 17:5, Phil. 2:7). As we have seen, this divine self-abasement was necessitated by the Father's decree that the Son should become the last Adam, the Head and Representative of the new family of God. To fulfill this role, the last Adam must become the Messiah. That is, he must be anointed with the Holy Spirit for the express purpose of serving God's people as their eternal prophet, priest, and king.

The second stage of the Son's humiliation is his *earthly work*. This he undertook almost entirely among the people of Israel, completing it in the short space of about three years. Officially, it began at Jesus' water baptism, when, in fulfillment of ancient prophecy, the Father anointed him with the Holy Spirit (Isaiah 42:1f, 61:1f, Mt. 3:13-17). Thus did God authorize and empower his Messiah to embark upon his three-fold earthly ministry.

As a *prophet*—or rather as the supreme Prophet—he would bring the fullness of God's truth to God's OT people (Mt. 23:8, John 1:9). In doing so, he would also perform many amazing miracles. In addition to helping the needy, these supernatural feats served as potent signs attesting to his divine nature, the truth of his message, and the character of the Kingdom he proclaimed—*a kingdom that he said was both present and yet to come* (John 10:37-38, Acts 2:22; Luke 17:20, Mark 14:25).

Acting as a *priest*, the Messiah would bring a message—and also an initial experience—of forgiveness to all who repented of their sins and trusted in him (Luke 5:17-26, 7:36ff). This he could do in virtue of his own perfect (and continually tested) righteousness, a righteousness that was transferable to all who believed in him. However, that righteousness was transferable only on the basis of something more fundamental still: the perfect sacrifice that he was soon to make on their behalf.

As a *king*, the Messiah stepped forward to rule, not politically over an Israelite theocracy, but spiritually over the powers of darkness, sickness, death, and—most importantly—the (formerly) rebellious wills of his own disciples (Luke 10:1-24; John 1:49, 8:31, 18:37, 20:28). Understanding all this to be the true meaning of his royalty, Jesus eschewed every effort to make him a temporal king (Mt. 21:1f, John 6:15f). In time, this refusal to take up the reins of temporal power would disillusion many of his followers, thereby contributing directly to his eventual rejection and death (Isaiah 53:3).

In passing, we should note here that the Messiah's work as prophet, priest, and king was by no means confined to his earthly ministry. As we are about to see, he would continue to occupy these high offices throughout the entire period of his exaltation, and even into eternity, where their deepest meaning would be fulfilled at last.

Jesus' three-fold earthly ministry was not the only work his Father called him to do. As we have seen, it was also necessary for him successfully to recapitulate the probation of the first Adam. Accordingly, he had to resist every temptation of Satan, and also live a life of complete obedience to the Law of Moses (Mt. 4:1-11, Gal. 4:4). Only thus could he attain the perfect righteousness that, in due season, God would bestow upon his believing people; only thus could he win the prize of eternal life that, as a gift to sinners who could never earn it, God would one day give to them as well.

The third stage of the Messiah's humiliation, and its nadir, is comprised of the dark events leading up to, and culminating in, his *atoning death* on a Roman cross. The former include his rejection by the rulers of Israel, betrayal at the hand of Judas, subjection to two unjust trials, gratuitous physical abuse at the hands of Jews and Romans, and open repudiation by the majority of the Jewish population, who preferred a thief, murderer, and insurrectionist to their own Messiah (Mt. 26-27, Mark 14-15, Luke 22-23, John 18-19). The depth of these humiliations is best beheld in the stunning cosmic inversions that they represent: here the creator is destroyed by the creature, the judge is condemned by the criminal, and the holy, wise, and merciful is mocked and spurned by the wicked, foolish, and cruel.

And yet the dregs of Christ's humiliation came not at the hand of men, but of God. He drank them between the sixth and the ninth hour, when darkness covered the face of the whole land; when the Father imputed the sins of his people to his own Son; when he turned his smiling face away and overshadowed the sacrificial lamb with his wrath and deep displeasure; when he condemned and sentenced him to death; and when he himself administered the punishment, sending him, as it were, into the very fires of hell—a hell of physical and spiritual agony that properly belonged to the beloved little flock for whom he so willingly endured it (Mt. 27:45-56, Mark 15:33-41, Luke 23:26-49, John 19:17-37).

Overwhelmed by the rays of divine truth and glory emanating from this stupendous transaction, hymn-writer Isaac Watts well captures not only the gravity and pathos of the event, but the spirit it was designed to evoke in God's own people:

> Well might the sun in darkness hide
> And shut his glories in,
> When Christ, the mighty Maker died,
> For man the creature's sin.
>
> Thus might I hide my blushing face
> While His dear cross appears,
> Dissolve my heart in thankfulness,
> And melt my eyes to tears.
>
> But drops of grief can ne'er repay
> The debt of love I owe:
> Here, Lord, I give myself away,
> 'Tis all that I can do.

Again, the NT regards Jesus' death as absolutely foundational, and so emphasizes it throughout. Here the last Adam undoes what the first Adam had done. Here he serves both as priest and sacrifice, offering himself once to God for all the sins of all his people of all times (Mark 10:45, John 10:11, Heb. 9:26). Here he satisfies God's justice, propitiates his wrath, and reconciles his people. And here he therefore paves the way for God to forgive, justify, adopt, indwell, transform, and rule over those people forever. The atoning death of Christ is foundational indeed, the very ground upon which the Kingdom of God will henceforth be built up, and upon which it will eternally stand (John 17:19, Rom. 8:34, 2 Cor. 5:12-21, Heb. 7:25, 9:24).[4]

2. THE MESSIAH'S EXALTATION

After his brief but profound humiliation, the Messiah entered the second phase of his work, his *exaltation*. It is glorious, indeed. As a consequence of his obedience unto death, the Father lifts the Son into heaven, makes him King of the universe, and commissions him personally to apply and consummate the cosmic redemption that he purchased with his own blood, (Phil. 2:9-11). Let us turn again to our time-line to explore this stupendous honor in further detail.

The Messiah's exaltation begins with his *resurrection* from the dead. As we have seen, the NT repeatedly declares that the Lord Jesus Christ rose from the dead on the third day after his crucifixion, left behind an empty tomb, and thereafter appeared to hundreds of eye witnesses chosen beforehand by God (Acts 10:41, 1 Cor. 15:1f). In the sight of the apostles, these appearances were intended as public testimony to the fact that their Master was and is the Son of God; that his death on the cross was not a punishment for his own sins (else he would have remained in the grave), but a sacrifice for his people's sins; and that God the Father had indeed accepted this sacrifice. With the resurrection, God therefore effectively sets forth on the stage of history the provision of the eternal covenant, the appointed object of saving faith. The resurrection publicly declares: Here is the God-Man, in whom alone men and women of all nations may find truth, righteousness, pardon, and resurrection life in the world to come. To receive him is to receive them all (Luke 24:25-26, 44-49; Rom. 1:1-6, 4:25, 1 Cor. 15).

The Messiah's exaltation continues with his *ascension*. This too was a public event, viewed by select disciples (Luke 24:50-53, Acts 1:9-10). Through it, we learn that heaven is a real place; that it is the proper abode of the divine Son, from which he descended for us and our salvation (John 3:13, 6:41); and that from that abode he will one day come again, not concealed in mortal weakness and humiliation, but revealed in divine power and splendor (Acts 1:10, 2 Thess. 1:3-12, Heb. 9:28). Importantly, the NT also casts the ascension as an integral part of the Messiah's priestly work. Here again he is seen as priest and sacrifice, only this time entering the Holiest Place of all (i.e., heaven) in behalf of his people, so that ever after they, like him, might receive a warm welcome at the throne of the Great Judge (Heb. 9:11-15, 24). The ascension also pertains to the Messiah's royal office. In it we see the humiliated savior now rising and returning triumphantly to the very throne of God, where he is about to be crowned High King of heaven and earth (Psalm 24, 2 Cor. 2:14, Eph. 4:7-9).

This brings us to the third stage of the Messiah's exaltation, his *session*. Here, in fulfillment of OT prophecy, he sits down at the right hand of God (Psalms 16:11, 110:1). As these texts show, in ancient times the king's right hand was the privileged place of *delegated authority*. Thus, the biblical imagery of Christ's session conveys precisely what the risen Jesus had said of himself, namely, that upon his return to heaven he would receive from the Father "all authority in heaven and on earth" (Mt. 28:18f). The session is, then, a kind of cosmic coronation, in which the entire universe experiences an ineffable transfer of divine sovereignty from the Father to the Son.

This transfer leads to the apex of the Messiah's exaltation, his *heavenly reign*, or what Jesus referred to as the Kingdom of the Son (Mt. 13:41, Luke 19:11f). Here again we have one of the great "mysteries" of NT revelation, namely, the idea that the Messiah's reign emanates from "the Jerusalem above" (i.e., heaven), and not from the Jerusalem below, as many OT prophecies of the Kingdom seemed to teach (Gal. 4:26, Heb. 12:22).[5] Again, the Father's high purpose for this reign was that the Son should enjoy the privileges and honors he was meant to enjoy from the very beginning: that he should be Head over all creation. To this end, he therefore grants that the Son should both administer and consummate the cosmic redemption that he himself purchased with his own blood. In short, Christ is henceforth the sovereign Lord of human history (Rev. 5, 6:1f). Even to the end of the age, he will reign so as to redeem; he will redeem so as to become Head; he will become Head so as to transform all beneath his reign into the glorious Kingdom God (Eph. 1:10, NIV)!

But concerning this heavenly reign, let us be more specific. Let us see how, precisely, the royal Messiah goes about heading up the universe under himself.

The story here begins when the heavenly King receives (authority over) the Holy Spirit from the Father (Luke 24:49, Acts 2:33). Shortly thereafter, on the feast day of Pentecost, he pours out the Spirit upon 120 of his praying disciples (John 16:7, Acts 1-2). Immediately, the Spirit-filled believers begin to preach Jesus as the Christ, as Savior and Lord. As they do so, the risen Lord himself brings many to faith (Acts 2:37, 4:4, etc.). This sets the pattern for his ministry throughout the remainder of the age: by the Spirit and through the Church, he henceforth brings the gospel not only to Israel, but also to all nations (John 16:8-15, Acts 2, Eph. 2:17, 1 Peter 1:12). Importantly, in this process *he puts all who hear on trial, testing their love of spiritual truth* (John 3:16-21). In the same process he also grants to God's chosen people all the rich fruits of his earthly work: new spiritual life, repentance and faith, forgiveness of sins, understanding of truth, transformation of character, equipment for service, a heart to worship, and much more (Acts 26:17-18,1 Cor. 1:30-31, Eph. 2:1-10, 4:1f, Gal. 4:6, Heb. 2:111-13). In short, the Messiah's heavenly mission is to gather the flock of God, to purify a special people for God's own possession (John 10:16, Eph. 5:25-27, Titus 2:11-14). Though they have never seen his face, these people have indeed come to know him, and have seen his work in their lives. Accordingly, they are ever growing in love for their heavenly prophet, priest, and king, and eagerly waiting for his soon return (1 Pet. 1:8f).

If the Messiah's heavenly reign is the apex of his exaltation, his *parousia*, or coming again, is its climax. This Greek word means "the arrival of a dignitary." As used in the NT, it speaks of the arrival of the divine Messiah, in power and visible glory, at the end of the present evil age. His purpose in that day will be two-fold: to judge and expel the wicked from God's presence, and to consummate God's plan for the redemption of his people and their world. To this end, the returning Messiah will raise the dead, judge all men and all angels, turn away the wicked into hell, destroy the present world by fire, glorify God's people, and completely refurbish their eternal home by creating new heavens and a new earth.[6]

Observe carefully that at the *parousia* the heading up of all things in and under God's Son is now complete (Eph. 1:10, Col. 1:18). Here the fallen world of Adam becomes the risen world of Jesus the Christ. Here both man and nature are freed from every remaining enemy, and filled with every promised friend. And here, with his mission now accomplished, the Son arrives at the final act of his heavenly reign: he delivers up all that he has won to the Father—a glorious new humanity and a glorious new universe: the completed Kingdom of God—and then submits himself once again to his authority. The Kingdom of the Son thus becomes the Kingdom of the Father, so that henceforth God may be all in all (1 Cor. 15:20-28).

> **SALVATION IS OUT OF THIS WORLD**
>
> *"He has rescued us from the domain of darkness and transferred us to the Kingdom of His beloved Son."* Col. 1:13
>
> **Wrath, Condemnation, Hell** | **Love, Pardon, Heaven**
>
> ADAM (Sin, Satan, Natural Evil) → CHRIST (Holiness, God, Christ, Natural Good)
>
> **DOMAIN OF DARKNESS** | **KINGDOM OF GOD**
>
> The New Testament represents salvation as a change of spiritual residence. Basically, it assumes that all people are born in Adam, and therefore in bondage to the whole spectrum of spiritual, physical, and divine enemies introduced by his fall. However, in conjunction with the preaching of the gospel, the exalted Christ sends forth the Holy Spirit to deliver a believing people out of Adam's fallen world and into his own, where they henceforth rest secure. During the present stage of the Era of Fulfillment, their blessings are largely spiritual. After the parousia they will be physical as well as spiritual. In other words, when Christ returns to make all things new, the redemption of the world that is in "in Christ" will be eternally complete.

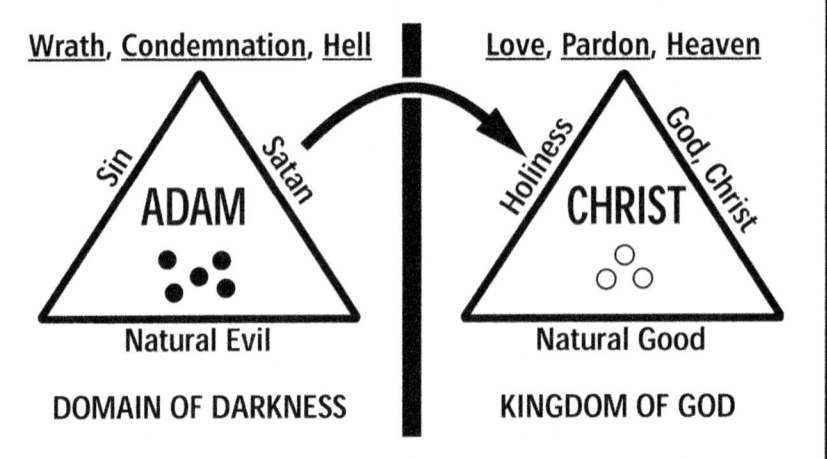

Comparing the Kingdoms

In their contemplation of the era of fulfillment, seekers will greatly benefit from comparing and contrasting the Kingdom of the Son and the Kingdom of the Father. Again, the two kingdoms are separate stages in the one Kingdom of God. Accordingly, they are *essentially* the same: both are spheres of deliverance and restoration, in which the sons and daughters of the Kingdom experience life in the Spirit under God's direct rule. Nevertheless, the two kingdoms differ in several important respects.

In the first stage—which Jesus called the Kingdom of the Son—God's reign is specially mediated through the exalted Messiah: he himself, at the Father's behest, is Lord, King, and Head of his people (Mt. 13:41, John 13:13, Acts 2:36, Eph. 1:22). Importantly, this reign is largely spiritual: it does not significantly affect the physical side of man or nature (Rom. 8:23, 2 Cor. 5:4). It is therefore hidden to the naked eye, though quite visible to the eye of faith (2 Cor. 4:18, Heb. 11:1f). It is temporary, having as its terminus the *parousia,* when the Son will deliver up his Kingdom to the Father (1 Cor. 15:28). For the saints, it is a time of struggle, opposition, humiliation, and hope, as they follow in the footsteps of their persecuted Master during the days of his flesh (Mt. 16:24, Rom. 8:17, Phil. 3:10, Rev. 11:7-10). As for seekers, it is a time of probation in which, beneath the preaching of the gospel, they are tested concerning their love of the truth about God (Mt. 16:15, John 3:16-21, 2 Thess. 2:10).

The Kingdom of the Father is different. Here too God's reign is mediated by the Messiah, yet in a manner that once again exalts the supreme sovereignty of the Father, (1 Cor 15:28, Rev. 11:15). This reign is not only spiritual, but physical as well: at the resurrection of the dead God will heal and glorify the entire creation (Rom. 8:18-23, Rev. 21:1-5). It is no longer hidden, but fully manifest: the pure in heart shall see God (Mt. 5:8, Col. 3:4, 1 John 3:2). It is not temporary, but permanent—a world without end (Mt. 25:34, 46). It is no longer a time of struggle and humiliation, but of rest and glory for all who have overcome (Mt. 5:3-12, Rom. 8:18,1 Peter 5:6). Importantly, it is no longer a (brief) season of proclamation and testing, but an eternal season of reward or retribution (Mt. 25:14-30, Rom. 2:1-16).

If, then, the Bible is true, it is clear that modern seekers are privileged to live at a very special time in history. Though they may not yet see or believe it, the Kingdom of God is "at hand," and "violent men," eager for the blessings of redemption, are forcing their way into it (Luke 16:16, NIV). It is a day of great opportunity, "the year of the Lord's favor," (Luke 4:19). But it is also a day that will not last forever. Seekers do well, then, to do what they do best: ask, seek, and knock until they hear, find, and enter in.

Conclusion

We have now examined the *soteriology* of Jesus of Nazareth, his teaching about salvation, his answer to the question, "What, if anything, can be done about evil, suffering, and death?" In it, we find Jesus giving a rich, complex, and profoundly hopeful reply. "Yes," he says, "something *can be done* about all these things, something *has been done,* something *is being done,* and something yet *remains to be done.* God's solution to the problem of evil, suffering, and death is his Kingdom. His Kingdom is his redemptive reign, a reign that entails *rescue* from every spiritual enemy and *restoration* to every blessing of eternal life. It is centered upon his Son, introduced by his Son, and exists for the glory and honor of his Son—as well as for the glory of the Father who sent him. It appears in two stages: a spiritual first, followed by a spiritual and a physical. It is the promise of an eternal covenant that was *planned* in eternity past; *promised, prefigured,* and *prepared for* throughout the era of preparation; and *previewed* in the earthly ministry of Jesus Christ, whose substitutionary life and death as the last Adam now make it possible for sinners to experience union with God and the blessings of his direct reign. Presently, it is spreading over the whole earth, as the exalted Christ sends his Church into all nations with good news about the world's divinely appointed prophet, priest, and king. One day it will be consummated, as the King descends from heaven to raise the dead, judge the world in righteousness, and create new heavens and a new earth, the eternal home the redeemed."

Seekers do well to ponder and evaluate this astonishing answer with the greatest care, since down through the centuries untold multitudes of their comrades have found it to be intuitive, reasonable, right, and hopeful in the extreme. Truly, in all world religion there is nothing quite like it. And if Jesus is telling us the truth, there never will be, not even to the end of the age.

Especially for Seekers

In his teaching about the Kingdom, Jesus presents us with a simple plan of salvation (i.e., the gospel, the covenant of grace), devised by a good God who is at work for the well being of his suffering creatures. Intuitively, we all hope for such a message from above. Jesus' tells us that God has sent one at last.

At points, this plan is indeed mysterious and surprising. Nevertheless, unlike pantheistic alternatives, it is both understandable and logical. Moreover, such reasonableness is enhanced by several lines of God-given evidence attesting to its truth, many of which God purposely supplied throughout the lengthy OT era of preparation. We have already seen how fabulously rich those lines of evidence are.

As to the "rightness" of this plan, some have asked if it is really just for one innocent man to take the place and punishment of many wicked. To this objection the Bible does not reply philosophically, but rather assumes that God alone is the final arbiter of justice, and that he does indeed reckon it a just thing that the sentence of his broken Law should fall upon one man acting in behalf of many others, *so long as that one man is the God-Man, his infinitely holy and righteous Son* (Deut. 32:4, Rom. 5:12-21, 2 Cor. 5:21, 1 Peter 1:19, 3:18, Rev. 5:1-8). In other words, the Bible concurs that an ordinary sinful man could not justly stand in for many sinners. It insists, however, that a divine, holy, and infinitely meritorious man may—and has.

As for hopefulness, Jesus' soteriology takes us beyond our fondest dreams to a vision of the perfect bliss of a perfect life with a perfect God in a perfect world—and all of this not just for a little while, nor intermittently in eternally recurring cycles (as in classical pantheism), but once and for all, forever. If, then, there is any flaw in this hope, it is that it seems too good to be true. But, says the Bible, *that* flaw is not in the hope itself, but in the eyes of those who look upon it thus. Happily, the Bible also says that God is well able to heal such eyes, so that his people will not only be able to see—but enthusiastically believe—*all* the good things that he has prepared for those who love him (1 Cor. 2:6-10, Eph. 1:15-23).

Unconditional Election

There is, however, one aspect of Jesus' teaching on salvation that strikes many people as morally objectionable: the assertion that God, before the creation of the world, chose only a particular portion of humanity for salvation, and that he sent his Son into the world to redeem these alone. Does the Bible really teach this? And if it does, how can God be just, loving, and good? History shows that these are difficult and controversial questions, not infrequently papered over with theological clichés or dodged altogether. But it is useless to try to avoid them, for the Bible itself raises them, and sooner or later thoughtful seekers will want to know the answers. Let us see, then, how the Bible might be of help to us on this score.

We begin with the question: Does the Bible really teach "unconditional election?" That is, does it really teach that God, before the creation of the world, elected a particular people to salvation, a decision based upon nothing whatsoever in them—neither their goodness, nor their wisdom, nor even their "free will choice"—but simply upon his mere "good pleasure?"

I would say that it does. I would also say, with John Calvin, that the classical expression of this doctrine is found in Ephesians 1:3-11, where the apostle states:

> (God) chose us in Him (i.e., Christ) before the foundation of the world, that we should be holy and blameless in His sight. In love, He predestined us to adoption as sons through Jesus Christ to Himself,

according to the good pleasure of His will, to the praise of the glory of His grace, which He freely bestowed upon us in the Beloved."
—Eph. 1:4-6

Here, Paul is trying to help the Ephesian Christians better understand their new relationship with Christ. In particular, he wants them to appreciate the fact that this relationship is a gift of God's *grace,* a manifestation of his "unmerited favor." Accordingly, he tells them that before the creation of the world God looked out over the sea of fallen humanity yet to come, set his redeeming love upon a chosen number of sinful men and women, and predestinated them to spiritual adoption into the Holy Family (i.e., the Holy Trinity) through the person and work of his incarnate Son, the Lord Jesus Christ (Rom. 8:29-30). Paul does not say that God chose them because he foreknew that they would choose Christ. Nor does he say that God chose them because he foreknew them as holy and blameless persons. To the contrary, Paul says he chose them so that, by being graciously drawn into a relationship with the holy and blameless Christ, they might *become* holy and blameless in his sight. Why, then, did God choose a people? And why is he now bringing them to Christ? Because, says Paul, he has set his redeeming love on them, because it pleases him to save them, and because their salvation will result in "the praise of the glory of His grace." In short, Paul says that unconditional election is *good:* good for the elect who will receive the unspeakably precious gift of the knowledge of the glory of God; and good for God, who will receive eternal thanks, praise, and adoration for sharing it with them.

In speaking thus, Paul was only elaborating upon the sayings of his Master. In the days of his flesh, Jesus often spoke of a special group of men and women whom his Father had planned to give him "out of the world." Consider, for example, the following words to the Pharisees:

> All that the Father gives Me will come to Me, and the one who comes to Me I will by no means cast out. For I have come down from heaven, not to do My own will, but the will of Him who sent Me. This is the will of the Father who sent Me, that of all He has given Me I should lose nothing, but should raise it up at the last day. And this is the will of Him who sent me, that everyone who beholds the Son and believes in Him may have everlasting life; and I will raise him up at the last day.
> —John 6:37-40; 10:29, 17:26

Here we find Jesus discussing the present and looking into the future. He begins by saying that the Father has chosen a special people to be gifts of love to his beloved Son. The choice was made before the foundation of the world, before the Son "came down out of heaven." Now that he is here, some of those chosen people have begun to come to him "out of the world." Moreover, in days ahead—after he has returned to heaven *via* the cross—many more will come, albeit in a different and more spiritual manner. Through the "foolishness of preaching"—and by the gracious, inward work of the Holy Spirit—they will "behold" in Jesus of Nazareth the very Son of God, and his appointed prophet, priest, and king (John 6:40, 1 Cor. 1:21). When they do, they will come to him, this time by faith and in prayer. And having come, he will by no means cast them out. To the contrary, he will faithfully love and guard all that the Father has given him until their redemption is complete at the resurrection on the last day.

It is, then, the united testimony of both Christ and the apostles that God has unconditionally chosen a particular people for salvation and adoption into the Holy Family (Deut. 7:7-8, 10:15, Isaiah 43:1-7, 16-21, John 15:16, Acts 13:38, Romans 8:29-30, 11:5-6, 1 Cor. 1:26-31, I Thess. 5:9, 2 Thess. 2:13, 1 Peter 1:1-2, 2:4-10).[7,8] In a moment, we will address the "rightness" of such a choice. But first, let us consider another closely related theme.

Definite Atonement

Running parallel to the doctrine of unconditional election is the historic Reformation teaching that in his death Christ made a "definite" or "particular" atonement. Among other things, this means that Jesus did not die on the cross for the sins of all people indiscriminately, but rather for those of the particular people given to him by the Father; that at the cross, God did not impute all the sins of all men to Christ, but only those of his elect; that Jesus did not die simply to make forgiveness *available* to anyone willing to come to him, but also (and most especially) to make it *inevitable* for those whom the Father would bring to him. In other words, according to this view, Jesus' death *actually* (and not just potentially) atoned for all the sins of a chosen people, thereby ensuring that in due season, despite their being spiritually dead in sin and unbelief, they would come to repentance, faith, and the eternal knowledge of God (1 Peter 3:18).

Though this nuanced view of the atonement is not widely preached today, many NT passages clearly affirm it. For example, the angel Gabriel appeared to Joseph, saying of the coming Christ child, "You shall call His name Jesus, for He will save His people from their sins" (Mt. 1:21). Again, Jesus said, "I am the Good Shepherd, and I know My own and My own know Me, even as the Father knows Me and I know the Father; and I lay down My life for the sheep" (John 10:10-18). Similarly, when he prayed to the Father about his imminent death, Jesus said of those whom God had given him, "And for their sakes I sanctify myself, that they themselves may be sanctified in the truth" (John 17:19). Building upon this view, the apostle Paul urged the Ephesian elders to "...shepherd the Church of God, which He purchased with His own blood" (Acts 20:28). Similarly, in his letter to the Ephesians, Paul exhorted the husbands to "...love your wives, just as Christ also loved the Church and gave Himself up for her, that He might sanctify her, having cleansed her by the washing of water with the word" (Eph. 5:25-33). Finally, we have this especially powerful passage from Paul's letter to the Romans:

> What then shall we say to these things? If God is for us, who can be against us? He who did not spare His own Son, but delivered Him up for us all, how shall He not also with Him freely give us all things. Who will bring a charge against God's elect? God is the one who justifies; who is the one who condemns? Christ Jesus is He who died, yes, rather who was raised, who is at the right hand of God, who also intercedes for us.
> —Rom. 8:31-39

Observe how this passage associates Christ's sacrifice strictly with the elect. For whom did God deliver up his Son? For whom did Christ die? For whom is he now interceding (for the forgiveness of sins) at the right hand of the Father (cf. John 17:9)? The answer is plain: for "us," for God's elect. We conclude, then, from this and many other such texts that the Father sent his Son to make a definite, effective atonement for the sins of his people, and for these alone. [9,10,11,12]

Is a God Who Chooses Just, Loving, and Good?

History and experience show that the biblical testimony about God's sovereign grace in salvation is difficult for people to receive. In particular, it raises questions in the minds of seekers and saints alike as to whether God is just, loving, and good. Happily, the Bible addresses all three. And not surprisingly, it is once again the apostle Paul who does the addressing. We find the most relevant text in Romans 9.

After affirming the doctrine of unconditional election, the apostle anticipates charges of divine injustice. When God chooses, does he do so unrighteously? To this rhetorical question, Paul replies:

> Certainly not! For He says to Moses, "I will have mercy on whom I will have mercy, and I will have compassion on whom I will have compassion." So then, it is not of him who runs, but of God shows mercy.
> —Rom. 9:14-16

WHAT, IF ANYTHING, CAN BE DONE?

Why, according to Paul, is election not unjust? *Because God is under no obligation to save a single sinner.* All are guilty, all are polluted, all are worthy of condemnation. Therefore, if strict justice were to be observed, all would perish. Far, then, from being an expression of divine injustice, election is actually an expression of the triumph of divine mercy and grace over judgment (James 2:13).

Someone may well reply, "Yes, election may be an expression of mercy and grace in the case of the elect, but what of poor sinners like Esau and Pharaoh, for whom Christ did not die, and from whom God chose to withhold the repentance and faith that leads to salvation? How loving and how kind was it of God to create them for the flames of hell?"

Paul answers these difficult questions as well, and with a notable sternness designed to remind sinful man of his "proper place:"

> But indeed, O man, who are you to reply against God? Will the thing formed say to him who formed it, "Why have you made me like this?" Does not the potter have a right over the clay, to make from the same lump one vessel for honor and another for dishonor? What if God, desiring to display His wrath and to make His power known, endured with much longsuffering the vessels of wrath prepared for destruction; and what if He did this so that He might make known the riches of His glory on the vessels of mercy, which He had prepared beforehand for glory...?
> —Rom. 9:20-23, NIV

Paul's answer to those who would put a sovereign God in the dock is simply to say that the sinful creature has no right to tell the holy creator how he should dispose of his own handiwork. Now as a matter of fact, God both loved and did good to Esau and Pharaoh, giving them life, breath, food, health, wealth, pleasure, power, and many other good things (Ps. 145:9, Mt. 5:43-8, Acts 17:25). Moreover, he also made himself known to them through nature and conscience, and strove with them by his Spirit, if perhaps they would repent of their own ways and choose his instead (Gen. 6:3, Acts 17:27, Rom. 1:18f). True, God could have granted them the necessary grace to turn to him; indeed, biblically it is safe to say that, at one level, he *wanted* them to turn to him (Ezek. 18:32, Mt. 23:37, Rom. 9:1-3, 10:1). But, says Paul, he wanted other things more, and so decided against it. In particular, he wanted to display his absolute sovereignty over sinners in such a way as to elicit the awe, fear, respect, love, and grateful praise of his elect for all eternity (Rom. 9:22-24, 11:36, Eph. 1:6, 12). Therefore, he decided not to save Esau and Pharaoh, but rather, in judgment and wrath, to make them foils for a show of his sovereign mercy and grace to Jacob, Israel, and the rest of his chosen people. If, then, for lofty reasons such as these, it pleased the divine potter to make of the same sinful lump some vessels for wrath and others for mercy, what right, asks Paul, have any of the pots to challenge his decision? Is the potter beholden to the pot? Can he not make of it what he wills?

Conclusion

I close here, as I did in the previous chapter, with words of warning and encouragement. The Bible's teaching on unconditional election and particular atonement—as unsettling as it can be to our weak and limited minds—was never meant to paralyze a seeker in his search for truth, and it must never be permitted to do so. Indeed, from one angle, it appears that these grand old "doctrines of grace" were actually meant to *stimulate* our search. For consider: would it not be an unspeakable blessing to know that one had been chosen for eternal life in God's Kingdom? Would that not afford, as the old Westminster Confession so richly puts it, "…matter for praise, reverence, and admiration of God; and for humility, diligence, and abundant consolation?" Well, the good news is that the Bible promises just such assurance to all who have seen and obeyed the truth of the gospel of Christ (Mt. 7:7, Rom. 8:15-18, Col. 2:2, 1 Thess. 1:2-5, 1 John 5:13). What's more, it promises to all who sincerely *want* to see the truth that they *will*. As Jesus himself put it, "If any man is willing to do His will, he shall know of the teaching, whether it is of God or whether I speak from Myself" (John 7:17; Mt. 7:7).

The implications of all this are crystal clear. In his evaluation of the Christian faith, the seeker need not entangle himself in the high mysteries of divine election. Rather, his task is simply to find out if the gospel is true—and then to obey it, if and when he sees that it is (Mark 1:15, Acts 17:30, 2 Thess. 1:8, 2:10). In other words, he must focus his attention, not on the paradigm of God's sovereignty in salvation, but on the paradigm of man's freedom on probation. He is to understand, as the Bible itself insists, that his life is a test of his love of the truth about God, and that he is to act accordingly.

Are you such a one? Are you willing to do God's will, even if it should mean abandoning your own worldview, and following Christ into his?

If so, Jesus says that you will find the truth (Mt. 7:7, John 7:17). And when you do find it, you may also find something more: that you have made your calling and election sure (2 Pet. 1:10).

CHAPTER 13

WHAT IS THE MEANING OF LIFE?

IT'S EASY TO be jealous of the oak trees. What marvelously purposeful lives they lead: feeding the air with oxygen, sheltering the birds in their boughs, supplying food for squirrels and wood for man, casting shade over the weary, holding firm the soil, and much more. But that is not the worst of it, for in addition to making such excellent contributions to the well being of others, the oak trees make their contributions unselfconsciously and in complete peace. They simply do what they do, never pausing even to *think* about their purpose in life, let alone anguish about whether or not they are fulfilling it as they should.

Alas, with us humans things are far different. Blessed—and often burdened—with the mystery of self-consciousness, we know intuitively that we (and all other beings) exist for a purpose. Yet even among those of us whose lives seem most purposeful—conscientious spouses and parents, diligent workers, model citizens—there is often a gnawing awareness that some higher purpose exists, a purpose that is both unseen and unfulfilled, yet also beckoning to be discovered. Naturally enough, this awareness moves us to ask questions that the oak trees cannot: Why am I here? What is the ultimate meaning of my life? Is there something more—something supremely important—that I should be doing? And if so, how can I find out what it is?

Happily, such questions contain yet another "hint of a heavenly hope." That is because in the very asking of them, we are bearing witness to the existence of a personal god. For if indeed there is a transcendent purpose for our lives—an *objective* purpose that we must discover, rather than a merely *subjective* purpose that we must heroically create—how could it exist apart from a transcendent purposer? Moreover, how could we even be asking about our purpose if the divine purposer were not, in some sense, *already* revealing it to us?

In this case, however, his revelation is quite peculiar. On the one hand, he somehow shows us that an ultimate meaning does indeed exist; yet on the other hand, he does *not* show us precisely what that meaning is! But why would the unknown god treat us this way? Why would he give, as it were, *a veiled revelation* of the meaning of life?

Most assuredly, the answer to this reasonable question is not that the unknown god means to torment us, for we have already seen that he is kind, not cruel. There is, however, another alternative, one that we have met time and again in our journey; namely, that he is testing us, and testing us with a view to our ultimate good. Does he whisper in the half-light? It is because he beckons to the full light. Does he fill our hearts with a hunger for high purpose? It is because he wants us to search for his Teacher, and to find in the palm of his hand one of his most precious gifts: a full and trustworthy revelation of the meaning of life.

Not surprisingly, Jesus of Nazareth offers just such a revelation. Moreover, he promises that all who receive it will see their lives become fabulously rich with meaning: ultimate meaning. Being fully fulfilled—and fully aware that they are—they will never again envy the oak trees.

Life's Ultimate Purpose

In teaching about the meaning of life, Jesus invited his disciples not only to hear his words but also to follow his example. Presenting himself as the last Adam—the Representative Man of the world to come—he purposely set forth his human life as the divine pattern for all. This is why he said, "A disciple is not above his teacher, but everyone who is perfectly trained will be like his teacher...As the Father has sent Me, I also send you...If you keep My commandments, you will abide in My love, just as I have kept my Father's commandments and abide in His love" (Luke 6:40, John 20:21, 15:10). In all such sayings, Jesus bids his followers to live as he lived. *His purpose for living was to become their purpose as well.*

But what exactly was his purpose? It is a question easily answered, and answered by Jesus himself: "My food is to do the will of Him who sent me, and to finish His work" (John 4:34). Jesus' ultimate purpose in life was to do the will of the Father. It was food to him: pleasurable, nourishing, and filling. It was his food at the beginning of his ministry, when, as a lad of twelve, he asked his anxious parents, "Did you not know that I must be about My Father's business" (Luke 2:49)? It was also his food at the end of his life, when he prayed, "I have glorified You on the earth; I have finished the work that You gave Me to do" (John 17:4). And it was his food all throughout the middle, when he said, "I must work the works of him who sent Me while it is day; the night is coming when no man can work" (John 9:4). The ultimate meaning of Jesus' life—and the secret food that brought him ultimate fulfillment—was to please and glorify his Father by doing his Father's will.

Here then—with a slight twist that we will discuss momentarily—is the biblical definition of the meaning of human life: *to please and glorify God by doing his will*. But this definition is only a beginning, since, like a shaft of sunlight, it contains a whole spectrum of implications that we must see and understand if it is to have practical value. Let us therefore briefly survey these implications, allowing Jesus himself to show us the way.

First, our definition implies that for a life to be ultimately meaningful, *one must know God*. Not just know *about* him, but also know him personally; *know him in the context of a personal relationship*. Jesus claimed precisely such a relationship for himself, saying to his opponents, "You have not known (God), but I know Him. And if I say, 'I do not know Him,' I shall be a liar like you; but I do know Him and keep His word" (John 8:55, 7:29, 17:4). Jesus' Father was not a theological abstraction, but a living person with whom he related intimately at all times.

Secondly, our definition implies that one must not only know God, but also *know his will*. In other words, for a man's life to be purposeful, God must reveal to that man the specific purpose(s) that he has ordained for him. This too was Jesus' experience, who said, "My food is to do the will of Him who sent Me...Truly, truly, I say to you, the Son can do nothing of Himself, but what He sees the Father doing; for whatever He does, the Son also does in like manner" (John 5:19-20, 30, 8:38, 17:3).

Thirdly, our definition implies that life's true meaning is never found in seeking one's *own* pleasure and honor (the natural bent of sinful man), but God's. Here again Jesus is the point man, telling his disciples that he did only those things that pleased the Father, and that his master passion in life was to see the Father's glorious beauty unveiled and admired among the sons of men. "He who speaks from himself seeks his own glory; but he who seeks the glory of the One who sent him is true, and no unrighteousness is in him" (John 7: 18, 8:29).

Finally—and quite paradoxically—our definition implies that the person who makes these things his ultimate ambition will receive back *from* God the very things that he seeks to give *to* God: pleasure, glory, and honor. So it was with Jesus. Pleasing the Father became his pleasant food and drink (John 4:31f). Pursuing the glory and honor of the Father led to glory and honor for the Son (John 13:32, Phil. 2:5-11). For Jesus, life in the will of God was not only meaningful, but delightful and eternally rewarding as well.

All of these implications—all of these pre-conditions for a meaningful life—Jesus offers to his disciples. He invites them into a relationship with God, to the knowledge of his will, to a life of pleasing and honoring him through obedience to his will, and to all the joy, fulfillment, and eternal reward that such a life will bring. "Whoever wishes to save his life shall lose it; but whoever loses his life for My sake shall find it" (Mt. 16:25).

These last words bring us to the twist that I mentioned above. For Jesus does not tell his disciples simply to *emulate* his relationship with the Father. Rather, he calls them into a relationship with the Father *by means of a relationship with himself* (John 14: 6, 1 John 2:23). They are to live *in* the Son, just as the Son lived *in* the Father (John 14:10-11). They are to take their cues from Christ, just as Christ took his cues from God. "As the Father has sent Me, I also send you…I am the true vine…Abide in Me, and I in you. As the branch cannot bear fruit of itself unless it abides in the vine, neither can you unless you abide in Me" (John 20:21, 15:1, 14). In this way, the Father's great purpose in creation and redemption is fulfilled at last. The Father calls the saints to life in his Son. As they respond, the Son becomes Head over all; all honor the Son even as they honor the Father; and the Father is thereby glorified in the Son (Mt. 11:25f, John 5:23, 14:13, Eph. 1:9-10, Col. 1:16). In short, for the disciples of Jesus, the ultimate meaning of life is to know, please, and glorify the Father by knowing, pleasing, and glorifying the Son.

Specific Purposes

In the teaching of Jesus and his apostles we learn that the ultimate purpose of life must be worked out in the context of several specific purposes. These may be conveniently categorized under four broad headings: purposes related to creation, fall, probation, and redemption. Let us briefly survey them now.

Creation

Jesus and the apostles never denigrated the purposes of God associated with creation, purposes revealed to man in the beginning. True, because of the fall, and because of God's ensuing redemptive program, the creation-related purposes must be re-prioritized, subordinated to higher purposes still. But they are never abrogated: everyday life—life as it began in Eden—must go on.

Among other things, this means that God's purpose for most people is that they should marry and raise a family. Indeed, this may be the primary means by which he populates his eternal Kingdom (Gen. 18:19, Psalm 78:1-8). As if, then, to signal the great importance of marriage, Jesus performed his first miracle at a wedding (John 2:1f), excoriated the Pharisees for their lax attitudes towards divorce (Mt. 5:31-32, 19:1f), and urged that little children should be permitted to come to him (Mt. 19:13-15). Yes, because of the exigencies of the Kingdom, some believers will be called to a life of celibacy (Mt. 19:12). And yes, all married couples must be on their guard, lest conjugal pressures and pleasures distract them from the work of the gospel (1 Cor. 7:25f). But having thus issued its caveats, the Bible persistently reckons family life as a great good (Psalm 127, Heb. 13:4). And because it remains one of God's great purposes for the world, it also remains a rich source of meaning and fulfillment.

Other creation purposes may also be briefly mentioned. For example, mankind is still under orders to "fill the earth and subdue it" (Gen. 1:28). Here we have the divine warrant for global exploration, as well as for all manner of domestic, scientific, technological, and entrepreneurial endeavor, so long as the fruits of such labors tend towards the glory of God and the good of the human race. Similarly, man is still called to exercise a loving stewardship over the earth—especially its animal life—so as to preserve for future generations the beauty and bounty of God's creation (Gen. 2:15).

Fall

God also purposes to address the affects of the fall, both redemptively and non-redemptively. One example of the latter is the institution of civil government, which God ordained early on for the restraint of sin and the administration of justice (Gen. 9:6, Rom. 13:1f). Notably, it is written that God puts a sword in the hands of civil servants for the express purpose of threatening and punishing evildoers (Rom. 13:4). This means that careers in government, law enforcement, and the military enjoy the divine imprimatur, and are therefore meaningful, fulfilling, and blessed to all who are called to them (see Mt. 8:1f, Luke 3:14).

As God acts forcefully through government to confront sin, he also acts mercifully through sundry human channels to alleviate suffering. One such channel is populated with healers—whether of diseased bodies, troubled minds, or broken relationships. Jesus—often referred to as the Great Physician—is widely regarded as their proto-type (Mt. 9:12). His ministry to the sick and injured has inspired multitudes to careers in the healing arts. Similarly, Jesus' special concern for the poor has inspired others to reach out to the needy with works of mercy. The Bible implicitly states that those who serve the poor in homeless shelters, orphanages, schools, prisons, crisis pregnancy centers, cottage industries, and the like, are doing the very work of the Lord (Micah 6:8, Mt. 25:31f, Luke 10:25). Such work is therefore meaningful indeed.

Probation

At all times and in all places, the God of Israel tests the children of men. It is one of his great purposes in the earth. The Psalmist writes, "The LORD is in His holy temple; the LORD'S throne is in heaven. His eyes behold, His eyelids try the sons of men" (Psalm 11:4). Wise Solomon observed, "The refining pot is for silver, and the furnace for gold, but the LORD tests the hearts" (Prov. 17:3). Speaking through his prophet Jeremiah, God himself said, "I, the LORD, search the heart; I test the mind, even to give to every man according to his ways, according to the fruit of his doings" (Jer. 17:10). This is God's way, his purpose for saint and sinner alike: to test their love of truth, righteousness, and God.

Jesus of Nazareth fully embraced this point of view. He taught that God is indeed testing mankind, and that taking and passing his test lies close to the very heart of the meaning of human existence.

Since his teachings on this subject are complex—and since they bear so heavily on the central theme of this book—we must wait until later to examine them more fully (chapters 18 and 19). Here, however, it is appropriate to note that Jesus does not simply reiterate OT teaching on this point. Rather, he declares that in these last days God is testing mankind in a new way: he is testing all men and all nations by means of the gospel (Mt. 28:18f).

Our survey of salvation history has already shown us how this occurs. After Jesus suffered, the Father raised him from the dead, caught him up into heaven, sat him down at his own right hand, and made him the High King of the cosmos. As Lord of all, he now sends the Spirit to his people, and his Spirit-led people to all nations. These in turn preach the gospel to every creature, the good news that God has sent his Son to unveil the truth about the questions of life, to supply forgiveness of sins, and to rule over transformed human hearts, both now and forever.

With the delivery of this message, the new "evangelical" test has begun. All who hear it must now decide whether or not these gospel messengers are telling them the truth. Furthermore, if they decide that they *are* telling them the truth, they must then decide whether or not they are willing to obey it. None of this will be easy. In fact, in most cases the gospel test will produce a definite spiritual crisis, for men are darkness, the gospel is light, and the two are perpetually at war (Eph. 5:8, John 1:4, 3:16f). Yet with God all things are possible, even to the extent that sinful men should see the light and bow to the truth (Mt. 19:26). In other words, some will indeed pass the test and receive its reward: eternal redemption. Having loved and obeyed the truth, they will inherit the eternal Kingdom of God.

Later on we will discuss these matters in greater detail. Here, however, it suffices to stress yet again that Jesus of Nazareth stands solidly with all his OT predecessors, affirming that the LORD God does indeed test the sons of men. In these last days he is doing so in a new way, through the gospel. The global gospel test is as important as it is difficult. On its other side waits eternal reward or eternal retribution, joy unspeakable or woe unending. Yes, says Jesus, life is a test. *And the primary meaning of human life—if not the ultimate—is to pass it.*

Redemption

Above all else, the Bible is a record of God's redemptive activity in the world. There we learn that the purpose nearest and dearest to his heart is redemptive: to rescue and restore a chosen people for the glory of his Son, and for the glory of God the Father, as well.

To accomplish this great goal, God is pleased to use his redeemed human servants. They are to be co-laborers with him, working towards the fulfillment of his redemptive plans (John 9:4, 1 Cor. 3:9). Jesus often called his disciples to this demanding work, and was at considerable pains to cast it as profoundly meaningful and richly rewarding. For example, having just preached the gospel to a Samaritan woman—and having experienced the blessedness of doing so—he said to his friends:

> Do you not say, "There are still four months and then comes the harvest"? Behold, I say to you, lift up your eyes and look at the fields, for they are already white for harvest! And he who reaps receives wages, and gathers fruit for eternal life, that both he who sows and he who reaps may rejoice together."
>
> —John 4:35-36

This Samaritan woman, says Jesus, is but a single stalk of wheat, but my speaking with her here is a fact of global significance. God has sown a people in the world, and I, their redeemer, have come to sow the gospel in the world. Therefore, now is the appointed time of God's harvest; now is the set time for his reapers to go forth to the work—to co-labor with the Father and the Son in the cause of the gospel, and to rejoice together with them as they do.

Jesus' mandate to his Church—that they should evangelize the world—requires that his servants embrace a new set of priorities. Domestic pleasures and temporal work remain meaningful, but must henceforth be subordinated to the more important work of the Kingdom. Jesus' himself stresses this point hyperbolically:

> Truly I say to you, there is no one who has left house or brothers or sisters or father or mother or wife or children or lands, for My sake and the gospel's, who shall not receive a hundredfold now, in this time, houses and brothers and sisters and mothers and children and lands, with persecutions—and in the age to come, eternal life.
> —Mark 10:29-30

This is not a call to the repudiation of God-given gifts and goods. It is a call to the subordination of those goods to a greater good: the progress of the gospel. Among some, the call will indeed mean celibacy (but never the abdication of existing marital or parental duties, 1 Tim. 5:8). Among others, it will mean forsaking lucrative employment for the far humbler wages of the gospel (Luke 5:11, 10:7, 1 Cor. 9:14, 1 Tim. 5:18). But among all it will mean holding this world's goods lightly, so that at a moment's notice one may embark to preach the good news (Mt. 19:21). Rich promises encourage God's wavering saints to answer this challenging call: he will supply their every need in this life, and abundantly reward their sacrifices in the next (Mt. 6:33, Luke 14:14, 1 Tim. 6:17-19).

God's redemptive purpose is not only advanced by evangelism, but also by a life of service to the brethren. The company of the redeemed is a family: sons and daughters through the Son, eternal children of the Father. Therefore, says Jesus, they are to love one another and, in manifold ways, to "wash one another's feet" (John 13:1f, 15:12, 17). The apostle Paul makes all of this quite practical, teaching that God has given specific spiritual gifts to each of his children (Rom. 12, Eph. 4, 1 Cor. 12-14). They are to use them in love, as servants, for the building up of the individual members of the Body of Christ, until the happy day when that Body becomes "a perfect man" (Eph. 4:12).

Other biblically mandated activities may be mentioned here as well: prayer (Mt. 6:9f, Eph. 4:18), worship (John 4:21-24, Eph. 5:19), and meditation upon the Word of God—all with a view to increased depths of understanding, holiness of life, and effectiveness of ministry (John 17:17, Rom. 12:1f). Together with evangelism and service to the brethren, such practices enable disciples to abide in intimate communion with Christ, bear much fruit, glorify God, and further his redemptive purposes in the world (John 15:1f). For Jesus of Nazareth, they are foundational elements of a meaningful life.

Managing the Meanings

By examining specific God-given purposes for man, we soon realize that it is not really possible to speak of "*the* meaning of life." There is not one meaning, but many—and it is no small part of the meaning of life to learn how to manage the many meanings well!

To manage them well means two things: to prioritize them and to keep them in balance. It is not acceptable simply to place them in a hierarchy and then to devote oneself to the top one or two. No, the Bible requires that we imitate Jesus, of whom it is written that he did *all* things well (Mark 7:37). Let us therefore conclude this chapter by hearing Jesus on life's priorities, and on how we may best keep them in balance.

The First Priority

It is clear that for Jesus, life's *first* priority is to pass the gospel test. The primacy of this purpose stems largely from the stakes involved. As Jesus put it, "What is a man profited if he gains the whole world and loses his soul? Or what will a man give in exchange for his soul" (Mt. 16:26)? What good does it do to devote one's life-energies to earthly things—to becoming rich, powerful, famous, secure, or comfortable—and then miss heaven for an eternity in hell? Priorities like this are not just skewed or inverted, but infinitely foolish (Mt. 22:1f, Luke 12:13f). The first priority, then, is to lift up one's eyes, to search out the truth about God, to consider and respond to the claims of Christ. To do so sincerely, with "a good and noble heart," will not only be to pass the test of life, but to see *all* the meaning of life opening up like a flower before one's wondering eyes (Luke 8:15, Mt. 13:16).

The Ultimate Priority

Among those whose eyes have thus been opened, the *ultimate* priority is henceforth to know God. This, as we saw earlier, is the biblical definition of eternal life, the *kind* of life God wants for his children: that they should know him, and Jesus Christ whom he has sent (John 17:3). Jesus elevates this priority above all others by teaching, urging, and warning his disciples to abide in him, since, apart from (the intimate knowledge of) him, they can do nothing (John 15:1f). The ultimate priority of the child of God is therefore carefully to maintain honest, intimate, open-hearted fellowship with God, so that he may hear God's voice and be led, effectively, into all God's work (Rev. 3:1-6).

The Pervasive Priority

This brings us to what might be called life's *pervasive* priority: that men should not only know God, but also seek to make him known in every venue of daily life. In other words, a concern for the advance of God's redemptive rule should pervade the outworking of every other purpose to which he may call us: marriage, parenting, friendship, work, recreation, community service, political engagement, etc. All such things are good, but they are goods pursued in a fallen world; goods pursued in the company of "neighbors" who must take and pass the test of life. Knowing this, the child of God is eager to serve faithfully as a gospel messenger—an ambassador of the High King of heaven—wherever he goes (Mt. 10:16-20, Eph. 6:20). Having himself passed the test of life, he earnestly desires to see others do the same.

Here, then, are Jesus' top three priorities for a meaningful life. Moreover, he assures us that when these are in place, all the others will fall into place as well. As he said, "Seek first the Kingdom of God and His righteousness, and all these things will be added to you" (Mt. 6:33).

Conclusion

Seekers hungry for the meaning of life will find Jesus' teaching on this theme both encouraging and challenging. As we have seen, he affirms that human life does indeed have a transcendent purpose, or rather many purposes; that these purposes are hidden in a divine purposer, but that they may be found in the teachings of the supreme prophet whom he has sent; and that once found and embraced, they will bring clarity, direction, challenge, adventure, fulfillment, joy, and eternal reward (Mt. 25:21, 23).

With promises like these in the offing, surely it would be wise—and meaningful in the extreme—for seekers to determine once for all if Jesus is telling us the truth.[1]

A MEANINGFUL LIFE

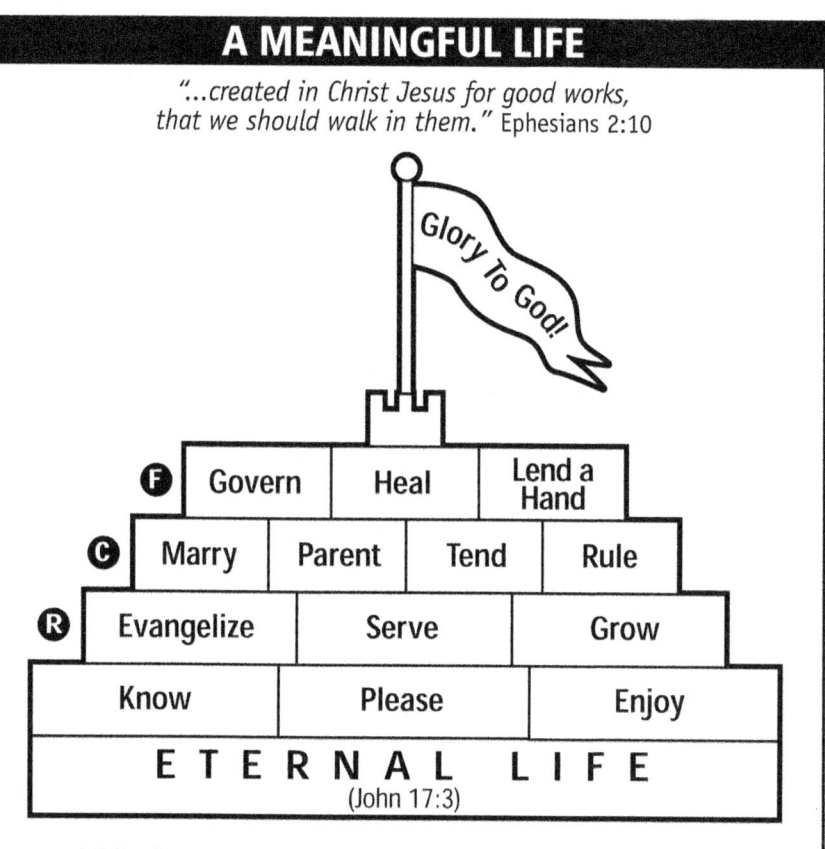

"...created in Christ Jesus for good works, that we should walk in them." Ephesians 2:10

```
                    Glory To God!
                    
        |  Govern  |  Heal  | Lend a Hand |
  (F)
        |  Marry  | Parent | Tend | Rule |
  (C)
        |  Evangelize  |  Serve  |  Grow  |
  (R)
        |    Know    |   Please   |   Enjoy   |
        
              E T E R N A L    L I F E
                        (John 17:3)
```

In biblical perspective, a meaningful life looks something like the castle pictured above. The foundation is the gift of eternal life, which Jesus defines as a personal knowledge of God and Christ through the Spirit. This supplies the Christian with a whole new motive for living: to know, please, and enjoy the triune God more and more each day. By studying the scriptures, he increasingly realizes how this is done: he must try to advance God's purposes in the world relative to redemption **(R)**, creation **(C)**, and fall **(F)**. Sensing his inadequacy for so great a task, he casts himself daily upon the Spirit, who gladly enables him to prioritize, balance, and fulfill these purposes according to his unique gifts and opportunities. In the way of obedience, the Christian now begins to feel that his life is becoming more meaningful. Indeed, he begins to feel it may even be bringing a little glory to God—the most meaningful thing of all.

CHAPTER 14

HOW SHOULD WE LIVE?

SOONER OR LATER we all will find ourselves in an ethical quandary. True, the morality of most attitudes and actions is fairly easy to discern: we know that we should be honest, humble, diligent, generous, and kind; that we should not murder, rape, lie, cheat, or steal, etc. But sometimes we are not so sure. For example, back in the late 60's many of us wondered if it was right to take hallucinogenic drugs in pursuit of spiritual experience; to engage in pre-marital sex; to fight in war; to work for a large corporation; to embrace the faith and morality of our parents, etc. These and other issues still excite lively debates. To judge from the abundance and intensity of those debates, people *often* find that it is hard to discern right from wrong.

Nor are our ethical quandaries simply confined to ascertaining what is good and what is bad. Suppose, for example, that we know we have done something wrong, but cannot seem to shake the guilt that we feel about it: What should we do? Or suppose that we find ourselves subject to imaginations, passions, or behaviors from which we now would like to be set free: Where should we turn? What if people in a given society sharply disagree about the morality of this or that public policy: How are we to discover a just solution? And even if we do discover it, how can we be sure it is fair to impose that solution on the minority who disagree?

Questions like these never go away. Generation after generation, mankind toils on in the half-light of ethical consciousness, certain about some things, uncertain about others; anxiously trying to know and do what is right, fearful of the consequences of erring and doing what is wrong.

In view of all this, it is hardly surprising that people often find themselves crying out for a teacher of true morality, for someone wiser than Solomon, for someone who can tell them once and for all exactly how they should live.

Does Jesus of Nazareth hear this cry? If he is God's appointed Teacher, he must. It is time now to see if he does.

Jesus on the Objective Moral Order

Earlier in our journey we found that conscience supplies us with a powerful hint of a heavenly hope. When carefully examined, conscience reveals that we live in an objective moral order whose elements include, 1) *moral absolutes, 2) moral obligation, and 3) a universal law of moral cause and effect*. But how, we asked, could such an intricate spiritual order possibly exist apart from a divine Orderer? Moreover, how could we *know* that it exists unless that Orderer was continually revealing it to us? Accordingly, we concluded that the objective moral order—as well as our innate knowledge of it—constitutes one of the great proofs for the existence of a supreme being; a god in whom we live and move and have our (moral) being; a god who definitely knows and cares about how we should live.

Jesus of Nazareth affirms these very things. Repeatedly, he tells us that there is indeed an objective moral order, that the God of Israel is its creator and sustainer, and that all men—both Jew and Gentile—must live in harmony with him by living in harmony with it.

This confidence is reflected in a poignant story related by Matthew, Mark, and Luke. As Jesus was journeying through Israel, a conscientious young man of some wealth and influence ran up to him, begging an audience. Having captured Jesus' attention, he asked him what he must do to inherit eternal life. In the manner of the OT prophets, Jesus replied, "You know the commandments. Do not commit adultery, do not murder, do not steal, do not bear false witness, do not defraud, honor your father and your mother" (Mark 10:19). For a young man schooled in the synagogues, this was familiar territory. Jesus was simply echoing Moses. It was as if he had said, "God laid down the Law at Sinai, giving our people specific commandments for the right ordering of our lives. If you obey those commandments, you will enjoy his blessings, both in this life and in the Kingdom to come."

Now if the story ended here, we would naturally be inclined to think that Jesus saw himself as still another Jewish moralist in a long line of the same. But it does not end here. Indeed, this was only beginning, for Jesus had something further—and much deeper—to say to this eager young seeker.

"Teacher," replied the rich young ruler, "all these things I have observed from my youth." So Jesus—knowing him better than he knew himself—answered, "One thing you lack. Go your way, sell whatever you have, give it to the poor, and you will have treasure in heaven. And come, take up the cross and follow me." A simple enough command. Yet, as Mark records, the words saddened the young ruler. Indeed, he went away grieved, for he had great possessions (Mark 10:17-22).

In this exchange, Jesus was being cruel in order to be kind. Yes, the young man was sincere, and therefore loved by Jesus (Mark 10:21). But he was also deceived. He thought he was living obediently to God's law, when in fact, because of his attachment to riches and their prerogatives, he had broken any number of God's commandments, especially those prohibiting covetousness and idolatry (Ex. 20:17, 3). Jesus' personal invitation—that he should sell all and follow the Messiah—was therefore shrewdly designed to show this man the painful truth about his spiritual condition. Though he turned away, the rich young ruler would have plenty to think about in the days ahead.

This story puts flesh and blood on a crucially important biblical teaching, repeated over and again throughout the NT: fallen, sinful man *cannot* properly align himself with the objective moral order; he *cannot* make himself righteous in God's sight. Many people, of course, do not even want to make themselves righteous. Of them, the Bible ominously declares, "There is no fear of God before their eyes" (Rom. 3:18). Others, like the proud Pharisee in Jesus' parable, think they are righteous simply because they are religious; not being spiritually minded, they are largely blind to the reality, depth, and ugliness of their sin (Luke 18:9-14, Rom. 8:5-8). Still others, having a genuine zeal for God and righteousness, find themselves ever-increasingly distressed to see how often they break the spirit, if not the letter, of the law. In the words of Paul, these people delight in God's Law inwardly, but they see another law at work in their members—a law of sin—bringing them into captivity to moral failure, spiritual frustration, and fear of divine retribution (Rom. 7:13-25, 8:15, Heb. 2:15). These, says the apostle, are God's "wretched men," from whose anguished spirit there eventually erupts a desperate cry: "Who will deliver me from this deadly sinful body" (Rom. 7:24)?

To read the gospels is to learn that Jesus likes wretched men. Indeed, he is at pains to produce as many of them as he can. Accordingly, in his teaching we find him setting the moral bar higher and higher, so that his hearer's resulting despair of themselves and their own righteousness may run deeper and deeper. Here, by the way, is one of the great motifs pervading Jesus' famous Sermon on the Mount. Men, he says, are not to break the least of God's commandments (Mt. 5:19). Their righteousness must exceed that of the Scribes and Pharisees (5:20). Those who hate their brother have already murdered him (5:22). Those who merely lust for a woman have already committed adultery with her in their heart (5:28). God's people (impossibly enough) are to love their enemies, pray for them, and do good to them (5:43-45). Indeed, they are to be perfect, even as their Heavenly Father is perfect (5:48)!

Here is the objective moral order with a vengeance. Here are commandments as lofty and holy as God himself; commandments too high for sinners even to see, let alone obey; commandments mighty to condemn, but powerless to transform or sanctify.

Seeing all these things, seekers may well ask, "But what good is a moral order like this? Why would Jesus—and the God who sent him—even bother to issue such commandments, if their net effect is simply to shut up poor sinners in a prison house of frustration, guilt, and despair?"

Jesus has an answer for this question, an answer as profound, hopeful, and astonishing as it is simple. "A moral order like this," he replies, "is actually very good, and commandments like these most excellent, if and when their deepest purpose is fulfilled. And their deepest purpose is fulfilled if and when they bring you to me."

Come Unto Me

How shall we live? We have just seen that Jesus replies first by saying we must live in harmony with the objective moral order. But how shall we who are sinful live in harmony with this order? Jesus answers a second time: "In and of yourself, you cannot. But you can, if you will come to me."

Here, then, is the moral genius of the faith that Jesus brings into the world; here is that which makes Christianity altogether unique among world religions. For Jesus is not like the former prophets, who simply exhorted Israel to repent and obey the Law of Moses. Still less is he like the scribes and Pharisees, who added hundreds of man-made rules and regulations to the Law, thus loading men down with burdens grievous to be borne (Mt. 23:4, Luke 11:46). Rather, he has deep compassion for struggling sinners (Mark 6:34). In that compassion he therefore offers them a completely new way of relating to the objective moral order, a way that brings life instead of death. What is that way? Jesus responds with words that have comforted multitudes down through the centuries:

> Come to Me, all you who labor and are heavy laden, and I will give you rest. Take My yoke upon you and learn from Me, for I am gentle and humble in heart, and you will find rest for your souls. For My yoke is easy and My burden is light.
>
> —Mt. 11:28-30

These words are, in essence, an invitation to a life of discipleship. Importantly, they come from the lips of one who saw himself as being fully divine, and therefore capable of welcoming sinners of all times and all places into a life-changing personal relationship with himself. In this relationship, he is to be the Master and they his obedient disciples: sinful human autonomy is banished forever. And this is all to the good, for henceforth the sinner's new master is not a band of deadly tyrants, but a compassionate King who is gentle and humble in heart. Moreover, he offers his subjects gifts: an easy yoke, a light burden, and eternal rest for their souls. It is a picture of weary sinners reconciled at last to the objective moral order because, somehow, they have been reconciled to its creator and sustainer: the LORD God, the holy one of Israel.

"Come unto me" is, then, the supreme commandment of Jesus' new way. It is, in an ultimate religious nutshell, his answer to the question, "How shall we live?" We should live, says Jesus, by coming to him, not just once, but over and again, for everything we need to live in harmony with God and God's will (John 6:29, Rev. 2:5).

But let us take a moment to unpack this nutshell. Let us look at some of the specific gifts that Jesus is prepared to bestow upon those who come to him; gifts that will enable them to live before a holy God in peace. As we proceed, please bear in mind what we learned in the previous section, namely, that this "coming" to Jesus is no longer physical, but spiritual. As Jesus himself anticipated, weary sinners must now come to him in prayer, crying out to the heavenly prophet, priest, and king who is seated at God's own right hand. When they do so in sincerity he will faithfully respond, giving them precious gifts by which they will become rightly related to God and to the objective moral order. Here are a few of the most important.

The Gift of Forgiveness

First, guilty sinners are to come to Jesus to receive *forgiveness*. Or, to use the favored biblical term, they are to turn to him for *justification*. Already Christ has so lived as to win a perfect righteousness for his people; already he has died for their sins, satisfying God's justice on their behalf. But in order to receive these precious gifts, sinners must come to him personally. To this end the Holy Spirit draws them, showing them the deity of Christ, his perfect righteousness, and the meaning of his substitutionary death for sin. In this heavenly light, they now see their own sin—as well as its dreadful consequences—and therefore turn away from their sin towards Christ, coming to him as Savior and Lord (John 1:12). When they do, immediately they are justified. Again, this important theological term means that *they are reckoned to be righteous in the sight of God and before his law.* They are forgiven all their sins: past, present, and future (Acts 13:38-39). They no longer abide under God's wrath (John 3:36, Eph. 2:3). They no longer stand condemned before his Law (Rom. 8:1f). They are delivered once for all from the peril of hell. Speaking of these rich blessings—and of the holy moment when God's children receive them—Jesus says:

> Truly, truly I say to you, he who hears My word and believes in Him who sent Me has everlasting life, and shall not come into judgment (i.e., condemnation), but has passed from death to life.
> —John 5:24

We see, then, that at the very moment of saving faith all the *divine* enemies incurred by sin are forever banished from the new disciple's life. Moreover, the blessedness of this new situation now registers in his conscience, so that, with unspeakable joy and relief, he experiences personal peace and reconciliation with God (Rom. 4:6, 5:1, Phil. 4:7). Very importantly, it is just here that we find the NT basis for a Christian's steadfast assurance, confidence, and joy. Because justification is a gift to be received and not a reward to be earned, disciples can *know*—and know *now*—that they are forgiven once and for all, and that they will therefore certainly enter heaven when they die (John 16:22, Rom. 5:1-2, 8:30. 1 John 5:13). Not surprisingly, the NT authors reckon divine justification among the greatest of all God's gifts, a veritable fountainhead of eternal thanksgiving and praise (Rom. 4:6f, 2 Cor. 9:15, Eph. 1:6).

The Gift of Spiritual Transformation

Secondly, the bound and broken are to come to Jesus for *spiritual transformation,* for *inward rescue and renewal.* As we saw earlier, the fallen sons of Adam are part of an evil world-system that is held in spiritual bondage to sin and Satan. Accordingly, they are not free to be what they were created to be, precisely because they are not free to know and obey their creator. However, Jesus promises, "If the Son shall make you free, you shall be free indeed" (John 8:36). Moreover, from his throne in heaven the King personally undertakes to make that promise attractive and real to his own people. Accordingly, he sends the Spirit to his elect, who opens their eyes to see that they can be free in Christ. Desiring this, they receive him (Christ) personally and are immediately liberated from the tyranny (though not from the presence and temptations) of sin and Satan

(Rom. 6:14, John 12:31, Col. 1:13). Moreover, in receiving Christ they also receive a new nature, a nature created by the indwelling Holy Spirit who will remain with them forever (John 14:16, Eph. 2:10). This new nature loves God (John 5:42, Rom. 5:5). It loves righteousness and holiness (1 John 3:9). It wants to know and obey the will of God (Ezek. 11:19, Heb. 8:7-13). It is infused with the very Spirit of the Son, who cries out, "Abba, Father" (Rom. 8:15, Gal. 4:6)! Here then is yet another way in which the heavenly Christ aligns his people with the objective moral order: he gives them a new heart, a heart that is ever inclined to love God and to do his will (Phil. 2:13, Heb. 10:5-10).

The Gift of Commandments

Thirdly, those groping for moral truth are to come and receive *commandments for all aspects of life*. Jesus does not suffer his disciples to walk on in shadow, but instead gives them a new law, "the Law of Christ" (Gal. 6:2). This law fulfills and supercedes the Law of Moses, and is therefore the definitive rule of action for God's people right up to the end of the age (Mt. 5:17, 9:17, Rom. 10:4, 1 Cor. 9:21, Heb. 8:13). It's essence is love: love of God and love of neighbor, a love that Jesus perfectly demonstrated in the days of his flesh when he went about ministering to the needy and doing his Father's will (Mt. 22:34-40, John 8:29, 14:31, Acts 10:38). Its form is the entire corpus of NT commandments, issued by Jesus and his writing apostles (e.g., Mt. 5-7, Col. 3-4). These commandments address a wide variety of attitudes and actions, either promoting or prohibiting them, so that disciples may be fully equipped to do God's will and therefore to enjoy his presence and blessing (Mt. 7:24f, Rom. 12:1-2, Eph. 5:17, 2 Tim. 3:16-17).

Very importantly, this law is *not* obeyed in order to gain acceptance with God. Acceptance with God is, as we just saw, a gift: it can never be earned, only received by receiving Christ (John 3:16, Gal. 2:16, Eph. 2:8-10, Titus 3:5). Why, then, are the disciples to obey Christ's new law? The NT offers many reasons: to express gratitude for the gift of salvation (Luke 7:47, 2 Cor. 9:15); to escape the power and presence of residual sin (Rom. 6, Col. 3); to draw closer to God (John 14:15, 21, 23-24); to discover and fulfill one's destiny (Phil. 3:12-14); to receive eternal rewards (Mt. 25:21); and above all, to bless the Lord (Phil. 3:12-13). The truth of the gospel casts out guilt and fear as the primary motives for moral action, supplanting them with love, gratitude, joy, and a childlike eagerness to please (1 John 4:18). Good news, indeed.

The Gift of Desire and Power for Obedience

The spiritually weak are to come to Jesus to receive *desire and power to keep his commandments.* Jesus himself warns that Christian discipleship is no cakewalk (Luke 14:25-33). Though the saints have a new nature, they continually wrestle against Satanic opposition, residual sin in their flesh, and worldly temptations (Gal. 5:16-17, Eph. 6:10f, 1 John 2:15). If and when these enemies gain the ascendance, disciples cannot do the (good) things they wish; they cannot fulfill the Law of Christ (Gal. 5:17). For this reason, Jesus urges and warns that they must "abide" in him at all times, that without him they can do nothing (Luke 14:34, John 15:1f). Practically, this means that they must come to him regularly in prayer, allowing him to renew their spiritual desire and fortitude by speaking to them in the Spirit through the Scriptures (Mt. 4:4, John 14:15-18, 2 Cor. 12:9). Thus does he secretly preserve and rekindle the hearts of his people, so that they will ever love God's law, and ever remain in close alignment with his objective moral order (Heb. 8:10).

The Gift of Cleansing and Renewal

Finally, Jesus encourages those who fail in the keeping of his commandments to come to him for *cleansing and renewal.* The NT is not naïve about the spiritual condition of God's people. Though they are new creations, they are not yet perfect creations (2 Cor. 5:17). Christ is slowly being formed within them (Gal. 4:19). They are gradually putting off the old (Adamic) man, and slowly putting on the new (Christ) (Col. 3:1-18). They are growing in understanding, godly character, and Christian service (2 Cor. 3:18, 2 Peter 3:18). But since this is a process, there will certainly be failures: the saints will stumble in many ways (Phil. 3:12f, James 3:2).

Yet even here, there is good news. For though Christ does indeed discipline his wayward sons and daughters, he will never leave nor forsake them (Heb. 12:1f, 13:5, Rev. 3:19). Having already forgiven them their sins, he will never again look upon them to condemn them. Nor will he let them fall again under the tyranny of sin (Rom. 6:14, 1 John 3:9, 5:18). Rather, the Good Shepherd will seek out his errant (and most unhappy) sheep, granting them repentance and moving them to return to him (Mt. 18:12, Acts 5:13, 11:18). Then, receiving their confession of sin, he will gladly cleanse their guilty conscience and renew their love, gratitude, and confidence in him (1 John 1:8-9). This, by the way, is what Jesus seems to have meant when he told his disciples that in order to abide in him they must eat his flesh and drink his blood (John 6:53-58). Over and again they are to come to him in prayer, humbly confessing their sins and appropriating by faith the forgiveness and inward renewal that he purchased for them with his broken body and shed blood. Because he is their omnipotent King—ruling forever in their hearts—he will surely see to it that they do this very thing (John 10:16).

Conclusion

As God's appointed Teacher must, Jesus of Nazareth does indeed answer the question, "How shall we live?" Yet we have seen that he does so in a manner most unexpected and altogether unique. He does not answer by simply laying down the law, urging compliance, threatening punishment, and promising reward. That way had been tried before and found wanting, due to the incorrigibility of sinful man (Heb. 8:7-13).

So Jesus does something new. He answers by laying down the law, and something else besides: his own life. In time, this sacrifice will enable his people fully to comply with the law. It will also enable them to be fully assured that they *have* escaped divine punishment and that they *will* receive an eternal reward. In other words, Jesus does not answer this question of life by *reinforcing* the objective moral order, but rather by *reconciling* his people to it. He relates them to the moral order in "a new and living way," a way that brings life rather than death (Heb. 10:20).

Observe, then, how comprehensively Jesus addresses every difficulty raised by the objective moral order. In his teaching, he articulates a new and fulsome body of divine law, so that men, nations, and entire civilizations need never again be in the dark about how they should live.[1] By his righteous life and atoning death, he justifies all who trust in him, reconciling them to this (oft-broken) law, and delivering them from its power to condemn. Moreover, through the gift of his indwelling Spirit, he breathes into his disciples a passionate love for his "easy yoke," the law of Christ. Henceforth, because of the Spirit's work within, this rule of life serves as a lofty goal towards which they may realistically strive, and also as a powerful instrument by which they will surely be made holy (Rom. 8:3-4).

How do people receive these great gifts? How do they learn to distinguish good and evil? How do they find forgiveness? How do they become better persons? Jesus makes it simple. To these and all other moral quandaries, he gives the same heart-warming reply: Come unto me.

Especially for Seekers

It is a matter of historical record that biblical law and ethics have, at least until recent times, served as the primary foundation for Western morality and jurisprudence. Even if unconsciously, we in Europe and America still pay tribute to the Judeo-Christian revelation whenever we appeal to a divine Sovereign as the ultimate basis for law, ethics, and civil government; when we insist upon a rule of law rather than a rule of kings or social elites; when we reckon men and nations to be responsible for their actions, and answerable to God for them; when we regard all persons as equal before the law, whether rich or poor, powerful or weak; when we strive to administer swift and proportionate punishments for law-breaking, not only as a matter of deterrence, but primarily as a matter of justice; when we specially enshrine the dignity and rights of each person or ethnic group; when we urge particular solicitude for the rights of women, children, the poor, the aged, the oppressed, and the socially displaced; when we proscribe and seriously penalize murder, kidnap, theft, perjury, slander, rape, adultery, and all forms of sexual deviancy; when we legally enforce the humane treatment of animals and a careful stewardship of the environment; and when, being convinced of the universality of divine law, we seek to eradicate unjust institutions in cultures beyond our own. In sum, history shows that under God biblical law and ethics powerfully engage, shape, and strengthen mankind's moral intuitions, so much so that they have radically transformed and civilized entire societies.

Critics sometimes complain, however, that at certain points God's laws and judgments seem cruel and/or unjust. Since these accusations have often troubled seekers, I want to conclude this portion of our journey by commenting briefly on what are probably the top four.

God's Command to Destroy the Seven Canaanite Nations

Prior to Israel's entering Canaan, God commanded Joshua to oversee the annihilation of the seven Canaanite nations. Men, women, children, flocks, and herds were all to be completely destroyed (Deut. 7:1-5, Josh. 6:15-21). God specifically commanded the Israelites to show these people no mercy. How can such severity be justified?

By way of response, let us note first of all that this war was unique. As a rule, Israel was to be a peace-loving nation. God positively forbade the accumulation of horses, or the fashioning of exotic weapons of warfare (Deut. 17:16). Though he did indeed authorize his people to defend themselves from invaders, they were not to invade other nations for the purpose of seeking territory, booty, or tribute. Moreover, when necessity forced them into war, they were to show mercy to women, children, and animals (Deut. 21:10-20). So again, the war against the Canaanites was something unique, a clear exception to the norm for Israel's conduct among the nations (Deut. 20:16-18).

Secondly, it must be understood that the Canaanites represented a serious threat to God's people and God's purposes. As we saw earlier, Israel was to be a kind of national incubator for the coming world redeemer. But what if the incubator itself were defiled by the egregious idolatry and depravity of Canaanite culture, thereby falling under divine judgment and possible destruction (Gen. 15:16, Lev. 18:24f)? It was, then, with a view to preserving the holiness of the Messiah's people, that God determined to judge, with exemplary severity, the unholiness of the inhabitants of their new homeland (Deut. 7:1-5).

Thirdly, it is arguable that this judgment represented a mercy to the Canaanite children. Their culture was thoroughly depraved, and soon they themselves would bear its imprint, if they didn't already. Since death must come to all, would it not be better for these children to die young and enter heaven, rather than to live long, sink further into depravity, and finally perish in hell? Suppose, then, that God did indeed take the souls of the dead Canaanite children to heaven, irrespective of their parent's immorality (see Deut. 1:39, Isaiah 7:15-16, Ezek. 18:1f, Jonah 4:11, Mark 10:13-14). Under such circumstances, who can reasonably deny that their death, far from being an injustice, was actually a mercy?

Finally, it appears that God intended the destruction of Canaan as a type. In this regard, it is very like the destruction of the world by water in the days of Noah, or the destruction of Sodom and Gomorrah by fire in the days of Abraham and Lot—*both of which calamities Jesus cited as types of the last judgment at his coming again in glory* (Luke 17:26-30). Guided by these precedents, we may therefore say, with the NT, that Canaan typifies the new and perfect world that Christ—God's latter day Joshua—will introduce at the end of the age (Romans 4:13, Phil. 3:21). It is, however, a world that must first be purged of every vestige of evil, so as to make it a fit habitation for God's glory and his glorified people (Mt. 13:40-43, 2 Thess. 1, 2 Peter 3:3-13, Rev. 19:11ff). In order, then, to picture this world—and the universal conflagration that must lead to it—God ordered Joshua to thoroughly purge Canaan before resettling it. This too may be seen as a mercy—a mercy to seekers and believers of all subsequent generations, who learn from this solemn story that they do well to fear the LORD, and to make their peace with his latter-day Joshua before he comes (Deut. 17:18-20).

Children Punished for the Sins of the Fathers?

As a motive to their spiritual obedience, the LORD declared to Israel that he is a jealous God, "...visiting the iniquity of the fathers on the children to the third and fourth generations of those who hate Me, but showing mercy to thousands, to those who love Me and keep My commandments" (Ex. 20:5). Does this mean that God punishes children for the sins of the fathers; and if so, how just is that?

In response, most commentators begin by pointing to Ezekiel 18:1-32, where God explicitly declares that, "The son shall not bear the guilt of the father, nor the father bear the guilt of the son. The righteousness of the righteous shall be upon himself, and the wickedness of the wicked shall be upon himself." The biblical rule, then, is that with respect to the guilt and punishment of sin, "Each man shall bear his own load" (Gal. 6:5). This does not mean, however, that children are not burdened with the negative consequences of their father's sins (e.g., poverty, shame, impaired health, etc.). In the Law, God therefore warns his people of this dreadful prospect, obviously intending to enlist parental affection and family honor as further motives to covenant loyalty to the LORD.

Also, if it seems unfair that children should suffer for their parent's ungodliness even to a limited extent, we should remember that the Bible repeatedly depicts God as being keenly attentive to the cries of the poor and needy (Deut. 10:18, Psalm 18). The suffering of the children of the wicked may therefore be carefully designed to elicit such cries, which in turn draws God near to them, and them away from the deadly paths of their parents. Here again we find that the judgments of the LORD are a great deep (Psalm 36:6), since they can reflect not only his wrath, but also the shadow of his hand extended in love and mercy.

Capital Punishment Under the Mosaic Law

Under the Mosaic Law, many crimes were capital offences. They included various "religious" sins such as idolatry, blasphemy, witchcraft, and Sabbath-breaking; and they also included various inter-personal sins, such as murder, kidnapping, incorrigible juvenile delinquency, adultery, rape, homosexual behavior, bestiality, and more. Many today, who cannot bring themselves even to sanction capital punishment in the case of murder, find the length of this list appalling (though only a century ago, even in many Western nations, it was actually far longer). Are we dealing here with cruel and unusual punishment, as was so typical of many ancient near Eastern societies?

In response, observe first that the number of capital offenses cited in the OT is actually smaller than those found in the legal codes of Israel's neighbors. Moreover, by insisting on a fair trial with two or more reliable witnesses, the Mosaic Law ensured that the administration of the death penalty was always a matter of divine justice, and never a matter of human vengeance, error, or caprice (Deut. 17:6). Also, it is noteworthy that the Mosaic Law, with a single exception, refuses to countenance punishment by mutilation (Deut. 25:11). This too separated Israel from most of her neighbors, whose tyrannical cruelty was renowned (Ex. 6:9, Jer. 6:23).

Secondly, it is clear that the OT norms cannot be adopted wholesale as a pattern for the nations of NT times. On the one hand, this is because the OT has been fulfilled in the New, *and is therefore obsolete* (Heb. 8:13). On the other hand, this is because the NT legislates exclusively for the Church, and never for the state. That is, it refuses to urge a Christian theocracy upon the Gentile nations, a mandate that would have entailed civil sanctions up to and including capital punishment for violations of NT law.

Practically speaking, this means that latter day governments *may* turn to the Old or New Testaments for guidance in formulating civil law; and indeed, various NT texts indicate that they probably *should*, especially since God designates civil magistrates as ministers of his justice (Mt. 5:18, Rom. 1:18f, 13:1f, 1 Tim. 1:3-11).

Nevertheless, in doing so they will have to be very careful.

Consider, for example, some of the distinctly "religious laws" of the OT. It is clear that Sabbath-breaking ought not to be a capital offense, since the NT regards the Sabbath as a temporary (and typological) ordinance, peculiar to OT times (Col. 2:16f, Heb. 4:1-10). Similarly, it is highly doubtful that blasphemy, idolatry, or even witchcraft should be punishable by death, since the culpability of these offenses in OT times arose precisely from their being committed by members of the OT covenant community, a community graced by the very presence of "the Holy One of Israel." Accordingly, if such laws are still to be enforced, they must be enforced *in the Church,* since the Church is the new covenant community, the new Israel of God (Gal. 6:16). And indeed, this is the position of the NT apostles, who specifically authorized Christian leaders to administer "spiritual capital punishment" (i.e., excommunication, in hopes of eventual repentance and restoration) upon all professing believers who persistently break NT religious (or interpersonal) laws (Mt. 18:15-20, 1 Cor. 5:9-13). But surely civil magistrates ought not physically to execute unbelievers for doing such things, since unbelievers claim no allegiance to the new covenant community at all. Thus, in the case of the OT *religious* laws, the words of the apostle would seem to apply: the Church judges those who are within, but God (and not the civil magistrates) judges those who are without (1 Cor. 5:13).

In the case of inter-personal sins, however, the situation is not so clear. Today, most citizens would still agree that pre-meditated murder is rightfully a capital offense. And one could argue biblically for drawing the line there, since prior to giving the Law to Israel, God designated murder as the only capital offense (Gen. 9:6). Paul, however, seems to affirm that other offenses are also worthy of death (Acts 25:11, 1 Tim. 1:3-11). Could it be, then, that the OT names them for us? Could it be that in some or even all such cases, justice is actually best served, protection best secured, deterrence best achieved, *and mercy best shown* by putting proven offenders swiftly to death?[2] True, most people today would balk at this suggestion. Yet most today are witnessing Western society's slow and deadly descent into sexual anarchy and gratuitous violence. Perhaps, then, if only for survival's sake, most will one day change their minds.[3]

Whatever the answer to these urgent practical questions, this much is clear: one of the chief functions of OT law was to demonstrate "the exceeding sinfulness of sin" in the sight of a holy God (Rom. 7:13). Always, he is just; always, he is merciful. But always, by his judicious administration of capital punishment in ancient Israel, he reminds the nations of this core biblical truth: "The wages of sin is death" (Rom. 6:23). It is, then, one of the Church's unavoidable duties to strive to see that truth enshrined in civil law. She must, however, remember that she has a higher calling still, which is to see it enshrined in the gospel. In other words, even to the end of the age the Church is to remind the world that there is a death penalty far worse than any that could befall our earthly bodies; and that there is a good and merciful God who will gladly enable us to escape it, if only we will trust in the One whom he sent to suffer it in our place (Mt. 10:28, Heb. 2:9, 14).

Slavery

From their reading of both the Old and New Testaments, many critics conclude that God not only refrained from condemning slavery, but actually viewed it as a societal norm. How, they ask, can he be good if he accepts and even institutionalizes slavery?

If by "slavery" we mean the right of one man to own another and to do with him as he pleases, the short answer to this question is that God does *not*, in any ultimate sense, accept or endorse slavery. We see this very clearly in the NT, where, according to Jesus and the apostles, we have God's "last word" on this subject. There we learn that the Son has come to set men free, chiefly from the tyranny of sin, but also from the tyranny of every human institution reared upon sin (John 8:36, 1 Cor. 15:24). Similarly, Paul says, "It was for freedom that Christ has set us free; therefore, do not...be subject again to a yoke of slavery" (Gal. 5:1). While his meaning here is spiritual, it entails that Christians must not become slaves of men (1 Cor. 7:23). Moreover, if, as slaves, they can become free, they should do so (1 Cor. 7:21). Yes, for pragmatic reasons connected with the spread of the gospel, some believers will have to abide awhile in their "calling" as slaves (1 Cor. 7:21-22, 1 Tim. 6:1-2). Furthermore, if this is their lot, they must serve their earthly masters from the heart, as unto the Lord himself, with the kind of submissive spirit that will commend their heavenly Master to all (Eph. 6:5-9). In doing so, however, they are to remember that slavery belongs only to this present evil age; that in its more oppressive forms it is a physical picture of mankind's spiritual servitude to sin and Satan (Mt. 12:29, John 8:34, Rom. 6:16f); that in its more benign forms it is a picture of the blessedness of servitude to the good Master above (Ex. 21:5-6, 1 Cor. 7:22, Col. 4:1); but that in any circumstance, it is only temporary. Yes, for the moment the merchants of "Babylon" (i.e., the fallen world system) continue their ugly traffic in "...cattle and sheep, horses and carriages, and bodies and souls of men" (Rev. 18:13). But one day soon the Lord God will consume their city with fire (Rev. 18:8). Then the form of this present world—including the slavery that more or less grievously disfigures it—will forever pass away (1 Cor. 7:31).

Once seen in the light of this definitive NT judgment, all other biblical texts dealing with slavery fall into proper perspective. True, the OT did articulate a body of law governing slavery. But again, this only means that God, desiring vividly to portray certain important truths about sin and redemption, elected temporarily to permit *and closely regulate* an institution that he planned ultimately to eradicate. Furthermore, the regulations themselves are noteworthy, manifesting great concern for the well being of every slave, whether foreign or native-born. For example, masters must rule their slaves with gentleness (Lev. 25:43, 46, 53). They must give female slaves their proper conjugal rights (Ex. 21:7-11). They must never acquire slaves by abduction, still less punish them by murder, both of which God declared to be capital offenses (Ex. 21:16, 20, Lev. 24:22). Enslaved debtors are to be released after six years (Ex. 21:2); those who voluntarily sell themselves into slavery must be released after 50 (Lev. 25:39-40), or upon payment to their master of the price of redemption (Lev. 25:47-53). Also, when a slave is freed, his master must send him away with ample provision for a fresh start in his tribal homeland (Ex. 21:2-6).

As we saw earlier, history abundantly confirms what the Bible itself teaches: the whole tenor of the Judeo-Christian scriptures is against slavery, not for it. The names of such human rights stalwarts as William Wilberforce, William Lloyd Garrison, Sojourner Truth, and Martin Luther King all remind us that, under God, the Bible and the Bible alone seems to have the power to kindle the insight, passion, and perseverance necessary for uprooting every form of slavery from the cultures of the world. While the task has taken too long—and will doubtless continue to occupy us for years to come—the great progress already made bodes well for the future. Indeed, it gives us a tantalizing glimpse of an altogether new world up ahead, one in which the Lord God Almighty has made *all* of his beloved children perfect slaves of his dear Son, and so free, free, free at last.

CHAPTER 15

WHAT HAPPENS WHEN WE DIE?

HUNDREDS OF YEARS before Jesus was born, the prophet Isaiah had this to say about the coming of the Messiah:

> The land of Zebulun and the land of Naphtali, the way of the sea, beyond the Jordan, Galilee of the Gentiles: the people who sit in darkness have seen a great light, and upon those who sit in the region and shadow of death, light has dawned.
> —Isaiah 9:1-2, Matthew 4:12-17

Truly, Isaiah's words are laden with divine compassion. God sees that the Gentiles, who have not yet received his revelation, are sitting in darkness. Moreover, he sees that they are sitting in the region and shadow of death, where the darkness is most fearsome. They do not know when, how, or why death entered the world. They do not know what happens at the moment of death: whether the lights go out, or whether they will continue to exist consciously in another world. And even if they do continue to exist, they do not know the condition in which they will find themselves: whether under eternal punishment for their evil deeds, or under eternal blessing for their good deeds, or waiting for still another go-around upon the earth. They do not know if they will ever see their spouse again, or their parents, or their children, or their friends. And finally, they do not know the One who has the answers to these questions. Yes, looking around and within, they see good evidence for an unknown god. But they cannot see what he will do with them at the moment of their death, when they fall into his hands.

So again, this prophecy is richly laden with compassion. It tells us that God cares about the Gentiles who sit despondently in the shadow of death. Moreover, because he cares, he soon will act. He will send his Messiah, who, like the rising sun, will shed the light of God's truth on the mystery of death.

In other words, the Messiah will be a Teacher, a Teacher appointed to tell us all what happens when we die. And in the case of those who put their trust in him, he will do something still more wonderful: he will *embolden* them to die. How? By bringing them to live with him in the region and shadow of *life*. In that holy place, they will never fear death again.

Jesus on the Mystery of Death

If Jesus of Nazareth is indeed God's Messiah, we may reasonably expect him to fulfill Isaiah's ancient prophecy by illuminating the mystery of death. In our journey thus far, we have already seen that he does. Here, however, we must probe his teaching on this weighty theme more thoroughly. In other words, we must now focus our attention on Jesus' *personal eschatology*, his view of the final condition—the eternal destiny—of individual human beings.

Let us begin by observing once again that Jesus saw man as a bi-partite being, a being composed of a physical body that is indwelt by a spiritual soul (Mt. 10:28). His teaching here accords perfectly with the Genesis creation narrative, where we learn that God first made man's body out of the dust of the earth, and then "breathed" a life-giving soul into him, so that he became a living human being (Gen. 2:7). Here we discover the divine norm for man, namely, that he should be a living soul, inhabiting and animating a living body, and thus dwelling with the living God in the world of nature, forever.

Jesus understood, however, that Adam's sin introduced a terrible departure from this norm (Gen. 2:15-17, 3:17-19, Rom. 5:12). Because of his disobedience in Eden, death entered the world in at least three different forms. First, there was *spiritual death*: the withdrawal of God's life-sustaining Spirit from the soul of man, so that henceforth it fell under the tyranny of sin (Gen. 6:5, Eph. 4:18). Secondly, there was *physical death*, which involved not only the (unnatural) separation of the soul from the body, but all the degenerative processes leading up to it: the burden of aging (James 2:26). Finally, there entered (the peril of) *eternal death*, a state in which unredeemed human beings are forever separated from the life-giving presence of God, and also exist, consciously, under positive punishments for their sins.

Believing all this, Jesus regarded death as an *enemy*. He would never, in the manner of many today, gloss over death by calling it "a part of life," or counsel men to "go gentle into that goodly night." To the contrary, he viewed death as an opponent of life, an unnatural interloper, an alien and evil presence in God's good world. True, God himself is the one who wisely ordained it as a consequence of sin. Yet he also hates it and plans to destroy it, as indeed the OT scriptures taught (Isaiah 25:7, Hosea 13:14). In this confidence, Jesus therefore stood firm against "the last enemy." In particular, he healed multitudes of sick and injured people who were threatened by death; he raised up not a few who had already succumbed to death; and he wept with those who were bereaved by death (John 11:35). Beyond this, he also earnestly taught about death—and not as a mere philosopher or scientist who is content to describe this spiritual scorpion, but as a divine savior, with authority and power to remove its sting once for all (Mt. 9:18-19, 23-25, Luke 7:11-15, John 11:1-44, 1 Cor. 15:26, 56-57).

Furthermore, unlike other religious leaders, Jesus taught on this subject as one who had perfect understanding of death and the after-life. He taught as one having authority (Mt. 7:29); as one who has come down from heaven itself (John 3:13); as one who knows what lies beyond death (Luke 16:19-26); as one who will personally rise to victory over death (John 10:18); as the one appointed by God to send every man to his eternal destiny at the moment of his death (John 5:16-30); and as the one who therefore holds the keys of death and Hades in his own hands (Rev. 1:18). In short, Jesus clearly projected himself to seekers as the one who brings God's full and final revelation about the mystery of death to all mankind.

Even the Jews, the privileged custodians of the oracles of God, had not yet received such a revelation. Yes, their prophets had paved the way. They had declared, for example, that at the moment of death the wicked descend into the Pit and *Sheol*, OT words that, in most contexts, conveyed the idea of a place of punishment lying somewhere beneath the earth (Deut. 32:22, Psalms 9:17, 55:15, Prov. 5:5, 15:11, Isaiah 14:9, Ezek. 31:15f; Num. 16:30, Job 33:18, 22, 24, 28, Isaiah 24:22). Similarly, the prophets had hinted broadly that at the moment of death the souls of the righteous ascend into heaven, where they behold the glory of God and, together with the holy angels, live with him in perfect joy (Psalms 16:11, 17:15, 73:24f, 139:8, Prov. 14:32, 15:24). Thus, like many Gentile nations, Israel had a definite awareness of an afterlife.

Yet the ancient biblical testimony, rich as it was, remained ambiguous. In some cases, for example, it was unclear whether *Sheol* meant "the grave" or an actual nether world (Job 17:13, 16, Psalm 16:10, 18:5, Isaiah 14:11, 38:10). In others, it seemed as if the dead were no longer conscious (Psalm 6:5, Isaiah 38:18). Yes, a number of passages clearly indicated that one day God would raise men from the dead (Job 19:26, Isaiah 25:17, 26:19, Dan. 12:2). But even these left readers uncertain as to when this great event would occur, who exactly would be raised, and what life would be like for those who were in that privileged number. Not surprisingly, then, by

Jesus' day this situation had given rise to a measure of doubt, confusion, and controversy about the nature of the soul, death, and the world beyond (Mt. 22:23-33). When at last he stepped out into his ministry, Jesus showed himself quite eager to dispel the confusion once and for all.

The Intermediate State

Jesus' teaching on death and the after-life is two-fold.

First, he shed fresh light on what theologians commonly refer to as *the intermediate state*. This may be defined as the condition of the soul after physical death and prior to the resurrection. On this fascinating theme, Jesus' story of the rich man and Lazarus is of special importance:

> There was a certain rich man who was clothed in purple and fine linen and fared sumptuously every day. But there was a certain beggar named Lazarus, full of sores, who was laid at his gate, desiring to be fed with the crumbs which fell from the rich man's table. Moreover, the dogs came and licked his sores.
>
> So it was that the beggar died and was carried by the angels to Abraham's bosom. The rich man also died and was buried. And being in torments in Hades, he lifted up his eyes and saw Abraham afar off, and Lazarus in his bosom. Then he cried and said, "Father Abraham, have mercy on me, and send Lazarus that he may dip the tip of his finger in water and cool my tongue; for I am tormented in this flame."
>
> But Abraham said, "Son, remember that in your lifetime you received your good things, and likewise Lazarus evil things; but now he is comforted and you are tormented. And besides all this, between us and you there is a great gulf fixed, so that those who want to pass from here to you cannot, nor can those from there pass to us."
>
> —Luke 16:19-26

Most commentators regard this story as a kind of parable, primarily because so many other biblical texts envision heaven as a true place above, and Hades as a true place beneath—hard cosmological facts implying that the rich man and Abraham could not really have held such a conversation. Nevertheless, it is clear that Jesus' intent was indeed to teach new and important truths regarding the intermediate state. Let us focus here on three.[1]

First, the story clearly teaches that death is not the end. As opposed to the philosophical naturalists, Jesus says that the lights do not go out when we die, but that the soul continues to exist—consciously—in another place and in another condition.

Secondly, it teaches that the soul, at the moment of death, goes to one of two possible destinations. In the case of the child of God, that destination is heaven (Mt. 5:3, 1 Cor. 1:26, James 2:5). Here, Jesus calls heaven "Abraham's bosom," a word-picture calculated to arouse in his Jewish audience comforting thoughts of heavenly fellowship with the heroes of their faith, including especially its ancient founder. Elsewhere, he refers to heaven as Paradise, another picturesque word recalling the serenity and delight of the Garden of Eden (Luke 23:43, 2 Cor. 12:4, Rev. 2:7).

As we saw earlier, heaven is best understood as a true place, a visionary world "above," where the holy angels and the departed sprits of the saints enjoy a continuous revelation of God, Christ, and divine truth (Heb. 12:22-24, Rev. 4-5). The NT is quite emphatic that at the moment of death believers enter heaven—possibly being carried there by holy angels—where they will henceforth enjoy manifold spiritual blessings, even as they wait eagerly for Christ's *parousia* and the resurrection of the dead at the end of the age (Luke 23:43, Phil. 1:19-26, 2 Cor. 5:5-8, Rev. 6:9, 20:4).[2]

In the parable, Jesus identifies the destination of the souls of the wicked as Hades. In one or two cases, this NT word seems to refer simply to the state of death (i.e., the state in which the soul is temporarily separated from the body, Acts 2:27, 31). As a rule, however, it refers to a true place beneath. Analogously to heaven, it is probably best to think of this "place" as an other-dimensional visionary world, a spiritual "abyss" where the souls of the wicked, along with a portion of the fallen angels, experience divine retribution for their sins (Mt. 11:23, Luke 8:31, Rev. 9:1-2, 20:1,3). Fundamentally, their punishment is two-fold. First, it involves loss: loss of all the "good things" (i.e., temporal blessings) that they enjoyed during their earthly life, as well as the loss of further opportunity to seek and find salvation (Luke 16:27-31). Secondly, it involves positive torments. These include darkness (2 Peter 2:4), (a consciousness of) some kind of fire (Luke 16:24), the proximity of demons (Rev. 18:2, 20:10), and dreadful apprehensions of the Day of Judgment still to come (Mt. 8:29).

Thirdly, we learn from this parable that at the moment of death the soul's destiny is sealed forever. As Jesus put it, God has fixed a "great gulf" between heaven and Hades. At death, the redeemed and the unredeemed embark on separate eternal destinies, and so are separated from one another forever (cf. Mt. 25:32f). Undoubtedly, this is why Jesus spoke so often and so forcefully about death and the after-life. In his thinking, there is no Purgatory—no place where the soul is temporarily purged under divine chastisements and then received into heaven.[3] Nor does the soul reincarnate, so as to work out its *karma* in one earthly life after another. Nor will people get a second chance to receive salvation after they die. Thus, for Jesus the truth is as simple as it is sobering: it is appointed to man once to die, and after that the judgment (Heb. 9:27). This means that earthly life is a unique—and very small—window of opportunity, a brief "year of the Lord's favor" in which men must settle their eternal destiny by deciding whether or not to follow the Messiah. In the case of those who do, even if they die, they will live forever (John 11:25-26, Rev. 20:5-6). In the case of those who do not, they will die in their sins, and henceforth be unable to come to him where he is (John 8:21-24). In sum, life is short, but it is long enough to prepare to die. And indeed, that is its main purpose. Paul's impassioned cry to the Corinthians therefore well expresses the mind and heart of his Master: "Behold, now is the acceptable time. Behold, now is the day of salvation" (Isaiah 49:8, 2 Cor. 6:20).

The Final State

Though the NT speaks from time to time about the intermediate state, its emphasis is upon the final state. Jesus' interpretation of the parable of the wheat and the tares gives us an important glimpse of this state, and of when and how it will begin:

> He who sows the good seed is the Son of Man. The field is the world, the good seeds are the sons of the kingdom, but the tares are the sons of the evil one. The enemy who sowed them is the devil, the harvest is the end of the age, and the reapers are the angels. Therefore as the tares are gathered and burned in the furnace, so it will be at the end of the age. The Son of Man will send out His angels, and they will gather out of His kingdom all things that offend, and those who practice lawlessness, and will cast them into the furnace of fire. There will be wailing and gnashing of teeth. Then the righteous will shine forth as the sun in the kingdom of their Father. He who has ears to hear, let him hear.
> —Mt. 13:39-43; Mt. 24:29-31, John 5:16-30

Here, in a few bold strokes, Jesus sketches for his disciples a basic picture of the consummation, the dramatic wrap-up of God's redemptive plan that will occur at the end of the age. Like the creation and the fall, it is one of the great transitional events in the history of the universe, an event of cosmic proportions. When it occurs, the intermediate state of the dead will draw to a close, and their final state will begin and endure forever.

Later on we will discuss a number of the texts that flesh out and illuminate the sketch found in this parable. Here, however, it suffices to observe that the final state comes quickly upon the heels of the Messiah's *parousia*, that is, *his bodily coming again in power and glory at the end of the age*. In that day, says the Bible, he himself will effect a single resurrection of all the human beings who have ever lived, as well as a bodily transformation of those who are alive at his appearing (Mt. 22:30, Luke 14:14, John 11:25, Acts 4:2, 24:15, 1 Cor. 15:21; John 5:25, Phil. 3:21, 1 Cor. 15:51-52, 1 Thess. 4:13-18). Then, by the hand of the holy angels, he will gather them all before his throne, lifting them into the darkened sky above, even as the earth beneath is dissolved by fire (2 Pet. 3:10-13, Rev. 20:11). With all the nations thus assembled before him, the Righteous Judge will weigh each man's life, determine his just recompense, separate the redeemed from the lost, and send each to his eternal destiny (Mt. 25:31-46, Rom. 14:10, 2 Cor. 5:10, Rev. 20:11-15). At this point, the final state for all rational moral agents—both human and angelic—begins.

The final state of the lost is terrifying to contemplate. Having been raised (or transformed), they are once again incarnate human beings, beings whom Christ himself—again by angelic agency—will cast into "the furnace of fire." This is the place of eternal punishment, also referred to in the Revelation as "the lake of fire" (Rev. 19:20, 20:10, 14). It will be created on the Day of Judgment (presumably by Christ), especially for Satan and his evil angels, but also for those rebellious humans who have spurned God's salvation (Mt. 22:1-14, 25:41, Rev. 20:10). Because the lost are said to go there bodily, this is a true place, apparently located close to the (new) earth (Rev. 14:10-11). Whether its fires are physical or spiritual (i.e., visionary), is unclear. As in *Hades*, its inhabitants experience loss, regret, torment, and, it would appear, a consciousness of God's wrath abiding upon them (John 3:36, Rom. 2:28, Rev. 19:9-20). In this "outer darkness" there is therefore weeping and gnashing of teeth, most especially at the terrible thought that such punishment will never end (Mt. 8:12, 22:13, Rev. 14:11). Tellingly, Jesus usually referred to this place as *Gehenna* (i.e., hell), a word whose Hebrew etymology identifies it as a kind of cosmic garbage dump, in which the refuse of the universe—both human and demonic—will burn forever just outside the City of God (Mt. 5:22, 29, 10:28, 18:9, 23:15, 33; Rev. 19:1-4, 22:15). Hell, therefore, becomes an eternal reminder to God's elect of his infinite holiness, perfect justice, and sovereign mercy. Seeing it, their grateful thought will ever be, "There, but for the grace of God, go I" (Eph. 1:6).

Concerning the final state of the redeemed, the Bible is more explicit. In the parable, Jesus says that they will shine forth like the sun in the Kingdom of their Father. Here he is envisioning the saints in new, glorified bodies, living under new heavens and upon a new earth (Isaiah 65:17, 66:22, 2 Pet. 3:13). Let us take a moment to consider each of these rich blessings.

As for the saints' resurrection bodies, they are necessary equipment, since flesh and blood, as presently constituted, are simply too frail to inherit the glories of the (consummated) Kingdom of God (1 Cor. 15:50). Above all, they will be like the body of the risen Christ, who is "the first-fruits of those who sleep," the divine prototype to which the new humanity shall be conformed in body, soul, and spirit (1 Cor. 15:20, Rom. 8:29, Phil. 3:21, 1 John 3:2). Jesus gives us glimpses of the resurrection body on the Mount of his Transfiguration (Mt. 17:1f), in his several resurrection appearances (Luke 24, John 21), and, to some extent, in his self-disclosure to John on the island of Patmos (Rev. 1:9ff). Paul affirms that the resurrection bodies of the saints will be incorruptible, immortal, powerful, Spirit-controlled, and radiant with the glory of God (1 Cor. 15:42f, Mt. 17:2, Rev. 1:9f). Being altogether perfected, both within and without, the saints will shine like the sun in its strength in the Kingdom of their Father (Dan. 12:3, Mt. 13:43, Rev. 1:16).

Concerning the saints' future dwelling-place, Jesus' parable implies what other NT texts make explicit, namely, that he himself will create it at his *parousia* (1 Cor. 15:25-28, Phil. 3:21, Rev. 1:18, 3:14, 22:13). The scenario appears to be as follows. As part of the last judgment, Christ will ignite a cosmic conflagration: the heavens will be dissolved by fire, and the elements will melt with fervent heat (2 Pet. 3:12). Then—again at Christ's word—a new earth will arise from the ashes of the old. After this, wedding bells begin to toll. Christ's Church—the Holy City, the New Jerusalem—descends to the earth, adorned as a Bride for her husband. She is without spot or wrinkle or any such thing, having the glory of God (Eph. 5:25-27, Rev. 21:1f). When her descent is complete, she is at home with her Beloved at last, and the eternal marriage supper of the Lamb begins (Mt. 22:1-14, Rev. 19:9).

Sparingly, the Bible reveals sundry physical features of the world to come. There will be no sun, moon, or stars, for God and Christ themselves, throughout a single eternal day, will be the light *in* all, and the light *of* all (Rev. 21:25, 22:5). There will be no more sea—though a world inwardly refreshed by the life-giving waters of the Spirit will doubtless be graced with physical analogues thereof: springs, streams, and rivers (Rev. 21:1; Isaiah 35:5-7, 41:17-20, Rev. 22:1). Animals will apparently be present, peacefully sharing with the family of man a new home of unimaginable Edenic beauty (Isaiah 11:6-9, 35:1ff, Rom. 8:19). While some interpreters have attempted to tease out of the Scriptures further details about the new earth, the Bible itself seems content to describe it in these few generalities. In doing so, it stirs the saints to a holy curiosity and an eager expectation of the secret glories that are yet to be revealed (1 Cor. 13:12, Rom. 8:18-25).

If, however, the physical details of the world to come remain largely concealed from their eyes, the saints may still comfort themselves in many general promises concerning the nature of the future Kingdom. For example, they may take hope and courage in the knowledge of what will *not* be there: the curse, sin, Satan, violence, war, sickness, pain, sorrow, and death (Isaiah 2:4, Rev. 20:10, 21:4). Similarly, they can rejoice in all that *will* be there: God, Christ, the Holy Spirit, the angelic hosts, multitudes of fellow-saints, light, life, purpose, service, righteousness, beauty, and joy (Rev. 21-22). It is the world of their dreams because it is the world of God's dreams; a world we all have dreamed of; a world in which, by God's grace, the real and the ideal have at last become one.

Especially for Seekers

Jesus' teaching about the after-life is highly intuitive. As we learn from ancient mythology and nearly all world religions, most people incline to the view that the soul survives death and goes on to live in a world beyond our own. Furthermore, most people feel it *should* go on, since justice requires that good or evil deeds not fully recompensed in this life should be so rewarded in the next. Jesus definitely agrees.

As for reasonableness, the Teacher's personal eschatology is both understandable and consistent. Moreover, it finds impressive empirical support in clinical experiments demonstrating the existence the soul, and also in scientific studies of "near death experiences" and related visions of heaven and hell.[4, 5, 6]

As for hopefulness, all agree that Jesus' teaching is fabulously rich—at least for those who stand with him as a friend. However, in the hearts of his enemies it only strikes terror, and quite reasonably so.

Eternal Punishment

This brings us to a much-needed discussion of one of the great scandals of Christianity: its doctrine of eternal punishment. And scandalous it is—so much so that it has caused many to run *away* from the faith, rather than *to* it. If this response is not reasonable, it is at least understandable. Who can fail to be shaken by the thought of anyone—even the chief of sinners—suffering the torments of hell forever? Moreover, beneath our initial revulsion at the thought of eternal punishment, there lurks a number of deep and gnawing theological questions. Is eternal punishment consistent with God's justice? How can the sins of one brief lifetime, however numerous or egregious, justly merit everlasting torment? Is eternal punishment consistent with God's love and goodness? How could his great Father heart allow him to impose such a terrible penalty on anyone? And finally, will not the brute fact of hell forever mar the blessedness of the saints? How will they be able to rejoice in heaven, knowing—and perhaps even witnessing—the sufferings of the damned?

In the face of such disturbing questions, the human mind, at least as presently constituted, recoils. Consequently—and not surprisingly—it is often tempted to race down miscellaneous paths of flight, seeking what it thinks to be a happier ending to the drama of salvation history.

Some, for example, argue that in the end all people will be saved, a view called *universalism*. Yet Jesus himself was clearly no universalist, saying that the gate is wide and the way broad that leads to destruction, and that many go in by it (Mt. 7:13-14, 24:51, 25:31-46, Rev. 22:15).

Others contend that the lost will not suffer consciously forever, but instead will (eventually) be "destroyed" by way of annihilation. Yet here too the Scriptures bar the way. John, for example, says of the lost that "the smoke of their torment ascends forever and ever," and that they have "no rest day or night" (Rev. 14:11). This echoes the words of his master, who described hell as a place "...where their worm does not die, and the fire is not quenched" (Mt. 24:51, Mark 9:46). It appears, then, that intellectual honesty requires us to admit that eternal punishment is indeed the teaching of the NT. Our only recourse is to try to understand it as best we can. Therefore, let us pause for a few biblically based reflections that may enable troubled seekers to reconcile themselves to this most challenging revelation.

Christian Severity?

To begin with, it is of some comfort to realize that Christianity is not alone in promulgating a doctrine of eternal punishment. Orthodox Judaism and Islam do the same. As for Eastern and New Age religions, they may, at first glance, seem to offer a "kinder, gentler" after-life in their doctrines of reincarnation and the final "salvation" (i.e., enlightenment) of all sentient beings. The truth, however, is that these faiths also envision "base" souls suffering in one or another of the several "hellish" planes that exist beyond our own. Furthermore, Eastern religions nearly always propound the idea of eternal recurrence. This means that even after the soul has completed its million-lifetime journey back to oneness with Big Mind, Big Mind will once again fall from its native oneness into a multiplicity of deluded and suffering sentient beings. And "he" will do so forever. The net result is that Eastern religion does indeed posit an eternity of (partially remitted) suffering *for everyone*. Whether this is in fact more hopeful (or more just or true) than the Christian scheme, every seeker must decide for himself.

Is Eternal Punishment Just?

Turning now to the Bible itself, let us probe a little further into the question of the justice of eternal punishment.

Observe first of all that the Bible repeatedly insists that *God is just*, that in him there is no darkness at all (Gen. 18:22-33, Deut. 32:4, 1 John 1:5, Rev. 15:3-4). If, then, a seeker becomes convinced that the Bible is God's Word, he must accept this affirmation as true, even if, in this or that particular case, it does not presently seem to be so. God is infinite, man finite (Job 38:2f). God's mind is pure, man's is stained and clouded by sin (Eph. 4:18). God knows all truth, man sees only some (1 Cor. 13:9, 12). Recognizing these things, those who honor the Bible as God's Word will prefer to doubt their own judgments rather than God's. It seems the only reasonable thing to do.

Observe also that the Bible insists that *retribution is just*. Retribution is, of course, simply recompense, or "payback," and in the biblical universe, payback is essential. Without it, there can be no justice. Indeed, one could argue that without it God cannot be God! This is because recompense belongs *essentially* to the way in which a sovereign and holy creator *must* relate to his free creatures if he is to continue being sovereign and holy.

In order to understand this crucial point, let us consider the example of an earthly father with his son. As we all know, a good father will teach his son the difference between right and wrong. Moreover, he will also clearly set forth the consequences of doing right and wrong, and will be faithful to administer those consequences as needed. Accordingly, he will praise and reward his son when he does what is good, but will also reprove and discipline him when he does what is evil. Concerning the latter, though he takes no pleasure in the disciplinary act itself, he will perform it anyway. Why? Because *not* to perform it would be to entangle himself in a positive evil of his own, namely, that he would now be unfaithful to his own word, and in clear violation of his parental duties. Indeed, such a failure would mean that he had actually abdicated his post as father and, in effect, made his rebellious son the "lord" of the family! Note carefully that in permitting all of this to happen, the father would also bring great dishonor upon himself and upon the family name. Foreseeing, then, the disastrous consequences of a failure to do his domestic duty, a good father realizes that he *must* discipline his son.

Biblically, the situation is much the same with God. Indeed, the scriptures teach that an earthly fathers' innate sense of obligation to govern his children actually flows from God himself; that it reflects and embodies

God's own sense of responsibility for the good government of the entire family of man (Prov. 3:11, Eph. 3:15, Heb. 12:1-11).

This divine responsibility is difficult but crucial to understand. It is based upon God's very nature, and also upon the nature of his relationship with his human children. Because they are *his* creatures, whatever they do necessarily reflects upon him, their creator. Therefore, desiring that their actions reflect upon him well, he "lays down the law," setting before them the path of a God-honoring life. But what if these free and accountable creatures choose not to walk that path? What if they choose to sin and rebel? At this point, a disaster of cosmic proportions threatens. For suppose that God, in the manner of a passive human father, were simply to turn a blind eye to their rebellion. Then the creator would in fact be yielding his rightful sovereignty to the creature. Moreover, he would also be subjecting himself to eternal shame, not only because his children's behavior reflected badly upon him, but also because he cared so little for his honor that he did nothing to protect it. In short, for God to overlook sin would be for him to deny his sovereignty, defile his glory, and therefore cease being God!

Needless to say, the Bible assures us that this *will not* happen because it *cannot* happen. In manifold ways, the scriptures tell us that God is a *very* good Father, fully committed to the preservation of his rulership and the honor of his family name. Accordingly, he enthusiastically assumes full responsibility for the moral government of his children. When they do his will and uphold his glory, he is well pleased to praise and reward them. But when they sin—when they threaten to *injure* the dignity of the Great King by challenging his natural right to reign over his own creatures—*then he must defend the integrity of his very being by injuring them in return* (Deut. 7:9-10, Mal. 1:14, Rom. 2:1-11, 12:19). Said the prophet Jeremiah, "The Lord is a God of recompense; he will fully repay" (Jer. 51:56; Prov. 12:14). Only through such an administration of justice—only through the "payback" of divine retribution—can God's glory be completely safeguarded.

These thoughts help us to see how eternal punishment—or eternal retribution—can be just. Suppose that a man sins. This responsible human creature—who ought to have honored his sovereign creator through obedience—has instead dishonored him through an act of rebellion. Observe carefully that this sin carries an eternal dimension, for it is an act that now threatens to mar God's glory *forever*. Moreover, unless the creator responds, it is an act that will, in some sense, *pain* him forever, for to all eternity he must suffer the sight of his glory being disfigured by it. To annihilate the sinner would do nothing at all to protect God's honor; indeed, it would only serve to dishonor him further by showing that he is either unwilling or unable to balance the scales properly and so protect his glory. How, then, is God to vindicate his sovereignty, maintain his honor, and deliver himself from eternal pain? In other words, how is he to go on being God? It appears that there is only one solution. *He must do to the sinner what the sinner would do to him: he must pain and dishonor him forever* (Dan. 12:2). Only thus is balance restored, only thus is justice done, only thus is the glory of God preserved forever.

But even this is not the end of the matter. For if a single sin merits such punishment, what of the sin of rejecting God's provision *for an entire lifetime of rebellion*? And according to the Bible, God has indeed made just such a provision for many. He has sent his Son, whose righteous life and atoning death secures redemption for any and all who are willing come to Christ (John 7:37, Rev. 22:17). He commands that this gospel be taken to all nations, and preached to every creature (Mt. 28:18f, Acts 1:8, Rom. 10:14-15). Moreover, out of love for all, he commands all everywhere to repent of their sins and believe the good news (Mark 1:15, Luke 14:23, Acts 17:30).

If, then, a man continually spurns this provision, he is effectively saying to God, "I will *never* obey You." His true intent is to remain autonomous forever, to rebel against God forever, to dishonor his sovereignty forever, and thus to pain him forever by staining his glory. Again, for God to annihilate such a one would actually be to reward him, since this painless "punishment" falls far short of what he justly deserves. But positively to afflict him forever would be to bestow upon him the same injury that he thought to bestow upon God (Luke 19:27, John 3:19, 2 Thess. 1:8). Thus, in hell the sinner gets exactly what he wants: eternal rebellion against God. But by casting the rebel into hell, God also gets what he wants, and what he needs in order to continue being God: the preservation of his glory forever through an administration of his perfect justice forever.

As regards God's justice, let us note also that Jesus foresaw degrees of punishment in hell, based upon the amount of spiritual light a person received and obeyed during his time upon the earth. Such texts reveal that God attends scrupulously to the demands of justice and equity in his every administration of retribution (Luke 12:47-48, 19:11-27, 1 Cor. 3:12-15).

One final point remains, a point that underscores the importance of our ever keeping in mind the biblical paradigm of man's freedom on probation. For while it is true that the Bible does indeed represent God and Christ as sending men to hell (Mt. 25:41, 46, Luke 12:5, John 5:27, 2 Peter 2:4-10), it also represents men *as sending themselves to hell*. The idea here is that God, by sentencing sinners to hell, is simply ratifying a judgment that they have already passed upon themselves. As Jesus put it, "This is the condemnation, that the light has come into the world, and men loved darkness rather than light, because their deeds were evil" (John 3:19). Similarly, Paul says to the recalcitrant Jews at Antioch, "It was necessary that the word of God should be spoken to you first; but since you reject it *and judge yourselves unworthy of everlasting life*, behold, we are turning to the Gentiles" (Acts 13:46). Again, such texts magnify the reality and seriousness of man's probation before God through the gospel. For both Jesus and Paul, the premise is that life is a test of one's love of God, truth, and righteousness; that men are given a *bona fide* opportunity to pass it; and that if they do not pass it, the fault is indeed their own (Luke 19:27, Acts 18:6, 2 Thess. 1:3-9). Is not such an arrangement just?

Is Eternal Punishment Consistent with God's Love and Goodness?

Many allege that eternal punishment is inconsistent with God's love and goodness. We have already seen, however, that in both of the biblical paradigms of God's dealings with mankind, these attributes shine forth.

As the divine Tester of his free creatures, God generously gives the wicked life. He gives them various temporal blessings. He gives them the spiritual light of nature and conscience. In many cases, he gives them the gospel, lovingly inviting them—indeed, commanding them—to come to Christ. Yet despite all these demonstrations of love and goodness, they choose to ignore and even scorn him.

Now it is true that in manifesting his ultimate sovereignty over the destinies of men, God elects not to set his redeeming love upon the reprobate (i.e., those whom he has decided to leave in their sins). And it is also true that this is hard to understand and to receive. Nevertheless, it is helpful to remember that God's decision in this matter was not made out of malice. Indeed, the Scriptures suggest that it was made with a certain sorrow and reluctance (Ezek. 18:32, Luke 13:34-35, Rom. 9:1-2, Phil. 3:17-19). Why, then, did he make it? Strange to tell, it appears that he made it out of his love and his goodness: love for the display of his sovereign grace, love for his chosen people, and love for the richness of their grateful worship through all eternity. Such things seemed good to God. Therefore, he determined to withhold his saving grace from the wicked, that they might freely choose to spurn the light and so condemn themselves to eternal punishment.

Will Hell Spoil Heaven?

Will the saints be offended by hell? Will the torments of the wicked grieve them forever? Here, the Bible answers with a clarion "no." God promises his people that in the world to come he will wipe away every tear from their eyes; that there will be no more sorrow or crying or pain, since the former things will have completely passed away (Rev. 21:4). So that the saints may enjoy this blessedness, God may cause them to forget the lost altogether (Isaiah 65:16-17). But if not, then the sight or the remembrance of their suffering may become an occasion, not for sorrow, but for a grateful admiration of the wisdom, justice, mercy, and grace of God. Admittedly, from our present vantage point such a response seems barely imaginable. But if, as the Bible teaches, God himself will eternally rejoice in his own judgments, it cannot be that his glorified saints—filled at last with the mind of Christ—will do any less (1 Cor. 2:16, Rev. 12:12, 15:3-4, 16:6, 18:20, 19:1-3).

Conclusion

In this chapter we have seen that Jesus of Nazareth does indeed tell us what will happen when we die. Though we may not fully understand his answer, or like certain parts of it, no one can say that he has not spoken clearly, reasonably, hopefully, and forcefully about the life to come. Moreover, in telling us about heaven and hell, he has gone on to tell us something even more important: how we may enter the former and escape the latter. Thus, Jesus' fulsome teaching on the after-life reaches its climax in one final statement, and in one final question based upon it:

> I am the resurrection and the life. He who believes in Me, though he may die, yet shall he live. And whoever lives and believes in Me shall never die. Do you believe this?
>
> —John 11:25-26

CHAPTER 16

WHERE IS HISTORY HEADING?

JUST AS AN individual can peer into his own personal future and ask, "What will happen when I die," so too can he peer into the cosmic future and ask, "Where is history heading; what does the future hold for the universe, life, and man?"

As he turns his gaze in this direction, it will not be long before a number of closely related questions spring to mind. Here is a sampling familiar to seekers acquainted with naturalistic, pantheistic, and theistic worldviews.

Will the human race, as most naturalistic philosophers assert, become extinct like so many other species have? Will the sun explode, and our earth perish in the resulting conflagration? Will our cooling universe become a cosmic dustbin, stripped of all order, beauty, life, and consciousness by the inexorable Second Law of Thermodynamics? Or, as other naturalists assert, will our (supposedly) expanding universe be captured by gravity, collapse into a tiny "singularity," explode again, evolve again, crunch again, and do the same thing over and over again, to all eternity?

On the other hand, could the Hindus and Buddhists be right when they teach that our so-called universe is actually a plane of consciousness, shared by a vast multitude of sentient beings; and that it is also an eternally recurring dream, cyclically springing in and out of the mind of Brahman, forever and ever?

Or are the New Agers closer to the mark, when, in their more linear view of cosmic history, they assert that the universe is god himself; that now, after so many billions of years of evolution, he (or she or it) is finally awakening to his true identity, with the result that a thoroughly divinized human race—the cutting edge of the evolutionary thrust—will soon have enough spiritual wisdom and power to create the world of its dreams?[1]

Or could it be that one of the theistic religions is correct, all of which share a rigorously linear view of history, looking for a coming day of God in which he will raise the dead, judge the world, and bring in the manifold blessings of his eternal Kingdom?

In asking these kinds of questions—and in considering the different answers given to them—seekers are venturing onto the terrain of *cosmic eschatology*. As a rule, they do so quite tentatively, feeling ill-equipped to address matters of such immense weight and complexity. If, however, the test perspective has gripped their imagination, they should be able to shake off many of their fears, understanding as they now do that the unknown god would not place such fascinating questions in our minds if he did not mean to answer them. Moreover, guided by that same perspective, they will know how to find the answers they need: they will actively seek out the world's greatest religious teachers, trying to determine who among them best answers the most daunting question of all, the question of the final destiny of the universe, life, and man.

Truly, this is a formidable challenge for any spiritual teacher. On the present leg of our journey, we will find out if Jesus of Nazareth rises to meet it.

The Teacher On Cosmic History

In previous chapters, we have seen that Jesus revealed to his disciples certain "mysteries of the Kingdom of God" (Mt. 13:16-17). That is, he undertook to unveil—once and for all—the complete truth about the course of salvation history. One important aspect of this teaching had to do with "things to come" (John 16:13, 1 Cor. 2:6-12, Eph. 1:15-18). Here Jesus taught on the whole spectrum of events that would occur after his return to heaven; that is, on events leading up to—and including—the appearing of the Kingdom of God in its final and eternal form. In other words, Jesus did indeed purport to bring to his disciples—and to all nations—God's very own cosmic eschatology (Rev. 1:8, 11-12, 17-20). We turn to it now.

Three Ages

In order to understand Jesus' teaching on this theme, we must again briefly survey his overall view of cosmic history. We will begin by introducing several new and important NT ideas pertaining to this theme.

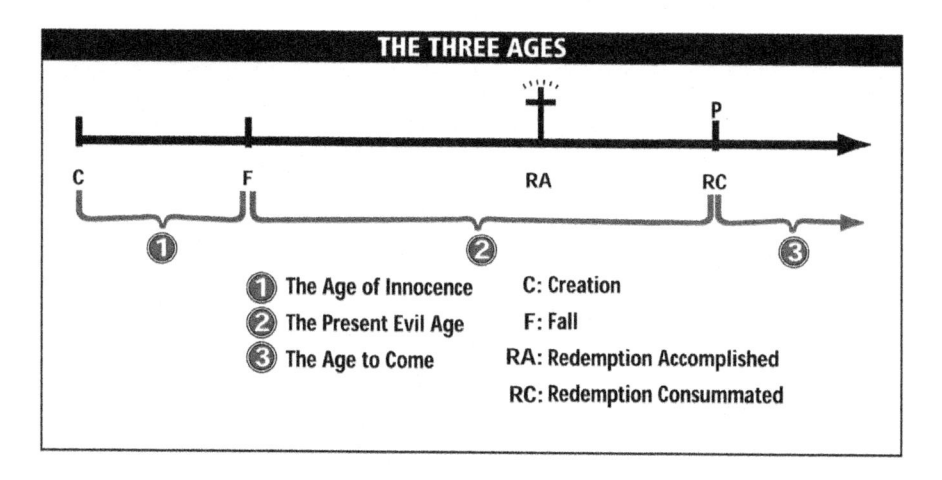

THE THREE AGES

① The Age of Innocence
② The Present Evil Age
③ The Age to Come

C: Creation
F: Fall
RA: Redemption Accomplished
RC: Redemption Consummated

Along with the OT, Jesus affirmed that cosmic history began at the creation, and that it will extend into eternity future. That history may be divided into three distinct ages (Greek: *aion*). The first was a very brief "age" of innocence and testing, the time between God's creation of the universe and Adam's fall. The second is "this present evil age," a lengthy period—also characterized by divine testing—that began with Adam's fall and continues until Christ's *parousia* (Gal. 1:4, Titus 2:12). Though God is very much at work in this era—especially since the first coming of Christ—it nonetheless remains fundamentally evil, since all throughout it the bulk of humanity remains dominated by "the god of this age" (Satan) and "the rulers of the darkness of this age" (Satan's demonic hosts) (2 Cor. 4:4, Eph. 6:12). Nevertheless, God gives us hope, a hope that will be fully realized in "the age to come." This age is of infinite duration, beginning at the *parousia* and extending throughout eternity future. For the saints, it is the age of eternal life, the age of the Kingdom of God in its full and final form. Jesus exhorts all who hear him to strive to attain to the resurrection of the righteous, and to the eternal glories of the age to come (Mt. 12:31-32, Mk. 10:29-31, Luke 20:34-36, Acts 26:6-7, Phil. 3:8-11).

Two Kingdoms

In his teaching about the three ages, we see that Jesus' idea of cosmic history is indeed linear; that he envisions history as moving towards a single, unending, pre-determined goal: the glorious Kingdom of God. But what of the history *leading up* to that Kingdom? Did Jesus and his apostles have anything to say about that? Indeed, they did. With the help of the diagram below, we will hear them on it now.

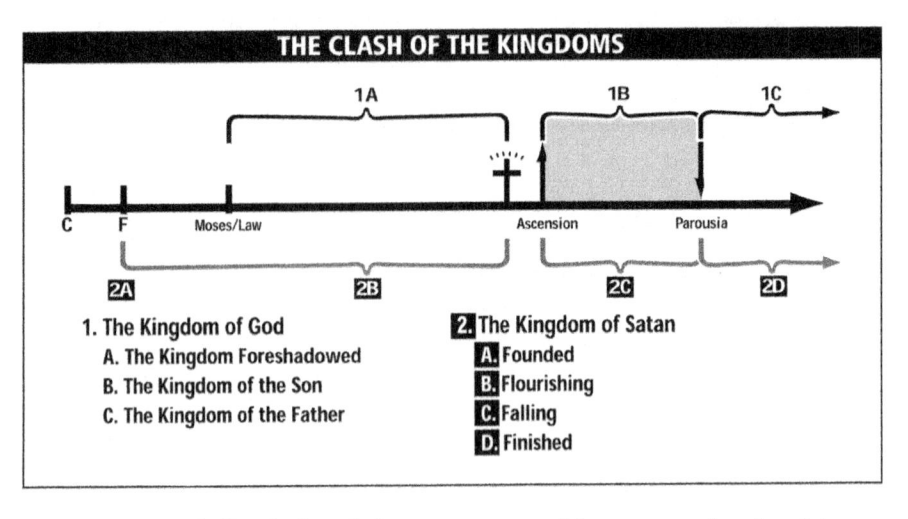

THE CLASH OF THE KINGDOMS

1. The Kingdom of God
  A. The Kingdom Foreshadowed
  B. The Kingdom of the Son
  C. The Kingdom of the Father

2. The Kingdom of Satan
  A. Founded
  B. Flourishing
  C. Falling
  D. Finished

Under the fuller light of the NT we are able to see salvation history as a great drama, *a drama that is most fruitfully portrayed as a clash of two kingdoms*. Each one merits close attention.

On the one hand, there is the kingdom of Satan. As we learned earlier, it was *founded* at the fall, when Adam effectively surrendered the family of man into the hand of God's adversary (Mt. 4:8-11). Prior to Christ's advent, Satan's kingdom *flourished* worldwide, though throughout this period—most especially in Israel—God preserved a remnant of redeemed humanity beneath his own spiritual rule (Ex. 19:6, Isaiah 14:12-21). Now, however, Christ has come, lived, died, and been exalted to God's right hand. As a result, Satan's kingdom is *falling*. This happens as the gospel goes forth into all the world, and as multitudes of believers from every tribe, tongue, people, and nation are transferred from the domain of darkness into the spiritual Kingdom of Christ (Luke 10:18, John 12:31, Col. 1:13, Rev. 7:9f, 12:7-12, 14:6). Satan's fall will be complete on the last day, when Christ, at his *parousia*, casts him into the lake of fire. At this point, his kingdom is *finished* forever (Rev. 11:15, 12:12, 20:10).

Locked in mortal combat with Satan's domain of darkness is the Kingdom of God. This kingdom, as we saw earlier, is best understood as the *direct reign of God over his creatures*, along with all of the *rescue* and *restoration* that such a reign entails. In OT times, God's Kingdom was *prefigured* by the nation of Israel, which God himself called "a kingdom of priests and a holy nation" (Ex. 19:6). Though God did not yet reside permanently in the hearts of all his people (Isaiah 32:15, Joel 2:28, John 7:39), he did dwell in their midst (Num. 5:3, 35:34), visit their leaders by his Spirit (Deut. 34:9, Judges 3:10, 1 Sam. 11:6), and actively seek to govern them through various laws and institutions (2 Chron. 30:12). In this manner the Israelite theocracy prefigured God's coming spiritual rule, as well as the chosen people who would be blessed to live beneath it (Num. 35:34, Jer. 31:31f, Ezek. 36:22-32, Joel 2:28). And again, it was during this era that the OT prophets—with ever-increasing frequency, specificity, and zeal—began to *promise* a future coming of the Kingdom of God.

In NT times, that promise is fulfilled. On the Day of Pentecost the exalted Christ pours out the Holy Spirit, with the result that the Kingdom has come at last (John 7:39, Acts 2:14f, Rev. 12:10). However, as Jesus taught his disciples, it does not appear all at once, but rather in two stages. First there is the *Kingdom of the Son,* in which the exalted Christ reigns invisibly, by the Spirit, over the hearts of his redeemed people in heaven and on earth (Mt. 13:36-43, Luke 19:11, Col. 3:1-4). This partial reign continues until the *parousia,* when, in fulfillment of God's redemptive plan, Christ will transform and glorify all (redeemed) things, thereby inaugurating the second and final stage of the Kingdom, the eternal *Kingdom of the Father* (1 Cor. 15:20-28).

Jesus' view of cosmic history speaks powerfully and probingly to seekers everywhere. For again, he sees the plain of human history as a spiritual battlefield, as the arena of a cosmic clash between two spiritual kings and two spiritual kingdoms. From the point of view of God's sovereignty, the end is not in doubt. But from the point of view of the test of life, each man—and each seeker—clearly has a decision to make: which king is he going to serve, and in whose army is he going to fight?

The Last Days

Jesus' teaching on the three ages and the two kingdoms prepares us to understand one of the Bible's most important eschatological expressions: *the last days.* As foretold by the OT prophets, the last days are the days in which God's redemptive rule will break into history, entering into sharp but ultimately triumphant conflict with the kingdoms of this world and their hidden spiritual ruler, the devil (Isaiah 2:2, 27:1f, Ezek. 38-89, Dan. 2:28, Hos. 3:5, Joel 2:28). Importantly, these are none other than the days of the Messiah, the chosen one through whom God will bring all his redemptive purposes to pass (Psalm 2, 110, Ezek. 36-39, Micah 2:13).

Convinced that they are now living in the last days, Christ and the NT writers describe their character in great detail. As to their length, though they are spoken of as "days," they will in fact last a long time, at least by human reckoning (Mt. 25:19, Luke 19:12, 2 Pet. 3:1-9). This is, by the way, one reason why the Revelation symbolizes their duration under such expansive numerical images such as 1260 days and 1000 years (Rev. 11:3, 12:6, 20:1-7).[2]

As to their character, they are fundamentally the days of Christ's heavenly reign, during which time his chief purpose is to apply and complete the redemption that he accomplished on earth through his righteous life and atoning death (Mt. 13:36-43, Luke 19:11:f, Acts 2:14-39, 1 Cor. 15:20f, Titus 2:14). Accordingly, these are also days of redemptive combat, during which the heavenly King now pours out his Spirit upon an earthly people, leading them into spiritual battle and enabling them, through the preaching of the gospel, to plunder Satan's household and capture his goods: the very souls of men (John 12:20-32, Acts 26:17-18, Col. 1:13, Eph. 6:10-20, Titus 2:13-14, Rev. 12). This means that they are days in which the present evil age has been *invaded* by the powers of the age to come (Heb. 6:6). Obviously, this spells big trouble for Satan. But it also spells trouble for the Church, which has now become the target of Satan's fury and cunning (Rev. 12). Thus, the last days are days of unavoidable conflict, peril, and difficulty (2 Tim. 3:1f, 2 Pet. 3:3). In the mystical language of the Revelation, they are the days of "the great tribulation" (Rev. 7:14). But the holy army can take heart: their King is in control of this war, its outcome is certain, and its end is soon to come (Rev. 3:11, 22:7, 12:1ff, 20:1ff).[3]

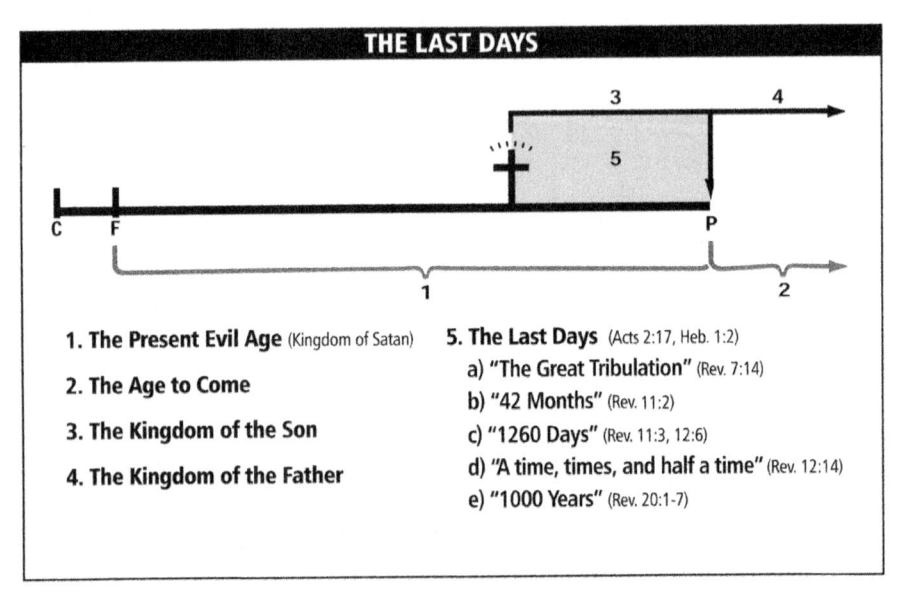

THE LAST DAYS

1. **The Present Evil Age** (Kingdom of Satan)
2. **The Age to Come**
3. **The Kingdom of the Son**
4. **The Kingdom of the Father**
5. **The Last Days** (Acts 2:17, Heb. 1:2)
   a) "The Great Tribulation" (Rev. 7:14)
   b) "42 Months" (Rev. 11:2)
   c) "1260 Days" (Rev. 11:3, 12:6)
   d) "A time, times, and half a time" (Rev. 12:14)
   e) "1000 Years" (Rev. 20:1-7)

The Teacher on the Consummation

In our journey so far, we have seen that Jesus gives us a comprehensive understanding of the flow of cosmic history, telling us that it is moving inexorably towards the advent of Kingdom of God. Furthermore, in speaking about this history, he focuses our eschatological attention on two key transitional events. The first is his righteous life and atoning death, both of which paved the way for the advent of the Spirit and the appearance of the first stage of the Kingdom, the Kingdom of the Son. The second transitional event—and our theme in the pages ahead—is what theologians refer to as *the consummation*. Centered upon the second coming of Christ in power and glory, the consummation is a stupendous cosmological hinge upon which the entire universe swings from the present evil age into the glorious age to come. Here we have the *grand finale* of salvation history, the last act in which God's redemptive purposes are fully revealed and finally brought to pass.

Very importantly, the consummation is also the climax of the Messiah's exaltation (Luke 19:11-27, Acts 3:19-21, 1 Cor. 15:20-28). As we saw earlier, even before the creation of the world the Father determined to reward his Son for the rigors of his humiliation by seating him at his own right hand, and by conferring upon him absolute cosmic sovereignty, so that he himself might fully complete his (the Father's) redemptive plan. Again, the final stage of this multi-faceted exaltation is the consummation. Here, the Messianic Son does indeed complete God's redemptive work at his glorious coming again at the end of the age. More than any other aspect of Christ's exaltation, this is a hugely *public* event, wherein the truth of his deity, gospel, and cosmic sovereignty will finally be vindicated, and the mouth of every opponent finally stopped. Here too is the fulfillment of one the Father's supreme purposes for the universe: that all sentient creatures should honor the Son even as they honor the Father (John 5:23). For this reason, it belongs essentially to the consummation that "…every knee should bow—of those in heaven, and of those on earth, and of those under the earth—and that every tongue should confess that Jesus Christ is Lord, to the glory of God the Father" (Phil. 2:5-11).

The Structure of the Consummation

According to the NT, God has structured the consummation with a view to enhancing the glory of his Son. Moreover, he has structured it in such a way as to supply a single, bright focus for the hopes of his people. That focus is the *parousia*.[4] Once again, this Greek word means "the arrival of a dignitary." At the *parousia*, then, the heavenly Dignitary, resplendent with divine glory, will arrive in the skies above the earth in order to perform all of the great eschatological acts by which God's redemptive plan will be brought to completion. In both the manner of his appearing and in the prerogatives accorded to him on that day, God will most highly exalt his Son.

By structuring the consummation in this way, God has made it easy and exciting for his people to envision where history is heading. For this reason, the apostle Paul aptly called the *parousia* "the blessed hope" of the saints:

> For the grace of God that brings salvation has appeared to all men, teaching us that, denying ungodliness and worldly lusts, we should live soberly, righteously, and godly in the present age, *looking for the blessed hope and glorious appearing of our great God and Savior, Jesus Christ,* who gave Himself for us, that He might redeem us from every lawless deed and purify for Himself His own special people, zealous for good works.
> —Titus 2:11-14

This rich passage, like many in the NT, frankly acknowledges the challenges of Christian discipleship in an age dominated by the powers of evil. But in order to encourage the saints to rise to the challenge, Paul gives them a great hope. It is the *parousia*, "...the appearing of our great God and Savior, Jesus Christ." It is a blessed hope, not least of all because God has made it clear, simple, and glorious: Christ will return *once* at the end of the age in order to perform all of the great eschatological acts, thereby bringing in the eternal Kingdom in its fullness (Mt. 24:27, 37, 39, 1 Thess. 3:13, 4:15, 2 Thess. 2:1, Heb. 9:28, James 5:7, 2 Pet. 3:12). This hope is also blessed because at the *parousia* so many wonderful things will happen, things that God has been pleased to reveal to his saints so that they can "look for" them with eager anticipation (1 Cor. 2:6-16, Rom. 8:19, 23, 25, Gal. 5:5, Phil. 3:20, Heb. 9:28). Yes, God has destined his children for a difficult journey through the wilderness of this world (1 Thess. 3:3, Rev. 12:13-17). But he will not leave them as orphans (John 14:18). Over and again he will come to them in the Spirit, using his written word to remind them of the *parousia* of his Son. Thus shall he fill them with fresh hope, so that they may confidently and joyfully journey on until the end (Acts 3:19, 1 Peter 1:3-9, Rev. 12:13-17).

Since the consummation is one of the most complex and fascinating themes of biblical revelation, let us devote the remainder of our chapter to examining its several elements in some detail. As we do, we shall see that each element involves its own particular kind of hope, and that all of these particular hopes, taken together, make the blessed hope blessed indeed.

The Signs of His Coming

Jesus and his apostles unveiled to the disciples a body of signs by which they might know that the *parousia* is drawing near. Strictly speaking, we cannot call these signs *elements* of the consummation. Nevertheless, because they are so closely associated with it, they merit special attention here.

On this score, Jesus himself led the way, speaking of most of the signs of his coming in his famous eschatological discourse on the Mount of Olives (Mt. 24, Mark 13, Luke 21). After his ascension and the outpouring of the Holy Spirit, the apostles would complete God's revelation on this theme, adding a few more signs and giving us a more nuanced picture of the events leading up to the end (Rom. 11, 2 Thess. 2, Rev. 6-20).

The NT distinguishes between two kinds of eschatological signs. On the one hand, there are what Jesus called "the beginning of birth pains" (Mt. 24:8). As with all the signs, these reflect the intensified clash of the two kingdoms now that Christ has entered the world and launched his redemptive assault on Satan's domain (Rev. 12). Accordingly, these signs appear all throughout "the great tribulation," that is, *throughout the entire course of the church era* (Rev. 7:1-8). They include what are manifestly judgments of God: wars, famines, earthquakes, pestilences, etc., but also the continual preaching of the gospel, by which sinners may understand the judgments for what they are, and flee from the far worse judgment they portend through repentance and faith towards Christ.

The signs also include what are manifestly acts of Satan: the emergence of false Christs and false prophets, the apostasy of false believers, and the persecution of true spiritual Church (Mt. 24:4-14, Rev. 6, 7, 11, 12, 13, 16, 20). Notably, Jesus tells his disciples, "Such things must happen, *but the end is still to come*" (Mt. 24:6). In other words, these are indeed signs that the end is fast approaching (Rev. 12:12), but also that the end is *not yet here*; it is not imminent. Accordingly, the wise disciple will not allow himself to be distracted by the "beginning of birth pains," but will rather stay focused on the work before him, which is, in essence, to preach the gospel.[5]

On the other hand, there are a few signs that will be historically unique. Since these will occur very near the end of the age, they do indeed herald the imminence of the *parousia*. Importantly, they will not enable believers to determine "the day or the hour" of their Master's return, only that it is quite near, even at the door (Mt. 24:32-36). Disciples are, then, to be on the lookout for (the confluence of) these special signs, and to take hope and courage when they see them on the horizon.

One such sign is *the completion of world evangelization*. As Jesus himself put it, "This gospel of the kingdom shall be preached in the whole world for a witness to all the nations, *and then the end shall come*" (Mt. 24:14). Accordingly, disciples are to keep close tabs on the state of the global harvest, and to rejoice in hope when they finally see thriving churches planted among "every tribe and tongue and people and nation" (Rev. 5:9).

Another such sign—closely related to the first—is *the conversion of the great mass of Jews*. According to the apostle Paul, this will occur near the end of the age, when the full number of elect Gentiles has finally come to Christ. At that time, God will graciously turn again to his ancient covenant people and graft them back into his vine through (God-given) faith in their Messiah. When he does, said the apostle, it will be nothing less than "life from the dead," this expression being an apparent reference to the general resurrection that Christ will bring to pass at his *parousia* (Gen. 45:1-15, Rom. 11:20-26).

A third sign of the nearness of the end is *the last battle* (Rev. 11:7-10, 16:12-16, 19:17-21, 20:7-10). This battle commences with the appearing of an individual whom Paul referred to as "the man of lawlessness," and whom John called "the antichrist" (2 Thess. 2:1f, 1 John 2:18). He will be a satanically energized world leader with pretensions to deity, who, by means of persuasive words and miraculous powers, will succeed in consolidating the fallen world-system around himself and against the people of God (Rev. 13:3). The resulting persecution, global in scale and ferocious in intensity, will culminate in the apparent demise of the true spiritual Church: she will lie "...dead in the street of the great city which mystically is called Sodom and Egypt, where also (her) Lord was crucified" (Rev. 11:7-10; Mt. 24:15, Rev. 16:12-16, 20:7-10). It was this final, end-time persecution—and not simply the destruction of Jerusalem—that Jesus had in view when he warned his disciples, saying, "For then there will be great tribulation, such as has not been since the beginning of the world until this time, no, nor ever shall be" (Mt. 24:21).[6, 7]

It should not be supposed, however, that the Church alone will endure the tribulation of those dark days. For God—responding to the final assault against his Christ, his truth, and his people—will now bring wave upon wave of judgment upon the rebellious nations. As the end draws near, these will increase in number and intensity, with less and less time between them for (a dangerously deceptive) "business as usual" (Mt. 24:36-44, 1 Thess. 5:1-3). These *stupendous disruptions in nature and society*—which mercifully trumpet a final warning to sinful humanity—are both "death throes" and "birth pangs." In other words, they are clear signs of the imminent destruction of Satan's kingdom, yet also of the imminent birth of God's (Mt. 24:8). Speaking of them, Jesus remarked as follows:

> And there will be signs in the sun, in the moon, and in the stars; and on the earth distress of nations, with perplexity; the sea and the waves roaring, men's hearts failing them from fear at the expectation of those things which are coming on the earth, for the powers of the heaven will

be shaken...And unless those days were shortened, no flesh would be saved; but for the elect's sake, those days will be shortened.
—Luke 21:25-26, Mt. 24: 21-22

It is easy to see why Jesus makes these signs of the end known to his disciples: how shall they endure such terrible tribulation unless they understand that it is all part of God's plan, that it will be ever so brief, and that it will both herald and trigger the return of their King—the one who will swiftly rescue his people from their enemies and richly reward them for their perseverance with the unspeakable joys of the Kingdom of God (2 Thess. 1:3-10, Rev. 11:11-19, 20:9-10, 21-22)? In other words, Jesus taught on the signs so as to give his people hope: hope of his *parousia*, and hope of all the rich blessings it would bring. As he himself said, "When you see these things begin to take place, straighten up, and lift up your heads, for your redemption is drawing near" (Luke 21:28)!

The Parousia

Here is the hub, the central element of the consummation, the core eschatological event that brings all the others to pass in quick succession. Many NT texts describe the *parousia*, but the most famous comes from Matthew's gospel:

> Immediately after the tribulation of those days, the sun will be darkened, and the moon will not give its light; the stars will fall from heaven, and the powers of the heavens will be shaken. Then the sign of the Son of Man will appear in heaven, and then all the tribes of the earth will mourn, and they will see the Son of Man coming on the clouds of heaven with power and great glory. And He will send His angels with a great sound of a trumpet, and they will gather together His elect from the four winds, from one end of the heaven to the other.
> —Matt. 24:29-31; 1 Thess. 4:13-18,
> 2 Thess. 1:3-10, Rev. 19:11-21

Clearly, Jesus' focus here is on the *parousia*, his arrival in glory in the skies above the earth. But even in this short text we see that his coming cannot be divorced from other elements of the consummation. Moreover, when we read this passage in context (Mt. 24-25)—and supplement it with material from other passages parallel to it—an altogether mind-boggling picture emerges: *the parousia involves nothing less than the centering of the entire universe around the glorified Son of God, with a view to its complete and ultimate restructuring at his own hand.*

Let us take a small moment to flesh out this very big idea.

Observe first that in order to set the stage for Christ's arrival, God (through Christ) literally extinguishes the sun, moon, and stars. This is high drama: blackest night falls upon the entire cosmos, so that all eyes may be turned upon the radiant body of him who comes their way in clouds of glory (Mt. 26:64, Acts 1:9-11, Rev. 1:7, 14:14f, 21:23). Note that the spiritual heaven itself has been emptied—or rather descends with Christ into the skies above the earth—since he comes not only with all of the holy angels, but also with the spirits of just men made perfect (Zech. 14:5, Mt. 25:31, 1 Thess. 3:13, 4:14, Heb. 12:23). As he draws near, there is a "cry of command," the voice of the archangel (Gabriel), and the sound of a trumpet (1 Thess 4:16). With this, Christ's final dealings with mankind begin: the dead are raised, the living are transformed, and all together are transported by the angels into the sky above, where they come before their King and Judge, sitting upon the throne of his glory (Mt. 25:31, Rev. 20:11).[8] Meanwhile, the earth below "flees from his face," which is to say that the world and its works are now consumed by fire (Rev. 20:11, 2 Peter 3:10). Hell suddenly appears (presumably in the vacancy of space), the final judgment is consummated, a new world is born, and the glorious Bride descends to her eternal home. The Kingdom of God in its fullness has come at last (Mt. 25:31f, Rev. 21:1f).

In this sketch of the consummation we see that the thrust of the *parousia* is essentially to reduce the universe as we now know it to a sea of men and angels, suspended in vacant space before the judgment seat of Christ, where they await, in awe and dread, the final disposition of all things. And herein will lie a consummate object lesson for every sentient being: the One now enthroned at the center of the universe is the One who has *always* been enthroned at the center of the Father's heart, and therefore at the center of his every purpose, plan, and work. In short, through the *parousia* both men and angels will behold the Son of God for who he is and for what God appointed him to be: the creator, sustainer, redeemer, judge, and re-creator of all. For the saints who eagerly await that day, the hope of seeing the Son in such great glory is a blessed hope indeed.

The Resurrection

The resurrection of the dead, promised by the ancient prophets and longed for by the OT saints, occurs at the *parousia* (Job 19:23-27, Psalm 16:10, Isaiah 25:6-8, 26:19, Dan. 12:2, Hosea 13:14, Acts 26:7). Christ himself will accomplish it. As Jesus put it, "Do not marvel at this; for the hour is coming in which all who are in the graves will hear the voice of the

Son of Man and come forth: those who have done good to the resurrection of life, and those who have done evil to the resurrection of condemnation" (John 5:28-29, Phil. 3:20-21). Observe from these words that there is but *one general resurrection*, for which reason Christ and the apostles repeatedly speak of it as *the* resurrection (Mt. 22:30, Luke 14:14, Acts 17:18, 24:15, Phil. 3:11). The saints look forward to it as the consummation of their redemption (John 11:24, Rom. 8:23, Phil. 3:11). In that day, their perfect spirits will be joined with perfect bodies, in which they will live forever. These bodies are like Christ's body: glorious, powerful, incorruptible, and immortal (Luke 20:35-36, Phil. 3:20-21). They are perfectly suited to the unimaginable glories of the world to come (1 Cor. 15:50). Interestingly, one of Israel's leading sects, the Sadducees, denied the bodily resurrection (Mark 12:18). The Athenians, at the sound of Paul's preaching, scoffed at the very idea (Acts 17:32). But Jesus rebukes them both, saying, "You are mistaken, knowing neither the Scriptures nor the power of God" (Mt. 22:29). The resurrection will abundantly vindicate both.

Saints living at the time of Christ's return will not be raised, but will be suddenly transformed and glorified. This amazing change, according to John, occurs at the very moment they behold their Lord coming in the sky. "Beloved, now we are the children of God, and it has not yet been revealed what we shall be; *but we know that when He is revealed, we shall be like Him, for we shall see Him as He is*" (1 John 3:2; 2 Cor. 3:18). Similarly, the apostle Paul declares: "Behold, I tell you a mystery: we shall not all sleep, but we shall all be changed—in a moment, in the twinkling of an eye, at the last trumpet. For the trumpet will sound, and the dead will be raised incorruptible, and we shall be changed" (1 Cor. 15:50-52, 1 Thess. 4:13-18). At the resurrection of the dead and the transformation of the living saints, Christ gathers together and glorifies the new human family of God forever.

In passing, we do well to note that the resurrection also includes an elevation, or "catching up," of risen humanity to meet the Lord in the sky. As we saw from the Olivet discourse, at his *parousia* Christ will send forth his angels to gather his elect from the four corners of the earth (Mt. 24:31, 1 Thess. 4:13-18). But as we saw from the parable of the wheat and the tares, he will also send forth his angels to gather up the wicked. These too are brought before the judgment seat of Christ (where *all* must appear), and then cast into the furnace of fire (Mt. 13:41-42, 2 Cor. 5:10, Rev. 14:14-16, 20:11-15). Thus, at the resurrection *all* are raised (or suddenly transformed), *all* are elevated, and *all* stand before Christ. In recent years, certain interpreters have argued that this elevation (sometimes referred to as "the rapture") affects only Christ's Church, occurs in secret, and is separated by seven years from his visible return in glory. But this view seriously departs both from the Bible and traditional Christian theology, as a careful study of the relevant texts will reveal (Mt. 24:29-31, 25:31ff, 1 Thess. 4:13-18, 2 Thess. 1, Rev. 14:14-20).[9]

The resurrection and its concomitants contribute abundantly to the saint's blessed hope. These amazing events promise a healthy new body, a joyful reunion with departed Christian loved ones, and the privilege of being *like* the Lord, *with* the Lord, forever.

The Last Judgment

The resurrection leads quickly to the last judgment. Again, Christ himself will administer it. Repeatedly, Jesus bade his disciples to envision him upon his Judgment Seat in the last day (Mt. 19:28, 25:31). He also said, "As the Father has life in Himself, so He has granted the Son to have life in Himself, and has given Him authority to execute judgment also, because He is the Son of Man" (John 5:26-27, 30; 2 Cor. 5:10). The judgment signals the end of all probation for the sons of Adam: there is no further opportunity for salvation, no further opportunity to earn rewards. As on the day of his death, so on the Day of Judgment: a man's destiny is sealed forever (John 8:24, Heb. 8:27, Rev. 20:11-15).

Christ administers the last judgment for two basic reasons. First, he effects a final separation of the saved from the lost. The saved will be included in God's Kingdom, the lost excluded from it, forever. These truths are vividly set forth in Jesus' Olivet Discourse, where he likens himself to a shepherd who, at the end of the age, will separate the sheep from the goats (Mt. 25:21ff). The one criterion for inclusion in God's Kingdom is personal faith in Christ (Mt. 11:28, 22:11-12, John 3:16f, 5:24, 6:29, Acts 16:31, 26:18, Rom. 3:28, 4:16, 5:1, Gal. 2:16, Eph. 2:8, Titus 3:4-5, etc.). When the books are opened, those who have trusted in him—and therefore lived for him—will find their names written in the Lamb's Book of Life (Rev. 20:12, 15)[10]. Theologians wrestle with the question of the eternal destiny of those who lived beyond the borders of Israel in OT times, and beyond the reach of the gospel in NT times.[11] Nevertheless, all who revere the Bible as God's word confess with Jesus that no one comes to the Father except through him (John 14:6), and that "He who has the Son has life; he who does not have the Son does not have life" (1 John 5:12).

The second purpose of the judgment is that Christ should bestow on all a just measure of reward or retribution. In the case of the saints, there is no retribution, since Christ has already received their punishment in his own person (1 Pet. 3:18). Indeed, this was his chief purpose in laying down his life a ransom for many, namely, that he should deliver them from the wrath to come (Mark 10:45, 1 Thess. 1:10). Believers do, however, receive rewards for all that they allowed Christ to accomplish through them during their days on earth, especially as their labors contributed to the advance of his Kingdom (Mt. 6:19-21, 25:14-30, Mark 10:29-31, John 15:1-8). Soberingly, Paul warns that at the last judgment spiritually negligent saints will find many of their works burning up like wood, hay, and stubble. Though they themselves will be saved, they have little reward (1 Cor. 3:15).

As for the lost, they must suffer retribution for their every evil deed. For their want of obedience to the gospel of Christ "...they will be punished with everlasting destruction away from the presence of the Lord and from the glory of His power" (2 Thess. 1:8-9). For their specific sins, they will suffer varying degrees of torment in hell, based upon all that they did or did not do during their time on earth (Mt. 12:36, Luke 12:47, 2 Cor. 5:10). Those who skirted Christ, trusting in their own righteousness to win heaven's favor, will be everlastingly dismayed to see how far short they fell of the one and only standard for salvation: the glory of God, offered to mankind in the Christ of God (Mt. 5:48, 22:11-12, Luke 18:9-14, Rom. 3:23, Phil. 3:8-9, Heb. 12:15).

Solemn as it is, the last judgment is also an integral part of the saints' blessed hope. Christ's disciples look forward to the day when their King will send forth judgment unto victory, when the scales will be balanced at last, when the righteous will receive their just reward, and the wicked their just desserts (Mt. 10:20, Rev. 15:3-4). They also look forward to receiving their own rewards, and to hearing these precious words from the Master's lips: "Well done, good and faithful servant" (Mt. 25:21). But knowing the true source of their righteousness, they mostly look forward to casting down their crowns at the feet of him who loved them and gave himself for them; the One who preserved them in holiness throughout their life on the earth, that he might present them faultless before the presence of his glory with exceeding joy (Gal. 2:20, Eph. 5:25-27, Jude 1:24, Rev. 4:10).

Cosmic Transformation

In order supremely to honor his Son, the Father has also conferred upon him the privilege of transforming the cosmos. This is the climax of Christ's *parousia*, the conclusion of his specifically redemptive acts. God has made him the Alpha and the Omega, the Beginning and the End (Rev. 1:8, 11). This means that the Father not only granted the Son to create the universe in the beginning, but also that he should re-create it in the end. Just as the returning Christ has authority to raise and transform the broken bodies of his saints, so too he has authority and power to subdue *all things* to himself, thereby liberating them from their subjection to futility, and lifting them into the freedom of the glory of the children of God (Rom. 8:20, 1 Cor. 15:20-28, Phil. 3:20-21).

This transformation is two-fold. It begins with what can only be called a cosmic conflagration, a universal meltdown in which, as Jesus predicted, heaven and earth shall pass away (Mt. 24:35). The most complete description of this awesome event is found in 2 Peter 3, where the apostle writes:

> But the day of the Lord will come like a thief, in which the heavens will pass away with a roar and the elements will be destroyed with intense heat, and the earth and its works will be burned up. Since all these things are to be destroyed in this way, what sort of people ought you to be in holy conduct and godliness, looking for and hastening the coming of the day of God, on account of which the heavens will be destroyed by burning, and the elements will melt with intense heat? But according to His promise, we look for new heavens and a new earth.
> —2 Peter 3:7, 10-13

Importantly, Peter is not looking here for the annihilation of the natural world, only its purging and restoration. Just as the ancient Flood cleansed the earth of sinners and paved the way for a new world, so it will be in the Day of the Lord, only moreso. In the conflagration, Christ will purge the natural order of every mark of sin, so that out of the very fires that consume "the former things" new heavens and a new earth may arise (Mt. 13:41-43, Luke 17:26f, 2 Pet. 3:3-6). Notably, Peter asserts that these fires are also ordained for the destruction (i.e., undoing and punishment) of ungodly men (2 Pet. 3:7). It appears, then, that in some small portion of the new heavens, flames of judgment will burn forever (Jude 7). This is *Gehenna*, or the Lake of Fire—the final destination of Satan, his demons, and all the people on earth who followed their ways (Mt. 25:41, Rev. 20:10).

The second stage of the transformation is what Jesus called "the regeneration," and what Peter called "the restoration of all things" (Mt. 19:28, Acts 3:21). It is, in essence, the formation of new heavens and a new earth, the recreation of the cosmos. Once and for all, Christ lifts the curse from the natural order, releasing it from its bondage to futility and its slavery to corruption (Rom. 8:18-25). Once and for all, he impresses upon it the forms and functions that perfectly reflect the will of God. As with the bodies of the saints, so with the world they shall inhabit: it is the same, yet different. The fundamentals remain: earth, sky, field, flower, fountain, man, and animal. Yet much is gone: sun, moon, stars, night, sea, desert, sickness, suffering, disaster, and death (Rev. 21:1-4). Though the Bible is reticent to describe the new world in detail, it assures us that it will be glorious beyond anything mortal man can ask or think (Rom. 8:18, 1 Cor. 13:12, Eph. 3:20). Thus, the doctrine of cosmic transformation contributes richly to the saint's blessed hope. It promises a new and beautiful world altogether purged of sin; an eternal home for the triune God and his extended family of redeemed men and holy angels.

The Delivering Up of the Kingdom

When the transformation is complete, one final act remains for Christ to perform: he must deliver up the Kingdom to his Father. Of this ultimate and mysterious transaction the apostle Paul writes as follows:

> For as in Adam all die, even so in Christ all shall be made alive. But each one in his own order: Christ the firstfruits, afterward those who are Christ's at his coming. Then comes the end, when he delivers the kingdom to God the Father, when he puts an end to all rule and all authority and power. For he must reign till he has put all enemies under his feet. The last enemy that will be destroyed is death. For "He has put all things under his feet" (Psalm 8:6). But when He says "all things are put under him," it is evident that He who put all things under him is excepted. Now when all things are made subject to him, then the Son himself will also be subjected to Him who put all things under him, that God may be all in all.
> —1 Cor. 15:22-28

Here, Paul's theme is the resurrection, but in discussing it he is moved to survey the entire course of the Messiah's reign. At the beginning of this reign, God the Father gave the Son all authority in heaven and earth, as well as a commission to subdue every enemy, to put all things under his feet (Psalm 2, 8, 110, Mt. 28:18, Eph. 1:15-22). Throughout the course of his reign he (Christ) did so victoriously, especially as he brought to himself a people for his own possession, changing their hearts and thereby making former enemies into eternal friends (Titus 2:11-14). One day, at the close of his reign (i.e., at his *parousia*), he will complete the work, defeating and banishing every remaining foe—spiritual, physical, or Satanic—from the new and glorious universe that he will create. The last of these enemies, says Paul, is death, which Christ will forever banish at the resurrection of the dead.

With this victory, the Messiah's work is finished. The Kingdom that the Father commissioned him to redeem and create stands complete before him: a new, glorified humanity, and a new, glorified world in which that humanity shall live. Yet one thing more remains, one final act of worship, one final acknowledgment of the One through whom he was able to accomplish it all: he must deliver his Kingdom up to the Father. He must give it back to the One who gave it to him (John 17:6). In other words, he must relinquish *this form* of his cosmic sovereignty, and freshly submit himself, his people, and his world to the Father's direct authority. He does this so that God the Father may be supremely glorified—that he may be all in all.[12] Because the Son loves the Father, he does so gladly (John 17:1).[13]

The delivering up of the Kingdom is "the consummation of the consummation." Not only this, it is the crowning touch upon the blessed hope of the saints. Mysterious as the great transaction is, they anticipate it with relish, knowing that herein the redemptive achievements of the Son are forever sealed, the Father fully glorified, and his eternal Kingdom introduced at last. Accordingly, even before it happens, they think they hear the Father saying to the Son precisely what the Son will say to them when their own labors are complete: "Well done, good and faithful Servant; enter into the joy of your Lord" (Mt. 25:31).

Especially for Seekers

In our survey of Jesus' cosmic eschatology, we have heard him say, "Yes, history is definitely heading somewhere. It is heading towards the consummation, and past that into the eternal Kingdom of God." This understanding of cosmic eschatology is, of course, shaped by his overall view of cosmic history. For Jesus and the apostles, history is actually "His Story"—a story written in eternity past by God himself. This story has many characters: divine, human, and angelic. It has many themes: the attributes and glory of God; the love of the Father for the Son; the love of the Son for the Father; the love of God for the world; the triumph of good over evil, truth over lies, humility over pride, etc.

But what especially concerns us here is that the story has a *plot*. There is a definite beginning, middle, and end. There is rising action, developing conflict, apparent defeat, and finally—in the dramatic closing scenes—sudden, unexpected deliverance and triumph. And for all who have played their part in the story honorably, there is something more: a happy ending.

In all of these things we see that Jesus' cosmic eschatology is thoroughly embedded in the mystery of *story*. This is why it resonates so deeply in our hearts. Intuitively, we feel that our own life is a story, and also that it is part of a much larger story—a universal story, even a divine story. Jesus confirms these intuitions. So too does world history subsequent to his first coming, which, to a mind schooled by the Bible, does indeed appear as the parallel development of two opposing kingdoms, kingdoms that are heading towards a final clash in the closing scenes of the cosmic drama. In other words, the actual course and character of world history since the days of Christ make it quite reasonable for us to believe that Jesus' cosmic eschatology is true.

Where his eschatology excels, however, is with respect to hope.

As we have seen, at its best naturalism offers us a short-term evolutionary promise of increased health and wealth, after which our essentially meaningless existence will sink into oblivion. Classical pantheism does indeed extend a more spiritual hope, promising that the family of man will one day attain corporate enlightenment. However, it immediately pollutes and effectively withdraws that hope with its doctrine of eternal recurrence, according to which human suffering will appear again and again in an infinite succession of universes. As for New Age pantheists, most of them would likely embrace the Hindu and Buddhist model, with the remainder trying as best they can to defend a more linear—and therefore more optimistic—conception of cosmic history. However, none of the New Agers are able to point to a trustworthy body of divine revelation that confirms their expectation and therefore grounds their hopes. Thus, viewed from the widest possible angle, the hope of the pantheist—whether classical or New Age—is finally engulfed in uncertainty or overwhelmed by despair.

Jesus, on the other hand, gives his obedient disciples "...*eternal* comfort and *good* hope by grace" (2 Thess. 2:16). Their hope is of life and blessing with God *forever*, in his eternal Kingdom. Moreover, the saints may look with hope upon *every* aspect of the consummation, not just the glories to follow. They hope to glorify Christ and advance his redemptive plan through their steadfastness in the midst of "the great tribulation" and "the last battle" (2 Thess. 1). They hope to behold his face at his appearing (1 John 3:2). They hope to see their beloved Master vindicated and honored as King of the whole universe (Phil. 2:5-11). They hope for perfect spiritual and physical wholeness, a wholeness bestowed upon them at the resurrection (1 Cor. 15, Col. 3:4). They hope for a joyful reunion with departed believing loved ones (1 Thess. 4:13-18). They hope to see perfect justice done at last (Mt. 25:41, Rom. 2:1-10). They hope to hear their gracious Judge commend them for lives well lived and for works well done (Mt. 25:21). They hope to see the realm of nature purified of every vestige of sin, and a beautiful new world arising out of the ashes of the old (2 Peter 3:10-13). And they hope to know, serve, and enjoy their triune God in that world forever (Rev. 21:9f).

Learning of all these hopes, many seekers will doubtless find themselves hoping they are true. Their path is plain: They must keep on seeking the truth about Jesus' cosmic eschatology until their hopes are dashed—or until they are blessed, thereafter becoming within them a perpetual spring of eager expectation, steady strength, and unspeakable joy.[14]

CHAPTER 17

HOW CAN WE FIND TRUSTWORTHY ANSWERS TO THE QUESTIONS OF LIFE?

IN OUR JOURNEY thus far, we have seen that the world needs a spiritual Teacher, a person or group of persons authorized by the unknown god to bring us trustworthy answers to the questions of life. We have also seen that Jesus of Nazareth is the world's outstanding candidate for this high office, in part because he is surrounded by a large, diverse, and historically credible body of supernatural signs. Moreover, having seated ourselves at his feet and heard him on the questions of life, we have found that he answers them comprehensively, authoritatively, and in a manner that is intuitive, reasonable, right, and full of hope. May we justly conclude, then, that this is God's appointed Teacher? With credentials like these, it would hardly seem fair to ask for more.

And yet there is indeed a further requirement: If Jesus really is the one true Teacher, then he must say so. In particular, he must tell us straightforwardly that he has received a commission from God to bring us the answers to the questions of life, and that the answers he brings are the truth, the whole truth, and nothing but the truth. Such, after all, is the job description of God's appointed Teacher—and it is inconceivable that the one who actually gets the job should not know it, or not tell us that it is so. To the contrary, out of love for the truth—and out of love for seekers of the truth—he would surely feel compelled to say, "My teaching brings you the one true worldview, all of God's answers to all of the questions of life. Any teaching that differs from mine—or purports to supercede it—is therefore either an error or a lie. Seeker, you have reached the end of your journey. My words are not only God's words, but also God's *last* words. Therefore, receive them, enjoy them, obey them—and live."

Would any human being dare to talk this way? Did Jesus of Nazareth? It is time to find out. In the present chapter, let us therefore ask Jesus, "How can we find reliable answers to the questions of life?" And let us see if he answers yet again by saying, "Come unto me."

A Teacher Promised

Seekers who believe that mankind needs a divinely authorized Teacher will find it more than interesting that in OT times the God of Israel promised to send one. The most ancient of these promises fell from the lips of Moses, who told his fellow Israelites, "The LORD your God will raise up for you a Prophet like me from your midst, from your brethren. Him you shall hear" (Deut. 18:15ff). In the days of Israel's sojourn in Canaan, this promise was partly fulfilled by a succession of prophets, through whom God did indeed speak directly to his covenant people. However, in the eyes of many interpreters, the saying also had another and much larger fulfillment: it spoke of God's Messiah, and of his role as Israel's supreme Prophet. For these interpreters—and they definitely included Jesus' apostles—Moses was *ultimately* speaking of the Messianic Prophet who would bring the fullness of God's truth to all nations (Acts 3:22, 2:29).

Later in Israel's history, God gave yet another promise of a latter-day world Teacher, this time through the pen of Isaiah. In the following words, so redolent of the mystery of the Trinity, we actually hear the voice of the Messiah himself, speaking of his forthcoming prophetic mission:

> And now the LORD says, who formed me from the womb to be His servant, to bring Jacob back to Him so that Israel may be gathered to Him (for I shall be glorious in the eyes of the LORD, and my God shall be my strength); indeed, He says, "It is too small a thing that you should be My servant to raise up the tribes of Jacob and to restore the preserved ones of Israel; I will also give you as a light to the Gentiles, that you may bring My salvation to the ends of the earth."
> —Isaiah 48:5-6; 9:1-2, 48:6

Here the Messiah speaks of a commission that he has received from the LORD, declaring that in days ahead he will brings the light of God's saving truth not only to Jacob, but to the Gentiles as well; that is, to all nations. Interestingly, Isaiah later assures his readers that the Gentiles will indeed come to that light as it shines forth into a sin-darkened world through the Spirit-anointed people of God (Isaiah 60:1-3).

Like Isaiah, the prophet Micah also wrote of a time when God would instruct the nations in his truth:

HOW CAN WE FIND TRUSTWORTHY ANSWERS TO THE QUESTIONS OF LIFE?

> Now it shall come to pass in the latter days that the mountain of the LORD'S house shall be established on the top of the mountains, and shall be exalted above the hills; and peoples shall flow to it. Many nations shall come and say, "Come, let us go up to the mountain of the LORD, to the house of the God of Jacob. He will teach us His ways, and we shall walk in His paths." For out of Zion the law (or *instruction*) shall go forth, and the word of the LORD from Jerusalem.
>
> —Micah 4:1-2

In this mysterious prophecy, Micah does not explicitly mention the Messiah. He does, however, speak of "the latter days," an expression that the Bible consistently associates with the Messiah's appearing (Ezek. 37:24-28, Hos. 3:5, Acts 2:14f, Heb. 1:1-4). In those days, says Micah, the Gentiles will turn from their idols to Israel's God. In those days, they will ascend his holy mountain, enter his house, and hear his law (or instruction). In those days, the nations will at last know and delight in his truth.

Reading this prophecy, many an OT Israelite must have asked, "How can such things be? How could so many millions of people gather on poor little Mt. Zion? How could they all enter a man-made temple that is smaller still? And how, precisely, shall the word of the LORD go forth? Will God speak it audibly, as he did at Sinai? Will he speak it through his Messiah? Will he speak it through the Messiah's servants? Or will he speak it personally and inwardly, to the heart of each man and woman? How, precisely, will he teach his truth to all nations in the last days?"

Yes, godly Jews from Micah's day onward must have puzzled long and hard over these words. In the end, however, they no doubt realized that they would simply have to wait for the answers to their questions. In particular, they would have to wait for the Messiah himself. When he comes, he will surely explain all.

A Promise Fulfilled

While sitting at Jesus' feet we have learned that he definitely thought of himself as the Messiah. This means, of course, that he also saw himself as fulfilling the OT promises of a latter day Prophet/Teacher who would bring the light of God's truth to the nations. But does the NT record of Jesus' words support this conclusion? As we are about to see, it does indeed, and not meagerly, but with an impressive abundance of richly illuminating texts. Let us look at a few of them now.

A Unique Teacher

Over and again, Jesus spoke of himself as a *teacher*. Indeed, after earning this title through the richness of his instruction, he not only commended his disciples for using it, but also identified his teaching as an essential aspect of his Messianic mission. "You call me Teacher and Lord," he observed, "and you say well, for so I am" (John 13:13; Mt. 8:19, 12:38, 19:16, Mark 9:38, 10:35). In fact, so powerful were his words that even his enemies grudgingly honored him by calling him "Rabbi" and "Teacher" (Mt. 12:38, 22:16, 22:24, Luke 11:45).

But beyond this, Jesus also saw himself as a *unique* teacher. This was clear from the very manner of his instruction: he did not appeal to the opinions of respected Jewish experts in the Law, but simply spoke as one having authority (Mark 1:22). Note also the implications of the following rebuke, sharply delivered to certain hostile Scribes and Pharisees: "The queen of the South will rise up in the judgment with this generation and condemn it, for she came from the ends of the earth to hear the wisdom of Solomon; and indeed, a greater than Solomon is here" (Mt. 12:42). Amazingly, Jesus here declares that he is wiser than the wisest man who ever lived (1 Kings 4:29f)! Moreover, he implies that even if the majority of Israelites will not own him as "a greater than Solomon"—in other words, as their supreme Teacher—Gentiles like the Queen of Sheba most certainly will (Mt. 8:11, Acts 28:27-28).

Bringing the Fullness of God's Revealed Truth

Jesus freely acknowledged that in OT times God had revealed a measure of his truth to Israel, and that the Jews were indeed the world's privileged custodians of the oracles of God (Deut. 4:7-8, Mt. 5:18, 11:13, 15:6, Mark 7:6-10, John 5:39-45, Rom. 3:2). Nevertheless, he insisted that that truth was incomplete. Moreover, he also insisted that it was *veiled*, and therefore imperfectly understood (John 5:36ff). Here, then, is why God had sent him: to *complete* his revelation to the world, and thereby to supply the missing key that would help his people grasp the true meaning of all that he had previously said.[1]

Jesus' convictions on this matter are on display in a large number of sayings. For example, he told his disciples that he was revealing to them *the mysteries of the Kingdom of God* (Mt. 13:16-17). As we have seen, this expression meant that he was now bringing them *definitive* light concerning the nature of the Kingdom, the manner of its advance in the earth, and the stages of its appearing. In other words, he was explaining to his followers

HOW CAN WE FIND TRUSTWORTHY ANSWERS TO THE QUESTIONS OF LIFE?

precisely how God would fulfill the OT prophecies of the Kingdom, *and how those prophecies should therefore be interpreted*. He was, then, bringing the *fullness* of God's truth about the supreme hope of the Jewish scriptures: the Kingdom of God.

Again, towards the end of his life, Jesus tells his disciples that in days to come he will enable them to understand *all things*. Already, he himself has given them much truth, "all the things" that the Father has been pleased to speak through him during his days upon the earth (John 15:15). But, he says, there is more to come, more that they are not yet "able to bear" (John 16:12). Therefore, after his departure to heaven, he will send them the Spirit of Truth, by whom he will *further* teach them (John 15:26, 16:12). In that day, they will know "all things" (John 14:25-26). This does not mean, of course, that they will become omniscient like God, but rather that they will know *all the truth that God is pleased to reveal to mankind, especially the truth about his redemptive plan*. Thus, through the agency of the Holy Spirit, the ascended Christ will himself complete the revelation of God's truth. And then, by the agency of his disciples, he will send it out into the entire world! More on this in just a moment.

Jesus also said, "For this cause I have come into the world, that I should bear witness to *the truth*" (John 18:37). By *the truth*, he meant *all* the truth: the fullness of God's revelation to the human race. This truth will set men free from the tyranny of sin (John 8:32). It will separate them from evil and bring them close to God (John 17:9). It will also go forth into all nations (Mt. 28:18f). If it were but partial truth, it could do none of these things. Since it is complete truth, it can do them all.

Because he purported to bring the fullness of God's truth, Jesus referred to his teaching as *a rock abiding*. In so speaking, he clearly anticipated that his words would be preserved, *and that they would henceforth become the one foundation upon which all people may safely build their lives, even to the end of the age*. This conviction is particularly clear from his closing words in the Sermon on the Mount, where he warns that only the doers of his "sayings," and not the hearers only, shall be able to endure the winds and rains by which God will most assuredly test the integrity of a man's life (Mt. 7:24-29). Believing this, he therefore commands his disciples to take those sayings to all nations, so that in the greatest gale of all—the Day of Judgment—men everywhere will be able to stand (Mt. 28:18f). Jesus' premise in all of this is clear: because he is now bringing the fullness of God's truth into the world, it is time that all the world should hear it and obey it, so that they may safely pass through the judgment and joyfully enter the Kingdom of God.

In this connection, we do well to note Jesus' short discourse to the Jews of Jerusalem, in which he declares that his words are nothing less than the God-given standard by which men of all nations shall be judged:

> He who believes in me believes not in me, but in Him who sent me. And he who sees me sees Him who sent me. I have come as light into the world, that whoever believes in me should not abide in darkness. And if anyone hears my words and does not believe, I do not judge him. For I did not come to judge the world but to save the world. He who rejects me and does not receive my words has that which judges him: *the word that I have spoken will judge him in the last day*. For I have not spoken on my own authority, but the Father who sent me gave me a command, what I should say and what I should speak. And I know that His command is everlasting life. Therefore, whatever I speak, just as the Father told Me, so I speak.
> —John 12:44-50

In this amazing text, Jesus clearly portrays himself as the Teacher *par excellence*. He is the very image of the Father, as well as the very voice of the Father, bringing the light and words of the Father to the whole world. Such words are definitive: even to the end of history they will offer eternal life to all who obey them, and warn of eternal death to all who reject them. However, *at* the end of history they will no longer offer or warn, but will rise up as the judge of all, and most especially of those who spurned them. Thus, in Jesus' mind, his teaching constitutes the whole of God's saving truth: right up to the Day of his return, the revelation he brings will continue to offer eternal life; after that, it will become the standard that determines the final outcome of the Day of Judgment.

Could any revelation be fuller than this? To a man, Jesus' apostles believed that it could not. His is a revelation given "once for all" (Jude 1:3). On earth he gave part of it; from heaven he gave the rest of it. Henceforth, the whole truth is out. The foundation having thus been laid, the temple of God is ready to rise upon it (Eph. 2:19-20, Heb. 1:1f). The Teacher has come, and the saints are to look for no other. Indeed, they are to be on their guard against other teachers—"false Christs," "false prophets," and "false teachers"—any who would try to supplant, supercede, or distort the definitive words of the true Christ and the true Teacher (Mt. 24:4-5, 24, 2 Pet. 2:1). In sum, the apostles affirm that Jesus of Nazareth is *the* Teacher, and that the truth he brings is *the* truth, whole and entire. Never in a million years would they think of abandoning him for another (John 6:68).

HOW CAN WE FIND TRUSTWORTHY ANSWERS TO THE QUESTIONS OF LIFE?

To All Mankind

Jesus looked for a day when his teaching would go out *to all mankind*. True, he told his disciples that he was sent only to the lost sheep of the house of Israel (Mt. 15:24). But on the very occasion when he said it, it was the faith of a *Gentile* woman that induced him to meet her need, despite the declared parameters of his mission (Mt. 15:21-28). Moreover, in meeting her need, he implicitly confirmed what, on other occasions, he explicitly stated: soon his message will reach the Gentiles because it was *meant* to reach the Gentiles (Mt. 8:11, Luke 13:29). In sum, Jesus himself trained his apostles to see that God was sending his truth to the Jew *first*, but *not* to the Jew *only* (Acts 3:26, Rom. 1:16). The significance of all this is clear and surpassingly important: *from the very beginning, Jesus definitely understood himself to be God's appointed Teacher to the whole human race.*

Quite a number of texts illustrate this crucial point. Echoing the prophet Isaiah, Jesus told the Jews, "I am the light of the world" (John 8:12; Luke 2:32). To the Gentile Pontius Pilate he said, "For this cause I was born, and for this cause I have come into the world, that I should bear witness to the truth. Everyone who is of the truth hears my voice" (John 18:37). To his closest Jewish disciples he said, "Other sheep I have which are not of this fold; them also I must bring, and they will hear my voice; and there will be one flock and one shepherd" (John 10:16). And in order to *effect* his vision of a single flock, he later commanded them, "Go therefore and make disciples of all nations, baptizing them in the name of the Father, and of the Son, and of the Holy Spirit, teaching them to observe all things that I commanded you; and lo, I am with you always, even to the end of the age" (Mt. 28:19ff; 10:18, Acts 22:21, 26:16-18). In these and many other such sayings, seekers of every nation, eager to find the unknown god's appointed Teacher, can indeed hear Jesus of Nazareth saying, "Come unto me" (Mt. 11:28, Rev. 14:6).

Even to the end of the Age

We have seen that Jesus presented himself as a unique teacher bringing the fullness of God's revealed truth to all nations. But he also said something more—something quite mysterious. Shortly before his death he commanded his disciples, "Do not be called teachers, for One is your Teacher, even the Christ" (Mt. 23:10). Here we see that Jesus both desired and intended to be the teacher of his people—Jew and Gentile alike—*even to the end of the age*. What could he have meant by this? How did he plan to accomplish such an amazing feat? Since the answers to these questions are important, fascinating, and challenging to understand, we must linger over them with extra care.

How the Teacher Teaches All Nations

How is it that Christ will be the *sole* teacher of his people? The NT responds to this question with many texts. One of the most concise, powerful, and picturesque is found in the Revelation, an extended vision given by Christ to the aged apostle John on the island of Patmos. Here are the first three verses of that amazing book:

> The Revelation of Jesus Christ, which God gave to Him to show His servants—things which must shortly take place. And He sent and signified it by His angel to his servant John, who bore witness to the word of God, and to the testimony of Jesus Christ, and to all things that he saw. Blessed is he who reads and those who hear the words of this prophecy, and keep those things which are written in it; for the time is near.
> —Rev. 1:1-3

This passage especially suits our purpose since it vividly depicts exactly *how* the God of the Bible likes to impart his truth to mankind. He likes to reveal it through what we might call *the great chain of revelation*. This chain is essentially a hierarchy of mediators. At the top of the hierarchy is *God*—that is, God the Father. He is, as it were, the fountainhead of all truth and divine revelation. In this case, the Father has given a revelation of present and future events to his exalted Son, the Lord Jesus *Christ*. Christ, in turn, "sends and signifies" the revelation through an *angel*. The angel then communicates it to the *apostle* John. And John, having borne witness to all that he saw and heard by writing it down, passes it along to Christ's "servants," to his *disciples* of all times and places (Rev. 1:1). Observe carefully that John's writing is *sacred scripture*. He calls it "the Word of God" and "the Testimony of Jesus Christ." It is normative writing, binding upon all Christians. They are to hear and obey the words of this prophecy, even until the end of the age. If they do, they will be blessed.

Observe also from Revelation 1:10 that when John received this amazing impartation he was "in the Spirit on the Lord's Day." We must, then, add *the Holy Spirit* to the great chain of revelation. When we do, we conclude from John's introduction that divine revelation comes from *God*, through *Christ*, through the *Holy Spirit*, (sometimes) through *holy angels*, through *apostles* (or prophets), and through *writing*, finally to reach its appointed destination: his *servants* or *disciples*. Once written down, this revelation becomes scripture. Henceforth, there is authoritative, inscripturated, divine truth in the world. Now all that remains is that the Spirit should give God's servants "an ear to hear;" that is, to understand what Christ is saying through the scriptures to all the churches (Rev. 2:7, 11, 17, 29, etc.).

HOW CAN WE FIND TRUSTWORTHY ANSWERS TO THE QUESTIONS OF LIFE?

Very importantly, this memorable passage actually supplies a vivid distillation of the way in which God, according the NT authors, teaches his people in "these last days." And how is that? Most simply stated, he teaches them through his Teacher. However, we must understand that when the Teacher teaches, he does so by administering God's truth in two distinct stages. First, he administers it as a *revelator,* thereafter he administers it as an *illuminator*. Let us pause to look at some further NT passages dealing with this fascinating two-fold theme.

The Teacher as Revelator

The story here begins at Jesus' baptism. Rising from the waters of the Jordan, he received from the Father a special anointing of the Holy Spirit. It was divine empowerment for his forthcoming ministry as Israel's Messianic prophet, priest, and king (Isaiah 42:1f, Mt. 3:16-17, Luke 3:22).

Having thus received the Spirit, from this time on the heavenly prophet began to teach. As a rule, he taught in parables, but explained their meaning privately to his disciples (Mark 4:1-34). In doing so, he saw himself as a mediator. He said, "I do nothing on my own, but I speak just what the Father has taught me" (John 8:28, 38, 15:15, 17:6-8). It is clear, however, that a man who speaks in this way is not just a mediator, but also a revelator. He is mediating divine revelation to men.

As we have seen, Jesus fully expected these revelations to reach the nations. Like a lamp, his truth was not brought into the house of this world to be hidden, but rather that all peoples might see by its light (Mark 4:21-22). If he whispered anything into the disciple's ears, it was only that they should one day shout it from the rooftops (Mt. 10:27, Luke 8:17). In sum, his ultimate purpose in coming down from heaven was to get God's truth *into* the world and *out to* the whole world (John 12:46).

Very importantly, Jesus declared that he would not complete his revelatory ministry during his brief stay on earth. He would not, because he could not. Why? Because what he had to reveal about the plan of redemption could not be fully understood until that redemption had been accomplished; what he had to reveal about the two-fold spiritual reign of God could not be grasped until the Spirit himself had come. Accordingly, he sought diligently to prepare his disciples for a future reception of further light:

> If you love me, keep My commandments. And I will pray the Father and He will give you another Helper, that He may abide with you forever, even the Spirit of Truth, whom the world cannot receive because it neither sees him nor knows him. But you know him, for He dwells with you and will be in you. I will not leave you orphans; I will come to you.

> These things I have spoken to you while being present with you. But the Helper, the Holy Spirit, whom the Father will send in My name, He will teach you all things, and bring to your remembrance all things that I said to you.
>
> I still have many things to say to you, but you cannot bear them now. However, when He, the Spirit of Truth has come, He will guide you into all truth. For He will not speak on His own authority, but whatever He hears He will speak; and He will tell you things to come. He will glorify Me, for he will take of what is Mine and declare it to you. All things that the Father has are Mine. Therefore I said He will take of Mine and declare it to you.
> —John 14:15-18, 25-26, 16:12-15

These rich words, taken from Jesus' Upper Room Discourse, were spoken only hours before his death (John 13-17). In them, he seeks to prepare, warn, and comfort his disciples by revealing things to come. With the benefit of hindsight, we can readily understand their meaning. "In days ahead," says Jesus, "I will return to heaven. Once there, I will ask the Father, and he will place the Holy Spirit in my custody. Soon afterwards, I will send him to you, and through him I will continue to teach you. I will enable you to remember all that I said to you on earth. I will enable you to communicate it to others. In time, I will even inspire some among you to commit it to writing. Through the Spirit, I will also reveal new truth, truth that I have yet to receive from my Father. When at last you have seen it, you will know all that he is pleased to reveal to mankind, including things yet to come. I will not leave you as orphans. I will come to you in the Spirit. I will teach you again. I will complete the revelation of God."

Reading the rest of the NT, we see that it happened just as Jesus said. After his exaltation to the Father's right hand, Christ did indeed receive the Spirit and pour him out upon the nascent Church (Acts 2:33). Then, as Peter and Paul's inspired sermons demonstrate, he opened his apostles' minds to understand the redemptive events that had just transpired in Israel, and enabled them to communicate all this in preaching (Luke 24:45, Acts 2, 3, 4, 10, 13, 17). Then, as the apostles preached, Christ also taught their audience, opening the hearts of many—both Jew and Gentile—to believe and obey their words (John 17: 20, Acts 2:37, 41, 10:1-48, 11:18, 16:14, 30). Moreover, after the people had believed, he continued to teach them, again using apostles, prophets, and teachers to deepen their understanding of the new faith (Acts 2:42, Acts 13:1, Acts 18:24f, 1 Cor. 12, 14).

As time passed and various pressing needs arose, the revelatory process finally reached its climax. Christ again moved upon certain of his apostles, this time enabling them to commit the new, God-given "traditions" to writing (1 Cor. 11:12, 2 Thess. 2:15). Accordingly, some penned *gospels*—accounts of the life and teachings of Christ. Others wrote *epistles*—letters to one or more of the new congregations, designed to articulate Christian truth, correct errors, and set forth the divine norms for personal and ecclesiastical conduct in the new era. Then, as the apostolic era drew to a close, the glorified Christ received the *Revelation* from his Father, and "sent and signified" it to his apostle John.

With this, the "canon" (i.e., the divinely authorized collection) of NT documents was complete. The heavenly prophet had finished his revelatory ministry. He had delivered the full measure of God's normative truth: like a newborn babe, it was out in the world, once and for all.

Very importantly, the teaching ministry of the heavenly Christ was still not done. It would, however, change in form. Henceforth, the *revelator* of God's truth must now serve as its *illuminator*. Since it is so vital to seekers, we must also explore this further ministry of the Teacher in some depth.[2,3,4]

The Teacher as Illuminator

We have seen that Jesus fully expected to teach his people even to the end of the age. The testimony of Christ's Church is that he has been doing so for centuries—even millennia—and that he will continue to do so forever. Such an amazing claim is sure to perk up the ears—and the hopes—of seekers who long for a personal inward experience of the unknown god, and for a personal inward assurance of his truth.

We can get a feel for the mystery of illumination by examining Luke's account of Jesus' first post-resurrection appearance to the assembled disciples. They are in a house in Jerusalem. All are astir. Their Master's tomb is empty, women have seen angels, Simon Peter has actually spoken with the risen Lord, and so too have two other disciples who have just joined them. Suddenly, Jesus appears in their midst. Stricken with fear, they think they are seeing a spirit. To ease their fears, and in order to persuade them otherwise, he invites them to look closely at his wounds, touch him, and even eat with him. At last they are satisfied that it really is the risen Lord. Then Luke writes as follows:

> And He said to them, "This is what I told you while I still was with you, that everything must be fulfilled that is written about me in the Law of Moses, the Prophets, and the Psalms."
>
> *And he opened their understanding that they might comprehend the scriptures.*
>
> Then He said to them, "Thus it is written that the Christ should suffer and rise from the dead the third day, and that repentance and remission of

sins should be preached in His name to all nations, beginning at Jerusalem. And you are witnesses of these things. Behold, I send the promise of My Father upon you; but tarry in the city (of Jerusalem) until you are endued with power from on high."
—Luke 24:44-49; 25-27, 32

Here, in a biblical nutshell, is the essence of illumination. *Illumination occurs as Christ, acting by the Holy Spirit, opens the understanding of his people so that they can comprehend and respond to the scriptures.* Keeping this definition in view, let us consider several important aspects of illumination more closely.

Necessary

First, the NT insists that illumination is *necessary*. Observe the gathered disciples. Even though they have been with Jesus for three years, they still are in the dark: their minds cannot understand spiritual things, including the scriptures. In part, this is simply because they are creatures of God, ever dependent upon him for spiritual light and life (John 15:1f). But in larger part, it is because they are *fallen* creatures, creatures whose minds are darkened by sin. Thus, unless God helps them, they will be like the Gentiles, "walking in the futility of their mind, having their understanding darkened, being alienated from the life of God, because of the ignorance that is in them, because of the hardening of their heart" (Eph. 4:17-18). They will remain mere "natural men," men in the state of nature to which Adam enslaved them, men who "…cannot receive the things of the Spirit of God…nor can they understand them, because they must be spiritually discerned" (1 Cor. 2:14). In short, to behold the spiritual truth revealed in scripture, God *must* give us eyes to see, and light by which to see it (Deut. 29:4). Illumination is necessary.

At the Hand of Christ

Secondly, illumination always comes *at the hand of Christ*. In our text, it is Jesus himself who opens the disciple's understanding through the mediating agency of the Holy Spirit (John 14:17). After his exaltation to heaven, he will continue to do the same. He will receive the Spirit, send the Spirit, and come to his people in the Spirit (Acts 2:33, John 14:18). Thus, under God the Father, he and he alone will remain the Teacher of all, even to the end of the age (Mt. 28:18ff).

Biblically Focused

As a rule, illumination *is biblically focused*. That is, when Christ illumines spiritual truth, he does so primarily through the scriptures. Our text reads, "He opened their minds *to understand the scriptures.*" What Luke means is that he opened their minds *to see the spiritual realities that stand behind the scriptures*, realities signified by the divine revelation that is contained in holy writ. For example, having now been illuminated, the disciples could see their crucified Lord in the OT Passover lamb, the scapegoat, and Isaiah's Suffering Servant (Exodus 12, Leviticus 16, Isaiah 53). Similarly, they could see his resurrection in Isaac's "return" from the dead, Jonah's escape from the belly of the whale, and David's cry of victory over death (Gen. 22, Jonah 2, Psalm 16). This is the very essence of illumination: Christ illuminating minds by illuminating spiritual realities at the hearing or reading of scripture. The implications here are truly mind-boggling: Christ can shine God's light on things above and things below; on things past, present, and future; on things within and things without; on anything and everything that would fill a seeker's eyes with the answers to the questions of life. In sum, through illumination, *Christ can shine God's light on reality as a whole, thereby imparting to his people the one true worldview.* Again, seekers should always remember that he does so primarily through his revealed word: he himself has ordained that illumination is biblically focused (John 17:17, Acts 20:32).

Purposeful

Finally, illumination is *purposeful*. We see this in Jesus' high priestly prayer, in which he concisely summarized the fundamental purpose of illumination: "Father,...sanctify them by Thy truth, thy word is truth" (John 17:17). Here, Jesus is looking into the future. He sees that God's word—his completed revelation—will soon be in the world. He asks that God will use it to "sanctify" his people. How will the Father answer that prayer; how will he sanctify his people? He will do so through his Son and by his Spirit. These two will illuminate the Word of God to the people of God in such a way that they will be sanctified unto God forever.

Since this idea is of supreme importance, let us delve into it a little further.

Sanctification, as we have seen, means "separation." Accordingly, God's purpose in illuminating his Word is that he should separate his people. This separation is two-fold. Initially, it means roughly the same thing as "salvation." A sinner comes into contact with "the word of the truth of the gospel" (Col. 1:5). As he does, Christ so illuminates the word that he sees the realities it proclaims, believes them, repents of his sin, and comes to trust the Savior. At that moment, this sinner is *definitively* sanctified: he is separated once and for all *from* Adam's evil nature and standing, *to* Christ's holy nature and standing. He is separated *from* the world, the flesh, and the devil, *to* the Father, the Son, and the Holy Spirit.

The NT supplies many examples of Christ using the Word to accomplish definitive sanctification. One of these involved a certain woman named Lydia, a seller of purple fabrics from the city of Thyatira. As a convert to Judaism, she was worshiping with some other women beside a river near Philippi. The apostle Paul joined them and preached the gospel to them. Then, says Luke, "The Lord opened her heart to heed the things spoken by Paul" (Acts 16:14). What exactly did the Lord do? He *illuminated* his word spoken through Paul, and *definitively sanctified* his new servant Lydia.

But sanctification is also *progressive*. Progressive sanctification has to do with spiritual growth, with progress in holiness. As we have seen, it is essentially three-fold. In progressive sanctification, the saints are continually separated from sin, unto God, in such a way that they grow in *knowledge*, *character*, and *service* in the advance of the Kingdom. Importantly, it is again Christ himself who accomplishes this sanctification, using the Word of God to teach, transform, and equip his people. The apostle Paul has this very thing in mind when he admonishes the Ephesian men as follows:

> Husbands, love your wives, just as Christ also loved the Church and gave Himself for her, that He might sanctify and cleanse her by the washing of water with the word, that He might present her to Himself a glorious church, not having spot or wrinkle or any such thing, but that she should be holy and without blemish.
> —Eph. 5:25-27

In this rich passage, Christ stands out as the illuminator of his people. In love, he has given himself for them. They are his Church, his beloved Bride. Having secured the Bride's forgiveness on earth, he is now free and eager to prepare her for heaven. He does so *from* heaven, cleansing her "by the washing of water with the word." That is, he so illuminates God's revelation—his inscripturated Word—that she is purified (and purifies herself) of every blemish in understanding, character, or conduct. So again, Christ himself is purposeful, and his work of illumination is purposeful. *From* heaven he is busy preparing his Bride *for* heaven, by continually illuminating and sanctifying her through the Word of God, (John 13:1-10).

HOW CAN WE FIND TRUSTWORTHY ANSWERS TO THE QUESTIONS OF LIFE?

HOW THE TEACHER TEACHES ALL MANKIND

"I am the Light of the world." John 8:12

GOD
↓
CHRIST
(The Heavenly Prophet / Teacher)
↓
THE SPIRIT OF TRUTH

REVELATION (completed) → Apostles → Scriptures

ILLUMINATION (continuing) → Disciples

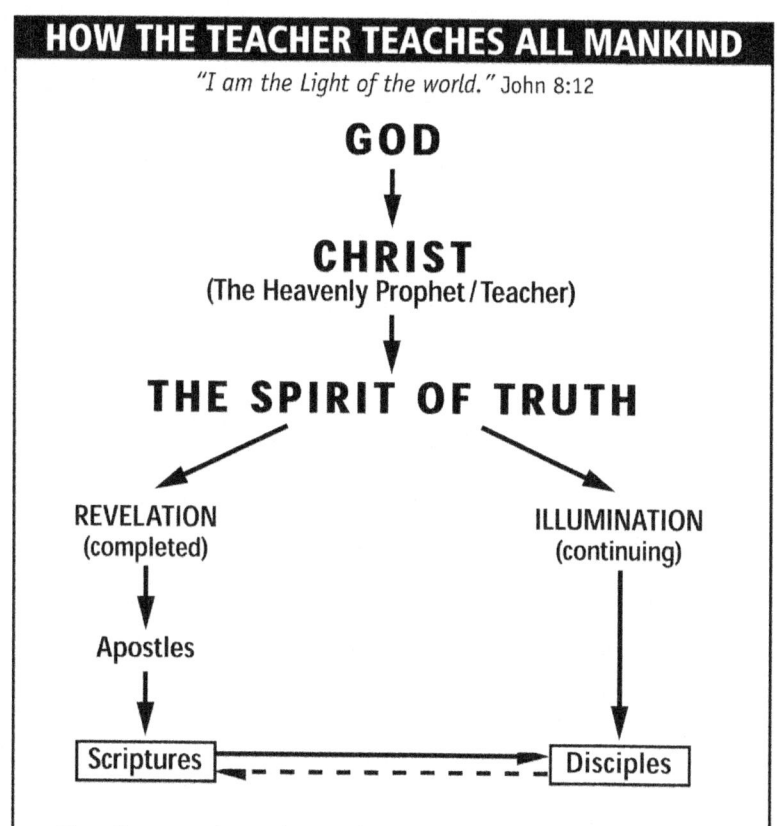

The diagram above depicts how the exalted Christ teaches all mankind. His method is essentially two-fold. First, he receives the fullness of divine truth from the Father, reveals it to his apostles by the Spirit, and inspires them to write it down once for all as Holy Scripture. At this point, his revelatory work is complete. Then, by means of the same Spirit, he sends his gospel messengers to all nations, illuminating the minds of his believing people to understand the scriptures. This prophetic work of illumination continues until his return in glory at the end of the age. Observe from the diagram that Christ normally illumines his disciples as they contemplate divine revelation. For now, it is in the Bible that they will best behold, enjoy, and grow in the things of God.

One is Your Teacher

Earlier, we heard Jesus tell his disciples, "Do not be called teachers, for One is your Teacher, even the Christ" (Mt. 23:10). Now we understand what he meant. He did not mean that he would leave his flock without teachers (Eph. 4:11). Nor did he mean that the sheep should not honor such teachers for their important work (Acts 13:1, 1 Tim. 2:7). He did mean, however, that no one should think of any *man* as his teacher, but that all should honor Christ as their true teacher, and their only teacher (1 Cor. 3:1-7, 1 John 2:27). Why? Because he alone has imparted the fullness of God's revelation to all mankind. He alone has authorized and inspired chosen men to inscripturate it. He alone illuminates its meaning to those who read and hear, inwardly unveiling the awesome reality of the things of God. And he alone enables them to respond as they should. So then, there is but one revelator, one illuminator, one Teacher. And according to Jesus, he is that one.

Especially for Seekers

We have reached the end of the third part of our Journey. In it, we have seen that Jesus addresses all the questions of life, that he answers them well, and that he does indeed identify himself as the one true Teacher come from God.

In light of all this, what is the seeker's next step? How shall he respond to claims and credentials so radical as these?

For some, the response will involve turning to the Bible with deepened interest. It will involve asking, "Is this book really everything that Jesus says it is? Is it really God's full and final revelation to mankind?"

But more than this, it may well involve turning to Jesus himself. For if things really are the way he says they are, *then there is no understanding the Bible without his help.* As it is written, he is the one who shuts, so that no one can open; and he is the one who opens, so that no one can shut (Rev. 3:7).

Perhaps, then, for some who have journeyed with me so far, a simple prayer is now in order. And perhaps it should go something like this: "Jesus, if what I have just read is true, I cannot understand spiritual things without your help. So please, send me your Spirit, open my mind, and illuminate me, that as I continue to read the Bible I may know with certainty who you are, and whether or not this book is indeed the very word of God."

ONE MAN'S JOURNEY:
A FURNACE FOR GOLD

The crucible for silver and the furnace for gold,
but the LORD tests the hearts.
—Proverbs 17:13

IT WAS A steep and winding road that led me to Father Gabriel Barry. Literally.

It began, I suppose, at the little Catholic seminary tucked away in the woods behind Dominican hospital in Santa Cruz. The lovely grounds were posted "No Trespassing," and since the facility seemed almost abandoned, I was reluctant to set foot on the property. In the end, however, my keen desire to find a knowledgeable priest overcame my fears, and I ventured onto the campus. After guiltily strolling around for a while, I finally plucked up my courage, entered one of the buildings, and wandered through the vacant halls. At last, from within a small office, I heard some sounds of life.

I no longer recall his name, but the cordial priest was all encouragement to the trembling seeker. I told him my story, emphasizing my deep involvement in Eastern religion, my attraction to Jesus, the mysterious gift of tears, and my desire to understand the meaning of what I was experiencing. When I finished, he seemed genuinely moved by what he had heard, and quite clear about what I should do. I must spend some time at the Benedictine monastery in Big Sur, the *New Camaldoli Hermitage*. In fact, if memory serves me, he called the hermitage then and there, arranging not only for my stay, but also for a visit with the abbot himself.

Only days later, I found myself on a narrow road traversing a 1,300-foot cliff overlooking the majestic Big Sur coastline. When at last I reached the top, I parked my car, visited with the guest director, and quietly slipped into an alien world whose basic forms and rhythms had been shaped some 800 years earlier!

The picturesque monastery, studded with small cells for twenty or thirty brothers, was structured for silence and contemplation. I was assigned a guesthouse where I could read, pray, and take my meals alone. I was allowed to walk the grounds but forbidden to speak with the monks. I was also welcomed to gather with the brothers for their many liturgical services. Though I understood this worship poorly, I participated faithfully—even at 2:00 A.M. matins! Perhaps among these ancient traditions and devoted men I could find the spiritual truth I longed for.

Early in my stay, the abbot visited my room. After hearing my story, he assured me that my experience with Jesus was a genuine gift of God. He invited me to spend some time praying, reading *The Boston Catechism* (a brief summary of Roman Catholic doctrine), and sharing in the liturgical life of the community. Then, after a few days, he would speak with me again. I was, of course, being encouraged to interpret my fledgling Christian experience in Catholic perspective—and was also being invited to make that community of faith my own. A bigger decision I had never faced.

The days went by. Though I practiced the recommended disciplines diligently, I had no noteworthy spiritual experiences. Indeed, my heart remained painfully divided. On the one hand, I was drawn to the Catholic Church. I liked its antiquity, its grandeur, its authority, its solemn rituals, its mystics, monastics, and saints—all of which seemed to promise a rich inheritance of truth and security to any potential son or daughter.

On the other hand, I simply wasn't sure that all this was true. *The Boston Catechism* was certainly impressive, and seemed reasonable enough to a biblical neophyte such as myself. But was the Catholic take on the Bible really correct? What about Protestant perspectives? More importantly, what about Eastern perspectives on God and salvation? What about all my friends on "the yogi trail"? Were they really deceived and eternally lost? If my heart was being drawn to Rome, it definitely remained tied to India as well.

And so I remained throughout the entire stay: curious, hungry, hopeful, and deeply divided. Exiting the chapel night by night, I would pause beneath the towering ocean firmament glistening with stars: so peaceful, so beautiful, so silent—and I, beneath it all, so very alone.

Finally, after about a week, I reached a decision. Everything seemed to favor it: my experience with Jesus, the uncanny way in which I had been guided to the monastery, the glory of Rome, and perhaps above all, my deep spiritual need for a place to call home. Yes, I still had many questions and reservations, but I convinced myself that under qualified spiritual care these would be quickly resolved. I decided to become a Roman Catholic Christian.

When I told the abbot, he was pleased, supportive, and ready with a plan. In anticipation of my water baptism and formal entrance into the

Church, he proposed that I meet regularly with his friend, Father Gabriel Barry, for a private catechism. I eagerly agreed, and soon thereafter found myself driving over the Santa Cruz Mountains to San Jose for my first session with the warm and thoughtful Irish Franciscan. We agreed that he would supply me with books and that we would meet weekly to discuss what I was learning. If all went well, I would be baptized, perhaps as soon as the coming Easter.

Needless to say, when this mentorship began in late 1970 I had the highest hopes. Surely, I thought, everything would now fall into place. Surely my questions about the biblical worldview would be answered. Surely my struggle to resolve the tensions between East and West would be laid to rest. Surely I was nearing the end of the road in my search for God and truth. Surely I was indeed coming home.

And surely—as events were soon to prove—I was greatly mistaken.

Between Two Worlds

I met with Father Barry for several months, peppering him with inquiries about Catholic answers to the questions of life. The more we visited, the more it became clear that the Christian religion was indeed radically different from Eastern religions. Father Barry, remaining true to most of the biblical fundamentals, refused to let me pull pantheistic rabbits out of the biblical hat. Kindly but firmly, he insisted, contrary to Eastern thought, that God is an infinite tri-personal Spirit, comprised of Father, Son, and Holy Spirit; that he transcends his creation, yet is also intimately and intricately related to it; that Adam and Eve were indeed true historical persons, the parents of the whole human race; that Satan and demonic powers were real and at work in the world; that man, having fallen in Adam, is born with a sin nature, and is guilty of individual sins emanating from it; that human beings will exist, consciously and for all eternity, either in heaven or in hell; and that Jesus of Nazareth—the incarnate Son of God—lived and died in order to save his believing people from the latter and bring them safely home to the former.

To my great consternation, I found that I could believe none of it. I simply could not see the truth—or the falsity—of these, the *prima facie* teachings of the Bible.

As a result, I found myself painfully suspended between two worlds. On the one hand, there was my homespun Eastern religion, the core of my present spiritual identity and the center of my most significant relationships. How could I altogether abandon it, especially in favor of a faith that increasingly struck me as incredible, narrow, frightening, and in some respects even repellent? On the other hand, there was the brute fact of my experience with Jesus. Because of it, I did indeed believe what the Bible said about the events of his life. I had seen his power, wisdom, goodness, and beauty. My heart had gone out to him in love. What did this experience mean? What was I to do with it? What was I to do with him?

Yes, the heavenly Tester had suspended me between two worlds, and was now watching to see what I would do. What *should* I have done? Today, it is easy to see the answer: I should have accepted his challenge. I should have loved the truth about Christianity enough to seek it out, whatever it was and however long it might take me to find it. But because I was afraid of what that truth might be—and also of what it might require of me—I did not. Accordingly, I decided to break off my relationship with Father Barry and to return to the practice of Zen Buddhism.

It was not too hard to construct a rationale for this intellectually dishonest move. To begin with, I seized upon the fact that Father Barry and certain modern Catholic theologians had endorsed theistic evolution. This departure from plain biblical teaching supplied a convenient solution to the apparent conflict between the Bible and Eastern religion. If the Bible had spoken metaphorically about the beginning (as Genesis certainly must have if cosmic evolution were true), then perhaps it had also spoken metaphorically— and pantheistically—about all the rest: the nature of God, man, sin, Christ, salvation, the afterlife, and so forth. Already, I had come upon biblical interpreters who taught this very thing. These proponents of "esoteric" Christianity argued, for example, that Jesus had secretly traveled to India in his youth; that his seemingly theistic teachings actually had a mystical, pantheistic sense; that he was, in fact, an *avatar*, a *boddhisattva*, an ascended Master: the greatest of all time, no doubt, but one among many, nonetheless. In my eastward leaning mind, all these strands of thought wove themselves into a plausible way of escape. I took it.

Again, with the benefit of hindsight it is now quite clear to me what happened at this critical juncture of my test: I "believed" all these things, not because I had *seen* that they were true, but because I *wanted* them to be true. In other words, at this decisive moment in my "search" for spiritual reality—when the gospel put me to the test by pressing for a deeper commitment to truth—I simply *decided* that pantheism was true, rather than try to discover whether or not it really was. It was a bad decision. Why? Because in that unspeakably consequential moment, I ceased to be a seeker of God's truth, and became instead a fabricator and defender of my own.

I believe I received a warning against doing so. It came one winter evening, shortly after I had decided to discontinue my studies with Father Barry. I was sitting comfortably in a couch at the Book Shop Santa Cruz, reading a volume of Zen meditations. Suddenly, I became aware of a band playing just outside the entrance to the store. Its members were singing Christian hymns while intermittently stepping forward to preach the gospel and testify about their personal experience with Christ. The Salvation Army was at war.

In mere seconds, my soul was also at war. For strange to tell, part of me was actually drawn to these people: I could see that they had deep spiritual assurance, joy, and an unnerving boldness to go public with their faith. Yet another part of me—the ruling part—would have none of it. I had been there and done that. I had rejected the fundamentalist take on Christianity. I had decided that orthodox Christians, while sincere, were sincerely deluded. How naive to think of God dualistically, as though he were a personal being separate from the world, separate from us!! Surely these relics of mankind's primitive religious consciousness were in egregious error. But if all of my philosophical reasonings were true, why did their singing and preaching bother me so?

Yes, on that memorable evening I once again came face to face with the painful truth: I was *still* a man suspended between two worlds. Though I could not see it clearly then, God himself, through the Salvation Army band, was showing me that I had not put the biblical Jesus behind me. Indeed, he was showing me that I *must* not put him behind me. Rather, I must continue to search until I could actually see for myself which version of Christianity—the biblical or the esoteric—was true.

But again, I did not want to search, because I did not want to see. And so, in order to escape the war within, I rose from my couch, exited the store, walked as quickly as I could past the little band, and was swallowed up into the night.

Descent into Darkness

The decision to re-immerse myself in Eastern religion was yet another milestone in my spiritual quest. Prior to that, things seemed to be going fairly well: I was confident about my journey and optimistic about quickly reaching its happy destination. However, after that decision, things became increasingly difficult. The difficulty was two-sided. On the one hand, I was continually plagued with doubts about the truth of pantheism. On the other, I was simultaneously haunted by suspicions of the truth of Christianity. My rejection of the orthodox Christ introduced me to these two unwelcome companions, companions who were ever at side during a three-year descent into darkness.

My recollection of those years is spotty. For the most part I remained in Santa Cruz, where my quest for enlightenment involved a daily routine of morning and evening meditation, extensive spiritual reading, long walks in the forest or on the beaches, periodic odd jobs, and occasional volunteer activities. Desiring to make some kind of contribution to the world around me, I again began writing poetry, hoping in this way to win others to an awareness of Big Mind and to the quest for mystical experience. My circle of friends remained small—confined almost exclusively to fellow-pilgrims of the Eastern way. Occasionally we would eat or walk together and discuss spiritual things. For the most part, however, I lived in solitude, believing that this narrow path was most conducive to the "mindfulness" that I hoped would soon flower into enlightenment.

Throughout this time I remained fairly faithful to my Zen practice, sometimes riding my bike across town to the Zendo twice a day for meditation. I did, however, continue to read widely in other mystical traditions. For example, I acquainted myself not only with Hinduism and Buddhism, but also with Taoism, Kabalistic Judaism, Christian mysticism, Islamic Sufism, American Transcendentalism, Theosophy, Christian Science, and the Unity School of Christianity. I was especially influenced by the writings of J. Krishnamurti, an Indian philosopher who strongly counseled seekers against adherence to traditional religious faiths and practices, arguing that these only entangled the (already divine) mind in dualistic thinking and desiring. But again, I did not pursue these studies with a spirit of genuine inquiry. Instead, I read selectively, in order to confirm what I already believed and what I wanted to believe. The intellectual dishonesty continued.

Haunted by Doubts

Because of this dishonesty, I became a haunted man. The specters that more or less continually intruded upon my troubled mind were threefold.

First, I was haunted by doubts about the truth of pantheism, doubts that came in several different forms. For example, I was often ambushed by the brute physicality of nature. Now even on a good day, it is hard to believe that the world is a dream. But when you can't get warm, or lie sick with intestinal flu, or fall off your motorcycle, it is virtually impossible. Like light and darkness, pain and pantheism cannot long dwell together in peace.

Similarly, I found myself almost always wrestling with the problem of evil. It was easy enough to scan the sky or the sea and say, "Yes, all is God." Or to peer into the throat of an orchid and say, "Yes, we are one." But such affirmations caught in my own throat when natural or moral evil unexpectedly intruded. I remember, for example, an afternoon in a San

Francisco cafeteria when I saw a poor man fall to the floor with an epileptic seizure and nearly drown in his own vomit. That lurid scene undid months of meditation and shook my pantheistic convictions to the core. And what about the dismal litany of distinctively moral evils: the rapes, thefts, tortures, murders, sexual perversions, lies, infidelities, treacheries, and all the rest? Was that God too? Was God really a cosmic sado-masochist, cruelly and criminally performing all these evil deeds upon himself? I tried to avoid this dreadful conclusion by affirming, nonsensically enough, that God was "beyond good and evil." But my heart would not buy it. Deep down, it knew full well that if all is God, then evil is God, and God is evil—at least in part. But it also knew that such things could not possibly be. Had I loved the truth, I would have listened to my heart and tried to learn from it. Because I did not, evil became a threat to my pantheistic faith: whenever I met it, I did not try to learn—I ran.

Still more doubts arose whenever I began to feel that I had a moral obligation to pursue a career by which I might better the world. And that happened a lot. To counter these impressions, I affirmed with my pantheistic teachers that all such pangs of conscience were really subtle forms of attachment to the good—an attachment that would only attract its opposite, evil, and further entangle me in the dualistic web of Maya. Better, then, to simplify one's life, work quietly and meditatively with one's hands, and keep oneself free from complicated moral projects that could only hinder the arrival of enlightenment.

The problem, however, was that my conscience refused to behave as if these notions were true. To the contrary, it kept urging me to get involved, to oppose evil, to promote good. It exhorted me to work for a better world and to eschew cowardly escapes from the imperfect one in which I happened to live. I tried, of course, to silence this voice with various rationalizations. But I could not. Indeed, if only temporarily, I occasionally gave in to it. Once, for example, I applied to a nursing school. Another time I volunteered to serve at Head Start. Still another time I explored post-graduate training in philosophy. Alas, they were pathetically short-lived ventures, soon cut off by the recurring thought that any such career would only delay my release from the fetters of this world. But the voice of conscience would not be cut off. Moreover, as it continued to reprove me in the depths of my heart, I began to wonder if this might not be the Hound of Heaven, the relentless voice of the living God himself.

Haunted by Jesus

During this time I was also haunted by Jesus. From the day I said goodbye to Father Barry, I simply could not escape him. It was as if something of Christ had been deposited deep beneath the pantheistic surface of my soul, something inexpungible and undying. To my recurring dismay, I found that any number of chance events could bring that subterranean deposit rushing to the surface.

When I was traveling in Mexico, for example, I spent a few weeks in the little town of San Miguel D'Allende. One day as I was passing the cathedral, I saw an old man at worship. Unashamed, he was kneeling on the steps that led up to the entrance of the church. What impressed me most about him was his spiritual fervor, reflected in the way that he fixed his eyes upon heaven and—with great, sweeping motions—repeatedly crossed himself. Suddenly, I realized that in my own life I had had only one spiritual experience that could even begin to elicit such devotion. Most assuredly, it had not come through the practice of Eastern religion.

On another occasion, this time in New Mexico, a group of us were camping. As we sat around the fire, a kindly looking man and his son asked if they could join us. After telling us how Christ had miraculously healed him from a major physical affliction, he and his boy began passing out gospel tracts. Immediately, I slipped away to my tent and spent a troubled half hour in meditation, trying to stanch the flow of unsettling thoughts and memories that his visit had induced. How amazing! Almost effortlessly this gentle evangelist had re-opened a gaping spiritual wound, a wound that no kind or quantity of eastern meditation could seem to heal.

Back in Santa Cruz, the haunting continued. I remember a serious young lady named Winn who frequently practiced Zen with our local group. One day, realizing that I had not seen her for some time, I asked my friend Bob what had become of her. "Oh, Winn became a Christian," he said. Needless to say, those words pierced me to the quick, eliciting unwelcome recollections of my own experience with Jesus, and of how—unlike Winn—I had declined to leave the world of Zen in order to enter his.

On another occasion, I was strolling along the beach and came upon an enthusiastic group of young people gathered at the sea's edge. Looking out into the water, I immediately realized what was going on, and just as immediately cut them a wide swath and quickly passed by. I had no desire whatsoever to get entangled in a baptism.

And then there was George. I met him one day on the campus of our local junior college. Standing in the midst of the quad, he kept raising his hands to heaven and shouting at the top of his voice, "Thank you, Jesus.

ONE MAN'S JOURNEY: A FURNACE FOR GOLD

Thank you, JESUS!" When I asked one of his companions to explain, she said that Christ had rescued him from a horrible trip on LSD, and that George had been praising him ever since. In the weeks to come, I would see George again, circulating among the cubicles of the library, quietly trying to win other students to faith in his Lord. He bothered me. True, he was a fanatic. But his behavior was undeniably that of someone who had had a profound religious experience: the kind of experience that could make a man quit his job, search out a priest, and plunge himself into the study of Christianity.

Yes, George bothered me, and Winn, and the Mexican peasant, and the Christians by the seashore, and Bibles on bookshelves, and crosses on steeples, and programs on the radio and TV, and ads in magazines, and so much more. As I said, I was a haunted man. And the message of the haunter was as simple as it was clear: Come back.

Haunted by Imminent Spiritual Collapse

The third haunting was the most frightening and painful of all. It occurred during the final months of my three-year journey into the depths of Eastern mysticism. During that time, I was increasingly haunted by the specter of a complete mental and spiritual collapse.

To understand what happened, you must first understand the premise, goal, and method Eastern spirituality. The premise, once again, is that all is one, and all is Big Mind. This entails that our natural sense of being a little mind—an individual person separate from other persons and other things—is a spiritual illusion, an illusion that keeps us from directly experiencing the reality of our divine nature. The goal, then, of Eastern spirituality is nothing so trivial as a mere calming of the individual mind, as some of its proponents disingenuously proclaim. No, the real goal is the *annihilation* of the individual mind—the extinction of the human personality altogether—so that Big Mind is all that remains. As guru Meher Baba once put it, "As long as the mind is there, the real 'I am God' state cannot be experienced. Therefore, the mind must go. We must attain this... annihilation of the mind during this life."

The method proposed for achieving all this, at least in the Zen tradition, is called *mindfulness*, or radically detached observation. Through the practice of Zazen, the meditator trains himself to become a passive spectator of all life; of all the upwellings of thought, emotion, and sensory perception that constitute the flow of daily human experience. In so doing, he is supposedly training himself to identify with the secret fountainhead of this flow: Big

Mind. Thus, the more detached and "mindful" the meditator becomes, the closer he gets to union with Big Mind.

In order to appreciate the danger of this practice, consider a humble illustration. Suppose you are sitting in meditation and the image of a potato chip floats succulently into your mind. You could, if you wished, immediately begin to imagine how nice it would be to have a whole bowl full of potato chips right after Zen practice. You could also think about where to buy them, what to dip them in, and whom you would like to eat them with. But all such imaginings would be most un-Zen-like. No, you must not let yourself get entangled in potato-chip-consciousness. Instead, you must train yourself to let such thoughts pass by. If clouds float through the sky, what is that to the sky? If thoughts of potato chips float through Big Mind, what is that to him?

This illustration is humorous, but the implications are not funny at all. For now suppose that as you sit in meditation there arise in your mind thoughts about practicing medicine among the poor, or taking a wife and raising a family, or the nature of the afterlife, or investigating the truth-claims of other world religions. If you are a fully persuaded pantheist, you must let these thoughts pass by as well. For why should big clouds bother Big Mind any more than little ones? And why, by following them into the realm of action, should Big Mind allow himself to get further entangled in the web of Maya? No, the proper strategy is to detach oneself from all such thoughts, questions, and pursuits, for it is only when these die that Big Mind's native awareness can once again spring to life.

It is clear, I trust, that such a worldview, buttressed by such a practice, tends not only to passivity and isolation, but ultimately to the atrophy and disintegration of a healthy personality. And for a zealous young seeker like myself—who practiced this kind of meditation with a vengeance—the disintegration was almost unto death.

The specter of psychological collapse began to haunt me in the spring of 1974, when I found myself increasingly plagued with certain frightening mental and spiritual experiences. My memory grew weaker and weaker. I became disoriented and indecisive. I was losing motivation, even for the smallest tasks such as maintaining the garden, repairing fixtures, visiting with friends, or taking walks. Waves of blank fear and anxiety periodically swept over me. At night on my bed, as I drifted off to sleep, I would sometimes begin to "soar," as if about to leave my body. (Once, in a hotel in Mexico, I believe I actually did leave my body, though the experience is too bizarre for me to relate here.) Waking from sleep, I would often see faces floating over my head, or human forms darting about the house. Once, as I sat in meditation, I began to sense the limits of my body falling away. I felt as if I were soaring upward and expanding outward all at the same time. In the back of my mind, something whispered, "This is it: enlightenment has come!" But realizing with sudden terror that I—Dean—might actually disappear forever, I quickly opened my eyes, jumped to my feet, and focused intently on my surroundings, all in a (successful) effort to force myself back into being myself. To this day, I do not know what would have happened if I had kept on.

And so, with the commencement of this final haunting, I entered a season of profound crisis. What were these phenomena? Were they really the death throes of the illusory self, a harbinger of final enlightenment? Or were they instead the warning signs of a terrible danger—signs that Eastern religion was, in the most radical sense imaginable, a dead end?

I was soon to find out, and in a manner that fills me with wonder to this very day.

PART 4

THE TEACHER ON THE TEST

CHAPTER 18

IS LIFE A TEST?

IN OUR JOURNEY to the meaning of life, we have traveled down many roads and lingered before many sights. It will serve us well to pause a moment to review our progress thus far.

In Part 1 we walked together through the natural, moral, and probationary orders, concluding from all we saw that life is—or may well be—a test; a test of our love of spiritual and philosophical truth, set before us by an infinite personal Spirit, an "unknown god."

Assuming this to be the case, we devoted Part 2 to searching for "god's appointed Teacher," the person, or group of persons, through whom the unknown god might be pleased to give us trustworthy answers to the questions of life. Having come to see that natural science and philosophy, despite the pretensions of some of their practitioners, cannot fill this exalted role, we realized we had but one choice left: to walk "the good rough road of revelation." Once upon it, we were surprised to discover something both fascinating and encouraging: a large, diverse, and historically credible body of supernatural signs, all pointing us to Jesus of Nazareth.

Accordingly, in Part 3 we did what the signs told us to do: we ascended the mount of Christianity, sat down at Jesus' feet, and listened long and hard to his teachings on the questions of life. As expected, he answered them all, and—in the eyes of many, at least—he answered them well: intuitively, reasonably, ethically, and in a manner that fills the heart with hope. As one of Jesus' own contemporaries said, "No man ever spoke like this man" (John 7:47)!

So, is our journey over? For some, it may well be, if indeed such seekers have become finders along the way. But for those who are still considering the claims of Christ, there may be two further questions they would like to hear Jesus address: *Is life really a test; and if so, how do we pass it?*

A God Who Tests His Children

Let us therefore embark on the fourth and final stage of our journey, the stage in which we examine Jesus' rich and nuanced teaching on these two important themes.

As a lover of the words of God, Jesus concurred with the Hebrew Scriptures: "The refining pot is for silver, and the furnace for gold, but the LORD tests the heart" (Psalm 17:3). He understood that God is a God who tests his children. It is his way with men, with angels, and even with his only-begotten Son (Job 7:17-18, Psalm 11:4, Prov. 17:3, Jer. 17:10, Mt. 4:1f).

OT history is replete with examples of this very thing. We have seen, for example, that God laid down the pattern for dealing with mankind in Eden, where he tested Adam and Eve at the Tree of the Knowledge of Good and Evil (Gen. 3). Subsequently, he tested Adam's sons, Abel and Cain, to see if they would worship him in a worthy manner (Gen. 4:1-8). He tested Noah's generation, to see if they would repent at the preaching of his faithful servant (Gen. 6, 2 Pet. 2:5). He (sorely) tested father Abraham, to see if he would love the Giver of his beloved son more than the son himself (Gen. 22:1f). He tested Joseph in the prisons of Egypt, to see if he would believe God's encouraging word more than the gloomy testimony of his own circumstances (Psalm 105:19). He tested Pharaoh by the message and miracles of Moses (Ex. 5-15). He tested Israel at Mt. Sinai, and at the borders of Canaan, and all throughout their journeys in the wilderness—tests that an entire generation largely failed (Ex. 20:20, Deut. 8:2, 16, Num. 13:1f, 1 Cor. 10:1f). He tested the Ninevites by the preaching of Jonah, and Jonah by the repentance of the Ninevites (Jonah 3, 4). He tested proud king Hezekiah by the worldly messengers from Babylon (2 Chron. 22:31). He tested the Hebrew exiles by the dainties of the king's palace, and also by the terrors of a fiery furnace (Dan. 1, 3). In these and many other such instances, we clearly see that the LORD God of Israel sits as a tester, refiner, and purifier of the souls of men (Mal. 3:3).

The definitive biblical treatment of God's probationary activity is found in the early chapters of Paul's letter to the Romans. Here the apostle expounds upon this theme at some length, elaborating the different ways in which God tests mankind throughout history. Before turning to Jesus' own words on the matter, it will prove helpful to consider first the later thoughts of his apostolic mouthpiece.

General Revelation

In Romans 1-3, Paul teaches that God tests his human creatures through two basic kinds of revelation. He begins with what theologians call *general revelation*. This term has a two-fold sense. Broadly speaking, it refers to God's revelation of certain *general spiritual truths* about himself, given to *mankind in general* (i.e., to *all* mankind). As we saw at the beginning of our journey, in general revelation God discloses himself through at least three fundamental media: *nature, conscience,* and *the questions of life*. His purpose in so doing is simple: he is testing people, to see if they will acknowledge him, obey him, and seek him out.

Paul begins by focusing on the realm of nature, declaring that God continually reveals his existence, eternity, power, wisdom, and goodness to all mankind through the natural order. Importantly, this revelation carries with it an immediate and inescapable sense of moral obligation: having seen something of the creator in his creation, men know full well that they ought to worship him and thank him for his many gifts, even if they do not know his name or the details of his will. Nevertheless, says Paul, as a rule they do not. Indeed, as a rule, they do precisely the opposite: they suppress their intuitive knowledge of God, turning instead to man-made idols, whether physical or spiritual. Not only so, they turn to various evil practices that their idolatry is designed to justify. Thus, they fail the test that general revelation puts before them, kindle God's wrath, lie under his condemnation, and therefore stand in desperate need of his forgiveness and heart-transforming power (Rom. 1:18f; cf. Psalm 19, Acts 14:17, 17:16ff).

Having discussed the natural order, Paul turns his attention to a second medium of general revelation, conscience (Rom. 2:1-16). He affirms that God has written his laws in the hearts of all. All know they ought to obey them. All realize that obedience means reward, and disobedience means retribution. In other words, all understand that they live in an objective moral order, an order created and sustained by a holy and sovereign god. This innate awareness of God as Moral Governor of the world also puts men to the test. Here, however, the test concerns their love of righteousness, and also of the Righteous Judge. But again, whether to a greater or a lesser degree, whether grossly or subtly, all spurn the voice of conscience and give themselves over to sinful passions. Accordingly, all now stand *further* condemned—not only as idolaters, but also as lawbreaking rebels. More than ever, they need the manifold blessings of redemption and reconciliation with God.

But what of the questions of life: Are they too a medium of general revelation? Admittedly, in Romans Paul does not *explicitly* say that they are.

Nevertheless, I would argue from the overall character of his teaching that he most certainly would. Why? *Because man's interaction with the questions of life leads to the same result as his interaction with nature and conscience: it gets him thinking about God.*

When we think about the ultimate reality, for example, we find that our mind refuses to concede this high honor to mere matter, but instead is positively inclined to look for a distinctly *spiritual* being above and behind all things. Similarly, when we think about origins, we are innately dissatisfied with the idea that the universe is eternal, but feel ourselves readily and repeatedly drawn to the idea of an infinite personal Creator. And much the same is true concerning the other questions of life: in contemplating their possible answers, we find that thoughts involving a spiritual supreme being continually suggest themselves. Indeed, in each and every case, theistically based answers seem far more reasonable, if not positively compelling. To whom, then, would the apostle ascribe the origin of the questions of life—and their inescapable spiritual overtones—if not to the God of Israel?

More than this, I think that Paul would also assert that God is *testing* us through the questions of life; that these questions do indeed lie at the heart of a probationary order. For if, as he asserts in Romans 1-2, God's self-revelation in nature and conscience is designed to promote worship, gratitude, and obedience, then surely his self-revelation in the questions of life must also have its own specific design: a search for his truth. On this view, the God of Israel himself is the one who deposits the questions in our hearts. He is the one who makes them existentially urgent. He is the one who associates the best possible answers with a living god. He is the one who encourages us to reach out to this god, whether by prayer, philosophical reflection, or diligent search for an authoritative spiritual Teacher whom he may have sent. And finally, *he is the one who eagerly waits to see if we will do these very things.*

Such speculations seem abundantly vindicated when we read of Paul's interaction with the Athenian philosophers. In his famous sermon on Mars Hill, he declared that God has created and providentially situated all persons and nations for one main purpose: "...so that they might seek God, in hopes that they might grope for him and find him, though he is not far from each one of us, for in him we live and move and have our being" (Acts 17:27-28). Would not such "seeking" and "groping" involve an honest interaction with the questions of life? Would it not involve a serious consideration of theistic answers? Would it not involve a fair-minded study of theistic revelations, and possibly even earnest prayer to the unknown god, whose help we would surely need to complete our quest for truth successfully?

We conclude, then, that the Bible does indeed encourage seekers to see God's hand in the questions of life, and to understand that through these questions he is testing us all concerning our love of spiritual and philosophical truth.

Special Revelation

Having spoken at length of general revelation—and also of the grave spiritual predicament that it creates for sinful mankind—Paul now turns to *special revelation*. This rich theological term also has a two-fold sense. On the one hand, such revelation is special because it comes to us in *special ways*. In other words, it does not come through nature, conscience, or philosophical intuition, but rather by theophany, vision, dream, angelic visitation, and divine utterance or verbal inspiration. That is, it comes in a *dramatically* supernatural manner. On the other hand, this kind of revelation is special because it brings to us certain *special truths,* truths of a specifically redemptive nature, truths that men cannot discover by means of general revelation. Importantly, the Bible indicates that down through the years God commanded certain chosen messengers (e.g., prophets, apostles, etc.) to preserve these redemptive revelations in writing for the benefit of future generations. As we are about to see, one result of this is that special revelation, just like general, puts men to the test. The gist of the test is simple: Will those who are privileged to receive God's special words about redemption honor him by obeying them? Also, will they thank him for them, and seek and worship him more than ever before (Psalm 27:8)?

In Romans, Paul begins his discussion of special revelation by citing the case of ethnic Israel. Having received the Mosaic Law, they are a highly favored nation, the privileged custodians of the very "oracles of God," by which oracles they may receive redemption and eternal life in the Kingdom to come (Rom. 3:2). Therefore, above all other peoples, they should be living in wisdom, holiness, and gratitude. Yet strange to tell, many of them violate it repeatedly; indeed, the Gentiles, who enjoy only general revelation, are sometimes more righteous than God's own covenant people! The Jews, then, have also fallen short, not only of general revelation, but of special as well. They too have failed the test. Accordingly, they too stand in dire need of reconciliation with God (Rom. 2:1-3:20).

Trial by the Light to Come

In our discussion so far, we have seen from Paul's teaching that God tests mankind in two basic ways: by general and special revelation. Observe, however, that in both cases the essence of the test remains the same. Always and everywhere, God tests sinful man by one fundamental and inescapable reality: *spiritual light*. Always and everywhere, he himself comes to them, shining into the darkness of their sinful souls, bidding them to worship, obey, and seek further light. How, then, are people to pass the test of life? The answer is clear and simple: when the light comes to them, they must come to the light!

As we saw earlier, the OT prophets looked for a day when the divine trial by light would take a new and definitive form; when Israel's God would test all men—both Jew and Gentile—by a *most* special revelation to the *whole* world. Again, this revelation would be granted in the days of the Messiah. He himself would bring it: first *to* Israel, but also *through* Israel to the ends of the earth (Isaiah 49:6, 51:4-5). He would send it by messengers, even to the farthest coastlands, so that all peoples could know at last the glory of Israel's God (Isaiah 66:19-21). Hearing it, they would rally to it, like an army to its banners (Isaiah 11:10). Indeed, as a result of this special revelation, they would throng to Zion, for there, in the house of the God of Jacob, the Messiah would teach it to them (Micah 4:1-2). Yes, said the prophets, a great light is coming (Isaiah 9:2). It will be God's ultimate light, a light that will test all nations, and a light that will redeem all who come—worshipfully and obediently—to the brightness of its rising (Isaiah 60:1-3).

All of this brings us back to Paul. For anyone who has read his sermon to the Athenian philosophers, or his letter to the Roman Christians, realizes that he can scarcely contain his enthusiasm for the message he is spreading. Why? Because he clearly believes—and therefore fervently proclaims—that now, in his own day, *the promised light has come*. That light is none other than Jesus himself, and the good news about all he has done to reconcile sinners to God. In sending forth this light, God has, of course, introduced a new and ultimate test to Jew and Gentile. But for Paul, that is all to the good, since Jews and Gentiles who have failed the former tests (and all have) now have a fresh opportunity to take the new. Moreover, those who pass this new test will be redeemed *once and for all*. That is, they will be rescued from every spiritual enemy, and restored to every spiritual blessing, *in such a way that they can never fail God's test again* (Rom. 3:19-31)! This was not simply Paul's theological understanding, but also his own personal spiritual experience. Therefore, with seemingly boundless gratitude, energy, and joy, he devoted the rest of his life to proclaiming the good news to the whole world.

In the pages ahead, we will call this good news—this most special light of divine revelation—*the gospel test*.

The Gospel Test

Many NT passages speak of the gospel test. There is one, however, that stands out above all the rest. Happily, it is a discourse of Jesus himself. Let us go, then, to the gospel of John, and hear him speak in his own words about the greatest test of all.

> There was a man of the Pharisees named Nicodemus, a ruler of the Jews. This man came to Jesus by night and said to Him, "Rabbi, we know that You are a teacher come from God; for no one can do these signs that You do unless God is with him."
>
> Jesus answered and said to him, "Truly, truly I say to you, unless one is born again, he cannot see the kingdom of God."
>
> Nicodemus said to Him, "How can a man be born when he is old? Can he enter a second time into his mother's womb and be born?"
>
> Jesus answered, "Truly, truly I say to you, unless one is born of water and the Spirit he cannot enter the kingdom of God. That which is born of the flesh is flesh, and that which is born of the Spirit is spirit. Do not marvel that I said to you, 'You must be born again.' The wind blows where it wishes, and you hear the sound of it, but cannot tell where it comes from and where it goes. So it is with everyone who is born of the Spirit."
>
> Nicodemus answered and said to Him, "How can these things be?"
>
> Jesus answered and said to him, "Are you the teacher of Israel, and do not know these things? Truly, truly, I say to you, we speak what we know and testify what we have seen, and you do not receive our witness. If I have told you earthly things and you do not believe, how will you believe if I tell you heavenly things?
>
> No one has ascended to heaven but he who came down from heaven, that is, the Son of Man. And as Moses lifted up the serpent in the wilderness, even so must the Son of man be lifted up, that whoever believes in him should have eternal life. For God so loved the world that He gave His only-begotten Son, that whoever believes in him should not perish but have everlasting life. For God did not send His Son into the world to condemn the world, but that the world through him might be saved. He who believes in him is not condemned; but he who does not believe is condemned already, because he has not believed in the name of the only-begotten Son of God. And this is the condemnation, that the light has come into the world, and men loved darkness rather than light, because their deeds were evil. For everyone practicing evil hates the light and does not come to the light, lest his deeds should be exposed. But he who does the truth comes to the light, that his deeds may be clearly seen, that they have been done in God."
>
> —John 3:1-21

In this famous passage Jesus declares that he is bringing a new and definitive spiritual test, not only to Israel, but also to the whole world. Let us first look at the gist of the new test, and then examine some of its key characteristics one by one.

Nicodemus, a secret disciple, has come to Jesus by night, seeking more light on the Kingdom of God. Indeed, he is wondering if Jesus himself might not be the Messianic king. Knowing his thoughts, Jesus answers in words that Nicodemus can barely understand, since he (Jesus) must speak of the Kingdom in terms of things yet to come: his own death upon a Roman cross, a global proclamation of the meaning of that death, and a mysterious work of the sovereign Spirit, by which alone men can see him (Jesus) as the divine prophet, priest, and heavenly king, and therefore gladly submit themselves to his spiritual reign.

Very importantly, Jesus here declares that God is about to test the whole world by means of a new revelation, by what he calls "the light." As the context indicates, the light is the good news about the life and death of God the Son, given in love to the world by God the Father. Soon, this light will go forth to men and nations everywhere. When it does, it will do just what God's light has always done: it will test their love of truth, righteousness, and the unknown god. When the light comes, it will divide. Some will hate and flee it—thereby showing their sinful love of darkness, failing the test, and condemning themselves to eternal death. Others, however, will come to the light—thereby showing a God-given love for spiritual reality, passing the test, and receiving the reward of eternal life. Clearly, then, Jesus is heralding a new day in God's dealings with mankind. Formerly, God tested the Gentiles by the light of nature, conscience, and the questions of life. Meanwhile, he further tested the Jews by the light of the Law and the Prophets. Now, however, there has been a change. Now he is testing both Jew and Gentile *by one and the same light:* the light of the gospel of Christ. And he shall continue to do so, even to the end of the age.

Here, then, is the gist of the gospel test. But since this test is so important—and since it lies so very close to the meaning of life—we must examine some of its key characteristics more closely. In so doing, we will use the passage from John as our base of operations, but look also at a number of other closely related NT texts.

It is Universal

First, the gospel test is universal. That is, through it God is not only testing Israel, but also all nations. This is why Jesus tells Nicodemus that God so loved *the world* that he sent his only-begotten Son (John 3:16).

This Son must be lifted up: not only on a cross in Palestine, but also in the preaching of the gospel to all nations (John 3:14, 12:32). Indeed, in several places in the gospels we find Jesus *commanding* this very thing (Mt. 28:18, Luke 24:46-48, Acts 1:8). Moreover, in the book of Acts we find his disciples *doing* this very thing (Acts 13ff). Paul, the "apostle to the Gentiles," was especially alive to the universality of the gospel test, declaring that he had personally received "grace and apostleship *for obedience to the faith among all nations,* for His name's sake" (Rom. 1:5, 16:26). For Paul, universal proclamation belonged to the very essence of "the mystery of godliness" (i.e., the latter-day revelation of God's saving truth). As he wrote to Timothy, his friend and colleague in evangelistic ministry, "He (God the Son) was manifested in the flesh, vindicated by the Spirit, seen by angels, *preached among the Gentiles, believed on in the world,* received up in glory" (1 Tim. 3:16). Thus, all the NT writers agree: in the preaching of the gospel, God is testing both Jew and Gentile concerning their love of truth, righteousness, and the ultimate spiritual reality (Acts 10:35, Rev. 7:9f).

It is Simple

Jesus' teachings have kept theologians pondering, writing, and debating for centuries. Peter confesses that Paul's letters contain some things "hard to understand" (2 Pet. 3:16). For many people, the Revelation is a closed book whose meaning is decipherable only by scholars or mystics. Yet the gospel—and the gospel test—is simple. To pass it, Nicodemus does not have to be a genius, or to be morally perfect, or to perform certain good works, or to follow the Law of Moses. All he must do is *believe* in the Son of God. As Jesus elsewhere put it, "This is the work of God, that you believe in Him whom He has sent" (John 6:29; cf., John 3:15-16, 18, Eph. 2:8-10, Tim. 2:8-11, Titus 3:5).

But what, precisely, do Jesus and the apostles mean by the word "believe"? Our passage—and others like it—teaches us that believing involves four basic components.

First, believing involves *seeing*. In particular, it involves seeing certain fundamental truths about *the person and work of the Messiah,* Jesus of Nazareth.

As to his person, believing involves *seeing his deity*—seeing that Jesus truly is the incarnate Son of the Father, the second person of the Holy Trinity, now in human flesh. Jesus had this kind of seeing in mind when he said, "For this is the will of My Father, that everyone who *beholds* the Son, and believes in Him, may have eternal life, and I myself will raise him up on the last day" (John 6:40, NAS). In the end, this kind of seeing is a gift of

God. Unless God illumines a man's mind, he cannot see who Jesus is. This is why Jesus told Nicodemus, "Unless one is born again, he cannot see the kingdom of heaven." He meant that unless God, by the Spirit, grants a man new spiritual life and insight, he cannot see Jesus' deity or the (spiritual) nature of his Kingdom. How, then, apart from such a gracious birth from above, can that man ever come to the King, and so enter into his Kingdom (John 3:5; Mt. 11:25ff)?

Believing also involves *seeing the meaning of the Messiah's work*, the significance of his life and death. In our passage, the emphasis falls upon his soon-coming death. Jesus tells Nicodemus that God so loved the world that he *gave* his only-begotten Son. Gave him to do what? Not simply to teach, says Jesus, but also to be lifted up on a cross for the sins of God's people everywhere.

To illustrate this point, Jesus turns to an OT type. He reminds Nicodemus of Israel's experience in the wilderness of Sinai, where God, reacting to the rebellion of his people, sent venomous serpents into the camp. Terrified and penitent, they pleaded for mercy. In response, God granted it, telling Moses to make a bronze serpent, suspend it on a pole, and elevate it for all to see. All who simply looked at the serpent would be healed.

Jesus recounts this story because it is about to be fulfilled. God is about to lift him up on a Roman cross, and thereafter in the preaching of that cross. Like the bronze serpent, he will become a substitute, bearing the sins of his people. All who look to him in faith will be forgiven and instantly healed. By seeing the holy and righteous one upon the cross, *and by seeing him punished for their sins,* they will receive pardon, righteousness, and eternal life (Num. 21:1f, John 3:14, Acts 3:14, 2 Cor. 5:21, 1 Pet. 2:24). If, then, it is done with true understanding, a simple look will save a soul.

Secondly, believing also involves *coming*. In our passage, Jesus says, "He who practices the truth *comes* to the light" (John 3:21). Elsewhere, he explicitly identifies himself as the light (John 8:12, 9:5). Therefore, believing involves *coming to Jesus,* something that he repeatedly commanded sinners to do, not hesitating to motivate them thereunto with rich promises and dire warnings (Mt. 11:28f, John 6:35, 8:21f). However, just as sinners cannot see who Jesus is without God's help, so too they cannot come to him without God's help. By their very nature, they are darkness, Christ is light, and darkness hates the light, and so refuses to come to it (John 3:20). Therefore, the Father must enable sinners to come to his Son; he must *draw* them to the light (John 6:44). Practically speaking, this means that God must give people a hatred for their sinful autonomy and rebellion, moving them to forsake it, and thereby granting them *repentance* (Acts 5:31, 11:18). It also means that he must give them a desire and love for his Son, thereby moving them to come to him, and to enter into a personal relationship with him. Most comfortingly, Jesus promises to all who enter this relationship that neither he nor his Father will ever cast them out (John 6:37, 10:28-30).

Thirdly, believing involves *trust*. Broadly speaking, a believer in Christ displays trust when he calms his every fear by resting confidently upon the promises of his all-powerful Lord (Mt. 8:23-27, 14:22-33). In our passage, however, Jesus has in mind a special kind of trust, a *redemptive* trust. He tells Nicodemus that whoever *believes* in God's Son will not perish, but have eternal life (John 3:16). Here, the word has the sense of *quietly resting upon* the Son, especially upon what he has done for his people in his own life and death. Such trust puts no confidence whatsoever in sinful man's character or accomplishments. Instead, it completely relies upon the holy character and accomplishments of God's Son for pardon, righteousness, and eternal life.

A simple illustration may prove helpful here. Imagine that the believer's life and destiny is a two-story house. In the miracle of salvation, God lifts the house from its old (Adamic) foundation, carries it over to his Son, and settles it down, once for all, upon him. Redemptive trust is in play when the believer sees this change and rejoices in it, henceforth relying exclusively upon the new foundation for his right standing before God. In his letter to the Philippians, the apostle Paul shows himself to be just such a man. In the Day of Judgment, he desires to be found *in Christ*, not having a righteousness of his own based upon the Law, but that which is through faith in Christ Jesus: the righteousness which comes from God on the basis of faith (Phil. 3:9). As Paul's words indicate, this is the kind of trust the Holy Spirit is eager to bless, granting Christ-dependent believers strength, confidence, and joy before God, even in the face of death and the final judgment (Rom. 8:15, 2 Tim. 1:7, Jude 1:24, 1 John 4:12-19, Jude 1:24).

Finally, to believe involves *obedience*. Jesus explains to Nicodemus that when the light shines, it implicitly issues a command—a command to come. To believe therefore means to obey that command and to come to Christ. As we have seen, the *initial* obedience and the *initial* coming are redemptive. They involve one's entering into an eternal relationship with Christ, trusting upon his perfect work, and thereby experiencing the joys of new life in the triune God. In short, they secure eternal life, once and for all. But coming and obeying must also be ongoing. The believer must *abide* in Christ, and *keep on* obeying, even to the end, (Mt. 24:13, John 8:31, 15:4). His deeds must *continue* to be done in God (John 3:21). As Jesus put it, "If you love Me, you will keep My commandments" (John 14:15). This is a both a command and a predictive prophecy. Those who love him *must* keep his commandments, and those who love him *will*.[1]

Here, then, is the essence of the gospel test. To pass it, one must believe in the Son of God. To believe is to see his divine nature and the meaning of his life and death. It is to forsake one's sinful autonomy, come into personal relationship with him, and remain in that relationship. It is to trust upon him, to cast the full weight of one's life—both this life and the life to come—upon who he is, what he said, and what he has done. And it is to obey: initially unto salvation, and then ongoingly unto growth in knowledge, character, and service. Among all who are truly born again, this obedience will continue, even if imperfectly, to the very end. He who began the good work, will keep on perfecting it until the day of Christ of Jesus (John 6:40, Phil. 1:6).

Simple.

But as we are about to see, by no means easy.

It is Difficult

The gospel test is difficult. Indeed, Jesus says, "With men, it is impossible—but with God, all things are possible" (Mark 10:27). So then, with God's help, one can pass this test. But even with God's help, no one will pass it without difficulty (Acts 14:22).

The difficulty does not flow from the God-ward side of the equation. As Jesus told Nicodemus, God so loved the world that he has given his only-begotten Son. As a result, he is now inviting—indeed, commanding—people everywhere to come to him (John 3:16, Acts 17:30). Moreover, he has made the way of salvation exceedingly simple. As the apostle Paul proclaimed to a humble jailer in Philippi, "Believe on the Lord Jesus Christ, and you will be saved" (Acts 16:31).

The difficulty, then, lies with not with God, but with man. And the root of the difficulty is that man, by nature, is darkness (John 3:19-21). In part, this means that he is spiritually destitute, *alienated from the life of God* (Eph. 4:8; Rom. 3:9, 7:18). As Jesus said to his unbelieving enemies, "I know you, that you do not have the love of God within you" (John 5:2). It also means that unregenerate man is *in bondage to sin, Satan, and the fallen world-system*. At the core of his being, he is a slave, driven along by selfishness, pride, and various kinds of lust (Eph. 2:1-3). What then if God should send the very light of heaven down into this hellhole of spiritual darkness? How is it possible that difficulties should not arise?

But let us be more specific. Using our passage, let us try to determine exactly what the difficulties of the gospel test are, why they arise, and how a seeker may best deal with them.

Jesus spoke to Nicodemus of light shining in the darkness (John 1:5, 3:19). The light is Christ himself, proclaimed in the gospel. The darkness is the fallen world of sinful men. Clearly, God intends that the two should interact.

Observe Jesus' assumption about the nature of this interaction. He assumes that when the light of the gospel reaches an individual sinner, *he will see that it is light;* he will see that the gospel is indeed truth come from God. Does this mean he sees that Jesus is the Son of God, and that his death on the cross is the divinely ordained sacrifice for the sins of men? Does it mean he understands his personal obligation to repent of his sin and come to the savior? Yes and no. Yes, because the Spirit of Truth bears witness to the truth of these great realities; no, because that same Spirit has not yet fully unveiled them to the sinner's understanding (Eph. 1:17-18). In other words, the sinner is walking in half-light, in shadow. He definitely sees something bright up ahead, but cannot make it out clearly. Accordingly, he also sees that *he has an obligation to seek out a fuller perception of it.* This means that he now faces a decision. He can follow the Spirit and *walk towards* the something up ahead in order to see for himself exactly what is there; or he can resist the Spirit, *turn away from* that something, and henceforth try to convince himself that there was nothing in front of him at all. At this crucial juncture, the gospel test has begun.

So too have the sinner's difficulties. The core difficulty is that by nature he does not *want* to see that the good news is true. Why? Because the good news contains so much bad news about himself! For example, it tells him that he is a mere creature (very bad news for people who like to think of themselves as god). It tells him that he is a spiritually defiled creature, a guilty creature, and a hell-bent creature. It wounds his pride, condemns his illicit pleasures, and threatens his lawlessness. It abases him, terrifies him, confuses him, and even repels him. Yes, it promises pardon, peace, and eternal life in God's family—precious gifts that, at one level, he may truly desire. Yet he understands well enough that such gifts will come at a cost: the cost of his very life. In other words, to receive them, he must humbly present his sinful, autonomous self to Christ for execution. Moreover, he must do so with the understanding that when he rises from his execution, he will no longer be his own god, but a bond-slave of the High King of heaven.

In sum, the gospel test is difficult because it always involves light shining into darkness, and because darkness always hates the light. But as we are about to see, the example of certain NT disciples offers instruction, encouragement, and hope to seekers everywhere. Moreover, the lesson of these disciple's lives is really quite simple: when the gospel comes knocking at a seeker's door, he only needs to open the door, walk straight into the light, and check out the truth of it for himself. Doing this one thing, he has done all he can do. Jesus promises that God will do the rest (Mt. 7:7, John 17:7).

It is Divisive

The gospel test is divisive. That is, its arrival upon the scene forces a spiritual decision which, at the end of the day, will neatly divide people into two groups, groups whose true character is revealed by their response to the coming of the light. Jesus speaks to Nicodemus about both groups.

The first is composed of the lovers of darkness. When the light of the gospel arrives and knocks at the door of their house, they will not open the door and go out to it. To the contrary, with bars and bolts they hastily fortify the house against entry. Inside are the treasures of darkness: illicit motives, passions, and patterns of conduct that the light requires them to leave behind. But lovers of darkness do not want to leave them behind, so they resolutely remain within.

Many of Nicodemus' colleagues fell into this category. From the very beginning, they refused to come to Jesus. Indeed, early on they even plotted to kill him (Mark 3:6, John 5:16). The pretext for their plotting was doctrinal aberration. They complained that Jesus worked on the Sabbath, and that he said that God was his Father (John 5:18). But their real motives were darkness itself: the love of money, pleasure, power, and the adulation of man (Mt. 21:38, 23:1ff, Luke 16:14). These "great men" understood perfectly well what Jesus' presence, teachings, and miracles implied: they must forsake all such deadly treasures, humble themselves, and seek further light from the Teacher sent by God, just as Nicodemus did. But because they loved the praise of man more than the praise of God, they did the opposite (John 5:44). They spurned the light, hated it, and even tried to extinguish it. Jesus reckoned this a suicidal response, one that only compounded their difficulties, leaving them in *deepest* darkness, henceforth to be haunted by doubt, fear, guilt, and the shadow of eternal condemnation.

The second group is composed of those who love and practice the truth. When the light arrives at their house, they too are tempted to bolt the door, for they too are attached to their own dark treasures. Yet these respond differently. Something about the light attracts them—so much so that, like curious children, they open the door, leave their treasures behind, and step outside for a better look. At first, they may see little, with the result that there is much stumbling, much intellectual and emotional difficulty. But despite the difficulties, they press on, seeking, asking, pondering, and even praying. As they do, the light grows brighter and brighter. Then, as if in the space of a single step, they enter the light and suddenly see things clearly. Seeing the world in God's light, they see it at last as it truly is.

Jesus' eleven disciples were such men. So too was Nicodemus. When the Teacher entered their lives, they understood little of his person and work. More often than not, he seemed to speak in riddles. Over and again, he threw them into confusion, doubt, helplessness, and fear. Yet even when the multitudes finally abandoned their enigmatic Rabbi, these faithful men stayed by his side, (Luke 22:28, John 6:68). Why? *Because their deeds were being done in God.* Secretly, graciously, mercifully, the Father himself kept drawing them to his Son (John 6:44; Mt. 11:25-30). And so, in due season, because of their God-given love for the truth, they came fully into the light. They beheld the world as it really was, and believed upon the Son of God unto the saving of their souls.

In passing, we do well here to look briefly at another of Jesus' sayings, one that richly illumines the divisiveness of the gospel test. He had just healed a blind man on the Sabbath. When certain Jewish authorities challenged him for doing so, he said, "For judgment (Greek: *krisis*) I have come into this world, that those who do not see may see, and that those who do see may be made blind" (John 9:39). Here we learn that the gospel is like a plow, slowly making its way through the whole earth. When it arrives in a given land, the people who are sitting in darkness see a great light—a gleaming blade—coming straight at them. Immediately, they are in a crisis. Now they must decide which side of the furrow they want to be on when the blade has passed through. Those who choose to love the truth are flung up into the air and cast into a land of bright light. Those who choose to cling to the darkness are flung up into the air and cast into a land of deeper darkness. Before the gospel test arrived, all lived in shadow; all were legally blind. Now that it has passed through, some see all things clearly, while the rest have become totally blind. For time and eternity, the gospel has divided them one from another.

Jesus often warns seekers about the divisiveness of the gospel test, for he knows that it is one of its most painful difficulties. Through the gospel, God tests men to see if their love of the truth is greater than their love (or fear) of man. It can even separate people from those who are nearest and dearest to them. In one of his sharpest sayings, Jesus put it this way:

> Do not think that I came to bring peace on earth. I did not come to bring peace, but a sword. For I have come to set a man against his father, a daughter against her mother, and a daughter-in-law against her mother-in-law. And a man's foes will be those of his own household. He

> who loves father or mother more than Me is not worthy of Me. And he who loves son or daughter more than Me is not worthy of Me. And he who does not take up his cross and follow after Me is not worthy of Me. He who finds his life will lose it, and he who loses his life for My sake will find it.
> —Mt. 10:34-39

We must interpret these words with great care. Jesus is no foe of domestic or civic tranquility. He bids us to honor our parents, care for our families, love our enemies, and be at peace with all men (Mt. 5:43-48, Mark 7:9-13, Rom. 12:18, 1 Tim. 5:8). But he recognizes that the "peace" of the fallen world-system is not based on God, truth, or righteousness. Rather, it is largely a false peace, based on self-interest and various lusts. As such, it is a peace that can quickly turn to war, especially when a spiritually awakened "loved one" dares to turn his back on the world-system so as to take up residence in the Kingdom of God. In other words, because the gospel effects precisely such a change of residence, it must break a false peace wherever it goes. It may arouse anger, alienation, and even persecution from those still remaining in the world. In short, the gospel divides the sons of light from the sons of darkness. Jesus desires seekers to understand and expect this. It is part of the cost of coming into the light (John 15:18-25).[2]

It is Redemptively Decisive

The gospel test is redemptively decisive. That is, this test—or rather one's response to it—determines the eternal destiny of all who take it. In our passage, Jesus is quite clear on this point. Again, his presupposition is that all are in darkness. All are guilty of Adam's (imputed) sin. All are guilty of their own sins. All have a fallen nature that inclines them to sin. Accordingly, none are fit for heaven, all are under wrath, and all are in danger of eternal punishment.

Now, however, the light has come into the world; now there is hope. In his Son, God has made a perfect provision for the rescue and restoration of sinners. All he requires is that they should believe on the Son. Those who believe will not perish, but have everlasting life (John 3:16). But the converse is also true: those who do not believe *will* perish; they will *not* have everlasting life. The Son is the *only* hope, the *only* provision. He alone is the way, the truth, and the life (John 14:6). He alone is the door into the Father's house (John 10:9). He alone is the perfect mediator between God and man (1 Tim. 2:5). Thus, in the gospel test God puts his Son—his sole provision for the redemption of sinners—squarely before men, and requires them to decide. *How* they decide will decide their eternal destiny.

It is Passed in a Moment of Time in This Life

The gospel test is—and must be—passed in a moment of time in this life. Moreover, God's children can *know* they have passed it. They can be sure in this life that they will live forever with God in the next.

From Jesus' conversation with Nicodemus, we learn how a sinner attains such blessed assurance. By God's providence, he comes into contact with the gospel. As he hears or reads about it, the Son of God is "lifted up" before his eyes. In other words, he is confronted with the core affirmations of the gospel: God's redemptive love for a sinful world, the all-sufficient gift of his only-begotten Son, and the simple requirement of believing on him for eternal life.

As the sinner hears of these things, a gentle wind begins to blow (John 3:8) Invisibly, yet quite noticeably, the sovereign Spirit draws near. The divine helper enters his heart, sensitizes his conscience, awakens spiritual hunger, arouses intellectual curiosity, and creates a strong suspicion of the truth of the gospel. One long dead in trespasses and sins is about to be born again.

A struggle ensues. At first, the sinner finds the gospel incredible, confusing, humiliating, and even frightening. It spells death to his way of looking at the world, his way of living his life. His every instinct is to run. Yet he does not run, or at least not for very long. For the more he thinks about the gospel (and he finds that he cannot stop thinking about it), the more it looks like light. The more he thinks about his present life, the more it looks like darkness. And the more he thinks about his future life, the more he thinks that he might like to live it in the light. And so, because there is nowhere else to turn, he turns towards the light. He has become like Moses, who, walking through the wilderness of Sinai, saw a burning bush that was not consumed, and said, "I will now turn aside and see this great sight" (Ex. 3:3).

And now another kind of walk begins, a search. He reads, he listens, he seeks out trustworthy authorities—all in an effort to find out the truth about the gospel. The more he searches, the brighter the light shines. The brighter the light shines, the more he searches. And then, in a manner that defies description, there comes the moment of seeing. Looking upon Jesus, he suddenly sees God the Son, veiled in human flesh. Looking upon the cross, he suddenly sees God the Father looming over it, hating sin, but loving sinners; judging Christ, but pardoning Christians; killing his own Son, but making many sons alive. Once again he is like Moses. Trembling with fear, filled with sorrow, yet thrilled with understanding and new hope, he now sees that he is standing on holy ground (Ex. 3:5). Moreover, he sees that on this ground there is but one thing left to do: come. He must come to Christ, call upon his name, prayerfully receive him, trust in his perfect work, and obediently submit himself to his benevolent rule. Being spiritually reborn, he *wants* to come. Wanting to come, he does. And when he does, Christ comes to him.

In that miraculous moment, things change once and for all, for time and for eternity. The NT is at no loss for words to describe the decisiveness of this change. The sinner is sealed forever with God's indwelling Holy Spirit (John 14:6, Eph. 1:13, 4:30). He passes from death to life (John 5:24, 1 John 3:14). He is lifted out of Adam and placed securely in Christ (1 Cor. 1:30-31). He is transferred from the domain of darkness into the Kingdom of God's beloved Son (Col. 1:13, 1 Pet. 2:9). He becomes a new creation in Christ Jesus (2 Cor. 5:17, Gal. 6:15). He is no longer in the world, but in the Church; and the Church is in God, and God is in the Church (John 14:23, 15:19, 1 John 14:23, Eph. 2:22). He is no longer under Satan, the ruler of this world, but under Christ, the High King of heaven (John 12:31, Eph. 1:22, Col. 2:6, 1 John 4:4). He is forgiven his sins, reconciled to God, justified before his Law, freed from condemnation, and delivered forever from the wrath to come (Acts 26:17-18, Rom. 5:1-2, 9-10, 8:1f).[3] He is no longer a slave, but a son (John 1:12, Eph. 1:5). And since he is a son, he is also an heir: an heir through Christ to the eternal Kingdom of God (Rom. 8:15, 17, 2 Cor. 1:20, Gal. 3:26 – 4:7).

Yes, says Jesus, great things happen when a sinner repents and believes. Small wonder, then, that when he does, there is joy unspeakable in the presence of the angels of God (Luke 15:7, 10). Why? Because an errant child was dead, but now is alive. Because he was lost, but now is found. Because he took the most important and difficult test of his life—the gospel test—and passed it (Luke 15:11-32).

Again, the NT is quite emphatic that believers in Christ not only *have* passed the gospel test, but also can *know* they have passed it. In other words, *it is normal for believers in Christ to have assurance of eternal life*. Such precious assurance is granted by the Holy Spirit, who immediately testifies in the new Christian's heart that he is a child of God, and if a child, then an heir to all the promises of God (Rom. 8:15-17, Gal. 4:6). This assurance increases over time, especially as he learns more about God's eternal love and purpose for his people (John 6:22-59, 10:1-30, Rom. 8:28-39, 1 Cor. 2:6-16, Eph. 1, Col. 2:1-3). It is strengthened as he examines his own life for the marks of a true believer: confidence that Jesus is the Son of God, zeal for progress in holiness, and a sincere love of the brethren (1 John 3:2, 9, 14; 4:7, 15; 5:13). Such assurance can indeed be shaken, whether by false teaching, personal sin, or divine testing (2 Thess. 2:2, James 1:2-8). But when discipline and testing have accomplished their perfect work, it is quickly restored. Jesus will not leave his children as orphans. As soon as the pruning is done, as soon as the chastening is complete, he will come to them in the Spirit, reassuring their hearts that they do indeed belong to him, that they always have, and that they always will (Acts 3:19, John 14:18, 15:1-2, Heb. 13:5).

It is Followed by Further Testing

When a sinner becomes a saint—when he has passed the gospel test—his days of testing are not over. Indeed, the NT casts the whole of his forthcoming Christian experience as an ongoing test: a test of his continuing love of truth, righteousness, and God. As we have seen, such testing is rich with the promise of eternal rewards.

How does God further test his redeemed people? He tests them by his word, to see if they will labor to understand, obey, and grow in it (John 14:23, 1 Peter 2:2).[4] He tests them by false teachers, to see if they can discern such imposters and even confront and discipline them when they rise up to lead the flock of God astray (1 Cor. 11:19, Rev. 2:2). He tests them with gifts and opportunities for service, to see if they will sacrifice temporary earthly comforts for eternal heavenly rewards (Mt. 25:14-30, 2 Cor. 2:12, Col. 4:3, 1 Tim. 6:17-19). He tests them by (permitting) worldly temptations, to see if they love holiness more than (illicit) pleasures (James 1:12-18, 2 Tim. 4:10, Rev. 17:4) He tests them by worldly persecutions, to see if they hate and fear compromise more than ridicule, ostracism, material loss, physical pain, or life itself (1 Pet. 4:12f). And the list goes on.

Such testing is richly purposeful. It provides the saints with a welcome opportunity to glorify their God and Savior, and to thank him for his gift of eternal life (John 21:19, Acts 5:41). It is fertile soil in which the rare and beautiful flowers of Christian wisdom, character, and effective ministry can grow to maturity (2 Cor. 1:3-7, James 1:2-4). It tends towards the salvation of sinners, since the weary of this world are often drawn to those who are manifestly enthusiastic about another (Mt. 27:54, Phil. 1:27-30, 2 Thess. 1:3-12). And again, it is God's chosen way of enabling his children to earn eternal rewards. For if, amidst the distractions of this life, they will respond to the upward call of God in Christ Jesus; if they will strive to discover and perform the good works that God has prepared for them beforehand; if they will deny themselves, take up their cross, and follow their Lord... then in that Day they will find that they have indeed laid a good foundation, upon which their eternal house shall rise up tall and strong (Phil. 3:14, Eph. 2:10, 1 Tim. 6:17-19). Small wonder, then, that Jesus calls that man blessed who enthusiastically welcomes the manifold tests of the Christian life (Mt. 5:3-12).

Yet important as all these tests are, seekers must always keep one great truth in mind: they are *not* redemptively decisive. To pass them is *not* to lay the foundation, but only to build upon it with gold, silver, and precious stones, thereby earning a heavenly reward. Moreover, to fail them is *not* to be removed from the foundation, but only to build with wood, hay, and stubble, thereby suffering loss of reward. The foundation itself is Christ. It was laid beneath the believer's life when he came to Christ, and those who have indeed come to him stand eternally secure upon it (1 Cor. 3:10-15). They have passed the one test that *is* redemptively decisive, the gospel test. It is, therefore, the first test, the all-important test, and the top priority test for every seeker of truth from the unknown god.

As such, it lies at the very heart of the meaning of life.

CHAPTER 19

IF SO, HOW CAN WE PASS?

IT IS WRITTEN of Jesus that when he saw the multitudes he was moved with compassion, for they were like sheep without a shepherd (Mt. 9:36). If, then, he is the divine, all-knowing Messiah that the Bible says he is, we may be sure that he also has compassion for seekers everywhere; that he both *knows* and *cares*.

He knows, for example that his Father has situated all men in a probationary order. He knows that they are troubled—sometimes even tormented—by the questions of life. He knows that they can see an unknown god in the wonders of nature; hear him in the whisperings of conscience; glimpse him in the amazing make-up of their own minds. He knows that they are inclined to search for this god, and also for a Teacher whom he might have sent: someone who can answer their questions, banish their fears, cleanse their conscience, and rightly relate them to their maker. He knows that through the gospel, his Father is even now sending word of this someone—and of all these precious gifts—to the nations. He knows that when this word arrives, it will produce a crisis; that it will put men to the test. And he knows that this test will be difficult, divisive, and eternally decisive.

Therefore, knowing all these things—and having taken a terrible test of his own—Jesus cares. He cares for each one who must take the gospel test, and he very much cares that he or she should pass it.

Such care is evident throughout the NT. There we hear Jesus speaking directly to seekers everywhere, giving them instructions, commands, warnings, and promises. In essence, his words revolve around two fundamental themes: the *actions* and the *attitudes* necessary for people to pass the gospel test. As we bring our journey to a close, let us briefly consider both.

Actions

We have seen that when God brings the gospel to a sinner's door, a crisis ensues. The sinner does not believe, and—left to himself—does not want to believe. But the Spirit of truth beckons, the sinner hears, and the gospel test begins.

As it begins—and as the responsive seeker begins searching the NT for more light—Jesus lovingly comes alongside, issuing two basic commands. Their design is as simple as it is important: that seekers should focus their attention on the *heart* of the gospel test, and that they should keep it there.

Find out Who I Am

In order to bring us to the heart of this test, Jesus' first command is, "Find out who I am." The centrality of this matter is especially clear from an episode recorded in three of the four gospels. Jesus and his disciples have arrived in the region of Caesarea Philippi. Suddenly, he turns to them and asks, "Who do men say that I, the Son of Man, am?" The disciples, fully abreast of the spectrum of popular opinion, reply, "Some say John the Baptist, some Elijah, and others Jeremiah, or one of the prophets." Then—no doubt looking them straight in the eyes—Jesus asks a question that will forever after echo down the corridors of time: "But who do *you* say that I am" (Mt.16:13-20)?

Here, indeed, is the central question; the question that, from Jesus' point of view, is the very gateway to eternal life; the question upon which seekers must therefore focus their attention; and the question upon which they must *keep* it focused until at last they have their answer.

Through the preaching of the gospel, Jesus asks this question of people today. As in NT times, they still respond with different opinions. Some say, for example, that Jesus was a man unknowable—a man whose true life and teachings now lie buried irrecoverably beneath a rubble of myth and legend. Others concede that he was indeed a true prophet, but a prophet later superceded by another prophet, or by a series of prophets. Others say he was an angel, the first created by Yahweh; an angel who, at Yahweh's bidding, finally took upon itself human flesh to die as a ransom for our sins. Others (of an essentially polytheistic persuasion) say that he was indeed a god, but only one among many; and that we, like him, may also become gods ourselves. Still others (this time of an essentially pantheistic persuasion) say he was an enlightened master, a mere mortal like us, but a very highly evolved one; indeed, a mere mortal who finally cast off the illusion of mortality, thereby attaining "god-consciousness," an ineffable, ongoing awareness that all is one, all is mind, and all is god.

And the list goes on.

Needless to say, modern seekers, diligently looking and listening for truth, will sooner or later hear all these voices. But then, over the din, they will hear another. This time it is the voice of Jesus himself, a voice that somehow sinks deeply into the seeker's ears when it says, "You have heard who *I* say that I am; you have heard who *men* say that I am. Now, who do *you* say that I am?"

Any search for the true answer to this question will inevitably carry a seeker into the depths of biblical revelation. In other words, he will find that he has no choice but to enter the biblical world and examine the biblical testimony concerning the person and work of Jesus of Nazareth. In particular, he must decide if the scriptures really do teach that the ultimate reality is an infinite, tri-personal Spirit; and that Jesus of Nazareth is the eternal Son of the Father, who was conceived by the Holy Spirit, born of a virgin, and lived among us in true human flesh. Also, he must decide if the Bible really does portray him as the divine redeemer; as God's supreme prophet, priest, and king; as the authorized teacher, savior, and spiritual ruler of all mankind.

As the seeker begins his journey into these forest deeps, Jesus again comes alongside, this time offering words of guidance and encouragement. He says, for example, "Ask, and it will be given to you; seek, and you will find; knock, and it will be opened to you" (Mt. 7:7). This promise is for all people, including those who are trying to determine Jesus' true identity. If they will but ask, they will receive the answer; if they will but seek, they will find the answer; if they will but knock, they will see a door opened, and the answer standing right before them.

Observe from these words that Jesus encourages an *active* pursuit of the truth about his identity. Yes, the Bible teaches that in the end it is the truth that comes to man; that it is God alone who opens a man's understanding to see the truth about Christ (Mt. 11:25f, Luke 24:45, Eph. 1:18). But it also teaches that the truth usually comes to a man as he is seeking it (Jer. 29:13, Mt. 13:45-6). So then, the seeker seeks because he is being sought; but as a rule, the seeker finds because he is actively seeking (John 4:23, Luke 15:1-10).

Happily, the practical outworkings of all this are few and simple. Jesus would have the seeker *search the Scriptures*, knowing that faith comes by hearing, and hearing by the Word of God (John 5:39, 17:17, Rom. 10:17). He would have them to *sit under the preaching of the gospel*, knowing that it pleases God, through the foolishness of the message preached, to open the eyes of the blind (1 Cor. 1:21). He would have them *seek out Christian leaders*, and also trusted Christian friends or acquaintances, knowing that any who come to his disciples are actually coming to him (Mt. 10:40, Acts 8:26-40, 2 Tim. 2:24f, 1 Pet. 3:15). And finally, he would have them to *pray*, even to himself. For example, speaking as a spiritual explorer rather than a convinced believer, a seeker might pray, "God, according to this book, Jesus of Nazareth is your Son. Please, show me what that means." Or he might pray, "Jesus, in your book it is written that you are God's only-begotten Son, and the Teacher of all your people. If this is so, then you are right here, right now; you can hear my prayer, and you can show me the truth. I humbly ask you to do so." If that prayer is sincere, then according to the Bible the answer is already on its way (Mt. 7:11).

Do What I Say

Jesus' second command is closely related to the first: *"When you do find out who I am, do what I tell you."*

Jesus issues this command on the premise that he is altogether divine, and that when a seeker sees this, he will also see what it entails: implicit obedience to the sovereign Christ. Moreover, he issues it on the premise that the seeker will *want* to obey him. This, as we have seen, belongs essentially to the character of the new birth: it creates within a seeker a new heart of love and submission towards Christ. Therefore, the seeker will *want* to call Jesus "Lord" (John 13:13, Rom. 10:9); he will *want* to keep his commandments (John 14:15); he will *want* to deny himself, take up his cross, and follow him daily (Mt. 16:24). So it was at the conversion of Saul of Tarsus. When the divine Christ revealed himself to this violent persecutor of his Church, the first words from Saul's trembling lips were, "Lord, what would you have me to do" (Acts 9:6)? The Lord gladly told him, and Saul gladly obeyed.

The first steps of this new obedience are also few and simple. Once a seeker sees who Christ is, he is to *come* to him (Mt. 11:28). Practically speaking, this means that he now opens up with Christ a life-long conversation in prayer. As he does, he will likely want first to *confess*, beneath the shadow of the cross, that he is indeed a sinner, that he is sorry for his sins, that he is eager to forsake them, and that he sees his need of the Savior (Luke 7:36f, 18:13, Acts 2:37, 1 John 1:9, 2 Cor. 7:10). But then, encouraged by Christ's many promises, he will gladly go on to *receive* him, prayerfully welcoming him into his heart and life as Teacher, Savior, and Lord (John 1:12). Finally, in order to complete the great transaction, he will search out, find, and affiliate himself with a trustworthy fellowship of believers. And there—in the presence of friends, loved ones, and members of his new spiritual family—he will be baptized in water. In so doing, he declares publicly—before God, men, and angels—that he has died to sin, risen to newness of life, and is now embarked upon a life-long journey of Christian discipleship that, by God's grace, will one day lead him into the eternal Kingdom of God (Mt. 28:18f, Acts 2:38, Rom. 6, 1 Tim. 6:12-13).[1]

Attitudes

Knowing that the gospel test measures a man's character, Jesus commends certain attitudes that are typically associated with good success in any spiritual endeavor. Here are a few that the NT considers important for all, both seeker and saint.

Love of Truth

First and foremost is the *love of truth*. This crucial posture is necessary because of the spiritual condition of unregenerate man, who, as saw earlier, is born in darkness. Therefore, when the gospel comes to him, he sees well enough that it is light, but not well enough to know with certainty that it is true. Accordingly, he faces a decision. He can ignore the light and content himself to remain in shadow, or he can do what the light implicitly demands: seek *more* light until he sees all things clearly. In other words, he can welcome the love of truth into his heart, and—*as an abiding principle of his entire spiritual life*—keep on loving truth until he finds it (2 Thess. 2:10).

For Jesus, the love of truth must become a seeker's guiding star, the master passion of his life. This is clear from many of his sayings. For example, he identifies as "the great (or foremost) commandment" these words from the Law of Moses: "You shall love the LORD your God with all your heart, with all your soul, and with all your mind" (Mt. 22:36-37). Here, Jesus is directly speaking to Jews, urging upon them a life-long devotion to Yahweh. But indirectly he is also speaking to seekers, urging them to love *the truth about the unknown god* with all their heart, soul, mind, and strength—and to keep on loving it till they find it. Moreover, Jesus here indicates that they do well to begin their search with the God of Israel, and also with the one who has openly declared that he is his appointed Teacher (Deut. 4:29, Jer. 29:13, John 8:12).

Similarly, Jesus declared that "Man shall not live by bread alone, but by every word that proceeds from the mouth of God" (Mt. 4:4). For the seeker, this is at once a word of instruction, a command, and a promise. It teaches him that he cannot hope to find inward fulfillment in the pursuit temporal and material goods; that he is by nature a spiritual being, a being meant to know God, hear his words, contemplate his truth, obey his will, and thrive under his blessing. Therefore, it implicitly commands the seeker to love and seek out the truth about the God of Israel. Moreover, it promises him that when he finds that truth, he will indeed find life.

The same exhortation to the love of truth appears in Jesus' brief dialogue with Pilate, where we hear him saying, "For this reason I was born, and for this I came into the world, to testify to the truth. Everyone on the side of the truth listens to me" (John 18:37). Here, Jesus issues a challenge, not only to Pilate, but to men everywhere. "Put yourself on the side of truth," he says. "Love the truth so much that you are willing to keep on seeking it until you find it. Do this, and you will find yourself listening to me. And in listening to me, you will find yourself hearing God's voice, God's truth" (John 14:6, Eph. 4:21).

Courage

As we saw earlier, when a seeker takes the gospel test he will face many difficulties. Likely as not, the difficulties will awaken many fears. These include fear of ridicule, hatred, and human rejection; fear of isolation from family, friends, colleagues, and the surrounding culture; fear of unemployability, poverty, injury, or death; fear of one's own sinfulness and helplessness; fear of spiritual failure; fear of God, fear of judgment, and fear of eternal punishment. In some cases, these fears are natural, being based on reality. In others they are unnatural, being based on a response to reality that is distorted by indwelling sin. But in all cases, they are part of the gospel test. Therefore, it will take courage—and encouragement—to pass that test.

Jesus gladly supplies both. The following story from Matthew's gospel shows us how he does it.

One night the disciples were caught in a windstorm on the Sea of Galilee. Suddenly, to their astonishment and dismay, they saw a human form walking towards them upon the water. "It is a spirit!" they cried. But then they heard the voice of their Master, speaking words that have comforted multitudes ever since: "Take courage," Jesus said. "It is I. Do not be afraid," (Mt. 14-22-23).

This episode contains precious encouragements for struggling seekers. It teaches them that Jesus is in their (stormy) test, that he means them well, that he understands their fears, and also that he understands how such fears can keep them from coming to the light. Therefore, he bluntly commands them *not* to fear. But more than this, he also *enables* them not to fear by skillfully dispensing instruction, promise, and warning in such a way as to encourage them. By means of pointed teachings—and graciously infused strength—he frees the seeker from fear so that he is henceforth free to seek on.

A single example of this pattern must suffice to show the Great Physician's skill in such spiritual surgery. Mindful of the grievous persecutions that were about to befall his disciples, Jesus said:

> And I say to you, My friends, do not be afraid of those who kill the body, and after that have no more that they can do. But I will show you whom you should fear. Fear Him who, after He has killed, has power to cast into hell. Yes, I say to you, fear Him! Are not five sparrows sold for two copper coins? And yet not one of them is forgotten before God. But the very hairs of your head are all numbered. Do not fear therefore; you are of more value than many sparrows...Fear not little flock. It is your Father's good pleasure to give you the kingdom.
> —Luke 12:4-7, 32

These words display an astonishing mix of realism, toughness, tenderness, warning, and encouragement. Jesus doesn't whitewash reality: persecutions will come, sometimes even unto death. If, then, for fear of such persecutions, a disciple is tempted to forsake God, let him remember to fear God even more, so that by means of the greater fear he may find courage to overcome the lesser. But better still, let him think on the goodness of his heavenly Father; on his unparalleled love for his people, his abiding presence, his constant watch-care, and his eagerness to see them persevere to the end so as to meet him in glory in his eternal Kingdom.

By many such words Jesus calls for courage in his disciples, even as he instills it, by his Spirit, into their trembling hearts. Speaking and working thus, he instills it into the trembling hearts of seekers as well.

Integrity

Jesus of Nazareth concurs with the Psalmist: "Light is sown for the righteous, and gladness for the upright in heart" (Psalm 97:11). If, then, a seeker hopes to pass the gospel test—if he hopes to learn from the unknown god whether or not the gospel is true—he must be a person of integrity.

Here, however, a *caveat* is very much in order. The kind of integrity a seeker needs is *not* sinless perfection; according to the scriptures, that kind of perfection long ago departed from the sons of Adam. Rather, the kind of integrity he needs is what the Bible calls *a perfect heart*. A perfect heart is a heart that sees and aspires to moral wholeness; a heart that is single-mindedly intent upon discovering and doing the will of God; a heart that grieves when it finds itself falling short, yet resolves to get up and try again, over and over again (1 Chron. 29:19, Isaiah 38:3, Psalm 110:2). David was asking God for a perfect heart when he cried, "Teach me Your way, O LORD, and I will walk in Your truth. *Unite* my heart to fear Your name," (Psalm 86:11).

We have already seen the importance of this kind of integrity in Jesus' discourse to Nicodemus. There he states that whoever practices the truth comes to the light, that it may be clearly seen that his deeds have been done in God (John 3:21). In this saying, Jesus has in mind a sincere seeker. God is already at work in his life, drawing him to the light of Christ and the gospel. How do we know God is at work? We know because this man is not like those who "practice evil," and who therefore show that they hate the light (John 3:20). No, he is a man who "practices truth," who does what is good, so far as he is able to see what is good in the light that has come to him from the holy God. In other words, he is a man whose conscience is waking from slumber; a man intent upon forsaking the evil that he now clearly sees in his heart and life; a man eager to know and do the will of the unknown god. In short, he is a man of integrity.

In yet another saying, Jesus is even more explicit about the importance of integrity in the search for truth. While speaking to certain Jewish leaders, he said, "My teaching is not Mine, but His who sent Me. If any man is willing to do His will, he shall know of the teaching, whether it is from God, or whether I speak from Myself" (John 7:16-17, NAS). Here Jesus asserts that his words are the very words of God. He recognizes that the Jews do not yet know this, *but insists that they can.* They need only have a "perfect" heart towards God. They need only be willing to discover and obey his will. Into such a heart, says Jesus, God will sow his light. To men and women of integrity, he will reveal his truth.

Soberingly, Jesus asserts that the Scribes and Pharisees—the religious leaders of the nation—failed to discern his identity because they were *not* men of integrity. He called them "whitewashed tombs." Yes, their scrupulously tended religious personas impressed the common people. But when Jesus looked beneath the surface, he only saw "uncleanness"—pride, avarice, hypocrisy, foolishness, willful blindness, extortion, and self-indulgence (Mt. 23:13-39). Again, Jesus was not looking for sinless perfection, only for a heart bent on obedience to God. But in the Pharisees he did not find such a heart, and so despaired of their ever coming to the knowledge of the truth. "I know you, that you do not have the love of God (or the love of the truth) in you...How can you believe (or find the truth), you who receive honor from one another and do not seek the honor that comes from the only God" (John 5:42, 45)?

Such words speak very practically to seekers everywhere. They urge them to believe something that they already know deep within: there is indeed a god-ordained connection between doing what is right and seeing what is true. Accordingly, earnest seekers of the truth about the gospel will listen carefully to the voice of conscience; they will consider thoughtfully the specific tenets of biblical morality; they will forsake any attitudes or actions that seem to be evil; and they will embrace any attitudes or actions that seem to be good. To the best of their ability they will walk in the light, so that they may advance in the light, so that one day they may finally see all things in the light (Isaiah 2:5, 1 John 1:7).

Humility

As Jesus' popularity grew, so too did his disciples' ambition. Their imaginations were enflamed with visions of their own glory in the coming Messianic kingdom. Finally, perhaps after quarreling over the matter, they came to the Master and asked, "Who then is greatest in the kingdom of heaven?" Summoning a little child and setting him in their midst, Jesus replied:

> Truly, I say to you, unless you are converted and become as little children, you will by no means enter the kingdom of heaven. Therefore, whoever humbles himself as this little child is the greatest in the kingdom of heaven. And whoever receives one little child like this in My name receives Me.
>
> —Mt. 18:1-5

As these probing words show, Jesus was troubled by the disciple's question. Their preoccupation with greatness revealed a worldly spirit, a spirit supremely embodied in the arrogant ambitions of Rome (Mt. 20:20-28). Now the infection was at work among his own disciples, driving them towards self-reliance, self-righteousness, self-exaltation, and—in essence—self-deification. Ironically, it was a spirit completely alien to the Kingdom they were proclaiming. Indeed, it was a spirit that could *exclude* them from the Kingdom they were proclaiming. It was the spirit of pride.

So Jesus addressed that spirit. With his eye upon events that would occur only after his death and resurrection, he graphically explained to these men what must happen to them if ever they were to enter the Kingdom, let alone rise to pre-eminence in it.

God must perform a work in their hearts. That work will begin when he converts them: when he turns them from their pride, draws them to his Son, and places them before the mirror of Christ's own person and work. There he will show them their separation from God, their sinful self-centeredness and lawlessness, their worthiness of judgment, their complete inability to save themselves, and their absolute dependence upon the mercy extended in Christ. There he will empty them, calm them, and silence them. And there, in the miracle of regeneration, he will turn them into children: children who see their absolute dependence upon God; children who are now willing to do the one thing that is necessary in order to live: gladly, gratefully, *receive*. To enter the Kingdom, says Jesus, a proud man must be humbled under the mighty hand of God. And when God's hand is thus stretched forth, he must also humble himself (James 4:10, 1 Pet. 5:6).

These words speak powerfully to the seeker, and to his need of humility in the search for truth. For example, if a seeker is a self-proclaimed atheist or agnostic, it will take humility to acknowledge the many signs of an unknown god at work in the world. If he has gone on to examine the evidence that identifies this god as the God of Israel, it will take humility to admit that the evidence is indeed weighty and worthy of careful consideration. And if he has come to understand the gist of the gospel, it will take *great* humility to wrestle honestly with its hard sayings about the exclusiveness of Christianity, the creatureliness and sinfulness of man, the ominous reality of divine judgment, and man's utter dependence upon Christ and Christ alone for salvation and eternal life.

But even this is not all. For what if, after sincerely considering the gospel, a seeker finds that he is *still* not sure? What if he sees that the gospel *may well be true*, but still cannot quite see clearly that it *really is true*? What if he knows he needs more light, but doesn't know where or how to get it? What, indeed, if he finds himself at his very wits end, feeling wretched, miserable, poor, blind, and desperately in need of *more* help (Psalm 107:27, Mark 9:24, Rev. 3:17)? What then?

Strange to tell, Jesus actually calls this man blessed. He is "poor in spirit," not because he is stupid or wicked or even insane (as indeed he may feel himself to be), but because (unbeknownst to him) God is drawing near, emptying him of his "riches"—his sinful pride and self-sufficiency—and preparing him in the darkness to receive the gift of his light (Mt. 5:3).

But as this poor seeker gropes in the shadow of God's outstretched hand, what, practically speaking, is he supposed to be doing? Jesus answers clearly: he is to humble himself yet again, and this in three fundamental ways.

First, he is to humble himself before Christ's people. This means that he is to seek out Christians, in order to see what kind of help, if any, they might be able to offer.[2] In Jesus' mind, his people are his spokesmen in the world. They are members of his own body, extensions of his very self. Therefore, to come to them is to come to him. And to come to them for help is to receive help from him (Mt. 10:40-42). The Ethiopian eunuch was one such man. Puzzled by what he was reading in the book of Isaiah, he humbly asked Philip the evangelist, "How can I (understand), unless someone guides me?" This great man sought help from Christ's lowly disciple. When he did, he got what he wanted—and much more—and went home rejoicing (Acts 8:26-40, 10-11).

Second, he is to humble himself before the Christian scriptures, the Bible. This does not mean, of course, that he must take a "leap of faith" and simply *decide* that the Bible is the God's Word. For the intellectually honest person, that is not an option. It does mean, however, that he will open himself to the possibility of being *shown* that the Bible is God's Word. He does this out of deference to the Teacher, who honored the OT scriptures as the foundation of God's Word, even as he heralded the (forthcoming) NT scriptures as the capstone of that Word. Moreover, he does it out of deference to Jesus' promises: that the God of Israel likes to sanctify his people by his Word; that the entrance of his word gives light; and that faith comes by hearing, and hearing by the Word about Christ (Isaiah 66:2, John 17:17, Psalm 119:130, Rom. 10:17). For all these reasons, then, the seeker will humble himself before the Bible *as if before the unknown god himself,* in order to see if, through the Bible, God might be pleased to reveal both himself and his truth.

Finally, the seeker will humble himself before God in prayer. Jesus himself encourages this very thing, urging men at every stage of their spiritual journey to ask, seek, and knock (Mt. 7:7). For the seeker, this means asking the God of the Bible to reveal himself, to disclose whether or not he really is the unknown god. Such prayers, which will doubtless be lifted up over and again, are not likely to be very polished. Indeed, they may seem quite messy, rather like the pitiful plea of that Jewish father who desperately sought Jesus' healing touch for his daughter: "Lord, I believe, help my unbelief" (Mark 9:24)! But if the God of the Bible is god, such prayers are actually quite powerful. They reflect a spiritual dependency that well accords with his original purpose for man, and they are therefore quite pleasing in his sight. The God of Israel delights to deliver the needy ones who cry out, the afflicted ones who have no one to help (Psalm 72:12). Let every struggling seeker take heart.

Perseverance

If life really is a test—and the gospel test its Mt. Everest—then it is reasonable to suppose that passing it will require perseverance. Indeed, perseverance belongs essentially to the very idea of a test. If the new alloy is to be used in space, it must persevere successfully under the stress of man-made heat, cold, pressure, and shaking. If the new pilot is to fly a passenger jet, he must persevere successfully under the man-made stress of a flight simulator. Similarly, if a seeker is to pass the gospel test, he must persevere in his search for truth under the God-ordained stress of obstacles, delays, setbacks, and discouragement. All along the way he will hear in one ear, "Give up," but in the other, "Keep going." We may reasonably expect that in order to pass, he will have to keep going.

By and large, Jesus confirms this expectation—yet not altogether. To understand this, let us look at three of his sayings. In the first two, we hear him urging seekers to persevere in their search for truth. But in the third, we hear him comfortingly remind them that in the last analysis success does not depend on man who wills, runs, seeks, or perseveres—but on God who shows mercy (Rom. 9:16).

We have met the first saying before, but I will cite it here in its most encouraging context:

> Keep on asking, and it will be given to you. Keep on seeking, and you will find. Keep on knocking, and it will be opened to you. For everyone who asks receives, and he who seeks finds, and to him who knocks it will be opened. Or what man is there among you who, if his son asks for bread, will give him a stone? Or if he asks for a fish, will he give him a serpent? If you then, being evil, know how to give good gifts to your children, how much more will your Father who is in heaven give good things to those who ask Him?
>
> —Mt. 7:7-11, Luke 11:13

Knowing the difficulties of the gospel test, Jesus here speaks directly to the seeker's heart. His words are rich with exhortation, instruction, and encouragement. Above all, they are to persevere. They are to keep on asking; keep on seeking; keep on knocking. And if God should seem at all to delay his response, they are to rekindle their courage at the fire of two great certainties. The first is that God, who cannot break his promises, *will* respond to those who seek—so long as they keep seeking. The second is that he will do so because he is good. Indeed, he is unimaginably good, better than the best earthly father the world has ever seen; more eager to give than the most generous parent the world has ever known (Luke 18:1f). To glimpse his goodness—and his good will towards every seeking child—is to find strength to keep on keeping on.

The second text, also found in the Sermon on the Mount, strikes a different note, a note of warning:

> Enter by the narrow gate. For wide is the gate and broad the way that leads to destruction, and there are many who go in by it. Because narrow is the gate and difficult is the way which leads to life, and there are few who find it.
> —Mt. 7:13-14, Luke 13:24

From our previous investigations we understand exactly what Jesus has in mind when he issues this solemn warning to all seekers. He knows that he himself is the narrow gate—the one and only door into God's Kingdom (John 14:6). He knows that it is difficult for sinners to find it and enter it—to see the true meaning of his person and work, and to respond accordingly. He knows that few actually do find it, but that all must: there is simply no other entrance into the city of God.

He also knows that in this fallen world system there will always be other gates—other religions and philosophies promising access to truth and salvation. He knows that multitudes will always be attracted to them, for they are not as narrow—not as difficult—as the true gate. He knows that the many gates are in fact one gate, for they all have their origin in one enemy, who has but one evil purpose (John 8:44, 10:10). And he knows that this one gate—so dangerously deceptive because of its great popularity—leads not to the city of God, but to the city of Destruction (Prov. 15:11, 27:20, 2 Thess. 1:9).

What, then, is the gist of this sobering exhortation? Let us hear it from Jesus himself: "*Agonize* to enter the narrow gate" (Luke 13:24). The seeker must spare no effort, he must pay any price. He must take his stand as a solitary individual before the towering mystery of the unknown god, and he must persevere until he finds and experiences the truth for himself. He dare not become indolent; he dare not yield to the prevailing philosophies and values of the world; he dare not become a reed shaken by the wind (Mt. 11:7, Eph. 4:14, Jude 1:12). He must take Jesus' words deeply to heart: the way that leads to life *is* narrow, and it *will* seem long, difficult, and lonely. But he must not leave it until he has found the narrow gate, passed through into the holy city, and there beheld its glorious precincts for himself. He must persevere until the end; until he knows that he knows that he knows he has found the truth.

In our final text, Jesus gives us two parables about the Kingdom of God, parables that should greatly encourage all who seek:

> Again, the kingdom of heaven is like treasure hidden in a field, which a man found and hid; and for joy over it he goes and sells all that he has and buys that field.
> Again, the kingdom of heaven is like a merchant seeking beautiful pearls, who, when he had found one pearl of great price, went and sold all that he had and bought it.
> —Mt. 13:44-46

As we saw earlier, the Kingdom of heaven is the direct reign of God over the hearts of men. Here, Jesus speaks of a day when this reign will indeed be in the world, but hidden—and therefore in need of being found. He has in view the days of "the Kingdom of the Son," days in which the gospel will be preached, God will draw near, and sinners—seeing the truth—will gladly respond by coming to his Son and submitting themselves to his rule. In fact, they will be so glad about finding the truth that they will "sell all." They will freely give up anything and everything that might keep them from possessing and enjoying the infinitely valuable treasure of eternal life.

Though seekers do not (yet) believe all these things, these two parables should much encourage them since they shed important light on *how* Jesus expected people to discover the truth of the gospel.

Consider first the parable of the pearl of great price. Here, the merchant seems to represent all who are *consciously* looking for God's truth. These are the spiritual vagabonds of our world, wandering from faith to faith, philosophy to philosophy, buying a pearl of wisdom here and a nugget of insight there, hoping one day to amass the fortune of truth. Observe that Jesus does not utterly discount the value of their holdings. He does, however, admonish that their quest is unfinished, and that their seeking must therefore continue. For there is indeed a pearl of great price, hidden somewhere in the marketplaces of this world. If they will keep seeking, they will find it. When they do, all that previously seemed to be gain will suddenly appear as loss in view of the surpassing worth of the immense fortune they now possess (Phil. 3:7-11).

Note, however, that there is hope even for those who do *not* seek. In the parable of the hidden treasure, we meet a man who is not questing for truth, but who, upon encountering it, recognizes it for what it is, sees its great value, and—just like the industrious merchant—goes and sells all he has to acquire it. Apparently, the apostle Paul was such a man. Far from seeking the truth of the gospel, he went about in a rage trying to destroy it. Yet when the truth suddenly revealed himself to Paul, he, like every seeker-turned-finder, instantly sold everything (Acts 9:1-30).

These two parables distil the mystery of man's relationship to God and truth. The first encourages seekers to seek, and to do so earnestly, faithfully, and confidently. But the second admonishes them never to do so in self-reliance or pride. For if those who were not seeking the truth found it, then it was actually the truth who sought and found them. And if such was the case among those who did not seek, then surely that must also be the case among those who do. So then, by all means let the seeker seek. And when he finds, by all means let him rejoice. But if he is at all inclined to boast, let him take care not to boast in himself, his seeking, or his perseverance. Rather, let him boast in a merciful and gracious God, by whose doing he is now in the Lord, and by whose doing he has now become a son and an heir to the unsearchable riches of Christ (John 15:16, 1 Cor. 1:30-31, Eph. 3:8, Rev. 3:17).[3]

Faith

Jesus of Nazareth is a great fan of faith. He urges his disciples to have it (Mark 11:22). He scolds them if they do not show it when they should (Luke 8:25). He marvels at it when he sees it expressed boldly (Mt. 8:10). He seeks to increase it (Luke 17:5f). He tests it, rewards it, and promises astonishing feats through it (Mt. 9:29; 15:28; Mt. 17:20, Luke 18:42). Jesus desires his disciples to have faith, and also to grow in faith, because he knows that without faith it is impossible to please God (Heb. 11:6).

But what exactly *is* faith? And what is its importance, if any, for those who are not (yet) Jesus' disciples; for those who are simply trying to find out the truth about God and the gospel?

As to the nature of biblical of faith, it is tersely defined for us in the NT letter to the Hebrews: "Faith is the assurance of things hoped for; the conviction of things not seen" (Heb. 11:1, NAS). Here we learn that faith is essentially "assurance" and "conviction." But where do such precious gifts come from? The answer, according to the NT, is that they come from God. They come as God *reveals* invisible spiritual realities to the human mind; as he makes things unseen by our naked eye visible to the eyes of our understanding (Rom. 1:20, Eph. 1:18). In other words, when God reveals truth, he creates faith. The man who *has* seen, *knows* he has seen, and henceforth can never (honestly) say that he has not seen. Vision has laid a bedrock for faith.

Faith, then, is a fruit of divine revelation in a man's heart. But it is more than that. For faith also involves *a right response* to that revelation. This is the practical thrust of Hebrews 11, and indeed of the whole epistle. Here the author urges his readers to continue in their new-found Christian faith; to respond to what God has shown them with *trust* and *obedience;* to trust in the complete sufficiency of Christ for all things, and to obey his various commands. Thus, biblical faith is a two-sided coin, a two-edged sword. *God creates it inwardly by revelation, and man shows it outwardly by a right response, by trust and obedience.* When both are present, faith is genuine and powerful, even to the saving of the soul (Heb. 11:1ff, James 2:14-26).

But how is all this relevant to a seeker, to someone who has not yet received a revelation of the truth of the gospel, or responded accordingly? To put the question in a slightly different way: What, if anything, would Jesus say to a seeker about faith?

To judge from the NT, he would say quite a bit.

First, he would say, *"You already have a little faith."* This is because the seeker *has* received a revelation—a revelation of the existence and activity of the unknown god. Moreover, he is now acting on that revelation: he is showing his faith by seeking more faith, more light, more truth about this god. And if he is doing so with a confidence that his search will not be in vain, then *great* is his faith, and ready to receive its just reward.

Secondly, Jesus would say, *"Faith will grow as you keep seeking light, and as you keep on doing what the light shows you to do."* We have already touched on this point—the need for perseverance and integrity in the search for God's truth. Importantly, the NT closely associates these two virtues with the gift of brighter light and larger faith. Jesus, for example, speaks of the spiritual rewards of integrity and obedience in these cryptic words:

> Consider carefully what you hear (or see). With the same measure you use, it will be measured to you; and to you who hear, more will be given. For whoever has, to him more will be given; but whoever does not have, even what he has will be taken away from him.
> —Mark 4:224-25

The idea here is that those who "consider carefully" what God has shown them *by acting upon it* will receive more light. Meanwhile, those who show their contempt for spiritual light by ignoring its practical ramifications will lose whatever light they may have. In short, Jesus closely associates growing wisdom with ongoing obedience.

In much the same way, the writer to the Hebrews speaks of the blessings of diligence in the pursuit of truth:

> Without faith, it is impossible to please Him, for he who comes to God must believe that He is, and that He is a rewarder of those who diligently seek Him.
>
> —Heb. 11:6

Does a seeker have faith in the existence of the unknown god? Then let him diligently seek out more truth about him. And if the unknown god is, in fact, the God of Israel, he will reward him with a revelation of that truth. The promise, then, is clear: God-given faith, acted upon in faith, will beget more God-given faith—faith that will bring good success in the test of life.

Finally, Jesus says, "*Faith will grow as you focus your attention upon the God of the Bible.*" Such attention is, of course, the attention of a true seeker, of someone who is genuinely open to the possibility that the biblical gospel is true, and willing to obey it if he finds out that it is. Jesus knows that such attention will engender more faith because he knows it will place the seeker in the gravitational field of the true God, who has promised to draw all sincere seekers closer and closer to himself, giving them more and more faith the nearer they come.

This persuasion is reflected in one of Jesus' most picturesque sayings, a saying that appears in the Sermon on the Mount:

> The lamp of the body is the eye. If therefore your eye is good, your whole body will be full of light. But if your eye is bad, your whole body will be full of darkness. If therefore the light that is in you is darkness, how great is that darkness!
>
> —Mt. 6:22-23

From the context, we learn that Jesus is urging his disciples to maintain right priorities. If they keep their eye on the King and the advance of his Kingdom, their whole life will be full of light. But if they divert their gaze to money and the things of this world, their lives will be filled with darkness (Mt. 6:33). Now it is easy to see how these words speak powerfully to seekers as well. In their case, Jesus is saying, "You too must keep your eye on the mark: the discovery of the truth about the unknown god. You will know you are near it when you find your body filling up with light. And you will find your body filling with light when you fix your eye upon the God of the Bible. Try it—openly and honestly—and you will see."

But how, practically speaking, is someone to do this? We have already discussed the answer. He is to train his eyes upon the Bible, reading it systematically, attending carefully (and even prayerfully) to its stories, precepts, types, shadows, prophecies, teachings, promises, and warnings.

As he reads, let him especially be on the look-out for the redeemer, the God-Man, the Messianic prophet, priest, and king; the One promised and prepared for in OT times, and celebrated and further anticipated in NT times. And while he is looking for Christ, let him also keep an eye out for the goodness of God: a God who is eagerly seeking a truth-loving people for his own possession; a God who takes pleasure in giving them the Kingdom; a God who has promised, in manifold times and ways, that all who ask will receive, all who seek will find, and all who knock will have the door opened to them (Jer. 29:13, Mt. 12:32, Mt. 7:7, Rev. 21:6, 22:17).

Yes, says Jesus, let a seeker train his eyes on all of this, and soon his body will be full of light—and full of faith, as well.

Out, Out, and Away!

The place was Jerusalem. The occasion: the feast of the Passover, the last that Jesus would ever celebrate. As John relates the story, certain Greeks—converts to Judaism—had come to worship at the feast. Having heard about Jesus, these earnest seekers were now seeking something more. At last they found Philip, one of Jesus' disciples, and said, "Sir, we would see Jesus." Philip told Andrew, and Andrew and Philip told Jesus. Listen carefully to Jesus' thought-provoking response:

> The hour has come that the Son of Man should be glorified. Truly, truly I say to you, unless a grain of wheat falls into the ground and dies, it remains alone; but if it dies, it produces much grain...Now is my soul troubled, and what shall I say? "Father, save Me from this hour?" But for this purpose I came to this hour. Father, glorify Your name."
> —John 12:23-24, 27

These words are full of pathos. When Jesus heard about the Greek seekers, he grew solemn—even troubled. The men were Gentiles, and the fact that they wanted to speak with him was a good sign—a sign that God was ripening the Gentile harvest, that his elect among the Gentiles were now ready to be reaped (John 4:35). But the good sign was also a bad, for it meant that Jesus' hour had come, the hour of his death. Yes, God's truth was about to go out into the nations. But before it could, the substance of that truth must be woven into the very fabric of history. In other words, the Messiah now must offer himself to Israel, suffer rejection, die as a ransom for the sins of his people, and rise again on the third day. Only then will the gospel be *complete;* only then will it be *ready* to go forth into the nations.

Seeing the sign of the Greeks—and seeing all it signified for the hours ahead—Jesus trembled.

Yet the Bible assures us that he also rejoiced. As we bring our journey to a close, it is important once again to remind ourselves why.

The NT declares that Jesus knew full well what was in man: the questions, the longings, the fears, the guilt, the (fragile) hope, the ever-present specter of despair—all the burdens of the great test of life. But he also knew what his Father was about to do. It was something new, something powerful, and something definitive: something that would lift the burdens of men once for all. God was about to fulfill his plan of redemption, complete his revelation to all mankind, and send the good news of both out into the whole wide world. The good news would arrive in the form of a test: the gospel test.

Looking ahead to the future, Jesus rejoiced to see the multitudes of people who would pass it. These would find trustworthy answers to the questions of life. They would receive forgiveness of sins. They would experience inward spiritual union with the triune God, a God who would fill their liberated souls with light, life, purpose, and joy. And at the end of their difficult days upon the earth, when it was time to engage the last enemy, they would do even that victoriously, seeing in the face of death itself nothing more than a doorway into the Jerusalem above and the company of its great King.

Yes, Jesus rejoiced. It was good that his life was about to fall as a seed into the ground. It was good that God's truth, presence, and healing power should no longer remain "alone," shut up in little Palestine. It was good that these rich blessings should now be sown in all the fields of the world. And it was good that they should produce a mighty crop of redeemed souls. At Philip's word about the Gentile seekers, Jesus did indeed tremble for himself, for his hour had come. But when he considered all that his death was about to accomplish for these very ones—and for a vast multitude like them—he took heart, knowing that *their* hour had come, as well. In showing him all these things, his Father had set before him a great joy. Because of that joy, Jesus willingly endured the sorrows of the cross (Heb. 12:1-2).

The New Testament, supplemented by Church history, reveals that it all came to pass just as Jesus had foreseen. After his passion and exaltation, the gospel test—in ever-widening circles—went out, out, and away. The heavenly stone first splashed into the lake on the day of Pentecost, when the apostle Peter, in the power of the freshly-come Holy Spirit, preached to his Jewish brothers in Jerusalem (Acts 2–4). Shortly after that, Christ's evangelists began fanning out, bringing the test to the cities of Judea. Next it arrived in Samaria, where, to the surprise of the apostles, many welcomed it with joy (Acts 8-9). Then, as a majority in Israel became hardened, it went out to the Gentiles (Acts 10-11). These too responded eagerly, so much so that dynamic churches soon sprang up in Asia (modern Turkey), Greece, and Italy. From these centers the gospel test would go still further out, eventually reaching Europe, Africa, India, China, Asia, and the America's. Moreover, it would go out not only in spoken word, but also in print, on tape, on film, on line, and over the airwaves. As it did, it would produce *very* much grain, just as Jesus had said.

And now, faithful companion, it has reached you—this time in a long book written by a fellow-seeker much like yourself. As he leaves you at the feet of Jesus, he does so with heart-felt gratitude for your willingness to journey so far together with him. He also does so with a sincere hope that on this journey you have indeed caught a glimpse—and perhaps even more than a glimpse—of the meaning of life in *The Test*.

ONE MAN'S JOURNEY:
THE THRILL OF THEM ALL

"I will come to you."
—John 14:18

AS I REACHED the nadir of my descent into darkness, the living God again drew near.

The great denouement began in the summer of 1974, when I ran into Linda at a local natural foods restaurant. She and I had been casual friends in college. Now we were two lonely singles, unexpectedly cheered to see one another again and to renew our friendship. In the weeks that followed our meeting, I sought her out. Soon a romance blossomed, so much so that we even began to talk of marriage. These conversations were not, however, without serious misgivings on my part. I was a committed Buddhist, she a half-hearted atheist. That unlikely combination was okay with her, but spiritually threatening to me. Was not marriage another entanglement in the web of Maya, a distraction from my supreme goal? Did I really want to postpone my enlightenment, and possibly incur still more incarnations, all for the passing pleasures of domesticity? Yet despite such misgivings, I hesitated to break off the relationship. I rather liked this entanglement. It brought us life, something neither of us had experienced for quite some time.

During the season of this troubled courtship, the heavenly Chessman put a crucial piece in play: Linda's mother, Louise. About 12 years previous, Louise had abandoned her spiritual roots in the mind sciences to become a Christian. Her atheist daughter, though duly respectful of Mom, would have nothing to do with her faith. I, on the other hand, was quite interested. Like Louise, I too had studied the mind sciences (pantheistic religions in Christian garb). Like her, I had also found that they failed to satisfy. And like her, I was now beginning to wonder if orthodox Christianity might be true after all. Whenever she visited, we talked at length and with much pleasure.

Interesting as our discussions were, Louise's most influential gift to me was two books: *The Hiding Place*, by Corrie Ten Boom, and *Ben Israel: The Odyssey of a Modern Jew*, by Art Katz. In the former, Corrie tells how her family—all members of the Dutch Resistance—sheltered persecuted Jews during the Nazi occupation of Holland. She also relates the terrible price they paid for doing it. This amazing story—so full of the clash of good and evil, vital biblical faith, amazing providence, and even divine miracle—seemed to open a window into heaven. Unsettling glimpses of a living God, active in history, again sent tremors through the foundations of my pantheistic soul.

The other book, also an autobiography, had, if possible, an even greater impact. Here I was introduced to Art Katz, a young, disillusioned Jewish intellectual, tramping his way across Europe to Israel, searching for he knew not what. However, the more I read of his story, the more I began to realize what was really happening: Someone was searching for him! How did I know that? Because, in a manner bordering on the uncanny, Art's path was continually intersecting with Christians. Moreover, whenever it did, these outspoken believers would unfailingly urge him to see in Jesus of Nazareth the spiritual reality that he was so desperately trying to find. The story of Art's eventual encounter with Christ in an out-of-the-way Pentecostal chapel in Jerusalem is, I think, one of the great modern testimonies of Christian conversion.

To my mind, these books had the ring of truth. Moreover, they prodded me to see my own spiritual odyssey in a fresh light. Could it be, as Corrie and Art had testified, that there really is a living God, an infinite personal Spirit? Could it be that he is active in people's lives today? Had his invisible hand been secretly at work in all my religious questing? Was his Spirit behind my previous experience with Jesus? And (heaven help me) was it his age-old enemy—secretly playing upon my own pride and spiritual dishonesty—who had kept me searching for God in the barren deserts of Eastern mysticism these four long years?

Having so zealously cultivated my pantheistic faith, such questions were indeed difficult to ask. Yet moved by a strange mixture of pain, dread, determination, and rising hope, I decided that I had to get the answers once and for all. The seeker within—long slumbering and nigh unto death—was born again.

Into His Marvelous Light

The remainder of the story is quickly told, for, as I have since learned, God is quickly found by those who are willing to submit themselves to his truth, and who make no attempts at all to negotiate the terms of surrender.

I took a leave of absence from my relationship with Linda, who graciously honored my request for time and solitude to explore these new ideas. I then arranged to meet with Art Katz during one of his upcoming speaking tours in California. As I awaited his arrival, I visited Christian bookstores and began to read voraciously. There was, for example, a book about the "Jesus Movement"—a Christian revival then in progress among countercultural youth. This study impressively confronted me with modern day miracles and powerful, life-changing conversions. I also read some books on biblical "eschatology"—theological discussions of future events surrounding the second coming of Christ. Through these writings I began to understand for the first time what Christians meant when they spoke of "the fear of the Lord." And there was, of course, the Bible itself, whose identity as the Word of God became increasingly clear to me through my discovery of various Old Testament Messianic types and prophecies.

Last but not least, I finally came into contact with some real flesh and blood Christians, folks like Arnie the carpenter whom I met quite "by chance" on a job site. Hearing the story of my search for God, he eagerly welcomed me into his home, taught me from the Scriptures, and lent me a number of helpful Christian books.

Sometime in early September of 1974, the great transition occurred at last: I became a believer, not in the Christ of the gurus, but in the Christ of the Bible. It happened as I read the Scriptures, read Christian books, talked with Arnie, and began to launch some pitifully inept prayers towards heaven. Amidst it all, an otherworldly light gradually filled my mind, opening it up in such a way that I could actually see, through the words of the Bible, the awesome spiritual realities to which those words had ever been pointing.

In essence, the heavenly sighting involved two great revelations.

First, it seemed to me that I could now behold the entire course of cosmic history—not in detail, but distilled into key transitional events that rose up like giant pillars all along the highway of time. These included the Creation, the test in Eden, the Fall, the Flood, the tower of Babel, Abraham, Moses, Israel, Christ, the Cross, the Resurrection, the Ascension, the expanding Church, the Second Coming, the Judgment, and the appearing of the consummated Kingdom of God in a new heaven and a new earth. In all of this, I also caught a glimpse of the Author of cosmic history—of him who is "from everlasting, to everlasting." I will never forget how this tiny peek at the immensity of time and eternity drained, as it were, every drop of color from my spiritual face.

Yet as impressive as this revelation was, it was all in preparation for a greater still. For no sooner had I beheld the panorama of cosmic history, than I found myself lingering before what manifestly lay at the center of that history: the Cross of Christ. And here, as seeing the unseen, I beheld and understood for the first time the towering realities of the gospel.

Above the cross, I saw God the Father: infinitely holy and sovereign, gazing down upon the slumping body of his Son—hating, sentencing, and punishing sin.

Upon the cross, I saw the Son himself—the Father's gracious and merciful gift of love—willingly enduring the dreadful consequences of that sin out of love for God and God's people.

Before the cross, I saw my own sinful self, and along with that, heaven above, hell beneath, and me suspended precariously between the two. I also saw the terrible urgency of calling upon the Savior, whose touch alone could seal me to the one and rescue me from the other, for time and eternity.

In short, through this climactic spiritual revelation of the cross, God altogether opened up the way of salvation—and my desperate need of salvation—to my astonished eyes.

So it had happened at last. Over the course of a few brief days filled with vision and insight, the battered seeker and mystic had finally reached his goal: he was enlightened. Not as he once had hoped for or expected, but enlightened nonetheless. For now—with his personality very much intact, and his every faculty trembling with the fear of the Lord—he had seen, under heaven's light, the truth about God, and God's true answers to the questions of life.

Unless You Become as Children

Yet for all this enlightenment, one crucial ingredient was still missing: I had not (so I thought) been "born again." Though I now fully believed that Jesus was God's Son, and though I had prayed (more than once) to receive him as Savior, I had had no experience of his coming to me; I had received no felt assurance that my sins were forgiven, and that he now lived inside me. My friend Arnie kept insisting that the true mark of salvation was not an emotional experience, but simple, God-given faith in Christ—a faith that he clearly saw in me. Today, I would probably agree. But back then, when I had only just awakened to the shockingly dangerous universe I inhabited, I felt myself almost palpably dangling over the fires of hell. If God were suddenly to let go, where would I land? Arnie's assurances notwithstanding, I felt I needed to grab onto something quickly!

And so, one Friday evening near the end of September, I paid a first-time visit to the Drug Abuse Prevention Center. It was located just down the street from me, in the old Twin Lakes Baptist Church building. Founded by the Reverend Gene Dawson—a Pentecostal pastor with a heart for youth—the DAPC was essentially a Christian commune. Its ministry was primarily to the casualties of the counterculture, young people living on the streets who were, more often than not, involved with drugs. Under Dawson's skilled leadership, many of them had found Christ and were now turning their lives around. At the time, I knew little about the DAPC. Still, I sensed that it might be just the place for me to find my own experience with the Lord, and along with that, the assurance of salvation I so deeply desired.

Picture, then, in a moment dripping with irony, the proud philosopher, poet, and mystic—the man who would be God—entering the foyer of the church and nervously looking about for someone, anyone— even a streetwise child—to take him by the hand and lead him to the feet of the King of the universe. As it happened, a streetwise child was exactly what he got.

After reconnoitering for a moment, I found my courage and approached a burly young man who looked to be in his mid-twenties. I introduced myself and briefly explained my reason for coming. "Hey Joe," he immediately yelled at the top of his voice, "come over here! This guy wants to get saved!" The gentleman-philosopher in me expected a little more in the way of intellectual ice breaking. I had to admit, however, that this plainspoken youth had definitely gotten to the heart of the matter.

And thus began the evening that I now mark as the beginning of my Christian life. Joe, it turned out, was something of a leader in the DAPC family, and also the adopted son of the Reverend Dawson. He had been rescued from much and given much. To say that he was fervent for Jesus would be an understatement of epic proportions.

Joe greeted me warmly and invited me to come with him to the back of the large sanctuary, where we could visit in private. He listened respectfully as I related the story of my last four years, told him of my recent awakening to Christ, and expressed my desire to be born again. When I had finished, he matter-of-factly rehearsed the biblical story of redemption, emphasizing that man's part in the great transaction is simply to call upon Jesus in faith, asking him to save us.

"Well," I said, "I believe all that, and I want him in my life. So what's next?"

Joe's reply was simple: "Let's pray."

His prayer, however, was anything but simple. He slid off the pew onto his knees, motioning for me to join him. When I did, he said, "I'll pray for a minute, then you go ahead." I agreed, and Joe began. Never in my born days had I heard the likes of it. No time taken to quiet himself, no hushed tones, no air of formality, no lengthy scriptural quotes—just the booming voice of a profoundly grateful young man, pouring out his heart to the Lord he loved.

He thanked Jesus for saving him. He thanked him for his adoptive dad. He thanked him for the DAPC family. He even prayed—much to my astonishment—in a strange language different from his own, exercising a spiritual gift that Pentecostals call glossolalia, or "speaking in tongues." Finally, arriving at the business at hand, he prayed for me, thanking Jesus for his work in my life and asking him to save me that very night. He then turned to me and said, "Now go ahead, brother, just tell him what's in your heart."

Well, at the end of so long a journey, in the presence of such unusual company, and at the feet of the High King of heaven, it is not so easy to "just tell him what's in your heart." But here is something encouraging that I have since learned about Jesus: on occasions like these, he only requires the tiniest step in his direction before he himself arrives on the scene to guide his tottering child into his waiting arms.

And so, almost before the first stammering sentence was out of my mouth, I felt myself altogether enveloped in the presence of the Spirit of Christ. And though I am reluctant to do so, I think it important to say that his presence was extraordinarily powerful; that it had a palpable physical impact. Indeed, beneath the weight of it, I immediately sank face down to the floor, feeling as if my body—quickly growing numb to its surroundings—were now super-charged with a current of spiritual electricity. This, I understood immediately, was the power that had created the universe, that now held it together, and that could—if its divine custodian so desired—destroy it in an instant. It had altogether pinned me to the floor, yet I felt neither pain nor danger, only infinite love.

And in this experience, it was the love—not the power—that stood out. As I have said, I hardly knew where to begin my prayer. But as Jesus' presence enfolded me, I realized above all that he was coming to me in love, embracing me in love, reassuring me in love, and rejoicing together with me in love. And so, being fully persuaded of his love, I completely broke, and with a flood of tears began pouring out my own heart in love to him. Skillfully and tenderly, the Savior was leading his penitent son to confess his sins, and to leave them, once and for all, with him.

What exactly I said, I cannot remember. I do know that I dwelt much on my quest for enlightenment, for here, in the presence of the Holy One of Israel, I felt almost palpably the absurdity, arrogance, ugliness, and cosmic impropriety of my trying to become God. Yes, I had acted partly in ignorance, but I still saw it as a monstrous sin. Therefore, I pleaded with the Lord to forgive me for it, keep me from it, and help me to walk humbly before the one true God all the rest of my days. I was not on my face for nothing.

How long I lay thus—held in Christ's embrace, confessing my sins, receiving his love—I do not know. However, when the great transaction was finally concluded, the weight of his presence began to lift. As it did, I regained consciousness of my surroundings and soon realized that Joe was gone. So I arose—visibly shaken, I'm sure—and sought him out. When at last I found him, I sheepishly asked what had happened to me.

"What happened?" he replied, with good-natured incredulity. "Brother, you just got saved!"

It was more of the signature DAPC bluntness, and once again it registered as a shock to my system. Yet deep down I knew he was right. For on this night, everything had indeed changed. Once and for all, I had exited the shadowy world of pantheism and entered the sunlit world of the Bible. Like the youth at the DAPC, it was a plainspoken world, where men talked bluntly about God and Satan, good and evil, heaven and hell, saved and unsaved. To a recovering mystic, it did indeed sound strange. But it was a world I would have to get used to, for it was the world in which I now lived.

After thanking Joe and arranging to visit with him again, I left the building. Outside, the air was warm and the sky cloudless. I stopped, looked up, scanned the stars, and realized with amazement that I had just met the One who created them all. How could I get to know him better? Would there be more experiences like this? What did he have in store for my future? Yet even as such questions multiplied in my mind, one thing—like the stars above—was already fixed and crystal clear: I had come the end of my journey. I had sought the truth and found it, I had sought for God and found him, and I had sought and found them both in the God-Man, Jesus Christ. He was the end of the line. Henceforth, there would be no new teachers, no greener spiritual grass, no further religious stops. Yes, I had much to learn, more to experience, and many things to do. But now, after four long and difficult years as a seeker, I rejoiced to know that by God's grace I had become a finder at last.

The Thrill of Them All

Today, more than thirty years later, I look back with amazement at all that has flowed, river-like, from the fountain of that one evening. I was soon baptized. I had the joy of seeing Linda come to faith in Jesus. Around the same time my brother, his wife, and Linda's sister also entered the Lord's fold. I began to meet and walk with my new family in Christ: a skilled and patient pastor, a close circle of new Christian friends, and a loving church family—all of whom stood by me during a long and exceedingly difficult season of spiritual healing.

When I finally realized that conjugal "entanglement" and the pleasures of domesticity were actually God's idea, Linda and I were married. There was work (in another bakery!), and later seminary, and later still a growing family, along with a miscellany of jobs and ministries by which I have tried to serve the Lord down through the years. And so, I trust, my life in Christ will continue: service, struggle, occasional failure, eventual victory—always by his grace, only by his grace, even to the end.

And the end, for us "baby-boomers," is not so far way. Indeed, these days I find myself thinking of it often, and also of the words to an old song we enjoyed many years ago:

> When my life is through,
> and the angels ask me to recall,
> the thrill of them all,
> I will tell them
> I remember you.

With wonder and gratitude, I find that I can sing this song with true gusto, for already I am quite clear about my own "thrill of them all."

But first, let me tell you what it will *not* be.

Most certainly it will not be my "career"—and odd, serpentine affair whose mark upon the sands of time will likely disappear mere seconds after I do. Nor will it be the rich years with my dear wife and our five precious children, though the thrills they have brought me are more than the hairs of my head and the sands of the seashore. Nor will it be the warm memories of fellowship with those few men whom I reckon as true bosom friends. It will not even be my humble but cherished insights into the Word of God, or the delightful opportunities I have had to share them with eager and appreciative students of Scripture.

No, for me the thrill of them all will always be that fateful Friday night at the DAPC, when the Unknown God became my heavenly Father; when he called for the best robe, put a ring on my finger, and crowned a poor, faltering philosopher with the true wisdom from above; when he granted a muddle-headed mystic that he should be lifted up into the waiting arms of his beloved Son, and thereby ushered once for all into the presence, knowledge, and family of the living God.

And now, dear fellow seeker, please hear well these few closing words. As long as eternity rolls, I will gladly confess to anyone willing to listen that my search for God was really his search for me. It was, as the Bible likes to put it, a gift, lest any man should boast. Yet for this very reason I do not hesitate to say, even now, that my erstwhile search for spiritual truth and reality was by far the noblest and most meaningful thing I ever did with my life. I am pleased and proud to have given myself to it, and heartily commend it to each and every soul.

For if, on that soon-coming day, I should be privileged to hear the Savior's words, "Well done, good and faithful servant," I will know exactly what he has in mind. He will have in mind the thrill of them all: the years I took—and the night I passed—the test.

APPENDICES

APPENDIX 1

TRADITIONAL EVIDENCES FOR THE DIVINE INSPIRATION OF THE BIBLE

THE CHART BELOW lists the main traditional evidences for the divine inspiration of the Bible. According to Christ and his apostles, the Spirit of Truth uses these evidences to bear witness to the truth of the Bible, to assure seekers that this is indeed the very Word of God (John 15:26, 16:13, Romans 10:17, 16:25ff, 1 Thess. 2:13). Numbers 1, 4, 5, 6, 7, 10, and 11 comprise the *internal evidences* of divine inspiration, since these are found within the Bible itself. Numbers 2, 3, 8, 9, and 12 comprise the *external evidences*, since these direct our attention to phenomena beyond the Bible that tend to confirm its message. In the course of our journey, I have emphasized evidence number 1, the supernatural unity of the Bible, partly because it includes several of the others (4, 5, 7, and 10), and partly because Jesus and the apostles seemed to like this evidence best of all (Luke 24:44-48, John 5:39, 45-47, Romans 5:25-27, 1 Peter 1:10-12). However, all the evidences are important, and all may reasonably be expected to surround the book that rightfully calls itself the Word of God (Mark 7:13, Luke 11:28, John 10:35, Acts 18:11, Romans 10:17, Revelation 1:2).

TRADITIONAL EVIDENCES FOR THE DIVINE INSPIRATION OF THE BIBLE

1. Supernatural unity

2. Historical accuracy

3. Scientific accuracy

4. Fulfilled types and prophecies

5. Philosophical depth

6. Moral grandeur

7. Literary beauty

8. Life-changing power

9. Civilizing influence

10. Testimony of Christ and the biblical authors

11. Trustworthiness of Christ and the biblical authors
    A. Character
    B. Sacrifice
    C. Miraculous attestation

12. Providential preservation
    A. Abundance of biblical manuscripts
    B. Quality of biblical manuscripts

APPENDIX 2

THE UNITY OF THE BIBLE

MANY BELIEVE THAT the multi-layered, Christ-centered unity of the Bible is the pre-eminent proof of its divine inspiration, authority, and trustworthiness. In this appendix, I offer a few words about the nature and spiritual significance of the phenomenon of unity. Then, in the outline that follows, I summarize various ways in which the Bible displays this telling characteristic.

The phenomenon of unity is inseparable from the phenomenon of *order*. We cannot behold unity unless we see it in an order of some kind. Webster defines an order as *a collection of component parts that has been integrated into a system by means of a definite plan*. A strand of DNA, a cell, a flower, an eye, an ear, a brain—all are examples of naturally occurring orders. They are collections of component parts, integrated into fantastically complex, beautiful, and functional systems according to a definite plan. Just to look at them is to know these orders could not possibly have arisen by accident. Self-evidently, they require and reveal a divine Orderer. Thus, they constitute one of the great proofs for the existence of a rational and powerful supreme being, a divine creator and preserver who is manifestly at work in the natural world.

The Bible too is an order, though of a different kind. Like an object in the fog, its orderliness requires some forward momentum on our part—some time and study—to be seen clearly. But if we are willing to spend the time and do the study, we will soon realize that—like the physical objects mentioned above—its many component parts are also woven into a fantastically complex, beautiful, and functional system by means of a rational plan. In fact, over time—and through God's gracious work of illumination—the Bible's unity will not only become evident, but compelling. Henceforth, it will no longer be possible to view this book as a random collection of Jewish myths and musings. Rather, we will see it as a *revelatory order*—the purposeful creation of a divine revealer of truth, reaching out in love to the nations. In other words, we will see the Bible as a gift from the unknown god, a gift in which he discloses not only his existence, wisdom, power, and goodness, *but also the much-needed and much-sought answers to the questions of life.*

The outline below is designed to display concisely the architecture and implications of the unity of the Bible. May it inspire you to keep walking through the fog until you behold that unity for yourself!

THE MANY-LAYERED CHRIST-CENTERED UNITY OF THE BIBLE

I. **MULTIPLICITY**
   A. 66 different books
   B. Written in 3 different languages (Hebrew, Aramaic, Greek)
   C. In 8 different literary genres
   D. By about 40 different authors
   E. Over the space of about 1600 years (ca. 1500 B.C. to 90 A.D.)
   F. Concerning thousands of persons, places, things, events, teachings, warnings, precepts, and promises

II. **UNITY**
   A. *One story* (the creation, fall, and redemption of man and the cosmos)
   B. About *one God* (the triune Yahweh: Father, Son and Holy Spirit)
   C. Administering *one plan of salvation* (an eternal covenant between God and man, veiled in the Old Testament, unveiled in the New)
   D. **Centered around *one Person* (the Redeemer, Jesus Christ: Divine-Human Prophet, Priest, and King)**
   E. Who is attested by *one (large and diverse) body of signs*
      1. Signs surrounding Jesus' birth
      2. Angelic visitation and testimony
      3. Theophany
      4. Miracles
      5. The Resurrection
      6. OT Messianic types

7. OT Messianic prophecies
8. The Church
F. Worshiped by *one people* (believing Jews and Gentiles of the past, present, and future)
G. According to *one (clear and comprehensive) worldview* (i.e., biblical answers to the ultimate questions of life)

III. IMPLICATIONS OF UNITY: THE BIBLE IS…
A. Divinely inspired (given by God through inspired men, 2 Tim. 3:16-17)
B. Inerrant (true in all it affirms, John 10:35, 17:17)
C. Complete (no more scriptural revelations to come, Eph. 2:19-22, Jude 1:3, Rev. 22:18-19)
D. Trustworthy (Mt. 7:24-28)
E. Authoritative (Mt. 7:29)
F. Sure to be Preserved (Mt. 24:36)
G. Sure to be Recognized as God's Word (Luke 24:45, 1 Thess. 2:13)
H. Infallible (certain to accomplish what it was sent out to do, Isaiah 55:11, Col. 1:3-6)

For further study, see Dean Davis, "One Shot, One Book, One God," *Christian Research Journal*, Vol. 27, No. 05, 2004. Available online at *www.equip.org*.

APPENDIX 3

TEN SIGNS OF A TEACHER COME FROM GOD

IN PART 2 of our journey, we examined a large and diverse body of supernatural signs, all of which point to Jesus of Nazareth and lend great credibility to his own testimony that he is God's appointed Teacher for the human race. We also saw that among all world religions, Christianity alone buttresses its truth claims by means of an appeal to God-given evidence: *the evidence of the signs*. For ease of reference—and because of its great importance to seekers—I have summarized this evidence under the ten categories found in the outline below.

TEN SIGNS OF A TEACHER COME FROM GOD

"The Lord himself will give you a sign!" Isaiah 7:14

I. SIGNS SURROUNDING JESUS' BIRTH
   Angelic Visitations and Testimony (Mt. 1, Lk. 1-2)
   The Virgin Birth (Isaiah 7, Mt. 1, Lk. 1)
   Revival of the Prophetic Spirit (Lk. 1)
   Journey of the Magi (Mt. 2)

II. THE MINISTRY OF JOHN THE BAPTIZER
   Predicted in OT (Isaiah 40, Mal.3)
   Fulfilled in NT (Mt.3, Mk.1, Lk.3, Jn.1,2)

III. ANGELIC VISITATIONS AND TESTIMONY
   Annunciations (Mt. 1, Lk. 1, 2)
   Temptation by Satan (Mt. 4, Lk. 4)
   Encounters with Demons (Mk.1, 5, Lk. 8)
   In Gethsemane (Lk. 22)
   At the Garden Tomb (Mt. 28)
   At the Ascension (Acts 1)

IV. THEOPHANIES
   At Jesus' Baptism (Mt. 3, Jn. 1)
   At Jesus' Transfiguration (Mt. 17, Lk. 9, Pet. 1)

V. MIRACLES
   Various Healings (Mt. 4, 8, 15)
   Exorcisms (Mt. 8, 15, Mk. 5)
   Power over Nature (Mk. 4, 6, Jn. 2)
   Resuscitations (Mt. 9, Lk. 7, Jn. 11)
   Clairvoyance (Mt. 17, Jn. 1)
   Predictive Prophecies (Mt. 24, Mk. 10, Lk. 21)

VI. THE RESURRECTION (Mt. 28, Mk. 16, Lk. 24, Jn. 20, 21)
   Predicted in OT (Psalm 2, 16, Isaiah 53, Hosea 6)
   Predicted by Christ (Mk. 9, 10, Jn. 2)
   Confirmed by Many Witnesses (Acts 1,10, 1 Cor. 15)

TEN SIGNS OF A TEACHER COME FROM GOD

VII. OT CHRISTOPHANIES
To Hagar (Gen. 16)
To Abraham (Gen. 22)
To Jacob (Gen 32)
To Moses (Ex. 4)
To Joshua (Josh 5)
To Daniel (Dan. 3)

VIII. OT MESSIANIC TYPES
Skins for Adam and Eve (Gen. 3; Rom. 3, Rev. 7)
Noah's Ark (Gen. 6-9; 1 Pt. 3, 2 Pt. 3)
Abraham and Isaac (Gen. 22; Heb. 11)
The Passover (Ex. 12; Mt. 26, Jn. 1, 19)
The Bronze Serpent (Num. 21, Jn. 3)
The Stricken Rock (Ex. 17; Jn. 4, 7, 1 Cor. 10)
The Scapegoat (Lev. 16; Heb. 10)
The Cluster of Grapes (Num. 13; Jn. 15)

IX. OT MESSIANIC PROPHECIES
Divine Pre-existence (Isaiah 7, 9, Micah 5; Jn. 1:1-3)
Virgin Birth (Isaiah 7; Mt. 1)
Born in Bethlehem (Micah 5; Mt. 2)
Miraculous Ministry to the Poor (Isaiah 49, 61; Lk. 4, 7)
Atoning Death (Psalm 69, Isaiah 53; Mt. 28)
Resurrection (Psalm 2, 16, Isaiah 53; Mt. 28)
Ascension (Psalm 68, Acts 1)
Heavenly Reign (Psalm 2, 110; Acts 2, 1 Cor. 15)
Second Coming in Glory (Isaiah 63, Mt. 24)
Eternal Dominion (Isaiah 9, Dan. 7; Rev. 11)

X. THE CHURCH
In Word (Mt. 28, Acts 1)
In Deed (Mt. 5)
In Transformed Character (Jn. 3, 2 Cor. 3, Col. 3)
In Perseverance (Mt. 16, Jn. 17)
In Growth (Mt. 13, Jn. 12)

APPENDIX 4

THE BIBLICAL WORLDVIEW

AS WE SAW at different stages of our journey, there is much good evidence to show that the Bible is indeed a trustworthy revelation from God, and that the worldview it proclaims is therefore true. In this appendix I briefly review that evidence, and then offer a chart summarizing the biblical worldview itself.

The Probationary Order

The first line of evidence favorable to the biblical worldview is *the probationary order*. Its elements include: 1) spiritually equipped human beings, 2) challenged by the (innate) questions of life, 3) ignorant of the answers, 4) situated in a manageably messy religious and philosophical world, and 5) free to seek the truth or not.

This complex and richly spiritual order clearly bears witness to a divine Tester, an unknown god in whom we live and move and have our religious and philosophical being. As we saw in chapters 13, 18, and 19, it appears that the LORD God of the Bible is this very being. In times past, he tested most people by revealing himself through nature, conscience, and the (largely unanswered) questions of life. Today he is testing all people by means of a completed revelation, which he gave through Jesus of Nazareth, and which Jesus' Church takes to the nations in the preaching of the gospel.

Who is this Jesus? Why did he come? Is the worldview that he brought to us true? These are the great questions raised by the presence of the gospel in the world. These are the great questions by which the LORD God of Israel now tests all mankind concerning their love of the truth.

The Natural Order

The second evidence favorable to the biblical worldview is *the natural order*. As we saw in chapter 2, this order exhibits dependency, order, and man-centeredness. Accordingly, it too bears witness to an infinite personal Spirit, a transcendent god who is at once powerful, wise, and good. In chapter 9, we saw that the Bible ascribes all these attributes (and more) to the LORD God of Israel, the Maker of heaven and earth.

The Objective Moral Order

The third line evidence is *the objective moral order*. Its elements include: 1) moral absolutes, 2) moral obligation, and 3) a law of moral cause and effect. Self-evidently, this order points to a holy and just Lawgiver, to a divine Moral Governor in whom we (along with our conscience) live and move and have our being. In chapters 9 and 14 we saw that the Bible depicts the LORD God of Israel in precisely this way. Moreover, it goes on to tell us of all that he has done in Christ to reconcile sinful men and women to his moral order, so that it no longer casts them down to eternal punishment, but rather calls them up to an eternal life of righteousness, peace, and joy in fellowship with him.

The (Supernatural) Evidence of the Signs

The fourth line of evidence is *the one large and diverse body of supernatural signs* pointing to, and converging in, Jesus of Nazareth. Very importantly, these signs (listed in Appendix 2) appear all along the highway of salvation history. That is, they appear before, at, and after Jesus' (first) coming into the world. This clearly marks them as the handiwork of a wise and sovereign God working through many men in all of history to promote his purposes, rather than as the handiwork of a few men working at a particular moment in history to promote their own purposes. As we saw in Part 2 of our journey, the one body of supernatural, Christ-centered signs is altogether unique in world religion. More than any other category of evidence, this one singles out Jesus of Nazareth as God's appointed Teacher to all mankind—and as much more, besides.

The (Providential) Evidence of History

The fifth line of evidence favorable to the biblical worldview is *the large body of literary and historical evidence that corroborates the historicity of the NT Jesus*. Unlike the signs, this evidence is not patently supernatural. It is, however, providential; indeed, it is so dramatically providential that in the end it appears to be supernatural. In other words, this evidence clearly reveals the hand of a sovereign God working through men and events to ensure the preservation and credibility of his testimony to Jesus, found in the four Gospels and the book of Acts.

As we saw in chapter 7, this evidence begins with the quality, quantity, and antiquity of the NT manuscripts. It includes the well-documented history of the emergence of the NT canon. It includes the many ways in which the NT record of Christ's life outstandingly meets the traditional criteria for trustworthy historical writing (i.e., the integrity and independence of the witnesses, the quality and harmony of their testimony, extra-biblical corroboration, etc.). And finally, it includes the intuitiveness and hopefulness of the miracles ascribed to Jesus. As one layer of such evidence descends upon another, it becomes increasingly difficult, if not impossible, to dismiss the NT Jesus as a mere legend.

Jesus' Answers to the Questions of Life

The final line of evidence consists of *Jesus' answers to the questions of life*. As we saw in Part 3 of our journey, they are quite comprehensive. That is, Jesus gives us richly nuanced responses to each and every ultimate question. Moreover, in the eyes of many people, his answers are intuitive, reasonable, "right," and hopeful—and far more so than those of any other religious teacher or world religion.

Conclusion

Is Jesus of Nazareth God's appointed Teacher? Has he really given us the one true worldview? In order to find out, each seeker will have to examine and evaluate these six lines of evidence for himself.

As he begins to do so, it is important that he ever bear in mind what we repeatedly saw in Parts 3 and 4 of our journey: Jesus offers us something more—and more precious—than the one true worldview. He offers us himself. And with himself, he offers us his Spirit, his Father, his pardon, his righteousness, his joy, his peace, his love, and his glorious Kingdom, both now and forever.

May these rich promises move every seeker to take the gospel test with all their heart, soul, mind, and strength—and to keep on taking it until they have passed!

THE BIBLICAL WORLD VIEW
Answers to Questions of Life

1. What is the ultimate reality?

The living God; an infinite personal Spirit; a holy trinity: Father, Son, and Holy Spirit. God is separate from his creation, but intimately and intricately related to it.

Mark 12:29-30; John 4:23-24, 14:15-18, 23-24, 16:13-15; Acts 17, 1 Pet. 1:1-2

2. What is the origin of the universe, life, and man?

The triune God created a good, fully formed, fully functioning, geocentric universe, especially for man, in six literal days.

Gen. 1, 2; Mark 10:5-10; John 1:1-3; 1 Cor. 8:6; Col. 1:15-18; Heb. 1:2, 11:1:3

3. What went wrong? Why are evil, suffering, and death in the world?

Adam's disobedience in Eden opened the door to indwelling sin, guilt, Satanic influence, a curse on nature, physical and spiritual death, and the peril of eternal punishment.

Gen. 3; Luke 4:6, John 8:44, Rom. 5:12, 8:18-21, Rev. 21:4, 22:3

4. What, if anything, can be done?

God's Part: God sent his Son to be the Last Adam, the holy prophet, priest, and king of his people. By his righteous life, atoning death, and resurrection, Christ did what the first Adam failed to do, and undid what the first Adam had done, thereby securing rescue, restoration, and eternal life for all who believe.

Mt. 23:8; Mark 10:45; John 3:16, 18:37; 1 Cor. 15:20-28; Rom. 5; Col. 1:13

Man's Part: Come to Christ personally, in repentance and faith; receive him, through prayer, as Savior and Lord; live with him day by day as his obedient friend and disciple.

Mt. 11:28-30, 28:18f; John 1:12, 3:16f, 6:29, 15:1f; Rom. 3:21f, Eph. 2:8-10, 1 John 1:9

THE BIBLICAL WORLD VIEW

5. What is the meaning of life?

To know, enjoy, please, and glorify God through obedience to his will, especially by receiving his Son and co-laboring with him in the advancement of his kingdom

Mt. 4:4, 5:14-16, 11:28f; Mark 10:28-31; John 3:16, 4:27f, 8:29, 15:1f, 17:3, Eph. 1:11-12

6. How shall we live?

According to God's will; by coming to his Son for pardon, spiritual renewal, and guidance for fruitful living.

Mt. 7:24-29, 9:36, 11:28f, 17:5, 28:18ff; John 3:16, 14:15, 15:1f, Rev. 3:18

7. What happens when we die?

The human spirit departs to Heaven or Hades, there to await the bodily resurrection at the end of the age.

Luke 16:19-21; Phil. 1:19-26; James 2:26; Rev. 6:9, 20:4

8. Where is history heading?

Towards the consummation: the bodily return of Christ in glory, the resurrection of the dead, the last judgment, the end of the world by fire, and the creation of new heavens and a new earth, the eternal home of the redeemed.

Mt. 13:40-43, 24, 25; John 5:24-29; Rom. 8:18-25; 1 Cor. 15; 1 Thess. 4; 2 Thess. 1, 2; 2 Pet. 3; Rev. 20:11-14, 21:9-22:5.

9. How can we find trustworthy answers to the questions of life?

Turn to God's appointed Teacher, Jesus Christ, who directs us to the Old and New Testaments for a full and final revelation of God's truth.

Mt. 23:8; Luke 24:44-49; John 14:6, 26, 15:1f, 18:37; Eph. 2:20, Jude 3.

APPENDIX 5

THE NATURALISTIC WORLDVIEW

THE CHART BELOW provides a concise summary of the modern naturalistic worldview. In evaluating this worldview, seekers should bear in mind the following three points discussed earlier in our journey.

First, naturalism is based upon the unprovable assumption that there is no god. For the naturalist, this assumption entails that the time/space/energy-matter continuum is the sole reality, and therefore the ultimate reality.

Secondly, it is primarily the naturalist's atheistic premise—and not logic, math, or science—that shapes or dictates his answers to the other questions of life. Moreover, it is this same premise—and not logic or hard evidence—that causes him to rule out divine revelation as a valid source of knowledge about the questions of life.

Finally, the presupposed atheism of the naturalist is sharply challenged by numerous features of the natural, moral, and probationary orders, all of which point to the existence, activity, and character of an unknown god; to an infinite personal Spirit who acts as the creator, sustainer, moral governor, and tester of all. Additional evidence—largely found in the Bible—indicates that this unknown god and the LORD God of Israel are one.

It appears, then, that there are many good reasons to doubt the naturalist's bedrock metaphysical assumption, and therefore the truthfulness of the worldview that he has built upon it.

For further study of the naturalistic worldview, see John Byl, *The Divine Challenge* (Banner of Truth, 2006); W. L. Craig and J. P. Moreland, *Naturalism: A Critical Analysis* (Routledge, 2000); Dean Davis, *In Search of the Beginning* (Pleasant Word, 2007); and David Noebel, *Understanding the Times* (Harvest House, 1997).

THE NATURALISTIC WORLDVIEW
Answers to Questions of Life

1. What is the ultimate reality?

Eternally existing matter; the time/space/energy-matter continuum, in one form or another. There are no supernatural beings (gods, angels, demons, souls, spiritual realms or forces).

2. What is the origin of the universe, life, and man?

The universe has no absolute beginning, but is eternal. About 15 billion years ago, it existed as a tiny "singularity." With the Big Bang, cosmic evolution began. Since then, time, chance, natural law, spontaneous generation, random mutation, and natural selection have produced the world as we now know it.

3. What went wrong? Why are evil, suffering, and death in the world?

Nothing went wrong. Natural evil, moral evil, suffering, and death are simply unpleasant parts of the way things are.

4. What, if anything, can be done?

Unless aliens arrive to help us, man must do whatever he can through science, technology, and social and political progress.

5. What is the meaning of life?

Human life has no transcendent meaning. Therefore, man must choose or create his own meaning: pleasure, prosperity, progress, etc.

6. How shall we live?

Since there is no god and no moral absolutes, man should live by whatever values he deems best for the survival, health, and pleasure of the human race.

THE NATURALISTIC WORLDVIEW

7. What happens when we die?

There is no soul or afterlife. Consciousness is a by-product of electro-chemical activity in the brain. When the brain dies, self-consciousness is extinguished. At death, the lights go out forever.

8. Where is history heading?

Probably towards cosmic heat death (linear view), possibly towards serial Big Bangs, followed by serial recurrences of cosmic evolution (cyclical view).

9. How can we find trustworthy answers to the questions of life.

Since god does not exist, naturalistic philosophy and scientific method supply all real knowledge.

Instances

Atomism, Materialism, Darwinism, Marxism-Leninism, Maoism, Secular Humanism

Exponents

Thales, Democritus, Lucretius, Hobbes, Darwin, Huxley, Nietzsche, Marx, Lenin, Mao, Crane, Dewey, London, Russell, Freud, Asimov, Skinner, Sagan, Gould, Kurtz, Nagel, Dawkins, Dennett

APPENDIX 6

THE PANTHEISTIC WORLDVIEW: EASTERN RELIGION

THE CHART BELOW summarizes the classic pantheistic worldview of the three main Eastern religions: Hinduism, Buddhism, and (to a certain extent) Taoism. There are, of course, important doctrinal differences between these faiths, a significant fact that logically calls into question the trustworthiness of at least two of them. Nevertheless, it is fair to say that in general they all answer the questions of life in the same basic manner.

At first glance, the classic pantheistic worldview seems to be more intuitive than the naturalist's. This is because it posits a *spiritual* ultimate reality, one that could conceivably explain the spiritual characteristics of the natural, moral, and probationary orders. However, by closely examining the pantheist's answers to the questions of life—and by keeping in mind what we have learned in our journey—seekers will find that in fact this is not the case.

For example, classical pantheism teaches that the ultimate reality is an infinite *impersonal* Spirit. But do the three orders that we studied really bear witness to an *impersonal* divine Spirit? Indeed, is an *impersonal* god even conceivable, let alone intuitively satisfying?

Again, classical pantheism teaches that in "the beginning" (a beginning that occurs over and again throughout eternity), Big Mind "fell" into a multitude of centers of conscious (sentient beings). This entails that: 1) the "physical" world is really a dream in our mind, and that our mind is really a dream in Big Mind; 2) all is Mind, all is god; 3) man is god. How intuitive are these assertions? Do the natural, moral, and probationary orders really point us in this direction?

Or again, classical pantheism teaches that when Big Mind fell into a multitude of sentient beings, "he" also fell into bondage to a *dualistic* consciousness of good and evil, pleasure and pain, life and death, etc.

Ethically, this entails that: 1) Big Mind is the *perpetrator* of moral and natural evil, 2) Big Mind is the *victim* of moral and natural evil, and 3) Big Mind *is* both good and evil. How well do these assertions harmonize with what we know about the unknown god from the objective moral order? Also, how does the god of pantheism differ from the God of the Bible on this score?

By asking questions like these as they work their way through the chart below, seekers will find that pantheistic answers to the other questions of life are just a problematic as the ones we have touched on here.

I close, however, with a *caveat*. While admitting that pantheism is disturbingly counterintuitive, unreasonable, ethically problematic, and fundamentally hopeless, thoughtful philosophers nevertheless understand that this worldview cannot be disproved by the unaided human mind. *It can, however, be disproved by a trustworthy divine revelation that teaches to the contrary.* And we have seen that the Bible is just such a revelation. Unlike the pantheistic scriptures (which do not even agree among themselves), its harmonious truth-claims are backed up by a compelling body of supernatural signs—a unified system of clear, God-given evidences by which we may reasonably and confidently believe that its doctrines are true. Moreover, its truth claims are also far more intuitive, reasonable, right, and hopeful than those of classical pantheism—and so all the more credible.

In short, the evidence convincingly declares that the Bible is true. But if the Bible is true, then pantheistic religions and philosophies are most certainly false.

THE PANTHEISTIC WORLDVIEW: EASTERN RELIGION
Answers to Questions of Life

1. **What is the ultimate reality?**

    An infinite, impersonal Spirit: Big Mind, Brahman, the Tao, Gaia, etc.

2. **What is the origin of the universe, life, and man?**

    A veil of illusion (*maya*) somehow fell over Big Mind, thereby "creating" a multitude of centers of consciousness, or sentient beings. These live on several different planes (of consciousness). The various planes, or worlds, are really dreams going on in Big Mind.

3. **What went wrong? Why are evil, suffering, and death in the world?**

    The fall of Big Mind produced consciousness; consciousness is always "dualistic." Therefore, sentient beings are always entangled in dualities: subject-object, good-evil, pleasure-suffering, life-death, etc.

4. **What, if anything, can be done?**

    Wake up! Sentient beings must transcend the suffering of dualistic consciousness through Enlightenment, Self-Realization, (re)union with Big Mind in its original state.

5. **What is the meaning of life?**

    To attain release from dualistic consciousness and the cycle of reincarnation (*samsara*) through complete union with Big Mind. The goal of life is Enlightenment, Nirvana, Yoga (union), Satori, etc.

6. **How shall we live?**

    In detachment from the illusory phenomena of this world; in harmony with nature; with respect for the law of karma (i.e., reward for good deeds, retribution for bad); by practicing mindfulness and meditation.

THE PANTHEISTIC WORLDVIEW: EASTERN RELIGION

7. What happens when we die?

At death, sentient beings experience consciousness on another plane, where (under reward or retribution for their karma) they await reincarnation upon the earth-plane. After many incarnations, they finally experience absorption into Big Mind.

8. Where is history heading?

After many billions of years, all sentient beings are absorbed back into Big Mind. Then Big Mind falls again, suffers again, struggles again, and awakens again. This cycle recurs forever.

9. How can we find trustworthy answers to the questions of life.

Turn to enlightened men: avatars, boddhisattvas, gurus, Zen masters, etc. Turn to the various pantheistic scriptures that they have written. Practice meditation.

Instances
Hinduism, Taoism, Buddhism

Exponents
Hinduism: Ramakrishna, Vivekananda, Aurobindo
Taoism: Lao Tzu, Chuang Tzu
Buddhism: Gotama, Milarepa, Wumen, Dogen, Suzuki

Representative Scriptures
Hinduism: *Upanishads, Bhagavad Gita*
Taoism: *Tao Te Ching, Chuang Tzu*
Buddhism: *Diamond Sutra, Heart Sutra, The Gateless Gate*, etc.

APPENDIX 7

THE PANTHEISTIC WORLDVIEW: THE NEW AGE

THE NEW AGE worldview is essentially an effort to synthesize ancient Eastern pantheism with modern Western evolutionism. As such, it has the same basic strength as classical pantheism: an underlying spirituality which at first glance seems to make sense of the natural, moral, and probationary orders. However, it also has the same weaknesses. For example, it fails to affirm what any viable spiritual worldview must affirm: an infinite *personal* god who rules over his creation. Moreover, by identifying its impersonal god with the phenomenal world, New Age theology, just like its classical counterpart, makes "him" both the author and the victim of moral and natural evil.

Importantly, the New Ager's attempt to embrace Western evolutionism does not enhance, but rather detracts from, the credibility of his worldview. In part, this is because the case for long-age cosmic evolution is so weak, while the case for recent biblical creation is so strong (see chapter 10). More important, however, is the fact that the New Age synthesis completely fails on metaphysical and theological grounds. This is because cosmic evolution requires human consciousness to evolve from some kind of pre-existing "stuff" (e.g., energy), whereas pantheism requires that all kinds of "stuff" be mere phenomena (i.e., dreams) in the mind of already existent sentient beings. In other words, it is impossible even to conceive, let alone to prove, the New Age origin of the universe, life, and man. Also, the New Age synthesis desperately needs what it cannot affirm: a *personal* god who plans and superintends the entire evolutionary process, from beginning to end.

For these and other reasons, it appears that New Age pantheism is even less intuitive and less credible than its classical Eastern counterparts.

For further discussion of pantheistic worldviews, see J. Ankerberg and J. Weldon, *Encyclopedia of New Age Beliefs* (Harvest House, 1996); D. Davis,

In Search of the Beginning (Pleasant Word, 2007); D. Noebel, *Understanding the Times* (Harvest House, 1994); J. Sire, *The Universe Next Door* (IVP, 1997).

THE PANTHEISTIC WORLDVIEW: THE NEW AGE
Answers to Questions of Life

1. What is the ultimate reality?

An infinite, impersonal Spirit (Big Mind); or, in panpsychism, a two-sided ultimate reality that is part mind, part matter (Mind/Matter).

2. What is the origin of the universe, life, and man?

Long ago, Big Mind turned itself into the evolving stuff of the universe, thereby launching an evolutionary journey to self-realization and global god-consciousness. Or, in panpsychism, eternal Mind/Matter for some reason begins to evolve towards god-consciousness.

3. What went wrong? Why are evil, suffering, and death in the world?

Nothing went wrong. Evil, suffering, and death are necessary but temporary elements in the evolutionary ascent to god-consciousness and universal perfection.

4. What, if anything, can be done?

Wake up! Realize our oneness with Big Mind (or Mind/Matter); cooperate with the evolutionary thrust of the universe; promote religious and social unity.

5. What is the meaning of life?

To awaken to one's own divine nature; to bring in the New Age of global unity and god-consciousness.

6. How shall we live?

Use meditation, creative visualization, and positive thinking to bring in world unity, health, and prosperity. Tolerate all views; do not judge. Live simply, mindfully, unselfishly, in harmony with nature.

APPENDIX 7: THE PANTHEISTIC WORLDVIEW: THE NEW AGE

THE PANTHEISTIC WORLDVIEW: THE NEW AGE

7. What happens when we die?

The self experiences consciousness on another plane, where (under reward or retribution for its karma) it awaits reincarnation upon earth so as to continue its evolutionary ascent to god-consciousness.

8. Where is history heading?

Toward a New Age of global god-consciousness, unity, health, and prosperity. Is this Age eternal? Will the evolutionary journey recur eternally? No one knows for sure.

9. How can we find trustworthy answers to the questions of life.

From ancient pantheistic scriptures; from "ascended masters" living on other planes, whose wisdom is mediated to us by "channelers" (i.e. psychics); from natural science and depth psychology; from personal mystical experience.

Instances
Theosophy, New Age philosophy, New Age Spiritism

Exponents
H. Blavatsky, A. Besant, J. Krishnamurti, A. Watts, R. Alpert (Ram Dass), M. Ferguson, F. Capra, D. Chopra, D. Spangler, J. White, K. Wilber, G. Zukav, E. Laszlo, P. Russell, C. De Quincy, S. Groff

Popular New Age Works:
The Phenomenon of Man, (de Chardin), *The Future of Man* (de Chardin), *The Aquarian Conspiracy* (Ferguson), *Revelation: The Birth of a New Age* (Spangler), *The Seat of the Soul* (Zukav), *The Dancing Wu Li Masters* (Zukav), *The Turning Point* (Capra), *A Course in Miracles* (Schucman), *Creative Visualization* (Gwain), *A Brief History of Everything* (Wilber)

APPENDIX 8

THE ISLAMIC WORLDVIEW

BECAUSE OF THE recent global resurgence of militant Islam, this appendix includes not only a lengthy chart summarizing the Islamic worldview, but also a fairly detailed evaluation of this large and growing theistic religion. Apart from parenthetical references to the Qur'an, my evaluation is not annotated. For a closer look at my source material, readers may consult the two excellent books noted at the end of this essay.

A Critical Evaluation of Islam

Islam is the world's second largest monotheistic religion. As such, it posits a single infinite personal Spirit (Allah) as the ultimate reality. This puts Islam in a good position to explain the natural, moral, and probationary orders, all of which point to just such a god.

Moreover, one can make a case that Mohammed attempted this very thing. For example, he often appealed to nature as a "sign" of the existence and power of Allah (17:44). He ascribed to Allah all the elements of the objective moral order: moral absolutes, moral obligation, and a law of moral cause and effect. And finally, he definitely viewed life as a test: a test of one's obedience to the revealed will of Allah. Thus, the Islamic worldview harmonizes fairly well with the three orders that point to the existence and activity of an unknown personal god.

There are, however, several additional considerations that should give seekers pause.

First, the Quranic treatment of the three orders is not nearly as extensive as that found in the Bible. More importantly still, the treatment that it does offer is drawn largely *from* the Bible. As a result, it is hard to find much that is innovative in the Quranic "revelations" about the three orders, while it is easy to see that they lack the theological richness and nuance of their biblical counterparts.

This fact is particularly evident with respect to the Islamic portrayal of the probationary order. As the chart indicates, the Qur'an makes life a simple test of our obedience to Allah's will, an obedience motivated by the fear of hell and the hope of heaven. The Bible, on the other hand, makes life a test of our love of spiritual truth, which, if passed, leads to an obedience motivated by love and gratitude to God, who, through Christ, has *already* delivered his people from hell, and granted them the gift of the (present) knowledge of himself, with the assurance of heaven besides. More on this below.

Like Judaism and Christianity, Islam also affirms the necessity of divine revelation for attaining trustworthy answers to the questions of life. In particular, it teaches that those revelations are found only in the Qur'an, since the teachings of the former prophets (including Moses and Jesus) have been lost, corrupted, and/or superceded. In short, Islam contends that Mohammed is god's appointed Teacher—the only one sent by Allah to all the nations—and that the Qur'an is his appointed book.

There are, however, several major problems with this view. Let us briefly survey each.

Problems With the Prophet

Muslims assert that Mohammed is the world's supreme prophet, bringing a full and final revelation of Allah's will. There are at least three good reasons to doubt the truth of this claim.

First, Mohammed is without attesting supernatural signs. As he himself admitted, he performed no miracles, even though he was pressed to do so by his contemporaries (2:23, 3:183, 4:153, 6:8-9, 17:88). This omission is all the more significant when we learn from the Qur'an that in times past Allah frequently confirmed the words of his messengers with miracles, and did so lavishly in the case of Jesus (2:87, 253; 5:10, 110, 112-114). Also, despite Muslim claims to the contrary, there is not a single Old or New Testament prophecy that points clearly to the person or work of Mohammed. In other words, the Bible is clearly a Christ-centered book, and just as clearly *not* a Mohammed-centered book. We see, then, why Mohammed lifted up the

APPENDIX 8: THE ISLAMIC WORLDVIEW

Qur'an as his one and only "miraculous" sign. He had to, since he had no others (3:181-4, 4:153, 6:8-9).

Secondly, Mohammed was a man of less than exemplary character. On this point, Islam itself teaches what common sense affirms: a true prophet must be sinless, or at least without major defects in character and behavior. Did Mohammed meet these criteria? For their part, critics cannot help but respond by citing a number of well-documented historical facts that raise serious questions.

For example, Mohammed had about 15 wives, though his own Qur'an limited a man to four (33:50). Some of these wives he ignored, others plotted against him, and one he took to himself when she was only nine years old.

After initially inculcating religious tolerance, Mohammed later expelled recalcitrant Jews, Christians, and pagans from their homelands, or else slew them outright. He subdued entire tribes at the edge of the sword. He raided caravans. He broke a peace treaty with the Meccans. He fought during the holy month, contrary to Quranic law. He endorsed lying, oath breaking, torture, and assassination, all in the name of Allah.

The Meccans, unimpressed with his claims to the prophetic office, charged him with plagiarizing Jewish, Christian, and pagan sources—a reasonable enough surmise, given that he frequently traveled as a merchant among all three of these people groups (16:103, 25:4f). Also, one of his early scribes, a man named Abdollah, eventually foreswore Islam, claiming that Mohammed had agreed to "improving" (i.e., changing) Allah's revelations at his (Abdollah's) suggestion.

Importantly, it appears that Mohammed himself was not unaware of his own moral lapses, frankly confessing that he too was a sinner who needed Allah's mercy (40:55, 47:19, 48:2). His life therefore stands in sharp contrast to the example, teaching, historical influence, and personal testimony of him who said, "Which of you convicts me of sin" (John 8:46)?

Finally, Mohammed's call and subsequent behavior evokes a strong suspicion of demonic influence. This suspicion arose early on, *even in Mohammed's own mind.* When the angel Gabriel first came to him, he (Gabriel) pressed him three times with a coverlet, "so tightly that I thought it was death." After this terrifying experience, Mohammed sought the comfort of his wife, Khadija, who tried to assuage his doubts about the source of the revelation and his fears of demonic deception.

Once, in order to divine from Allah the truth about the faithfulness of his wife Aishah, Mohammed fell into convulsions, and then, before a terrified audience, awoke from his trance with beads of sweat covering his forehead.

On yet another occasion, he set forth a revelation permitting intercession to three pagan deities. Realizing from his disciple's shocked reaction that he had just contradicted earlier sayings condemning idolatry, he later declared that Satan had deceived him, that the offending "Satanic verses" were henceforth canceled, and that new ones had been given to supplant the old.

Finally, it is noteworthy that Mohammed claimed to speak to the dead, and that he sometimes prayed for the dead in a local cemetery.

In contrast to all this, we learn from the NT that Jesus expressed no doubt whatsoever about the divine source of his revelations, heard directly from his Father (rather than angelic mediators), and took great pleasure (rather than terror) in doing so. Much the same was true of the other biblical prophets, who, it should be noted, were strictly forbidden to engage in spiritism (Deut. 18:9-14).

Summing up, we have seen that Mohammed has no body of supernatural signs to attest to his revelations, that he was not a man of outstanding moral character, and that there is a definite suspicion of demonic activity in his life and religious teaching. Is it likely that the unknown god would appoint such a man as this to be his Teacher to the entire human race?

Problems With the Qur'an

These considerations lead us to a discussion of the Qur'an itself. Muslim apologists regard this book as nothing less than a miracle; a full and final divine revelation for all mankind; a "necessary attribute" of Allah's own mind; a revelation perfectly transmitted through the angel Gabriel and the apostle Mohammed, perfectly preserved for all time (39:1-2, 43:3-4, 55:1-2, 85:21-22).

But again, there are good reasons to doubt these lofty claims. Here, I will focus on two.

First, the traditional evidences for the divine inspiration of the Qur'an do not stand up under scrutiny. For example, it is argued that the beautiful literary style, diction, and structure of the Qur'an are quite miraculous, and therefore proofs of its divine inspiration. But literary excellence hardly qualifies as a miracle, still less as a proof of divine inspiration. Furthermore, many question the Qur'an's literary quality, citing its "obtuse" (i.e., non-chronological) arrangement, its many grammatical irregularities, and its ponderous and confusing diction. Also, if literary excellence points to divine inspiration, then surely the Bible is even more divinely inspired, since it is a much larger book that displays a far greater variety of literary genres, all of which are executed with consummate literary skill.

Again, it is asserted that the Qur'an has been preserved free from change or error since the beginning. Now even if this were true, it would prove neither divine inspiration nor special providential oversight, since

APPENDIX 8: THE ISLAMIC WORLDVIEW

many non-inspired books have been well preserved. But as a matter of fact, it is not true. Prior to Uthman's 7th century recension, there were a number of different versions of the Qur'an in use. Indeed, it was their many discordant readings that led to Uthman's recension in the first place, *and to the mandatory destruction of the all the rest*. This is why Shiite Muslim's, to this very day, allege a tendentious editing of the standard Sunni Qur'an, and why alternative texts of the Qur'an still remain in use.

Muslim apologists also point to what they call the fulfilled prophecies of the Qur'an. These, however, are precious few, and hardly prophetic in the traditional biblical sense. Instead of being detailed predictions of specific historical events, they are largely generic promises, usually of future victories over the unbelievers. Even the Quranic prediction of Rome's forthcoming defeat of Persia is more in the nature of an educated guess than a true prophecy (30:2-4). Most fair-minded investigators would therefore agree that nothing in the Qur'an remotely compares with Daniel's detailed prophecies of the four coming world empires, or with Jesus' minute predictions of his imminent death and resurrection, or with his warning about the destruction of Jerusalem that would soon follow (Dan. 2, 4, Mt. 20:17-19, 24:1ff).

Finally, these same apologists contend that the "unity" or internal consistency of the Qur'an proves its divine inspiration. But again, while internal consistency is doubtless a necessary *mark* of divine inspiration, it cannot be said to *prove* it. Many internally consistent books are not inspired, and some are even full of lies. As a matter of fact, however, the Qur'an is not internally consistent. For example, the infamous "sword verse" authorizing the execution of unbelievers (9:5) contradicts approximately 120 other passages commending religious tolerance (2:256). Some texts affirm that Christians will enter Paradise (2:62, 5:69), others that they will go to hell (3:85, 5:72). One passage enjoins the stoning of adulterers, while another prescribes punishment by 100 stripes (24:2). Mohammed, aware of such contradictions, attempted to solve them by propounding a doctrine of "abrogation," declaring that Allah occasionally sets aside earlier revelations by means of later (2:106). However, this maneuver only aggravated the problem, since he himself had given revelations insisting that there can be no change in Allah's words (10:64, 6:34)!

In passing, it is worth noting here that Caner and Caner have found at least 14 Quranic contradictions, most of which are not resolvable by an appeal to abrogation. For example, surah 2:29 states that Allah created the earth first and then the heavens; surah 79:27-30 says the opposite. Again, surah 21:76 says that all of Noah's family survived the Flood; surah 11:42-43 says that one son drowned. And again, surah 22:47 says that one of Allah's days equals a thousand human years; surah 70:4 says that one such day equals 50,000 years. If, then, internal consistency is a mark of divine inspiration, the evidence speaks loudly against the divine inspiration of the Qur'an.

Secondly, the Bible contradicts the Qur'an—and the Bible does display supernatural evidence of divine inspiration. In the body of *The Test* I have discussed this evidence at great length, placing special emphasis upon the multi-layered, Christ-centered unity of the Bible, a unity that shows itself dramatically in OT Messianic christophanies, types, and prophecies. The Qur'an, being set forth by one man over the space of 23 years, and not by some 40 different men over the space of some 1600 years, displays no such unity, and is therefore without supernatural attestation. This crucial difference entails that when the Qur'an contradicts or speaks against the trustworthiness of the Bible, it is not reasonable to believe those accusations. On the other hand, it also entails that when the Bible contradicts Quranic declarations, it *is* reasonable to believe the Bible.

And the Bible *does* contradict the Qur'an, both in matters of historical fact and doctrine. Caner and Caner again give us a sampling of the former. The Qur'an states, for example, that Pharaoh's wife adopted Moses (28:9); that Christians worship three gods, one of whom is Mary (5:116); that a Samaritan made the golden calf (20:85-97); that Abraham offered Ishmael rather than Isaac as a sacrifice to Allah (37:100-111); that Saul, rather than Gideon, led Israel to war against the Midianites (2:249); and that Judas (or some other surrogate of Jesus) was crucified by Pilate (4:157). Those who know the Bible well know that it belies all of these assertions, and that a number of them involve serious historical anachronisms.

As for matters of doctrine, it is true that the Bible and the Qur'an do display some broad similarities. Both affirm, for example, a monotheistic view of the ultimate reality; a supernatural creation in six days (though one Quranic text says eight); the existence of angels, Satan, and demons; the probation of Adam and Eve in Eden; sin, judgment, and salvation; revelation, prophets, and divine law; and finally, reward and retribution in the world to come.

Nevertheless, despite these broad similarities (which, again, many critics trace to plagiarism), there are actually a great many differences, *and differences that are of great importance*. In our next section, we will look at just a few.

Summing up, in this section we have found that a supernaturally attested Bible contradicts the Qur'an at many points—and that the Qur'an also contradicts itself. How reasonable is it, then, to believe that the Qur'an is divinely inspired?

Problems With Islamic Answers To the Questions of Life

Let us conclude our evaluation of the Islamic worldview with a few words about its answers to what are arguably the four most important questions of life.

The Ultimate Reality

As we have seen, Islam has a fairly intuitive view of the ultimate reality, positing an infinite personal Spirit who, in some respects, is like the God of the Bible. However, for a number of reasons Allah fails to satisfy completely. First, it is impossible to know much about him, since, according to Islamic theology, we ourselves are *not* created in his image and likeness (i.e., he is not like us), and since his many names do not describe his nature, but only his will.

Secondly, the Qur'an portrays Allah as a distant sovereign. He is, above all else, the lofty moral governor of the universe, but never a loving heavenly Father who desires intimate fellowship with his human children. In other words, the Islamic view of the ultimate reality offers seekers no hope of something they deeply long for: inward spiritual union and relationship with their creator. Sufism, with its emphasis upon mystical experience of the imminent Allah, attempts to rectify this defect of Islamic theology, but this sect is generally regarded as being beyond the pale of orthodoxy.

What Went Wrong?

To this troubling question of life, the basic Islamic answer is, "Nothing *went* wrong: Adam's sin did not ruin the human heart, nor did it affect the realm of nature. Rather, things *go* wrong whenever men (or *jinn*) misuse their freedom to transgress Allah's will."

But for a number of reasons, this answer is problematic.

First, by divorcing natural evil from Adam's sin, it makes Allah the *author* of all natural evil, including death.

Secondly, it offers no real explanation for sinful acts. How can "freedom" lead to rape, theft, murder, pride, hatred, or foolishness? How can forgetfulness or carelessness or external pressures do the same? No, evil acts clearly flow from evil passions, passions lodged deep within the human heart, just as the Bible says they do (Mark 7:21f).

Thirdly, this answer trivializes sin, being content to view it only in terms of outward acts of transgression, rather than in terms of *an innate hostility to God that produces outward acts of transgression* (Mt. 7:15-20, Rom. 3:9-20, 8:7). Moreover, it offers no hope of personal deliverance from sin, since it does not even acknowledge that such a principle exists in the human heart.

Finally, this answer severely undermines the possibility of assurance of salvation. Why? Because in tracing sin and guilt exclusively to each individual, Islam leaves each individual alone before Allah, wondering if his good deeds will outweigh his bad on the Day of Judgment. The Bible, on the other hand, traces sin and guilt to the person and work of the first Adam, a bad Head; but it offers each individual salvation through the person and work the last Adam, a good Head. In other words, by propounding a doctrine of representative headship, the Bible makes assurance of salvation possible and available through simple faith in Christ, an all-sufficient source of righteousness and pardon. But because Islam explicitly rejects the doctrine of representative headship, it shuts up Muslims to their own good works, *and therefore to a life of fear that those works are insufficient to save them from the wrath to come.* More on this in a moment.

We find, then, that the Islamic theology of the origin and nature evil is defective at many points—points upon which the Bible not only speaks differently, but far more reasonably and with far greater hope.

What Can Be Done?

On the godward side of the equation, the Islamic solution to the problem of evil, suffering, and death is Paradise, which Allah will bestow upon his resurrected followers as a reward for their obedience in this life. On the manward side, the solution is for people to remember Allah, and to do his revealed will, especially by embracing the five articles of faith, and by practicing the five pillars of Islam. If, on the Day of Judgment, one's good deeds in these areas outweigh his bad, Allah will welcome him into the heavenly garden. If not, he will cast him into hell. Here then is a simple system of salvation by good works, one that has seemed reasonable and attractive to many people. However, for several weighty reasons, seekers should pause for second look.

First, this scheme of salvation appears to involve a defective view of divine acceptance. Yes, it is natural enough for us to *hope* that our good deeds will somehow cancel our bad. But the persistent testimony of our conscience is that our bad deeds *always* demand punishment, *no matter how many good deeds we may have done.* Will a judge remit the death penalty of a proven murderer, simply because hitherto he has been a model citizen? As

APPENDIX 8: THE ISLAMIC WORLDVIEW

this question shows, moral intuition insists that justice be done in *all* cases; that the unknown god, in order to remain just, cannot simply overlook or counterbalance a transgression, but must actually punish it. Importantly, Islam itself seems to acknowledge this very thing, asserting that all believers must suffer in the grave or spend some time in hell (19:71). It appears, then, that the true balm for a troubled conscience is not a vague hope that in the end our good deeds might outweigh our bad, but a confident assurance that god will punish someone (or something) else for our sins, so that he may *justly* forgive us and accept us. Unfortunately, Allah himself rules out this option, saying, "No bearer of a burden can bear the burden of another" (17:15, 35:18). But the God of the Bible rules it in, saying, "Christ suffered once for sins, the just for the unjust, that he might bring us to God" (1 Pet. 3:18, Rom. 3:21-26).

Secondly, as a general rule, Islamic teaching on salvation does not offer eternal security to believers. This is intrinsic to its theology, and in more ways than one. The believer cannot know if Allah has chosen him for final salvation (17:3). He cannot know if he has met, or will meet, the conditions for salvation, which is a preponderance of good deeds over bad. He may fear that he has committed one or more of the unpardonable sins mentioned in the Qur'an and the Hadith (4:48, 116; Hadith 2:375, 460, 448). He may also wonder (and fear) how long he must suffer in the grave or in hell before Allah takes him to Paradise. In view of all this, it is hardly surprising to learn that Mohammed himself did not know what Allah would do with him (Hadith 1:35)! If, then, eternal security is really important to a Muslim, his only recourse is to engage in *jihad* and to die as a martyr to Allah's cause. According to the Qur'an, this is the only good work that guarantees instant and perpetual access to Paradise (3:157-8, 169; Hadith 1:35).

Importantly, in all of this we see that the Muslim stands on far different ground than the Christian. The Christian views salvation as a gift to be received rather than a reward to be earned. Moreover, he is *presently* assured by the Holy Spirit that Christ has *already* paid the penalty for his sins, so that at the moment of death he *will* be in heaven with his Lord (John 1:12, 5:24, Rom. 8:16, 2 Cor. 5:8, Eph. 2:8, Col. 2:2, 1 John 5:13). Indeed, it is because the believer is *already* seated in heavenly places with Christ that he can *now* exult confidently in the hope of the glory that is yet to be revealed (Rom. 5:1-2, 8:18, Eph. 2:6). Needless to say, many a troubled Muslim, fearful of the Day of Judgment, has found promises like these to be "good news from a distant land" (Prov. 25:25).

How Can We Find Answers to the Questions of Life?

We have seen that Islam points seekers of religious and philosophical truth to Mohammed and the Qur'an. But for the many reasons discussed above, it does not appear that these are reliable sources of divine revelation. What is needed, then, is a Teacher and a Book that really are surrounded by a credible body of supernatural signs; that maintain the highest ethical standards; that supply intuitive, reasonable, right, and hopeful answers to all the questions of life; and that have won a large following of satisfied disciples, disciples who manifest the abiding love, joy, and peace that the knowledge of the truth must ever bring.

May all who read these pages keep up their search for that special Teacher and that special Book until at last they have found them both!

For further study, see Caner and Caner, *Unveiling Islam* (Kregel, 2002); and N. Geisler and A. Saleeb, *Answering Islam* (Baker, 2002).

THE ISLAMIC WORLD VIEW
Answers to Questions of Life

1. What is the ultimate reality?

Allah, an infinite personal Spirit. His key attributes are unity (he has no "companions"), self-existence, eternity, omniscience, omnipresence, omnipotence, and absolute sovereignty over all creatures and events. His 99 names reveal much about his will, but nothing of his ineffable nature. Man can know *about* the transcendent Allah through the Qur'an, but cannot know him personally by inward spiritual experience.

Scriptures: Surahs 2:255; 59:22-24; 112

2. What is the origin of the universe, life, and man?

Allah created the seven heavens, the earth, the angels, the *jinn* (lesser spirits with free will), man, and all other creatures in six days. He created Adam and Eve in the heavenly Eden, and then put them on earth to be his vice-regents. Man has the gift of knowledge, will, and power for action from Allah, but is not created in his image and likeness, which are humanly unknowable.

Scriptures: Surahs 10:3; 17:44; 25:61; 32:4; 41:12; 55:3-7

3. What went wrong? Why are evil, suffering, and death in the world?

Natural evil on earth (e.g., sickness, injury, death, natural disasters, etc.) comes from Allah, often as an expression of his wrath and judgment. Moral evil in men and the jinn comes from weakness, carelessness, forgetfulness, the pressure of external circumstances, and the misuse of freedom. Satan (a *jinn*) sinned in Eden because he would not bow down to Adam. Adam and Eve sinned in Eden when they listened to the proud and deceitful Satan. Adam's sin did not damage his spiritual integrity, nor influence the natural order. All human beings are born good, with a clean slate. Man does not need a new nature from Allah; rather, he needs to remember Allah and to seek his forgiveness and favor through obedience to his laws.

Scriptures: Surahs 2:30-35; 7:12-25; 18:50; 32:9; 38:71-77; 72:11

THE ISLAMIC WORLD VIEW

4. What, if anything, can be done?

On the last day, Allah will destroy the earth, punish the wicked, and admit his obedient servants into Paradise, where they will enjoy physical and spiritual pleasures forever. Therefore, men must use this life to prepare for the next by embracing right belief (*iman*) and performing right actions (*amal*). If, at the end, their good deeds outweigh their bad, they will escape hell and enter heaven. As a rule, no one can know beforehand if they have done enough good to earn Paradise. However, salvation is sure for those who engage in jihad, (i.e., those who fight and die for Allah and Islam).

Scriptures: Surahs 2:207; 3:157-8, 195; 4:57; 17:13-14; 23:102-3; 39:61; Hadith 1:35, 5:2666

5. What is the meaning of life?

Allah created man to be his vice-regent and servant on the earth, but many have strayed from this calling and are in danger of judgment. Therefore, the main purpose of this life is to prepare for the next through obedience to Allah in right belief and right action. Also, since Allah desires to rule over all mankind, Muslims should strive to spread submission to his will (*islam*) to all nations, by persuasion if possible, by force if necessary.

Scriptures: Surahs 2:190-193, 216; 4:74-5, 95, 101; 8:65; 9:5; 17:10, 70; 22:36; 47:4; 49:13; 51:56

6. How shall we live?

All the ancient prophets answer this question the same way: believe and confess the oneness and sole deity of Allah, submit to his laws, and do good in this life with a view to gaining heaven in the next. However, since the message of the earlier prophets has been lost and/or corrupted, men must now live according to Allah's full and

THE ISLAMIC WORLD VIEW

final revelation, the Qur'an. In particular, they must embrace the five articles of faith: belief in Allah, angels, the prophets, the Qur'an, and the resurrection on the last day (some add to this list *qadar/kismet:* absolute predestination). They must also embrace the five pillars of right action: a confession of faith in Allah, (daily) prayer, (yearly) fasting, almsgiving, and (a once in a life-time) pilgrimage to Mecca. These and other good actions are said to earn the believer a place in heaven.

Scriptures: 1:2-4; 2:3-4, 25-26, 43, 83, 183-185, 207; 3:16-17; 10:9; 11:14; 13:36; 16:90; 20:14-15; 23:102-103; 32:15-16; 39:61; 52:21

7. What happens when we die?

At death the soul leaves the body and is carried heavenward by its assigned angels. Believers receive a brief glimpse of Paradise, then return to the grave where their angels first interrogate them and then subject them to mild punishments. Thereafter, some wander the earth, others enter heaven, others sleep. The souls of unbelievers are rebuffed at heaven's gates, then return to the grave for their own angelic interrogation, and are thereafter subjected to miscellaneous torments and terrifying glimpses of hell. All souls await the resurrection and judgment of the last day.

Scriptures: 6:93; 7:40; 8:5; 56:83

8. Where is history heading?

The Qur'an does not give a clear answer, but the following traditional sketch is popular. History is linear, heading towards the resurrection, the last judgment, and eternity in Paradise or in the fires of hell. In "the final hour" the *Dajjal* (i.e., the antichrist) will arise to lead many astray even as much of the world descends into gross wickedness. Terrible signs will appear in the sky and upon the earth. At this time, Jesus will descend from heaven—or, according to

THE ISLAMIC WORLD VIEW

Shiite beliefs, the twelfth imam (the *Mahdi*) will come out of hiding. After destroying the *Dajjal*, he will establish Islam throughout the earth, then die and be buried. After that, the heavenly trumpet will sound, the dead will rise, and the whole world will bow in awe—possibly for a thousand years or more—before Allah's throne. At the judgment, the angels will weigh men's deeds in the scales and Muhammad will intercede for sinners. The wicked will be cast into hell while believers safely cross the *sirat* (a narrow bridge over hell) into Paradise. Once there, they will enjoy the physical and spiritual pleasures of Paradise forever. In time, Allah will display his mercy by rescuing some from hell and bringing them to Paradise.

Scriptures: Surahs 20:15; 33:63, 66; 37:23-24; 39:68; 69:13-16, 18-31; 81:1-3, 6, 14; 82:1-5

9. How can we find trustworthy answers to the questions of life.

In his mercy, Allah sends prophets to all the peoples of the world. Those prophets who have given us written revelations include the biblical authors (e.g., Moses, David, Jesus) and Muhammad (the Qur'an). However, the Bible was intended only for the Jews, whereas the Qur'an is intended for the whole world. Also, the original books of the Bible have been lost and/or corrupted. Hence, Allah's full and final truth is now available only in the Qur'an, which stands eternal in heaven. Though the Hadith and the Sunna did not come by way of direct revelation, they faithfully preserve for us many of Muhammad's words and deeds. Therefore, they are valuable in helping us to interpret and apply the broad principles of the Qur'an.

Scriptures: Surahs 10:47; 16:36; 40:15; 43:3; 85:21-22

ENDNOTES

Chapter 1: Life: A Mess or a Test?

1. Throughout this book I use the words *god* or *unknown god* to refer generically to the Supreme Being, the object of mankind's inquiries and speculations about an ultimate spiritual reality. On the other hand, I use the word *God* when referring to the god of the Bible. In so doing, I am using the word as the Bible does (and as we in the West have traditionally done)—as a proper name, the English equivalent of the Hebrew *Elohim* and of the Greek *Theos*. Thus, God is the god of the Hebrew-Christian Scriptures. Though a bit irksome at first, this distinction will prove quite helpful in the pages ahead.

2. In the war of the worldviews, the question of the beginning is of crucial importance, especially today when so many people have rejected the traditional biblical cosmogony in favor of some form of cosmic evolution. Feeling this keenly, I spent several years outside my educational comfort zone, studying and writing about cosmology. The resulting book is, like this one, dedicated to seekers. See Dean Davis, *In Search of the Beginning: A Seeker's Journey to the Origin of the Universe, Life, and Man*, (Pleasant Word, 2007).

3. The rather imposing English word *eschatology* comes from the Greek *eschatos*, meaning *last*. Hence, eschatology is simply the study of "the last things." More particularly, *personal eschatology* deals with the last things in the life of an individual human being; *cosmic eschatology* deals with the last things in the history of the universe.

4. The following quotations from philosopher Walter Anderson will give you a feel for postmodern thinking. Note carefully his implied endorsement of "incredulity toward metanarratives," postmodern lingo

for disbelief in objective truth, absolute values, and therefore the power of religion or philosophy to discover them.

> Surrounded by so many "truths," we cannot help but revise our concept of truth itself, our beliefs about belief. More and more people are becoming accustomed to the idea that, as philosopher Richard Rorty puts it, truth is made rather than found...A metanarrative is a story of mythic proportions, a story big enough and meaningful enough to pull together philosophy and research and politics and art, relate them to one another, and above all give them a unifying sense of direction...Examples are the Christian religious story of God's will being worked out on Earth, the Marxist political story of class conflict and revolution, and the Enlightenment's intellectual story of rational progress... The postmodern era may be defined as a time of "incredulity toward metanarratives," all of them...This does not mean that all people have ceased to believe in all stories, but rather that the stories aren't working so well anymore, in part because there are too many of them, and we all know it (Walter Anderson, *The Truth about Truth*, (G.P. Putnam's Sons, 1995)).

5. In the following excerpt, C. S. Lewis concludes from our experience with natural hungers that the hunger for heaven is a good sign that heaven exists. Much the same may be said about our hunger for truth and spiritual fulfillment.

> Creatures are not born with desires unless satisfaction for those desires exists. A baby feels hunger; well, there is such a thing as food. A duckling wants to swim; well, there is such a thing as water. Men feel sexual desire; well, there is such a thing as sex. If I find in myself a desire that no experience in this world can satisfy, the most probable explanation is that I was made for another world (C.S. Lewis, *Mere Christianity* (Harper, San Francisco, 2001)).

6. As mentioned in the text, this list includes several men who were philosophical Deists. Deists believed in an infinite personal god, yet not the God of the Bible or any other revealed religion. Kant, Voltaire, Rousseau, Thomas Paine, and Thomas Jefferson all fall into this category.

7. For a handy comparison of the three main worldviews, see the various appendices at the back of this book. See also Dean Halverson, ed., *The Compact Guide to World Religions* (Bethany House, 1996).

8. Some philosophers and theologians posit two ultimate realities, a view that is called *metaphysical dualism*. Plato and Aristotle are sometimes called *complementary dualists* because they believed in two closely related and complementary eternal realities: god and matter. On the other hand, the

Persian theologian Zoroaster is called a *competing dualist* because he believed in two spiritual supreme beings—one good and the other evil—which are at war with each other eternally. But again, history shows that metaphysical dualism is rare, since the human mind so strongly inclines towards the idea of a single ultimate reality.

9. A little reflection suggests that the three basic worldviews can, in principle, be reduced to two. This is because in considering the nature of the ultimate reality, the human mind is really trying to decide between two—and only two—irreducible and irreconcilable options: an impersonal *it* or a personal *he*. In other words, the real choice is between *naturalism* and *theism*. Pantheism, which at first glance seems like a viable third option, turns out to be an unstable—and ultimately inconceivable—hybrid of the other two. This is why it is not uncommon to find pantheists who in one breath speak of the ultimate reality as an *impersonal cosmic consciousness* and then in the next as a *him* or a *her*. Their tendency is to oscillate between the two metaphysical poles. But since the theistic pole is far more satisfying to the needs and inclinations of the heart, their overall drift is usually towards the personal god of theism.

10. It is very important to understand that postmodernism is not a worldview. A worldview, as we have seen, supplies answers to the questions of life and then synthesizes them into a picture of reality as a whole. Postmodernism, on the other hand, says that there are no such answers, or that if there are, we cannot know them: therefore no such picture is possible for us. Observe, however, that in so speaking, postmodernists cannot keep themselves from doing the very thing they say is impossible: making declarative statements about what is philosophically the case, about what is objectively true. The very fact that they stay up nights and write books is an excellent piece of evidence for one of the key insights and premises of the test perspective: *the human mind, by its very constitution, is truth-oriented.* It cannot help but think in terms of what is true and false. This constitution speaks up loudly in favor of a divine creator who has instilled in man a desire to know and express objective truth, and who equips him to find it. This in turn speaks up loudly in favor of the thesis that objective truth exists, waiting to be found by all who love it enough to seek it until they find it.

Chapter 2: Hints of a Heavenly Hope: Nature

1. See Walt Brown, *In the Beginning: Compelling Evidence for Creation and the Flood*, (CSC Books, 2001), pp. 21-23, 67. This outstanding collection of creationist evidences is available online at www.creationscience.com.

2. Over the last 200 years, chemists have discovered an astonishing orderliness underlying the world of physical things. This order is impressively depicted in the Periodic Table, a teaching device that systematically arranges and categorizes the 103 atomic elements known to man. In particular, the table arranges the elements in such a way that we can see how similarities among the members of each group (e.g., alkali, metal, noble gas, rare earth, etc.) are based upon similarities in their atomic structure. Interestingly, one of its creators, Dmitri Mendeleev, used the table to predict the properties of three as yet undiscovered elements. Between 1875 and 1886 the three elements were finally discovered and did indeed display the properties he predicted. Clearly, the atomic world is rational; and if rational, then a testimony to a rational supreme being.

3. Biological taxonomy—the orderly classification of living beings according to kingdom, phylum, class, order, family, genus, and species—would not be possible if life itself were not thus arranged hierarchically. Interestingly, the founder of modern taxonomy, Carolus Linnaeus, was a biblical creationist, avowedly seeking to understand the rational plan according to which the creator had fashioned all living beings.

4. As I learned from examining seashells, the symmetry of biological forms (e.g., radial, bilateral, spherical, explosive, etc.) can be breathtakingly beautiful. The poet William Blake famously captured the spiritual impact and significance of nature's symmetry when he wrote:

> Tiger! Tiger! burning bright
> In the forests of the night,
> What immortal hand or eye
> Could frame thy fearful symmetry?

5. This interview is found in a *Back to Genesis* article written by John D. Morris, (El Cajon, CA., Institute for Creation Research, 2000). It is available at www.icr.org. Notably, the complex orderliness of living things has roused many a modern skeptic from his naturalistic slumbers. An outstanding case in point is Dr. Anthony Flew, arguably the most influential atheistic philosopher of the 20th century. Having rejected all the classical proofs for the existence of a god for over 60 years, he finally found, at age 81, that the complexity of life (and especially of the DNA molecule) compelled him to embrace the theistic position. Writes Flew:

Science has shown, by the almost unbelievable complexity of the arrangements that are needed to produce life, that intelligence must have been involved. I have been persuaded that it is simply out of the question that the first living matter evolved out of dead matter and then developed into an extraordinarily complicated creature. My whole life has been guided by the principle of Plato's Socrates: follow the evidence wherever it leads. The conclusion is: there must have been some intelligence. (See, Gene Veith, "Flew the Coop," *World Magazine*, December 26, 2004).

6. When god "speaks" his truth to the scientific mind, he often uses the language of mathematics. That is, having endowed man with mathematical ability, he progressively enables him to see that the structures, motions, and relations of the natural world can best be described in mathematical terms (i.e., by means of arithmetic, geometry, algebra, probability, calculus, etc.). Reflection shows that mathematics— and the mathematics of nature—are mysterious, transcendent entities, incomprehensible apart from the place of their origin: the mind of the unknown god. For more on the spiritual implications of mathematics, see John Byl, *The Divine Challenge* (Banner of Truth, 2004), and Larry Zimmerman, *Truth and the Transcendent* (available at www.answersingenesis.org).

7. Is the intelligibility of nature designed to move us to a contemplation of god? Dr. Michael Gore would likely answer yes. In a television interview he was questioned about the mysterious Fibonacci sequence, which is generated simply by adding the two previous numbers (0, 1, 1, 2, 3, 5, 8, 13, 21, etc.). Elements of this sequence pop up all throughout nature. For example, the seeds in the head of a sunflower are arranged in two sets of spirals, one going clockwise, the other counter-clockwise. Amazingly, the numbers of the spirals in the two sets are always Fibonacci numbers (e.g., 34 and 55, 55 and 89, 89 and 144). The same pattern is observable in pinecones, shells, animal horns, and leaf buds on a stem. Also, when we divide a number in the Fibonacci sequence by its predecessor, the result (after the first four numbers) always hovers around 1.62. Fascinatingly, this is precisely the ratio of the two sides of the so-called Golden Rectangle, regarded from ancient times as the rectangle most pleasing to the human eye. Apparently it is pleasing to the creator's eye too, since the width of a DNA molecule is 21 angstroms and the length of one full turn of its spiral 34 angstroms—both Fibonacci numbers! In other words, the DNA molecule is literally one long stack of golden rectangles.

Asked to explain all this, Dr. Gore replied,

> "I personally believe there is some greater deity that's organized it. Everything is too cleverly organized, as far as I'm concerned, to have just happened by chance. Whether you say all this was constructed by god, or whether you believe in some other way of doing it, I'm not quite sure. But yes, I think there is some power behind it all, but what it is, I have no idea."

See the article *Golden Numbers*, by Carl Wieland and Russell Grigg, www.answersingenesis.org. See also the article *Shapes, Patterns, and the Divine Proportion in God's Creation*, by Fred Wilson, www.icr.org.

8. To say that human admiration of the creator of natural beauty is a reflection of god's own admiration of himself seems to invite charges of narcissism in the deity. However, it is actually quite reasonable for god to admire himself since, as the sole repository and creator of beauty, he is the one *rightfully* to be admired. By contrast, it would indeed be narcissistic for Mozart to admire himself for having created a beautiful symphony, if in fact he had simply received the symphony from god above. Rather, he, along with his audiences, should admire (i.e., worship) the one who gave it to him. In other words, because god is the beautiful creator of all beauty, his self-admiration is permissible, since it is simply according to truth. Man's self-admiration is not, since it is according to error or lie. Furthermore, if god is a trinity of divine persons, as Christianity teaches, we can make even better sense of god admiring god, since now we can think of this as one divine person (e.g., the Holy Spirit) admiring the person and work of another (e.g., God the Father or God the Son), even as he enables us, the beholders of that work, to do the same.

9. See the article by Don De Young, *The Universe is Finely Tuned for Life*, www.answersingenesis.org. See also Lee Strobel, *The Case for the Creator* (Zondervan, 2004), chapter 6; and *The Privileged Planet* (Illustra Media), a film available at the website of the Discovery Institute or www.amazon.com.

10. Robert Jastrow, *The Astronomer and God: Intellectuals Speak Out About God* (Regnery Gateway, 1984), pp. 19-20.

11. For a survey of various evidences favoring the man-centered-ness of the cosmos, see Dean Davis, *In Search of the Beginning: A Seeker's Journey to the Origin of the Universe, Life, and Man,* (Pleasant Word, 2007), chapters 2, 5, and 6.

Chapter 3: Hints of a Heavenly Hope: Conscience

1. It is true, of course, that our conscience may be burdened with a false sense of moral obligation or a false sense of guilt. For example, a woman in India may feel obligated to destroy herself on the funeral pyre of her dead husband, when in fact the objective moral law demands nothing of the kind. Similarly, a woman in Africa may feel obligated to submit to the ritual of female circumcision. But cases like these do not prove that *all* sense moral obligation is untethered to objective moral law, only some. Moreover, a false sense of moral obligation is often *based* upon a true, yet distorted by ignorance or error. Thus, the woman in India may rightly feel an obligation to honor her husband, or to try to secure his happiness in the afterlife, yet wrongly feel that such ends are properly served by her killing herself. Yes, our sense of moral obligation is sometimes distorted—a curious human frailty that definitely requires an explanation. But again, this does not mean there is no such thing as moral obligation, only that we must do all we can to ascertain the true obligations—the true moral laws—by which we are to live.

2. Our overall experience of the moral order also involves a crucial *subjective* element: *free moral agency*. Free moral agency may be defined as *the uniquely human ability to choose between two or more options, based solely upon one's own values, judgments, and desires*. Concerning this definition, two important observations may be made.

First, it is free moral agency that, among other things, distinguishes man from the animals. Unlike animals, man alone is conscious of the elements of the objective moral order; man alone is conscious of his ability to decide for or against them; and man alone is therefore morally responsible for what he does. This is why man alone struggles over the morality of his decisions. As the poet Szymborska humorously put it:

> The buzzard never says it is to blame,
> The panther wouldn't know what scruples mean.
> When the piranha strikes, it feels no shame,
> If snakes had hands, they'd claim their hands were clean.

As creatures of pure instinct without self-consciousness or free moral agency, the animals do not worry about their choices, nor are they morally responsible for them. The situation is far different for man.

Secondly, our definition implies that free moral agency is not inconsistent with a certain kind of determinism, *since a person's decisions are ultimately determined by his own judgments and desires.* Intuitively, we know this is true. We know that our decisions do not pop up out of a psychological vacuum; rather, they are motivated. They spring forth from the totality of who we are: our understanding, our values, and our inclinations. In short, they spring from our character. Yet these decisions are still rightly said to be free, since they are determined *solely* by our own judgments and desires, and not by anyone or anything external to us. Such freedom is an important element of our overall sense of personal responsibility. If someone forces me to take LSD, I am not responsible for my decision. But if I myself choose to do so, being constrained by nothing other than my own values, judgments, and desires, then I am responsible for what I have done, and I know it.

3. It is important to understand that our common sense view of the natural world—that it exists objectively, independently of our minds—cannot be proven by the mind itself. How can we *ever* observe the world unless we are first conscious of it, unless we first have it, in some sense, in our minds? In other words, we are *always* "stuck in our heads," and the world as well—an unnerving thought that has inclined not a few towards pantheism. It is true, of course, that common sense loudly testifies in favor of an objective outer world, and of an objective moral order as well. And I would argue that it is always wise to listen hard to the testimony of common sense. Nevertheless, in the end there is really only one way to know *for sure* if both orders are objectively real: we must have a revelation on these matters, a revelation from the unknown god. See chapters 9 and 10 for more.

4. For a critique of this position, see Dean Davis, *In Search of the Beginning,* (Pleasant Word, 2007), chapter 3.

5. Cited in Josh McDowell, *The New Evidence That Demands a Verdict,* (Nelson, 1999), p. 618.

6. The phrase is the title of a thoughtful book by J. Budziszewski, *What We Can't Not Know*, (Spence, 2003).

7. This cartoon is especially useful in helping us to reconcile the law of moral cause and effect with the pervasive and disturbing reality of earthly injustice. For again, the cartoon affirms what moral intuition inclines us to believe: if justice is not done in this life, it certainly will be done in the next. However, the prospect of a future judgment raises yet another troubling question: how can folks who are moral failures (a mathematical set that includes the whole human race) hope to escape retribution in the

life to come? Happily, we will soon hear from a Teacher who supplied an astonishing solution to that problem, a solution that allows a holy and sovereign god to forgive fallible men, all the while preserving the integrity of the OMO inviolate.

8. In this and the previous two chapters we have focused on three large-scale hints of a heavenly hope: the probationary, natural, and moral orders. Very importantly, in each case the discussion brought us face to face with a fourth and equally large-scale hint: *the human mind.*

Here we meet the Achilles heel of all naturalistic philosophy. Because of its implicit atheism, naturalism simply cannot explain the origin of the human mind, nor the astonishing variety and efficacy of its faculties. Why? Because mere matter—being in and of itself unconscious—cannot give rise to consciousness (or to life, either). That this is true is powerfully borne home to us by a deep, immediate, inescapable, and undeniable awareness of the fact that these two realities—mind and matter—are absolutely *heterogeneous*. That is, they have two completely different natures. In particular, the brain (i.e., the matter most closely associated with the mind) is a *physical* something, whereas the mind is a *spiritual* or *metaphysical* something. We can observe and handle the brain, but not the mind. Unlike the brain (or any other physical object), our minds cannot even be located in time and space. The mind is not part of nature at all. In fact, the mind is so supernatural that somehow it can take all of nature into itself, most especially when it is doing science, philosophy, and theology! So again, before the mystery of the human mind naturalism arrives at its philosophical Waterloo.

As for pantheism, it goes to the opposite extreme, being so impressed by mind that it seeks to collapse nature itself into consciousness—the physical into the spiritual—so that the entire cosmos becomes a mere dream. The problem here, however, is that by their very nature our minds balk at denying the objective existence of the external physical world, and balk still more at turning absolutely everything—matter, mind, body, soul, self, good, evil, etc.—into (manifestations of) god. We know ourselves—and the unknown god—far too well for that!

The conclusion, then, is that the human mind—along with the amazing spectrum of its functions (e.g., sensory perception, reason, language, logic, mathematics, imagination, emotion, and scientific, philosophical, and artistic creativity)—finds its best explanation at the proto-type and fountainhead of all such faculties: an infinite personal spirit who is the creator and sustainer of them all. Accordingly, the human mind—interacting as it does with an objectively real and ordered external world—is certainly among the top three or four evidences for the truth of the theistic worldview. It is a most powerful hint of a heavenly hope.

See John Byl, *The Divine Challenge*, chapter 14. Also, Lee Strobel, *The Case for the Creator*, chapter 10.

Chapter 4: In Search of the Teacher

1. Observe carefully that the standard of truth set up by logical positivists is self-refuting. They assert that a statement is meaningless unless it can be empirically verified. But this statement itself cannot be empirically verified. Therefore, by positivist standards, it is meaningless.

2. Because naturalism and scientism now reign supreme in most of our public schools, science students are not permitted to get involved in the great debate about cosmic origins that now rages in the culture at large. That is, they are not permitted to examine scientific evidence unfavorable to naturalistic evolution, or favorable to divine creation. Also, they are not permitted to consider non-scientific lines of evidence that point clearly to the existence of an infinite personal god who is active in the world. Yes, these lines of evidence are historical, religious, and philosophical in nature (e.g., various lines of evidence showing the trustworthiness of the biblical stories of creation, fall, flood, and dispersion at Babel). But by what law have they become unmentionable in a science class? Etymologically, the word "science" simply means "knowledge," not "knowledge exclusively gained by scientific method." If, then, science, in the most fundamental sense of the word, is the search for true knowledge about the universe (e.g., its origin, structure, purpose, destiny, spiritual components, etc.), why shouldn't science students be exposed to any and all kinds of knowledge that might help them reach their goal?

3. These quotes were included in an article written by Dr. George Fox, entitled "The Philosopher's Dilemma!" It appeared in *The Grace Messenger Newsletter*, (Fall, 2000). For a copy, contact Grace School of Theology, 40 Cleveland Road, Pleasant Hill, CA 94523.

4. As my definition indicates, when using the word *theism* I have in mind *monotheism*, the belief that the ultimate reality is a *single* infinite personal spirit; that there is but *one true god*. Most theologians use the word in this sense. There are, of course, still many polytheists in the world, folks who believe in the existence of many different personal gods. Seekers should understand, however, that most polytheists are really pantheists,

since they believe that the gods originally sprang from a single, impersonal, divine Spirit or Mind (e.g., Brahman).

5. Though Mormonism claims that its god is the God of the Bible, careful investigation will show that this religion does not properly fall into the category of biblical theism, since it is actually a polytheistic rather than a monotheistic faith. For more on Mormon theology, see A Hoekema, *Mormonism,* (Eerdmans, 1963), and James R. White, *Is the Mormon My Brother?* (Harvest House, 1997).

6. For charts comparing and contrasting the tenets of the main religions and worldviews, see the appendices in the back of this book. See also, Dean Halverson, *The Compact Guide to World Religions* (Harvest House, 1996).

7. Freud's disciple, Carl Jung, also denied the objective existence of spiritual beings. For Jung, god, angels, demons, fairies, dragons, etc., are all "archetypes." Archetypes are primitive modes of thought, stored up in a kind of racial memory bank that Jung called "the collective unconscious." Largely pictorial, these archetypes are inherited from our ancestors who, we are told, personified natural processes and inward psychological states in terms of what we now call mythological concepts. Thus, for Jung, evil spirits are mythical personifications of the darker side of our animal nature and ancestry.

Importantly, some Western pantheists, building upon Jung's theories, postulate that the collective unconscious is in fact what the Hindu's call Brahman, the spiritual ground of all sentient beings and all phenomenal worlds. Like Jung, they too teach that evil spirits have no objective existence, but are mere "shadow" and illusion. In the moment of enlightenment, they say, the seeker-mystic will realize that the demons with which he has done battle have no objective existence at all.

This pantheistic version of Jung's psychology has attracted many New Age seekers of a mystical bent. If you are among them, I would again urge you to ascertain the truth or falsity of (Jungian) pantheism *before* you embark upon mystical practices, rather than after, when the consequences of doing so may be dire.

For a thought-provoking study of the psychology of atheism, see R. C. Sproul, *If There's a God, Why are There Atheists?* (Ligonier Ministries, 1997).

8. Even on Hindu and New Age premises, seekers are wise to be cautious about channeled revelations. What if base (i.e., karmically undeveloped) spirits, bound by ignorance or malevolence, are behind them?

Would anything they say be trustworthy? Interestingly, hard experience has brought certain New Age leaders to this very conclusion. Some years back, a spirit channeled by J. Z. Knight (called *Ramtha*) gave false predictions of coming natural catastrophes. After a number of credulous followers responded by relocating to the Pacific Northwest, New Age spokesman Craig Lee concluded, "Many now speculate that whatever (positive) energy came through J. Z. Knight has either shifted, departed, or been replaced by a less benign entity." See Elliot Miller, *A Crash Course on the New Age Movement*, (Grand Rapids, MI, Baker Book House), p. 152.

9. *Crash Course*, p. 126. Schucman's story alerts us to a fact that seekers must not ignore: *unfailingly*, spiritism harms those who practice it. I myself have seen chilling advertisements in New Age journals, offering assistance to troubled channelers who are unable to get rid of now-unwelcome spirits. Robert Shell, a New Age leader with a cautious and scientific bent, has observed the same. After two years of research into spiritism, he concluded as follows:

> It seems that at any given point in history, these entities, whatever they are, couch themselves in the form most likely to be accepted by the mind they contact. Thus, the occultist has his invocations of spirits, good and evil; and the Saucerian has his space people. However, on one point only can we look to the literature and be certain: *that such contacts are always detrimental to the physical and the mental well-being of the contactee*." (See *Crash Course*, p. 181).

It appears, then, that if disembodied spirits really do exist, at least some of them are unwelcome, ignorant, duplicitous, malicious, and harmful. Knowing this to be the case, how wise can it be for seekers to look to them as sources of divine truth?

Chapter 5: Window on a World of Signs

1. For more on the unity of the Bible, see Dean Davis, "One Shot, One Book, One God," *Journal of the Christian Research Institute*, (December, 2004). Available at www.equip.org. Also, see appendix 5.

2. The literary unity of the Bible is vividly seen in the way it begins and ends. It begins with Genesis, the book of beginnings. It ends with Revelation, the book of the end, the consummation. Roughly in the middle it gives us the four gospels, containing the life story of him whom the NT reveals as both the creator and the consummator, the Alpha and the Omega, the beginning and the end (Rev. 22:13). Observe also how this literary unity

ENDNOTES

521

implies that the biblical canon is closed—that the Bible is now complete, with no more books to be added. Why would God add another chapter, when he has already so clearly written the last?

3. Unlike myth and legend, the biblical story is so thoroughly embedded in historical narrative that it positively invites historians and archeologists to check out its accuracy. When they do, they consistently find—as archeologist Nelson Gleuck once put it—that the Bible has "an almost incredibly accurate historical memory." For more on this topic, see chapter 7.

4. The NT doctrine of the Holy Trinity is seen vividly in Mt. 3:13-17, 28:18ff, John 14:15-19, 23-24, 16:13-15, 17:20-21, 2 Cor. 13:14, 1 Pet. 1:1-2. For more on this theme, see chapter 9.

5. Christian interpreters find both hints and explicit affirmations of the divine nature of the Messiah throughout the OT. See Psalms 2, 110; Isaiah 7:14, 9:6-7, Jer. 23:5; Dan. 7:9-14; Micah 5:2; Malachi 3:1.

NT passages affirming or implying the deity of Jesus of Nazareth include Mt. 1:23, 11:25ff, 22:41-46, 24:30-31, 28:20; Mark 2:1-12; John 1, 5:16-33, 6:44, 8:46, 8:58, 9:35-36, 16:30, 15:5, 20:28; Philippians 2, Colossians 1, Hebrews 1-2, Revelation 1-3.

6. An American analogue to Mohammed is Joseph Smith, the founder of Mormonism. Smith claimed that he received visitations from God the Father, Jesus Christ, and the angel Moroni, through whom he was designated as a prophet. Though he did not claim that his resultant writings supplanted Christianity, he did claim that they reinterpreted it definitively. The problem, however, is that the Bible itself anticipates no writing prophets after those who lived in Jesus' day and who completed the NT scriptures (Eph. 3:5). Indeed, it solemnly warns against anyone trying to add anything whatsoever to a revelation that has been given "once for all" to the saints (Jude 1:3, Rev. 22:18).

7. In virtue of its impressive unity, the Bible may be called a *revelatory order*. Just like the natural, moral, and probationary orders, it brings together a number of different elements and integrates them into a system (or order) by means of a rational plan. But if the rational orderliness of the natural, moral, and probationary orders marks them as the handiwork of the unknown god, to whom shall we trace the rational orderliness of the revelatory order that is the Bible?

522 THE TEST

Chapter 6: First Look

1. Rumors about Jesus' unusual birth circulated freely even in his own day. Far from investigating them open-mindedly, the Pharisees assumed the worst, concluding that he was the son of a Samaritan, born of fornication (John 8:41, 48).

2. For some fascinating OT accounts of angelic visitations, see Gen. 12:2, 191f, 28:12, 2 Samuel 24:16, 2 Kings 6:17, Daniel 9:21.

3. For some OT accounts of theophanies, see Genesis 18:1f, Ex. 3:2f, 33:9, 34:5f. See also the section on christophanies in chapter 8.

4. From the second to the fifth centuries, a rather large number of spurious gospels (and epistles) circulated freely throughout the Roman world. Christians knew them to be spurious because, relative to the canonical gospels, they were clearly fanciful, heretical, or both. The fancy usually appeared in their miracle stories, which had Jesus turning stones into birds, or emerging from the tomb as a giant. Even today, such stories are easily identifiable as legend, since they are not imbedded in trustworthy historical narrative, and since they are silly, purposeless, and unworthy of the unknown god.

5. Just as the evangelists were eager to establish the historicity of Jesus' resurrection, so too were they were eager to establish the historicity of his death. For them, it was important that Jesus died, and important that people *know* he died. This is because they viewed death as the one true penalty for sin (Gen. 2:17), and Jesus' (substitutionary) death as the one true penalty for his people's sins. Therefore, if he did not die, his people are still in their sins. And if his people are not *sure* that he died, then they are not sure that their sins are forgiven. Here, then, is one of the reasons for the detailed gospel descriptions of Jesus' suffering, death, burial, and three-days in the grave (Mt. 27:45-66, John 19:31-42, 1 Cor. 15:3-8). The evangelists desired all to know with certainty that he truly died, truly rose, and therefore truly redeemed his own.

6. My sketch of Jesus' post-resurrection appearances is based on the following key NT texts: Mt. 28, Mark 16, Luke 24, John 20-21, Acts 1:1-9, 1 Cor. 15:1-11. Observe in the last of these that the risen and glorified Jesus, after his ascension, showed himself one final time to the apostle Paul.

7. In OT times, Elijah raised a widow's son to life (1 Kings 17:17-24), and his successor, Elisha, did the same for the son of his patroness (2 Kings 4:29-37). The patriarch Enoch, of whom it is written that he walked with

God, did not see death, "for God took him" (Gen 5:24, Heb. 11:5). Nor did Elijah, who was taken up bodily into heaven in a chariot of fire (2 Kings 2:1-12). The latter was an especially powerful type of Christ, who was himself taken up bodily into heaven, and who also sent down a mantle of spiritual power upon his successors, the disciples (Acts 1:6-11, 2:1f).

8. According to the Qur'an, the angel Gabriel visited the aging Mohammed in Mecca, seated him upon a spirit-horse named Burak, and took him first to Sinai, then to Bethlehem, and finally to heaven for an audience with the spiritual heroes of old. After this, he returned to earth, where he eventually died. This so-called Ascension of Mohammed differs significantly from the ascension of Jesus. Most importantly, Jesus' ascension followed his resurrection from the dead. Mohammed's did not. Indeed, in Mohammed's case, it was a prelude to his death. Also, Jesus' ascension was seen by many eyewitnesses. Mohammed's was not, and is even reckoned by many Muslims today as having been a dream or a vision, and not a bodily ascension at all. For these and other reasons, Jesus' ascension has no historical analogue, and therefore remains in a class by itself.

9. See Acts 2:25-28, 13:13-41, 1 Cor. 15:20-28, Eph. 1:18-23, 4:7-10, Heb. 1:5, 5:5-6. In each of these passages, the speaker/writer cites or alludes to OT prophecies of Christ's resurrection and/or ascension. For other OT hints and prophecies of the risen Christ see Gen. 22:13 (with Heb. 11:19), Ex. 19:11, Lev. 19:16, 1 Sam. 20:5, 2 Kings 6:1-7, Job 19:25, Isaiah 53:11 (NIV), Hosea 6:2.

Chapter 7: The Great Debate

1. Josh McDowell, *The New Evidence That Demands a Verdict*, (Nelson, 1999), p. 353. This well-organized and comprehensive treatment of Christian apologetics (i.e., the defense of the faith) is, in my judgment, the single most useful book of its kind on the market today. Loaded with interesting insights and quotations.

2. *Evidence*, p. 552.

3. *Evidence*, p. 557.

4. *Evidence*, p. 356.

5. For a thorough, critical discussion of various naturalistic theories of Jesus' resurrection, see *Evidence*, pp. 257-284.

6. In an excellent short essay on the trustworthiness of the Bible, Dr. Norman Geisler explains how the abundance of NT manuscripts enables scholars to determine with a high degree of accuracy which reading, among several variants, is genuine. This means we can *know* that we have the original manuscripts, and also that we can identify them with almost 100% confidence. See *Compact Guide to World Religions*, (Bethany House, 1996), pp. 258-260.

7. From ca. 150 A.D. on, the NT was translated into different languages, such a Latin, Syriac, and Egyptian. Like the Greek manuscripts themselves, these ancient versions all resemble one another closely, thereby adding yet another layer of testimony to the integrity of the NT. See *Evidence*, pp. 41-42.

8. *Evidence*, pp. 37-38.

9. For an enlightening discussion of the Council of Nicea (A.D. 325) and its alleged role in establishing the NT canon, see Erwin Lutzer, *The DaVinci Deception*, (Tyndale, 2006), pp. 1-24. Lutzer also offers a thorough discussion of Gnosticism, explaining why the early Church fathers rejected the Gnostic gospels.

10. For further discussion of the formation of the NT canon of scripture, see chapter 16 of *The Test*.

11. Here are Irenaeus' words concerning the four-fold gospel:

> For as there are four quarters of the world in which we live, and four universal winds, and as the Church is dispersed over all the earth, and the gospel is the pillar and base of the Church and the breath of life, so it is natural that it should have four pillars, breathing immortality from every quarter and kindling the life of men anew. Whence it is manifest that the Word, the architect of all things, who sits upon the cherubim and holds all things together, having been manifested to men, has given us the gospel in fourfold form, but held together by one Spirit. *Evidence*, pp. 53-54.

12. NT textual scholar Bruce Metzger writes, "So extensive are these citations (i.e., patristic references to the canonical NT books) that if all other sources for our knowledge of the text of the NT were destroyed, they would be sufficient alone for the reconstruction of practically the entire NT." *Evidence*, p. 43.

13. McDowell identifies a number of pressures leading to the official canonization of the 27 NT books. These include the rise of heretics, the circulation of spurious writings, the need of missionaries to know which

books to translate into other languages, and persecution over possession of biblical books. *Evidence,* p. 23.

14. In a number of the NT epistles we find the apostles reacting to the proto-Gnostic teaching that was cropping up in and around the new churches. These include Colossians, 1 and 2 Timothy, 2 Peter, 1 John, and Jude.

15. This quote is found in an interesting article by James Holden, "Mary Magdalene's Modern Makeover," *Journal of the Christian Research Institute,* (Vol. 29/No.02/2006), pp. 6-8. Holden impressively demonstrates how heterogeneous the Gnostic beliefs really were.

16. Some liberal critics hypothesize that the anonymous "redactors" (i.e., editors/authors) of the gospels traditionally ascribed to Matthew and Luke actually wove popular oral gospel traditions around an old collection of Jesus' sayings called "Q". However, there is no historical evidence for Q, nor for any gospel redactors other than Matthew, Mark, Luke, and John themselves.

17. In their treatment of apparent discrepancies, liberals and conservatives reveal once again how their differing presuppositions lead them to differing interpretive approaches and conclusions. Not believing in its divine inspiration, liberals have little reason to give the Bible the benefit of the doubt, or to look for plausible solutions to its problem passages. For them, the best explanation for an apparent discrepancy is that it *is* a discrepancy. Conservatives, on the other hand, having examined the various evidences for the Bible's divine inspiration—and having found them compelling—conclude that this book *cannot* contain errors in what it affirms, since errancy is logically inconsistent with divine inspiration. Therefore, they view apparent discrepancies *as* apparent only. Moreover, their presuppositions lead them to search out reasonable explanations for the problem passages, since biblical inerrancy persuades them that such explanations must exist. These solutions cannot, of course, be considered inspired or inerrant, since they are, after all, only speculations. Still, speculations can actually be quite reasonable, and therefore quite helpful in bolstering faith. Practically speaking, all of this means that seekers cannot allow apparent discrepancies to overthrow their confidence in the Bible until they have honestly interacted with the various evidences for its divine inspiration. For more, see pp. 144-155, and also Appendix 1.

18. Down through the years many Christian apologists have carefully studied the alleged historical, ethical, and theological contradictions of

the Bible. Though they do not claim to have solved every problem, they all agree that most are easily explained, and that the rest can and will be, one day. Some of the better books in this category include John W. Haley, *Alleged Discrepancies of the Bible* (Baker, 1977); Norman Geisler and Thomas Howe, *When Critics Ask*, (Victor Books, 1992); and Gleason Archer, *The New International Encyclopedia of Bible Difficulties*, (Zondervan, 2001).

19. There are three main naturalistic accounts of Jesus' resurrection: 1) he "swooned" and later revived, 2) the disciples hallucinated the risen Christ, or 3) the disciples fabricated a Messianic lie. Each of them runs afoul of one indisputable historical fact: *all the disciples* fervently believed that Jesus truly rose from the dead, *and all of them,* in the face of much suffering, *kept believing it* until the (violent) end of their lives. Could a revived Jesus, or an hallucinated Jesus, or a fictitious Jesus elicit such longstanding devotion, moral transformation, and deep self-sacrifice? It is a question for every seeker to ponder long and hard.

20. For further discussion of the extra-biblical testimony about Jesus and the early Christians, see *Evidence*, pp. 53-60.

21. This quote appears in Lee Strobel, *The Case for Christ*, (Zondervan, 1998), p. 115.

22. For a recent survey of biblical archeology, including archeological finds related to the NT era, see A. Hoerth and J. McRay, *Bible Archaeology: An Exploration of the History and Culture of Early Civilizations,* (Baker, 2006). In this connection, we do well to note that the primary extra-biblical scripture of the Latter Day Saints, *The Book of Mormon*, is altogether without the kind of historical and archeological corroboration that the Bible enjoys and that seekers would reasonably expect to find in a book that truly gives us "another testament" of Jesus Christ. Furthermore, like *The Qur'an, The Book of Mormon* is plagued with various anachronisms and historical inaccuracies. Such phenomena do not speak well for the divine inspiration of either. See Gleason Archer Jr., *A Survey of Old Testament Introduction,* (Moody, 1974), Appendices 2 and 3.

23. For further comments on Luke the historian, see *Evidence,* pp. 62-66.

24. For further discussion of Paul's early witness to Jesus' resurrection, see *The Case for Christ*, pp. 308-315.

ENDNOTES

Chapter 8: Second Look

1. Though in strictness it cannot be held to contain christophanies, there is a fourth category of OT passages that may fairly be said to reveal the divine Son of God. I refer to those texts in which God speaks in the plural, using the pronoun "us." In Genesis 1 we come upon the first instance of this curious phenomenon:

> Then God said, "Let Us make man in Our image, according to Our likeness; let them have dominion over the fish of the sea, over the birds of the air, over the cattle, over all the earth, and over every creeping thing that creeps upon the earth" (Gen. 1:26, 3:22, Isaiah 6:8).

Some assert that in using the plural personal pronoun, God here speaks as "heaven's King in company with heaven's hosts." Yet nowhere else does the Bible portray the angels as agents of creation; to the contrary, they are consistently depicted as God's creatures, never as his fellow-creators (Psalm 148, Ezek. 28:13, Col. 1:15-16). Thus, both the pronoun itself and the contexts in which it appears give us a glimpse of *plurality within the godhead*. The NT affirms and unveils this plurality more fully, identifying the three divine Persons who constitute the godhead as Father, Son, and Holy Spirit. In so doing, it also enables us to understand the many trinitarian glimmers that we find throughout the OT.

2. Other alleged OT types of Jesus and his work include Jacob's ladder (Genesis 28), the scapegoat for sin (Leviticus 16), Aaron's rod (Numbers 17), Rahab's scarlet cord (Joshua 2), and a great many OT persons, such as Joseph, Aaron, Joshua, Boaz, David, Solomon, Elijah, Jonah, Ezra, Nehemiah, and more.

3. In chapter 12 we will examine the hugely important biblical theme of the Kingdom of God in further detail.

4. In Isaiah 9:6 it is written that the Messiah will be called Everlasting Father (Heb., "Father of Eternity; Father of the ages"). On the face of it, this name appears to identify the Messiah as the first person of the Holy Trinity rather than the second, the Son. Theologians advance two main solutions to this apparent contradiction. Some argue that the purpose of the passage is to describe the *roles* that the divine Messiah will fill when he rescues his people from oppression and establishes his everlasting Kingdom. As Wonderful Counselor, he will be their wisdom. As Mighty God, he will be their deliverer, strength, and protector. As Prince of Peace he will be their rest and security. Analogously, as Everlasting Father he will be their

source of life and provision. Eternally, the Messianic Son will be as a father to his people, mediating to them the spiritual life that he himself receives from his own Father (John 5:26, 1 Cor. 4:15). Other interpreters, such as Calvin, see Isaiah using the word father to identify the coming Redeemer as the divine *author* of eternal life for his people. By his work, Christ will be the father or progenitor of the eternal future—the endless ages—that his redeemed people will spend in company with him. Says Calvin, "The name *Father* is put for *Author*, because Christ preserves the existence of his Church through all ages, and bestows immortality on the Body and on the individual members" (John Calvin, *Calvin's Commentaries: Isaiah*, Baker, 1984, p. 311).

5. For an informative and moving medical perspective on Jesus' death, see *The Case for Christ*, pp. 255-274.

6. According to Genesis 14, in Abraham's day Melchizedek was a king of Salem (i.e., ancient Jerusalem) and a priest of "the most high God." Because the Bible reveals nothing about his origin or destiny, he became, for both Old and New Testament writers, a type of the Messiah as *a royal and eternal priest*. Christian interpreters see the Lord Jesus Christ as God's eternal High Priest and King, and therefore as the latter-day Melchizedek who fulfills the Messianic promise contained in Psalm 110. For more, see Heb. 5:1-11, 6:19-20, 7:1f.

7. For further discussion of OT Messianic prophecies, see *Evidence*, chapter 8, pp. 164-202.

8. Material for this section is drawn from an excellent short article by Christian apologist Greg Koukl, called "Christianity's Real Record." Visit www.str.org. Also, for a spirited response to charges that moral failure in the Christian Church is somehow endemic to the faith rather than contrary to it, see Vincent Carroll and David Shifflett, *Christianity On Trial*, (Encounter Books, 2001).

9. Herbert Kane, *Understanding Christian Missions*, (Baker, 1974), p. 159.

10. See James and Marti Hefley, *By Their Blood*, (Grand Rapids, MI, Baker Books, 1979), pp. 9-11.

11. For an impressive overview of current state of Christ's Church in each of the countries of the world, see P. Johnstone and J. Mandryk, *Operation World*, (WEC International, 2001).

ENDNOTES

Chapter 9: What is the Ultimate Reality?

1. The biblical understanding of God's spirituality is fundamentally different from that of pantheism. For the theist, spirit (whether human, angelic, or divine) can be related to matter, but is different from it; for the pantheist, spirit manifests itself *as* (what we call) matter. For the theist, the divine Spirit is absolutely without form; for the pantheist, spirit is the hidden reality behind all form. For the pantheist, god is therefore visible in and under all forms. But for a theist like Paul, God is "...the invisible God...dwelling in unapproachable light, whom no man has seen or can see," (1 Tim. 1:17, 6:15-16).

2. Israel's God displays gender, but in a manner that calls for extra discussion and careful discernment.

Let us begin with the biblical data. In the OT, God consistently reveals himself—whether in word or vision—as a "he," but never as a "she" or an "it" (Ex. 15:3, Isaiah 6:1f, 42:13, Ezek. 1:26). In the NT, Jesus advances this paradigm by introducing us to God the *Father*, and also to God the *Son*, who, for important reasons, has entered the world as a man, and not as a woman (Rom. 5:12f, 1 Cor. 11:1f, 15:22). Moreover, in teaching about the Holy Spirit, Jesus always refers to him as a "he." Thus, the biblical pattern is both clear and consistent, offering little encouragement to those who would "update" God by re-naming him Father/Mother, or Holy Parent.

The question arises, however, as to *why* God reveals himself in masculine categories. The answer is not, of course, that he has a man's body, for God is, as we have seen, an infinite personal spirit. But if he (Christ now excepted) does not have a man's body, then *in what sense* is he a he?

The answer is found *in the nature of God's spiritual relationship to his creation and his people.* Specifically, he is their progenitor, their provider, their protector, and their rightful "head" or ruler. Knowing, therefore, that human wives and children, by his own design, will instinctively relate to their earthly husbands and/or fathers in terms of these roles, God reveals himself to his people as their heavenly Husband and heavenly Father (Isaiah 54:5, Hosea 2:16, 2 Cor. 11:2, Mt. 25:1, Rev. 21:2). In other words, he reveals himself as male—and institutes male headship among his human creatures—because he would train his people to relate to him as their spiritual Head: as the loving, all-sufficient creator, sustainer, and sovereign ruler, to whom they may confidently look for their every need.

If, however, we seek to understand God's gender, not in terms of his role-relationship to his people, but rather in terms of his own intrinsic nature, then, in faithfulness to the biblical language itself, we should *still* think of him as a he, *but as an altogether unique he: a he who contains within himself all of the characteristics that we humans identify as masculine and feminine.* This would include not only such attributes as authority, power, and rulership, but also love, compassion, tenderness, and a heart for the nurture of his children (1 Thess. 2:6-12).

The words of the creation narrative itself reflect this perfect confluence of the masculine and the feminine in God: "So God created man in His own image; in the image of God He created him; *male and female He created them*" (Gen. 1:27). Here we learn that (non-physical) masculine and feminine traits belong to the very image of God. This may illuminate the manner in which he created the sexes: first, he created Adam, the repository of the more "masculine" side of his nature; then, *discerning an imperfection in the full display of his glory*, he created Eve, the repository of the more "feminine" side of his nature. Their union in marriage therefore gives a complete picture of God's manifold "gender," as well as a display of the union of Christ and his Church (Gen. 2:18-20, 1 Cor. 11:1ff, Eph. 5:22-33, 1 Thess. 2:6-12).

Interestingly, Jesus teaches that in the resurrection marriage and procreation will be abolished forever (Luke 20:27-40). Does this mean that the sexes themselves will be abolished? At the physical level, perhaps. But even so, "male and female" would still live on together in the hearts of the perfected saints, just as they ever have in the heart of their all-inclusive God.

3. The immutable God of the Bible stands in sharp contrast to the mutable god of classical pantheism, who is a being eternally in flux, at one moment lapsing from blissful unity into painful self-consciousness, at the next toiling to escape it, and at the next returning to its primordial unity once again, etc. Much the same is true of New Age pantheism, in which god is ever evolving towards more sophisticated levels of outward form and inward consciousness. All this flows, of course, from pantheism's identification of the "creator" with his (or its) ever-changing creation.

4. In his perpetual omniscience, Israel's God again differs from the god of pantheism. By slipping into a dream of creatureliness, the latter exists more or less continually in a state of ignorance. He/it is ignorant of his own nature, the nature of the world, his past, and his future. This is a god who mysteriously forgets, slowly learns, briefly understands, and then (in the case of classical pantheism) mysteriously forgets again. By identifying god and man, pantheism winds up subjecting god to the intellectual limitations of man.

5. Israel's God has infinite power at his disposal at all times. The god of classical pantheism, on the other hand, is powerless, since "he" is an impersonal being subject to a law of eternal recurrence. Meanwhile, the

ENDNOTES

evolving god of New Age pantheism is powerful only at the end of "his" cosmic journey, when he attains "god-consciousness" in man. Will he fall again into ignorance and begin still another evolutionary journey? It's anyone's guess.

6. In the OT, God is occasionally referred to as Israel's father, a predicate that spotlights his role as the loving creator, protector, and provider of his people (Deut. 1:30, Psalm 103:13, Is. 63:16, 64:8). But nowhere in the OT does God *name* himself Father, or invite his people to address him as such. Not surprisingly, then, Jesus met with bewilderment and resistance when he attempted to do this very thing.

7. This is in contrast to the behavior of Jesus' disciples who, when worshiped as gods by other men, fiercely protested what they took to be an act of blasphemy (Acts 10:24-26, 14:8-18).

8. For explicit NT references to the Holy Trinity, see Mt. 3:13-17, 28:18ff; Acts 2:32f, 10:36f, Rom. 8:9f, 15:16, 1 Cor. 12:4-6, 2 Cor. 13:14, Eph. 2:18, 3:14f, 4:4-6, 2 Thess. 2:13f, Titus 3:4f, Heb. 9:14, 1 Peter 1:1-2, Jude 20, Rev.1:4-6.

The OT intimates the tri-unity of God in at least six different ways. 1) The Hebrew word for "God" (*Elohim*) is a plural noun. Thus, it could well be rendered "gods" (Psalm 82:6). Interestingly, this has led some people to translate the *Shema* as follows: "Hear O Israel, Yahweh our Gods is Yahweh a unity" (Deut. 6:4). 2) In several OT passages, the divine Agent is spoken of as "Us" (Gen. 1:26, 3:22, 11:7). 3) Passages referencing the Angel of the LORD clearly point to a plurality within the godhead (see the section on christophanies in chapter 8). 4) God commanded Israel's priests to speak a triune blessing over his people (Num. 6:22-7). 5) In his vision of the glory of God, Isaiah saw seraphim (i.e., angels). Each of them had three sets of wings, and they all cried out day and night, saying "Holy, holy, holy is the LORD of hosts" (Isaiah 6:1-3)! Why such a prominent emphasis on the number three? 6) Like the christophanies, many OT Messianic prophecies hint at plurality within the godhead; some even refer explicitly to a divine Son (Psalm 2, 110, Isaiah 48:16, 61:1, 63:8-11, Dan. 7:9-14, Zech. 13:7, Mal. 3:1f).

9. See Gen. 22:1f, Eph. 5:22-6:8, Heb. 12:3-11.

10. The NT writers often distinguish God from Jesus Christ (see 1 Cor. 12:4-6, 2 Cor 13:14, I Pet. 1:2f, etc.). They are not, however, denying Christ's deity. Rather, they are simply using the word "God" in a special NT sense, a sense introduced by their Master himself in order to designate

the Father as the supreme "Head" of the Holy Family (Mt. 6:25-34, John 20:17; 1 Cor. 11:3). Therefore, with notable exceptions (e.g., John 1:1, 20:28, Rom. 9:5, 2 Pet. 1:1), the apostles usually spoke of the Father as "God" or "God the Father," and of Jesus Christ as "Lord," (Rom. 1:7, 1 Cor. 1:3, 1 Pet. 1:3, etc.). This pattern allows them tersely to acknowledge the ultimate sovereignty of the Father, without in any way denying the full deity of the Son and the Spirit.

11. Since the Council of Nicea (AD 325), the majority opinion of the Christian Church has been that the trinitarian hierarchy is rooted in the "ontological" relationship of the three persons ("ontology" being the study of the origin and nature of a particular being). Thus, with respect to the triune godhead it is held that the Son is subordinate to the Father because, necessarily and from all eternity, the Father "begets" or "generates" the Son (John 1:14, 18; 3:16, 18; 5:26; 1 John 4:9, 5:18). Similarly, the Spirit is subordinate to the Father and Son because, necessarily and from all eternity, the Father and the Son "send forth" the Spirit, so that he "proceeds" from them both (John 15:26). Observe carefully from these nuanced definitions that even if the Son and the Spirit in some sense derive their (unique manner of) being from one or two divine Others, they are nevertheless *not* created beings, since, again, they both exist necessarily and eternally, just like the Father, and share with him all of the attributes of the one (triune) God. For more, see Louis Berkhoff, *Systematic Theology* (Eerdmans, 1941), pp. 90-99. Also, for a close study of the theologically crucial Greek word *monogenes* (rendered by some translators as "only begotten" and by others as "one and only"), visit the blog of Lee Irons at www.upper-register.com, s.v., eternal generation.

12. For more on Jesus' teaching about the ultimate reality, see J. I. Packer, *Knowing God* (Inter Varsity Press); A. W. Tozer, *The Knowledge of the Holy* (Christian Books). My discussion of the attributes of God is highly indebted to Louis Berkhoff, *Systematic Theology* (Eerdmans, 1941), pp. 52-90.

Chapter 10: What is the Origin of the Universe, Life, and Man?

1. See Mt. 23:35, Mk. 2:27, Luke 17:26-27, John 8:4; 1 Cor. 11:1f, 2 Cor. 4:6, Eph. 5:30-31, 1 Tim. 2:13-14, 2 Peter 3:4-5.

2. According to a popular modern view, "the waters above the expanse" were something historically unique: a canopy of water vapor that surrounded the earth from its creation up to the time of the Flood. One of its chief defenders, Henry Morris, points out that this hypothesis goes far

toward explaining a number of important biblical and natural phenomena. They include the apparent lack of rain before the Flood (Gen. 2:5, 7:4); the daily mist (or springs) that watered the antediluvian lands (Gen. 2:6); the waters that fell for forty days and nights when, at the time of the Flood, "the windows of heaven were opened" (Gen. 7:11, 8:2); the late appearance of the first rainbow (Gen. 9:13f); the tropical climate of the ancient earth (including the Arctic and Antarctic regions), presumed to be the result of a greenhouse effect induced by the vapor canopy; the great longevity of antediluvian man (Gen. 5); and the greater size of most animals prior to the Flood. (See Morris, "Let the Word of God Be True," *Acts and Facts*, January, 2003.)

It should be noted, however, that capable creationist critics have found this view both scientifically and biblically wanting. See Walt Brown, *In the Beginning*, (CSC, 2001), pp. 260-268; also, D. Kelly, *Creation and Change*, (Mentor, 2002), pp. 182-185.

3. For a basic introduction to the biblical and scientific case for radical geocentricity, see Dean Davis, *In Search of the Beginning* (ISB) (Pleasant Word, 2007), pp. 264-317. Also, see Dean's short article, *The Case for Cosmic Geocentricity*, available at http://www.clr4u.org/writings/essays/345.html. For in-depth study, see Robert Sungenis and Robert Bennett, *Galileo Was Wrong*, available at www.geocentrism.com. Also, be sure to visit www.geocentricity.com, www.veritas-catholic.blogspot.com, and http://reformation.edu/scripture-science-stott/geo/index.htm.

4. In Ecclesiastes 3:2 (NIV), we find Solomon asking, "Who knows if the spirit of a man rises upwards and if the spirit of the animal goes down into the earth?" Though he cannot tell where it goes, Solomon definitely knows the animal has a spirit.

5. It is noteworthy that the apostle Paul often appealed to the beginning when he supplied Christians with ethical guidelines for relations between the sexes. As for Jesus, so for Paul: creation norms determine ethical norms (1 Cor. 11:1f, Eph. 5:22f, 1 Tim. 2:8f).

6. Bible-believing scientists of the past include such notables as Isaac Newton (physics), Johann Kepler (astronomy), Robert Boyle (chemistry), Lord Kelvin (thermodynamics), Louis Pasteur (bacteriology), Matthew Maury (oceanography), Michael Faraday (electromagnetics), Clerk Maxwell (electrodynamics), John Ray (biology), and Carlous Linnaeus (taxonomy). See H. Morris, *The Biblical Basis for Modern Science*, (Baker, 1999), p. 30.

See also pp. 463-5, where he lists more than 60 outstanding creationist scientists.

7. Numerous biblical passages depict the world as a theatre in which man is tested and observed by powers beyond his ken. See 2 Chron. 6:9, Job 1-2, Psalm 14:2, Mt. 18:10, 1 Cor. 4:9.

8. Speaking of Christ's return, which in the mind of certain early critics was late in coming, the apostle Peter writes, "But do not let this one fact escape your notice, beloved, that with the Lord one day is as a thousand years, and a thousand years as one day" (2 Peter 3:8). Seizing upon these words, some modern interpreters argue that the "days" of Gen. 1 may not be solar days after all, but "divine" days: long periods of time, perhaps even millions or billions of years. However, for reasons already discussed above, it is clear that the days of creation are indeed to be understood as solar days. Peter's point here is simply that God's *consciousness* of time is different than ours, so that what seems slow to us may seem quick to him. This does not mean, however, that God's *reckoning* of (intervals of) time is different than ours, especially when he speaks to us in his word about the beginning of astronomical time and the (daily) stages of the creation of his world.

9. Down through the years, various interpreters have attempted reconcile millions of years and/or cosmic evolution with an inspired Bible. For a critical survey of the different views (e.g., theistic evolution, the gap theory, the framework hypothesis, progressive creation, etc.), see Henry and John Morris, *The Modern Creation Trilogy* (MCT), (Master Books, 1996), Vol. 1, pp. 35-64. The following remarks by progressive creationist Pattle Pun demonstrate how these interpreters readily admit the plain sense of Genesis 1, but feel pressured by purely scientific considerations to adopt another non-literal view:

> It is apparent that the most straightforward understanding of the Genesis record, without regard to hermeneutical considerations suggested by science, is that God created heaven and earth in six solar days, that man was created in the sixth day, and that death and chaos entered the world after the Fall of Adam and Eve. (*Journal of the American Scientific Affiliation*, March, 1987).

10. Progressive Creationism is a semi-biblical cosmogony developed by astronomer Hugh Ross. Ross argues that after the Big Bang, God creatively intervened at several different stages of universal history in order to produce the world as we now know it. See *The Genesis Question* (NavPress, 2001)

and *A Matter of Days* (NavPress, 2004). For a thorough critique of this popular view, see Jonathan Sarfati, *Refuting Compromise*, (Master Books, 2004).

11. A possible exception to this general rule is the ongoing creation of the spirits of living beings at the time of their conception (see Psalms 104:27-30, 139:13-16).

12. For a rich meditation on the meaning of the Sabbath day, see Douglas Kelly, *Creation and Change*, (Mentor, 1997), pp. 237-252.

13. John Byl, *God and Cosmos*, (Banner of Truth, 2001), p. 167-171; ISB, chapter 5.

14. In his second letter to the Corinthians, Paul writes, "I know a man in Christ who fourteen years ago—whether in the body I do not know, or out of the body I do not know, God knows—such a man was caught up to the third Heaven...caught up into Paradise" (2 Cor. 12:2-4). Observe from this cryptic testimony that for Paul a man *can* be in his body and in heaven (Paradise) at the same time! Importantly, this is not to say that heaven is *merely* a visionary experience in someone's mind, that it is not a true place after all. It is to say, however, that *shared visionary experience belongs essentially to the nature of heaven*. Thus, the Holy Spirit, by means of an extended vision, enabled Paul briefly to share something of the goings on in heaven, wherever heaven may be. The lesson of the passage, then, is that its visionary nature is *more* essential to heaven than its place, so much so that, God willing, the saints and angels *can* experience heaven *wherever* they happen to be.

15. Romans 1:20. This approach to interpreting biblical visions is helpful for understanding the meaning of the Revelation, which, like all apocalyptic literature, communicates essentially spiritual truths under physical, earthly imagery.

16. In the Revelation, Christ also refers to himself as "The Beginning of the creation of God" (Rev. 3:14). Some have interpreted this to mean that he is the first (angelic) creature God made. But because so many other passages clearly designate Christ as the creator of all things (including the angels), this view is impossible. There is, however, a solution. The word here translated as "Beginning" (Greek, *arche*) can also mean *origin* or *source*. Translating it thus, the passage has the glorified Christ identifying himself as the Source—which is to say, the Creator—of the universe.

17. Again, the Latin word for knowledge—and the root of our English word "science"—is *scientia*. Here, language itself is telling us something important: a true "scientist" is one who desires to find knowledge, *not just one kind of knowledge* (e.g., knowledge derived by scientific method). In other words, he is willing to quarry for truth in *any* mine, even in the depths of divine revelation. The great Swiss mathematician, Leonard Euler (1707-1783), showed himself to be one such a scientist when he wrote:

> In our researches into the phenomena of the visible world we are subject to weaknesses and inconsistencies so humiliating that a (divine) revelation is absolutely necessary to us. We ought to avail ourselves of it with the most powerful veneration (cited in ISB, p. 352).

18. I am indebted to Henry and John Morris for the three-fold rubric under which I discuss the scientific evidences favorable to creationism. See Morris and Morris, *The Modern Creation Trilogy*, vol. 2, (Master Books, 1996).

19. By "biological evolution" is meant a net increase in genetic material resulting in the appearance of new biological structures. Again, such evolution has never been seen, nor has it been produced in a laboratory. Note also that according to this definition, "micro-evolution" is not evolution at all. That is because what scientists call "microevolution" is really only *adaptation*: small changes in an organism (e.g., a darkened wing, an enlarged beak, etc.) resulting from special combinations of *pre-existing* genetic materials in the parents, as well as from environmental conditions favorable to their retention (i.e., natural selection). Evolutionists would like us to think that "microevolution" is a species of "macroevolution," and therefore a proof of the latter. But again, the truth is that it is not evolution at all.

20. Over 500 Ph. D's working around the world in various disciplines have signed the following Scientific Dissent from Darwinism:

> We are skeptical of claims for the ability of random mutation and natural selection to account for the complexity of life. Careful examination of the evidence for Darwinism should be encouraged.

The statement, with a list of signatories, may be viewed at www.discovery.org. See also www.cosmologystatement.org for a similar declaration of skepticism about the Big Bang hypothesis.

21. Observational evidence of a sudden catastrophic restructuring of the surface of the Earth caused by the release of vast quantities of subterranean waters (and resulting in the fossilized geological column) abounds.

It includes: 1) soft-tissue fossils (e.g., jellyfish), 2) "live action fossils" (e.g., fish eating fish), 3) polystrate fossils (e.g., trees passing vertically through several layers of sedimentary rock), 4) delicate imprints between strata, 5) the absence of chemical erosion atop strata, 6) upwarped and folded strata, 7) vast animal graveyards (even in the arctic regions), 8) marine fossils (including whales!) and pillow lava on mountaintops (pillow lava only forms under water), 9) the Grand Canyon (both layers and cut), and 10) over 200 flood legends worldwide. Such phenomena clearly speak up in favor of a global Flood, and also against the widely held assumption that geological structures evolved slowly over millions of years.

Observe also how biblical texts dealing with the Flood are designed not only to enable God's people to understand the face of the world as we now know it, but also to interpret it to their contemporaries. For what, in the end, is the *meaning* of fossilized creatures, salinized oceans, infertile deserts, uninhabitable mountain ranges and arctic regions, and (perhaps) the four seasons themselves, with their burdensome extremes of hot and cold? Is it not that they all constitute, after the curse, a further wounding and defacement of the Earth; a further divine judgment upon man's sin; a further warning against such sin; and a solemn foreshadowing of a further—and far worse—judgment still to come (2 Peter 3)? In sum, the God of the Bible clearly intends that his cosmogony of the Flood (and of the Fall and the Dispersion at Babel) should be proclaimed by his people, with a view to the advance of his redemptive purposes in the Earth.

For an extended discussion of the age of the universe, life, and man, see ISB, p. 317f. See also the accompanying notes that will guide you to numerous books and articles on this fascinating subject.

22. See Bill Cooper, *After the Flood* (New Wine Press, 1995).

23. For an interesting look at North and South American legends that closely parallel the biblical stories of creation, fall, flood, and the dispersion at Babel, see Bill Johnson's article, "American Genesis: The Cosmological Beliefs of the Indians," (Impact, March, 2004). This is available at www.icr.org.

24. For a general introduction to biblical cosmology, seekers may begin with *The New Answers Book* (Master Books, 2007) and *In Search of the Beginning* (Pleasant Word, 2007). Also, they may profitably browse the following creationist web sites: http://www.creationscience.com, www.answersingenesis.org, www.icr.org, and http://reformation.edu/resources/index.htm

Chapter 11: What, If Anything, Went Wrong?

1. In the Bible, the number forty is often associated with divine testing. Moses, for example, was on Mount Sinai forty days and forty nights, while Israel's faithfulness was being tested on the plain below (Ex. 16:35). God tested Israel in the wilderness for forty years (Deut. 8:2). Under Jonah's preaching, he tested the penitence of the Ninevites for forty days. Could it be, then, that God intended Adam's probation to last forty days? Though we cannot be sure, this seems probable, since Jesus, retracing Adam's probationary footsteps in Eden, was himself tested in the wilderness for forty days (Mt. 4:2).

2. In describing the elements of eternal life, the NT helps us envision the manifold blessings that Adam would have inherited if he had eaten first from the Tree of Life. He would have received the Holy Spirit as an eternal indwelling Helper (John 14:17). He would have been introduced to the mystery of the Holy Trinity (Mt. 11:27, Eph. 2:18). He would have come into the knowledge of the Son of God, and also under his rule, for God the Father had created all things *for* him (Col. 1:16, Heb. 1:2). Moreover, in receiving all of this for himself, Adam also would have received it for his children (Heb. 2:13). Henceforth, he and his growing family would have worked together towards the fulfillment of the dominion mandate (John 4:27-38, 1 Cor. 3:9). Then, at the end of the age, when all was accomplished, God the Son would have glorified both man and nature, immersing them still more fully in the power and presence God (Isaiah 11:9, 40: 40:5, Mt. 13:43). In that glorious new world, the extended Holy Family would have lived forever.

3. When Eve ate, nothing happened. She certainly did not die, nor, apparently, did she even feel remorse. Here is proof that Adam was indeed her head, her proxy before God. Though she sinned, the sin was not imputed to her, for God had not issued his warning to Eve, but to Adam. If, however, Adam were to sin, he would sin for her, and for her offspring as well. And great indeed would be the consequences of that sin.

4. The butterfly in our garden supplies a good example of the biblical idea of true freedom. If a child catches this butterfly in a net, we feel sad because it is no longer free. If the child releases it, we are happy since now it is free again. But in what, precisely, are we rejoicing? We are rejoicing in the fact that that the butterfly can now do, without hindrance, what it was *meant* to do: *fly, in response to the promptings of its own God-given nature.* Can the butterfly spin another cocoon over itself, or roar like a lion, or do calculus? No, it is not free to do those things, for it is limited by its butterfly

nature. We might even say that it is a slave to its butterfly nature. Yet so long as the butterfly can "do its own thing" without hindrance—so long as it can feed and fly and bless a watching world—we do not regard it as a slave, but as free.

So it is, says the Bible, with man. Even in Eden, he was not an autonomous being. There were many things he could not be or do. He was a (mutable) slave to the good human nature that God had given him, and so he was happy and free. After his sin, however, he was no longer happy or truly free. Indeed, there is a sense in which he was no longer even human, since he was no longer the man God meant him to be. If, however, God were somehow to release him from the net of sin, fill him with his Spirit, restore him to his true humanity, and send him soaring heavenward upon the winds of a new, God-given nature—then, says the Bible, he would still not be autonomous, but he would be free indeed (John 8:31-36, Rom. 6:15-23, 2 Cor. 3:17)!

5. An important further consequence of sin, and therefore of the fall, was the advent of civil government. God instituted it in seed form after the Flood, when he prescribed capital punishment for murder among Noah's offspring (Gen. 9:5-7). Later, he himself created a more elaborate system in the ancient Israelite theocracy. Later still, in Paul's letter to the Romans, he supplies a definitive revelation of the purpose, prerogatives, and (limited) authority of civil government: God himself has mandated it for all nations; its narrow but vital purpose is to administer (retributive) justice (i.e., to encourage the good, but especially to judge and punish the evil); to this end, rulers are divinely authorized to use force, up to and including capital punishment (Rom. 13:1-4); therefore all people should respect the powers that be, and willingly pay taxes for their support (Rom. 13:5-7).

Having its mandate from above, civil government is not a law unto itself, but remains accountable to God. Therefore rulers must dispense justice impartially and avoid every taint of corruption (Lev. 19:15, Deut. 16:19). They must not transgress their proper sphere by usurping the God-given prerogatives of the patriarchal family: material provision, the education of children, personal self-defense, etc., (Eph. 5:22-6:4, 1 Tim. 5:8; Gen. 14, 1 Sam. 30). Similarly, they must not usurp the prerogatives of the Church: spiritual instruction, oversight of divine worship, church discipline, etc., (1 Cor. 6:1-11, Eph. 4:1-16, 2 Thess. 2, 1 Tim. 2, 3). And they must not wage imperialistic wars of aggression, "…removing the boundaries of the peoples and plundering their treasures" (Isaiah 10:12-14; cf. Acts 17:26).

Governments that persist in doing such things have lost their divine mandate and are subject to God's judgment, usually at the hands of other governments (Isaiah 10, Jer. 46-51, Amos 1-2, Psalm 82). Individual citizens have a positive obligation to resist the evil decrees of evil governments (Acts 4:19-20, 5:29). In dire circumstances, this principle appears to justify secession from, and/or "revolution" against, such governments, the change being accomplished, ideally, through the popular formation of a new, alternative government dedicated to the administration of true justice, and therefore divinely authorized to defend its citizens against any retaliatory aggression that may ensue (Judges 3:7-16:31, 1 Kings 12:1-24). Near the end of the age, in a final embodiment of the ancient Babylonian impulse (Gen. 11:1-9), civil government, in violation of God's ordinances, will become global, theocratic, tyrannical, and violently hostile to God, Christ, and the Church (2 Thess. 2, Rev. 11:7, 13:1ff, 17:1f, 19:19, 20:7-10). The return of Jesus in final judgment will bring it to an end once for all, even as the saints rejoice to see the kingdoms of this world become the Kingdom of their Lord and of his Christ (Rev. 11:15).

Thus, in biblical perspective, civil government is a *temporary* historical phenomenon altogether tied to the presence of sin in the world. Before the fall, it was not necessary; since the fall, it has been; at the coming of Christ, when sin is eradicated completely, it no longer will be (Rom. 13:1f, 1 Cor. 15:24, Rev. 11:15).

6. Importantly, the Bible teaches that God's wrath falls in judgment upon *every* sin (Eccl. 12:14, Titus 2:14). It does not, however, fall in one way only. In the case of God's enemies, it falls upon their own heads. But in the case of his friends, it falls upon another head—Jesus Christ, the representative head of his people (Gal. 3:13). Thus, in the biblical universe, justice is *always* done, but not always upon those by whom injustice was committed.

7. Cited in Robert Velarde, "Greatness and Wretchedness: The Usefulness of Pascal's Argument in Apologetics," *Journal of the Christian Research Institute*, (Vol. 27, #02), pp. 34-40.

8. Bob and Cecelia Brown, "The Power of the Creation Message," Impact Article #284, www.icr.org.

9. In chapter 18 we will see that God tests the children of Adam in different ways at different times. Today, the divine test comes to mankind primarily in the gospel. When it does, it requires him to search out its truth and to receive or reject Christ. Here, men are actually choosing which head they desire to live under: the first Adam, who bequeaths to them eternal death, or the last Adam, who bequeaths to them eternal life. More on this in later chapters.

10. Critics of the Intelligent Design Movement (ID) point to apparent flaws in the biological structure of men and animals, and also to so-called "defense/attack structures" (fangs, claws, stingers, venom, etc.), asking derisively how much intelligence or goodness these phenomena reveal. Unfortunately, proponents of ID, having decided to eschew any appeal to divine revelation, cannot give a satisfactory answer. Biblical creationists, however, respond immediately by directing such critics to the fall, and in particular to its impact upon the physiology of living beings. Their contention, based upon biblical revelation, is that life does indeed display intelligent design—and that in its apparent defects it displays intelligent judgment, as well. For a helpful essay illustrating this approach, see the chapter on defense/attack structures in *The New Answers Book* (Master Books, 2007), p. 259f.

11. In this paragraph, I have joined with the Bible in assuming that all people are "free," not just Adam in his innocence, but even Adam's fallen offspring in their sin. But again, it is important carefully to define the word "free." As we have already seen, Adam in his innocence was a (mutable) slave to his good nature (a fact that makes his rebellion difficult, if not impossible, for us to understand, (Mt. 7:17-20)). As for Adam's fallen children, they too are slaves, but now to a sinful nature (John 8:34, Romans 6:1f). Furthermore, there is a sense in which all creatures are "slaves" to what God has foreordained, for God has foreordained all things. So then, in biblical perspective, no one but God is free in an absolute sense. Yet all are "free" in this limited sense: they choose what they choose, and do what they do, *as an expression of their own will*. To state the case negatively, no one—neither God nor the devil—coerces them to do anything other than what they themselves want to do. Accordingly, we may say that God tests Adam's fallen children in pretty much the same way he tested their innocent father. Through nature, conscience, and the Bible, he makes his existence, character, and commandments known in their sin-darkened souls, beckoning them to seek out a fuller perception of his truth. And they are free to do so, if only they will.

12. Jonathan Edwards, inquiring as to why a holy God would decree and permit sin to enter his universe, argues as follows:

> It is a proper and excellent thing for infinite glory to shine forth; and for the same reason, it is proper that the shining forth of God's glory should be complete; that is, that all parts of his glory should shine forth, that every beauty should be proportionately effulgent, that the beholder may have a proper notion of God. It is not proper that one glory should be exceedingly manifested, and another not at all...

> Thus, it is necessary that God's awful majesty, his authority and dreadful greatness, justice, and holiness should be manifested. But this could not be unless sin and punishment had been decreed; otherwise, the shining forth of God's glory would be very imperfect, both because these parts of the divine glory would not shine forth as the others do, and also the glory of his goodness, love, and holiness would be faint without them; nay, they could scarcely shine forth at all.
>
> If it were not right that God should decree and permit and punish sin, there could be no manifestation of God's holiness in hatred of sin, or in showing any preference, in his providence, for godliness before it. There would be no manifestation of God's grace or true goodness, if there was no sin to be pardoned, no misery to be saved from. However much happiness he bestowed, his goodness would not be so much prized and admired...
>
> So evil is necessary, in order to the highest happiness of the creature, and the completeness of that communication of God, for which he made the world; because the creature's happiness consists in the knowledge of God and the sense of his love. And if the knowledge of him be imperfect, the happiness of the creature must be proportionately imperfect (Cited in John Piper, *Desiring God* (Multnomah, 2003), p. 350).

13. In discussing the biblical teaching about God's will, theologians often employ a useful distinction. On the one hand, they speak of God's "will of purpose" or his "decretive will." These phrases point to everything that God, in eternity past, willed or decreed to occur in history (Eph. 1:11). Apart from what already *has* happened, or from what the scriptures predict *will* happen, God's will of purpose lies hidden from man. On the other hand, they speak of God's "will of precept" or his "moral will." These phrases point to God's rule of action for the sons of men. This will is partly revealed in human conscience, and more fully revealed in the Bible. Also, the Spirit reveals the particulars of God's will to the believer's heart (e.g., whether he should marry, where he should live, what he should do for a living, etc.). Importantly, the biblical writers urge the saints to live under the shadow of both wills. They are to understand and rejoice in God's great, good, and infallible purpose for his people. But far from letting such knowledge lull them into passivity, they are to express gratitude for their part in his purpose by zealously conforming their own wills to his life-giving precepts.

14. Cited in L. Boettner, *The Reformed Doctrine of Predestination*, (Presbyterian and Reformed, 1932), P. 242. Similarly, John Piper writes:

> He (Jonathan Edwards) uses the analogy of the way the sun brings about light and warmth by its essential nature, but brings about dark and cold by dropping below the horizon. "If the sun were the proper cause of cold and darkness," he says, "it would be the fountain of these things, as it

is the fountain of light and heat; and then something might be argued from the nature of cold and darkness, to a likeness of nature in the sun." In other words, "...sin is not the fruit of any positive agency or influence of the most High, but on the contrary, arises from the withholding of his action and energy, and under certain circumstances necessarily follows on the want of his influence (John Piper, *Desiring God*, (Multnomah, 2003), p. 348).

15. For a fuller discussion of God's decrees and the problem of evil, see Louis Berkhoff, *Systematic Theology*, (Eerdmans, 1977), pp. 100-108; John Frame, *Apologetics to the Glory of God* (Presbyterian and Reformed, 1994), chapters 6, 7; *Evangelical Dictionary of Theology*, (Baker, 2001), s.v. "Decrees of God"

16. For two principal reasons, the biblical doctrine of predestination cannot be identified as fatalism. First, the Bible places a wise, powerful, and benevolent *personal* god above all events, not an uncaring, impersonal force, as in the case of fatalism. And secondly, it does *not* view divine predestination as inconsistent with human responsibility for obedience to God's will of precept. This is why the Bible pointedly reproves the very attitudes that fatalism tends to foster: resignation, passivity, laziness, and despair (Mt. 25:26, Rom. 12:11, 1 Cor. 15:58, Gal. 6:9). Indeed, the biblical revelation of God's sovereignty is clearly designed, not to *paralyze* a believer's will, but to *energize* it. The saints now have a purpose in life. Before the foundation of the world, the sovereign God prepared specific good works for each of them to walk in (Eph. 2:10). Accordingly, they must "lay hold of that for which Christ Jesus laid hold of (them)." They must, "work out their salvation in fear and trembling" (Phil. 2:12, 3:12). Yes, God has decreed great things for his people. Therefore, they must use their newfound freedom in Christ to find them, choose them, and enjoy all the blessings that a passionate doing of them is sure to bring (Gal. 5:13, 1 Pet. 2:16).

Chapter 12: What, If Anything, Can Be Done?

1. For a look at the King's family tree, see Mt. 1:1-16 and Luke 3:23-38. Matthew's genealogy is stylized and partial, going back to Abraham; Luke's is complete, going all the way back to Adam. From Joseph to David the names in the two genealogies differ markedly. One time-honored solution to this problem is to say that Matthew traces Jesus' lineage from his father (Joseph) to Solomon, to David, and finally to Abraham, thus showing him to be *the promised Messiah*. Meanwhile, Luke is said to trace it from his mother (Mary) to Nathan, to David, and all the way back to Adam, thus

showing him to be *the perfect man* (see Norman Geisler and Thomas Howe, *When Critics Ask*, Victor Books, 1992, pp. 385-386). In favor of this view is the fact that Luke shows a keen interest in, and intimate acquaintance with, Mary. However, in his genealogy he not only says nothing about Mary, but also explicitly states that Heli is *Joseph's* father. Accordingly, other scholars propose that Luke—for reasons unexplained—elected to trace Jesus' lineage through the line of Nathan (another son of Bathsheba). Also, they say Jacob (Joseph's father in Matthew) actually died childless, while Jacob's younger brother, Heli (Joseph's father in Luke), was Joseph's biological father. On this view, Matthew is therefore seen to be focusing on Jesus' *legal* parentage, while Luke is seen to be focusing on his *biological* parentage (see *New Bible Dictionary*, s.v. "Genealogy of Jesus Christ," Eerdmans, 1979). However, the great difficulty here is to understand why Luke elected to trace Jesus' family tree through Nathan rather than Solomon. Also, if Jacob and Heli were brothers, sons of the same father, how is it that they have two different family trees? It may be, then, that the traditional view is best after all, *if we may assume* that Heli was, a) Mary's biological father and Joseph's adoptive father, or, b) Joseph and Mary's adoptive father. Whatever the final solution may be, it is clear enough that Luke, a scrupulous and trustworthy historian, was not simply pulling names out of thin air. Accordingly, the puzzling differences in the genealogies not only disprove collusion, but actually lend them an air of verisimilitude.

2. Though the OT administrations of the eternal covenant did indeed bring those who obeyed into the covenant of grace, the vehicles by which God administered it were *intrinsically* powerless to accomplish his redemptive purpose. For example, the animal that God killed, and the skins that he draped over Adam's shoulders, had no power to cover his sins. The ark that Noah constructed had no power to carry his soul safely through the flood of God's wrath at the Last Judgment. The son that God promised to believing Abraham had no power to open the portals of heaven to his father. The priests and the animal sacrifices offered under the Mosaic Law had no power to put away transgressions (Heb. 10:1-4). If, then, all of these earthly types *did* have power to redeem, it was solely in virtue of their connection with the heavenly realities that they symbolized. That is, it was in virtue of their connection with Christ. This, by the way, is why God went to considerable lengths to show the *imperfection, impotence, and impermanence* of the OT Law. The writer to the Hebrews makes much of these things, fearing that the new Jewish Christians of his own day might be tempted to abandon Christ and the new covenant (the body of truth) in favor of Moses and the old covenant (mere shadows of truth). For example, he points out that under

the Law many mortal priests offered many animal sacrifices, not only for the people, but also for themselves. Christ, on the other hand, is the one immortal priest who offered one human sacrifice, not for his own sinless self, but solely for his sinful people (Heb. 7). For this reason, the whole Mosaic Law, now being fulfilled in Christ, is obsolete (Heb. 8). Therefore, any Jewish Christian who returns to it is actually trying to enter the Kingdom by living under the Ten Commandments *without the benefit of a God-approved sacrifice for his inevitable failures to do so*. Long ago at Sinai God showed what kind of welcome such a one may expect to receive (Heb. 12:18-24).

3. While the era of promise and preparation lasted some 4000 years, the OT scriptures focus largely on the much shorter period of Israel's nationhood (ca. 1500 B.C. to 400 B.C.). This is purposeful, since one of God's main concerns in OT times was to provide, through his dealings with Israel, *a picture of his coming Kingdom; a set of earthly, physical images, by which he would later describe his heavenly, spiritual Kingdom*. Such, in any case, was the conviction of Jesus and his apostles. For example, they saw Canaan as a picture (or type) of a fully restored cosmos (Rom. 4:13; Rev. 21:1f); Mount Zion as a picture of heaven, and of the heavenly world still to come (Heb. 12:22, Rev. 14:1); earthly prophets, priests, and kings (especially Melchizedek, David, and Solomon) as pictures of the heavenly Messiah in his various offices (Acts 3:22, Heb. 7, Rev. 19:16); animal sacrifices as pictures of Christ crucified (Heb. 9, 10); Israel as a picture of God's eternal people, both Jew and Gentile (Gal. 3:29, 6:16, 1 Pet. 2:4-10,); the temple (where God's glory resided) as a picture of the Christ's body, the Church, indwelt by God's Spirit (John 2:19f, 2 Cor. 6:16, Eph. 2:21), etc. Israel itself was not the Kingdom of God; indeed, the prophets find in her history of moral failure a powerful proof of the *need* of his Kingdom (Jer. 31:31f). But for all her faults, she was indeed a *picture* of the Kingdom; a picture of a chosen race, a royal priesthood, a holy nation, a people for God's own possession—both Jew and Gentile—who will one day live forever under a new heaven and in a new earth (1 Pet. 1:9-10).

4. For further study of the atonement wrought by Christ, see C. J. Mahaney, *Living the Cross-centered Life* (Multnomah, 2006); S. Jeffery, M. Ovey, A. Sach, and J. Piper, *Pierced for Our Transgressions* (Crossway, 2007); Leon Morris, *The Cross in the New Testament* (Eerdmans, 1999); and R. C. Sproul, *The Truth of the Cross* (Reformation Trust, 2007).

5. OT Kingdom prophecy, being NT truth mystically cloaked in imagery drawn from Israel's life under the Law, largely cast the coming Kingdom as *an eternal, universal, theocracy, mediated by Israel's Messiah and*

the Mosaic Law (Psalm 2, 22:27-28, 110; Isaiah 9:6-7, 11:1-10; Jer. 33:14-18, Ezek. 37:24-28, 40-48; Micah 4:1-3, Haggai 2:6-9, Zech. 14:8-9, 16-21). Jesus and the apostles, however, insist that these prophecies are spiritually fulfilled in the one spiritual Kingdom that unfolds in two stages. First, there is the Kingdom of the Son, whose reign emanates from heaven, is effected by the secret workings of the Spirit, and is therefore essentially inward. Then, after Christ's return, comes the eternal Kingdom of the Father. Here, the divine reign falls upon the realm of nature as well, leading to eternal life under new heavens and in a new earth (2 Pet. 3:13, Rev. 21:1). For further study on this important theme, see Mt. 13:36-43, Luke 19:11f, Acts 2:14-39, 3:11-26, 1 Cor. 15:20-28, Eph. 1.

6. In chapter 16 we will discuss the events surrounding the *parousia* in greater detail and give scriptural citations for more study.

7. Some biblical interpreters assert that God elected sinners to salvation "conditionally;" that he chose them in eternity past based upon his foreknowledge of the fact that one day they would freely choose him. But for many reasons, this view is untenable. First, there is not a single NT passage that teaches it. The best candidate is Romans 8:29, which states: "Those whom he foreknew, he also predestined to be conformed to the image of his Son..." However, this verse says nothing about God's foreknowing future attitudes, decisions, or actions; instead, it simply depicts him as foreknowing *persons*. The thought, then, is that those whom God *chose* beforehand—*those whom he knew beforehand as the ones he would make his own*—he predestined to be conformed to Christ (Amos 3:2, John 10:27). So here too the Bible teaches unconditional election. The doctrine of conditional election creates additional problems, as well. For example, it contradicts and destroys the very idea of divine election by making man's free-will choice of God the decisive factor in redemption; by effectively making man his own savior and God a helpless bystander who could, in principle, wind up with no people at all. Also, far from representing God's plans as being based on his foreknowledge, the Bible repeatedly represents his foreknowledge as being based upon his eternal plans (and the subsequent providence in which he will work out those plans) (Isaiah 37:26, 46:9f, Lam. 2:17, etc.)! Finally, we must ask: Upon what foreknown virtues in man could God possibly base his decision to save a sinner, seeing that apart from the gracious operation of his Spirit, there is, in fallen man, "no good thing," (Rom. 7:18, 3:10-18)? If the children of Adam, apart from God's grace, really are "slaves to sin" and "dead in trespasses and sins," is not conditional election based upon foreseen freedom, virtue, and desire for God ruled out by the Bible itself (John 8:34, Rom. 7:14, Eph. 2:5)?

For more, see J. Boice and P. Ryken, *The Doctrines of Grace* (Crossway, 2002), pp. 99-101.

8. The corollary and obverse of election is "reprobation," or the doctrine that God has effectively appointed certain people (and angels) to eternal destruction, since he decided, in eternity past, not to redeem them, but to leave them in their sins, exposed to his wrath and just retribution. While the Bible's emphasis naturally falls upon God's mercy and grace in election, it does not hesitate also to teach divine reprobation as well (Ex. 9:16, Prov. 16:4, Malachi 1:2-3, John 17:12, Rom. 9:6-18, 1 Thess. 5:9, 1 Peter 2:7-8, 2 Peter 2:12, Jude 4). See *The Doctrines of Grace*, pp. 101-107.

9. The OT contains a number of passages pointing to the Messiah's definite atonement. One thinks, for example, of the blood of the original Passover lambs, which was ordained only for the deliverance of the sons of Israel, and not for the sons of Egypt (Ex. 11-12). One thinks also of the High Priest (Aaron), whose breastplate was adorned with twelve stones, each with one of the names of the twelve sons of Israel written upon it. God said of him, "So Aaron shall bear the names of the sons of Israel on the breastplate of judgment over his heart, when he goes into the holy place, as a memorial before the LORD continually" (Ex. 28:15-30). Here is a powerful OT picture of Christ, entering and interceding in heaven for the forgiveness of a chosen people, for whom alone he has made his sacrifice (Heb. 9:24). Finally, we have the great Messianic prophecy of Isaiah, who said of the coming Servant Priest, "He was taken from prison and from judgment, and who will declare His generation? For He was cut off from the land of the living; *for the transgressions of My people He was stricken*... By His knowledge My righteous Servant shall justify many, for He shall bear their iniquities" (Isaiah 53:8, 11).

10. There are a number of NT passages in which it is stated or implied that Christ died for "all" (2 Cor. 5:14-15, 1 Tim. 2:5-6), "all men" (John 12:32, Rom. 5:18, Titus 2:11), "the world" (2 Cor. 5:19), or "the whole world" (1 John 2:2). Appealing to these, some have argued that Christ's atonement was universal: that it paid for all the sins of all men indiscriminately; that the lost do not benefit from this atonement simply because they freely choose not to. But for many reasons this view is problematic. First, it directly contradicts the clearer and more numerous texts that teach a definite and efficacious atonement. Secondly, it means that Christ did not die for the (rampant) sin of unbelief, and therefore did not really die for all sins. Thirdly, it means that all will be saved, for how could God justly require sins to be punished twice: once in the person of his Son, and once

again in the person of the (unrepentant) sinner himself? Yet it is clear from scripture that all will not be saved (Mt. 25, 2 Thess. 1, Rev. 20). And finally, it means that, in principle, Christ's death could completely fail in its purpose, since all men, if so inclined, could reject his sacrifice. Yet turning to the NT we find that Jesus anticipates no such failure, neither total nor even partial, but confidently affirms that he *will* bring to himself every sheep for whom he has died, and that there *shall* be one flock with one shepherd (John 10:14-16). Therefore, the passages supposedly teaching a universal atonement must have another meaning. Happily, when we read them in their contexts, we see clearly that they do. "All," for example, can refer to all the elect (2 Cor. 5:14-15), or to all classes and categories of people (1 Tim. 2:5-6, Titus 2:11). Similarly, "the world" can refer to the (new) world in Christ (2 Cor. 5:19), or to the world of all nations (and not just "us" apostles or Jews) (1 John 2:2). For an extended discussion of these and other such passages, see Robert Reymond, *A New Systematic Theology of the Christian Faith,* (Nelson, 1998), pp. 683-702).

11. Opponents of a definite atonement ask how God can sincerely offer Christ to all, or command all to repent and trust in Christ, if in fact Christ did not die for all (John 3:16, Acts 17:30, Rom. 1:1-7, 2 Thess. 1:8, 1 Pet. 4:17). Though the Bible does not specifically address this reasonable question, its use of the two paradigms discussed earlier offers considerable help. If we view the preaching of the gospel from the point of view of man's freedom on probation, we can say that in it God sincerely offers Christ to all men and commands them to turn to him because: a) Christ's atoning sacrifice is, from one point of view, *sufficient* for all, since the sins of one, some, or all people are equally punishable by death (being equally transgressions of God's Law and injurious to his glory); and since Christ, in actually paying the penalty of death for *some* people, could not have died less had he paid it for one, or more had he paid it for all; b) it is the natural obligation of all of Christ's creatures to submit themselves to their sovereign creator and Lord, and c) God sincerely *desires* them to do so (Mt. 23:37-39, Rom. 9:1-5, 10:1, 1 Tim. 2:4?). However, if we view gospel preaching from the point of view of God's sovereign action in history, we can say that, beyond simply appealing to man's will, he also uses such preaching to apply an atonement that was *efficient* only for his elect, since theirs were the only sins he imputed to Christ. In other words, the sovereign God uses preaching to *bring* his people to Christ, and to bring the fruits of Christ's work to his people. We find, then, that the two biblical paradigms do indeed offer us some help in addressing this difficult question. We do well, however, to remember that the philosophical harmony of the two paradigms is itself shrouded in mystery,

so that our answer to this and other similar questions may, for the moment, be incomplete.

12. Critics sometimes ask why, if the God of the Bible is real, so few people believe in him. The doctrines of unconditional election and definite atonement supply the answer. The ongoing historical fact of faithful Christians co-existing in the world beside people of other faiths or of no faith offers empirical evidence for the truth that it has pleased God to take a little flock out of the world, a chosen people for his name (Luke 12:32, Acts 15:14).

Chapter 13: What is the Meaning of Life?

1. For more on the meaning of life see J. Piper, *Don't Waste Your Life* (Crossway); R. C. Sproul Jr., ed. *Vanity and Meaning* (Baker).

Chapter 14: How Shall We Live?

1. The New Testament issues a remarkably comprehensive body of moral norms that, with preliminary light from the OT, supply general principles and specific precepts for the right ordering of sexual expression, marriage, parenting, inter-personal relationships, money-management, business, law, government, international relations, military action, and more. Confident of this, Jesus likens his teachings to the one rock upon which men (and nations) may safely build their lives (Mt. 7:24-27). Paul affirms this very thing, saying that the Scriptures are sufficient to equip God's children "for every good work" (2 Tim. 3:16-17). Peter agrees, declaring that Christ has given his people "all things that pertain to life and godliness" (2 Peter 1:3). In short, the NT writers are certain that God, in Christ, has shown us how to live, once and for all.

2. Biblically, the state is never to pervert justice, whether by favoring the rich and the powerful or the poor and the weak (Lev. 19:15, Deut. 1:17). In particular, it is never to void or mitigate proper penalties, since the state is not to be the instrument of God's compassion, but of his judgments. The instrument of God's compassion is his Church, which he sends to the prisoners with the good news of redemption through Christ (Mt. 25:36). If the guilty receive it gladly, judgment may fall upon their bodies, but never upon their ransomed souls.

3. In chapter 7 of his excellent book, *The Goodness of God* (IVP, 1974), Gordon Wenham argues that capital punishment may be far more merciful

than the living death of a protracted imprisonment. He points out that OT law conspicuously omits to mention imprisonment as a proper penalty for crime, preferring instead various forms of physical restitution, corporal punishment, and, in the worst-case scenarios, the death penalty. On this view, the true path of wisdom in dealing with modern crime would be to return to a basically OT system of punishments, even as society expresses compassion for lawbreakers by encouraging contact with Christians, who bring them the good news of pardon and new spiritual life through faith in Christ and God.

Chapter 15: What Happens When We Die?

1. Some interpreters cite Luke 16:19f, Eph. 4:7-10, 1 Pet. 3:18-20, and various OT texts to argue that in OT times the spirits of the dead *all* went to the nether world (i.e., *Sheol*). According to this view, Sheol was divided into two compartments: Hades (a place of torments) and Abraham's Bosom (a place of comfort, in which the saints awaited the opening of heaven by Christ's sacrifice). But the weight of the biblical evidence speaks against this view. As we have seen, there are many OT passages implying that at death the OT saints entered heaven. Likewise, there are not a few NT passages that imply the same (Mt. 17:3, Luke 20:27-40, Heb. 12:22-23). The text in Ephesians simply refers to Christ's descent (*via* incarnation) from heaven to earth, and from earth to the grave. 1 Peter 3:18-20 does not teach that Christ personally descended into *Sheol* to preach to the spirits imprisoned there (why would the spirits of the righteous be imprisoned?). Rather, it teaches that *through the Spirit* (and also through Noah) the Son of God long ago preached to Noah's rebellious generation, who are *now* in prison (i.e., Hades) awaiting final judgment, (see NAS). Luke 16:19f must be interpreted in light of all this, and therefore parabolically, along the lines suggested above.

2. A number of NT texts speak of the dead saints as being "asleep," or "asleep in Jesus" (John 11:13, 1 Cor. 11:30, 15:51, 1 Thess. 4:14). This has led some to suggest that at the moment of death their souls fall into unconsciousness, and that they continue thus until their awakening at the resurrection. But this view is contradicted by the many NT texts, already cited, depicting the departed saints as consciously enjoying the glories of heaven. We must conclude, then, that in speaking of the "sleep" of the departed Christian, the apostles are simply trying to comfort the living with certain important truths about the dead. The death of their loved ones is not the last word. The separation of their soul from their body is

not permanent. Their dead bodies are really only sleeping. At Jesus' soon return, when the resurrection shall occur, they will "awaken" and rise again to eternal life (1 Thess. 4:13-18).

3. Over the course of centuries, Roman Catholic and Orthodox churches have developed and taught the doctrine of Purgatory. These churches contend that during some portion of the intermediate state the saints go to a special place where they are punished for various post-baptismal sins, and thereby purified for their eventual entrance into heaven. But this idea (along with grievous ecclesiastical abuses to which it has given rise) has no foundation in the NT, and is, at many points, positively contradicted by it. Above all, the doctrine of Purgatory confuses punishment with chastisement (or discipline). The Bible teaches that there is only one punishment for sin (i.e., death), and that Christ has already received that punishment on behalf of his people (Rom. 8:3-4, 1 Peter. 3:18). In the moment that the saints place their trust in him and his finished work, they are forgiven of *all* their sins (past, present, and future) and therefore *welcomed into eternal fellowship with the triune God* (John 5:24, Acts 13:39, Rom. 5:1f, Eph. 1:6). As the apostle Paul puts it, they are *already* "seated in heavenly places in Christ" (Eph. 2:6). Yes, for the remainder of their days on earth they are indeed subject to various trials. But these are not punishments for sin, only disciplinary providences, wisely administered by a loving Father who is preparing them to be a worthy Bride for his Son (John 15:1-2, Eph. 5:25f, James 1:2f, 1 Pet. 1:3-9, Heb. 12:1f, Rev. 3:19). The NT insists, however, that this purification will be completed at the moment of death, when the souls of the redeemed immediately enter heaven. Henceforth, they are "the spirits of just men made perfect," worshiping their Lord in robes of righteousness that are white, bright, and clean (Heb. 12:22-24, Rev. 4:4, 6:11, 19:14).

4. In recent years various clinical experiments have persuaded a number of eminent neurophysiologists to abandon their naturalistic view of consciousness—namely, that consciousness is a bi-product of chemical activity in the brain, and that it ceases with the death of the human organism. One of them, Wilder Penfield, concluded from his work with epileptics that cortical stimulation can trigger only a very limited set of human responses, and that it is therefore necessary to posit a "non-physical reality" that interacts with the brain so as to produce the full range of mental and physical capacity. Oxford physiologist and Nobel laureate Charles Sherrington, towards the end of his life, came to the same conclusion, confessing, "For me now, the only reality is the human soul." His student, John Eccles, followed suit, saying, "I am constrained to believe that there is what we might call

a supernatural origin of my unique self-conscious mind, or my unique self-hood or soul." We find, then, that weighty scientific evidence supports our common-sense notion that body and soul are two distinct entities; that the one is natural (physical) and the other supernatural (spiritual); and that while the one is most certainly *related* to the other, neither can be *reduced* to the other. In short, the evidence favors the "dualistic" (or "two-part") man of biblical theism, and not the "monistic" (or "one part") man of naturalism or pantheism. For more, see Lee Strobel, *The Case for the Creator*, (Zondervan, 2004), chapter 11; John Byl, *The Divine Challenge*, (Banner of Truth, 2005), pp. 82-109, 237-253.

5. Modern parapsychological research has produced intriguing evidence, not only for the existence of the soul, but also for its survival after death. In one influential study of 63 heart-attack victims, "About ten percent reported having well-structured, lucid thought processes, with memory formation and reasoning, *during the time that their brains were not functioning.*" At the very least, this means that the soul is not a bi-product or "epiphenomenon" of brain processes. In another study, one woman reported that during her near-death experience (NDE) she saw a tennis shoe on the hospital roof—a shoe that later investigation proved to be really there! The objective truth of her vision would certainly seem to support the idea that she left her body, and that the soul, in principle, can exist separately from the body. It is true, of course, that such experiences (which are numerous) do not conclusively prove the existence of an after-life. In the very nature of the case, "conclusive proof" is available only to those who have departed their bodies once for all, either into oblivion or into another world beyond this one. Nevertheless, like the proverbial smoke whose presence ever signals fire, NDE's do provide, in the words of philosopher J. P. Moreland, "...at least a minimalist case for consciousness surviving death." See *Case for the Creator*, pp. 250-257. Also, Don Piper, *90 Minutes in Heaven* (Flemming H. Revell, 2004).

6. In many popular works produced by parapsychologists and psychics, the after-life is represented as a realm of light that all persons will enter, irrespective of their faith in Christ. As a rule, it is portrayed as a kind of "world between worlds," a place where souls go to learn essential spiritual lessons before returning again to the earth *via* re-incarnation. This is, of course, the Hindu/Buddhist/New Age view of the after-life, a view that is taught in their respective sacred writings and "confirmed" by so-called "spirit-guides" who have communicated with us through channelers or the near dead. Here, however, Christian observers urge great caution, since the Bible warns that Satan, desiring to eclipse the vital importance of the person and work of Christ

in salvation, can appear to men as "an angel of light" imparting spurious religious experience and "truth" (Mt. 4:1-11, 2 Cor. 11:14). Moreover, they note that still other researchers report "near-hell" experiences, *from which faith in Christ is experienced as the only avenue of escape*. Again, NDE's are not conclusive evidence of an after-life, but neither are they insignificant. Perhaps, then, their chief practical value lies in this, that they tend to move seekers to take a closer look at the teachings of the one man who, alone among the world's spiritual teachers, is said to have risen from the *really* dead unto eternal life. If anyone should know about the after-life, it would be him! For an excellent survey of NDE's in biblical perspective, see Doug Groothuis, *Deceived by the Light*, (Harvest House, 1984).

Chapter 16: Where is History Heading?

1. New Age theologian Scott Peck writes, "God wants us to become himself (or herself, or itself). We are growing towards godhood. God is the goal of evolution. It is God who is the source of the evolutionary force, and God who is the destination. This is what we mean when we say he is the Alpha and the Omega, the beginning and the end." Cited in David Noebel, *Understanding the Times* (ACSI Publishing, 1995), p. 353.

2. In the Revelation, the apostle John uses several different expressions to refer to the period of time between Christ's first and second advents (i.e., the last days). In Rev. 7:14 he calls it "the great tribulation," a phrase by which the entire Church era is identified as a time of persecution and suffering for true believers in Christ. Elsewhere, he refers to it as "forty-two months," "1260 days," and "a time, times, and a half a time," (Rev. 11:2-3, 12:6, 14). All of these numeric symbols hearken back to Elijah's difficult three and a half years in the wilderness, where he hid from the persecutions of Ahab and Jezebel. Accordingly, they identify the last days as a *pre-determined and relatively brief* season of hardship for Christ's persecuted Church (1 Kings 17:1f, James 5:17, Rev. 12). In Rev. 20, the last days are said to endure for "1000 years," (Rev. 20:2-5, 7). This numeric symbol speaks of *God-ordained completeness* (10x10x10) and *temporal magnitude*. Accordingly, it teaches us that Christ's heavenly reign (and therefore the period between his two advents) will last a *long* time, but only as long as it takes for the triune God *fully* to administer his redemptive plan (Luke 19:11-12). Experience abundantly shows that a literal interpretation of these numbers is a formula for confusion and controversy. The approach here suggested, which is consistent with the symbolic character of the Revelation, is therefore much to be preferred. (See Rev. 1:1, where it is written that that

Christ's angel *signified* the Revelation to the apostle John. In other words, it is a book of signs or symbols). For an excellent commentary on the Revelation, see William Hendriksen, *More Than Conquerors*, (Baker, 1997).

3. The heavenly reign of Christ is the much-neglected key to understanding The Revelation. The truth of this is seen in both the contents and structure of the book. We may very simply describe them as follows:

In chapter 1 we have John's *Vision of the Heavenly King*.

In chapters 2-3 we have *The Heavenly King's Messages to the Seven Churches*.

In chapters 4-5 we have *The Heavenly King's Investiture*—his commissioning, authorization, and empowerment from the Father to apply and complete the redemption accomplished by his humiliation (Mt. 28:18f).

In chapters 6-20—the bulk of the book—we have *The Course of the Heavenly King's Reign*. Very importantly, this is described six separate times, in six parallel, large-scale visions that employ symbolic imagery drawn largely from the OT: They are: 1) *The Vision of the Six Seals* (chapter 6, followed by a sneak preview of the final state in chapter 7); 2) *The Vision of the Seven Trumpets* (chapters 8-11); 3) *The Vision of the Dragon and his Helpers vs. the Heavenly Woman* (chapters 12-14); 4) *The Vision of the Seven Bowls of God's Wrath* (chapters 15-16); 5) *The Vision of the Harlot, the Beast, and the Fall of Babylon* (chapters 17-19); and 6) *The Vision of the 1000 Year Heavenly Reign of Christ* (chapter 20).

Again, each of these visions describes the entire course of the King's heavenly reign, sometimes with special emphasis on events that will occur near the end of the age. They reveal to the saints the kinds of trials and temptations they may expect at the hands of a Satanically dominated world system, yet also assure them that their sovereign King is actually in control of all things, and that he will faithfully strengthen, guide, and preserve them for the Kingdom soon to come. *That this is the true structure of chapters 6-20 is clear from the fact that towards the end of each of the six visions, John gives us a symbolic description of Christ's coming again in judgment at the end of the age—at the end of his heavenly reign.*

This paves the way for the happy, climactic vision of chapters 21-22, where we read of *The Heavenly King's Re-creation of the Cosmos*, and of the new heavenly homeland that he has prepared for his own.

Once the reader sees that this is indeed the structure of The Revelation—and once he understands that the book's basic purpose is to describe, under largely OT symbolism, the course of the heavenly King's heavenly reign vis-à-vis friend and foe—then a hitherto closed book is opened once and for all.

For more on this subject (which richly repays close study), see *More Than Conquerors*, pp. 7-34.

4. Along with *parousia*, the NT uses two other Greek words to describe Christ's coming again in glory. The first is *apokalupsis* (i.e., revelation), a word that conveys the idea of Christ's coming out of hiding (1 Cor. 1:7, 2 Thess. 1:7, 1 Peter 4:13). The second is *epiphaneia* (i.e., appearing, manifestation), a word that emphasizes the showing forth of Christ's glory (2 Thess. 2:8, 1 Tim. 6:4, 2 Tim. 1:10, 4:1, Titus 2:3). Even a cursory examination of the relevant texts will show that the NT uses these terms basically interchangeably. From slightly different angles, all three words describe the same one glorious event.

5. The Olivet Discourse has proven difficult to interpret. Was Jesus speaking here of the destruction of Jerusalem in 70 A.D., or of "the great tribulation" (i.e., the entire course of the Church era, Rev. 7:14), or of "the *greatest* tribulation" that will occur at the end of the present evil age (Mt. 24:3; cf., Mt. 13:39-43, 49-50, Gal. 1:4, Titus 2:11f)? For many scholars, the answer is: "Yes—for he was speaking of all three!" For the following reasons, I concur.

First, Jesus gave this discourse by way of response to his disciple's question about *two* distinct events (now separated by two millennia): the destruction of the Jewish temple, and his return in visible glory at the end of the present evil age (Mt. 24:3). Accordingly, we may assume that his response was cast in such a way as to speak not only to those who would (soon) experience the destruction of Jerusalem, but also to *all* who would look for his coming and the signs that would herald it. In other words, we may assume that Jesus here speaks not only to the twelve, but also to *all* of his disciples of *all* times.

Secondly, Jesus' predecessors, the OT prophets, commonly did this very thing. That is, in a single prophecy they would actually be referring to two or even three widely separated historical events, *since the events, though different, manifested a common nature or character*. This pattern is especially evident in certain OT prophecies of the "Day of the Lord," in which the prophets are clearly speaking not only of an imminent local judgment, but also of an ultimate global judgment (see Isaiah 2: 5-22, 13, Joel 2:1-20, Zeph. 1). Following this ancient precedent in his Olivet Discourse, Jesus therefore skillfully chose his prophetic words so as to speak relevantly to *all* of his disciples of *all* generations: to those who would live to see Titus' invasion; to those born after them who must endure like tribulations throughout the entire church era; and (especially) to those born near the end of the age, who will experience unprecedented tribulation just prior to Christ's coming again.

Keeping all this in mind, we are better able to understand a passage that has stumbled many biblical readers:

> Now learn a parable from the fig tree: when its branch has already become tender and puts forth its leaves, you know that summer is near. Even so you too, when you see all these things, recognize that He is near, right at the door. Truly, I say to you, this generation will not pass away until all these things take place (Mt. 24:22-34; Mark 13:28-32).

By "all these things" Jesus clearly means the signs of which he has just been speaking—*but not* the *parousia* itself (see Mark 13:29-30). By "this generation" he seems to mean not only the generation of (unbelieving) Jews amongst whom he and the disciples were presently living, but also the "generation" of unbelieving mankind among whom all the rest of his disciples would live till the end of the age. Accordingly, it is certainly true that the first generation of disciples *did* see all the signs, and that at that time their Lord was near (Mark 13:29). But subsequent generations of Christians have seen them as well, in times when their Lord was nearer still. Moreover, the last generation of Christians will see them *on an unprecedented scale*, and at a time when their Lord will not only be *at* the door, but *coming through* it!

Summing up, in the Olivet Discourse Jesus actually speaks to all generations of believers because his words will be fulfilled in all generations—and *fully* fulfilled in the last (to which he specially alludes in Mt. 24:13-14, 15, 21-22, 29). There are, then, no grounds for saying, as some have, that Jesus was in error about the time of his *parousia* and/or the signs that would precede and herald it (vv.32-35). Still less are there grounds for saying, as others (called *full preterists*) do, that his *parousia* occurred in 70 A.D., and along with it all the other elements of the consummation (e.g., the resurrection, the end of the world, the new heavens and a new earth), albeit in a spiritual rather than a physical sense.

6. Under symbolic imagery that would be meaningful to ancient Israel, the OT predicts the last battle in portions of chapters 9, 11 and 12 of the book of Daniel, and also in Ezekiel 38-39, and Zech. 12-14.

7. Concerning the Satanically energized ruler who will lead the end-time revolt against God, it is noteworthy that this "son of destruction" and "man of lawlessness" is an *antichrist* in the fullest possible sense (2 Thess. 2:3, 1 John 2:18). That is, he is both *against* Christ and *instead of* Christ, just as the two-fold meaning of the Greek word *anti* implies. When he appears, he will both *oppose* Christ (and his Church) and *impersonate*

ENDNOTES

Christ (2 Thess. 2:4). The latter was particularly on Paul's mind when he wrote to the Thessalonians about the *coming* (Greek: *parousia*) of the man of lawlessness (2:9), his *revelation* to the world (2:3, 8), the *miraculous signs and wonders* (2:9) that Satan will enable him to perform, the way in which these will seem to confirm both his *pretensions to deity* (2:4) and his *false gospel* (2:11), and the *world-wide following* that will result from it all (2:10-12). Very importantly, only one group of people on earth will be able to discern and resist this powerful Satanic caricature of the true Christ and the true gospel: those who "receive the love the truth" (2:10).

8. There are a number of NT passages indicating that all humanity must stand before the *throne* (Mt. 25:31, Rev. 20:4) or *judgment seat* (Rom. 14:10, 2 Cor. 5:10) of Christ for judgment. While it is not impossible that Jesus and his apostles are here speaking of a physical throne, it seems more likely that the throne is visionary in nature, or that it is simply a picture (symbol) of the absolute sovereignty of the High King of Heaven, especially as this will be manifested at the last judgment. (See Mt. 13:36-43, in which the mention of Christ's throne is conspicuously absent.)

9. The view under discussion in this paragraph is called Dispensationalism, a system of biblical interpretation developed in England in the late 19th century by John Darby, a leader of the Plymouth Brethren movement. Though still popular today in some evangelical circles, Darby's system has become increasingly controversial, since it is actually quite foreign to classical Protestant theology. For an excellent short discussion, see A. Hoekema, *The Bible and the Future* (Eerdmans, 1979), pp. 194-223. For a close study of "the rapture," see G. E. Ladd, *The Blessed Hope* (Eerdmans, 1956).

10. At first glance, Jesus' parable of the sheep and the goats (Mt. 25:31ff) seems to teach final salvation by good works done for his "brethren" (25:40). Who are Jesus' brethren, and how can we square this parable with the abundance of other sayings—many from the lips of Jesus himself—to the effect that salvation is *not* by works, but by simple faith in Christ and what *he* has done in behalf of his people? Theologian George Ladd replies as follows:

> Jesus used a parabolic incident of the nightly separation of sheep and goats to tell his disciples that they have a mission to the nations of the world. The destiny of men will be determined by the way they treat Jesus' representatives—his brethren (Mt. 12:50). They are to go as itinerant preachers, finding lodging and food from those who receive them (Mt. 10:8-11). However, they will meet persecution and imprisonment (Mt.

10:17-18). Those who receive these preachers and treat them well in reality receive Christ: "He who receives you receives me" (Mt. 10:40). Those who reject these preachers and treat them ill do so because they are rejecting their message, and in doing so reject Christ. Judgment awaits them (Mt. 10:14-15). The destiny of the nations will be determined by the way they respond to Jesus' representatives. This is not a program of eschatology, but a practical parable of human destiny (George Ladd, *A Theology of the New Testament*, (Eerdmans, 1974), p. 206).

Interpreted thus, the parable does not contradict salvation by grace through faith in Christ's work, but actually confirms it.

11. The Bible insists that all have sinned, and that there is no salvation for any human being apart from faith in Christ (John 3:16, 6:29, 14:6, Acts 4:12, 16:13, Eph. 2:8, 1 John 5:12, etc.). But what of those who never heard of Christ, whether in Old Testament times or in New? Are all these people necessarily lost? Understandably, this is a common question among seekers; it is also one upon which thoughtful biblical interpreters disagree. Some, citing Mt. 28:18f and Romans 10:14-17, insist that God makes Christ and the gospel known strictly through evangelism; that contact with a human preacher is therefore yet another demonstration of his providence and sovereign grace; and that to deny the necessity of evangelistic contact is to undermine the urgency of world missions. Others, granting that evangelism is indeed God's norm—and a norm to be taken with utmost seriousness—nevertheless urge that the crux of the matter is repentance and faith towards Christ, and not necessarily faith in Christ preached by Christians. Accordingly, they ask: Could God send an angel to preach Christ (Luke 2:11, Acts 10:1-8)? Could he preach Christ by giving a dream (Daniel 2, Mt. 1:20-21)? Could he, by giving a vision to a Gentile spiritual leader, awaken faith in a coming savior among some remote tribe, a tribe that, in partial ignorance of his identity, nevertheless worships the Great Spirit? Could God bestow forgiveness of sins upon those who, in repentance and faith, offer animal sacrifices to a Great Spirit or an Unknown God? Would not such sacrifices be essentially the same as those offered by the godly Israelites of OT times, and therefore an expression of implicit faith in the One who alone could fulfill them? The test perspective suggests a yes answer to these questions. For there, the assumption is that God is pleased to test each and every sinner, giving them a *bona fide* opportunity to love truth over lies, good over evil, and God and Christ over self—and so to be saved (John 3:17f, Acts17:26-28, Rom. 2:13,15, 26-29). If, then, a kind, merciful, and sometimes unpredictable God occasionally chooses to do all this in an unorthodox way, why should any Christian object? The Christian's job, it

ENDNOTES   559

would appear, is simply to attend to the orthodox way, by doing his part to carry the light of the gospel to all nations.

12. What does Paul mean when he says that Christ will deliver up the Kingdom to the Father, and freshly subject himself to him, *so that God may be all in all?* The thought here seems to be that the Son, having fulfilled the redemptive work of his mediatorial reign, is now eager to lay down his special authority at the feet of the One who gave it to him, *so that God the Father may be, and be glorified as, the Supreme Sovereign of the universe.* This calls to mind the final days of Jesus' earthly ministry, when he asked the Father to glorify the Son, so that the Son might glorify the Father (John 17:1). Here, in the delivering up of the Kingdom, we see that prayer being answered, and being answered by Jesus himself!

13. Numerous biblical texts affirm that Christ will reign forever over his people (Daniel 2:44, 7:14, 27, Luke 1:13, 2 Peter 1:11, Rev. 11:15). These make it clear that the delivering up of the Kingdom does not *terminate* the Son's sovereignty, but rather—in a manner that defies complete description—*subordinates and transforms* it once for all.

14. For an excellent, in-depth survey of biblical teaching on cosmic history, along with a critical evaluation of different views, see Anthony Hoekema, *The Bible and the Future* (Eerdmans, 1979). Also, see Kim Riddlebarger, *A Case for Amillenialism: Understanding the End Times* (Baker, 2006)

Chapter 17: How Can We Find Trustworthy Answers to the Questions of Life?

1. In the Sermon on the Mount, Jesus elucidates the subtle relationship between the old revelation that God gave to Israel through Moses, and the new revelation that God is giving to the Church through himself. Both men are prophets, both are priests, both are mediators of covenants. But the latter is greater than the former, since what the latter brings *fulfills* and *illuminates* what the former taught in ignorance of its deeper meaning. Thus, Jesus tells his disciples, "Truly, I say to you, till heaven and earth pass away, not one jot or one tittle will by any means pass from the law till all is fulfilled" (Mt. 5:18). Here, Jesus certainly does not mean that the Mosaic Law will remain in force until the consummation: as he said elsewhere, the wine of the new covenant requires new wineskins—and this entails discarding the old (Mt. 9:17, Heb. 8:13). What he means, then, is that the old covenant is about to be fulfilled and superceded by the new, so that *in its new form*

it will continue in force until the consummation and beyond (Mt. 5:17). Though the butterfly looks quite different from the caterpillar, in truth not a jot or a tittle of the insect has passed away. It is the same creature, only in its new and final form. And again, observe from this illustration that the old form cannot really be understood except in the fuller light of the new. It is only as we ride upon the wings of the NT butterfly that we can look back and see the meaning of the OT caterpillar, since now we know all that the OT caterpillar was meant to be!

2. Christ's apostles definitely saw themselves as an integral part of the revelatory process. For example, Paul told the Galatians that he had not received "his gospel" from man, but directly from Jesus Christ by special revelation (Gal. 1:11-24). Similarly, he urged the Ephesians to accept his teaching, since God, by direct revelation, had made known to him (and to all of Christ's holy apostles and prophets) the "mysteries" of redemption, mysteries that in other ages had been hidden from men and angels, but are now revealed to all men (and angels!) through the Church (Eph. 3:1-13). Such texts could be greatly multiplied (Mt. 16:18-19, 1 Cor. 2:6-16, 1 Thess. 2:13, 2 Pet. 1:12-21, 1 John 1:1-4. 4:6, Rev. 1:1f). Again, we learn from them that the apostles understood themselves as chosen vessels of Christ, bringing God's definitive revelation into the world once for all.

3. Importantly, the apostles also knew that in committing Christ's revelation to writing they were creating *scripture*—divinely inspired documents that would become the rule of faith and conduct for God's people (2 Thess. 2:15, 1 Cor 14:37, 2 Pet. 1:12-15, 3:14-16, Rev. 1:11). Moreover, they knew they were not only creating scripture, but also *completing* it! Through them, God was delivering his truth, *once and for all* to the saints (Jude 1:3). Accordingly, when they passed from the scene, no further normative revelations would be given—but their inscripturated words would remain (2 Pet. 1:12-15). These would become the continuing foundation for Christ's Church, the authoritative standard for the saints of all times and places (Mt. 16:17-19, Eph. 2:20, 3:5). On that foundation the Church would rise, led by men who loved, preached, and taught "the word," (Acts 20:32, 2 Tim. 2:2). It would become "the pillar and support of the truth" to all nations (1 Tim. 3:15). Indeed, it would become a holy temple, a dwelling-place of God by the Spirit (Eph. 2:19-22). And in that temple—just as the ancient prophets had promised—the heavenly Teacher would teach the peoples daily, opening their minds to understand the scriptures, instructing them, transforming them, and equipping them, even unto the end of the age (Micah 4:1-2, Mt. 26:55, Mark 13:30, Luke 24:45).

ENDNOTES

4. For a brief history of the canonization of the NT, see chapter 7. Here we do well to remember that most Christians see their Teacher as having been integrally involved in the canonization process. In other words, they claim that part of the Teacher's heavenly ministry was to enable a second generation of Christian leaders to recognize the true apostolic writings, and thereby to distinguish the true from the false (John 16:13, 1 Cor. 12:10, Heb. 5:14, 1 John 4:1f). Historically, this took place as second century pastors prayerfully worked out the criteria for accepting any alleged NT writing as genuine. As we have seen, these criteria included early and widespread usage, apostolicity, authoritativeness, doctrinal integrity, and the witness of the Holy Spirit. By such criteria, the Teacher taught his leaders to recognize, fence off, and preserve God's completed revelation for all future generations.

Chapter 18: Is Life a Test?

1. In this life, such obedience will not be perfect. Nevertheless, because it is his destiny, perfection remains the goal of the child of God, in whose heart there now burns a desire to please the Father and to grow closer to him through greater conformity to his will (Phil. 2:13, 3:12-16, Heb. 8:7-13).

2. In NT perspective, to abandon the world system for Christ's sake is not to betray family or friends, but to love them. By making a costly decision for the sake of truth, the disciple is showing his loved ones the value of truth, and thereby drawing them to it. Interestingly, Jesus himself had to walk down this difficult road. By turns, the members of his own family thought him a fake or a madman (Mark 3:21, John 7:1-9). Yet through costly obedience to his Father, he won them at last to the gospel and eternal life (Mt. 12:46-50).

3. In James 2:14-26, the apostle discourses on the importance of good works in the Christian life. In vv. 21 and 24 he even states that men—including father Abraham—are justified by works and not by faith alone. How can this be reconciled with the numerous NT passages that seem to teach the exact opposite: that men can *only* be justified (i.e., declared righteous by God) through faith in Christ's work in their behalf, and *never* by their own works (e.g., John 3:16, 5:24, 6:40, Acts 16:31, Rom. 3:19-31, Eph. 2:8-10, Titus 3:4-7)? Theologian J. I. Packer supplies a concise and insightful answer:

> In James 2:21, 24-25 (the word justification) refers to the *proof* of man's acceptance with God that is given when his actions show that he has the kind of living, working faith to which God imputes righteousness. James'

statement that Christians, like Abraham, are justified by works (v. 24) is not contrary to Paul's insistence that Christians, like Abraham, are justified by faith (Rom.3:28; 4:1-5), but is complementary to it. James himself quotes Genesis 15:6 for exactly the same purpose as Paul does—to show that it was faith which secured Abraham's acceptance as righteous (v. 23; cf. Rom. 4:3-25; Gal. 3:6-9). The justification that concerns James is not the believer's original acceptance by God, but the subsequent *vindication* of his profession of faith by his life. It is in terminology, not thought, that James differs from Paul (James Packer, *Evangelical Dictionary of Theology*, s.v. *Justification*, (Baker, 2001), p. 643).

4. The test perspective helps us understand the scandal of theological schisms in the Church of Jesus Christ. "How can it be," ask seekers and critics, "that Christians are so divided theologically? If they really do have God's true revelation, as well as the Spirit of Truth to help them understand it, why can't they seem to agree?"

The answer to these excellent questions begins with an important observation: as a matter of fact, the vast majority of Christians *do* agree on the fundamentals of the faith. They all affirm, for example, that God is a Holy Trinity; that in the beginning he created the universe, life, and man, *ex nihilo;* that the world fell into evil, suffering, and death through the sin of Adam; that redemption is accomplished through the person and work of Jesus Christ; that redemption is received through personal faith in him; that there is a heaven above, a hell beneath, and a new world coming at the return of Christ, etc. In other words, *generally speaking*, Bible-believing Christians give the same basic answers to the questions of life.

Beyond the basics, however, there are indeed frequent points of disagreement. For example, Christians engage in lively debates over the time and manner of the creation; predestination and free will; the proper candidates for—and the mode of—water baptism; the nature and purpose of the Lord's Supper; the structure of church government; the roles of men and women in the church and the family; the nature and perpetuity of various spiritual gifts; the time, manner, and events associated with Christ's coming again at the end of the age, etc.

These disagreements arise for different reasons. In some cases, it is because the biblical teaching is sketchy; in others, because it is difficult to understand; in others, because it is difficult to receive; in others, because the world-system has mounted an especially sharp attack on the matter at hand. But whatever the cause, history plainly reveals that doctrinal controversy is a permanent companion to Christ's Church as she makes her pilgrimage through the wilderness of this world.

Seekers should realize, however, that controversies do not arise because God is hiding his truth. Rather, they arise because he is testing his spiritually growing people to see if they love his truth enough seek it out with diligence, humility, and complete dependence upon the Spirit of wisdom and revelation (Mt. 7:7, John 16:13, Eph. 1:17, 4:11-16, 2 Tim. 2:7). The biblical promise is quite clear: "If any of you lacks wisdom, let him ask of God, who gives to all liberally and without reproach, and it *will* be given to him" (James 1:5). If, then, disagreements arise, it is because some teachers have not asked God for wisdom or waited for his answer, while others have. When, therefore, teachers begin to disagree, hearers are forced to seek out the truth for themselves, so as to know which, if any, of the contesting parties God has truly taught. Thus, in his wisdom God permits a measure of doctrinal error (and even intentional deception) to trouble his Church, that he might test his people concerning their love of truth—and richly bless those who pass (Deut. 13:3, Acts 17:11, 1 Cor. 11:9).

Chapter 19: If So, How Can We Pass?

1. Focusing on a small handful of NT texts (Acts 2:38, 22:16, Romans 6:3-4, 1 Peter 3:21), some have argued that it is actually in and through the act of water baptism that God justifies (believing) sinners and/or bestows the gift of the Spirit upon them. However, the NT itself rules out this understanding, since, in a far greater number of texts, it teaches that God saves sinners *prior* to water baptism, sovereignly visiting them by his Spirit, granting them new spiritual life, and thereby creating in them repentance and (saving) faith towards Christ, all under the preaching of the gospel (John 3:3, 5, 16, 5:24, 6:40, Acts 16:14, 31, Rom. 3:19-31, 10:19, Eph. 2:8-10, 1 Peter 1:23). It is, then, by means of his prior work of *spiritually* baptizing sinners into Christ—of inwardly crucifying their sin nature, raising them to newness of life, and washing away their sins--that God makes them viable candidates for the physical rite of initiation that pictures these things to a watching world (John 13:8, Acts 22:16, Romans 6:3-4).

Once we have understood all this, we can see that in the four texts mentioned above the preachers are using a kind of spiritual shorthand; they are using verbiage from the rite of Christian conversion (baptism) to describe the spiritual dynamics of Christian conversion itself, or to call men to it. Will water baptism really effect the forgiveness of sins, and really secure the gift of the Holy Spirit for Peter's Jewish neighbors? No, but repentance and faith towards Christ will, both of which he urges them obediently to express in water baptism (Acts 2:38; cf. Luke 24:7, Acts 3:19, where, tellingly, water baptism is not mentioned at all). Can water baptism really wash away Paul's sins? No, but faith in Christ, which must now be expressed in water baptism, can (Acts 22:16). Along these lines, observe in 1 Peter 3:21 how the apostle is actually at pains to avoid any confusion in this matter. Yes, he asserts that "baptism now saves you." However, he immediately qualifies and clarifies this, directing his reader's attention away from the cleansing of the outer man by water to the spiritually cleansing faith of the inner man who, through baptism, expresses his gratitude to God for the gift of a good conscience granted through the death and resurrection of Christ—and who also pledges to keep that conscience clean in days ahead. In sum, it is not water baptism that saves, justifies, or secures the gift of the Spirit, but the sovereign, saving work of God in a sinner's heart—a work that is pictured by baptism, and a work to which, in baptism, the sinner obediently, gratefully, and gladly responds.

2. Seekers may wish, for example, to visit different churches in their area, listen to the pastors preach, and make an appointment to talk with those leaders to whom they are drawn. They could invite a Christian friend or neighbor over for coffee and a heart-to-heart conversation. Christian radio offers some excellent Bible teaching over the air (and some not-so-excellent, as well). Quality Christian bookstores provide thoughtful volumes on virtually any subject of spiritual interest. There are number of fine Christian websites, including: 1) www.ligonier.org, 2) www.desiringgod.org, 3) www.aomin.org, 4) www.equip.org, 5) www.family.org, and 6) www.enjoyinggodministries.com. Finally, for a list of books adapted specially to the needs of modern seekers, please see the select bibliography at the end of this book.

3. In the following quotation, observe how seeker George Lucas, the producer of the *Star Wars* saga, recognizes the need of diligence in the search for truth. Observe also that he definitely sees life as a test.

> I wanted to make the films so that young people would begin to ask questions about the mystery. Not having enough interest in the mysteries of life to ask the question, "Is there a god or is there not a god,"—that, for me, is the worst thing that can happen. I think you should have an opinion about that. Or you should be saying, "I'm looking. I'm very curious about this, and I'm going to continue to look until I can find an answer. And if I can't find an answer, then I'll die trying."

SELECT BIBLIOGRAPHY

1. Ankerberg, J. and Weldon, J., *The Encyclopedia of New Age Beliefs* (Harvest House, 1996)
2. Berkhoff, L., *Systematic Theology* (Eerdmans, 1941)
3. Boice, J. M., *Foundations of the Christian Faith* (IVP, 1986)
4. Boice, J. M. and Ryken, P., *The Doctrines of Grace* (Crossway, 2002)
5. Brown, C., *Philosophy and the Christian Faith* (IVP, 1968)
6. Brown, W., *In the Beginning*, 8th Edition (CSC Books, 2008)
7. Byl, J., *God and Cosmos* (Banner of Truth, 2001)
8. Byl, J., *The Divine Challenge* (Banner of Truth, 2004)
9. Cairns, E., *Christianity through the Centuries* (Zondervan, 1981)
10. Caner, E. M. and Caner E. F., *Unveiling Islam* (Kregel, 2002)
11. Clowney, E., *The Unfolding Mystery* (Presbyterian and Reformed, 1988)
12. Davis, D., *In Search of the Beginning* (Pleasant Word, 2007)
13. Elwell, W., ed., *Evangelical Dictionary of Theology* (Baker, 1984)
14. Geisler, N. and Howe, T., *When Critics Ask* (Victor, 1992)
15. Geisler, N. and Nix, E., *A General Introduction to the Bible* (Moody, 1968)
16. N. Geisler, A. Saleeb, *Answering Islam* (Baker, 2002)
17. Halverson, C., ed., *The Compact Guide to World Religions* (Harvest House, 1996)
18. Ham, K., ed., *The New Answers Book* (Master Books, 2006)
19. Hendriksen, Wm., *More Than Conquerors* (Baker, 1982)
20. Hoekema, A., *The Bible and the Future* (Eerdmans, 1979)
21. McDowell, J., *The New Evidence That Demands a Verdict* (Nelson, 1999)
22. Noebel, D., *Understanding the Times* (Harvest House, 2004)
23. Packer, J. I., *Evangelism and the Sovereignty of God* (IVP, 2008)
24. Packer, J. I., *Knowing God* (IVP, 1973)

25. Reymond, R., *A New Systematic Theology of the Christian Faith* (Nelson, 1998)
26. Sarfati, J., *Refuting Compromise* (Master Books, 2004)
27. Sire, J., *The Universe Next Door* (IVP, 1997)
28. Strobel, L., *The Case for Christ* (Zondervan, 1998)
29. Strobel, L., *The Case for Faith* (Zondervan, 2000)
30. Veith, G. E., *Postmodern Times* (Crossway, 1994)
31. Zacharias, R., *Jesus Among Other Gods* (Word, 2000)
32. Zacharias, R., *Light in the Shadow of Jihad* (Multnomah, 2002)
33. Zacharias, R., *The Lotus and the Cross* (Multnomah, 2001)

To order additional copies of this book,
please visit www.redemption-press.com

REDEMPTION ◗ PRESS